THE POSTAGE STAMPS
AND POSTAL HISTORY
OF CANADA

Winthrop S. Boggs

The Postage Stamps and Postal History of Canada

Winthrop S. Boggs

QUARTERMAN PUBLICATIONS, INC.
Lawrence, Massachusetts

Copyright 1945 by Chambers Publishing Company

Copyright © 1974 by Quarterman Publications, Inc.

All rights reserved. This impression may not be reproduced in any form without written permission.

This Quarterman edition is a republication of the original edition published in 1945 by Chambers Publishing Company and contains Volume I of the original in its entirety and excerpted portions of Volume II. A new foreword and a section comprising author's revisions has been added.

International Standard Book Number: 0-88000-042-2
Library of Congress Catalog Card Number: 74-79893

Printed in the United States of America.

Quarterman Publications, Inc.
5 South Union Street
Lawrence, Massachusetts 01843

FOREWORD

Canadian philately has been singularly fortunate in the quality of the collectors and the students it has attracted. Amongst the latter none ranks higher than the late Winthrop S. Boggs, whose *Postage Stamps and Postal History of Canada* remains after almost three decades unsurpassed. Others have since explored in greater detail certain facets of the field, yet Boggs, many will concur, retains his primacy—not least, one ventures to observe, because his work is far easier to use and to move around in. It is safe to say that collectors will continue to consult it first, and only then, if need be, go on to more recent publications.

For those of us who did not know Mr Boggs personally, the work must represent the man. Others have paid tribute to him as an individual, notably Mr Harrison D. S. Haverbeck in an appreciation in *The Collectors Club Philatelist* for July, 1973, whilst Mr Boggs's own "A Philatelic Autobiography" published in the same journal in 1958, on the occasion of his receiving the Club's Alfred F. Lichtenstein Memorial Award, gives a bare outline of his career. Yet it is his writings that will endure and reveal his inner self.

Here perhaps the most salient feature is his modesty. Though it is conceivably possible that he sometimes may have seemed impatient or stubborn with others who did not think as he did, he may be forgiven, for they in turn may not have brought to the matter at hand the depth of knowledge, experience, enthusiasm, or dedication that he possessed. But as an author he displays the genuine humility of the true scholar, though in the absence of advanced academic training and degrees he would have made no claim to being one. Yet without all this he nonetheless achieved the finest aims of the professional historian, by diligently ferreting out relevant information, consulting authorities to whose aid he pays generous tribute, providing pertinent documentation, and organizing his materials clearly and meaningfully. That he brought to his tasks an acute intelligence he would pass over: he would no doubt have merely said that the facts and the conclusions he offered spoke objectively for themselves.

The same modesty perhaps prevented his resting on his laurels following the publication of the work. Instead he continued to amend and emend, recording the corrections and addenda the publishers now make available. In turn, we can ourselves but feel humble at the debt we owe the man.

Boston, Massachusetts
May 1974

John Alden
Keeper of Rare Books
Boston Public Library

PUBLISHER'S NOTE

Long out of print, Winthrop Boggs' masterly work on Canada has become one of the most sought-after items in all philatelic literature, as collectors have become increasingly aware of its merits and of Canada's stamps and postal history.

The work as published made no pretentions to typographic distinction, and its production reflected war-time restrictions. To reproduce it, using the resources of modern technology, a single volume appeared to provide the best economic compromise and yet reach the collector. To further this end in this reprint, we have omitted most of the material in the original Volume II. Some sections, specifically, Appendices A, F, J, N, P and Q, have been retained as relatively important to the needs of the collector. We acknowledge that we may be open to criticism in this decision, yet we believe it was justified.

However, we have provided as addenda a compilation of the annotations scattered in the copy of Volume I which belonged to Boggs himself, acquired as Lot #924 in the H. R. Harmer auction of Boggs' philatelic holdings held in New York, January 31, 1974. His notes have been painstakingly transcribed — possibly not without error — and in published form should provide a sound basis for further investigation. Those pages for which addendum material exists are indicated by an asterisk adjacent to the page number. It has not been feasible, unfortunately, to provide separate notations in the text to indicate the existence of each individual correction or comment in this addendum.

We take great pleasure in being able not only to make available this established classic in reprint form but also to extend its scope.

PREFACE

This book represents the labor of many months intensive study of the stamps and postal history of Canada, combined with over thirty years' experience in studying, analyzing and handling stamps generally. It was undertaken with the intention of compiling a compact and accurate handbook for collectors of Canadian postage stamps, and cancellations.

The extensive literature on the subject led us to suppose that there would be little need or place for original research on what appeared to be a well worn theme. It soon became manifest, however, not only that the history of the postal service and postal issues of Canada had not been written, but that to a surprising extent was not even known. Although many issues of these stamps and postal markings have been exhaustively discussed, we found that nearly every point would have to be carefully investigated anew, while with regard to some of the supposedly well written up fields various collateral problems still awaited solution. Such questions, arising one by one, necessitated unforeseen and tedious investigation, the accumulation and examination of thousands of stamps and covers, and the study of a vast mass of documents, reports, and letters, some of it in distant libraries and archives; plus a voluminous correspondence with those generously assisting this work. In addition difficulties arising out of war time conditions have delayed the appearance of this work, a considerable portion of which was already written when it was originally announced for publication early in 1943.

In dealing with a subject so extensive and with material so copious, it has proved no easy task to keep the book within reasonable bounds. Conclusions which are stated in a sentence, or data which are epitomized in a single column of a table, frequently represent the results of prolonged research and many hours of study. The enormous mass of stamps, covers, documents and literature at our command has been carefully sifted, and with very few exceptions personally examined. The few exceptions have been studied and reported by competent men whose names and reputations are known to every philatelist.

The difficulty of compressing essential details into small compass has been chiefly met by presenting much of the data in tabular form, or placing the documentation in various appendices. These numerous appendices will be found by the serious student to be of primary importance. It will probably be a matter of surprise that so much of this material has never been published, or if published, only in various official reports. However, it is probably true that even the existence of such documents has not been known by philatelists generally.

We would remind our readers that every portion of this work has been carefully planned. The scope is intentionally broad, particularly in the historical aspects, so necessary for a full appreciation of the reasons for much that otherwise remains unexplained or only partly understood. Every effort has been made to present a well integrated and closely knit body of information which we hope will furnish the basis for further research by other students. As we do not collect, nor have any personal interest in the stamps of Canada beyond the study of them, our approach has been without any preconceived theories or notions to defend. We have been motivated solely by a desire to examine the facts as we have found them, and to present these facts, with such conclusions as can be reasonably drawn from them. Where we conflict with other students such disagreement is based solely on the evidence, and is in no way influenced by personal feelings.

In the acknowledgments we have expressed our gratitude to those who have personally helped us, and in the Bibliography we credit those whose writings have been of assistance.

That there are errors in this book we have no doubt, the omissions are acutely felt, and the inadequacy of the treatment of certain phases is readily admitted. Some of this is intentional as explained in the introduction, some due to the lamentable lack of definite information; plus the human tendency to err. By the standards of today's philatelic writing it can by no means be considered "the last word." Such a claim would be manifestly absurd. Practically every chapter covers a field that warrants a handbook in itself. Future years may see the appearance of such books.

It is therefore with mixed feelings of pleasure and regret that we lay our pen down; pleasure in being able to turn to other urgent work, and regret at leaving so many problems unsolved.

WINTHROP S. BOGGS.

St. Matthias Day
February 25, 1944.

INTRODUCTION

In presenting this book to the philatelic public in general, and to students of the Stamps and Postal History of Canada in particular, some words of explanation as to the origin, scope and underlying principles seem appropriate.

The idea of a revision of the material embodied in Mr. Clifton A. Howe's great work, plus the results of studies by other students since 1911, had been broached during the International Philatelic Exhibition in New York, in 1926. Some progress was made on this proposed book, but with the exception of Senator Calder's articles on the 1859 issue, nothing has been published along the lines of Mr. Howe's original work of 1911.

Mr. Howe's classic work still remains a standard book for all students of Canada. Rarely, if ever, has philatelic knowledge and literary excellence been so ably combined. Although almost thirty-five years have passed since its publication practically all the data and conclusions therein are still valid, and, as we amply show, the conclusions in some instances were amazingly accurate in spite of sparse data as compared with the wealth of material available to us.

When we began the compilation of data, and the study of stamps, covers, documents, etc., we were fortunate in having not only permission to use all the material gathered in preparation for the book proposed in 1926, but also, as our acknowledgments show, the unstinted co-operation of the leading authorities, not only in Philately, but in many fields of endeavor. We on our part had certain definite ideas as to the scope and plan of our work and in this regard we offer the following statements:

As the title implies this book is primarily concerned with the Postage Stamps and Postal Development of Canada. No explanation therefore is necessary for omitting revenue stamps. The issues of the Provinces of British Columbia, New Brunswick, Nova Scotia and Prince Edward Island are studies in themselves, and are touched on only insofar as they are reflected in the operation of the Canada Post Office, while the stamps and postal history of Newfoundland have been covered in a previous work.

Within these limitations, however, there is a vast amount of data and we were faced with the task of sifting this material, to keep the book within reasonable bounds. It was necessary, therefore, to establish principles to aid us in this selection of what to omit and what to include, as follows:

First:—By what authority was the stamp or marking issued, and what was its franking power? Our decision was to confine our study to items issued by the Post Office authorities, and with franking power throughout the jurisdiction of the issuing authority.

Second:—What is the general philatelic importance of the varieties or group discussed. This of course is an extremely variable factor, and what may be of significance in one issue may, contrariwise, be of little importance in another. This is further complicated by various opinions as to what is of philatelic significance. We have endeavored to be judicious in our choice, but are fully conscious of being unable to please everyone.

From the first of the principles briefly stated above, it can be readily seen that Locals, Semi-Official Airmails (which are a peculiarly limited type of local), etc., do not meet the requirements as outlined, whereas Metered Mail merits attention, such impressions being under the rigid supervision of the Post Office, and the franking power equal to that of other forms of stamps.

The Postage Dues, Special Delivery and Official Seals, while having limited or no franking power, were issued by the Post Office Department, and custom sanctions their inclusion.

From the second principle briefly given, we can say that the philatelic importance of varieties, generally speaking has become less significant in more recent years. The increased technical excellence in stamp production has tended to eliminate many of the varieties so dear to the heart of the collector.

Notice for instance the comparative rarity of re-entries on the 20th century stamps, as compared with those occurring on the stamps of the earlier years. This, coupled with the increasingly broad scope of the philatelic press, especially during the last two decades, provides readily available documentation for these issues. The establishment of the Philatelic Agency has also made much official information easily obtainable. As a consequence our treatment of these issues is not as full as some might like, but we are sure than even the most ardent collector of modern stamps will concede the reasonableness of our position.

When we come to the postal markings and cancellations our policy is along similar lines. We feel that Robson Lowe coined a happy phrase in terming the early "Paid" and similar markings as "Handstruck Postage Stamps," and we have unhesitatingly adopted that term in discussing these interesting forerunners of the adhesive stamp.

Our first thought in classifying the postal markings has been to study those supplied by the Post Office to the various Postmasters, and then those which are the product of the local postmaster, or advertising marks of no significance to the Postal Service. These principles are fully discussed in the introductory remarks on cancellations.

With respect to prices and valuations. Where necessary we have given definite figures. This is true in the case of the Handstruck Stamps, Essays, Proofs, Postal Stationery, etc., where there is no standard catalogue generally in use. Those groups, however, which are listed in either the Standard Postage Stamp Catalogue, published by Scott Publications, New York, or Stanley Gibbons Postage Stamp Catalogue, published by Stanley Gibbons, Ltd., London, Eng., are valued by a factor system, explained on a later page. The objection that this is too complicated to be understood, can be countered by the thought that anyone with enough intelligence to use this book should be intelligent enough to interpret the factor values. Futhermore, this system has two distinct advantages, viz: The relative values are constant, so that regardless of changes in the market the factors are the same, and the necessity of frequent revisions unnecessary; and by using Scott and S. G. numbers as a guide the tables are available to anyone with a catalogue or price list with these numbers as a basis. Whether John Doe's or Richard Roe's list are used the factors still apply.

The plan of the book is rather obvious, but the special groups have been taken up in the order of the appearance of the adhesive stamps. Thus the Registration stamps come first, followed by the Special Delivery, Postage Dues, etc. Each group, however, is preceded by the Handstruck forerunners, where they are known, to emphasize the historical continuity and development of each service.

Every effort has been made to make the arrangement as logical and consistent as possible throughout, but one of the fascinations, or should we say exasperations, of philately is its inconsistency!

The Appendices are voluminous, and could have been more so, but we confined most of them to the 19th Century for reasons noted previously. Enough, however, has been given so that students may test the validity and reasonableness of many of our conclusions. In so far as possible the source of our information has been stated, but in some instances it has been necessary to merely state that the facts are from sources that are reliable, but which at this time cannot be divulged. We plead the indulgence of our readers in these instances.

In conclusion we wish to say that this book is by no means the final word on many aspects of Canada's Philately, but simply an attempt to place in compact and readily available form, data for other students to continue investigations in their respective fields of research, and to stimulate further study of their collections.

THE AUTHOR

ACKNOWLEDGMENTS

It is a great pleasure as well as a source of pride and satisfaction to express publicly my gratitude and appreciation (albeit inadequately) to the persons named below who have so generously and graciously given of their time and knowledge; have loaned their most prized philatelic possessions for examination and illustration; have given permission to use information which is the result of many months or even years of study and research; or have assisted us in numerous other ways all of which are reflected in the content and arrangement of this book. Briefly we ask those who have made this book possible to take well merited "curtain calls."

First and foremost a debt of gratitude is owed, not only by us, but by all collectors and students of the stamps and postal history of Canada, a debt that can never be fully repaid, to

ALFRED F. LICHTENSTEIN
OF RED BANK, N. J.

whose magnificent collection of Canada, and authoritative knowledge was so freely placed at our disposal; which, coupled with the great mass of data so generously turned over to us has made it possible for our fellow philatelists to enjoy, and we venture to say rejoice in the flood of light thrown on all Canadian issues, and more particularly on the stamps issued before Confederation in 1867.

SENATOR JAMES A. CALDER, of Ottawa, and Regina. Another gentleman whose generosity has made possible the publication of much of the data on the Provincial Issues. All serious philatelists are greatly indebted to Senator Calder for his painstaking search and study of the Official records, as well as his magnificent work on the 1859 Issue; work which represents philately at its finest. In connection with these studies Senator Calder was awarded a Palm of Honor at the International Philatelic Exhibition, New York, in 1926. Later, at different times, he was awarded the three Medals of the Royal Philatelic Society, London.

MR. EUGENE N. COSTALES, Rockville Centre, N. Y., who was of great assistance in compiling the many tables; permitted free access to his unrivalled file of reference material; the unlimited use of his splendid philatelic library; the benefits of his vast fund of knowledge, the result of many years study and handling of stamps; as well as many other kindnesses too numerous to memtion.

MR. SPENCER ANDERSON, New York, N. Y. His fine stock of Canada was open to us, and of his staff MR. WILLIS CHENEY spent much time in going over material, making notes, and giving us other assistance.

MR. STANLEY B. ASHBROOK, Fort Thomas, Ky., for the loan of material for illustration as well as data on some obscure points of postal history.

MR. JERE HESS BARR, Reading, Pa., for the loan of items for illustration as well as many helpful suggestions.

MR. SIDNEY F. BARRETT, New York, N. Y., for his encouragement and helpful suggestions; as well as the loan of items for illustration.

MR. J. MURRAY BARTELS, New York, N. Y. This great authority of envelopes gave freely of his vast knowledge of United States and Canadian postal stationery, especially in regard to data concerning George F. Nesbitt, as well as loaning material for study on numerous points.

DR. JULIAN BLANCHARD, New York, N. Y., for the loan of many of the British American Bank Note Co. proofs, for suggestions and encouragement, and for his invaluable assistance in the complation and interpretation of statistical data.

MR. THOMAS E. BOGGS of Syracuse, N. Y., for the loan of a number of unusual early covers.

Mr. Nelson S. Bond, Roanoke, Va. His comprehensive list of Postal Stationery was most helpful, and his valuable study of the coils, booklets, and other data was generously placed at my disposal. His constructive criticism was of great assistance, especially from the viewpoint of what the collectors of Canada are looking for in the way of information.

Mr. Clarence W. Brazer, New York, N. Y. To him we owe the greatest part of the information we have concerning the engravers and printers, the designers and artists, and the essays and proofs of all Canadian issues. His Catalog of Essays for U. S. Adhesive Stamps published by the American Philatelic Society was of great assistance, and our chapter on the engravers and printers is largely from his magnificent historical study now appearing serially in the Collectors Club Philatelist.

Mr. David H. Burr, Gioversville, N. Y. This well known authority on postal stationery give us aid on the postal stationery chapter which was invaluable, as well as many suggestions, and help in numerous other ways concerning the planning of this book.

Mr. Frank Campbell, Royal Oak, Mich. His assistance was of great aid in the solution of some of the problems concerning the 1912-26 issues, and also the precancels.

Dr. Kenneth M. Day, Pittsburgh, Pa., for his kindness in sending us his fine collection of the Large and Small Queens, replete with re-entries, plate flaws, etc.; which were of great assistance in settling many of the problems surrounding these issues.

Mr. George R. M. Ewing, New York, N. Y., for data on the modern issues, particularly the 1930-35 series.

Mr. Carroll J. Frost, Ridgefield, N. J. For his assistance on the Canadian Railway Mail Service, including a complete set of the Official Schedules of 1942.

Professor R. DeL. French, McGill University, Montreal, P.Q. Generously turned over the revised Postal Stationery Catalogue for incorporation herein, and answered many of my queries, as well as reading the proofs of the postal stationery section.

The Late Mr. Gerard Gilbert, New York, and formerly Paris, France. This well known philatelist (who was in charge of the disposal of the great Ferrari Collection), was kindness itself in his many helpful suggestions, and his persistent ferreting out of some obscure points concerning the early issues. It was typical of him to give us many hours of his time in examining stamps, and discussing the problems surrounding them. His genial, urbane, and witty manner was always pleasant and it was a privilege to hear his wisdom on philatelic matters. We regret his passing and our inadequate tribute; such men as Gerard Gilbert are all too few in this world.

Mr. James Hallstein, Brooklyn, N. Y. His comprehensive collection of Canadian postal stationery was of great help in checking much of the published data on this interesting field.

Mr. Gordon Harmer, New York, N. Y., kindly loaned a number of unusual items for illustration, as well as called attention to several items of interest in the sales under his supervision.

Mr. Henry Harmer, New York, N. Y., generously loaned his well known collection of counterfeits and fakes, and was of assistance to us in several other ways.

Mr. C. F. Harwood, Tenafly, N. J., graciously loaned us a number of covers for illustration, and gave us a number of valuable suggestions.

Lt. Harrison D. S. Haverbeck, U.S.N.R., for his search through various records and newspapers for data on the Pence Issue.

Mr. Berton Hoover, New York, N. Y. for his assistance on the precancels, and permission to use such material as necessary from the Canadian Precancel Catalog.

Dr. Dard Hunter, of the Massachusetts Institute of Technology, Cambridge, Mass. This noted authority on paper and printing, very kindly assisted us in the solution of a number of problems in these fields of reasearch, as well as loaning material for illustration.

Mr. Ernest A. Kehr, New York, N. Y. The stamp editor of the New York Herald Tribune, opened his files to us, and also took many of the photographs which contribute greatly to this book.

Mr. A. L. Macready, Cobden, Ont., the publisher of "Popular Stamps" readily gave us permission to use such data that we found useful in his excellent little magazine.

Mr. George C. Marler, Montreal, P. Q. The authority on the 1912-26 issues unhesitatingly gave of his fund of knowledge on this most complicated series, as well as reading the proofs of that chapter.

Mr. Thomas F. Morris, Jr., New York, N. Y., loaned his fine collection of Canadian essays and proofs, as well as giving us considerable data on these interesting items. Mr. Morris' practical knowledge of the work of bank note engravers was of great assistance in the solution of many of the problems relating to plates, and plate varieties. Mr. Morris' father was an engraver, and at one time the chief of the engraving division of the Bureau of Engraving and Printing, Washington, D. C.

Mr. Pfeifer, Verona, N. J., a practical printer of many years experience who was of great aid in a number of problems of typography and similar processes.

Mr. Ruben C. Pierce, Dalton, Mass., the secretary of the famous Crane Paper Co., cordially assisted us in the analysis of the paper of the Pence issues.

Mr. Elliott Perry, Westfield, N. J., from whom we received many suggestions, constructive criticisms, and helpful information as well as a great deal of philatelic data from his vast store of such material, which did much to clarify and settle many disputed points, as well as placing the archives of *Pat Paragraphs* at our disposal.

Mr. Arthur Rankin, and Mr. Percy L. D. Rankin, Hamilton, Ont. To thank these gentlemen individually is difficult as they work so closely together. The Rankin brothers loaned us their fine collection of cancellations, and Mr. Arthur made the tedious search in the files of the *Hamilton Argus* for 1851 for items relating to stamps and postal history, and secured information on the U. E. Loyalists. Mr. Percy followed up my queries and patiently carried on a lengthy correspondence with me, as well as loaning me several items for illustration.

Lt. A. J. H. Richardson, R.C.N.R., Ottawa, Ont. His search in the Archives of Canada for data was of tremendous value, and his patient study of documents, led to much new data being discovered, as well as clearing up many points that were somewhat obscure.

Prof. A. V. Richardson, Lennoxville, P. Q., for his co-operation on the railway cancellations, and proof reading of this section, as well as many helpful suggestions.

Mr. Lawrence D. Shoemaker, Lakewood, Ohio, who placed at my disposal his file of material on the large and small Queens, and the 1912-26 issues, as well as spending much time in working on many of the problems of the Dominion Issues to 1912, and correlating the data on the 19th century cancellations.

Mr. Edward Stern, New York, N. Y., for the loan of many items for illustration and suggestions as to listings.

Capt. G. Nowell Usticke, New York, N. Y., loaned us many fine items for illustration as well as placing at our disposal the fine stock of Stanley Gibbons, Inc., New York, in which much of interest was found.

We are also indebted to the following publishers for permission to use material we saw fit to use from their various publications:

Mr. Franklin Bruns, Jr., editor of the Collector's Club Philatelist, and stamp editor of the New York Sun, for permission to use much of the material in Mr. Clarence Brazer's work on the engraving firms, appearing serially in that invaluable publication, as well as for other helpful suggestions, and the loan of material.

Mr. Hugh M. Clark, New York, N. Y., and The Catalogue Listing Committee of the Bureau Issues Association for permission to adapt the "Information for Collectors" in the "United States Stamp Catalogue", familiarly known as the "Specialized U. S.".

Messrs. Alfred A. Knopf, New York, N. Y., for permission to quote from "Paper-Making, The History and Technique of an Ancient Craft" by Dard Hunter, in Appendix P.

Mr. Harry L. Lindquist, New York, N. Y., generously permitted the use of much material on the various Canadian issues that appeared in the Stamp Specialist and Stamps Magazine.

Dr. Stephen G. Rich, Verona, N. J., who gave us helpful suggestions, and much sound advice, as well as generously permitting the use of any of his published material in various magazines, particularly in *Postal Markings*.

Mr. Prescott H. Thorp, Netcong, N. J., graciously granted us permission to use whatever we deemed of value from his magnificent new "Bartels Catalogue of U. S. Stamped Envelopes, Fifth Edition, Thorp, 1943."

Further we wish to express our gratitude to the following organizations for their work and aid:

Chase National Bank, Money Exhibit, particularly Mr. M. B. Schumacher, who had photographs made of various items on exhibit.

The Collector's Club, New York, N. Y., for the loan of the very fine collection of Large Queen issues; bequeathed by the late Mr. Charles Lathrop Pack.

The Post Office Department of Canada, the officials of which we found always courteous and helpful, and we especially wish to mention Mr. A. Stanley Deaville, and Mr. H. E. Atwater, both of whom are familiar to philatelists.

There are also several gentlemen who prefer to remain anonymous, a choice we regretfully concur with, but whose aid nevertheless was of great importance.

Our thanks must also go to the following who kindly loaned material or made suggestions which, while not large in themselves contributed to the completion of this work, and it would have been poorer without their assistance: Burger Bros., New York, N. Y.; Mr. Chas. L. Brisley, Detroit, Mich.; Mr. Cleveland Cady, Tenafly, N. J.; Mr. Elliott G. Corin, Glen Ridge, N. J.; Mr. Leslie A. Davenport, Toronto, Ont.; Mr. Sidney Harris, Brooklyn, N. Y.; Miss Althea Harvey, Windsor, Conn.; Mr. Herman Herst, Jr., New York, N. Y.; Mr. J. C. Martin, New York, N. Y.; Mr. W. L. L. Peltz, Albany, N. Y.; Lt. Sherman E. Rogers, Great Neck, L I., N. Y.; Mr. J. N. Sissons, Toronto, Ont., Mr. Paul Wise, New York, N. Y.; Mr. Ezra Cole, Nyack, N. Y.; Mr. E. M. Kemeny, Newark, N. J.

Last but not least a brief and inadequate appreciation in mentioning Mr. Theodore L. Chambers, of the publisher's firm, for his aid throughout this work, every page of which shows evidence of his care and attention, as well as his patience in handling masses of copy, complicated tables, complex revisions and corrections. In addition we were the recipient of many other kindnesses too numerous to mention without seeming to indulge in flattery.

To these people and organizations goes the credit for whatever virtues this book may possess, its faults however, are ours, and our alone.

THE AUTHOR

THE SYSTEM OF NUMBERING AND CLASSIFICATION EXPLAINED

Each classification of material listed herein has received an appropriate symbol *EXCEPT THE REGULARLY ISSUED POSTAGE STAMPS,* which are numbered in BOLD FACE without any prefix.

Each symbol, as nearly as possible suggests the classification in which the item belongs.

The principal classifications, alphabetically arranged are as follows:

Prefix AM is for Airmail Stamps.
Prefix BK is for Booklet Panes.
Prefix C is for Coil Stamps.
Prefix E is for Essays.
Prefix EM is for Exchange Markings.
Prefix H is for Handstruck Stamps.
Prefix LC is for Letter Cards.
Prefix MI is for Meter Indicia.
Prefix O is for Ocean Mail.
Prefix OS is for Official Seals.
Prefix P is for Proofs.
Prefix PB is for Postal Bands.
Prefix PC is for Postal Cards.
Prefix PD is for Postage Due Stamps.
Prefix PM is for Postal Markings.
Prefix PS is for Envelopes.
Prefix PW is for Publishers' Wrappers.
Prefix R is for Registered Letter Stamps.
Prefix S is for Specimens.
Prefix SD is for Special Delivery Stamps.
Prefix SM is for Manufacturers Samples.
Prefix TC is for Trial Color Proof.
Prefix WT is for War Tax Stamps.

The combination of two prefixes still further identifies certain items, thus:—

PPS is Proof of Postal Stationery.
EPS is Essay for Postal Stationery.
HPD is Handstuck Postage Due.
    etc.

The agreement of any number or classification with that of any other system or catalogue or price list is purely coincidental.

THE TABULAR INFORMATION AND FACTOR SYSTEM EXPLAINED

In order to present much of the data herein in compact form, a great deal of this important information has been given in tabular form. Also many of the tables have the values of the items given in terms of factors. We herewith explain the use and application of the symbols in these tables.

In the listings of the regular stamps, and those listed in the standard catalogues will be found two columns at the extreme right of the table giving the Scott and S. G. numbers of the stamp which is used as a basis for values. Thus Scott #22 may be the basis for the factors of multiplication in determining the value of other items in the table. "N" is the "Normal" or common stamp which is the basis referred to previously. Thus "N" is whatever the price given in any particular price list or catalogue is stated to be. If a variety has a factor of 3, then the normal price should be multiplied by that figure. Let us assume that $2.50 is the Catalogue price for N, then a variety with the factor 3 would be 3 x $2.50 or $7.50. A block may have a factor of 30. Thus if $2.00 is the price for a normal, then a block of four would be 30 x $2.00 or $60.00. In case where two factors are involved, such as a variety on cover then the most desirable factor should be given full value and the result multiplied by *one-half* of the less desirable factor, provided that the final result is not absurd, such as 50 x 25 = 1250 for a basic value of $1.00.

As will be noted most of the tables are divided vertically into a number of columns each with a symbol, numeral, or letter. The numbering of any item therefore should be suffixed by the column symbol. Thus a number 18C may indicate #18—Column C a certain type of paper or perforation. A variety of 18—thus 18aC would show it to be say an imperforate but on paper listed in column C. *Particular attention and care should be taken to use the proper upper and lower case letters, numerals, etc.,* so that no confusion will be caused *in* referring to such numbers.

An "x" in a price or value column indicates that such an item has **been noted, but insufficient data is available to warrant a valuation. It does NOT necessarily mean that the particular item is rare.**

FUNDAMENTAL INFORMATION FOR COLLECTORS OF CANADA

Index of Fundamental Information for Collectors of Canada

The index lists all terms with explanation or designates proper subject under which the explanation may be found.

Arrows .... See Plate Markings, Plate Diagrams
Batonne' Paper .... See Paper
Bi-colored Stamps .... See Printing
Bi-sects—Stamps cut in half so that each portion prepaid postage, used in emergencies where no stamps of the lower denomination were available. These may be cut diagonally, horizontally, or vertically. See below.

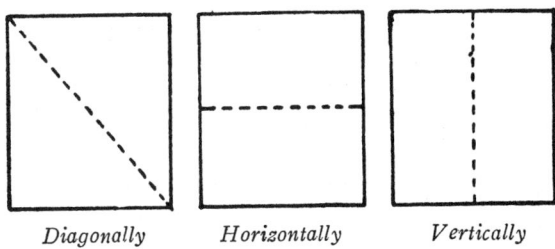

Diagonally *Horizontally* *Vertically*

Blocks .... See Plate
Booklet Panes .... See Plate, Plate Diagrams
Booklets .... See Plate, Plate Diagrams

Cancellations .... See Postal Markings
Coils .... See Plate
Color Trials .... See Printing
Commemorative Stamps—Special stamps issued to commemorate some event of local, national or historical importance. As a rule stamps of this class are in use for only a limited period and frequently they are in concurrent use with the ordinary series. Canadian Commemoratives begin with the Jubilee Issue of 1897.
Compound Perforation .... See Perforations
Corner Blocks .... See Plate
Cracked Plate .... See Plate
Crystallization Cracks .... See Plate
Curvature Cracks .... See Plate
Cut Square—A term adopted to designate an envelope stamp cut rectangularly from the envelope, or post card.

Diagonal Half .... See Bi-sect
Die .... See Plate
Double Impression .... See Printing
Double Paper .... See Paper
Double Perforation .... See Perforations
Double Transfer .... See Plate
Dry Print .... See Printing

Embossed Printing .... See Printing
Engraving .... See Printing

Error—A stamp is called an error when it differs from the normal variety by some mistake or omission in the inscription, color, paper, impression, watermark, or perforation.

Essay ....See Printing

First Day Cover—A philatelic term to designate the use of a certain stamp (on cover) on the first day of sale at a place officially designated for such sale and so postmarked.

Flat Plate Printing ....See Printing
Flat Press Printing..See Printing
Gripper Cracks ....See Plate
Guide Dots ....See Plate
Guide Lines ....See Plate Markings, Plate Diagrams
Guide Line Blocks..See Plate
Gutter ....See Plate Markings, Plate Diagrams
Handstruck Stamps..See Postal Markings
Hidden Plate Number ....See Plate
Horizontal Half ....See Bi-sect

Imperforate ....See Perforations
Imprint ....See Plate Markings, Plate Diagrams
Imprint Blocks...See Plate, Plate Diagrams
India Paper ....See Paper
Intaglio ....See Printing
Inverted Center ....See Printing
Joint Line Pair...See Plate
Laid Paper ....See Paper
Line Engraved ....See Printing
Line Pair ....See Plate
Lithography ....See Printing

Manila Paper ....See Paper
Margin ....See Plate Markings
Margin Blocks ....See Plate
Margin Block with Arrow ....See Plate, Plate Diagrams
Margin Block with Imprint.......................................See Plate, Plate Diagrams
Margin Block with Plate No..See Plate
Margin Block with Plate Letter..See Plate
Meter ....See Metered Mail
Offset ....See Printing

Original Gum—A stamp is described as "O.G." (original gum) when it has the original gum as applied at the time it was issued.

Overprint ....See Printing

Pair Imperf. Between..See Perforations
Pane ....See Plate
Part Perforate ....See Perforations
Paste-Up ....See Plate
Paste-Up Pair ....See Plate

Patriotic Covers—Envelopes of the Boer War Period showing patriotic designs or verses. Occasionally U. S. Patriotics of the Civil War period were used in Canada in the 1860's.

Pelure Paper ....See Paper
Plate Arrangement ....See Plate, Plate Diagrams
Plate Flaws ....See Plate
Plates for Stamp Booklets ....See Plate, Plate Diagrams
Plates for Coil Stamps..See Plate, Plate Diagrams
Plate Markings ....See Plate, Printing, Plate Diagrams
Plate Numbers ....See Plate, Plate Diagrams
Postal Markings, History of ....See Postal Markings
Postmarks ....See Postal Markings

Printing, Kinds of ....See Printing
Printing Order ....See Printing, Plate Diagrams
Printed on Both Sides ....See Printing
Proofs ....See Printing
Propaganda Covers—Envelopes carrying inscriptions appertaining to Cheaper Postage, Temperance, Anglo-Saxon Unity, etc.
Railroad Postmarks ....See Postal Markings
Receiving Mark ....See Postal Markings
Recess ....See Printing
Recut ....See Plate
Recutting ....See Plate
Re-engraved ....See Plate
Re-entry ....See Plate
Registry Markings ....See Plate Markings, Plate Diagrams
Relief ....See Plate
Reprints ....See Printing
Retouch ....See Plate
Rotary Press Printings ....See Printing
Rough Perforation ....See Perforations
Rouletting ....See Perforations

Se-tenant—(French—"joined together"). Used in speaking of an unsevered pair of stamps of different values or of different design, with different types of surcharge, or differing in some manner.
Sheet ....See Plate, Plate Diagrams
Ship Postmarks ....See Postal Markings
Short Transfer ....See Plate
Slogans ....See Postal Markings
Stampless Covers—Prior to the issuance of Canadian Government adhesive postage stamps, and until 1875, letters were mailed "collect" or, postage was prepaid in cash. In such instances the covers often bear in addition to the town postmark notations such as "Paid," "Paid 10," etc. See Handstruck Stamps.
  While many of these covers have no great commercial value they are of historical value to collectors interested in the postal history and operations of the Canadian Post Office Department.
Stitch Watermark ....See Paper
Strip—A number of unsevered stamps forming a vertical or horizontal row.
Surcharges ....See Printing

Tete-beche—A French term applied to stamps printed upside down in relation to one another. Tete-beche stamps must be collected in pairs, as when separated the stamps will show no peculiarity.
Tied On ....See Postal Markings
Transfer ....See Plate
Transfer Roll ....See Plate
Triple Transfer ....See Plate
Type—Generally means the design of the stamp. It may be used when two stamps are described as being of the same type, and it would mean that the design of both is identical, though they may differ as regards color, paper, perforation or value.
  Also may have reference to the printer's type used in making an overprint.
  As used in Handbook refers to minor differences and to illustrations of stamps.
Type Set ....See Printing
Typography ....See Printing
Vertical Half ....See Bi-sect
Watermarks ....See Paper
Worn Plate ....See Plate, Printing
Wove Paper ....See Paper

EXPLANATION OF TERMS

Grouped under subjects in the following order:

    I.   Plate.
   II.   Printing.
  III. Paper.
  IV. Perforations.
   V.   Postal Markings and Cancellations.

Section I-A. Plate—Line Engraving (Intaglio, Recess).
The Process.

1. *Die.* Making the *"die"* is the initial operation. The *"die"* is a small flat piece of soft steel on which the subject (design) is recess engraved in reverse by engraving tools and etching. After the engraving is completed, the *"die"* is hardened to withstand the stress of subsequent operations.

2. *Transfer Roll.* The next operation is the making of the *"transfer roll"* which, as its name implies, is the medium used to transfer the subject from the *"die"* to the *"plate."* A blank roll of soft steel, mounted on a mandrel, is placed under the bearers of a *"transfer press,"* so as to allow it to roll freely on its axis. The hardened *"die"* is placed on the bed of the press and the face of the roll is brought to bear on the *"die"* under pressure. The bed is then rocked back and forth under increasing pressure until the soft steel of the roll is forced into every line of the *"die."* The resulting impression on the roll is known as a *"relief"* or a *"relief transfer";* and several *"reliefs"* are usually rocked in on each roll. After the required *"reliefs"* have been made, the roll is hardened.

3. *Relief.* A *"relief"* is the normal reproduction of the design on the *"die"* in reverse. A *"defective relief,"* caused by a minute piece of foreign material lodging on the *"die,"* may occur during the *"rocking in"* process, or from other causes. Imperfections in the steel of the transfer roll may also result in a breaking away of parts of the design; and if the damaged relief is continued in use it will transfer a repeating defect to the plate. Also, reliefs are sometimes deliberately altered. *"Broken relief"* and *"altered relief"* are terms used to designate these changed conditions.

4. *Plate.* A flat piece of soft steel replaces the *"die"* on the bed of the transfer press and one of the *"reliefs"* on the transfer roll is brought to bear on it. The position on the plate is determined by *"position dots,"* which have been lightly marked on the plate in advance. After the position of the *"relief"* is determined, pressure is brought to bear and, by following the same method used in the making of the transfer roll, a *"transfer"* is entered, which reproduces in reverse every detail of the design of the *"relief."* As many *"transfers"* are entered on the plate as there are to be subjects.

The operation of transferring the design to a plate is known as "Siderography" and the operator is a "siderographer."

After the required *"transfers"* have been entered, the position dots, layout dots and lines, scratches, etc. are generally burnished out; and any required "guide lines," "plate numbers" or other marginal markings are added. A *proof* impression is then taken and if "certified" (approved), the plate is machined for fitting to the press, hardened and sent to the plate vault as being ready for use. The early plates, however, were not hardened and could therefore be re-cut or re-entered to sharpen the impressions.

Rotary press plates, after being certified, require additional machining. They are curved to fit the press cylinder and "gripper slots" are cut into the back of each plate to receive the "grippers," which hold the plate securely in the press, after which the plate is hardened.

The present practice of chromium plating the steel plates reduces wear and secures increased production, as the plates may be replated many times. This process was introduced in 1927.

5. *Transfer.* An impression entered on the plate by the transfer roll. A *"relief transfer"* is also made when entering the design of the die on the transfer roll.

6. *Double Transfer or Re-entry.* A term used to describe the condition of a *"transfer"* on a plate that shows evidences of a duplication of all, or a portion of the design. It is usually the result of the changing of the registration between the *"relief"* and the *"plate"* during the rolling in of the original entry. It is sometimes necessary to remove the original *"transfer"* from a plate and enter the *"relief"* a second time, when the finished re-transfer shows indications of the original *"transfer,"* due to incomplete erasure, the result is also a *"double transfer."*

7. *Triple Transfer.* Similar to a *"double transfer"* but showing evidences of a third entry or two duplications.

8. *Re-entry.* When executing a *"re-entry,"* the transfer roll is reapplied to the plate at some time after it has been put to press. Thus, worn-out designs may be resharpened by carefully re-entering the transfer roll. If not very carefully entered, the registration will not be true and a *"double transfer"* will result. With the protective qualities of "chrome plating" it is no longer necessary to resharpen the plate. In fact—after a plate has been curved for the rotary press it is impossible to make a re-entry.

9. *Short Transfer.* It sometimes happens that the transfer roll is not rocked its entire length in the entering of a transfer on a plate, with the result that the finished transfer fails to show the complete design. This is known as a *"short transfer"* and the plate of the 3d 1851 has several examples of this.

10. *Re-engraved.* A term used in connection with *"line engraving."* Either the die that has been used to make a plate or the plate itself may have its "temper" drawn (softened) and be re-cut. The resulting impressions from such re-engraved die or plate may differ very slightly from the original issue, and are known as "re-engraved."

11. *Re-cut.* A "re-cut" is line strengthening or altering by use of an engraving tool on unhardened plates.

12. *Re-touching.* A "re-touch" is line strengthening or altering by means of etching.

Section I-B. Plate—Arrangement (See Also Plate Diagrams Appendix Q).

1. *Arrangement.* The first engraved plates used to produce Canadian postage stamps in 1851 contained 200 subjects. The number of subjects to a plate varied between 100 and 200 subjects until the Jubilee issue of 1897, when 50 subject plates were first laid down. Since that time, the size of plate has varied considerably. These are duly noted in the respective issues.

2. *Plate-Marking.* The name of the manufacturer, plate number, denomination, lines, arrows, or any other marking not part of the stamp design appearing on the plate. (See Section I-D.)

3. *Sheet.* In single color printings the impression from a plate is termed a *"sheet."* A *"sheet"* of bi-colored stamps requires the impressions from two plates, one for each color.

4. *Pane.* A pane is a portion of the original sheet as cut for sale at the post offices. A pane may be an entire sheet where the plate is small, or it may be a half or quarter of a sheet where the plate is large.

Panes are classified according to their position on the printed sheet by being designated "U.L." (Upper Left), "U.R." (Upper Right), "L.L." (Lower Left) and "L.R." (Lower Right). Where only two panes appear on a sheet, they are designated "R" (Right), "L" (Left), "T" (Top) or "B" (Bottom), depending on whether the sheet is divided vertically or horizontally.

To fix the location of a particular stamp on any pane, the pane is held with the subjects in the normal position and a number is given to each stamp starting with the first stamp in the upper left corner and proceeding horizontally to the right, then starting on the second row at the left and across to the right, and so on to the last stamp in the lower right corner. All references to the plate positions are to the printed sheet.

5. *Plates for Stamp Booklets.* These are illustrated and fully described on the pages showing plate layouts, Appendix Q.

6. *Booklets.* These are stamps issued in small booklets for the convenience of users. They are sold by the Post Office Department at a small premium. Booklets are supplied in panes of four or six stamps each.

7. *Booklet Panes.* Small panes (of four or six stamps) especially printed and cut to be sold in booklets. Panes are straight-edged on bottom and both sides but perforated between the stamps. See: "Booklets."

Section I-C. Coil Stamps.

1. *Coils.* Stamps issued by the Canadian P. O. Department in rolls for use in affixing or vending machines. Perforated horizontally or vertically only.

2. *Line Pair.* Pair of stamps with guide line between. See: Guide Lines.

3. *Joint Line Pair.* On rotary coils a line of color (not a "guide line") shows between the stamps where the curved rotary plates meet or join on the press.

4. *Paste-Up Pair.* Pairs of stamps at the junction *(paste-up)* of two sheets of flat plate printings joined for making coil stamps.

5. *Hidden Plate Number.* Plate number hidden by a *"paste-up,"* on flat plate printings.

6. *Coil Plate Numbers.* Rather scarce as plate numbers on "coil" sheets are placed so as to be cut off when the rotary sheets are cut into coils. The only times they are found is when the sheets were cut off-center.

Section I-D. Plate Markings.

1. *Guide Lines.* Horizontal or vertical colored lines between the stamps, and extending wholly or partially across the sheet are known as *"guide lines,"* and serve as guides for the operators of perforating machines, or to indicate the line of separation of the sheet into panes.

2. *Gutters.* Ordinarily when guide lines are used to divide the sheet into panes the spaces between the panes are not greater than the space between any other of the stamps on the sheet. On some plates, however, a wide space or *"Gutter,"* is left between the panes and on such plates the "guide lines" usually do not appear.

A block of stamps showing this wide space running between is called a "Gutter Block."

3. *Arrows.* On certain issues guide lines were not used but marginal arrow shaped markings, known as *"arrows,"* were substituted, and served the same purpose as the guide lines.

A marginal block of 4 stamps showing the *"arrow"* centered at one edge is called an *"Arrow"* Block. But the number of stamps in the block need not necessarily be limited to four.

4. *Registry Markings.* Various shaped marks used as an aid in properly registering the frame and vignette impressions of bi-colored stamps. In the Handbook listing these *"registry markings"* are referred to as *"register marks."*

5. *Imprint.* The name of the producer of the stamps, appearing on the sheet margins sometimes adjoining the plate numbers, when such are put on the plate. All Imprints listed in the Handbook are numbered for convenience of identification.

A block of stamps with the sheet margin attached, on which appears the "imprint" is known as an "Imprint Block." Imprints are generally collected in blocks of six, or of sufficient size to include the entire imprint. Needless to say this does not apply to early issues where singles showing part of imprint are of importance.

6. *Plate Numbers or Letters.* Serial numbers or letters assigned to plates, appearing on one or more margins of the sheet or pane to identify the plate.

A marginal block of 6 or 8 stamps with the plate number centered in the adjoining sheet margin is the usual manner of collecting flat plate numbers, and is known as a "plate block." Rotary press plate numbers are collected in blocks of 4 with the number, on the attached sheet margin, appearing opposite one of the corners of the block. Plate numbers take a further designation from the position on the sheet on which they appear, thus there would be U.L. (Upper Left), etc.

7. *"C.S." and "C."* Indicate that the plate is made of "Chrome Steel."

8. *"PO"* followed by a number in reverse (1903-12) on the printed sheet is for "Printing Order" number. Later the printing order number was regularly entered near the top imprint, or at the lower left of the plate.

9. *"Top."* A marking on the top and bottom sheet margin of printings from certain King Edward VII plates.

10. *Initials.* Initials in sheet margins of 20th century issues were used to identify individuals in the Bank Note plant, who participated in the production or use of the plates.

11. *Margin.* The border outside the printed design of a stamp, or the similar border of a sheet of stamps A block of stamps from the top, side or bottom of a sheet or pane to which is attached the margin is known as a *"Margin Block."* A block of stamps from the corner of a sheet with full margins attached to two adjoining sides is known as a *"Corner Block."*

Note. In the foregoing, we have designated that a certain number of stamps make up an Arrow or Plate Number Block. Naturally any block of stamps, no matter how large or small, which had an arrow or a plate number on its margin would be designated by that name. But, the general practice is to collect flat Plate Numbers in margin blocks of 6 or 8 and Arrow Blocks in margin blocks of 4. Plate Number Blocks from rotary press printings are generally collected in blocks of 4 as the plate number usually occurs on the side of the stamp at the upper or lower corners of the sheet.

Section II-A. Printing.

1. *Methods Used.* The methods employed in producing Canadian stamps include two of the basic forms of printing, viz.: "Intaglio," and "Typography."

2. *Intaglio-Engraved or Recess.* In this process the ink is received and held in lines depressed below the surface of the plate, and in printing from these plates the damp paper is forced down into the depressed lines and retains the color. In consequence the lines on the face of the stamp are slightly raised and when seen from the back of the stamp are slightly depressed.

3. *Inking the Plate.* The plate on the press has to be kept warm and this is done in various ways on the different types of press which we will describe in due course. The ink is applied to the plate in such a manner as to force it into the recessed lines of the design. There are automatic inking arrangements on the power presses, but, generally speaking the hand dabber is the most effective. This literally punches the ink into the lines. After the ink has been applied so as to fully charge the recessed lines, all the surplus ink on the surface of the plate has to be removed by wiping, and the plate is then polished with the palm of the hand. The human hand is unrivalled as a polishing medium, and the operator before applying his hand covers it with some whiting or chalk. In wiping and polishing care has to be exercised to avoid removing any of the ink from the sunken lines.

Because of the necessity of the paper being forced into the lines to "pull" the ink it cannot be too strongly emphasized that many impressions from so-called *worn* plates are simply due to poor inking, dry paper, poor plate wiping, caking of the ink or chalk in the lines of the engravings, as well as other causes.

In order that this be clearly understood we take the liberty of quoting Senator J. A. Calder on the subject. He says (on page 43 et seq.) in his book "SOME PHASES OF THE CANADA '59 ISSUE":

"In continuing to work on the problem there was always present a feeling that a *shade* was a very illusive sort of intangible thing that was most difficult to keep fixed. Time and again, when clear definite proof existed from dated material that a printing had been made in a certain colour (or a shade thereof) at a certain definite period of time, other stamps would persist in continuing to bob up in the same period that simply would not fit in. These "off" shades in many cases differed but slightly—but there were many marked types that continued to be very troublesome.

As a consequence of this perplexing situation it was for the first time realized that if progress was to be made it could only be done through intimate contact with a pressman and his tools. Fortunately there was located in Ottawa in actual use by the Canadian Bank Note Co., an old hand press of much the same type as that used between 1859 and 1868 for the printing of the Canadian stamps of that period. There followed two days of observation and study of all the printing processes of this press from the making of the batch of ink to be used to the drying of the printed sheets. As a consequence of this study many difficulties disappeared, *and it was clearly seen and definitely established that from the same batch of ink, properly made and uniformly mixed, it was possible to produce a variety of shades the extremes of which had but slight if any resemblance, except that they might be referred to as red, or green, etc., as the case might be.*

In order that this haphazard production of shades *from the same ink* may be understood it is first necessary to define what may be called a normally printed stamp of that period. To produce such a stamp the following requirements were essential and had to be strictly adhered to:

(a) the preparation of a batch of ink of the correct consistency, properly made and uniformly and thoroughly mixed;

(b) making certain that the engraved lines on the plate were open and not clogged up with dried-up old ink;

(c) daubing the ink on the plate in such a manner as to make certain that all the hollows of the engraved lines were completely filled;

(d) by using cheese-cloth or its equivalent the thorough removal of all surplus ink from the surface of the plate, thereby leaving ink in the engraved lines only;

(e) a systematic and complete burnishing of the plate with the palm of the hand to make certain that a thin sheet or scum of ink was not left on the surface;

(f) the proper fixing of the plate in the press with the necessary preparations and adjustments to ensure that the pressure between plate and sheet would be just sufficient and no more or no less;

(g) the dampening of the sheets to be printed to such a degree—not too wet or too dry—as would enable them to take from the plate the correct quantity of ink;

(h) making certain that in the printing of a sheet of paper the time of contact between the plate and the sheet would be just right—not too long or short;

(i) the removal of the printed sheets from the press and their proper drying in the correct way.

Should all these details in printing a series of sheets be attended to carefully and correctly—the resulting stamps would all be of the same colour and shade. The so-called normally printed stamps thus produced are always bright in colour and shade. Those portions of the design that are free from engraved lines and that are not intended to be inked are always distinctly white when paper of this colour is used. As a general rule stamps thus printed are much scarcer than all other types.

Whenever a departure—through carelessness or neglect—was made from any of the printing processes or arrangements referred to, the result was always a sheet of stamps of a different shade. If the departure was slight the variation in shade would be so slight that it would not likely be discernible. On the other hand, if the departure was marked a distinct shade would be the result. Between these extremes, as well as through various combinations of defects in these printing processes, there was ample scope to produce a variety of shades from the one batch of ink used.

It can be readily understood that in the actual production of these stamps during the 1859-67 period the pressman on the work was not particularly interested in normally printed stamps. His task was to get the job done, and if negligence or carelessness crept into some of his operations and arrangements it was quite excusable." Furthermore it is generally known that in those days almost every printer made his own color, grinding the material himself and producing thereby his own ink. If for any reason the colors were not properly mixed or the ink was not sufficiently well made, an excess of oil might get on the plate, leaving too much pigment on the press roller. This produced a watery appearance, and weak color.

From the above it can thus be seen that care should be taken in dating and classifying shades, and that where the change is not intentional the value of various shades is a matter for the collector to decide.

We refer our readers to Chapter on the Small Queens Issues, where leaves from the printers ink mixing book are illustrated.

4. *Lithography.* A common and the cheapest process for printing stamps. In this method the design is drawn by hand or transferred from an original engraving to the surface of a lithographic stone or metal plate in greasy ink. The stone or plate is wet with an acid fluid, which causes it to repel the printing ink except on the greasy lines of the design. A fine lithographic print closely resembles an engraving, but the lines are not raised on the face or depressed on the back, and there is usually a duller appearance in the lithograph than in the engraving. Passing the edge of the finger nail lightly over the lines of the design will sometimes assist in distinguishing a lithographed from an engraved stamp. Up to now this method has not been used for Canadian stamps.

5. *Offset.* See "Printed on Both Sides."

6. *Typography.* The exact reverse of engraved plate printing. In this process the parts of the design which are to show in color are left at the original level of the plate and the spaces between are cut away. The ink is applied to the raised lines on the plate and the pressure of printing forces these lines, more or less, into the paper, impressing the colored lines of the face of the stamp and slightly raising them on the back of the stamp. In practice a large number of electrotypes of the original are made and assembled together into a plate with the requisite number of designs for printing a sheet of stamps. Stamps printed by this process show great uniformity, and the process is cheaper than intaglio printing. Used for postal stationery and surcharges or overprints.

7. *Embossed Printing.* A method in which the design is sunk in the metal of the die and the printing is done against a yielding platen such as linoleum or leather, which is forced up into the depression of the die, thus forming the design on the paper in relief. Embossing may be done without color, or with part color and part colorless, as the Canadian stamped envelopes.

Section II-B. Printing—Terms Used.

1. *Bi-Colored Stamps.* Those printed in two colors, in which a central picture in one color is surrounded by ornamental inscription or framing of another color. In bi-colored stamps two printings are required, and if the sheet is fed to the press in reversed position, after one color has been printed, the part printed in the second color will, of course, be upside down and the stamps will have "inverted centers."

2. *Color Trials.* These printings in various colors made to facilitate selection of color for the issued stamps.

3. *Double Impression.* A second impression of a stamp over the original impression, should not be confused with a "double transfer" which is a plate

imperfection and does not show a doubling of the entire design. A double impression shows every line clearly doubled. See: "Printed on Both Sides."

4. *Essay.* A design submitted in stamp form but not necessarily accepted for issuance. Printings in various colors other than the issued stamp are known as "Color Trials." See: "Color Trials."

5. *Inverted Center.* A stamp with the center printed upside down in relation to the rest of the design. See: "Bi-colored Stamps."

6. *Flat Plate Printing.* See: "Flat Press Printing."

7. *Flat Press Printing.* Stamp printed on the ordinary flat-bed press, as distinguished from rotary press printing. See: "Plate."

8. *Overprint.* (Commonly called *"Surcharge"*). Any word, inscription or device printed across the face of a stamp altering its use, or its locality, or overprinted for a special purpose, as "World's Grain Exhibition & Conference Regina 1933" in honor of the International Grain Congress, etc. See: "Surcharge."

9. *Printed on Both Sides.* Occasionally a sheet of stamps already printed will, through error, be turned over and passed through the press a second time, thus creating the rare "printed on both sides" variety. This is often confused with an *offset* which occurs when sheets of stamps are stacked while the ink is still wet. There is, however, an outstanding difference; the *"printed on both sides" variety shows a positive design (all inscriptions reading correctly) on both sides of the paper. An "offset" shows a reverse impression on the back of the stamp, that is, all wording, etc., reading backwards.* See: "Double Impression."

10. *Proofs.* Trial printings of a stamp made from the original die or the finished plate. Those from the *die* are *Die Proofs,* while those from the plate are *Plate Proofs.*

11. *Reprints.* Impressions from the original plates, blocks, or stones, from which the original stamps were printed, taken after the issuance of the stamps to post offices had ceased and their use for postal use had been voided. Notably the 1860 envelopes reprinted in 1868.

12. *Rotary Press Printings.* These are stamps which have been printed on a rotary type press from curved plates as compared to stamps printed from flat plates on a flat bed press. See: "Plate."

13. *Surcharge.* An overprint which alters the face value or denomination of the stamp to which it was applied. Most Canadian "surcharges" are typographed. See: "Overprints."

14. *Type Set.* Made from movable type. Printed from ordinary printer's type, just as a book or newspaper is printed. Sometimes electrotype or stereotype plates are made.

Section II-C. Printing—Common Flaws.

1. *Cracked Plate.* A term to describe stamps which show evidences that the plate, from which they were printed, was cracked.

Plate cracks arise from various causes, each resulting in a different formation of the crack and its intensity. Cracks in the older issues are largely due to too-quick immersion in the cooling bath when being tempered. These cracks are known as crystallization cracks. A jagged line running generally in one direction and most often in the gutter between stamps is due to the stress of the steel during the rolling in or transferring process.

In curved plates (rotary) there are two types of cracks. One is the bending or curving crack, which is quite marked and always runs in the direction in which the plate is curved.

The second type, which is the "Gripper Crack" and is caused by the cracking of the plate over the slots cut in the under side of the plate, which receive the "grippers" that fasten the plate to the press. These occur only on curved plates and are to be found in the row of stamps adjacent to the plate joint, and appear on the printed impression as light irregular colored lines generally parallel to the plate joint line.

2. *Rosette Crack.* A cluster of fine cracks radiating from a central point in irregular lines. Usually caused by the plate receiving a blow.
3. *Scratched Plate.* Caused by foreign matter scratching the plate. These are usually too minor to mention. See: "Gouge."
4. *Gouge.* Exceptionally heavy scratch or dent and may be caused by a tool falling on the plate, usually short in length. The "Weeping Princess" variety is a notable example.
5. *Surface Stains.* Irregular circular marks resembling the outline of a pond on a map, sometimes called "splashes" Authorities differ as to the cause and they are too minor to list.

Section III-A. Paper.

(See also Appendix P).

Paper consists of vegetable fibres, linen, cotton, straw, wood and certain grasses, which, after being pulped and bleached, are spread evenly and thinly, by hand or machinery first upon a wire cloth. The resultant film consolidates into a wet web of pulp, which being passed to felt cloths and through other processes becomes a sheet of paper. This is then finished and cut into sheets for printing. Any coloring is added to the pulp mixture before it is run on the wire cloths, or the mould is diped in it.

1. *The Texture of the Paper.* The wire cloth is the most important part of the machine, or mould, in the case of handmade paper, from the philatelic point of view, as it is upon the texture of this wire cloth that the character of paper depends, and it is on this that the "watermark" designs are introduced. Wove paper is produced when the wire cloth is evenly interwoven and the paper shows scarcely any sign of the texture except when magnified, when small diamond or square shaped specks betray the crossing of the wire lines, forming small diamond or square shaper interstices. *Laid* paper is produced when the wire cloth is composed of regular lines running longitudinally and close together crossed at wide intervals by other wires, which keep the wire cloth flat and even. The lines, both longitudinal and cross ones, show in the paper when finished.

2. *Wove.* When the wire of the mould or of the dandy-roll is woven like cloth instead of in parallel lines (as in *laid*) the paper produced is known as *wove.* The wires of the mould or dandy-roll for wove paper are finer and cross each other diagonally, and a close examination or an enlargement of the paper texture will reveal tiny diamond-shaped interstices formed by the crossing of the wires. May be either hand made or machine made.

3. *Laid Paper.* When the wire forming the base of the mould (in hand made paper) is composed of parallel lines set close together the resulting paper is termed "laid," in contradistinction to wove (q.v.). In all cases of laid papers there are tying wires crossing the ordinary waterlines to keep the wires level, and these show more prominently than the laid lines. The lines close together are known as *vergeures*, while the lines crossing at wide intervals are *batonne' lines.* Modern *laid papers* are produced by machine and are really wove papers watermarked with lines to simulate the old hand made laid papers.

4. *Pelure.* This refers to the substance rather than the texture and is a term used by philatelists, evidently taken from the French word *pelure,* signifying a paring, skin, peel; pointing to a very thin (about .002" thick), strong and hard paper such as is found in some of the early stamps of the South African Republic, Arequipa (Peru), New Zealand, etc. It differs from tissue in its hardness, tissue always being soft and porous. It may be wove or laid. The very thin papers of the Pence stamps are sometimes termed "pelure."

5. *Manila.* Manila paper is a coarse paper made of manila hemp fibre. It is used for cheaper grades of envelopes and newspaper wrappers. It is usually of a light brown color and may be wove or laid.

6. *India Paper.* A thin handmade paper about .0025" thick. It varies in thickness in the sheet and shows small defects, such as air gaps which resemble pin holes, light spots, fibres, etc. It is white to yellowish in color. Immersion

in water is very injurious. Older writers called it Proof Paper. It is particularly suited for sinking into the lines of a steel plate engraved in recess, and extracts a maximum of ink without smearing. Die proofs and plate proofs of postage stamps are generally printed on this paper, which shows off the engraving at its best.

7. *Bond Paper.* A thin tough crisp wove paper, made from linen, and resembling the paper on which the issued stamps were printed. White or grayish in color. Usually about .003″ thick. Used frequently for proof impressions, as it takes an impression similar to the paper actually used on the issued stamps. Known in the trade as "Bank Note" paper.

8. *Double Paper.* Rotary press printings are occasionally found printed on a double sheet of paper. The web of paper used on these presses must be continuous, therefore any break in the process of manufacture must be lapped and pasted. This overlapping portion when printed, is known as a *"Double Paper"* variety. Examples of this overlap occuring on paper for flat press printings are also known.

Paper is also distinguished as thick or thin, hard or soft, and by its color, as bluish, yellowish, greenish, etc.

Section III-B. Paper—Watermarks.

1. Closely allied to the paper, as they are usually formed in the process of manufacturing the paper. Watermarks of Canada consist of the words *E & G Bothwell, Clutha Mills* (1868), *Alexander Pirie & Sons* (1873), *Ca PO D* (1860), or *U S PO D* (1868) and are composed of double-lined letters. They are formed of wire or cut from metal and soldered to a roll under which the pulp is passed. The action of these is similar to the wires causing the "laid" lines, the designs making thin places in the paper which show by transmitting light. The best method to detect them is to lay the stamp face down on a tray with a black background and immerse in benzine (petroleum ether), which brings up the watermark in dark lines against a lighter background.

All watermarks listed in the Handbook are numbered for convenience of identification.

Paper watermarked *USPOD* was used for the reprints of the 1860 envelopes.

2. *Stitch Watermark.* A type of watermark consisting of a row of short parallel lines. This is caused by the stitches, which join the ends of the band on which the paper pulp is first formed, or in a handmade paper it is due to repairs to the screen of the mould. "Stitch watermarks" have been found on a great many issues and may exist on all.

Stitch Watermark

Section IV Perforations.

1. *Perforation.* The chief style of separation of stamps, and the one which today is in almost universal use, is called "perforating." By this process the paper between the stamps is cut away in a line of holes, usually round, leaving little bridges of paper between the stamps to hold them together until they are to be separated. These little bridges are called the teeth of the perforation, and of course project from the stamp when it is torn from the sheet. As the

gauge of the perforation is often a guide to the date of issue of the stamp, it is necessary to measure them and describe them by a gauge number. Thus we say a stamp is perforated 12 or 13½. This does not mean that there are 12 or 13½ perforations on the side or end of the stamp, but that 12 or 13½ perforations can be counted in the space of two centimeters. This space has been arbitrarily adopted by philatelists the world over as the length in which perforation shall be measured, and the number of perforations in two centimeters is called the gauge of that perforation. Thus a stamp perforated 12 would have perforations so spaced, that twelve of them would measure exactly two centimeters. Canadian stamps from 1859 to 1912 were usually perforated 12, or 11½ x 12, and give readily obtainable material for testing the above rule.

2. *Perforation Gauge.* Gauge for measuring perforations as above. An *accurately printed gauge* is a necessity for every collector.

3. *Rough Perforation.* Holes not clean cut, but with small discs of paper still filling them.

4. *Compound Perforation.* Where perforations at the top and bottom differ from the perforations at the sides In describing "compound perforations" the gauge of the top is given first, then the sides.

5. *Double Perforations.* Often found on early Canadian revenue stamps and occasionally on regular postage issues, double perforations being applied in error. They do not command any premium over catalogue prices of properly perforated stamps.

6. *Imperforate.* Stamps without perforations, rouletting or other forms of separation between them.

7. *Part-Perforate.* Stamps with perforations on the two opposite sides, the other two sides remaining imperforate.

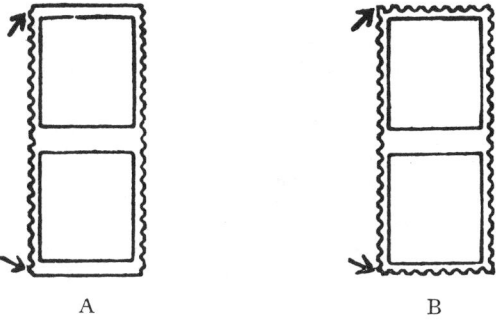

A B

8. *Vertical Pair Imperforate Horizontally.* (Type A) This indicates that the pair is fully perforated vertically but is imperforate horizontally.

9. *Horizontal Pair Imperforate Vertically.* (Type A) This indicates that the pair is fully perforated horizontally but is imperforate vertically.

10. *Vertical Pair Imperforate Between.* (Type B) This indicates that the vertical pair is fully perforated at the top, sides and bottom but is imperforate between the stamps.

11. *Horizontal Pair Imperforate Between.* (Type B) This indicates that the horizontal pair is fully perforated at the top, sides and bottom but is imperforate between the stamps.

The distinction between imperforate horizontally or vertically, and imperforate between should be clearly understood to avoid confusion.

12. *Rouletting.* Short consecutive cuts in the paper to facilitate separation of the stamps, made with a toothed wheel or disc. Experimental roulettes are known on the 3d 1851.

Section V. Postal Markings.

1. Postal markings are those marks placed by the post office of this or other countries on the stamp or cover or both, which indicate mailing place of a letter, date, rate, route, accounting between post offices, etc.

They had their beginning in what is now the Dominion of Canada during the Colonial period when Benjamin Franklin, Deputy Postmaster General for the English Crown in 1765, appointed Hugh Finlay Postmaster of the Northern District of America and introduced at the Montreal and Quebec post offices a straight line type of handstamp.

Some of these early Colonial letters carry a marking of a circular type containing the month in abbreviated form as "IV" for July and the day. These circles are about 15mm. diameter, and are known as Bishop marks, after Postmaster General Henry Bishop of England, who invented the postmark. (See Chapter II).

As Finlay's post office activities increased, some of the other important towns or cities of the 1765-1800 period employed handstamps, and among those are found straight line markings from Halifax, St. John, N. B., Three Rivers, etc.

Straight line types, plus manuscript markings to indicate rates, were quite normal up to the early 1800's when oval and circular types came into use.

It was not, however, until the 3d and 6d post office period (effective April 6, 1851), that handstamps began to be used in almost every post office and these "3" and "6" marks are of all sorts and styles and often bring sad moments to attic searchers who, never having seen a stampless cover, imagine they have found an unusual item in a letter written at Montreal or some other large town, with a fancy "3" or "6" at the upper right corner of the letter or envelope.

Envelopes did not come into general postal use until about 1844 or 1845. Possibly the main reason was that letters sent through the mails were charged "per single letter rate" which considered each piece of paper as a "single letter" and so required postage, until 1844.

In the period from 1850 to 1880 many post offices employed cancellers cut from wood or cork and of fanciful designs such as, Stars, Masonic signs, Flags, Letters, etc. These are listed in this Handbook in a separate section as they owe their origin to the whim of some individual and have no postal significance. Sometimes these designs were symbolical of the towns of their origin.

From the beginning the handstamped and machine type of cancellations were standardized by the Post Office Department and supplied to the various post offices, when required. The Post Office Department contracted with several firms to supply cancelling devices.

2. *Postmarks.* Markings to indicate the office of origin, or manner of the postal conveyance. Generally speaking the postmark refers to the post office of origin; but sometimes there are also receiving postmarks of the post office of destination or of transit. Other post office markings include: *Advertised, Forwarded, Mail Route, Missent, Paid, More to Pay, Registered, Too Late, etc.,* etc. Postmarks often serve also to cancel postage stamps with or without additional obliterating cancels.

3. *Cancellations.* A cancellation is a postal marking which cancels the stamp, making its further use impossible. As used in the listings in this Handbook, cancellations include both postmarks used as cancellations, and obliterations intended primarily to cancel (or "kill") the stamp.

4. *Free.* Handstamp generally used on free, franked mail. Occasionally seen on early adhesives of Canada used as a cancelling device.

5. *Railroad Postmarks.* Markings indicating carriage of mail by railroads. Railroads began to carry mail from their very beginnings. The railroad postmarks of the 1850 period and later usually carried the name of the railroad.

Modern railroad marks such as "T.P.O." (Traveling Post Office) or "R.P.O." (Railway Post Office) indicate transportation by railroad cars on designated routes and distributing mail in transit.

6. *Way Markings.* Way letters are such letters as are received by a mail-carrier on his way between post offices, and which he is to deliver at the first post office he comes to; and the postmaster is to inquire of him at what places he received them, and in his post bills charge the postage from those respective places to the offices at which they are to be finally delivered, writing the word "Way" against such charges in his bills. The word *"Way"* is also to be written or stamped upon each letter. If the letter is exempt from postage it should be marked "Free." This system was in operation in Nova Scotia and New Brunswick particularly.

Receiving Mark. Impression placed on the back of envelopes by the receiving office to indicate name of office and date of arrival. Also known as "backstamp."

7. *River Packet Marking.* A vessel under contract to carry river mail.

8. *Packet Marking.* A packet boat is literally a boat under contract to carry the mails. Several St. Lawrence River and Ottawa River boats had packet markings.

9. *Ship Postmarks.* Postal markings indicating arrival on a private (i.e., not under contract to carry mails) ship. This marking was applied to letters delivered by such ships to the post office at their port of entry as required by law, for which they received a fee and the letters were taxed with a specified fee for the service in place of the ordinary postage.

Packet, Steam, Way, etc., postmarks indicate transit by way rider or vessels on interior waterways. These marks were used in the Canadian postal service as early as 1800, possibly earlier, and continued in use for many years. On stamps and covers franked by stamps they usually read: *Boat, Packet, Ship, River Mail, Steam, Steamer, Steamboat, etc.*

10. *Target or Concentric Ring Cancellations.* Commonest type of obliteration on early Canadian stamps. There are several varieties of these cancellations, most of which were supplied by the contractors for cancellations.

11. *Paid Markings.* Generally consist of the word "PAID," sometimes within a frame, indicating regular postage prepaid by the sender of a letter. They are found as separate handstamps, within town or city postmarks, and as a part of obliterating cancels. In each case the "paid" marking may be used with or without an accompanying or combined rate numeral indication.

12. *Precancels.* These are stamps having cancellations applied before the mailing of the article on which they prepay postage. As a rule, these are cancelled with a distinctive device, most commonly consisting of the names of a city and state between two lines, either printed, rubber stamped. Several different styles of overprint are known.

13. *Metered Mail.* Mail franked by envelopes, or strips of gummed paper on which has been impressed by a machine an indicia indicating the amount of postage, the indicia form requiring the approval of the Post Office Department, and the machines are under strict control and regulation as to use.

14. *Tied-on.* A stamp is "tied-on" when the cancellation (or the postmark) extends from the stamp to the envelope.

CONTENTS

	Page
Preface	vii
Introduction	ix
Acknowledgments	xi
System of Numbering and Classification Explained	xv
The Tabular and Factor System Explained	xvi
Fundamental Information for Collectors of Canada	xvii
Map Illustrating Postal System of Canada	xxxvi
Chapter I. Early Postal History. 1608-1851.	1
Chapter II. Early Postal Markings. 1864-1800.	15
Chapter III. Manuscript and Handstruck Stamps. 1795-1875	23
Chapter IV. Handstruck Postage or Postage Due Stamps	35
Chapter V. Handstruck Ocean Mail Stamps.	41
Chapter VI. Postal Relations Between Canada and the United States. 1792-1883.	43
Chapter VII. Printers of Canadian Stamps and Postal Stationery	89
Chapter VIII. The Pence Issues	119
A. Laid Paper. 1851.	119
B. Three and Six Pence on Wove Paper. 1852.	141
C. The Additional Values of 1855-57.	149
D. Perforated "Pence" Stamps	167
E. The Post Contempory Proofs and Other Impressions	173
Chapter IX. The Decimal Currency Issue of 1859.	181
Chapter X. Introduction to the Queen's Head Issues of 1868-97	221
Chapter XI. The Large Queen Designs. 1868	237
Chapter XII. The Small Queen Designs of 1870-93.	267
A. The First Ottawa Printings. 1870-74.	273
B. The Montreal Printings. 1874-87.	282
C. The Second Ottawa Printings. 1887-97.	291
D. Additional Values of 1893	299
E. Canada Bank Note Engraving Co. Essays	300
F. Small Queen Bisects.	301
G. The Imperfs.	305
Chapter XIII. Introduction to Issues Produced by American Bank Note Co. and Its Subsidiary Canadian Bank Note Co. 1897-1929	315
Chapter XIV. The Diamond Jubilee Issue of 1897.	317
Chapter XV. The Maple Leaf Issue of 1897.	321
Chapter XVI. The "Numeral" Issue of 1898	329
Chapter XVII. Port Hood Provisionals	335
Chapter XVIII. Special Issues of 1898-99.	339
A. Imperial Penny Postage Issue of 1898	339
B. The "Two Cents" on "Three Cents" Provisionals of 1899	343
Chapter XIX. King Edward VII Issue	345
Chapter XX. King George V Issues of 1911-28	361
Chapter XXI. Scroll Issue of 1928-29	387
Chapter XXII. Issues Engraved and Printed by the British American Bank Note Co.	391
A. The Arch and Maple Leaf Issue. 1930-31	391
B. The Georges Cartier Stamp. 1931	400
C. The 3c on 2c Surcharge of 1932	400
D. The Medallion Issue of 1932	401
Chapter XXIII. Dated Die Issues of 1935-43	403
A. King George V. 1935	403
B. King George VI. 1937-38	408
C. Unissued King Edward VIII Stamps	411
D. 1942 War Effort Issue	411

	Page
Chapter XXIV. The 20th Century Commemorative Issues	415
I. The Quebec Tercentenary Issue. 1908	417
II. Unissued Commemoratives of 1914	422
III. The Confederation and Historical Issue	424
V. The 1933-34 Commemoratives	429
VI. The 1935-39 Commemoratives	436
Chapter XXV. The Booklet Issues	441
Chapter XXVI. Registered Letter Stamps	457
A. Handstruck Registered Stamps. 1841-55	457
B. 1865 Essay for Adhesive Registered Letter Stamps	463
C. Adhesive Registered Letter Stamps. 1875-93.	469
Chapter XXVII. Special Delivery Stamps. 1898-1942	475
Chapter XXVIII. The Postage Due Stamps	481
A. Handstruck Postage Dues	481
B. Short Paid Ocean Mail Letters	485
C. The Adhesive Postage Dues	486
Chapter XXIX. The War Tax Stamps. 1915-16	491
Chapter XXX. Air Mail Stamps	497
Chapter XXXI. The Postal Stationery	503
A. Nesbitt Envelopes. 1860-68	507
Chapter XXXII. The Envelopes and Wrappers of the Dominion, 1875-1944	517
A. Dominion Envelopes	517
B. Postal Bands and Publisher's Wrappers	532
Chapter XXXIII. Post Cards and Letter Cards	535
I. The Line Engraved Cards	535
II. The Typographed Post Cards	542
III. Letter Cards	557
Chapter XXXIV. The Obliterations and Cancellations	559
Chapter XXXV. Imperial and Provincial Markings	567
Straight Line and Circular Town Marks	567
Too Late and Way Letter	579
Advertised	580
Forwarded and Missent	581
Concentric Ring Obliterations	582
Target Cancellations	590
Ring Numerals	593
Toronto Obliterators	606
Seal Obliterators	607
Chapter XXXVI. The Postmarks and Cancellations of the Dominion. 1868-1900	609
Numerals	610
Duplex or Killer Cancellations	625
Crown Obliterators	626
Registered Markings	629
Non-Official Obliterators	630
Military Markings	642
Express Company Cancellations	647
Chapter XXXVII. The Railroad Postmarks. 1853-1943	649
Chapter XXXVIII. Steamboat and Steamship Markings	681
Chapter XXXIX. Development of the Northwest	689
Chapter XL. Stamps, Covers and Seals of the Dead Letter Office	715
Chapter XLI. The Handstruck and Punched Official Stamps	721
Chapter XLII. Precancelled Stamps	729
Chapter XLIII. Meter Imprinted Postage Stamps	737
Chapter XLIV. Bogus and Questionable Items	747
Bibliography	750
Index	753

VOLUME I

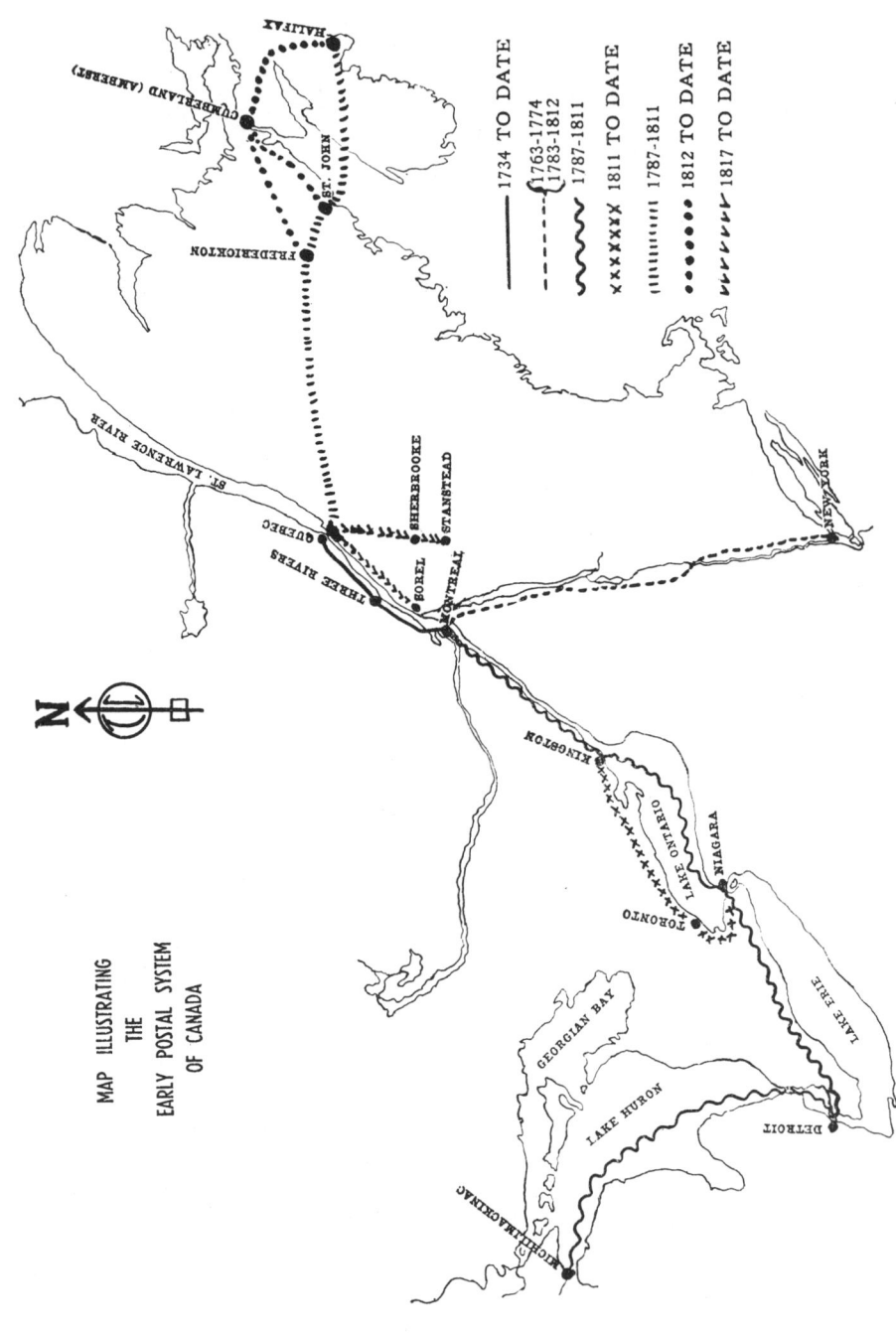

Chapter I

EARLY POSTAL HISTORY OF CANADA
1608-1851

The postal history of Canada previous to the formation of the Dominion is divisible into three distinct periods as follows:
I. French Control—1608-July 1763.
II. British Control—August 1763-April 5, 1851.
III. Provincial Control—April 6, 1851 to March 31, 1868.

Beginning April 1, 1868, the postal system was operated by the newly formed Dominion of Canada.

I. French Control 1608-July 1763

Although the French explorers led by Jacques Cartier in 1534 were the first to sail up the St. Lawrence and claim the country for France, it was not until 1608 that a permanent settlement at the Indian village of Stadacona was made by Samuel de Champlain. This grew to be the present City of Quebec. In 1642 Maisonneuve with some fifty colonists founded the City of Montreal. Communication between the settlements at Quebec and Montreal was by river, or less frequently by Indian trail.

The earliest reference we have been able to trace of courier service is 1705 when there were regular couriers who carried the Governor's despatches within the Colony, and also conveyed private letters for a fee. As there were no roads then the couriers travelled by boat.

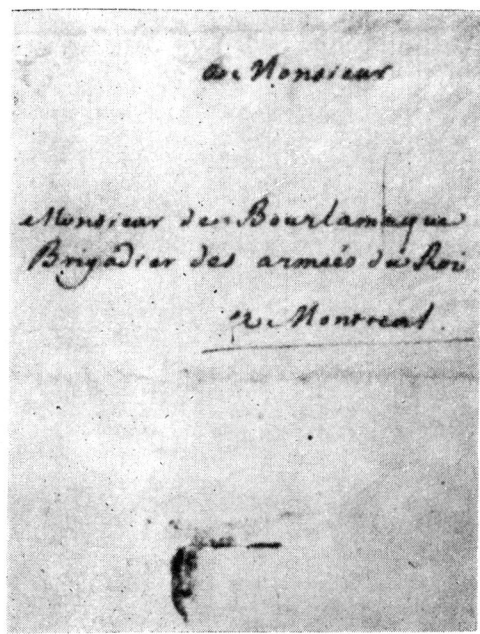

Fig. 1. French Regime. Letter carrier by courier from Quebec to Mons. de Bourlamay, Montreal.

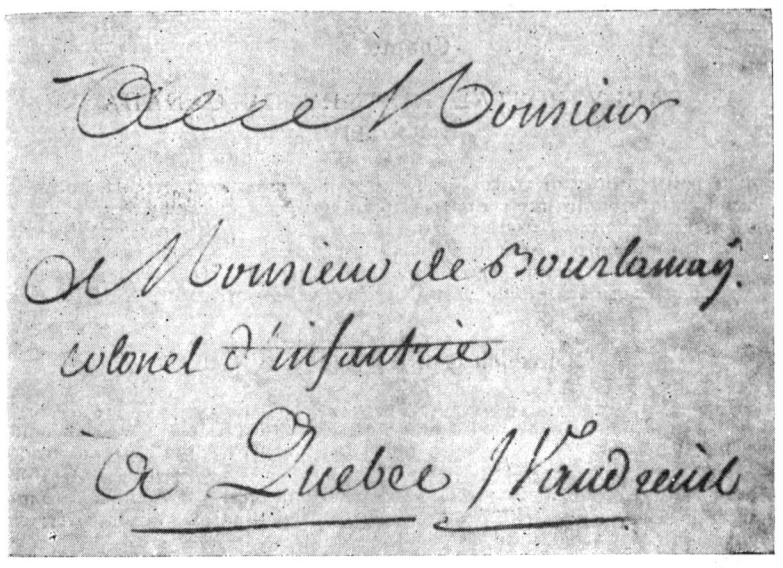

Fig. 2. French Regime. Another letter to Mons. de Bourlamay, now in Quebec. Franked by the Governor, "J. Vaudreuil" (Marquis de Vaudreuil, Governor 1755-1763).

In 1721 one Nicholas Lanoullier, a treasury clerk, proposed that a postal system similar to that in France be established. However, the expense involved in the construction of a road between Quebec and Montreal was too great to incur at the time. A few years later, however, the road was decided upon and in 1734 it was opened. Post houses were established at nine mile intervals and ferries put into operation across the larger rivers. Although the courier service, as heretofore, was primarily for government despatches, the couriers were allowed to take any letters that might be entrusted to them by private persons.

The fees were ten sols (10c) from Quebec to Montreal and vice versa, five sols (5c) to Three Rivers, with proportionate rates to other settlements.

This was the maximum extent of the Postal Service in Canada during the French control.

Communication with France was maintained by permitting letters to go free between Quebec and La Rochelle, while letters to Paris and vice versa would be conveyed from La Rochelle on payment of a fee of seven sols (7c). Letters to any other place in Canada or France had to be handled by private arrangements. This system was in operation as early as 1723, and was irregular, depending entirely on the ships that called at Quebec and La Rochelle.

Letters of this period are recognizable only by the superscription and contents, there being no postmarks. It seems superfluous to remark that such letters are rare, most of them being in various official archives, or museums.

Brief Note on the Military Postal Service of 1760-1763.

The British were successful in occupying Canada as early as 1760, having taken Montreal on the 8th of September, 1759, and Wolfe defeated Montcalm, and took possession of the city and Citadel of Quebec on September 17 of the same year.

A rudimentary postal service was established almost immediately, as reference is made in General Thomas Gage's letters to its existence in the winter of 1759-60. On November 2, 1761, Gage, who was Governor of Montreal, wrote to Sir Jeffrey Amherst as follows:

> "No letters have been received from (New) York, later than yours of the 6th Ulmo, which has occasioned some Applications both from Military & Civil; I write to Colo. Young by this Opportunity, as they must stick either at the point (Crown Point) or Albany. As we have never before been so long, without receiving a post. There being no Rangers now here, by whose means the Communication was preserved last Winter. I propose when Lake Champlain is shut, to take some Canadiens into the Service, & keep up a Regular Communication with Crown Point, once every Fortnight, during the next Winter. And if the Commanders of Crown Point & Albany will give the usual orders to forward the Mails from Post to Post, we shall have the same regular Correspondence with the Provinces, as the last Winter."

Approximately two months later Gage again mentions the postal service in a letter to Amherst, from Montreal, December 29, 1761:

> "From the very severe weather we have had for some time past, I Judge all the waters betwixt Canada & New York must be now passable. This River has been froze for some Days & there is no doubt of Lake Champlain being in the same state; I therefore send off the Montreal Bag tomorrow for Crown-Point by a Soldier & a [French] Canadian, & propose to repeat the same about once a Fortnight, during the Winter. I write to Lieut. Colo. Elliott to desire Him to get the Baggs forwarded from Post to Post to Albany, as usually practiced, by which means a regular Communication may be kept up till the middle of March."

On February 17, 1762, Gage complains to Amherst of the poor service:

> "Our Communication with the Point is bad, but the People I have in Pay, contrive to do their Business very well; it's a tedious Journey, generally taking eight or nine Days."

This Military postal system functioned between Quebec and Montreal, and Montreal and Albany, until the establishment of Civil government in 1763.

II. Postal Service Under the Control of the General Post Office, London, August 1763-April 5, 1851

Shortly after the signing of the Peace Treaty in 1763 which ceded Canada to the British, London merchants interested in the Canadian trade urged the British Government to establish regular service between New York and Quebec, a desire that was heartily supported by the Governor of the Province of Canada.

Accordingly the Government instructed the Postmasters General of the American Colonies, Messrs. Benjamin Franklin and William Foxcroft, to survey a route between New York and Quebec. This they proceeded to do, and upon reaching Quebec in August, 1763, they met a young Scotchman, Hugh Finlay, who offered to conduct a regular post between Quebec and Montreal, assuming all risks, for a commission of 20% of the revenue collected, and a monopoly of licensing persons to provide horses and conveyances for travellers. Furthermore these licensees, termed "maitres de poste," were paid 2d a mile for providing horses and carriages for the mail couriers.

When Finlay first took control of the Canadian system the legal basis for his operations was Section 4 of the Act of the 9th of Anne (1710) which like so many legislative enactments did not fully cover all points, and in the case of the North American Colonies the Act failed to prescribe rates for distances over 100 miles, with the result that there were no legal rates between Quebec and Montreal or Montreal and New York. The legal rate for 100 miles was

3

6d, and Finlay was keen enough to see that low rates would increase the volume of mail handled by the post and accordingly set the rate at 8d on the Montreal-Quebec route.

The rate to New York, however, was high, being 2sh from Montreal and 3sh from Quebec.

These high charges were protested by the colonists, who were fully supported in their pleas by the governors, with the result that in 1765 the Act of 1710 was amended[1] and the charges on letters from Montreal to New York were reduced to 1sh, while from Quebec it was only 1sh-4d. Furthermore Halifax, which had had a post office since 1755, was greatly benefited by a new rate of 4d per single letter between any two seaports in America.

In addition, the local rates were made 8d up to 200 miles, and 2d for each additional 100 miles.

In a report to his superiors (1766) Finlay said:

> That the Establishment of a Post Office in Canada from Quebec to Montreal, is found to be of the greatest utility to His Majesty's Service, by the Speed, Safety and Regularity with which all Military Orders have been conveyed in the Mails: the like benefits have accrued to the Commercial Interest, and both the Services would suffer exceedingly if any Interruption should arise in the mode of forwarding these Mails, which Duty is well performed at present at the cheap rate of Six pence p League, by a set of Men stiled Maitres de Postes, as they are also appointed by a law of the Province to furnish Relais to Travellers at one Shilling P League.
>
> HUGH FINLAY[2]

These "Relais" or couriers were obtained by advertising in the newspapers. We quote such an advertisement which appeared in May, 1765:[3]

May 23, 1765

Any Person willing to engage himself as a Rider between the Post Office of Quebec and Montreal, is desired to give in his proposals to HUGH FINLAY, at this Office, or at the Office at Montreal, to JOHN THOMSON. THE RIDER is to set out from Quebec every Monday at 12 o'clock, and must be in Montreal at 12. He is to set out from Montreal on Thursday at 12 and must be in Quebec on Saturday at 12———. He is to furnish himself with Horses.

The Mail for New York will be made up on Monday the 27th Instant.

The first mail vehicle used in Canada was called a caleche, and besides the courier and mail bag two passengers might contrive to get in. The 180 miles between Montreal and Quebec was served by twenty-seven maitres de poste and two post offices, one at Three Rivers (103)[4] and one at Berthier (57). There were also six ferries on the route, the one at Three Rivers being three miles wide. Service was once a week, every Monday from Quebec, and every Thursday from Montreal. The journey took about forty hours, and the rate for a single letter was 8d and proportionately less for the intermediate offices. William Gray was the first postmaster of Montreal.

Furthermore a monthly courier service was established between Montreal and New York to connect with the British Packets running from England to New York. About a year later the service was increased to twice a month in the summer, as the quotation from the "Hardwicke Papers" shows:

> From Quebec to Albany 450 miles From Albany to New York 150. A Post goes once a Fortnight in the summer every month in the winter from Quebeck to N.Y. thro' Montreal, Crown Point and Albany. A

---
1. Appendix A #1.
2. Canadian Archives, Shelburne Manuscripts LXVI 59.
3. Quebec Gazette.
4. AUTHOR'S NOTE: Numerals in parentheses indicate miles from Montreal, unless noted "Q" indicating distance from Quebec.

Pacquet is made up every 2d Saturday in the month for New York by which letters may be forwarded to Quebec[5].

The earliest notice we have been able to find is dated August 1, 1764, and is as follows:

"POST OFFICE, Quebec, August 1st, 1764.

"The Post for New York sets out on the first and third Monday of every month. All persons are intreated to put their letters into the Office before 10 o'clock, as the bag is shut at that hour precisely, and Letters cannot possibly be taken in a moment after.

"The Post returns from Montreal every Saturday at 11 o'clock at which hour the Letters will be delivered out, and attendance given till two, when those remaining will be delivered to the Penny Post."[6]

A notice of December 20, 1764, is as follows:

POST-OFFICE, December 20, 1764

THE MAIL for *Britain,* via New-York, will be made up on Monday the 31st Cur. at 12 o'clock. All letters for England must pay the Postage from this place to New-York, otherwise they cannot be forwarded.

There is now in the Office several letters for England, which have not been paid for[6a].

Under Finlay's regime letters to England had to be prepaid.

Finlay maintained a zealous supervision over the postal service, and issued many directions, notices, and regulations; for instance:

February 16, 1767

MANY complaints have been made by the Publick of the Irregularity of the Post-men between Quebec and Montreal. Complaints have been made also by the Post-Men, of Persons riding Post: It is necessary therefore to inform the Public, That from this Day the different Post-Houses are to be on the same footing with the Post-Houses in Britain, as regulated by an Act of Parliament, made in the 9th Year of the Reign of Queen Anne. And as many Persons riding Post impose on the Post-Men, threaten and abuse them, contrary to all Law, I have ordered every Post-Man to hang up in his House exposed to view, Abstracts from the above Act, relative to Post-Men and Persons riding Post; also the Distance between each stage, with the Fare affixed, so that for the future there may no Disputes arise between the Post-Men and Persons riding Post.

Abstracts from the aforesaid ACT

"The Post-Master-General, and the respective Deputies or Substitutes of such Post-Master-General, and no other Person or Persons whatsoever, shall prepare and provide Horses and Furniture to let to hire, unto all or any Person or Persons riding Post by Commission or without.

"And in Regard that the said Post-Master-General and his deputies are obliged, as well for performing the Duties of the several Stages, as for furnishing such as ride Post with Horses, to be at a great Charge to maintain a convenient Number of Servants and Horses, *Be it Enacted, by the Authority aforesaid,* That it shall and may be lawful to and for each Post-Master-General and his Deputies, to ask, demand, take and receive of every Person that he or they shall furnish and provide with horses and Furniture, or with Horses, Furniture and Guide, to ride Post in any of the Post Roads as aforesaid, Three Pence of British Money[6b] for each and every Horse Hire, or Postage, for every

---
5. Canadian Archives, Hardwicke Papers 35914, 9.
6. Quebec Gazette. Is the "Penny Post" referred to the earliest in N. A.?
6a. Quebec Gazette.
6b. Note the expression "British Money".

English Mile, and Four Pence of like Money for the Person riding as Guide for every Stage[7].

Again he advertised the appointment of a Master of the Post House in Quebec as follows:

Post-House, April 2, 1767

CHARLES LORTIE, at St. John's-Gate, being appointed Master of the Post House in this city, will furnish all Persons, riding Post to Montreal, with Horses and Carriages, at a Minute's Warning to carry them to the next Stage[8].

The delivery of letters was at the Post Office, and if not called for runners would be sent out later. There was undoubtedly a fee for such delivery. This may be considered as the earliest carrier service, which apparently had been going for some years. A typical notice follows:

Post-Office, July 23, 1767

LETTERS arriving on Wednesdays will be delivered at this office precisely at Ten o'clock; none can be sent out by the Runner till Six o'clock in the Evening. Every Person expecting Letters will be so obliging as to send for them.

HUGH FINLAY, Postmaster[9]

The Post was so convenient that many used it also as a means of conveying goods. This practice so delayed the mail that it had to be stopped, but an enterprising party by the name of Sills immediately established an *Express*[10] between Quebec and Montreal. This began in December, 1768. It is interesting to observe the final "N.B." From this notice we may assume that Sills was the founder of the Express business in North America and not Harnden as is generally supposed.

December 15, 1768

WHEREAS many PARCELS, BUNDLES, &C. HAVE been frequently sent to the Post House in this city, to be carried to Montreal by the Courrier who goes with the Mail; but it being found that the mail is subject to be retarded by such a Practice, no Parcel or Bundle can for the future be sent by that conveyance, the Courier being forbid to take Charge of them: Therefore, for the Conveniency of those who may have Occasion to send small Parcels, to Montreal, Three-Rivers, or any part of the road, a cover'd Slay will be sent to Montreal, next week from the Post House here, and continue to go every fortnight during the winter Season, to perform the Journey (Weather permitting) in four Days; those therefore who may want to send small Bales, Bundles, Parcels, &c. may have them carried on moderate Terms, and carefully delivered, by their most obedient Servant,

S. SILLS

N.B. Whatever Effects are sent from hence will be enter'd in a Book, and Receipts taken on their Delivery to prevent any Mistakes that may Happen.

Quebec, 14th December, 1768[11].

By 1770 the necessity for branch routes was beginning to be felt. The newspapers of March that year carried this enlightening advertisement:

March 22, 1770

Any Person willing to contract with this Office, for carrying the mails from Montreal to Skene's-Borough, once every Fort-night, may

---

7. Quebec Gazette.
8. Quebec Gazette.
9. Quebec Gazette. The "Penny Post" referred to before, is mentioned here as being "sent out by Runner."
10. Webster's New International Dictionary defines an Express as "A company or system for the prompt and safe transportation of parcels, money, or goods; as, to send a package by express.
11. Quebec Gazette.

give in his Proposals here, or to Mr. John Thomson, at the Post-Office in Montreal, on or before the 20th of April next[12].

The public was apparently just as dilatory in 1771 as in 1767, for in January, 1771, the following long notice was published in the newspapers:

POST-OFFICE, January 3, 1771

All persons, who expect Letters by the Post, are entreated to send for them to the office on Wednesday. Those which may remain uncalled for on the Day of the Courier's Arrival, shall be sent out next Morning, to be delivered by the Runner.

Should Letters be sent to the office after 12 oclock on Thursday to be forwarded by Post, the Public is hereby advertised that they cannot be sent by that day's mail, but must remain in the Office until the Thursday following.

Such Letters as are to be left at any Place on the Road between Quebec and Three-Rivers, or Three-Rivers and Montreal, cannot be forwarded unless the Postage is paid where they are put in: When thus frank'd they are left with the Masters of the Post-Houses, nearest the places to which they are directed, and there remain until called for, so that the Country Traders and others expecting Letters from Quebec, Montreal or Three-Rivers, know where and on what Days to send for them to the nearest Maitre de Poste, commission'd from this Office[13].

Further expansion of the Postal Service is shown by another advertisement, viz.:

Jan. 16, 1772

TO PREVENT MISCARRIAGE OF LETTERS, AND TO FACILITATE Correspondence with the Corn-countrys round Berthier and Sorrel, a By-Office is established at BERTHIER, where the Mail from QUEBEC AND THREE-RIVERS will be delivered every Friday afternoon, and the Mail from Montreal every Tuesday afternoon; the Mails from thence for Quebec and Three Rivers will be made up and dispatched on every MONDAY AFTERNOON, at 4 o'clock, and for MONTREAL on Friday AFTERNOON, at the same hour; So that all Persons in the Parishes near BERTHIER, viz. St. Francois, Maska, Sorrell, St. Denis, &c. &c. expecting Letters from QUEBEC OR MONTREAL, will now know when and where to receive them . . . .

It has been represented that a Post is much wanted by the Parishes below Quebec as far as the River des Loups: Any Person willing to make an Agreement with this Office to set out from hence on every other Thursday at 12 o'clock, may apply on or before Monday next to know the Conditions that he is to perform, and to fix a Price for his Service[14].

In January, 1774, Finlay was made "Deputy Postmaster" for the Northern District of America, and also retained the benefits of the P. M. of Quebec. August of that year saw the Quebec-Montreal service increased to twice weekly as announced in the newspapers:

Aug. 11, 1774

IT IS IMAGINED, THAT TWO POSTS WEEKLY BETWEEN THIS place and Montreal, will be of advantage to the Publick; for that end, a mail for Montreal will be made up at this Office every Monday morning at nine o'clock, the door of the Office will not be shut at that hour. But all letters coming late into the Office will remain to be forwarded at the usual hour on the Thursday follow-

---

12. Quebec Gazette.
13. Quebec Gazette.
14. Quebec Gazette.

ing; And the same method will be followed on Thursday; the letters coming late that day will be forwarded on the Monday after.

The Post that leaves Quebec on Monday, will arrive at Montreal on Wednesday, and the Post that leaves this on Thursday, will as formerly arrive on Saturday at Montreal.

The Post will return from Montreal to this place on Wednesdays and Saturday.

It is hoped that those, who wish that this regulation may continue, will discourage the private conveyance of letters[15].

The last paragraph shows that the Post Office was meeting competition. Although Finlay retained the Postmastership of Quebec as well as being Deputy Postmaster for the Northern District of America, he apparently delegated the actual administration of the Quebec Post Office to a subordinate, who in 1774 was James Jeffry, signer of the newspaper advertisement, quoted herewith:

December 29, 1774

POST-OFFICE, Quebec, December 28.

EVERY MONDAY AT 2 o'clock, a Mail will be made up at this Office for New-York, to be forwarded from Montreal of the Wednesday Evening following, by way of Lake George; and every Thursday as formerly, a New-York Mail will be made up and dispatch'd from hence at 2 o'clock, and from Montreal on the Saturday Evening following, by way of Skenesborough.

For the Conveniency of all Persons who may have Concerns on La Champlain, or between the Lake and Albany, an office is established at Crown-point, and another at Fort Edward[16].

JAMES JEFFRY

The practice of sneaking a letter in a parcel was evidently quite prevalent as the following indicates:

POST-OFFICE, January 9, 1777

PARCELS OR BUNDLES GIVEN IN CHARGE TO THE Courier, must be inspected at this office—A letter, or any written Paper found in any such bundle or Parcel will subject the whole to Postage.

All sealed Parcels or Packets will be forwarded in the mail[17].

A minor change in the route between Quebec and Montreal became effective on October 1, 1778.

POST-OFFICE, Quebec, 1st September, 1778

IT IS HIS EXCELLENCY THE GOVERNOR'S PLEASURE, THAT Post-houses be established by Lorette, Champigny, St. Ange and the upper concessions of St. Augustin, in order to avoid the inconveniences which attend travelling the lower road by Cap-rouge and also to avoid the difficulty found in passing thro' Maskinonge' woods where from the nature of the ground it is impossible to keep the road in repair, that the Post pass by the upper road thro' the Lonmiere.

In obedience to His Excellency's commands, this is to give notice to all persons, that from the first day of October, His Majesty's Couriers will pass by this new route, and for the speedy conveyance of those who travel in Post every necessary conveniency will be found at the Post-houses to be establish'd. Information shall be timeously given to the Publick of the distance of the first stage from town.

Those whom it may concern will observe that the road by Ste. Foix, Cap-rouge and St. Augustin, by the river side, is not to be reckoned a Post-road after the first day of next month[18].

---

15. Quebec Gazette.
16. Quebec Gazette.
17. Quebec Gazette.
18. Quebec Gazette.

Later the public was advised of the "Maitres de Poste" on the new route, viz:

September 17, 1778

THE PUBLIC IS HEREBY ADVERTISED THAT ON AND AFTER the first day of October next, all persons travelling Post between Quebec and Montreal will be supplied with Horses and Carriages at the first Stage distant three leagues from Quebec, kept by Ignace Allin of old Lorette—who will drive three leagues farther to the stage kept by Augustine Desfoix in the parish of St. Augustin— Desfoix drives to the former Post-house in the parish of Pointe aux Trembles kept by Jean Mercure[19].

The disturbances in the Colonies which eventually became the American Revolution soon made the New York route impossible, and it was therefore suspended. Lack of support from the Governor made it impracticable to continue any service except between Montreal and Quebec, with the result that it was not until 1783 that there was any postal connection with the outside world.

Shortly after the close of the American Revolution the New York to Montreal route was again in operation. However, the experience during the period 1775-1783 showed the necessity for an all-British route between Quebec and Halifax, and accordingly in 1787 a mail route between these two cities was put in operation. The route was by Rivere du Loup near Grand Portage where the couriers exchanged mails. From thence it went to Fredericton by the Madawaska and the Grand Falls. At Fredericton a fresh courier took the mails by sloop to Digby, thence overland to Halifax via Annapolis. This route was 663 miles long and was operated monthly in winter and semi-monthly in summer, the couriers taking twenty-one to thirty-one days in summer, and thirty-five to forty-five days in winter. These trips cost about £100 each, far more than the revenue warranted.

Upper Canada was served until 1787 by an annual mail known as the "Yearly Express" and run primarily for keeping the military posts and frontier settlements in touch with headquarters. This route followed the St. Lawrence to Kingston, thence across Lake Ontario to Niagara, and then overland to Detroit, and north on Lakes Huron to Michilimackinac at the junction of Lakes Huron and Michigan.

In 1789 post offices were opened at Lachine (8), Cedars (29), Coteau (38), Charlottenburg, Cornwall (68), New Johnston, Lancaster, Osnabruck, Augusta, Elizabethtown (now Brockville—125) and Kingston (173).

By 1791 the Quebec-Halifax route was served every five days in summer, and monthly in winter, while the western offices had a mail from Quebec the first Monday in each month. The Gaspe and Baie des Chaleurs districts were given mails "as the need and occasion arises."

In 1792 the first postal agreement between the United States and Canada was concluded, and the U. S. Post Office agreed to convey the British mails arriving at New York in a sealed bag to Burlington, Vt., where a Canadian courier took it on to Montreal. First trips were semi-monthly, but in 1797 these trips became weekly. (See Chapter VI on U. S.-Canada Mails).

Service west of Kingston had been haphazard but finally in 1799 or 1800 a post office was established at Toronto (then known as York) with William Willcox as first postmaster.

It is sad to relate that after many years of faithful service to Canada, and through causes mostly beyond his control Finlay was indebted to the Postmaster General, London, for the sum of £1,408, which he was unable to pay, and was therefore dismissed as a defaulter in October, 1799. Finlay was supported in Canada by the lieutenant governor, and the leading merchants, but judgment nevertheless was obtained against him. He died in 1801 at the age of seventy-two, and it was not until 1830 that Finlay's uncollectible debt was finally wiped off the books.

1800 was also notable for the fact that Finlay was succeeded by John Heriot.

---

19. Quebec Gazette.

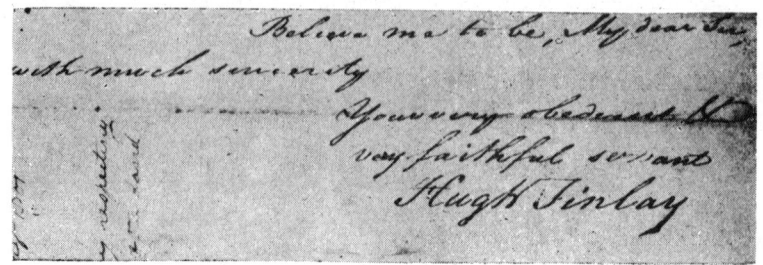

Fig. 3. Signature of "Hugh Finlay" on a letter written shortly before his death, 1801.

Heriot had authority to extend new routes and offices but only if such extensions of the service would in his opinion pay for themselves. The postage rates were nominally based on Act of the 5th George III (1765), but since the routes had never been accurately measured the rates were merely guesswork.

Heriot was in a difficult position. Legally he could take orders only from the London General Post Office, but he was under constant pressure from the Canadian people for extensions and improvements in the service. There had been a great influx of immigrants in Upper Canada particularly of Loyalists from the United States who had supported the Crown during the American Revolution. Furthermore it was important that the Government keep in contact with these people.

This situation led to an anomalous system in which the colonists made grants to aid the establishment of post offices and routes, but under the law could have no voice in the administration of the post office however much they might contribute to its support.

However, in spite of these difficulties, by 1811 couriers were taking the mails from Kingston to Niagara via York (Toronto) with branches to Sandwich and Amherstburg as the volume of letters warranted. In 1815 the route from Montreal to Kingston was by coach, and thence by horseback or sleigh to Niagara via Toronto and Hamilton. The branch lines were served by foot couriers.

Lower Canada was little changed, the system consisting of a semi-weekly service between Montreal and Quebec, and a semi-monthly summer, or monthly winter service between Quebec and Fredericton. From thence to St. John and Halifax on a weekly basis.

The war of 1812 between the United States and Great Britain made it necessary to change the Quebec-Halifax route. Formerly it went to St. John along the St. John River, then across the Bay of Fundy to Annapolis and thence to Halifax. From 1812 on it went across country to Cumberland (now Amherst), thence to Halifax. A branch route ran from the main route at Sussexvale (now Sussex) and took the St. John mail.

The New York mail was completely suspended, and the service between Montreal and Quebec became daily instead of semi-weekly.

Fig. 4. Signature of Daniel Sutherland, Deputy Postmaster General, 1816-1827.

In 1816 George Heriot resigned and in April of that year, Daniel Sutherland, who had been postmaster of Montreal since 1807 was appointed Postmaster General of Canada, with the support of the Governors of Upper and Lower

Canada. With this support he was able to expand the Post Office, in spite of the hostility of the legislatures, and the fact that in the year of his appointment Nova Scotia and Prince Edward Island were taken from his control.

That same year an office was opened in Belleville, Ont. (220) (then Bay of Quinte, and followed in 1817 by the Port Hope, Ont., office (271) (then known as Toronto), and Stanstead, Que. (165Q) in the Eastern counties. In 1819 offices were opened at St. Eustache, Que. (17), St. Andrews, Que. (40), Grenville, Que. (57), Hawkesbury, Ont. (54), Hull, Ont. (118), just across the river from Ottawa, Coburg, Ont. (264), (then known as Hamilton), and Sherbrooke, Que. (147Q). In 1825 Hamilton, Ont. (373), London, Ont. (453), Brantford, Ont. (399) and St. Thomas, Ont. (362) offices were opened. About this time offices were also established at Perth, Ont. (140), Lanark, Ont. (151), Richmond, Ont. (145), Dundas, Ont. (380), Grimsby, Ont. (390), St. Catharines, Ont., (405), Niagara, Ont. (430), Queenston, Ont. (440), Victoria, Ont. (423), Port Talbot, Ont. (470), Burford, Ont. (410), Woodstock, Ont. (425) and Delaware, Ont. (465).

During Sutherland's administration agitation for a postal system under the direct control of the provinces continued and in March, 1820, the House of Assembly of Upper Canada passed a resolution condemning the administration of the postal service.

The Legal Officers for the Crown advised the Post Office that it would be unwise to contest the colonists' complaints which were based on "no tax shall be levied on the people of this country except such as shall be appropriated for the public use and accounted for by the legislature" (31 Geo. III (1801) Cap. 31) and the Declaratory Act (18 Geo. III, (1778) Cap. 12) in which the Home Government disclaimed the right to impose on a colony any duty, tax, or assessment except where necessary for the regulation of commerce.

To get around this difficulty an act was passed (4 Will IV, Cap. 7) in 1834 giving the administration in London sole control, but allowing the local legislatures to fix the postage rates, and any surplus revenue should be divided between the provinces. This bill was to take effect if passed by the Provincial Legislatures as well as the British Parliament. This was not accomplished as three local legislatures rejected it, while two offered substitute bills which were unacceptable to the other Provinces and London.

During this period of negotiation Daniel Sutherland retired in 1827, to be succeeded by his son-in-law Thomas Allen Stayner, who remained in office until midnight April 5th, 1851, when Canada assumed the operation of her own postal system.

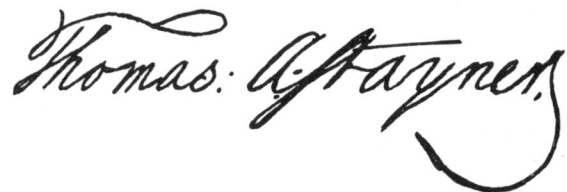

Fig. 5. Signature of Thomas Allen Stayner, Deputy Postmaster General, 1827-1851.

Stayner was the last, and was undoubtedly the most brilliant of the officers under the General Post Office in London.

Fortunately the General Post Office had loosened the reins with which it controlled the previous Deputy Postmaster Generals, so that Stayner had more authority with which to deal with the postal system of which he was the nominal head. His executive capacity was enormous.

He opened a post office at Guelph in 1827, and was warned by the home authorities that approval would depend on financial results. Some months later he established between St. Johns and St. Andrews, N. B., an additional courier, thereby making the exchange of mails with the U. S. more frequent. This action brought a rebuke, but Stayner was fully justified. By this time his

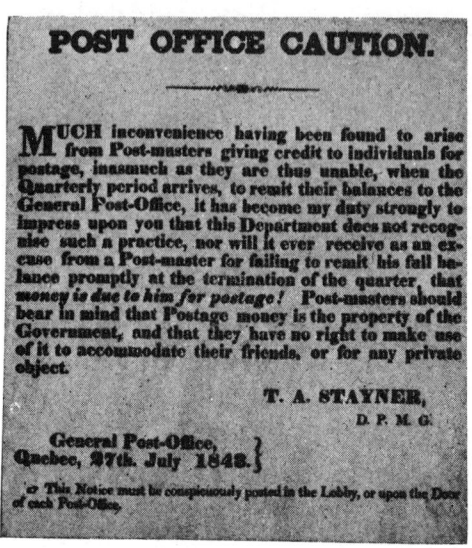

Fig. 6. Post Office order sent to all Postmasters by Stayner in 1843.

success and his report pointing out that practically every town and village in the United States had a daily mail, which excited the discontent of the populace with the comparative infrequency of the Canadian service, plus the request that he be allowed to expand the service and increase the frequency of the courier's trips, whenever he thought conditions warranted carried great weight with the home authorities.

Stayner was fortunate enough to have impressed his superiors in London of his discretion, and the Postmaster General was under an increasing sense of the weakness of his legal authority over the colonial postal systems. Accordingly Francis Freeling, Secretary of the G. P. O., in a letter dated August 7, 1830, receipt of which was most gratifying, urged him (Stayner) to make it his study to extend the postal system in all directions where the formations of new towns and settlements justified.

Stayner's Commission of 1827 included Upper and Lower Canada and New Brunswick. In 1828, however, the New Brunswick service was transferred to Nova Scotia.

At the time Stayner assumed control of the Canadian postal system it was still comparatively simple. The main line ran from Halifax to Niagara and Amherstburg on the western boundaries of Upper Canada. From Halifax to Niagara was 1,356 miles, while to Amherstburg 1,516 miles. Between Halifax and Quebec the courier travelled weekly each way, between Quebec and Montreal service five times weekly each way. From Montreal to Niagara and Amherstburg there were semi-weekly trips.

In addition to the main line there were six branch lines. Two were from Three Rivers, one to Sorel via Nicolet, running semi-weekly. The other to Sherbrooke and Stanstead where an exchange with the U. S. mails was made. This was a weekly service.

As an example of how primitive conditions were Stayner tells us that in 1835 the Montreal Post Office was on the second floor of a building between the printing plant of the Quebec *Gazette* and a boarding house. Beneath was a dry goods store. To get to the office the public had to grope up a rickety and dark flight of stairs, and then through a small room half filled with firewood and junk!

Stayner issued detailed instructions to postmasters[20], telling them when to make up their accounts, how to postmark their letters, handling of letterbills, disposition of undeliverable letters, missent mails, assistants, etc. His instructions were clear, and he followed them up[21].

During his regime the registration system was introduced in December, 1840. Three years later the basis for rating letters was changed from the number of sheets of paper to weight, which was the subject of a circular sent out by Stayner, December 1, 1843, from Quebec[22].

Fig. 7. James Morris, First Postmaster General of the Canada Post Office Department. Appointed February 22, 1851, effective April 6, 1851 to August 16, 1853 inclusive, at a salary of £1000 per annum. His residence was Brockville, Ont., and he was a member of the Legislative Council.

The changes made in the Post Office Laws of the United States effective July 1, 1 45, were the subject of a long order from Stayner to his staff[23].

In 1847 the practice of putting mail clerks on board steamers plying between Montreal and Toronto was begun[24] and the "Steamboat Letter" came into being.

Stayner's last order was issued from Montreal on the 14th of March 1851[25], notifying the postmasters that the transfer of the Post Office to Provincial Control would take place on April 6, 1851, and that James Morris would be the new Postmaster General.

Stayner continued as Deputy Postmaster General until the operation of the Post Office was transferred to the Provincial Government on April 6, 1851, under the terms of the Post Office Act passed in August, 1850[26], and the Proclamation of the Governor General, April 5, 1851.

---

20. Appendix B #1, et seq.
21. Appendix B #3, 4, etc.
22. Append'x B #11.
23. Appendix D #2.
24. Appendix B #14.
25. Appendix B #16.
26. Appendix A #4.

Chapter II

EARLY POSTAL MARKINGS
1764-1800

The earliest postal markings were the straight line markings of Quebec and Montreal. They were introduced by Finlay in 1764, following the custom of the other American Colonies, and under the direction of Benjamin Franklin. These straight line markings had been used in New York as early as 1756, and the inclusion of Canada in the American Colonial postal system resulted in the adoption of similar practices.

We list herewith such markings that are known to us and the entire subject is worth careful investigation by students of Canadian postal history.

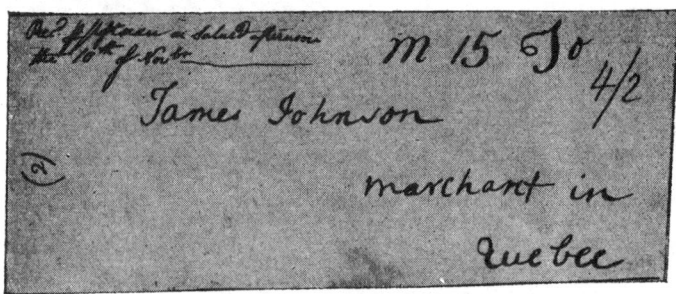

Fig. 1.
One of the Earliest Covers Known from British North America.
A Letter from Montreal to Quebec, November, 1764.
"M 15 To"—Montreal 15 Grains of Silver and Rated 4/2 on Arrival in Quebec.
Notation: "Recd. p postman on Saturd afternoon the 10th of Novbr."

Fig. 2. Type PM2 on Letter from Montreal to Quebec, 1774.

The earliest markings were in manuscript, as follows:
    B—Berthier.
    M—Montreal.
    Q—Quebec.
    T—Three Rivers.

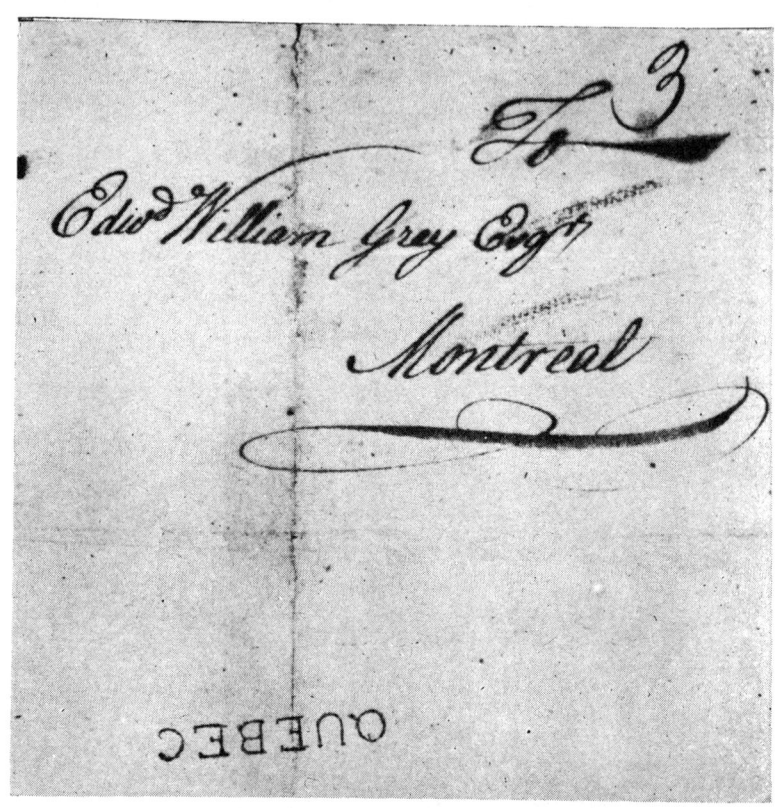

Fig. 3. 1765. Face and Back of Letter Showing Straight Line "Quebec," Type PM1.

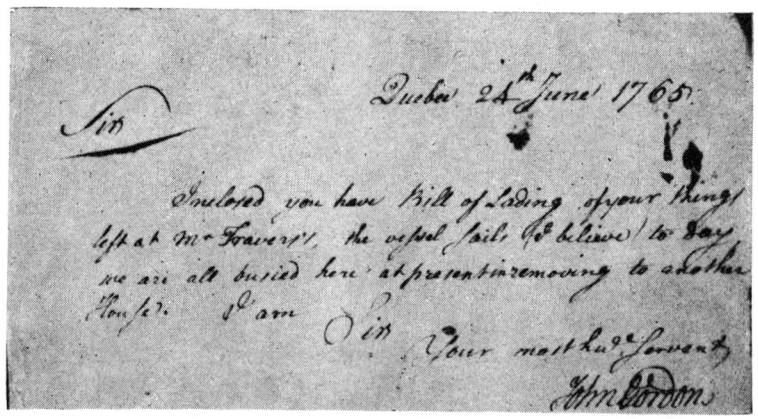

Fig. 4. Contents of the above Letter.

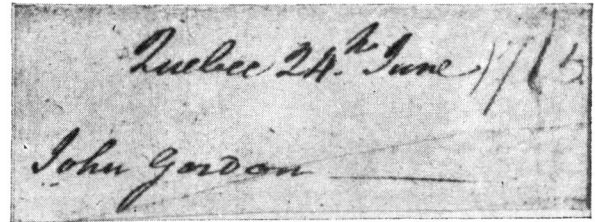

Fig. 5. Endorsement, by Addressee, of letter in Fig. 4.

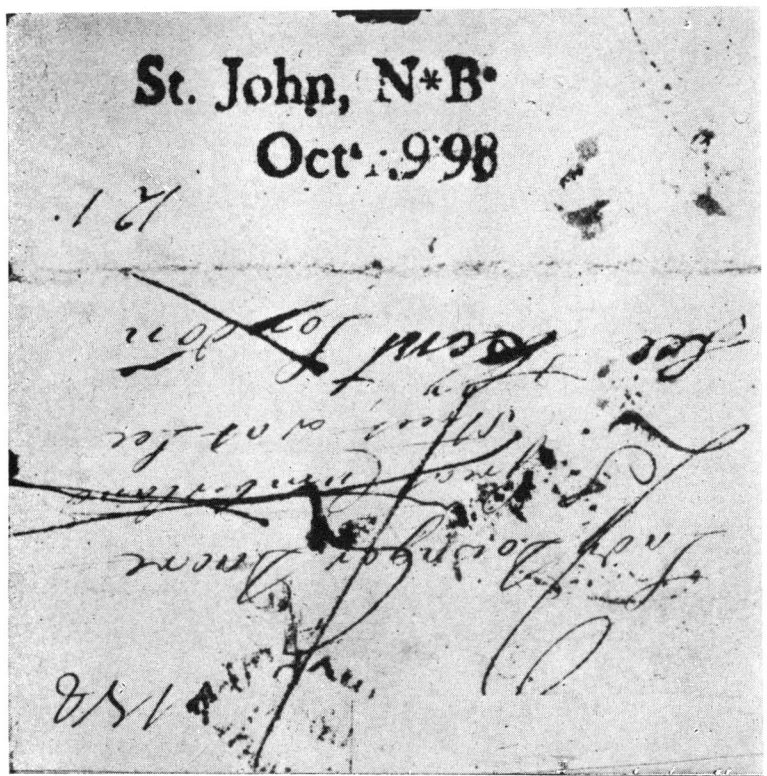

Fig. 6. St. John, N. B., Oct. 9, 1798. One Star—One Stop. Type PM10b.

Sometimes the name of the town is written out. Paid letters would be marked "M Paid 2-16" and the receiving office would not write in any rate. These manuscript markings continued in use for about twenty years, although special markings were introduced by Finlay in Quebec early in 1765.

A. Straight Line Postmarks

Introduced by Hugh Finlay, 1765-1799

QUEBEC
Type PM1

MONTREAL
OCTOBER, 15.
Type PM3

See Page 15, Fig. 2. for Type PM2.

MONTREAL
Type PM4, PM14-20

THREE RIVERS
Type PM5

Montreal
FEB,y'.13;
Type PM6.
Eight types, varying in punctuation.

HALIFAX
DEC 11·99
Type PM12.

Type PM7.

St. John. N. B.
August, 18, 1804
Type PM10.

MONTREAL
MARCH, 7
Type PM8, a, b, c.

ST JOHN N: B
NOV 27 93
Type PM9.

REFERENCE LIST

Type		Date	Color	Value
PM1	QUEBEC	June 1765-1828	black	50.00
PM2	(Montreal) M.2:16 (Fig. 2)	June 1774	red	x
PM3	MONTREAL (Month and day)	Oct. 1774	black	x
PM4	MONTREAL (no date)	Sept. 1777-84	black	50.00
PM5	THREE RIVERS	Jan. 1782	black	x
	a. " " (no stars)	1791-1828	black	x
PM6	Montreal (Month & Day) Apr. 1785-Oct. 1789		black	x
	a. With year date	Feb.y 1785	black	x
PM7	HALIFAX N.S. (Framed)	June 1786	black	40.00
PM8	MONTREAL (Month & Day) May 1789-Apr. 1799		black	x
	a. With year "99	Aug.-Dec. 1799	black	x
	b. With year "1800" or "1801"	Mar. 1800-Oct. 1801	black	x
	c. Whole marking in one line with year in full	Nov.-Dec. 1801	black	x
PM9	ST. JOHN N.B.	1793-94	black	50.00
PM10	St. John N. B. and date	1795-96	black	35.00
	a. With stars instead of stops	1797-1824	black	25.00
	b. With one star and one stop (Fig. 6)	1798	black	x
PM11	Halifax (Double lined frame)	1795	black	50.00

Type PM11

Type PM12

Type PM13 has no frame.

Type					
PM12	HALIFAX (Single line frame)	Aug. 1797-1799	black	50.00
PM13	HALIFAX (No frame)	1799-1816	black	25.00
PM14	BERTHIER	1787-1829	black	x
PM15	DUNDAS	1799-1829	black	x
PM16	HALIFAX	1799-1816	black	25.00
PM17	KINGSTON	1799-1829	black	x
PM18	MONTREAL	1777-1829	red	x
PM19	SANDWICH	1799-1829	black	x
PM20	YORK (later Toronto)	1799-1828	black	x

B. Circular Postmarks
Introduced by Hugh Finlay 1765-1800

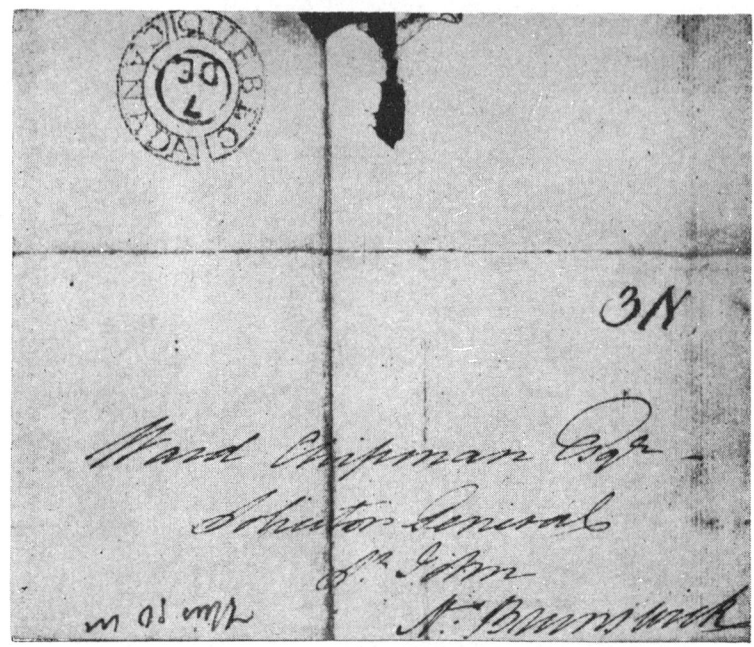

Fig. 7. Letter Showing Type PM24 With Bishop Mark Type 1.

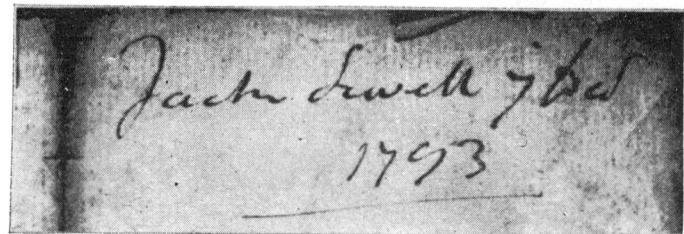

Fig. 8. Endorsement "Jackson Lowell, 7 Dec. 1793" on the above.

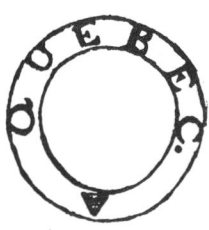

Type PM22
The triangle does not show in most impressions.

Type PM23

Type PM24 Type PM25
With Year Date

REFERENCE LIST.

PM22	QUEBEC	Nov. 1780-1788	black	25.00
	a. With Bishop Mark on letter also	1788	black	30.00
	b. With Bishop Mark in center of postmark Fig.(9)	1781-89	black	50.00
PM23	HALIFAX N. SCOTIA	Apr. 1788-1792	black	35.00
	a. Month with Capital letter		black	x
	b. Month all caps like "HALIFAX"		black	x
	c. Date in full thus "1792"		black	x
PM24	QUEBEC CANADA with Bishop Mark	Sep. 1791	black	x
PM25	QUEBEC with Bishop Mark	Sep. 1791-1797	black	x

Fig. 9. Entire Cover (1788) Showing Type PM22b (Retouched) and Type 2 Bishop Mark. About One-Half Actual Size.

From 1801 the town marks become more or less conventional and quite common. There is one outstanding exception and that is the Triangular Mark used by Quebec in 1841. (See Chapter on Cancellations for a discussion of the later Postmarks).

The Bishop Mark[1] was introduced in America in about 1750, and was first used in New York. A similar type was used in Quebec from about 1775. The Bishop Mark was also intended to be used in conjunction with types PM22, to PM25.

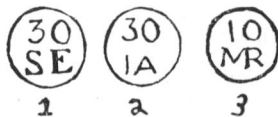

Three types of Bishop marks were used in Quebec:

    Type 1 with PM22 and PM24   1776-1794
    Type 2 with PM 22   1781-1789
    Type 3 with PM22   1792-1797

The historical interest of these early postal markings is great, and with the opening of the 19th century covers bearing various postmarks, etc., become more frequent.

The postal services of Prince Edward Island and Nova Scotia were separated from Canada in 1816. In 1828 the New Brunswick service was transferred to Nova Scotia. Postal markings of these colonies from the dates mentioned to the formation of the Dominion properly belong to the postal history of the self governing colonies.

---

1 Note on the Bishop Mark: The Bishop Mark was the invention of Henry Bishop, Postmaster General under Charles II, 1660-1663. In reply to charges of mismanagement he wrote (among other things) "A stamp is invented that is putt upon every letter shewing the day of the moneth that every letter comes to the office, so that no Letter Carryer may dare detayne a letter from post to post: which before was usual." Bishop died March 23, 1692, and buried in Henfield, Sussex, England.

Chapter III

THE MANUSCRIPT AND HANDSTRUCK POSTAGE STAMPS OF 1795-1875

These are actually the first postage stamps, as these markings were only struck on letters which were prepaid. Some of the types were made locally but most types were issued by the G.P.O., London, until 1851, when the Canadian Post Office contracted directly with John Francis of London, the contractor for the British Post Office, to furnish such markings as were needed[1]. Manuscript markings are known as early as 1764. (See Chapter II, Fig. 1).

General Issues

These types were supplied to a number of offices or for general use in one office. They have no indication as to office of use, but the superscription of the letter will usually be sufficient to allocate any particular marking.

We have given the post office from which many of the types are known to have been used, but the existence of any type from other offices or the discovery of earlier dates should occasion no surprise, nor should the occurence of colors other than listed be unusual, as we merely list items we have seen or have been reliably reported.

The chief purpose of giving a post office from which the type is known is to give it an identification independent of any numbering system.

The prices are for reasonably clear strikes on entire letters or covers. Fronts of letters or covers are worth about 30% of the price quoted while cut squares only rate about 10% of the quotations. Letters or covers bearing adhesive stamps on which these markings are struck while of interest and great historical importance, nevertheless reduce to Handstruck Stamp to a postal marking. Such letters and covers carry an additional premium of about 20% of the value listed for the handstruck item.

For example:

H36 On entire letter or envelope	—	2.50
On Front only	—	.75
Cut Square	—	.25
On cover with adhesive stamp	—	.50 + value of cover

The rate of postage is frequently added in manuscript or struck with a handstamp. (See note page 40.)

A. General Issues

    P<small>AID</small>.   paid

Type H1   Type H2   Type H3   Type H4

REFERENCE LIST

#	Date	Red	Black[2]	Post Office
H1	Sep. 1790-Apr. 1792		25.00	Halifax, N. S.
H2	1795-Dec. 1815	10.00	x	Fredericton, N. B.
H3	July 1818-Sept. 1824		x	Niagara, U. C.
H4	July 1826		x	L'Assomption, L. C.

1. Appendix E #1, 2.
2. Appendix B, #3, 4. From this it can be seen that from 1839 black on Paid letters was against the regulations.

#	Date	Color		Post Office
		Red	Black	
H5	Oct. 1838	2.50		Cornwall, U. C.
H6	Aug. 1842	1.50		Montreal, L. C.
H7	Nov. 1842	3.50		Amherstburg, U. C.
H8	Dec. 1842	1.50		Montreal, L. C.
H9	May 1843	1.25	1.50	Kingston, U. C.
H10	Sept. 1843	1.50		Dundas, U. C.
H11	Feb. 1848	1.75		Three Rivers, L. C.
H12	Dec. 1848		1.25	Howard, U. C.
H13	Jul 1850	1.50		Coburg, U. C.
H14	Apr. 1851	.50	.50	Montreal, L. C.
H15	Jan. 1852	1.25		Hamilton, U. C.
H16	Oct. 1853	1.50		Guelph, U. C.
H17	Apr. 1854	2.00		St. Denis L. C.
H18	July 1855	1.00		Montreal, L. C.
H19	July 1855	1.50		Silver Creek
H20	Aug. 1855	1.50		St. Benoit, L. C.
H21	Mar. 1858	1.00		St. Agatha, L. C.
H22	Jul. 1858 (Page 25)	1.25		Windsor, U. C.
H23	Sept. 1858	.50	.50	Note
H24	Jan. 1859	.50	.50	Note
H25	July 1859	3.50		Note
H26	Jan. 1866	.50	.50	Galt, U. C.
H27	18—	1.50		Note
H28	18— (Page 25)	1.50		Windsor, U. C.

Note: Types H23, H24, and H25 were in general use and may be found from many offices.

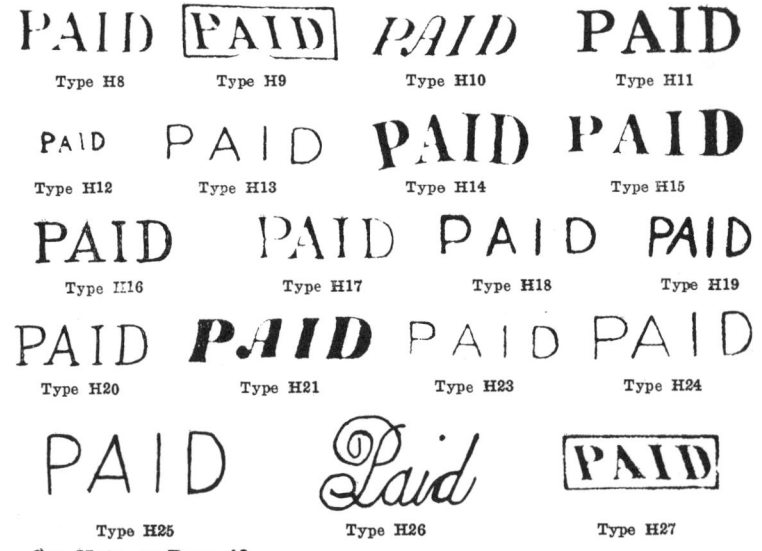

See Note on Page 40.

 Type H22

 Type H28

B. City Types

These types include the name of the Post Office at which they were used.

Type H29 — POST-OFFICE SHELBURNE

Type H30 — QUEBEC PAID

Type H31 — PAID AT QUEBEC.L.C.

Type H32a — MONTREAL PAID AU25 1846 CANADA

Type H32b — MONTREAL PAID JU22 1861 CANADA

Type H33 — TORONTO-CANADA SP 6 1853 PAID

Type H34 — PAID AT HAMILTON MY 16 1851 C W

Type H35 — PAID OC 28 1853 QUEBEC.L.C.

Type H36 — TORONTO.C.W. SEP 15 1855 Paid

Type H37   Type H38   Type H39

Type H40   Type H41

REFERENCE LIST

#	Date	Post Office		Red	Black	Note
H29a	1795-1824	SHELBURNE	Date in center in ms.		20.00	Note 1
H30	1815-30	QUEBEC		35.00	20.00	
H31	1842-50	QUEBEC		10.00		Note 2
H32a	Aug. 1844-69	MONTREAL		1.50	1.25	Note 3
b	Jun 1861—	Larger lettering		1.00		
H33	Feb. 1851-60	TORONTO		2.00	2.50	
H34	May 1851-	HAMILTON		2.50	3.00	
H35	Oct. 1853	QUEBEC		1.50		
H36	Aug. 1855	TORONTO		2.50		
H37	Dec. 1855	OTTAWA		2.25		
H38	Mar. 1861	TORONTO		2.00		
H39	July 1862	TORONTO		2.25		
H40	Apr. 1863	TORONTO		2.00		
H41	Oct. 1866	TORONTO		1.50		

Note 1. This was used until 1833, but any date after 1816 belongs to the Nova Scotia P.O. which was separated from Canada that year. Although the word "Paid" does not appear on this type nevertheless it only occurs on prepaid letters.

Note 2. The crowned circle type was registered at the G.P.O., London, Jan. 13, 1842. Machine made of brass. This type of stamp was supplied to all ports served by the British Mail Boats under the reforms of the packet service introduced by J. McQueen in conjunction with the Royal Mail Steam Packet Co.
Instructions were issued on December 22, 1841, by the G.P.O., London, which included the following:
"Letters . . . . . must be distinctly stamped by you on the sealed side with the stamp to be furnished for that purpose showing the name of the Port from whence despatched and the date when posted."

Note 3. Commonly called "tombstone type." Originally issued by the G.P.O., London.

C. Hand Struck "PAID" Stamps With Value Expressed in PENCE

General Issues[1]

With value expressed 1d, 3d, etc.

Type H42

Type H43a   Type H43b   Type H43c   Type H43d

Type H44

Type H45

Type H46a   Type H46b   Type H46c

REFERENCE LIST

#		Date	Red	Color Black	Blue	P. O.
H42	1d	Oct. 1853		3.50		TORONTO
H43a-d	3d	Oct. 1851	1.50	1.00	3.00	Note 1.
H44	3d	May 1853		5.00		Gananoque, U. C.
H45	3d	Mar. 1859		X		Warsaw, U. C.
H46a-c	6d	Aug. 1851	2.00	2.50	5.00	Note 1.

Note 1. The Types of #H43, and #H46 vary in the size of the circle and type of lettering. They were used in many offices.

1. See Appendix F, Table A.

D. With Value Expressed in Numerals Only.

Type H47

Type H48

Type H49

Type H50

Type H51

Type H52

Type H53

Type H54

Type H55

Type H56

Type H57
Type H57a—"6" 24mm high

Type H57b

Type H58

See Note on Page 40.

REFERENCE LIST

3d

		Color		
		Red	Black	Post Office
H47	Oct. 1851	6.00	5.00	Gananoque, U. C.
H48	June 1854	3.00		Lonsdale, U. C.
H49	Nov. 1854	3.00		Kincardine, U. C.
H50	Jan. 1855	5.00		Nelson, U. C.
H51	May 1857	3.00		Wallaceburg, U. C.
H52	Aug. 1857	3.50		Pefferlaw, U. C.
H53	Feb. 1858	5.00		Delaware, U. C.
H54	Oct. 1858	2.50		Babcaygeon, U. C.
H55	Dec. 1859	2.50		Warwick, L. C.

6d

H56	185-		2.50	3.00	
H57	185-		2.50	3.00	
H57a	Nov. 1858	"6" 24mm high.	x		Ormstown, L. C.

9d

H57b	Feb. 1855 (Note)	x		Kincardine, U. C.
H58	Apr. 1835	x		Buckingham, L. C.

Note: #57b may be a "6" inverted in error.

E. City Types

Type H59   Type H61

Type H60a   Type H60b   Type H60c

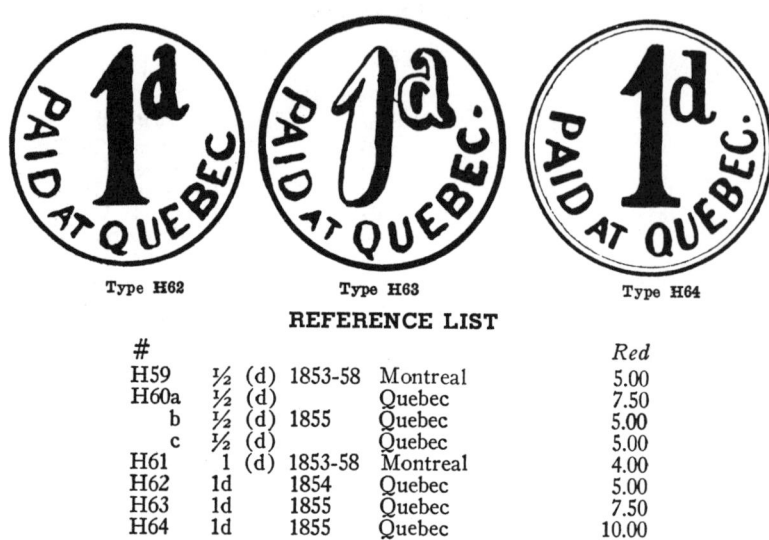

Type H62   Type H63   Type H64

REFERENCE LIST

#					Red
H59	½	(d)	1853-58	Montreal	5.00
H60a	½	(d)		Quebec	7.50
b	½	(d)	1855	Quebec	5.00
c	½	(d)		Quebec	5.00
H61	1	(d)	1853-58	Montreal	4.00
H62	1d		1854	Quebec	5.00
H63	1d		1855	Quebec	7.50
H64	1d		1855	Quebec	10.00

F. The Decimal Currency Handstruck Stamps

In 1859 the currency was placed on a decimal basis—3d being equal to 5c. Although a penalty of 2 cents was levied on unpaid letters, the postage could be paid in cash as before. Letters were then struck with "Paid 5," "PAID 10," etc.

1. General Issues

Single Rate
Types H65a to 65aa

PAID 5   PAID 5   PAID 5
a   b   c

PAID 5   PAID 5   PAID 5
d   e   f

PAID 5   PAID 5   PAID 5
g   h   i

PAID 5   PAID 5
j   k

30 *

PAID 5
l

PAID 5
m

PAID 5
n

PAID 5
o

PAID 5
p

PAID 5
q

PAID 5
r

PAID 5
s

PAID 5
t

PAID 5
u

PAID 5
v

PAID 5
w

PAID 5
x

PAID 5
y

PAID 5
z

PAID 5
aa

These were extensively used in many offices from July 1, 1859 to Oct. 1, 1875. On Oct. 1, 1875 prepayment by adhesive stamps became compulsory.
See Note on Page 40.

Double Rate

PAID 10 PAID 10
H66a   H66b

Triple Rate

H67

REFERENCE LIST

			Red	Black	Blue
H65a to aa	1859-1875		2.50	2.50	3.50
H66a, b	1859-1875		2.50	2.50	4.00
H67	1859-75	(TORONTO)	5.00		

For rate markings see Chapter IV where these are listed and discussed. Unpaid markings will be found in Chapter on "The Handstruck Postage Due Stamps."

2. Paid 5—Special Types

Type H68a

PAID 5   PAID 5

Type H68b   Type H68c

   PAID 5

Type H68d   Type H68e

See Note on Page 40.

Type H68f   Type H68g

Type H69

Type H70

REFERENCE LIST

#		Red	
H68a	1859	2.50	Charleston, L. C.
H68b	Sep. 1861	2.50	Williamstown, U. C.
H68c	Nov. 1861	6.00	Craigleith, U. C.
H69	Jan. 1862	7.50	Nissouri, U. C.
H70	Oct. 1862	6.00	Kingston, U. C.
H68d	Nov. 1864	2.00	Oakland, U. C.
H68e	Jan. 1866	2.50	Oil Springs, C. W.
H68f	Mar. 1866	3.00	Brougham (Note)
H68g	Mar. 1867	(7.50)	

Note: Type H68g is in green.

G. The Handstruck United States Stamps.

These rather unusual, if not unique, stamps were used at various offices from 1830 at least, and until November 15, 1847 (Appendix D #3 and #4). Although we have examined many hundreds of stampless covers of Canada, we have only noted a dozen examples of these markings.

H-US1—Oval Double Line "Niagara U. Canada Paid to New York" and Ms. 25 on entire Letter from York 21 Jan 1830 to London, Eng. Note Ms. "Paid 9 & 1/3". All Markings in Red.

H-US4.

REFERENCE LIST

#	Date		Red	City
H-US 1	1830		x	Niagara
H-US 2	1836	"PAID 9 & 25"	x	Toronto[1]
H-US 3	1837	"PAID 7 & 25"	x	Toronto[1]
H-US 4	1847		50.00	Montreal[2]

The postmasters of these and other offices were also postmasters for the United States in those towns. These handstruck stamps are therefore of peculiar interest in being equally handstruck United States Postage Stamps *used only outside the country!*

---

1. See Fig. 3A, 3B Page 61.
2. See also Fig. 15 Page 67, and Fig. 16, Page 68.

Chapter IV

THE HANDSTRUCK POSTAGE OR POSTAGE DUE STAMPS[1]

This class of handstruck stamp has commonly been referred to heretofore as "rating" stamps. While it is true that these stamps show the amount of charges on a letter, nevertheless they can be considered as handstruck stamps. If struck in *red* they are usually on PREPAID LETTERS, while if struck in *black* they usually indicate charges to be collected—that is POSTAGE DUE stamps[2]. Struck on adhesive stamps they are rare.

Ia. Pence Stamps—With Currency Expressed

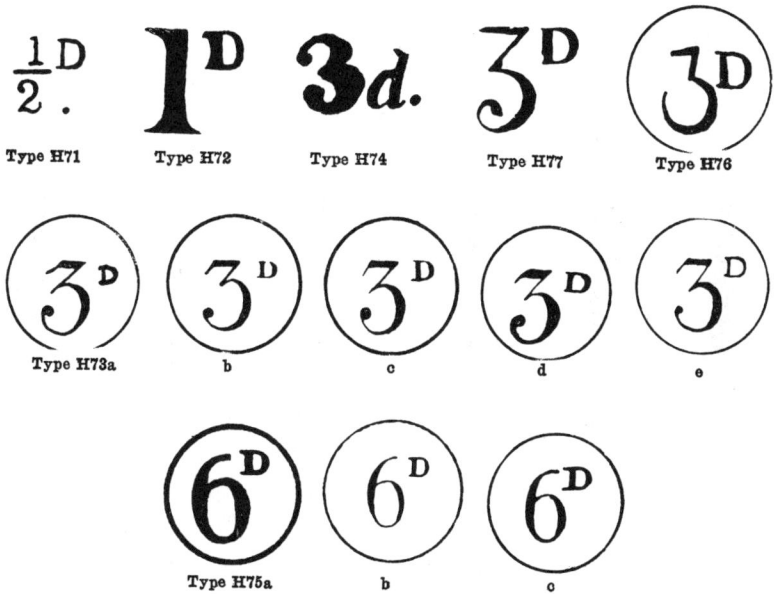

REFERENCE LIST

#	Denom. & Date	A. Red	B. Black	Post Office
H71	½d 1852		7.50	Toronto
H72	1d 1852		5.00	Toronto
H73a-e	3d 1852	2.50	1.25	General use
H74	3d May 1852			New Carlisle, L.C.
H75a-c	6d 1852	2.50	2.00	General use
H76	3d 1855			
H77	3d 1856	7.50		Norwood

1. See Appendix F, Table A.
2. Appendix B, #18, Sec. 22, Page 9-B.

Ib. Pence Stamps—No Currency Expressed

½ (d)

Type H77   Type H78   Type H79   Type H80   Type H81   Type H82

REFERENCE LIST

#	Date		A. Red	B. Black	Post Office
H77	1852			2.50	Toronto
H78	1852			2.50	Toronto
H79	1852			2.50	Montreal
H80	1852			2.50	Quebec
H81	1853			2.75	Toronto
H82	1859			3.00	Toronto

1 (d)

Type H83   Type H84   Type H85   Type H86   Type H87   Type H88

REFERENCE LIST

#	Date	A. Red	B. Black	Post Office
H83	1851-8		1.00	General use
H84	Aug. 1852		1.25	Quebec, L.C.
H85	Feb. 1853		1.00	Montreal, L.C.
H86	Sep. 1854		1.25	General use
H87	Feb. 1855		1.00	Toronto, U.C.
H88	Jul. 1858		1.25	Quebec, L.C.

3 (d)

Type H89

See Note on Page 40.

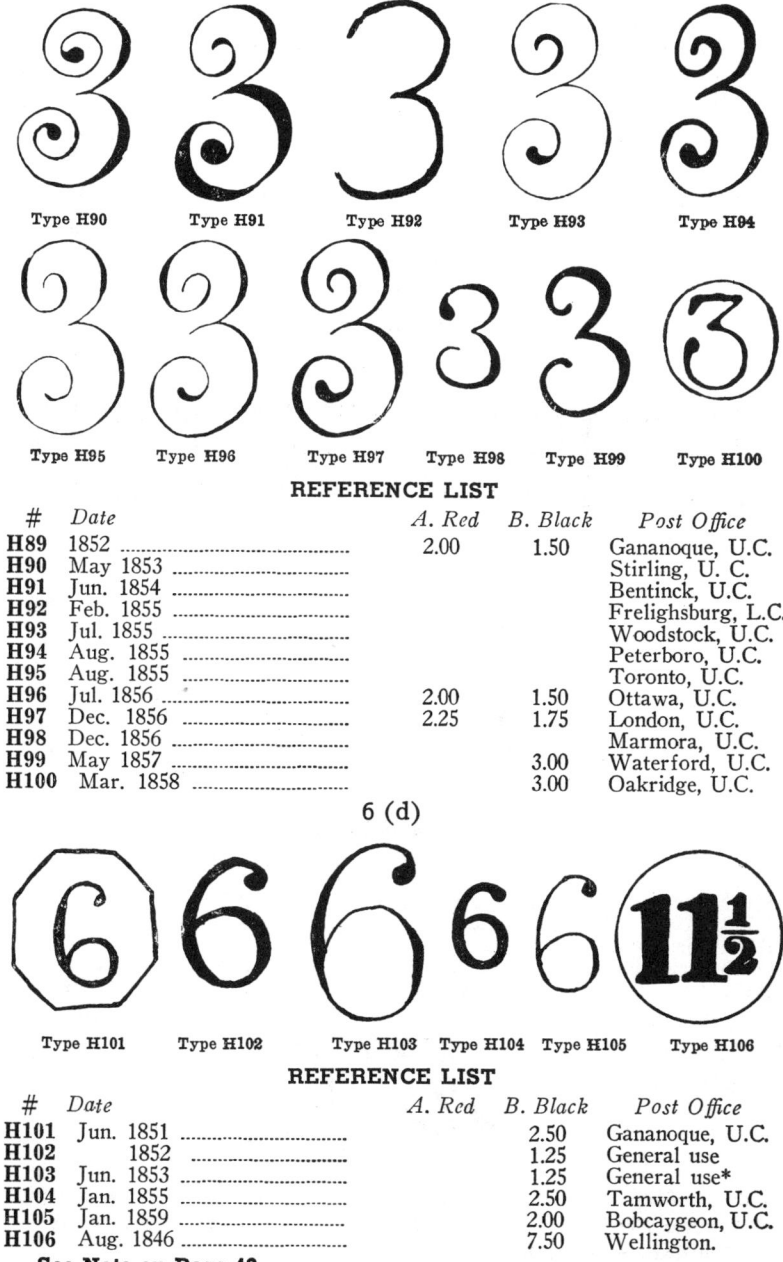

Type H90 Type H91 Type H92 Type H93 Type H94

Type H95 Type H96 Type H97 Type H98 Type H99 Type H100

REFERENCE LIST

#	Date	A. Red	B. Black	Post Office
H89	1852	2.00	1.50	Gananoque, U.C.
H90	May 1853			Stirling, U. C.
H91	Jun. 1854			Bentinck, U.C.
H92	Feb. 1855			Frelighsburg, L.C.
H93	Jul. 1855			Woodstock, U.C.
H94	Aug. 1855			Peterboro, U.C.
H95	Aug. 1855			Toronto, U.C.
H96	Jul. 1856	2.00	1.50	Ottawa, U.C.
H97	Dec. 1856	2.25	1.75	London, U.C.
H98	Dec. 1856			Marmora, U.C.
H99	May 1857		3.00	Waterford, U.C.
H100	Mar. 1858		3.00	Oakridge, U.C.

6 (d)

Type H101 Type H102 Type H103 Type H104 Type H105 Type H106

REFERENCE LIST

#	Date	A. Red	B. Black	Post Office
H101	Jun. 1851		2.50	Gananoque, U.C.
H102	1852		1.25	General use
H103	Jun. 1853		1.25	General use*
H104	Jan. 1855		2.50	Tamworth, U.C.
H105	Jan. 1859		2.00	Bobcaygeon, U.C.
H106	Aug. 1846		7.50	Wellington.

See Note on Page 40.

*See Type H57a. Varies somewhat in thickness.

II. Decimal Currency

The decimal currency system became the legal system in Canada on July 1, 1859[1]. From that date various handstruck stamps appeared until 1875 when prepayment by adhesive stamps or stamped envelopes became compulsory[2]. Most of these are unpaid stamps, but some may be found in red. Those with the word "unpaid" will be found in the Chapter on the Handstruck Postage Dues.

IIa. Decimal Currency—Value Expressed in "C" or "Ct"

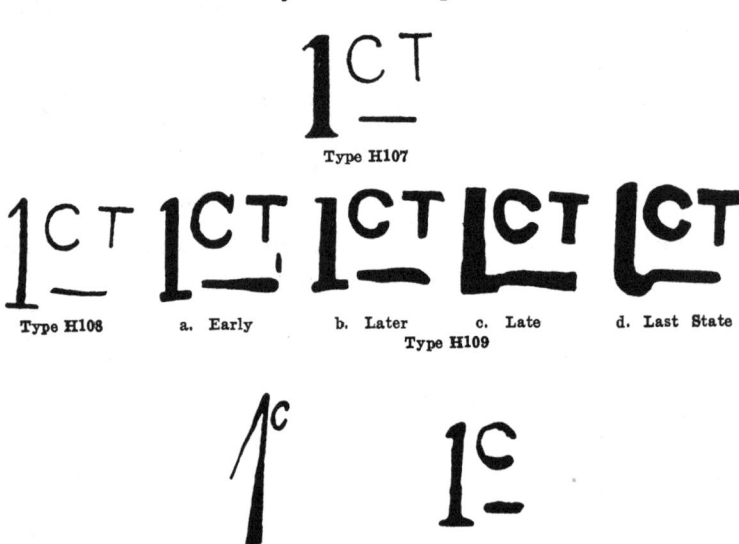

Type H107

Type H108   a. Early   b. Later   c. Late   d. Last State
                         Type H109

Type H110   Type H111

REFERENCE LIST

#	Date		A. Red	B. Black	Post Office
H107	Aug. 1859		2.50		Toronto
H108	Aug. 1859			3.00	
H109	Feb. 1861		2.50		Toronto
H110	Jun. 1863		2.50		Montreal
H111	1860 (?)		2.00		General use

Type H112

#	Date		A. Red	B. Black	Post Office
H112	Apr. 1863			1.50	Paris, C. W.

See Note on Page 40.

---
1. Appendix B #31.
2. Appendix A #13.

IIb. Decimal Currency. Figures of Value Only

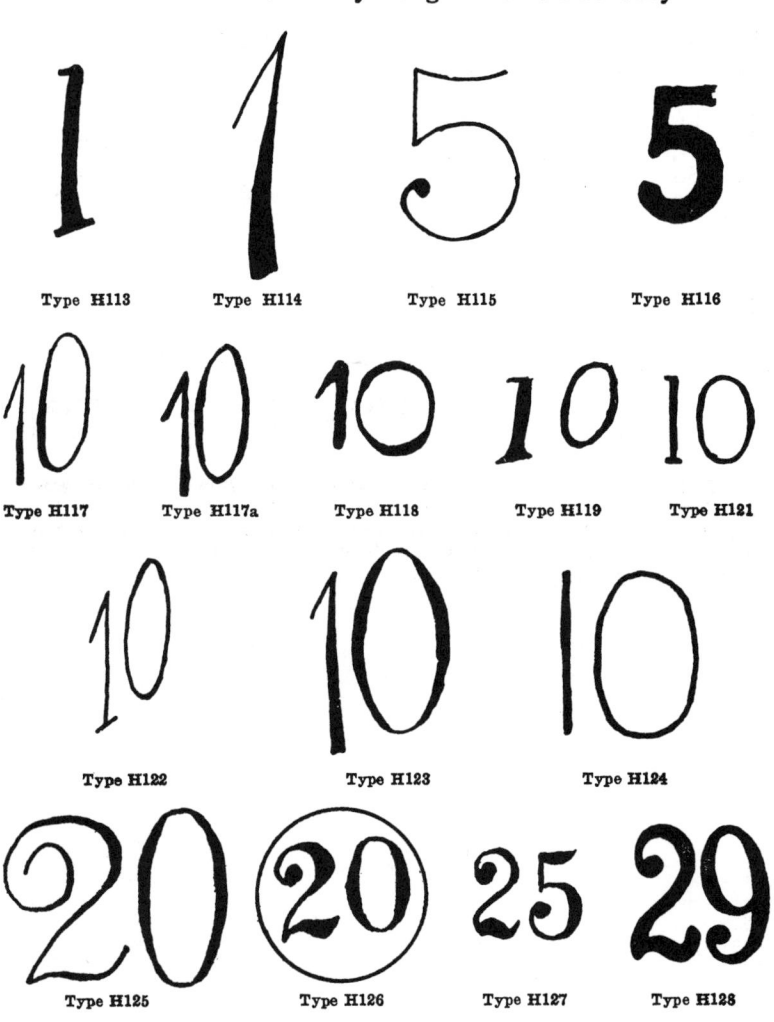

Type H113   Type H114   Type H115   Type H116

Type H117   Type H117a   Type H118   Type H119   Type H121

Type H122   Type H123   Type H124

Type H125   Type H126   Type H127   Type H128

REFERENCE LIST

1 (c)

#	Date	A. Red	B. Black	Post Office
H113	Dec. 1859		x	Montreal
H114	Oct. 1865		x	Ottawa

5 (c)

#	Date	A. Red	B. Black	Post Office
H115	Jul. 1863		2.50	Montreal
H116	Apr. 1868		3.50	Alsa Grand, C.W.

See Note on Page 40.

10 (c)

#	Date	A. Red	B. Black	Post Office
H117	1859		x	
H117a	Jan. 1860		2.00	Toronto
H118	Apr. 1861		2.00	Quebec
H119	Feb. 1865		2.00	
H121	Feb. 1865		2.00	Fort William, L.
H122	Sep. 1865		3.00	Morrisburg
H123	Apr. 1868		2.00	Peterboro, C. W.
H124	Feb. 1870		2.00	Quebec (?)

20 (c)

#	Date	A. Red	B. Black	Post Office
H125	Jan. 1860		R	
H126			R	

25 (c)

#	Date	A. Red	B. Black	Post Office
H127	Feb. 1863		R	Clifton

29 (c)

#	Date	A. Red	B. Black	Post Office
H128	Jan. 1860		R	London, Toronto

NOTE: Various combinations of "Paid" and rate marks are known, thus Type H16 plus Type H105 each struck separately may occur on the same cover and mislead the tyro into believing a new type has been found. Care should be taken therefore to consider all the possibilities before making such a conclusion.

Chapter V

THE HANDSTRUCK OCEAN MAIL STAMPS[1]

In 1840 Samuel Cunard entered into a contract with the admiralty to provide two trips monthly each way between Liverpool, Halifax, and Boston, and Liverpool, Picton and Quebec. The payment was £55,000 per annum. Shortly after an additional £5,000 per annum was aded on the consideration that the steamers should leave the American ports as well as Liverpool on fixed dates.

The first trip was made by the "Brittannia" which left Liverpool on July 1, 1840, arriving Halifax twelve and a half days later. The mails reached Quebec in eighteen days from Liverpool.

The rate for letters was set on July 6, 1840, at 1sh.2d sterling, equivalent 1sh4d currency. Paid letters were to be marked in red, in both sterling and currency, while unpaid letters were to be marked in black in sterling only.

H-01

In March, 1854, the Imperial authorities reduced the rate to 8d stg.; 10d cy by British Packet to New York, and 6dstg.; 7½d cy if by Canadian Packet via Quebec or Halifax,[2] and the rate was marked in sterling or currency, or both.

H-02

Type H-03

Type H-04

---
1. See Appendix F, Table A.
2. Appendix M #2.

10ᵈCʸ   *10ᵈCʸ*

Type H-05   Type H-06

REFERENCE LIST

			A. Red	B. Black	
H-O1	1840-54	½ stg. PAID ¼ cy.......			
H-O2	1854-	6d stg.	2.50	2.50	
H-O3	1854-	8d stg. paid 10 cy............	15.00	12.50	Quebec
H-O4	1854-	PAID 8d stg...................	3.00	3.00	Kingston
H-O5		PAID 6d Stg.....................	x	x	Quebec
H-O6		7½d cy.	x	x	Quebec
H-O7	1854-	10 cy.	2.50	2.50	
H-O8	1854-	10 cy.	3.50	3.50	

There were a number of markings used on unpaid letters from England. These will be found in the chapter on "The Handstruck Postage Due Stamps," section on Ocean Mails (q.v.).

Chapter VI

POSTAL RELATIONS BETWEEN CANADA AND THE UNITED STATES
1792-1883

Introductory Remarks

The first postal convention between Canada and the United States was concluded in 1792. Under its terms letters *from Canada to the United States had to be prepaid to the lines,* but the United States charge could be prepaid or it was collected from the addressee. On the other hand *letters from the United States to Canada could be prepaid to the lines, or sent entirely unpaid,* the Canadian Post Office acting as agent for the United States Post Office. The United States Post Office, however, did not allow any of its offices to act as an agent for the Canadian Post Office Department. A rather anomalous situation to say the least!

Since the Canadian Post Office was acting as an agent for the United States Post Office in collecting postage due on letters from the United States, it was soon agreed that it (the Canadian Post Office) could also collect the United States Postage on letters sent from Canada, and since the Deputy Postmaster General received 20% commission on such collections, it was a lucrative business, although only quasi-legal[1].

It is quite true that the General Post Office in London protested strongly but the legal situation at the time was so confused that Sutherland and later Stayner continued the arrangement until January 5, 1844, when Stayner, the Deputy P. M. G., was placed on a straight salary of £2500 per annum. The arrangement was not upset in its actual operation but the 20% commission went into the Post Office revenue, instead of into the private income of the Deputy Postmaster General, and Postmasters at the Exchange Offices[1a]. The next important event affecting Canadian-American postal relations was the Act of Congress passed March 3, 1845, effective July 1, 1845, which reduced the rates of postage in the United States to 5c per half ounce for distances up to 300 miles, and 10c per half ounce for distances over 300 miles. This Act of Congress was the subject of a long Department Order by Stayner dated 5th June, 1845[2], in which he calls attention to the difference in the scale of progression of the American rates as compared with the system then in force in Canada.

Under the new laws a ½ oz. letter from Montreal to New York would be charged 4½d Canadian, plus 10c American=6d, or a total of 10½d. Postage to the lines had to be prepaid but United States postage could be prepaid or not as the sender desired.

The first general issue of United States stamps was made on July 1, 1847, being the well known 5c and 10c (Scott #28 and 29).

This was of no immediate importance in Canada, but it was quickly realized that the issue of United States stamps made it of no advantage to the Canadian Post Office to act as agent for the United States Post Office any longer. Accordingly an official circular was sent out by Stayner, dated 25th of Oct., 1847, wherein he states that *no American postage* is to be collected on and after the 16th of November, 1847[3]. The following day a special circular was sent to Frontier Postmasters, advising them of the change in the handling of mails across the border[4].

1. "History of the P. O. in B. N. A." by William Smith.
1a. See page 58 for further details of Exchange offices.
2. Appendix D #2.
3. Appendix D #3.
4. Appendix D #4.

Fig. A. Post Office Notice of 1846 concerning letters to the United States.

From this it will be seen that in order to prepay the United States Postage on a letter from Canada to the United States on and after the 16th of November, 1847, it was necessary to have United States stamps affixed. It will be observed that all such letters also had to be prepaid to the lines.

This arrangement continued until the 14th of May, 1849[5], which was the date of settling the details of an agreement proclaimed on the 15th of February, 1849, by President Polk, announcing the ratification of a convention concerning the postal arrangements between the United States, Great Britain, and the British North American Colonies[6]. Articles XIII and XIV of this convention state that letters between the United States and Canada "shall be charged according to the rates of postage" . . . "for inland letters," and that the rates of postage "shall be combined into one rate, of which *payment in advance shall be optional.*"

The transfer of the Canadian Post Office from Imperial to Provincial control on April 6, 1851 necessitated that arrangements be made to continue the interchange of mail between Canada and the United States. This was covered by Department Order No. 1[7], which continued the arrangements as before with the necessary modifications in rates as governed by the various Acts and regulations of the Canadian Government.

Paragraph #4 specifically states that the rates include the *whole charge* from any place in Canada to any place in the United States, and paragraph #6 states that prepayment is optional. It was necessary, however, to prepay in full, or to forward entirely unpaid, that is, partial payment was not allowed[8].

On the 10th of June, 1851, the United States agreed to a rate of 1d, (2c) for letters between Canada and the United States where the only transportation was the ferry, or a short land journey over the International Boundary between the two points[9], an arrangement which continued until February 1, 1875[10].

The special ferriage rate was the continuation of a practice which had been in use for many years. See Figure 1A which illustrates a letter from Madison, N. Y. to Chippewa, N. C. in which "Ferriage" is 2d of a total of 18 pence or 1sh6p.

It will be noted that the P. L. & R. of the United States for 1852 (April 3), Section 341[11] gives a list of exchange offices, and Section 343[12] instructs on the handling or *paid* or *unpaid* letters.

This arrangement of optional prepayment of letters *to or from* Canada and the United States continued until the "Postal Arrangement" of 1875[13], when prepayment became compulsory[14], although from April 1, 1868, a fine of four cents was levied on *unpaid* letters, as prepaid letters were reduced to 6 cents per ½ oz. on that date. On March 1, 1888, a new treaty became effective, which abrogated the 1875 convention. The new treaty was very similar to the previous convention, and was primarily made to make the postal relations conform to Articles V and VI of the Universal Postal Union Agreement of 1878, and amendments thereto of 1885.

Section A. Canada Exchange Markings.

Imperial Control

These markings were applied to letters *from Canada* to the United States by the Canadian Exchange offices.

The first type, a two line marking, was introduced by Hugh Finlay in 1792 and was struck on letters that had been paid to the lines only. Letters that had

---
5. Appendix D #5 Note 2.
6. Appendix D #5.
7. Appendix D #6.
8. Appendix D #6, 17, 20.
9. Appendix D #16.
10. Appendix D #34.
11. Appendix D #41.
12. Appendix D #43.
13. Appendix D #34.
14. By cash or stamps until October 1, 1875, then by stamps only. Appendix B, #40 paragraph 6.

been paid through of course were not marked other than "PAID", "Paid to New York", or "U.S.P. Paid" etc. The mails were exchanged at Burlington, Vt. The marking illustrated below is very rare.

AMERICAN INLAND POSTAGE DUE ☞

Type EMD1.

EMD1 "AMERICAN INLAND POSTAGE DUE ☞" 50.00

Under the agreement of March 25, 1851, effective April 6, 1851, letters from Canada were to be marked "Canada", or "Canada 10 cts". Conversely letters from the United States were to be marked "U. States" or "U. States 6d". (Appendix D #6 paragraph 9; #11; #43).

Provincial Control

THE EXCHANGE MARKINGS OF 1851-1875[1]

NOTE: There are no doubt types not listed here. These markings were hand cut and may vary considerably in length and other dimensions. Markings used at the New Brunswick-Maine, and Nova Scotia Exchange Offices are not listed.

1. No rate expressed

Struck in red on PAID letters, and in black on UNPAID letters.

A. Arc Types

Type Ia. April 1851.   Type Ib. May 1851.   Type Ic. June 1851.

NOTE. Type Ia was supplied by Rawdon, Wright, Hatch & Edson. (Appendix H #2, 3) Types Ib, and Ic are obviously locally cut attempts to duplicate Type Ia.

B. Straight Line Types

CANADA

Type II. October 1853.

2. Rate Expressed, "10", "10 cts" or "10 cents"

A. Straight Line Types with "PAID."

CANADA   CANADA   CANADA
PAID 10 Cts   PAID 10 cts.   PAID 10 Cts

Type IIIa. General use from 1852.   Type IIIb. Toronto 1852   Type IIIc.

---
1. See Appendix F, Table C.

PAID
CANADA-10-CENTS
Type IIIe. "CANADA" in Serifed letters and "PAID 10CTS" upright. See Fig. 50

B. Without "PAID"

CANADA. 10 Cts. CANADA 10 cts.
Type IVa. October 1851.   Type IVb. November 1851.

CANADA 10 Cts. CANADA 10 Cts.
Type IVc. December 1851.   Type IVd. March 1856.

CANADA·10·Cts CANADA-10 CENTS
Type IVe. September 1855.   Type IVf. March 1852.

CANADA 10
Type IVg. "Cts" Omitted.

C. Oval, Circular and Miscellaneous Types

Type Va. Windsor. September 1856.

Type Vb. Ribbon Shaped Type, used in Toronto, 1851.

Section B. United States Exchange Markings

Struck on letters *from* the United States to Canada by the United States Exchange Offices.

1. No currency expressed

A. Straight Line Types

U.STATES
Type I. Buffalo. 1859.

B. Arc Types

For Paid (Red) or Unpaid Letters (Black).

Type IIa. Buffalo. 1851.   Type IIb. Ogdensburgh. 1851. Shield slanting to left, Rouses Point 1852.   Type IIc. Buffalo. 1853.

NOTE: Types IIa, and IIc may sometimes have the rate "6", "15" or "20" stamped under the curve. This was added separately in most instances. The length of the arc varies from 30 to 35 mm.

C. Oval or Circular Types

Type III. Buffalo. 1861.

Similar types, but with inner circle dotted were used at New Brunswick-Maine Exchange Offices.

2. Rate Expressed in Pence

A. Straight Line Types

PAID

UNITED STATES PAID 6
Type IVa. Lewiston. 1860.

UNPAID

UNITED STATES 6ᴅ
Type IVb. Lewiston. 1858.

Ud. STATES 6D.
Similar to IVb But in One Line With
"UNITED" Abbreviated to "Ud."
Type IVc. Buffalo. 1852.

B. Arc Types
PAID

Type Va. Buffalo.
1864.

Type Vb. Buffalo.
1854.

Type Vc. Buffalo.

UNPAID

Type Vd. Buffalo.

Type Ve. Buffalo.

C. Oval or Circular Types

Type VIa. Lewiston.
1858.

Type VIb-I. Detroit.
1858.
Type VIc. Double Lined Oval.

Type VIb-II. Detroit.

3. Rate Expressed in Decimal Currency

A. Straight Line Types

PAID

Type VIIa. Lewiston.
1860.

UNPAID

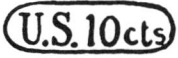
Type VIIb. Lewiston.
1864.

B. Arc Types

PAID (in red)   UNPAID (in black)

Type VIIIa. Detroit or
Sault Ste Marie. 1860.

Type VIIIb. Buffalo.
1854.

C. Oval and Circular Types

Type IXa-I. 1865.   Type IXb. Port Huron, Mich. 1853.   Type IXa-II. 1862.

Canadian Exchange Markings

			Red	Black	Value (any color)
EM-C	Type	Ia	x	x	2.50
		b		x	5.00
		c	x	x	10.00
EM-C	Type	II	x	x	2.50
EM-C	Type	IIIa	x	x	2.00
		b	x		2.00
		c	x		2.00
		d	x		2.00
		e	x		2.50
EM-C	Type	IVa		x	1.50
		b		x	1.50
		c		x	1.50
		d		x	1.50
		e		x	2.00
		f		x	1.75
		g		x	2.00
EM-C	Type	Va	x	x	2.50
		b		x	10.00

United States Exchange Markings

			Red	Black	Blue	Value (any color)
EM-US	Type	I	x	x		5.00
EM-US	Type	IIa	x	x	x	5.00
		b	x			5.00
		c	x			3.50
EM-US	Type	III	x	x		3.00
EM-US	Type	IVa	x			2.00
		b	x			2.50
		c	x			2.00
EM-US	Type	Va	x			2.50
		b	x			2.50
		c	x			3.00
		d		x		3.00
		e		x		3.00
EM-US	Type	VIa	x	x		3.50
		b	x	x		3.50
EM-US	Type	VIIa	x			3.50
		b		x		3.00
EM-US	Type	VIIIa	x			3.00
		b		x		2.50
EM-US	Type	IXa	x			2.50
		b	x			5.00

Section C. United States Rate Markings on Covers From Canada

The markings illustrated herewith, are, strictly speaking, United States markings and occur on many covers carried only in the United States Mails.

However, covers from Canada also frequently have these rate markings which are often of considerable help in the correct classification of such covers.

According to the P. L. & R. they were to be struck in red on a PAID letter, and black on an UNPAID letter (Appendix D #40, #43).

NOTE: These markings add 25 cents to 50 cents to value of a cover.

United States Rate Markings
1845-1868

"10" Cents

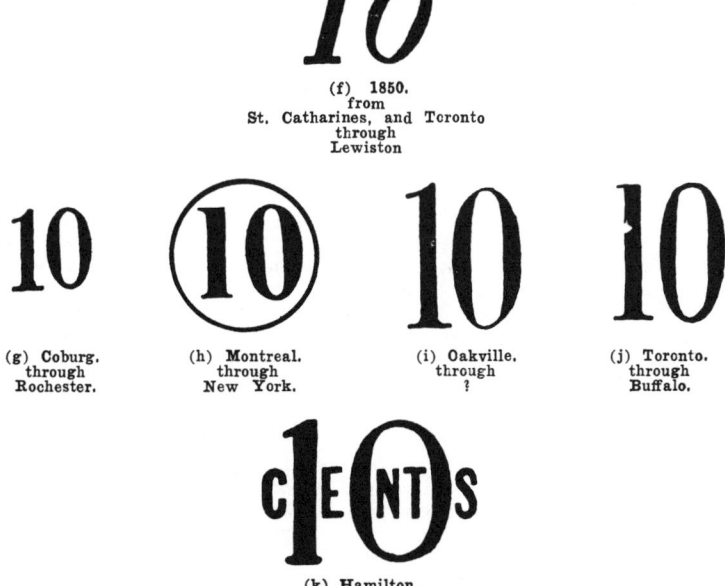

(a) 1848. On Letter from Niagara through Youngstown

(b) 1848.

(c) 1849.

(d) 1851. Kingston through Cape Vincent

(e) 1857.

Note: The "X" mark was sometimes struck twice to denote twenty cents on double weight letters.

(f) 1850. from St. Catharines, and Toronto through Lewiston

(g) Coburg. through Rochester.

(h) Montreal. through New York.

(i) Oakville. through ?

(j) Toronto. through Buffalo.

(k) Hamilton.

51 *

"20" Cents

20
1847.
(a) Kingston.
through
Cape Vincent.

20
1845.
(b) Montreal.
through
New York.

20
(c) 1850.
Coburg.
through
Rochester.

20
(b) 1851.

(e) 1854. Montreal through Portland, Me. Similar to (c) but Larger.

20
1850.
(f) St. Catharines.
through
Lewiston.

20
1858.
(g) Windsor.
through
Detroit.

Note: The "X" as mentioned above was sometimes struck twice to indicate "twenty cents".

Section D. The Classification of Covers From Canada to the United States

The procedure necessary to correctly classify a cover from Canada to the United States, or vice versa, should be so carefully outlined that collectors may, in the vast majority of the instances, do so quickly and accurately. There are, however, always certain exceptions, which require careful study and a thorough familiarity with the postal arrangements and mail routes of the time to arrive at any conclusion concerning them.

However, the procedure outlined in the following paragraphs should be helpful in most instances.

The first consideration is the date of the letter or cover.

First. If before *May 14, 1849*, inclusive, the Canadian postage must be prepaid to the line.

Second. If before *June 1, 1792*, the United States postage is UNPAID as it was not possible until 1792 to prepay the United States postage.

Third. If *between June 1, 1792, and November 15, 1847*, inclusive, the Canadian postage must be prepaid, but the United States postage could be PAID OR NOT at the option of the sender. *From July 1, 1847 United States stamps could be used to prepay the United States postage;* in other words stamps were equivalent to cash (Appendix D #45).

Fourth. If *between November 16, 1847, and May 14, 1849,* the Canadian postage must be prepaid, *but the United States postage could not be prepaid at Canadian offices,* althrough United States stamps could be affixed to be treated by the United States postal officials as they saw fit.

Fifth. If *between May 15, 1849, and April 5, 1851,* inclusive, the letter *could be prepaid through or not at all;* that is partial prepayment was not permitted. However, stamps were accepted as prepayment, and 1847 United States stamps occur on covers of this period. In addition large commercial firms and banks with charge accounts in both countries sent letters "Paid to the lines" which was credited to the Canadian offices, and the United States offices, respectively.

Sixth. From *April 6, 1851,* the date when Provincial control began the same conditions were in effect until June 30, 1851. The period of SIXTY NINE DAYS, from *April 23, 1851,* (when the 3d beaver was issued) *to June 30, 1851,* was the only time that United States and Canadian stamps could be used on the same cover and comply with the regulations.

Seventh. From *July 1, 1851,* the whole or through rate of 6d or 10c per half ounce could be paid in Canadian stamps or cash. The use of United States stamps was not countenanced although Canadian postmasters in handling letters with United States stamps affixed were to treat the letter as *UNPAID, and not to cancel the United States stamps,* but to allow them to be accepted or refused by the United States Postal Officials as they saw fit (see fourth).

Since *July 1, 1851,* was the date of the new reduced rates in the United States of 3c per ½ oz., it follows that the combination of a 3d beaver and a 3c 1851 was against the regulations, such covers that are known with this combination having been passed in error; negligence, or being treated as UNPAID by the Canadian postmasters. (See Fig. 46).

The points discussed are set forth in the tabulation on page 54.

Having classified the cover by the seven periods discussed the question of rates should then be examined. The postage rates in Canada and the United States varied at different times, and the method of computing rates also varied. These factors have to be carefully considered in arriving at conclusions as to the use, and correctness of the markings on any cover.

The Canadian rates are given first:

CANADA RATES

(All dates are inclusive)

TABLE 1

June 1, 1792 to January 4, 1844

up to 60 Miles   4d Stg. per single sheet of paper.
60 to 100 Miles   6d Stg. per single sheet of paper.
101 to 200 Miles   8d Stg. per single sheet of paper.
201 to 300 Miles   10d Stg. per single sheet of paper.

And 2d Stg. for each additional 100 Miles or fraction thereof.

Note: *We give the rates in Sterling as the exchange rate between Sterling and Currency fluctuated somewhat.* In the 1840's and 1850's 4d Stg.$=$4½d cy; 8d Stg.$=$9d cy; 10d Stg.$=$11½d cy. These rates appear commonly on many covers of that period.

TABLE 2

January 5, 1844 to April 5, 1851

The rates remained the same, but were calculated by *weight.* One rate for each ½ oz. or fraction thereof.

TABLE 3A

April 6, 1851 to June 30, 1859

6d per ½ oz. or fraction; whole charge to the United States, except the Pacific Coast (6d$=$10c). Pacific Coast 9d per ½ oz. (9d$=$15c).

TABLE 3B

July 1, 1859 to March 31, 1868

Same rates as table 3a but in decimal currency:

10c per ½ oz. or fraction; whole charge to the United States, except the Pacific Coast. 15c per ½ oz. to the Pacific Coast.

CANADA TABLE 4—UNITED STATES TABLE 10

April 1, 1868 to January 31, 1875

Irrespective of distance. { 6c per ½ oz. prepaid
                            { 10c per ½ oz. unpaid

TABULATION OF POSTAGE PREPAYMENT OF CANADA-UNITED STATES MAILS—1783-1875

PERIOD	Canadian Postage	United States Postage	NOTES
1. Previous to June 1, 1792	PAID IN CASH	UNPAID	United States Postage could *not* be paid.
2. June 1, 1792 to June 30, 1847	PAID IN CASH	PAID IN CASH or UNPAID	
3. July 1, 1847 to Nov. 15, 1847	PAID IN CASH	PAID IN CASH or Stamps or UNPAID	
4. Nov. 16, 1847 to May 14, 1849	PAID IN CASH or UNPAID	PAID IN STAMPS only or UNPAID	United States postage could *not* be paid in *cash*.
5. May 15, 1849 to April 5, 1851	PAID IN CASH or UNPAID	PAID IN CASH or Stamps or UNPAID	Payment could be all cash, or cash and stamps.
6. April 6, 1851 to June 30, 1851	PAID IN CASH or Canadian Stamps from April 23, 1851 or UNPAID	PAID IN CASH or U. S. Stamps or UNPAID	Payment could be all cash, cash and stamps, or all stamps[1].
7. July 1, 1851 to Oct. 1, 1875	PAID IN CASH or Canadian Stamps or UNPAID	PAID IN CASH or Canadian Stamps or UNPAID	All cash or all stamps[2].

Remarks: Previous to May 15, 1849 it was not possible for a person to prepay the Canadian postage from the United States; in other words from 1792 a Canadian could prepay a letter through to its destination in the United States, but it was not until 1849 that the reverse was possible, letters posted in the United States could only be prepaid to the border prior to that time.

1. This is the only period when combination use of U. S. and Canadian Stamps was permissible by the regulations.
2. Combination usage was against the regulations although examples are known (See Fig. 46.)

CANADA TABLE 5—UNITED STATES TABLE 11
February 1, 1875 to September 30, 1883

3c per ½ oz. irrespective of distance, prepayment compulsory, but short paid letters forwarded and charged deficiency.

The February 1, 1875 Convention agreed that the domestic rate of each country should apply to letters to the respective parties.

We note however the following changes: On October 1, 1883 the United States rate became 2c per ½ oz., but letters *from* Canada still required 3c; and on July 1, 1885 the United States 2c rate was made per ounce instead of per ½ oz. the Canadian rates remaining unchanged.

Effective May 8, 1889 the Canadian rates were based upon one oz. or fraction, the fee remaining at 3c. (Appendix B #50). United States and Canadian rates again became uniform on January 1, 1899. Several changes have taken place since then, and at the time of writing letters to Canada are 3c per oz. while from Canada the rate is 4c per oz.

The relationship between the various rates in effect is as follows:

	Canada Table	United States Table
June 1, 1792 to April (16?) 1799	1	1
April (17?) 1799 to January 31, 1815	1	2
February 1, 1815 to March 31, 1816	1	3
April 1, 1816 to April 30, 1816	1	4
May 1, 1816 to March (10?) 1825	1	5
March (11?) 1825 to January 4, 1844	1	6
January 5, 1844 to June 30, 1845	2	6
July 1, 1845 to April 5, 1851	2	7
April 6, 1851 to June 30, 1851	3A	7
July 1, 1851 to March 31, 1868	3A, 3B	8,9
April 1, 1868 to January 31, 1875	4	10
February 1, 1875 to September 30, 1883	5	11

Note: 1. From July 1, 1845 to April 5, 1851 the rate of progression of increase in charges for overweight letters differed (Appendix D #2), a factor which should be taken into consideration when calculating rates on letters of this period.

2. From January 5, 1844 to June 30, 1845 Canadian rates were calculated by weight, while United States rates were by sheets of paper. It is therefore possible to have a single rate in Canada and a double or triple rate in the United States, during this period of a year and a half.

3. The rates effective February 1, 1875 were according to a postal agreement which established that the domestic rate would apply to letters to the respective parties. (Appendix D #34, Art. IV).

UNITED STATES RATES

TABLE 1

The act of February 20, 1792, 1 Stat. 235 and 238 fixed the following rates of postage, to take effect June 1, 1792:

For every single letter conveyed not exceeding 30 miles, 6 cents;
over 30 miles and not exceeding 60 miles, 8 cents;
over 60 miles and not exceeding 100 miles, 10 cents;
over 100 miles and not exceeding 150 miles, 12½ cents;
over 150 miles and not exceeding 200 miles, 15 cents;
over 200 miles and not exceeding 250 miles, 17 cents;
over 250 miles and not exceeding 350 miles, 20 cents;
over 350 miles and not exceeding 450 miles,, 22 cents;
over 450 miles, 25 cents;
and every double letter, double said rates; every triple letter, triple said rates;

and every packet weighing 1 ounce avoirdupois to pay at the rate of four single letters for each ounce, and in that proportion for any greater weight.

TABLE 2

Act of March 2, 1799 (1 Stat. 734, 738-740) Effective April (17?) 1799:
For every letter composed of a single sheet of paper, conveyed not exceeding 40 miles, 8 cents;
    over 40 miles and not exceeding 90 miles, 10 cents;
    over 90 miles and not exceeding 150 miles, 12½ cents;
    over 150 miles and not exceeding 300 miles, 17 cents;
    over 300 miles and not exceeding 500 miles, 20 cents;
    over 500 miles, 25 cents;
and every double letter, or two pieces of paper, double said rates; every triple letter, or three pieces of paper, triple rates; and for every packet composed of four or more pieces of paper, or other thing, and weighing 1 ounce avoirdupois, quadruple such rates, and in that proportion for any greater weight.

Any packet which weighs more than 3 pounds shall not be accepted for mailing.

Note:—The War of 1812 began June 19, 1812, and ended February 18, 1814.

TABLE 3

Act of December 23, 1814. (3 Stat. 159). February 1, 1815 to March 31, 1816).
Not over 40 miles..12 cents per single letter;
    over 40 miles but not over 90 miles, 15 cents per single letter;
    over 90 miles but not over 150 miles, 18¾ cents per single letter;
    over 150 miles but not over 300 miles, 25½ cents per single letter;
    over 300 miles but not over 500 miles, 30 cents per single letter;
    over 500 miles..37½ cents per single letter.
It will be noted that this is a 50% increase in the rates.

TABLE 4

Act of February 1, 1816 (3 Stat. 252):
Repeals from March 31, 1816, so much of the act of December 23, 1814, as increases the rates of postage 50 per cent.

For every letter composed of a single sheet of paper, conveyed
Not exceeding 40 miles.. 8 cents;
    over 40 miles and not exceeding 90 miles, 10 cents;
    over 90 miles and not exceeding 150 miles, 12½ cents;
    over 150 miles and not exceeding 300 miles, 17 cents;
    over 300 miles and not exceeding 500 miles, 20 cents;
    over 500 miles..25 cents;
and every double letter or two pieces of paper, double said rates; every triple letter, or three pieces of paper, triple rates; and for every packet composed of four or more pieces of paper, or other thing, and weighing 1 ounce avoirdupois, quadruple said rates, and in that proportion for any greater weight.

Any packet which weighs more than 3 pounds shall not be accepted for mailing.

TABLE 5

Act of April 9, 1816 (3 Stat. 264):
Fixes, from May 1, 1816, the folowing rates of postage on letters and packets:

For every letter composed of a single sheet of paper, conveyed
Not exceeding 30 miles.. 6 cents;
    over 30 miles and not exceeding 80 miles, 10 cents;
    over 80 miles and not exceeding 150 miles, 12½ cents;
    over 150 miles and not exceeding 400 miles, 18½ cents;
    over 400 miles.. 25 cents;

and every double letter, or two pieces of paper, double said rates; every triple letter, or three pieces of paper, triple said rates; and for every packet composed of four or more pieces of paper, or one or more articles, and weighing 1 ounce avoidupois, quadruple those rates, and in that proportion for all greater weights.

TABLE 6

Act of March 3, 1825 (4 Stat. 105, 111, 112, 114): Effective March (11?) 1825:

Repeals all former acts and parts of acts which have been passed for the establishment and regulation of the General Post Office and fixes the following rates of postage:

For every letter composed of a single sheet of paper conveyed
Not exceeding 30 miles.................................... 6 cents;
    over 30 miles and not exceeding 80 miles, 10 cents;
    over 80 miles and not exceeding 150 miles, 12½ cents;
    over 150 miles and not exceeding 400 miles, 18¾ cents;
    over 400 miles.................................25 cents;
and every double letter, or two pieces of paper, double said rates; every triple letter, or three pieces of paper, triple said rates; every packet of four or more pieces of paper, or one or more other articles, and weighing 1 ounce avoirdupois, quadruple said rates, and in that proportion for all greater weights.

Any packet which weighs more than 3 pounds shall not be accepted for mailing.

TABLE 7

(Rates calculated by weight)

Act of March 3, 1845 (5 Stat. 733, 737): By weight:

From and after July 1, 1845, in lieu of the rates of postage now established by law, there shall be charged the following rates:

For every single letter, in manuscript or marks or signs, conveyed under 300 miles, 5 cents; over 300 miles, 10 cents; double letter, double rates; treble letter, treble rates; quadruple letter, quadruple rates; and every letter or parcel not exceeding one-half ounce in weight shall be deemed a single letter, and every additional weight of one-half ounce or less shall be charged with an additional single postage. Drop letters shall be charged a postage rate of 2 cents each.

Any packet weighing more than 3 pounds shall not be accepted for mailing.

TABLE 8

Act of March 3, 1851 (9 Stat. 587-589):

From and after June 30, 1851, in lieu of the rates of postage now established by law, there shall be charged the following rates:

For every single letter in writing, marks, or signs, conveyed not exceeding 3,000 miles, if prepaid, 3 cents; if not prepaid, 5 cents, and for any greater distance double said rates; double letter, double rates; treble letter, treble rates; quadruple letter, quadruple rates; and every letter or parcel not exceeding half an ounce in weight shall be deemed a single letter, and every additional weight of half an ounce or less shall be charged with an additional rate. Drop letters, 1 cent each.

Rate to or from Canada 10c per ½ oz., or fraction; to the Pacific Coast 15c per ½ oz. or fraction; *prepayment optional.*

TABLE 9

Act of March 3, 1855 (10 Stat. 641):

In lieu of the rates of postage now established by law there shall be charge the following rates, effective April 1, 1855:

For every single letter in manuscript, or paper of any kind in writing, marks, or signs, conveyed in the mail not exceeding 3,000 miles, 3 cents; and for any greater distance, 10 cents; double letter, double rates; treble letter, treble rates; quadruple letter, quadruple rates; every letter or parcel not exceeding one-half ounce in weight shall be deemed a single letter; and every additional weight of half an ounce or less shall be charged with an additional rate; *the foregoing rates to be prepaid, except on letters to and from a foreign country.*

Drop letters shall be charged with postage at the rate of 1 cent each.

Note: This act made the prepayment of domestic postage compulsory except on drop letters, but letters to or from a foreign country could be prepaid or not at the option of the sender, thus in the case of Canada continuing the arrangement agreed upon by the two Post Office Departments March 25, 1851, effective April 6, 1851, but subject to provisions of postal treaties.

From 1868 to 1883 the Canadian and United States tables can be combined. See Canada Tables 4 and 5.

United States Postmasters of Canadian Post Offices—1791-1844

There is definite evidence in the records that from June 1792 to January 5, 1844 inclusive either the Deputy Postmaster, or the Postmasters of certain Canadian offices were also Postmasters for the United States Post Office Department. We list below such offices that we know were exchange offices during this period, the earliest date we have noted it as a United States office, and the Postmaster to whom the commissions were paid:

Office	Date — Postmaster	Amount of Commissions from U.S.P.O. in 1840-1841
Kingston	1823-38 John Macauly	
	1839-43 Robert Deacon	999.03
Brockville	1839-40 T. A. Stayner, D.P.M.G.	
	1841-43 Henry Jones	81.98[1]
Montreal	1835-41 T. A. Stayner, D.P.M.G.	1611.76[1]
Moose River	1839-40 T. A. Stayner, D.P.M.G.	
Niagara	1835-40 T. A. Stayner, D.P.M.G.	
	1841-43 Alexander Davidson	173.05[1]
Prescott	1835-40 T. A. Stayner, D.P.M.G.	
	1841-43 Alpheus Jones	174.54[1]
Quebec	1841-43 T. A. Stayner, D.P.M.G.	735.90[1]
Queenstown	1835-40 T. A. Stayner, D.P.M.G.	
	1841-43 John Stayner (Son of T. A. Stayner)	1899.63[1]
Sandwich; from 1843	1841-43 Edward Holland	43.21[2]
Windsor[3]	1843-..... J. C. Ritter	
Stanstead	1835-40 T. A. Stayner, D.P.M.G.	
	1841-43 P. Hubbard, Jr.	283.29[1]
Woodstock	1839-43 T. A. Stayner, D.P.M.G.	
Toronto	1843-43 Charles Berczy	834.39[1]

1. For nine months.
2. For six months.
3. Exchanged with Detroit.

Prior to the individual postmasters receiving commissions all the proceeds from United States postage went to the Deputy Postmaster General, personally. From January 5, 1844, all such revenue went into the general funds of the Imperial Post Office and were credited to the Canada division. All payments, however, were made to the Deputy Postmaster General of Canada.

Section of Illustrations of Canada - United States, and United States - Canada Covers, Showing How the Rates and Regulations Worked in Actual Practice

NOTE: The "Approximate value" is intended as a guide to similar covers. Since nearly all covers of this type have some distinctive characteristic—no hard and fast rules can be laid down. For example Fig. 4 has a value peculiarly its own because of its historic significance although similar covers are only worth about $5.00.

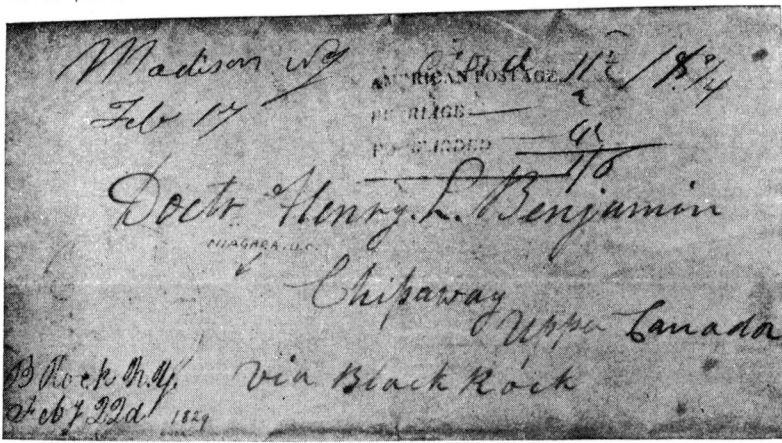

Fig. 1A. "Madison NY Feb 17" 1829 Ms. postmark to Chippewa, U. C. "via Black Rock". Exchanged through "B Rock N. Y. Feb'y 22d" and "Niagara U C" where it was struck with the itemized marking:
"American Postage 11½d"
"Ferriage 2d"
"Forwarded 4½d"
Note also Ms. "18¾" for the American Postage. This is a very rare marking, all markings in black—an unpaid letter. Canada rates Table 1. United States rates, Table 6. Approximate value $50.00.

Fig. 1B. An entire letter from Eastport, Me, Sept 16, 1830 to Ancaster U.C. via New York. All markings in red. Note rare itemized two line marking
"American Postage 1/3"
"British do 6½"
1/9½
Passed through "New York Nov 1", and "Niagara U. C. Nov 8 1830". Also an unpaid letter. Approximate value $35.00.

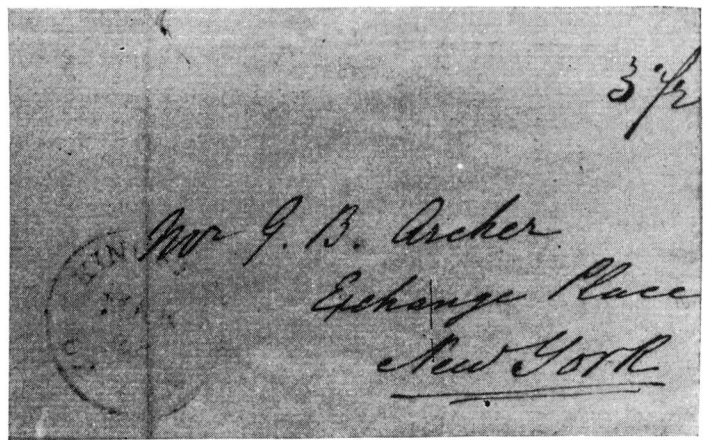

Fig. 2. "Kingston, U P Can Mar 26 1831" (Type Ia) in red. Note "37½" in manuscript. This was the double United States rate to New York. No Canadian charge as the Postmaster was also a United States Postmaster. Towns separated by only a ferry or land journey of a mile or so could send a letter to Canada or the United States, paying only the rate of the country of destination. Thus a letter from Cape Vincent, N. Y., could be sent to any place in Canada up to 60 miles for "4½d" equals 7½ cents, instead of 4½d plus 6 cents. This practice continued with changes made necessary by alteration of the rates. Approximate value $5.00.

Fig. 3. "Montreal L. C. JY 10 1835" (Type IIa) and "PAID" in red. Manuscript "4½"d Canadian rate to the lines. United States clerk at Philadelphia struck out the "PAID" of the Montreal Office, and wrote "25" cents due for a letter conveyed over 400 miles. Canada Rates, Table 1. NOTE United States Rates, Table 6. Approximate value $3.00

Fig. 3A. Toronto 1836-37. Note "PAID 7 & 25" and "PAID 9 & 25" (H-US2, H-US3) showing both Canadian and United States Postage paid. Canada Rates Table 1. United States Rates Table 6.

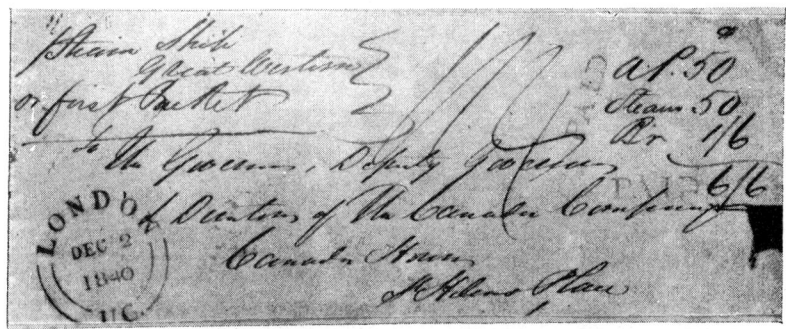

Fig. 3B. "London Dec 2, 1840" with "PAID" struck twice and Ms. sum of postage: AP50; Steam 50; Br 1/6; i e. American postage 50 cents, steamship 50 cents; and Canadian postage 1sh-6p. Total 6/6. All markings in red. A double letter. Compare this with Fig. 1A, 1B, and 9.

Fig. 4. "Montreal JY 15 1837" and "PAID" in red. Manuscript "4½"d. to Kingston, New York, where the United States clerk struck out the "PAID 4½" and charged the letter "18¾" cents due. Forwarded from "New York Jul 24" 1837 to Philadelphia, rated "12½" cents. This is historically a most interesting letter from David Smillie in Montreal to his brother James, the famous vignette engraver. As requested in the letter James Smillie forwarded it to the other brother, William Smillie, who at that time was an engraver with Draper, Toppan & Co., Philadelphia. Mr. William Smillie in 1866, with Alfred Jones, and Henry Earle, Sr., founded the British American Bank Note Co., noted for printing the Large and Small Queen Issues, 1867-97, as well as much other work for the Dominion up to the present time. Notice that James in forwarding the letter carefully obliterated the Montreal postmark (Type IIa) with fine strokes, characteristic of an engraver. Approximate value of similar cover $5.00

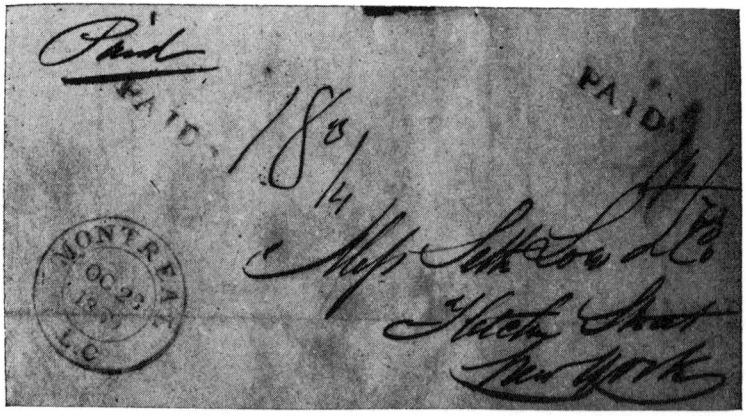

Fig. 5 PAID all the way through. "Montreal Oc 23 1839" (Type IIa) and two "PAID" marks all in red. The "4½"d is the Canadian rate to the lines, and the "18¾" is the United States rate from the lines to New York. Canada Rates Table 1. United States Rate Table 6. Approximate value $5.00.

Fig. 6. "Montreal Oc 22 1842 (Type IIIc) to New York. "Paid 4½"d to the lines. The United States Clerk at New York struck out the "PAID" and rated the letter "18¾" cents due, the rate on a letter conveyed between 150 and 400 miles. It is interesting to note that "D. S. Kennedy, Esqr," was the agent for the Bank of Montreal, and later agent for the Canada Post Office Department among his numerous other interests (Appendix H, #1 et seq.) Canada Rates Table 1. United States Rates Table 6. Approximate value $2.50

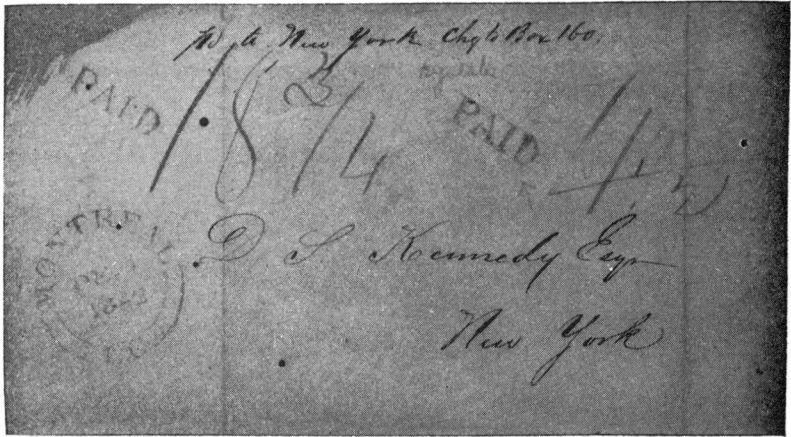

Fig. 7. "Montreal DE 1 1842" (Type IIIc) to New York. "Paid 18¾" cents, United States rate, and "PAID 4½"d Canadian rate. Note manuscript "Pd to New York, Chg to Box 160". (Box 160 was "C. Dorwin" money and exchange broker, 20½ St. Francis Xavier St., Montreal). Canada Rates Table 1. United States Rates Table 6. Approximate value $3.50.

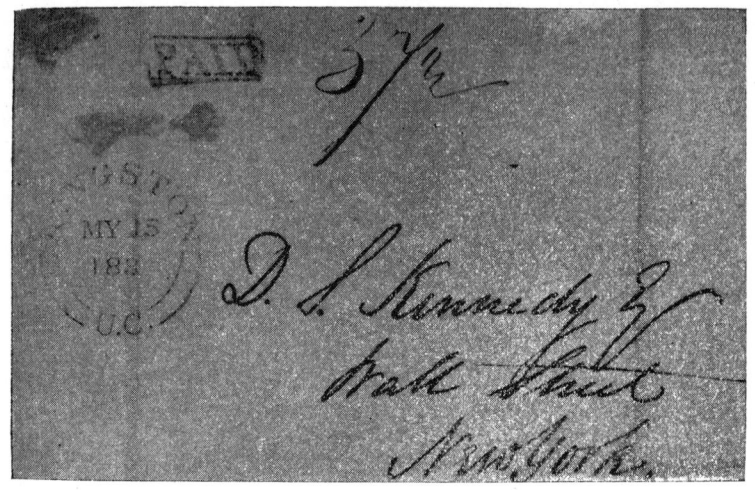

Fig. 8. "Kingston My 15 183", (1843), Type IIIc) to New York. Note "37½", double rate from Kingston. Since the Kingston P. M. was also P. M. for the United States there was no Canadian charge (see Fig. 2). Approximate value $7.50

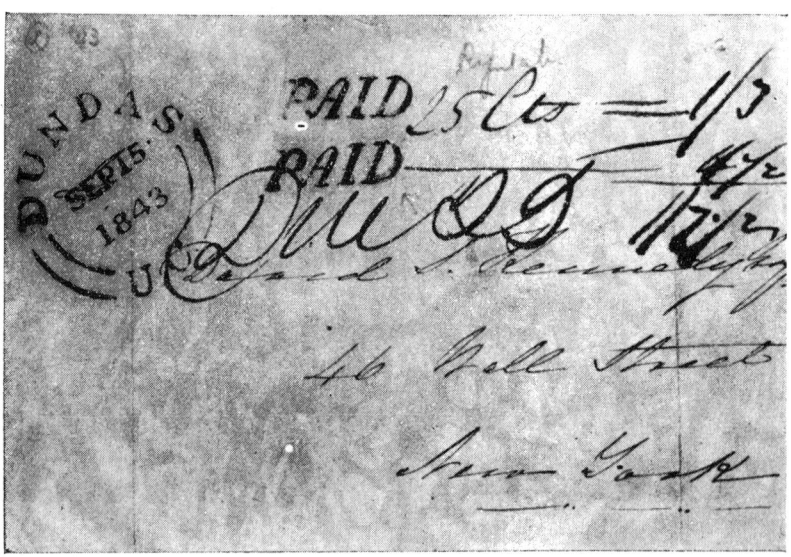

Fig. 9 "Dundas U. C. Sep 15 1843" (Type IIIc) to New York. "PAID 25 cts equals 1/3" for United States postage. "PAID equals 4½" for Canadian rate to the lines. Total "1/7½". United States clerk rated the letter "Due 25" as it was a double letter according to the United States regulations, at that time. Canada Rates Table 1. United States Rates Table 6. Approximate value $10.00

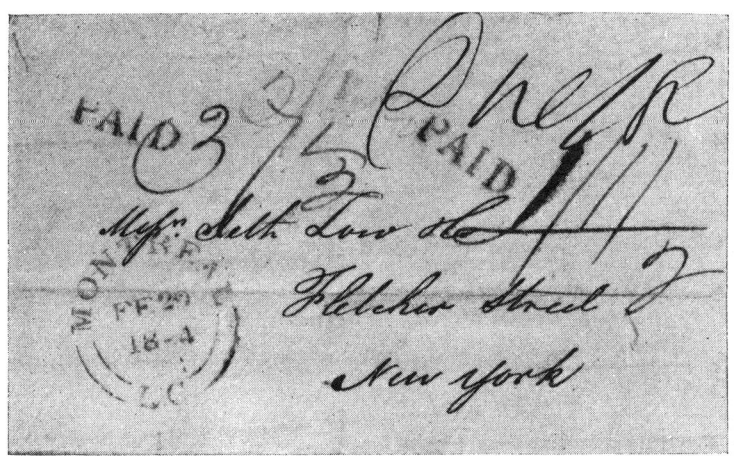

Fig. 10 "Montreal Feb 29 1844" (Type IIIc) Leap year, to New York. PAID through, but "Due 18¾" cents. From January 5, 1844, Canada rates were on the basis of weight, but the United States rates were still figured on the old basis of sheets of paper. The sender paid double the United States rates, but the contents of the letter enclosing TWO drafts, made it a triple letter, hence the "18¾" cents due. Canada Rates Table 2. United States Rates Table 6. Approximate value $5.00.

Fig. 11. "Montreal Jul 3 1844" (Type IIIc) to New York. "Paid" to the lines "4½"d. The New York clerk struck out the "PAID" and rated it as a double letter "37½" cents due. Canada Rates Table 2. United States Rates Table 6. Approximate value $2.50.

Fig. 12. "Montreal Oct 29 1844" (Type IIIc). Similar to Fig. 11, but a "single" letter all the way through. Note that this was a "charge account" in Canada as the inscription "Box 70 J. C & Co. lines" shows ("J. C & Co." was John Carter, chemist and druggist 136 St. Paul St.) Canada Rates Table 2. United States Rates Table 6. Approximate value $2.50

Fig. 13. "Quebec Sp 26 1845" (Type IIIc) to New York. Note manuscript endorsement, "Paid" and "Pd to New York". Struck with Quebec Crowned Circle (H31) in red, twice, with "11½"d for Canadian postage, and "10" cents for United States postage. From July 1 1845 United States rates were also figured on the basis of weight, but at a different scale of progression than that of Canada (Appendix D #2). Canada Rates Table 2. United States Rates Table 7. Approximate value $25.00

Fig. 14. "Montreal De 22 1846" (Type IV) "Paid 4½"d to the lines. The New York clerk struck out the "Paid" and rated the letter "10" cents. From David Smillie to his brother William C. Smillie who then was at 31 Wall Street, New York. As noted under Fig. 4, William C. Smillie founded the British American Bank Note Co. in 1866. Canada Rates Table 2. United States Rates Table 7. Approxmiate value $2.00

Fig. 15. "MONTREAL PAID JU 4 1847 CANADA" (Type H32a), also struck at the same time with the circular red handstruck "U. States Postage PAID" (H-US4) stamp. This was a double weight letter as evidenced by the "20" cents and the "9"d. Note manuscript "Pd to NYork Box 160" ("Box 160" was "C. Dorwin, exchange & money broker, 25 St. Francis Xavier St.) indicating a "charge account." We have seen a similar cover dated "Se 8 1847" with the same marking, rated "4½"d and "10" cents, charged to "Box 98." "Box 98" was Bank of Montreal. Canada Rates Table 2. United States Rates Table 7. Approximate value $50.00

Fig. 16. 10c 1847 lightly struck with 16 lines red grid, and used from "Montreal SP 3 1847" (Type H&2a) and also struck with U. STATES POSTAGE PAID (H-US4) "and Money Letter" all in red. A rare and interesting cover. Canada Rates Table 2. United States Rates Table 7. Approximate value $400.00.

Fig. 17. "Niagara C. W. Oc 18, 1847" (Type IV) to New York. Exchanged through Youngstown. Note "PAID 10", which was charged to "66+a45"—the account of the Niagara Harbor and Dock Co. No Canadian charge (see Figs. 2 and 8). Approximate value $5.00.

Fig. 18. "MONTREAL AU 13 1847" (Type IV) and paid through to New York, as shown by "PAID 10" cents, and "PAID 4½"d. Canada Rates Table 2. United States Rates Table 7. Approximate value $5.00.

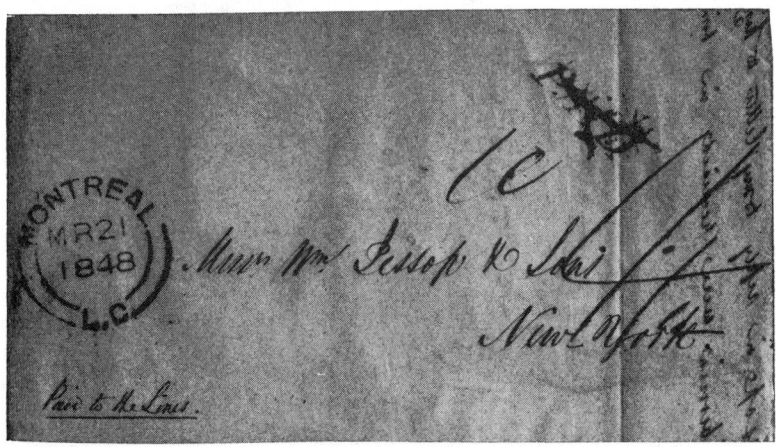

Fig. 19. "MONTREAL MR 21 1848 (Type IV) "Paid to the lines". United States postage could NOT be prepaid in cash (Nov. 16, 1847 to May 14, 1849, Appendix D #3, 4, and 5). New York clerk struck out the "PAID" and rated the letter "10" cents. Canada Rates Table 2. United States Rates Table 7. Approximate value $2.50.

Fig. 20. "TORONTO U. C. AP 21 1848" (Type IV) to New York. "Paid to the lines No. 20", ("No. 20" was the Commercial Bank, Midland District, Toronto Office) and charged "4½"d as required. Vertical pair of 5c. 1847's pen struck by clerk at "Lewiston, N. Y. Apr 23" who also struck out the "PAID" of Toronto. Canada Rates Table 2. United States Rates Table 7.
Approximate value $225.00.

Fig. 21. "Quebec No 7 1848" (Type IV) and manuscript notation "Paid No 15 to the lines". ("No 15" was the Bank of Montreal, Quebec office). Struck with Crowned Circle (H31), in red, and rated "1/11", that is 1sh 11 pence, double letter rate. The New York clerk rated it "20" cents due. Canada Rates Table 2. United States Rates Table 7.
Approximate value $12.50.

Fig. 22. "Bytown, U. C., MAR 2 1849" (Type IIIc) (OTTAWA). "Paid 9"d to the lines as required by the regulations. Sender affixed two 5c 1847's to pay the United States postage. The clerk at New York cancelled the stamps with the "10" rating mark, and also struck out the "PAID" with the same mark. This was a single rate letter but as Ottawa was more than 100 miles, but less than 200 miles from the border the letter was rated "9"d. Canada Rates Table 2. United States Rates Table 7.
Approximate value $225.00.

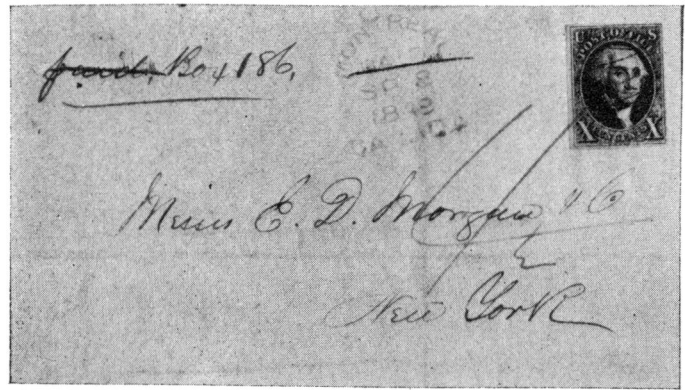

Fig. 23. "Montreal PAID SP8 1849 Canada" (H32a) in red, and manuscript "4½" tieing the 10c 1847, which paid the United States charge to New York. The New York clerk struck out the "Paid" both on the Postmark, and on the manuscript "Paid, Box 186" ("Box 186" was Gillespie, Moffat & Co. Importers and General Merchants, 132 St. Paul St.), and at the same time lightly penmarked the stamp, all in the same blue ink. Canada Rates Table 2. United States Rates Table 7. Approximate value $250.00.

Fig. 24. "Quebec L. C. Oc 3 1849" (Type IIIc) to New York. Struck with crowned circle (H31) in red and Ms. "11½"d. Two 5c 1847's affixed to pay United States postage, which were struck "10" by the New York clerk. Canada Rates Table 2. United States Rates Table 7.
Approximate value $250.00

Fig. 25. "Quebec L.C. DE 12, 1849" (Type IIIc) to New York. Crowned circle (H31) in red and "11½"d rating for postage "paid to the lines No. 94" United States postage paid by two 5c 1847's (one of which has been removed as can be seen by the blot that marks the lower edge). The Quebec clerk apparently cancelled the stamps also as this was a "Money" letter, and from May 15, 1849, letters could be prepaid through in cash or stamps (Appendix D #5). Canada Rates Table 2. United States Rates Table 7.
Approximate value $100.00

Fig. 26. "MONTREAL DE 14 1849" (Type IV) to New York. "PAID 4½"d, and 5c 1847 affixed at Montreal. The New York clerk struck out the "PAID" and cancelled the stamp with "10", and rated the letter as "Due 5" the amount short paid from Montreal. Canada Rates Table 2. United States Rates Table 7.
Approximate value $300.00.

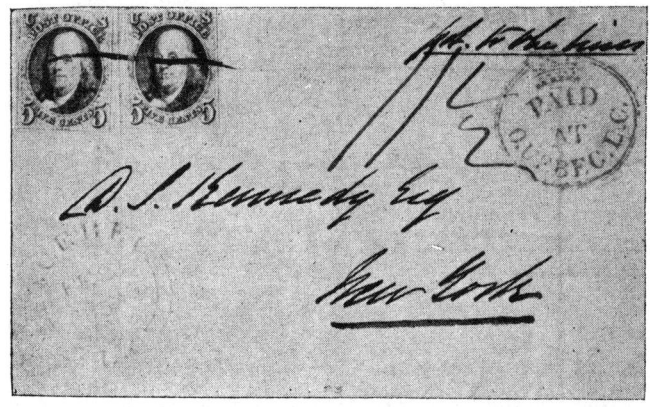

Fig. 27. "Quebec, L. C. Fe 23 1850" (Type IIIc) to New York. Quebec crowned circle (H31) and ms. "11½"d. "Paid to the lines." Two 5c 1847 affixed at Quebec. Upon arrival in New York the clerk drew the blue penmark across the stamps. Canada Rates Table 2. United States Rates Table 7. Approximate value $250.00.

Fig. 27A. Unusual instance of a 5c 1847 paying the correct rate from Canada. "Montreal MY 4 1850" to Buffalo. Canadian rate "4½" pence to the lines, the 5c 1847 affixed in Canada, paid the United States postage to Buffalo which was just under 300 miles, and therefore the rate was 5c. Exchanged at "Whitehall N. Y. May 6" where the clerk cancelled the stamp. Canada Rates Table 2. United States Rates Table 7. Approximate value $200.00.

Fig. 28. "Coburg U. C. Jul 17 1850" (Type IIIc) to New York. Exchanged at "Lewiston, N. Y. Jul 19". Struck "PAID 9" for over 100 miles but less than 200 miles in Canada. The "Paid" was crossed out at the Lewiston office which rated it "10" cents to New York. Note Manuscript "Paid Box 50 CHM" (Box 50 was Bank of Montreal, Chas H. Morgan, Agent). Canada Rates Table 2. United States Rates Table 7. Approximate value $5.00

Fig. 29. A "Money Letter", "Hamilton JU 22, 1850" (Type IV) to New York. Note manuscript "Money" and "Paid to Lines Box 102 G.J.G.", ("Box 102" was the Commercial Bank, Midland District, Hamilton Office). Also "Rec" (Recorded), probably by the Lewiston clerk who struck out the "PAID" and rated it "10" cents for United States postage. At the time the clerk wrote "Rec" he checked it against the money letter way bill, as can be seen by check mark in lower left corner. Canada Rates Table 2. United States Rates Table 7. Approximate value $5.00

Fig. 30. "Quebec L. C. Au 25, 1850" (Type IIIc) to New York. Struck with Quebec crowned circle (H31) in red and rated "11½"d. 1847 10c paid the United States postage, and was cancelled by the New York clerk with the "20" rate mark in black. Canada Rates Table 2. United States Rates Table 7. Approximate value $325.00.

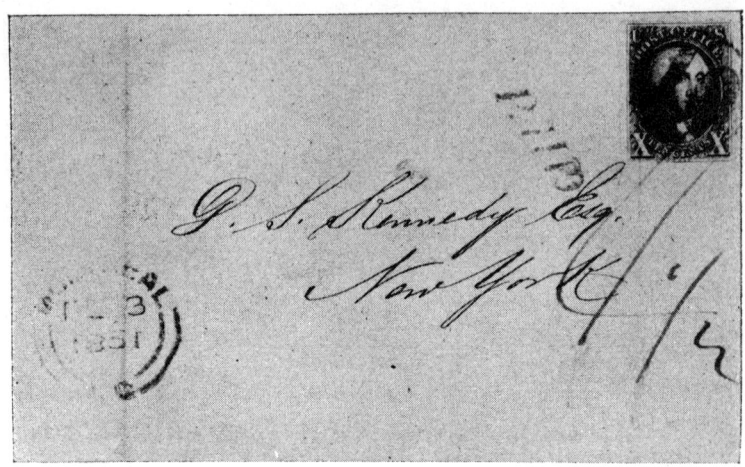

Fig. 31. "Montreal L. C. Fe 3, 1851" (Type IV) to New York. Struck "Paid" and manuscript "4½"d Canadian rate. Note that "4½" ties the 10c 1847, which paid the United States charge. In New York the clerk struck it with the "10" in circle. All markings in red.
Canada Rates Table 2. United States Rates Table 7.
Approximate value $300.00.

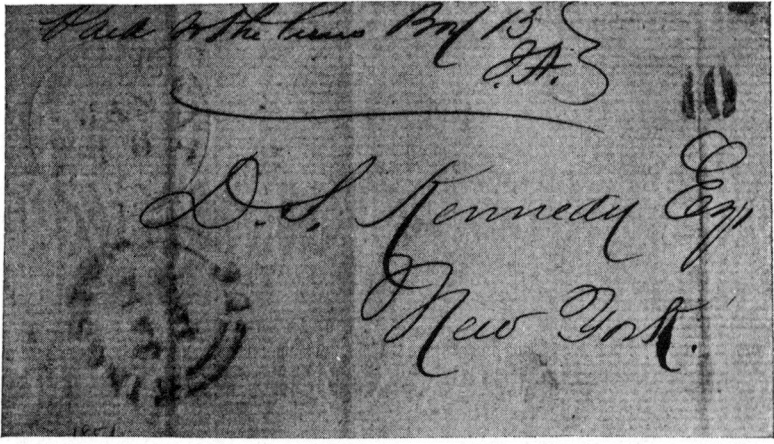

Fig. 32. "Kingston, U. C JA 14 1851" (Type IIIc) via Cape Vincent, where it was struck "10" in red; to New York. This being a "charge acount" the letter was charged to "Box 13" (Bank of Montreal, Kingston Office). Since the Kingston Postmaster was also the U. S. Postmaster, there was no Canadian charge. Approximate value $5.00.

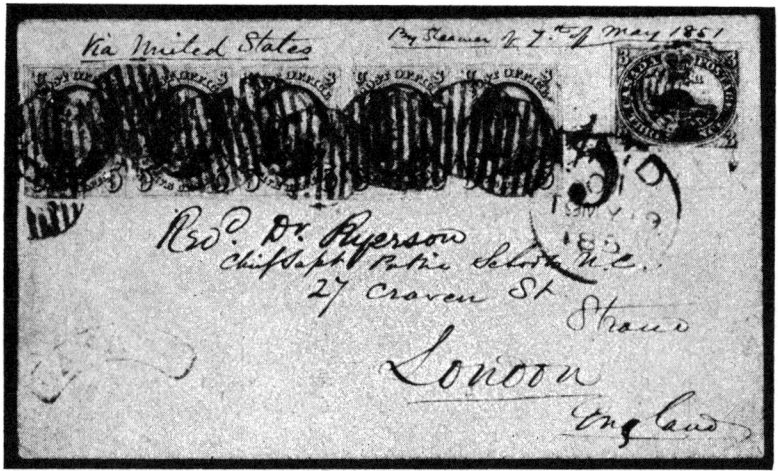

Fig. 33. This remarkable cover is one of the rare examples of the CORRECT combination usage of the 3d Beaver and the 5c 1847. The 3d was issued April 23, 1851, and as noted the letter was to go "By Steamer of 7th of May 1851". Probably left Toronto about May 1, 1851, and is therefore an early use of the Beaver stamp. The strip of five 5c 1847's paid the rate to England. Note also the "Canada" exchange marking, and that the stamps are tied by the London receiving mark "PAID 19MY19 1851", showing that it made the steamer as directed. All markings in red. Canada Rates Table 3. United States Rates Table 7.

Fig. 34. The extreamely rare example of the 3d Beaver and 5c 1847 used FROM the United States. "Rochester May 4" 1851 in red. U. S. clerk then struck the 1847 U. S. stamp, and also the Canadian 3d Beaver, with the red grid cancel. Note "U. States" in arc, also struck in red. Exchanged through "Queenston May 6" which is struck in black. Canada Rates Table 3. United States Rates Table 7. Approximate value $500.00.

Fig. 35. Another example of the CORRECT usage of the 3d Beaver and the 5c 1847. The rate was ten cents, and the stamps were used from "Kingston U. C JU 4 1851" (Type IIIc) to ANY PLACE in the United States except the Pacific coast. Note that both stamps are tied by the typical concentric ring obliteration of Canada in black. The postmark and "10" are in red as they should be on a PREPAID LETTER, both being struck at Kingston, the Canadian exchange office. In other words the above represents the through rate of 10c and not 3d to the lines plus 5c up to 300 miles as might be supposed. Canada Rates Table 3. United States Rates Table 7. Approximate value $300.00.

Fig. 36. Another example of the CORRECT USAGE of the 3d Beaver and the 5c 1847 stamps. From "Montreal Ju 8 1851" (Type IV) to New York. Both stamps tied by concentric ring obliterator of Canada in black, and upon arrival in New York struck with the curved "PAID" in red, again tying the stamp. Note "Canada" exchange marking and manuscript notation "p paid", for "postage paid". This paid the 10c rate and was not 3d to the lines and 5c for up to 300 miles. Canada Rates Table 3. United States Rates Table 7. (See also Fig. 52). Approximate value $400.00.

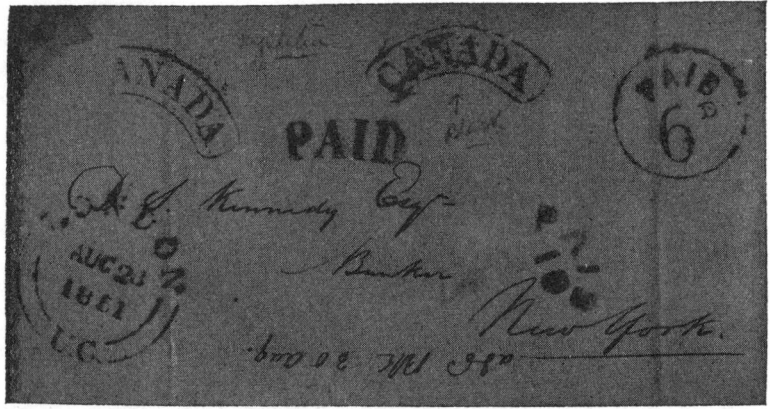

Fig. 37. "LONDON U. C. Aug 23 1851" (Type IIIc) to New York. Struck in black and red "CANADA" exchange marking. Black town mark, red handstruck "Paid 6d". Exchanged at "Hamilton C. W. Aug 24 1851" backstamp, and also struck "PAID 10" in blue. Canada Rates Table 3. United States Rates Table 8. Approximate value $7.50

Fig. 38. "Montreal L. C Oc 24 1851" (Type IV) to New York. Double weight, unpaid. Montreal clerk rated it "1/-", and the New York clerk struck the "20" in black as the amount due. The "Canada" exchange marking is in black also. Canada Rates Table 3. United States Rates Table 8. Approximate value $5.00

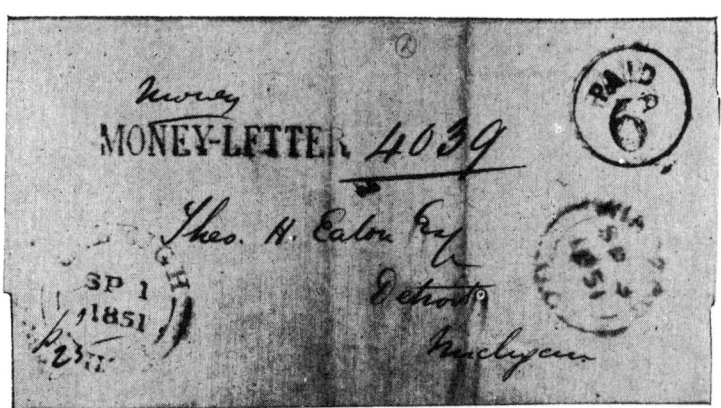

Fig. 39. "Raleigh U. C. Sp 1, 1851" (Type IIIa) to Detroit, Mich., via Windsor. This was a "Money Letter", and was paid, as per red "Paid 6d". Raleigh, U. C., was the old name for the Chatham Post Office. As per agreement of March 25, 1851, effective April 6, 1851, the through rate was 6d; equals 10c. (Appendix D #6). Canada Rates Table 3. United States Rates Table 8. Approximate value $15.00.

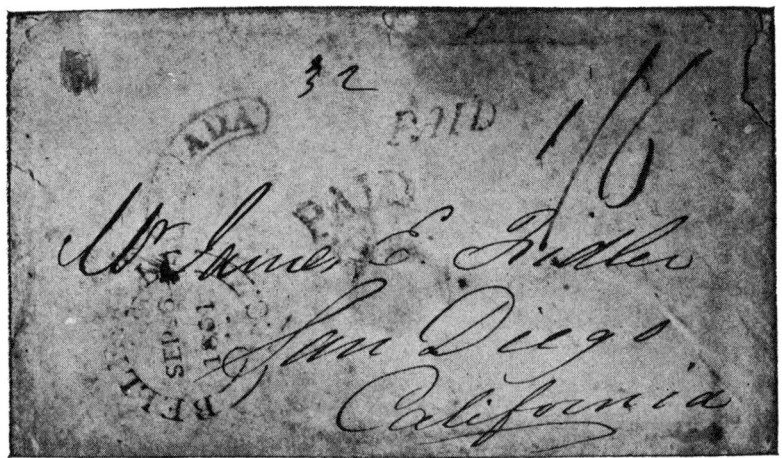

Fig. 40. Cover from "Belleville U. C. SEP 26 1851" (Type IIIa) via Toronto (backstamped "Toronto-Canada SP 28 1851"), and New York (Note curved "PAID") to San Diego, California. This was a letter weighing over ½ ounce, hence the rating "Paid 1/6", the double rate to the Pacific coast (See Appendix D #6 paragraph 3). The United States clerk made the "32" cents notation, which was equivalent to "1/6" Canadian currency. Canada Rates Table 3, United States Rates Table 8. Approximate value $25.00

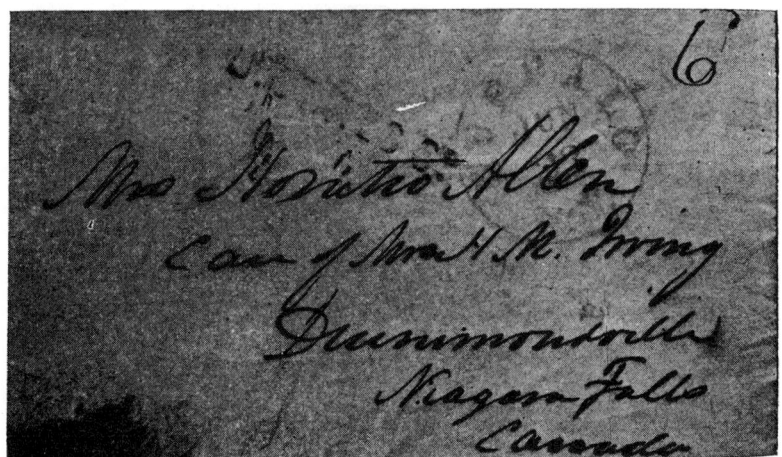

Fig. 41. Entire letter from "New York Saturday" to Drummondville. Blue "Buffalo N. Y. Jun 23", black "Ud STATES 6d", backstamped in black "Queenston U. C. Ju 23 1852" and "Drummondville U. C Ju 23 1852". Note manuscript "6d" alco in black by Drummondville postmaster. This letter is historically interesting as it is from Horatio Allen, who assembled the "Stourbridge Lion" a locomotive brought from England in 1829, for the Deleware & Hudson Co. Allen later became chief engineer of the South Carolina R. R. and was prominent in early railroad developement in America. Canada Rates Table 3. United States Rates Table 8. Approximate value of similar cover $2.50

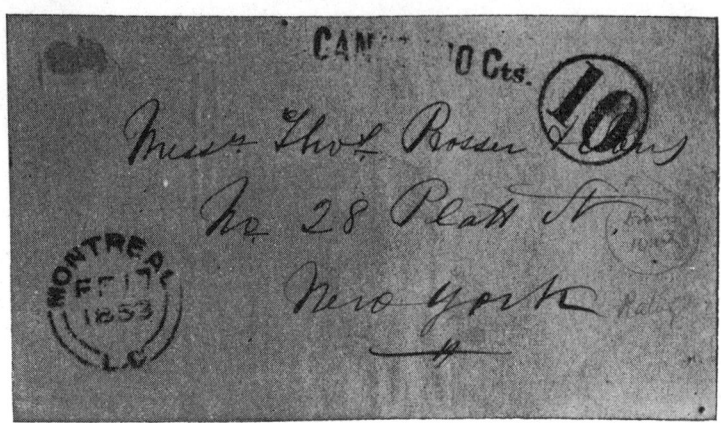

Fig. 42. "Montreal, L. C. FE 17, 1853" (Type IV) to New York. Unpaid and therefore struck in black "CANADA 10 Cts" (Type IVc). The New York clerk struck the black "10", for the 10 cents due. Canada Rates Table 3. United States Rates Table 8. Approximate value $5.00.

Fig. 43. It was the practice in those days to run "charge accounts" with the large commercial houses who settled their accounts quarterly. The cover illustrated above is one of these "charge" letters. Note oval cachet "Paid Drawer 14 Y.J.&Co." (Y.J.&Co. was "Young, Janes & Co." general merchants.) and also straight line "Grand Trunk Railway" both in bright carmine red, and struck by the sender. The "6d" and the Montreal markings are in dull brick red. Canada Rates Table 3. United States Rates Table 8. Approximate value $50.00.

Fig. 44. "City of Ottawa U. C DE 11 1855" (H37) to New Hampshire. Note "PAID 6" and "Canada" in red. Exchanged at Ogdensburg, N. Y. DEC 12" where it was also struck "10" in red. This indicates that unless the exchange marking embodies the word "Canada Paid" or "Canada 10", etc, it is probably a United States marking. Canada Rates Table 3. United States Rates Table 8. Approximate value $7.50.

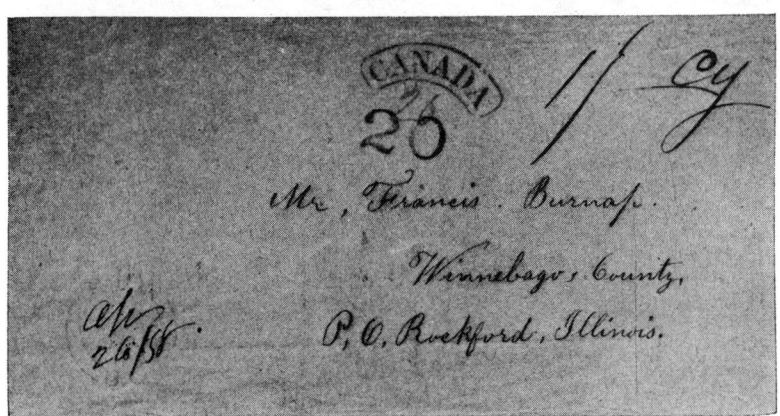

Fig. 45. "LONDON, C. W. Apr. 26 1858" to Illinois via "Windsor C. W. Ap 27 1858" both backstamped in black. "Canada" and "20" both black. Note manuscript "1/-cy" and "20". The handstruck "20" was applied at Windsor the exchange office. A double weight letter. Canada Rates Table 3. United States Rates Table 8. Approximate value $10.00.

Fig. 46. Two examples of incorrect usage of United States and Canadian stamps in combination. Both covers are from "Dundas U. C" in 1856. First cover struck "Canada Paid 10 c'ts" (Type IIIb) in red, contrary to instructions (Appendix D #17, 18, 19, and 47) which show that only the Canadian stamp should have been cancelled. The second cover was correctly handled in that it was struck "6d" in black, and "CANADA 10 cts" (Type IIc) as unpaid, both stamps being cancelled, although the United States Post Office accepted the letter as paid (Appendix D #17, 18, 19, and 47). Letters from the United States to Canada bearing similar combinations are also contrary to instructions, and when struck with black Canadian markings show that they were treated as unpaid.

Fig. 47. Four 3c, 1851 paying the rate from "St. Thomas U. C Oc 21 58" to Buffalo. This is an instance of the postmaster not following instructions. He should have forwarded the letter as unpaid, and not cancelled the stamps, leaving it to the United Staes Post Office to accept or reject the stamps as payment (Appendix D #19, 47). Overpayment of two cents was probably due to the lack of stamps of 1c, 5c, or 10c to make up the proper rate. Canada Rates Table 3. United States Rates Table 8

Fig. 48. "U. STATES" exchange mark of Buffalo (Type VIIIb), in black on an unpaid letter to Canada. Canada Rates Table 3B. United States Rates Table 8
Approximate value $5.00.

Fig. 49. "U. States" (Type IIc) and pen struck 6d on letter from Leyard, Conn. to Perth, C. W. Struck 6d in black and rated "10" (cents) due.

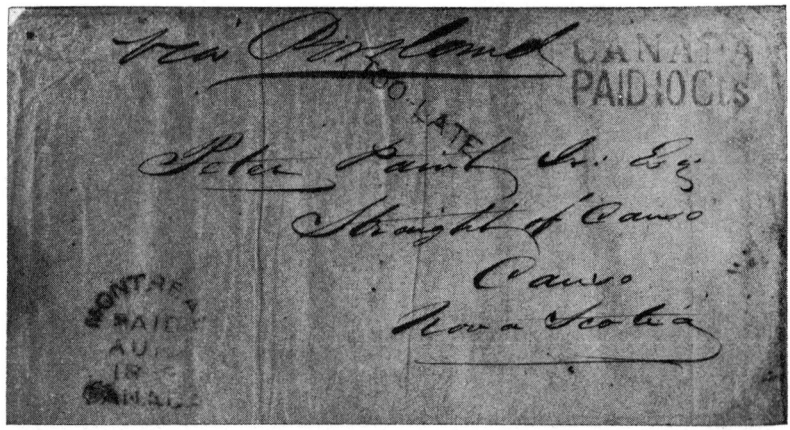

Fig. 50. "Montreal PAID Au 16 1863 Canada" (H32b) in red, and "Too Late" in black. Note Exchange marking, also in red "CANADA PAID 10 Cts" Type IIIe. This is a Nova Scotia letter. It could have gone to Nova Scotia for 5c, but the sender preferred to pay the 10c as "via Portland" was quicker. Arrived "Ship Harbor C. B Aug 26 63". (From James Mitchell & Co. Commission Merchants.) Canada Rates Table 8B. United States Rates Table 8 Approximate value $10.00.

Two Items Illustrating Odd Points.

Fig. 51. "York Nov 5" 1832 to London, Eng., "via New York". Note Ms. "9 & 25". Exchange through Lewiston, where the U. S. Postmaster struck the straight line "U. S. P. Paid 25" at the right. All markings in red. (See Particularly Figs. 1A, 1B, 3A, 3B.) Since this marking was struck by the United States Postmaster it has not the significance that the markings listed on page 34.

Fig. 52. "Quebec L. C Sep 23 1851" (Type IIIc) to New York. Amount of postage represented correct but United States stamp was not supposed to be used. Nevertheless it was duly accepted and represents unusually late use of 5c 1847—(which had been demonetized).

Chapter VII

THE PRINTERS OF CANADIAN STAMPS AND POSTAL STATIONERY*

The process of designing, engraving and printing Canadian adhesive stamps has, without exception, been identical with the production of bank-notes, in order to safeguard against counterfeiting. Some of the same designers and engravers work alternately on postage stamps, revenue stamps, bank-notes and other securities, such as bonds and certificates, so that what applies historically to one applies equally to the other, with the exception that ONLY THOSE QUALIFIED TO PRODUCE THE MOST DELICATE WORK WERE ENGAGED UPON POSTAGE STAMPS, DUE TO THE NECESSITY OF FINE WORK IN A SMALL AREA.

Prior to the close of the American Civil War (1861-65) most of the banks throughout the world issued their own engraved bank-notes, so that engraving of bank-notes, and works of art, before the development of photography, attracted many eminent artists. Some of these combined with engraving firms including also clever inventors who did much to advance the art of engraving. Patents such as Mathew's "green tint" gave their firms particular advantages over competitors, and a high degree of skill amongst designers and engravers developed from the competition of the times.

All Candian adhesive stamps and most of the Canadian revenue stamps, as well as some of the postal stationery, are from line engravings produced by private engraving firms.

Engraved dies are the valuable stock in trade of these firms. They are re-used, re-engraved and combined in new forms for new uses. Parts of the designs of U. S. and Canadian stamps may be traced from the work of the firm (as on bank-notes) which produced the original die, through their successors under other firm names. It is therefore desirable to trace the history of the firms who produced these stamps from their antecedents to their successors, who inherited the dies. For this reason the parts of Canadian stamps not definitely known as the work of a particular engraver may have originated with any of the firms' antecedents skilled in that line of work. The early firms were partnerships composed of experts of various skills in engraving. These later developed into Companies. Bank-notes, etc., produced by these firms usually contain the firm name or "IMPRINT."

Jacob Perkins

Jacob Perkins—Engraver, was born July 9, 1776, at Newburyport, Mass., and died in Scotland July 13, 1849. In 1816 he joined the Philadelphia firm of Murray, Draper, Fairman & Co., and by his mechanical talent, revolutionized the process of engraving and printing. Prior to that time engraving of bank notes was done on copper, a process which permitted about 5000 impressions to be made from a single plate. Perkins invented what were known as "stereotyped steel plates," from which about 30,000 impressions might be made. He also invented the transfer press and the process of "Transfering" of engraved work from one piece of metal to another piece of metal, which he called a "Siderographic" process. His invention made it possible for the soft steel surface of a transfer roll to take up reliefs from the hardened steel die, and, after hardening the transfer roll, to transfer the engraving to a soft steel plate, thus making duplication possible. To this invention we credit the producing of 100 or more duplicates of the original engraving on a steel plate, that eventually in 1840, made possible the first issue of British postage stamps. In conjunction with Asa Spencer, Perkins is also said to have perfected the application of lathe work

---

* Most of the data in this chapter is from the very fine "Historical Catalog of U. S. Stamp Essays and Proofs" (appearing serially in the Collector's Club Philatelist since 1938), by Dr. Clarence W. Brazer the well known authority on Essays and Proofs.

89

producing colorless engraved lines, oval or circular geometric patterns and combining various pieces of such work upon the same plates, whether flat, convex or concave. The lathe was originally invented by Christian Gobrecht. Perkins' idea was perfected by Spencer and in later times further perfected by Cyrus Durand.

Fig. 1. Jacob Perkins.
Inventor of the Perkins "Siderographik" method of transferring a design from a steel die to a steel plate, known as the Perkins Mill and Die Process.

The reputation of MURRAY, DRAPER, FAIRMAN & CO. was such, particularly after Jacob Perkins had joined them in 1816, that Sir Charles Bagot, the British Minister resident at Washington, urged the firm in 1818 to go to Europe for the purpose of offering their services to the Bank of England, whose notes had been recently counterfeited. Perkins' plates were then considered impossible of imitation by counterfeiters. Those plates were composed of steel blocks covered with engraving consisting principally of the denomination repeated in very small letters. Mr. Perkins was also the first to make and employ a roller for applying the ink to the engraved bank plate, instead of a dabber, which had been formerly used; the roller distributed the ink over the surface of the plates with greater regularity and evenness.

The suggestion of Sir Charles Bagot being favorably received, two members of the firm, Messrs. Fairman and Perkins, accompanied by Asa Spencer and Charles Toppan, with Machinists, went to England where they arrived in June 1819, the other partners remaining in Philadelphia.

Thomas F. Morris, Jr., says:

"This one man played a more important part in the historical background of bank-note work than any other person. His career was spectacular. During his youth, while employed as a goldsmith, he gave evidence of initiative and inventive ability, and on the death of the proprietor of the shop, Perkins assumed charge of the business when only fifteen years of age. Seven years later he was commissioned by the State of Massachusetts to engrave dies for copper coinage. It is recorded that the old Massachusetts cents with the Indian and the eagle were coined from the Perkins original die. He then became interested in the technical problems of bank-note engraving, and having moved to Philadelphia in 1814, he met GIDEON FAIRMAN. of the well-known bank-note firm of MURRAY, DRAPER, FAIRMAN & COMPANY. During this early period the banks throughout the country were considerably alarmed by the increase in spurious money being made by unscrupulous persons and many banks were forced to close their doors. With the same resourcefulness which characterized his earlier efforts, he perfected a machine, which was patented some fifteen years later, one claim of which read " 'Essentially founded upon the assumption that the bank-note may be made to contain so great a quantity and variety of work, extremely difficult of imitation, that a single note so made would cost the counterfeiter more than he could obtain by passing hundreds of them.'" This machine now commonly known as the Transfer Press, revolutionized the bank-note industry of that period in that it was possible by such process to make fac-similes from the original."

"There are many inventions credited to him—such as an improved paddle wheel, method of warming and ventilating rooms, an instrument to indicate the speed of moving vessels (and depth of water under them), and many other numerous devices. Perkins was awarded several gold medals by Engineering Societies in England for his pioneer work in the advancement of science. He continued in his business activities until his 70th year. The name of Perkins and his inventive genius add much color to the history and development of the process by which the government and the banknote companies can produce many thousands of stamps in a single hour."

So much for the inventor of the process of producing stamps by line engraving. Because of the beauty of the process it can truthfully be said that one of the principal charms of the stamps of Canada is the beauty of their design and reproduction which in the case of adhesives as mentioned before, has always been by the line engraved process, technically known as the Perkins Mill and Die process.

The Engraving Firms.

The various firms printing the adhesive stamps of Canada have been as follows:

1. Mar. 27, 1851[1] to April 30, 1858—Rawdon, Wright, Hatch and Edson, New York.
2. May 1, 1858 to December 4, 1867—The American Bank Note Co., New York.
3. From October 22, 1867, to April 22, 1897[2]—British American Bank Note Co., Ottawa until late in 1874; then Montreal until late 1887; from early 1888 at Ottawa again.
4. May 1, 1897 to December 31, 1922—American Bank Note Co., Ottawa.
5. January 1, 1923 to March 31, 1930—Canadian Bank Note Co., Ottawa[3].
6. April 1, 1930 to March 31, 1935—British American Bank Note Co., Ottawa.
7. April 1, 1935 to date—Canadian Bank Note Co., Ottawa[3].

We proceed to a discussion of these firms and their relation to Canadian stamps.

1. Rawdon, Wright, Hatch & Edson.

This firm was well known in Canada, as their active agent, George Mathews of their Montreal office, had secured a number of contracts from the various Canadian banks, for bank notes as well as printing debentures for various counties. Besides the first stamps used in Canada were the 5c and 10c 1847 issue of the United States which were also products of Rawdon, Wright, Hatch & Edson, and proof of their ability in postage stamp production.

The firm was formed in March 1, 1832, as Rawdon, Wright, Hatch & Co., and in 1847 the name was changed to Rawdon, Wright, Hatch and Edson.

The pedigree of the firm is as follows:

1826-   TRACY R. EDSON, Engraver, New York City.

1816-1817 RALPH RAWDON, Engraver, 8 Liberty St., Albany, N. Y.
1818-1823? RAWDON, BALCH & CO., Engravers, 55 State St., Albany, N. Y. (Ralph Rawdon and Vistus Balch).

---
1. Appendix H #1.
2. Appendix H #117. Appendix O Part I #5.
3. NOTE: The Canadian Bank Note Co. is the wholly owned subsidiary of the American Bank Note Co. For practical purposes, therefore, the same concern has printed Canada's stamps from 1851 to 1867, from 1897 to 1930, and from 1935 to date.

1823-1834 RAWDON, CLARK & CO., Engravers, 55 State St., Albany, N. Y. (Ralph Rawdon and Ashbel Clark).

1835- RAWDON, WRIGHT, HATCH & EDSON, Engravers, 55 State St., Albany, N. Y. (All residents of New York City).
1828-1831 RAWDON, WRIGHT & CO., Engravers, 35 Merchants Exc., N. Y. (Ralph Rawdon and Neziah Wright).
1832-1834 RAWDON, WRIGHT, HATCH & CO., Engravers, 35 Merchants Exc., N. Y. (Ralph Rawdon, Neziah Wright and George W. Hatch).
1835- RAWDON, WRIGHT, HATCH & EDSON, Engravers. (Tracy R. Edson had this address from 1834 to 1837).
1836-1839 RAWDON, WRIGHT & HATCH, Engravers, 30 Wall St. (Freeman Rawdon). (In 1838 Tracy R. Edson, 205 Pearl St.).
1840-1841 RAWDON, WRIGHT & HATCH, 48 Merchants Exchange.
1842- RAWDON, WRIGHT, HATCH & SMILLIE, Engravers, 48 Merchants Exc. (James Smillie).
1843-1846 RAWDON, WRIGHT & HATCH, Bank Note Engravers, 48 Merchants Exchange.
1847-1858 RAWDON, WRIGHT, HATCH & EDSON, Bank Note Engravers, 48 Merchants Exchange. (Some work from July 5, 1851, to Sept. 30, 1857, was by Rawdon, Wright & Co., and in 1852 and 1854 by Rawdon, Wright, Hatch & Co. They absorbed The New England Bank Note Co. of Boston, Mass., May 1, 1848).
1858- AMERICAN BANK NOTE CO., Bank Note Engravers, 48 Merchants Exchange.

This famous firm, which in 1851 produced the first Canadian Government stamps, had its 1818 roots in Rawdon, Balch & Co. and Rawdon, Clark & Co.

Fig. 2. Tracy Robinson Edson.
Guiding Genius in R. W. H. & E. and prime mover in the formation of the American Bank Note Co. (Photo Courtesy Geo. E. McCabe).

Fig. 3. Geo. W. Hatch.
Member of the firm of R.W.H. & E., and President of the A. B. N. Co., 1863 to 1866.

in Albany, N. Y. where they maintained an office in 1835 and again in 1852 and 1853, but opened an office in New York in 1828.

They also had branch offices in Albany, and one in New Orleans which was supervised by Tracy R. Edson while he was absent from New York from 1837 to 1847. James P. Major the designer spent three winters in this office after 1840. On May 1, 1848 they absorbed the New England Bank Note Co. of Boston which was founded in 1833 by a certain Pendleton.

George W. Hatch was President of the American Bank Note Co. from 1863 to 1866 when he died on Feb. 13, at Dobbs Ferry, N. Y.

We give herewith a brief biographical sketch of the members of the firm and others who were of importance in the production of Canadian stamps.

Ralph Rawdon, Designer and Engraver (1790 -1860?). In 1813 Ralph Rawdon was engraving in a very crude manner in Cheshire, Conn., where he was associated in this work with Thomas Kensett, the father of the American artist. About 1816 Rawdon removed to Albany, N. Y., where he engraved stipple portraits over his own name, and with his brother Freeman Rawdon, and Asaph Willard he was in the bank note and general engraving business in that city.

He was a member of the firm of *Rawdon, Wright & Co.* in New York from 1828 to 1835 after which he was with *N. & S. S. Jocelyn* for two years. From 1841 he was with *Rawdon, Wright & Hatch* at least until 1846. In 1852 he is listed as a Broker at the Coal Mine Co. Office, 71 Merchants Exc., *but from 1853 he was continuously an Engraver with Rawdon, Wright, Hatch & Edson until 1858 when they consolidated into the American Bank Note Co. in their old premises, 48 Merchants Exchange.* In 1859 his address was 75 Merchants Exchange which was several doors away, as Treasurer of the Coal Mine Co. He was not a member of the firm of *Rawdon, Wright, Hatch & Edson* when they consolidated into the *American Bank Note Co.* since on January 1, 1852 new articles of copartnership were effected as shown by the following entry made that day on Page 55 of the R. W. H. & E. Ledger:

"The Capital Stock of Rawdon, Wright, Hatch & Edson consists of all the Bedpieces, Rolls, Machinery, Paper, Furniture and fixtures contained in or appertaining to the Offices of the said firm, at New York, Albany, Cincinnati & New Orleans, (as more fully set forth in the Inventory of Permanent Stock

Book) together with the Good Will of all the said establishments. Also of the equal undivided one half interest in all the Bedpieces, Rolls, Machinery, Paper, Furniture & fixtures (as also more fully set forth in said Inventory Permanent Stock Books) together with the Good Will, of the New England Bank Note Company at Boston.

Said Capital Stock belong equally to Freeman Rawdon, Neziah Wright, George W. Hatch and Tracy R. Edson, and all future additions to the same made during the continuance of their Copartnership, shall be made at the joint expense of, and, (together with the Good Will), shall in like manner belong equally to the above named Copartners, in accordance with the terms of Certain Articles of Copartnership between them, dated, New York 1st January 1852."

Freeman Rawdon, Pictorial Engraver—Born in Tolland, Conn., in 1804 and died Sept. 21, 1859, in New York. He was a pupil of his brother Ralph Rawdon, an engraver, then of Albany, N. Y. From about 1825 he was with the firm of *Rawdon, Clark & Co.,* of Albany, N. Y., and from 1838 of *Rawdon, Wright & Hatch* (and successors) of New York, at which time he was living with George W. Hatch. In 1850 he became interested in a Coal Mine Co. and had offices at 71 Merchants Exchange until 1854, but also retained his interests in his Bank Note Engraving firm until it consolidated, and he became one of the founders of the *American Bank Note Co.* in his old premises, in 1859. He was one of the few engravers to sign vignettes.

Neziah Wright, Engraver (1805?-1863?). While the name of Wright was used by *Rawdon, Wright & Co.* and their successors from 1828, there is no engraver of that name in the New York directories that can be identified as a member of that firm until 1838. Neziah Wright may have remained in Albany until that time when he is listed (at the firm's address) from 1838 to 1858 when they consolidated into the *American Bank Note Co.* at the same address. In 1859 he is listed as Treasurer of the latter company, having been the first to

Fig. 4. JAS. P. MAJOR
Designer for R. W. H. & E., and A. B. N. Co.
Photo Courtesy Thomas F. Morris.

hold that office upon the consolidation in May, 1858. He retired from the firm in 1862 because of bad health.

George Whitfield Hatch, Designer and Vignette Engraver. Born April 27, 1804, in Johnstown, New York; died at Dobbs Ferry, N. Y., in 1866. Mr. Hatch was one of the first students of the National Academy of Design in 1826, and for a time he was a pupil of A. B. Durand. He was a good line-engraver, and in 1827 he was designing and engraving bank-note vignettes in Albany and in New York City. While he engraved portraits, landscape plates, and subject plates for the "Annuals" his signed work is not plentiful.

In 1827-8 he was engraving with *A. B. & C. Durand, Wright and Co.* and in 1829 with *Durand, Perkins & Co.* In 1831 he formed a partnership with James Smillie at 48 Wall St. and from 1832 he was continuously a member of the firm of *Rawdon, Wright, Hatch & Co.* and their successors until they consolidated into the American Bank Note Co. in 1858.

Tracy Robinson Edson, Bank Note Engraver. Born at Fly Creek, Otsego County, N. Y., on December 12, 1809, and died in New York on November 29, 1881.

After leaving school Tracy R. Edson was for a time engaged in commercial work and then went to Albany where he learned engraving with *Rawdon, Clark & Co.* He went to the New York office of the firm in 1827.

In 1832, Tracy R. Edson began his successful business career in New York, where on March 1 he joined a banknote engraving partnership with Freeman Rawdon and George Whitfield Hatch as the firm of *Rawdon, Wright, Hatch & Co.* of 35 Merchants Exchange, of New York and with Ralph Rawdon, Ashbel Clark and Neziah Wright as the frm of *Rawdon, Clark & Co.* of Albany, N. Y. Each original firm was to conduct business in its respective city. He established for *Rawdon, Wright & Hatch* their branch offices in New Orleans, Cincinnati, Boston and Philadelphia.

While these branches were being established the firm became financially embarrassed, and a failure seemed absolutely certain. Edson was recalled to New York in 1847 and became business manager of the firm. He skillfully averted the impending catastrophe and in the end brought fortunes of very considerable proportions to the partners.

In 1858 he wrote a booklet entitled "New Security for Protecting Bank Notes from Alterations" published by *Rawdon, Wright, Hatch & Edson*. It described a new green and black ink that, when printed partly over the usual black engraving ink and photographed, looked alike thus preventing photographic counterfeiting of engravings in these two colors. He was President of the American Bank Note Co. from 1860 to 1863. When he retired from the Presidency of the American Bank Note Co. he retained an active interest in the management until about 1875 and only retired from the Board upon the 1879 consolidation.

One of R. W. H. & E.'s important employees was *James Parsons Major,* Script Engraver and Designer. Born at Frome, Somersetshire, England, May 13, 1818, and died at Somerville, N. J., Oct. 17, 1900. He emigrated to Brooklyn, N. Y., in 1833, where he resided until 1872 and for over 55 years he was in charge of the engraving and modeling department of *Rawdon, Wright & Co.,* and their successors including the *American Bank Note Co.*

Through the courtesy of his grandson George Wyckoff Major Clark, Esq., we give below quotations from James Parsons Majors autobiography, written in 1900, in a paper which Mr. Clark read at the New York International Stamp Exhibition in 1936. (TIPEX). We quote:—

" 'In 1836 Mons. Halbert obtained me an engagement with the old established firm of *Rawdon, Wright & Hatch,* Banknote Engravers, who, before the big fire (1845) occupied a good part of the old Exchange, and who were then located in Pine Street near Broadway, awaiting the completion of a building on the N. E. corner of Wall and William Streets, which we afterwards occupied during the entire construction of the present building (now known as National City Bank). Some sections of this building were purposely planned for the use of *Rawdon, Wright & Hatch.*

" 'On my 21st birthday I made an engagement with *Rawdon, Wright & Hatch* for a term of years, followed by others from time to time up to the first formation of the *American Bank Note Co.* This consolidation embraced the various banknote firms then extant—year 1858. After a rest of two or three months, I returned to the *American Bank Note Company,* who, in the meantime, had moved the engraving department to other new apartments, especially constructed on the main roof of the Exchange, gaining thereby increased light and room. The transferring department also occupied rooms on this floor which extended, I think, the full Wall Street front.

" 'In 1879 the last consolidation was effected, embracing the National Banknote Co. organized 1863 [1859]. The resources of these establishments were of such extreme value both in quantity and value as to add very materially to the excellence of the artistic and mechanical work now produced by the *American Bank Note Company.*

" 'After leaving the Exchange in Wall Street, *The American Bank Note Company* occupied a large portion of the marble building—N. E. corner Broadway and Liberty Street. (New York City).

" 'During the lapse of time, many dear friends, employers and associates, have passed away from earthly desires and cares. Especially dear to memory are Messrs. Rawdon, Wright & Hatch. At their hands I was ever the recipient of kind and generous treatment, a source of never failing pride and gratification today when recalling youthful days. I also retain a pleasing remembrance of the several gentlemen who have succeeded to the management of the *American Bank Note Company.* To complete a summary of my business career, a few additional lines are required. To wit, that for many years prior to the first consolidation of banknote companies, my position was modeller and also superintendent of the engraving department of Rawdon, Wright & Hatch. The modelling or designing branch I continued to hold until 1895, when on solicitation I returned to my favourite branch of script engraving and so continued until warned by Dame Nature to rest my hard worked eyes.

" 'While engaged in the Exchange with *Rawdon, Wright & Hatch,* a Mr. Crome was engaged as designer of vignettes. He was a quiet, unassuming man and well liked.

"In the early 1840's James P. Major passed three winter seasons in New Orleans in accordance with an arrangement with *Rawdon, Wright & Hatch.* Although only 22 years old at that time he apparently had become quite skilled and also had the confidence of his firm. 'James did not much wish to go there but there was but little chance of work in New York. At present things are very bad and by going he secures work for twelve months. Several offered to go for half the salary, but he had the preference.' Robert Moore and his brother John, designers, were also employed by Rawdon, Wright & Hatch under Mr. Major and Robert Moore went to New Orleans with him. James P. Major married Mary Ann Wright and Robert Moore married her sister, Susie Wright.

"One of his brothers-in-law was Alfred Jones, a member of the National Academy. Mr. Jones was connected for many years with the *American Bank Note Company* and the *British American Bank Note Company.* He was one of the most accomplished portrait engravers of his period.

"As to Mr. Major's work on the engraving of stamps. The 1845 New York postmaster stamp, the first United States stamps issued in 1847, and the first Canadian stamps, issued in 1851 were the work of *Rawdon, Wright, Hatch & Edson,* the 1847 stamps containing the four initials of the firms. At that time, according to his own story, Mr. Major was the modeller and head of the engraving department of that firm.

"Several years before my grandfather's death he gave to my sister, who is older than I, a number of choice engraver's proofs of stamps and admonished her that they should be treasured and should never leave the family.

"These proofs included interesting proofs of the early Canadian stamps of 1851, 1855, and 1859 Beaver 3 pence, Prince Albert 6 pence, Victoria 6 pence, 12 pence, one half penny, 2 cents, X cents; the 1860 stamps of New Brunswick

5 cents Victoria, X cents; and the early stamps of Nova Scotia 8½ cents Victoria, 10 cents Victoria, 12½ cents Victoria; as well as of Newfoundland 2 cents green, 5 cents brown, 12 cents garter. It might well be that Mr. Major designed and partly executed many of these early stamps, but of that I have no definite knowledge.

"This gives a hurried but fair idea of one of the most virile and versatile engravers of the period from 1840 to 1890—fifty years and more of life devoted to the maintenance and development of the highest ideals of a steel engraver."

The circular issued in 1853 by Rawdon, Wright, Hatch & Edson, which we illustrate (Fig. 5) is quoted in full herewith.

BANK NOTE ENGRAVING
Rawdon, Wright, Hatch & Edson
No. 48 Merchants Exchange
New York:
Offices at Albany, Cincinnatti & New Orleans
also at
Boston.
Under the name of—
The New England Bank Note Company.
Since May 1, 1848.

The undersigned are prepared, at either of the above places, to execute all orders for Bank Note Engraving and Printing, with promptitude and fidelity, and ample provision is made for the safety of all plates and impressions entrusted to their care. Their specimens embrace a great variety of vignettes and Ornamental Diework, suitable for Bank Notes, Bonds, Bills of Exchange, Bills of Lading, Deposit & Stock Certificates, Diplomas, Checks &c. accumulated at great expense and illustrating almost every subject connected with the business of the country: and the superiority of their style of work as affording the best possible security against counterfeiting, is established by the success of their efforts, which have been devoted to the attainment of that object, during an experience of thirty years past.

BANK NOTE PAPER, of the best quality at Manufacturers prices[4].

RAWDON, WRIGHT, HATCH & EDSON
Bank Note Engravers
No. 48 Merchants Exchange,
New York.

TERMS:

For Engraving 4 Bank Notes on Steel,		$500.00
" do 4 do Copper		300.00
" do 4 Combination Backs $100. to		250.00
" Retouching plates after first wear, one half the above prices.		
" Printing plate 4 Bank Notes, per 1,000 impresns		25.00
" do 2 do		15.00
" do 4 Combination Backs,		20.00
" do 2 do		15.00
" do 4 Typographical Red denominations,		12.50
" do 2 or 1 do		10.00
" Bank Note Paper, per 1000 sheets,		22.50

Bank Note Plates, engraved by us only on the express condition that they are to be printed by us. Steel Plates, (other than Bank Note Plates), having Bank Note work on them, engraved by us only on the express condition that they are never to be taken out of our possession. Steel Bank Note Plates engraved and printed by us, are warranted to give 30,000 good impressions before, and 25,000 do. after retouching. Copper do. 3,000 before, and 2,000 do. after retouching.

Author's Note— The sentence "steel plates other than Bank Note Plates having Bank Note Work on them,"—refers to postage Stamp Plates.

---

4. This was Willcox's paper. Appendix P #2, #6, et seq.

Circular Issued by Rawdon, Wright, Hatch & Edson in 1853 and 1854.

Dated "Jany 1854"

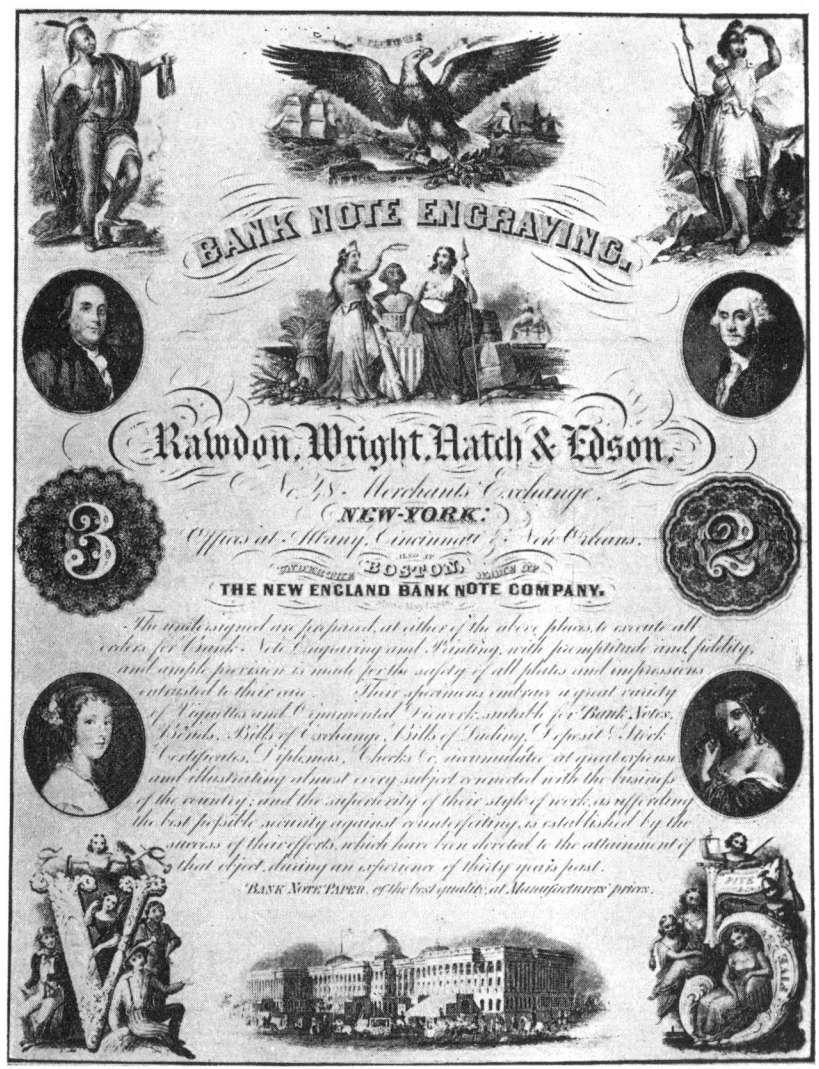

FIG. 5.

Circular Issued by Rawdon, Wright, Hatch & Edson in 1853 and 1854.

Dated "Jany 1854"

FIG. 5.

Fig. 6. Entrance to Merchants Exchange, where Rawdon, Wright, Hatch & Edson, and later (1858) the American Bank Note Co. was located. The building later became the U. S. Custom House, and is now the head office of the National City Bank. This and other illustrations of the American Bank Note Co. are from Harpers New Monthly Magazine for February 1862.

2. American Bank Note Co.

Until this time all bank note engraving firms were partnerships, composed entirely of skilled artists, practical engravers and agents actually engaged in production of the business. The *American Bank Note Co.* agreement was eventually signed by all the 25 partners on April 29th, 1858, to become effective two days later on May 1st, as shown by the following copy of the Articles of Association, which Mr. Brazer had the good fortune to obtain from George E. McCabe of Troy, Pa. This was found not far from Tracy R. Edson's old home town in New York state among some of his old papers and correspondence, others of which will be quoted later. The original agreement is beautifully handwritten in the old style (fs for ss) on twelve foolscap pages and the signatures are all exceptionally bold.

Mr. Major mentions the formation of the American Bank Note Co. in 1858. We quote herewith some extracts from the

Articles of Association of American Bank Note Co.

Whereas We

Freeman Rawdon
Neziah Wright
George W. Hatch
Tracy R. Edson
Charles Toppan
Samuel H. Carpenter
Henry E. Saulnier
Charles T. Carpenter
Samuel H. Carpenter, Jr.
Moseley I. Danforth
Edward J. Danforth
Henry Perkins
J. Dorsey Bald

William Cousland
Edward A. Moss
Albert G. Goodall
Frederick E. Bliss
Nathaniel Jocelyn
Robert Draper
Charles Welsh
Simeon S. Jocelyn, Jr.
John G. Wellstood
DeWitt C. Hay
William H. Whiting
John E. Gavit

Fig. 7. Engraving Room, showing Engravers working on dies.

Fig. 8. Geometric Lathe at left and Transferring Press at right.

as copartnership firms and individuals heretofore and at present engaged in the business of Bank Note Engraving and Printing are desirous of uniting and consolidating our said business, and the talents, skill and good will of our respective establishments, and also all the machinery, tools, instruments and implements of our art and trade, furniture, materials and effects, as possessed and used by us in our respective establishments, with all our facilities of business, into one concern, for the purpose of imparting greater energy, skill and efficiency to the exercise of the said art, trade and business of Bank Note Engraving and Printing and the business collateral thereto, or connected therewith, and for our united advantage and profit, as well as for the greater security of the public, believing that the same can be attained in no other way: Now, for the carrying out of the said objects, and defining our rights and regulating our conduct in the premises, we, the undersigned, the original proprietors, corporations and projectors of the Company hereinafter named, do mutually undertake, covenant and agree, to and with each other, as follows:

First.—That from and after the first day of May 1858, the business of bank note engraving and printing, and its collateral branches, for our own account, and in our and each of our establishments, shall cease; and that we will not, either as members of any firm, or association, or individually, carry on, or be interested in the business of bank note engraving, or printing, or any business collateral thereto, viz. The engraving or printing of Government, State or Corporation Bonds, or Securities, Certificates of Stock or Deposit, Checks, Drafts, Bills of Exchange, Labels or Postage Stamps, involving in their production the use of steel dies, and transferring therefrom according to the current practice of the several bank note engraving houses parties hereto, except as herein provided. But such business in said respective establishments, shall be transacted for the present, and till other premises are provided by the Company hereinafter named, in the premises now occupied by the said firms, and the leases of said premises, shall be transferred to and assumed by said Company.

Second:—We agree that upon signing these articles, all the machinery, presses, tools, instruments and implements, plates and dies, stock of materials, furniture and effects belonging to our said establishments in the business of bank note engraving and printing, the same being guaranteed as free from all encumbrance or lien, or the business collateral thereto, and also all orders and contracts for such engraving and printing in our said establishments, shall be, and by virtue of these articles, are transferred and assigned to the Trustees of the Company incorporated as the "American Bank Note Company." But this does not include debts due to such parties or firms, up to the time these articles are to take effect, nor bank note paper, moneys or securities, and all unfinished orders or contracts in progress, are to be and are hereby transferred to the said Company and taken and estimated at a fair valuation for the work already done.

Third:—We agree that, as full compensation and consideration for such sale, transfer and assignment, we will accept and receive from said Trustees, subject and in reference to these Articles of Association, the stock of the said Company, which shall be issued by the said Company pursuant to the provisions of the amendatory act of the Legislature of the State of New York, passed June 7th, 1853, to the general law of voluntary corporations, passed February 17th, 1848, the said stock to be issued and delivered to and held by us, subject to the provisions and covenants and agreements in these articles contained, and to be issued to us in the amounts in the next succeeding article (Fourth) herein specified, to wit.

Fourth—

To Rawdon, Wright, Hatch & Edson	5,951	Shares.
To Toppan, Carpenter & Co.	5,577	Shares.
To Danforth, Perkins & Co.	5,428	Shares.
To Bald, Cousland & Co.	3,312	Shares.
To Jocelyn, Draper, Welsh & Co.	2,092	Shares.
To Wellstood, Hay & Whiting	2,042	Shares.
To John E. Gavit	498	Shares.

Fig. 9. Die Hardening Furnaces.

Fig. 10. Transferring Room, showing Transfer Presses, and Geometric Lathes.

The amount of the said shares so issued and delivered to each firm or individual shall represent the estimated and agreed value of the property, business, contracts, &c., sold and transferred by them to the said Company; and the whole number of such shares so to be issued for the property &c. as aforesaid shall amount to 24,900 shares and no more.

Nothing however in these articles contained shall prevent the assignments and transfer by Rawdon, Wright, Hatch & Edson to Isaac Cary and George Mathews, of such number of shares of the stock of the Company as said Rawdon, Wright, Hatch & Edson shall appropriate to them for their interests in the firm of Rawdon, Wright, Hatch & Edson; and upon signing these articles, and receiving said shares said Cary and Mathews may become parties to these articles of association, with the same benefits and the same obligations as the original parties hereto.

Seventh:—Such of the parties hereto as desire to be employed in their profession and art of bank-note engraving and printing, or the various departments thereof, may be employed by the Company, at such prices and on such terms as shall be agreed upon, and a preference shall always be given to the parties hereto in any professional work or business to be performed by, or for said Company; but this provision is not to prevent the employment and hiring by the Company of artists and professional engravers and printers, and other persons who are not parties to this agreement.

Tenth:—Other parties than the original parties to these articles may become parties hereto, in the following manner, and in no other manner. First. By a vote of four-fifths of all parties to this agreement, counting by shares, each share to count one vote. Second. By becoming a purchaser of at least ten shares of stock in the Company, to be held subject to these articles. Third. By signing these articles and sealing. All these acts shall be necessary to enable any one to become a party thereto, other than the original parties.

Eleventh:—The parties hereto have unanimously agreed, and do hereby agree, that the following named persons be and they are nominated and appointed, as the Trustees of the said Company, and named in the Certificate of Incorporation, viz.:

Fig. 11. Press Room showing Hand Presses and Operators.

Fig. 12. Plate Vault. Plates for stamps and banknotes were stored in this room. At the time this engraving was made the American Bank Note Co. was supplying stamps to Canada, New Brunswick, and Nova Scotia.

Freeman Rawdon	Edward J. Danforth
Tracy R. Edson	J. Dorsey Bald
Charles Toppan	Nathaniel Jocelyn
Samuel H. Carpenter	William H. Whiting
Mosley I. Danforth	

and to them or their substitutes or successors, to be from time to time appointed, as herein provided for, we, the parties hereto, and each of us for ourselves, our personal representatives and assigns, have granted, and do hereby mutually and irrevocably grant, full power and authority to transact all the business of the said Company, and to exercise every power and privilege in respect thereto, which the parties hereto, or any of them, or any person claiming under them, or any or either of them, could exercise if personally present; and every person substituted or appointed by the said Board of Trustees, or who may be substituted, or appointed in any other legal manner, according to these articles, shall possess the same authority in all respects, as that which was committed to the Trustees whose place he shall supply, and shall hold his office by the same tenure.

x   x   x   x   x   x   x   x

In Witness whereof we, the parties hereto, have hereto set our hands and seals this twenty-ninth day of April in the year of our Lord Eighteen hundred and fifty-eight.

Freeman Rawdon	seal	Wm. Cousland	seal
Neziah Wright	seal	Edward A. Moss	seal
Geo. W. Hatch	seal	Albert G. Goodall	seal
Tracy R. Edson	seal	Frederic E. Bliss	seal
Chas. Toppan	seal	Nathaniel Jocelyn	seal
S. H. Carpenter	seal	Robert Draper	seal

NOTE: The first signers were the firm of R. W. H. & E. (Bold type ours).

H. E. Saulnier	seal	Chas. Welsh	seal
C. T. Carpenter pr S. H. Carpenter	seal	Simeon S. Jocelyn Jr.	seal
S. H. Carpenter Jr.	seal	John G. Wellstood	seal
M. I. Danforth	seal	De Witt C. Hay	seal
Edward J. Danforth	seal	William H. Whiting	seal
Henry Perkins	seal	Jno. E. Gavit	seal
J. D. Bald	seal		

Extracts from the Report of Head of the Business Department
Tracy R. Edson

Four months after formation of the Company, on September 1, 1858, Edson submitted to the Board of Trustees a lengthy and legibly hand written Report. He first defined the duties of the Board as not executive but legislative, to make rules and determine policies to be executed by the appointed officers, and then proceeded to report on what had transpired during the three months past.

George Mathews* in charge of the Montreal Branch agreed to a modification of his contract permitting the Company "to meet any competition which may arise"—"particularly in Canada West provided his rights as Patentee of the Green Tint are respected."

The Canada Post Office Department accepted a proposal of Rawdon, Wright, Hatch & Edson to perforate their stamps for an additional compensation of 5 cents per 1000 and Rawdon, Wright, Hatch & Edson on July 21, 1858 ordered a perforating machine for $500, to be delivered early in September. The machine, however, was not in working order until November, 1858[5].

On May 16, 1860 the following executives were elected by the Board of Directors:—

Tracy R. Edson—President.
Moseley I. Danforth—Vice Pres. & Supervisor of Designs and Models.
Nathaniel Jocelyn—Supervisor of the Art Department.
De Witt C. Hay—Supervisor of Pictorial Department.
John G. Wellstood—Supt. of Letter Engraving Dept.
Henry E. Saulnier—Supt. of Transferring Dept.
C. L. Van Zandt—Supt. of Printing Dept.
Neziah Wright—Supervisor of Lettering & Transferring.

F. O. C. Darley was re-engaged as designer of vignettes on March 14, 1861.

This firm continued to print the stamps for the Canadian Post Office Department under the terms of the original contract of R.W.H. & E. until the formation of the Dominion, when the British American Bank Note Company secured the contract which it held until 1897. (See below).

The next important event in the history of the relations between the American Bank Note Co. and the Canadian Post Office was the establishment of

The Ottawa Branch

In September, 1896, tenders were called for by the Dominion Government for the engraving and printing of the Dominion Bank Notes, *postage and revenue stamps, etc. One of the requirements of the contract was that the work should be done in Ottawa*. Accordingly upon being awarded the contract the American Bank Note Co. immediately began the construction of a plant especially for the business at 224 Wellington St., Ottawa. Additions to this plant were made in 1904, 1907, and 1914. The original contract was for five and a quarter years. It was renewed until 1930 when the British American Bank Note Co. secured the business of printing postage stamps[6].

---

* NOTE: George Mathews of R.W.H.&E's. Montreal office was the owner of a patented "indestructible green tint" which was used extensively on Bank Notes, both by the American Bank Note Co., and the British American Bank Note Co. and known as "Canada Bank Note Printing Tint." The Canada Directory for 1851-2 lists George Mathews as an "engraver on steel, copper and wood, and lithographer and printer, 19 Great St. James St.", Montreal.

5. Appendix H #65 and #72.
6. The details of these contracts are discussed in "Introduction to the issues, Engraved and Printed by the American Bank Note Co., 1897-1930", etc.

Announcement of the Formation of the American Bank Note Co.

American Bank-Note Company.

NEW-YORK, MAY 1ST, 1858.

For the purpose of placing the Bank Note Currency of the country upon a basis of greater security, with the same features of stability and perpetuity that appertain to Banking Institutions, the undersigned, being all the firms now engaged in the business of **BANK-NOTE ENGRAVING AND PRINTING** in the United States, respectfully give notice that they have associated themselves together under the style of the **American Bank-Note Company**, and have been duly incorporated by Law.

This Company offers to the public important advantages.

It combines the greatest skill and experience with the most perfect division of labor.

It brings to bear all improvements in machinery.

It offers the opportunity of selection from the whole material now in use.

It gives the greatest possible security by the superior perfection of work.

It places the business on a permanent footing, protecting the community against contingencies that might arise from the dissolution or derangement of any particular firm.

The business will be continued, as heretofore, at New-York, Philadelphia, Boston, Montreal, Albany, Cincinnati, Chicago and New-Orleans.

The following are the names of the Trustees appointed under the Act, viz:

> FREEMAN RAWDON,
> TRACY R. EDSON,
> CHARLES TOPPAN,
> SAMUEL H. CARPENTER,
> MOSELEY I. DANFORTH,
> EDWARD J. DANFORTH,
> J. DORSEY BALD,
> NATHANIEL JOCELYN,
> WILLIAM H. WHITING

Until arrangements are completed for the concentration of the business, orders may be addressed to the respective firms, each of which, representing this Company, will hereafter afford to **Banking Institutions** the aggregate advantages, responsibilities and safeguards possessed by all the Houses composing this Corporation. Their prices will remain the same as heretofore

Very Respectfully,

RAWDON, WRIGHT, HATCH & EDSON,
New-York, Montreal, Cincinnati and New-Orleans,
and with ISAAC CARY, *The New-England Bank Note Co., Boston.*
GEORGE MATTHEWS, *Montreal.*

TOPPAN, CARPENTER & CO.,
New-York, Philadelphia, Cincinnati and Boston.

DANFORTH, PERKINS & CO.,
(Late DANFORTH, WRIGHT & CO.,)
New-York, Philadelphia, Cincinnati and Boston.

BALD, COUSLAND & CO.,
New-York and Philadelphia.

JOCELYN, DRAPER, WELSH & CO., *New-York,*
DRAPER, WELSH & CO., *Philadelphia.*
New-York, Philadelphia and Boston.

WELLSTOOD, HAY & WHITING,
New-York and Chicago.

JOHN E. GAVIT,
Albany.

In 1923 this branch of the American Bank Note Co. became the Canadian Bank Note Co., Ltd., a wholly owned subsidiary of the parent company. The present concern again secured the Postage Stamp Contract in 1935 and this contract is still in effect at the time of writing.

3. British American Bank Note Co.

Late in 1867 the British American Bank Note Co. of Montreal and Ottawa began engraving and printing the postage stamps of the newly formed Dominion of Canada. The officers were William C. Smillie, President; Alfred Jones, vice-president and secretary; and Henry Earle, Sr., treasurer. Later Earle became secretary as well as treasurer. G. B. Burland was general manager. The company had two offices, one at Ottawa and one at Montreal. The printing of the bonds, notes, currency and stamps for the Dominion was done at Ottawa under the supervision of a government agent, until late in 1874, when the Ottawa plant was closed and all work was done in Montreal.

Upon renewal of the contract in 1887 the company moved the stamp and security printing to Ottawa again as required by the Government.

These contracts are discussed in greater detail in the Chapter "Introduction to the Large and Small Queen Design Issue".

We quote an announcement sent out by the firm in 1870 to prospective customers.

British American Bank Note Co.
INCORPORATED BY LETTERS PATENT—CAPITAL $100,000

Sir:

We take the liberty of submitting for your inspection the within specimens of our engraving and would respectfully ask your support for the enterprize in which we have embarked. We hope it may commend itself as one that proposes good to the Country, as well in the advancement of Art as in the encouragement of Home Industry.

Long and intimate practical experience as Artists & Owners in similar Companies of the United States, establishes our competency; and the *patronage of the Government of Canada in the execution of Provincial Notes, Stamps, Bonds, &c.* endorses our responsibility.

In the ownership of the Canadian Patent Green Tint we possess exclusive advantage as against the alteration and photographing of Bank Notes, and are enabled from the facilities at our command in an already large and growing stock of Vignettes, Lathe Work and other material, to promise ready fulfilment of any orders with which we may be favored, in a style of excellence & at such rates as should prove satisfactory.

Very respectfully,

JANUARY 1, 1870   ENG. BY W. C. SMILLIE

NOTE: Italics are ours.

This announcement is in script letter and was engraved by William Cumming Smillie.

Brief biographical notes of the various members of the firm at the time of its formation are herewith given:

William Cumming Smillie, Script Letter Engraver. Born in Edinburgh, Scotland, Sept. 23, 1813. Died July 2, 1908, at Poughkeepsie, N. Y. Wm. C. Smillie was a brother of James Smillie and came to Canada with his father's family in 1821. After working at silver-engraving for a time in Quebec, he came to New York in 1830. He early turned his attention to bank-note engraving and was connected with several bank-note companies; the last of which, EDMONDS, JONES & SMILLIE, was later absorbed by the American Bank Note Company.

The United States Postage Stamp contract of June 10, 1851, discloses that W. C. Smillie was at that time a member of the firm of TOPPAN, CARPENTER,

Fig. 13. W. C. SMILLIE
President of the British-American Bank Note Co., 1867.
Photo Courtesy Theodore H. Saulnier.

Fig. 14. ALFRED JONES
Vice-President of the British-American Bank Note Co., 1867.
Photo Courtesy Thomas F. Morris.

Fig. 15. HENRY EARLE, SR.
Secretary and Treasurer of the B. A. B. N. Co., 1867.
Photo Courtesy Adelaide L. Earle.

CASILEAR & CO. of Philadelphia, but the directories of that city from 1848 to 1860 do not include his name. He was probably at that time the New York (though possibly the Boston) representative of the firm, as his signature (as was also that of John W. Casilear) was witnessed by others than the witnesses of the Philadelphia members of the firm.

From 1836 he was continuously with the New York offices of *Draper, Toppan, Longacre & Co.; Draper, Toppan & Co.; Toppan, Carpenter & Co.* and *Toppan, Carpenter, Casilear & Co.* He became a member of the New York branch of the firm from 1848 to 1856, when he became associated with *Edmunds, Jones & Smillie* until they consolidated with the *American Bank Note Co.* (1859). He married a sister of Henry Earle, also a letter engraver with *Toppan, Carpenter & Co.*

"From a letter written in 1897 to Joseph Willcox from Wm. C. Smillie we quote the following:

'I began in the office of Rawdon, Wright & Hatch, as nearly as I can recollect, in the year 1834 in the old Exchange Building in Wall St., New York, and remained with them a year; after which I was in the employ of Casilear, Durand, Burton & Edmunds, until the failure of that firm in about a year later. *During this time I had the pleasure of becoming intimate with your father, James M. Willcox, who had supplied the firm with large quantities of his paper, which was highly thought of*[7]. I ought not to go on without paying a well deserved compliment to the memory of the dear old gentleman, whom I had learned to love for his genial heart and temper, and profoundly to respect him for his high principles of honor. I have been frequently at Ivy Mills [Delaware County, Pa.] with my friend Saulnier.

'In 1836 I began an engagement with Charles Toppan, with whom John Draper had but a short time previously formed a partnership, associating with them also Joseph (James B.) Longacre under the firm name of Draper, Toppan, Longacre & Co. After a term of 12 years employment with this company, during which time Samuel Carpenter joined the firm, I was admitted as a partner in 1848, by the kind cooperation of Mr. Saulnier. I was a letter engraver, in connection with Mr. Toppan, from 1836 to 1857. I sold my interest in the firm of Toppan, Carpenter & Co. to Mr. Samuel Carpenter in 1856. In 1858 I became associated, with Edmunds & Jones, in the firm of Edmunds, Jones & Smillie. Before we got well started we were taken into the American Bank Note Company, with whom I remained 5 years (1863). I am now 84 years old."

---

7. See Chapter on The Pence Issues, and Appendix P #2,, #6 et seq.

In 1866 he secured a contract to engrave the paper currency of the Canadian government, and for this purpose he established a bank-note engraving business in Montreal, and Ottawa, together with Alfred Jones and Henry Earl, being president of the concern.

Alfred Jones, Portrait & Pictorial Engraver (1819-1900). Born in Liverpool, England, April 7, 1819; accidentally killed by taxicab in New York, April 18, 1900. Mr. Jones came to the United States as a very young man and in 1834 he was apprenticed to the engraving firm of *Rawdon, Wright, Hatch & Edson* first in Albany, N. Y., and later in New York City.

About 1841 Alfred Jones began engraving over his own name, and in 1846-47 he visited England to perfect himself in his art, and he there worked under some of the best London masters and made the acquaintance of a number of prominent English engravers of that period. Upon his return to New York he engaged in business for himself and he also worked for other engravers. Being himself an admirable line-engraver, about 1850 Mr. Jones worked almost exclusively in bank-note engraving, and to this branch of his profession he devoted the remainder of his life.

In 1842 he was with *Sherman & Smith* but engraving independently from 1843 to 1858 at 34 Liberty St. He married Louisa Major, sister of James J. Major and lived in Yonkers, N. Y.

In 1857 with Charles Edmonds and Wm. C. Smillie he formed the short-life firm of *"Edmonds, Jones and Smillie."* In 1866 he was the president of the *United States Bank Note Co.* of New York; **and in 1868-70 he was vice-president of the British American Bank Note Co. of Montreal and Ottawa, Mr. William C. Smillie being the president. Later in life he worked independently, chiefly for the American Bank Note Co.**

As a line-engraver Mr. Jones had few, if any, superiors, in America; and his large plate of "The Image Breaker" published by the American Art Union in 1850, is deservedly recognized as one of the best engravings ever produced in America. Mr. Jones continued to engrave with undiminished skill up to the time of his death.

It will be seen that apparently Edmonds did not go with Jones and Smillie to Canada. They were, however, accompanied by a brilliant engraver:

Henry Earle, Letter Engraver and Designer. Born Mar. 1, 1827; died Oct. 12,

Fig. 16. JOHN EARLE
Brother of Henry Earle, Sr., and Inventor of Pantograph Engraving Machine, Which B A. B. N. Co. Used.
Photo Courtesy of Adelaide L. Earle.

Fig. 17. Business card of the British-American Bank Note Co., about 1867. Pale brown net work, black lettering on white glazed card. Note early type of imprint, which is known on the 1c, 3c, and 6c Large Queen plates, and on at least one 3c Small Queen plate.

Fig. 18. Smaller card, about 1870. Note that G. B. Burland was Manager, and W. C. Smillie was President.

Fig. 19. Card, about 1876, showing G. B. Burland as President and W. C. Smillie as Vice-Pres.

Fig. 20. Card of about 1883. Note that Mr. W. C. Smillie's name no longer appears. He left the British American Bank Note Co. 1882 to join the newly formed "Canada Bank Note Engraving and Printing Co."

Fig. 21. Letter head of the British American Bank Note Co. dated 1881. We have seen this letter head dated 1876. Note the Queen's Head vignette as used on the 1868-97 stamps.

Fig. 22. Modern letter head of 1906. Note Queen's head vignette was still in use.

1914. He was born in Philadelphia, the son of John H. Earle, proprietor of the famous Earle's Art Galleries. He began engraving under the eminent letter engraver Charles Tappan about 1840, and was with *Toppan, Carpenter & Co.* in Philadelphia until about 1861. He is listed in the directory at *Toppan, Carpenter, Casilear & Co.,* 76 Walnut St. from 1853 to 1858 and then with the *American Bank Note Co.,* where he for a time engraved and designed in their office in the Trinity Bldg., New York City. **Henry Earle's sister married Wm. C. Smillie, Letter Engraver with Toppan, Carpenter & Co., and both Smillie and Earle were founders of the British American Bank Note Co. of Canada when the Canadian Government decided their work should no longer be done in New York. He was secretary and treasurer of the British American Bank Note Co. in 1867.**

Henry Earle's "Scrap Book" which has passed through Mr. Brazer's hands, is endorsed on the by leaf "Henry Earle, from his father, Oct. 2, 1879" (probably his son) and contained 81 die proofs of bank note vignettes mostly with imprint of "British American Bank Note Co.—Montreal & Ottawa"; 41 bank note proofs of the Bank of Canada from 1870 to 1879 and some other Canadian, German and Greek banknotes; **49 Canadian Revenue proofs; 38 Canadian Postage die proofs of the 1868 and 1872 issues,** 2 Canada Postcard proofs of similar design, the Canada Officially Sealed proof, **Prince Edward Island 1870 4½p die trial color lake, and 3 engraved cards of the B. A. B. N. Co.**

An accompanying Album contained 183 die proofs of bank note vignettes by Toppan, Carpenter & Co.; Rawdon, Wright, Hatch & Edson; American Bank Note Co., etc.; 4 proofs of bank notes, **102 proofs of Canada, Manitoba, Ottawa, Ontario and Quebec Revenue Stamps;** and 19 proofs of landscape engravings by Sir Charles Heath (2), James Smillie (5), Bartlett (12), one by T. Macklin dated Jan. 18, 1873 and one by P. J. Louthdour dated Nov. 30, 1875.

John Earle, Square Letter Engraver (1830-1905), was born August 18, 1830 in Philadelphia, Pa. He was a younger brother of Henry Earle, Letter Engraver (born March 1, 1827, in Philadelphia) and an elder brother of William H. Earle, Vignette Engraver, born August 11, 1832, in Philadelphia.

John Earle was taught square letter engraving by his famous brother, Henry Earle, at Toppan, Carpenter & Co. in Philadelphia, where he engraved continuously, and with their United States stamp engraving successors, Butler and Carpenter and Joseph R. Carpenter, and probably in 1876 with their successor, the Philadelphia Bank Note Co. Later he engraved in the Philadelphia plant of the American Bank Note Co. **He patented a pantograph engraving machine prior to 1891, by which amateurs produced and automatically spaced several styles of square and script lettering, borders, counters, and tints that seemed incredible, until witnessed. This machine was sold after his death to the American Bank Note Co. The Canadian patent was sold to the British American Bank Note Co. of Montreal.** John Earle's sister, Agnes Earle (b. Sept. 28, 1825) married Wm. C. Smillie, Letter Engraver, whose scrap book of engraved lettering was later given to Howard I. Earle by his aunt, Agnes Smillie. It contained cards and letter heads of engravers and engraving firms, from which, Mr. Brazer obtained much information through the kindness of Adelaide Louis Earle, daughter of John Earle. He died at Primos, Pa., January 26, 1905.

It is not generally known that the British American Bank Note Company lost its contract in 1891 to *The Canada Bank Note Engraving and Printing Co.,* which was formed in 1882. This concern was prepared to go ahead and fulfill its agreement when it was purchased by the British American Bank Note Co., which assumed the contract and continued to supply the small queen's head stamps until April 22, 1897, when it finally ceased printing stamps for the Post Office Department of Canada, the American Bank Note Company having secured the contract, beginning May 1, 1897[8].

---

8. See "Introduction to the Issues Engraved and Printed by the American Bank Note Co., 1897-1930", etc.

The Canada Bank Note Engraving and Printing Co., which was located at 526 Craig St., Montreal, had as officers in 1882 Geo. E. Desbarats, president; Wm. C. Smillie, vice-president; G. H. Dreschel, secretary-treasurer. In 1889 Mr. Smillie returned to the B. A. B. N. Co.

For the period of five years, from April 1, 1930, to March 31, 1935, the British American Bank Note Co., Ltd., Ottawa, held the postage stamp contract. Although it no longer prints the postage stamps the firm still prints all the Revenue stamps for the Dominion Government, as well as much other work of a like nature.

Fig. 23. Business card of the "The Canada Bank Note Co. Ltd.", about 1885. Note that W. C. Smillie was vice-president. Mr. Smillie returned to the B. A. B. N. Co. in 1889. Brown on pale green glazed card.

Fig. 24. Letter head of the Canada Bank Note Engraving and Printing Co. in the 1880's. Note that "William C. Smillie" was vice-president.

4. The National Bank Note Co.

This firm was formed in 1859 and was printing the United States stamps in 1867. when the Dominion Government was in the market for a new series of stamps and securities. The National Bank Note Company submitted an essay, the frame of which was by Douglas S. Ronaldson, vignette by Alfred Jones.

Fig. 25. D. S. Ronaldson.
Engraver of frame for Essay by National Bank Note Co., in 1867.

Douglas E. Ronaldson, Letter and Ornamental Engraver (1848?-1902?). In July, 1868, he was engraving for the National Bank Note Co. and continued with them at least until 1872. He probably continued with the N. B. N. Co. until the consolidation in 1878 with the American Bank Note Co. for whom he engraved at least until 1894. From 1897 until he died he was engraving for the Bureau of Engraving & Printing in Washington. See Chapter on the Large and Small Queen Designs of 1868-1897.

The engravers and printers of the postal stationery are fully discussed in the chapter on these interesting issues.

Proclamation by the Governor General Transferring the Management of the Inland Posts to the Provincial Government.

Province of Canada.

By His Excellency the Right Honorable JAMES, EARL OF ELGIN AND KINCARDINE, Knight of the Most Ancient and Most Noble Order of the Thistle, Governor General of British North America, and Captain General and Governor in Chief in and over the Provinces of Canada, Nova Scotia, New Brunswick, and the Island of Prince Edward, and Vice Admiral of the same, &c. &c. &c.

To all to whom these presents shall come, or whom the same may concern—GREETING:

A PROCLAMATION.

WHEREAS in and by an Act of the Parliament of this Province made and passed in the Session held in the Thirteenth and Fourteenth Years of Her Majesty's Reign, Chaptered Seventeen, and intitled, *An Act to provide for the transfer of the management of the Inland Posts to the Provincial Government and for the Regulation of the said Department,* it is amongst other things enacted, that the said Act shall come into force at and from the time when the assent of Her Majesty thereto with the advice of Her Privy Council shall be proclaimed in this Province, or at such subsequent time as in the order of Her Majesty in Council by which the assent of the said Act may be signified, shall be fixed in that behalf and not before. AND WHEREAS the Act hereinbefore mentioned has been duly submitted to Her Majesty in Her Privy Council for the assent of Her Majesty thereto, and that thereupon by an order in Council bearing date at Windsor, on the TWELFTH day of DECEMBER, in the Year of Our Lord, One thousand eight hundred and fifty, Her Majesty by and with the advice of Her Privy Council did assent to the said Act, and did order that such assent should be, and be proclaimed in the said Province as soon as might be. Now KNOW YE that I, JAMES, EARL OF ELGIN AND KINCARDINE, Governor General of the said Province of Canada, in compliance with the said Act and in obedience to the said order of Her Majesty in Her Privy Council, do issue the present Proclamation for the purpose of proclaiming Her Majesty's assent to the said Act so intituled as aforesaid, *An Act to provide for the transfer of the management of the Inland Posts to the Provincial Government and for the Regulation of the said Department,* and of promulgating the said Act so assented to by Her Majesty in Council as aforesaid; of all which Her Majesty's Loving Subjects and all others whom it doth or may concern, are hereby required to take notice and govern themselves accordingly.

GIVEN under my Hand and Seal at Arms, at Toronto, this FIFTH day of APRIL, in the year of Our Lord, one thousand eight hundred and fifty-one, and in the Fourteenth year of Her Majesty's Reign.

By Command,   ELGIN AND KINCARDINE.
J. LESLIE, *Secretary*.

["The Canada Gazette," Extra, No. 515. Toronto, April 7, 1851]

(The heading is from a die proof on india, of die #119, British American Bank Company, engraved about 1875).

Chapter VIII

THE PENCE ISSUES

SECTION A.   1851—LAID PAPER

Three Pence, Six Pence, and Twelve Pence

The first "adhesive postage labels"[1] to be issued in British North America appeared in April, 1851, and were issued by the Post Office Department of Canada.

Official mention of adhesive stamps for the prepayment of postage first occurs in the Journals of the Legislative Assembly of Canada, where under the date of May 22, 1849, we read a resolution was made "That postage stamps for prepayment be allowed and that Colonial stamps be engraved." This was passed May 25, 1849, and received the approval of the Legislative Council the following day[2].

The contract for the printing of these labels was given to the well known firm of engravers, Rawdon, Wright, Hatch, & Edson[3], of New York, who were contractors to the Canadian Government for debentures, as well as bank note engravers for several Canadian banks. They also at that time had the contract for printing postage stamps for the United States Post Office Department[4].

It was decided that the first series should consist of three denominations, namely 3d, 6d, and 12d to pay the rate as follows:

> 3d per ½ oz. in Canada, and (after July 6, 1851) to New Brunswick, Nova Scotia, and Prince Edward Island.
>
> 6d per ½ oz. to the United States (except the Pacific Coast) and double weight domestic letters.
>
> 12d per ½ oz. to Newfoundland, or the British West Indies via Halifax and Liverpool; double weight letters to the United States; or quadruple rate domestic letters[4a].

Before it was decided to have the work done by Rawdon, Wright, Hatch and Edson, two essays had been prepared by Sandford Fleming, civil engineer and surveyor, as per entry in his diary for Monday, February 24, 1851, which reads "Breakfasted at Ellah's Hotel[5] with Mr. Rutten & Honble Jas Morris, Postmaster General. Designing postage stamps for him[5a]."

These essays were of two denominations, 3d, and 1s., both similar in design (Fig. 1).

1. This was the official name given to Stamps by the British Post Office.
2. The Resolutions are printed in full in Appendix A, #3A.
3. Appendix H, #1, and 11 to 16 inclus.
4. Append'x H. #1.
4a. Appendix B #17, Paragraphs 1, 5 #18, Paragraphs 58, 63, 70
5. Ellah's Hotel was run by a Mrs. Ellah, and was located at 72 King St. West, Toronto.
5a. Appendix Vol. II, Page XIV.

SANDFORD FLEMING

From "Sandford Fleming, Empire Builder", by J. Lawrence Burpee, Oxford University Press, 1915

Portrait Made About 1858.

A lithographic plate was made by Mr. (James) Ellis[6] and a number of stamps printed. The fact that these stamps were not engraved was undoubtedly the chief reason for the Post Office authorities declining to use them[6a].

Essays

DIE PROOFS

E1   E2

Fig. 1.
Sandford Fleming's Essay for the Three Pence, and the One Shilling.

REFERENCE LIST

DESIGNED AND ENGRAVED BY SANDFORD FLEMING, FEB. 1851[7]

These are very rare.

E1. 3d black on thin brittle yellowish paper.
E2. 1s black on thin brittle yellowish paper.

None of the specimens printed by Mr. Ellis appear to have survived, although the example now or formerly possessed by H. Borden Clarke of Ottawa may be from this plate. (See Illustration Vol. II Page XIV).

Sandford Fleming's design was accepted for the 3d, but as the other two denominations were chiefly for letters going out of the country it was deemed more fitting that they should bear the effigy of the sovereigns.

The pending issue of the stamps was noted in the well known "Order No. 4,"[8]

It is interesting to observe that the Beaver stamp was the first adhesive stamp to picture an animal[9], and until 1939 the only one to picture a rodent[10].

The dies were engraved on steel by Alfred Jones[11], under the supervision of James Parsons Major[12]. Steel transfer rolls bearing one relief were used to lay down a steel plate[13] of two hundred subjects for each denomination.

Although these stamps were produced by the foremost Bank Note engravers of the day there was some criticism of them mostly from political motives. A sample quotation will show the caliber of the animadversions:

> "We may mention, that on examining the *three pence* stamp got from New York, the public will be surprised to find that the work gererally is not so well done as that on the plate first engraved in Toronto; that there is no engine ruling upon it, nor is there anything about it to prevent its being forged. Cheerfully would we submit, to competent

---

6. "The British Colonist", Toronto, June 9, 1851.
6a. Appendix H #3.
7. Sandford Fleming was born in Kirkaldy, Scotland January 7, 1827 and died in Halifax, N. S. on July 22, 1915. He was one of Canada's outstanding citizens.
8. Appendix B, #21.
9. The Mulready envelope pictures a number of animals, and the N. S. W. Letter Sheets of 1838 bear armorial creatures.
10. In 1939 Bolivia issued 60c and 75c stamps picturing a Chinchilla; a rodent.
11. See Chapter VII, Page 110.
12. See Chapter VII, Page 94.
13. Appendix H, #16, 17.

Pence Issues on Laid Paper

THE ILLUSTRATIONS ARE SELF EXPLANATORY. THE 12p PAIR IS #60, 70 LEFT PANE.

judges, for their opinion, as to the relative merits of the New York plate and that done here."[13a]

The finished stamps were furnished at the rate of 20c per thousand[14], the dies, rolls and plates being furnished without cost to the Post Office Department of Canada[15].

The preparation of the stamps in 1851 was as shown herewith:

Denom. & Color	Ordered	Die	Plate Proof	First Delivery	Quantity
3d red	Mar. 27	April 5	April 7	April 15	100,000
6d lilac	Mar. 27	April 23	April 28	May 2	100,400
12d black	Mar. 27	April 23	May 8	May 14	51,000

The colors given are the official colors as named by the contractors.

Proofs

CONTEMPORARY DIE PROOFS. 1851.

On Thin Wove

We have never seen die proofs of these stamps, and list them here for puroses of record as we know they were made.

D1a. 3d red. April 5, 1851
D2a. 6d lilac. April 23, 1851
D3a. 12d gray black. April 23, 1851.

CONTEMPORARY PLATE PROOFS (Rare)

P1a. 3d black on thin card
P1b. 3d black on india
P1c. 3d red on india
P2a. 6d black on india
P2b. 6d dark gray on india
P2c. 6d purple on india
P3a. 12d black on india

Blocks 6 to 8 times normal.

Proofs on other papers, in other colors, are post contemporary proofs made from the original dies or plates for various purposes, such as official records, samples, or for advertising. They will be found listed on page 173f.f. Contemporary plate proofs on india, sometimes mounted on card were overprinted "SPECIMEN."

"Specimen" Stamps
(These are scarce)

Fig. 2.

Position of Overprint

H—Horizontal=At bottom of stamp.
V—Vertical=Reading up.
D—Diagonal=Southwest to northeast.

13a. "The British Colonist", Toronto, May 9, 1851. This is possibly the type of criticism that P.M.G. Morris was referring to in his letter to R.W.H.&E. May 17, 1851 (Appendix H #10). "The British Colonist" was an opposition paper. Its criticisms therefore are to be discounted somewhat.
14. Appendix H #16.
15. Appendix H #16.

Fig. 4. View of Mill Where Paper for Pence Stamps Was Made Until 1857.

The overprint is typographed in a setting of 100 subjects (10 x 10) and shows slight variations in size being 2½ - 2¾ mm. high, by 20½ - 21 mm. long, in the horizontal and vertical overprints.

The diagonal overprint was another setting of 100 (10 x 10), the length is 23 mm. and the letters are 3 mm. high.

Overprint

		^{w}Carmine	^{y}Yellow	^{z}Green
S1a.	3d black	D	H	—
b.	3d red	H	—	H
S2a.	6d black	V	V	—
b.	6d gray	V,D	V	V
c.	6d blue gray	V	V	—
d.	6d blue	V	—	—
e.	6d red lilac	V	—	—
S3a.	12d black	V,D	—	V

Blocks 6 to 8 times normal.

See also section E—Post Contemporary Proofs, page 173 f.f.

Fig. 3. Portrait of James Willcox, Owner of Ivy Mills.

The Paper

The first deliveries were printed on a crisp laid paper, horizontal in the case of the 3d, and vertical in the other two values. It varies somewhat in thickness, from almost pelure to a rather stout substance. The color is grayish to white. This is a hand-made paper, supplied by the famous Ivy Mills, of Chester, Pa., which specialized in Bank Note Papers[16].

The laid lines are sometimes so faint as to be barely discernible, but when the stamp is viewed by reflected rather than transmitted light the laid lines can usually be seen. Examples are known however which apparently show no laid lines. The paper is characteristic, however, and in the case of the 6d, copies on semi-transparent paper may be considered as on laid.

---

16. Appendix P #6.

Any 3d stamp used before April 25, 1852, must be on laid paper, and any 6d stamp used before March 21, 1855, also must be on laid paper[17]. The delivery of the 12d included several sheets on thin wove to replace the poor impressions made on the laid paper. The impressions on the thin wove were not satisfactory and on May 8, 1851, a proof sheet on thicker wove was sent to the Postmaster General in Toronto, where it was afterwards postally used. (Fig. 9).

The Plates

The plates were of unhardened steel[18] and consisted of two hundred subjects, arranged in two panes of 100 (10 x 10) separated by a gutter 10-10½ mm. wide. Owing to the horizontal format of the 3d the panes were arranged one above the other, the gutter being horizontal, thus corresponding to the right and left panes of the 6d, and 12d. From this it will be seen that the 3d plate was 10 x 20, while the other two were 20 x 10[19]. During the printings on laid paper the plates had no imprints[20].

THE THREE PENCE

This popular stamp has been studied by many philatelists, and its numerous varieties are a fascinating field with much still to be learned.

Before describing the plate varieties we wish to briefly discuss the well known "flaw" or "cut" which shows on all the subjects of the 3d plate, more or less clearly, especially the fine impressions on machine made paper after 1857 (q.v.). On the proofs this flaw also shows very clearly, particularly when in black.

The flaw does *not* appear on the die proofs, and neither does it show on the die proofs of the 5c 1859, the die for which was the 3p die suitably altered.

This flaw is therefore a "relief flaw" or "relief break" which occurred on the transfer roll. Since the lines on the transfer roll are raised (that is the relief on the transfer roll is similar to the finished stamp), it follows that the breaking of any of these delicate lines will result in a "white" line or break showing on the printed stamp. Traces of color may be due to ink smearing across the break and being transferred to the paper during printing.

The fact that all the stamps on the plate show this flaw is sufficient evidence that only one relief was used in making the plate, as it is extremely improbable that two reliefs would show exactly the same flaw. Futhermore the evidence given on page 217 conclusively shows that only one relief was on the transfer roll.

The "Relief Break" on the Transfer Roll of the Three Pence

Fig. 5. Emphasized Diagram of "Relief Break".

---

17. Appendix H #44.
18. Appendix H #16, etc.
19. Appendix Q #1.
20. The printing area of the three plates was 403-407 x 236-241 mm. including the gutter between the panes.

Plate Varieties

THREE PENCE

The plate of the 3d is notable for several prominent varieties, illustrated herewith:

Re-entries: Pane A (Upper Pane)

No. 47. This is the Major Re-entry.

No. 80. Similar to Re-entry #47 but Upper "3s" Do Not Show Traces of Doubling.

No. 34. Doubling of Lines Below "REE PENC," and Lower "3's". This is Frequently Confused with #47.

No. 91. Pearls of Crown Show Doubling.

Other Varieties: Pane A (Upper Pane)

No. 56. Small Loop in Frame Line Under "P" of "Pence."

No. 88. Short Transfer. Right Frame Missing.

The following varieties while minor are worthy of note:
#33 Minor Re-entry. Line through top of "PE" and below "PE" of "PENCE" in white oval. Right top frame line missing.
See section on wove paper stamps for illustration of #31 with flaws at lower right.

Re-entries: Pane B (Lower Pane)

No. 42. Doubling of Line Opposite "TAGE."

No. 53. "V.R." Re-entry.

No. 61. The Major Re-entry on this Pane. Doubling of Line Above Crown, and Below "REE".

No. 65. Lower Left Corner Re-entry.

Other Varieties: Pane B (Lower Pane)

No. 15. Recut at Right of Crown.

No. 20. Flaw in Upper Right "3."

The following varieties are also worthy of note:
#12 Short Transfer. Frame missing from bottom left to center.
#30 Dot in lower right corner near "3".
#66 Entire left portion of stamp weak. This is an exceptionally fine example of a SHORT TRANSFER.

THE SIX PENCE

There are no plate varieties of importance. Proof impressions are known which show a number of re-entries, but none of these exist on the issued stamps. It is possible that the plate was re-entered before the proofs were pulled, as it is known that proofs were made in 1858 or 1859 for the purposes of record.

Nevertheless on clearly printed examples the following minor varieties may be noted:

LEFT PANE

#15 Left frame line very weak. Top frame line very weak at left.
#22 Blurred mark from upper left "6" to final "A" of "CANADA".

RIGHT PANE

#2 Top frame recut.
#5 Dot above top frame at left.
#33 Horizontal guide line through stamp, bisecting it.
#57 Left and right frame lines very weak or missing in lower half of stamp.

THE TWELVE PENCE

This plate was extensively re-entered, so much so in fact that a normal is rarer than one showing evidence of re-entering. At least one triple entry is known. The stamp is so rare however, that a discussion of the re-entries and plate flaws is purely academic so far as the average student is concerned.

The chief interest centers around the problem of papers, and there was considerable discussion in the early days as to whether this stamp actually occurs on wove paper.

Although there was but one delivery of this stamp, we are able to show that there was more than one printing. From the extensive correspondence between the contractors and the Post Office Department (given in extenso in Appendix H), we quote:[20a]

Hon. James Morris, P.M.G.
Toronto, C. W.   May 8th 1851
"Enclosed we hand you a proof impression of the twelve pence stamp plate, which we hope will be found satisfactory—the stamps would have been sent on Saturday next, but on examining them we found them so badly printed that they will have to be reprinted, and the present ones destroyed. They will be sent on Wednesday next.
Very respectfully, Sir,
Your Obedient Servants,
(Signed) Rawdon, Wright, Hatch & Edson."

A few days later the shipment of twelve pence stamps was sent as this letter shows:

Hon. James Morris, P.M.G.
Toronto, C. W.   May 14, 1851
"We sent you by mail this day, a package containing 50,000 twelve pence stamps, which completes your order for three, six and twelve

---

20a. The three letters quoted herewith were found by us after Editing Appendix H. Delete note 11 to Appendix H #10, Page 5-H.

Fig. 6. Left Half of Pane A Overprinted "Specimen" in Red. (S1-BW).

pence stamps. Please have the kindness to acknowledge receipt of this package sent, and oblige,
>Yours respectfully,
>(Signed) Rawdon, Wright, Hatch & Edson."

As noted in Appendix H #10, 51,000 stamps were sent and R. W. H. & E. replied to the query as follows:

Hon. James Morris, P.M.G.
Toronto, C. W.   May 23rd 1851

"We are in receipt of your favor of the 17th inst., and agreeable to your request we have this day deposited with D. S. Kennedy, Esq. for safe-keeping, the plates and dies of the three, six and twelve pence stamps.

In regard to the excess which you mention in the number of stamps received over the number advised, our foreman put these in the package to make up for any impressions that might be found defective in parts, in consequence of the gum adhering to the face of the stamps. The number thus added was marked on each package, and was separated by a slip of paper from the remainder in the same manner. In any future impressions, it will be advisable to use a little heavier paper that is more opaque, as we find the present paper too thin and transparent."

>Yours respectfully,
>(Signed) Rawdon, Wright, Hatch & Edson.

The solution of the problem therefore would appear to be somewhat as follows: There were sent out, besides the 50,000 stamps, "A proof imprint of the Twelve Pence stamp Plate", also the 1000 stamps which the printer added to make up for any possible deficient copies. It is quite probable that the extra five sheets were from the first printing.

Another point to consider, which a glance at the proof sheets readily shows is that these are printed in black, the same color as the originals, and on account of the poor workmanship in making up the plate many of the copies have a blurred apperance.

We have clearly shown, that there was more than one printing of the Twelve Pence, and therefore, there is a distinct possibility of different paper, and besides we have positive evidence that the delivery made on May 14, contained both printings. In addition there was a proof sheet sent on May 8. This accounts for Mr. Pack's statement *(London Philatelist, Volume 16, Page 144)*, in which he mentioned that he was told part of the Twelve Pence Canada, which had been for sale at the Hamilton Post Office, were on wove paper, and he was convinced this was the case.

Furthermore, Mr. Howes in referring to a meeting of the Philatelic Society of London, May 4, 1888[21], mentions the following:

>Mr. G. Ranson, showed an undoubted postmarked specimen of the Twelve Pence Canada, printed on stout wove paper.
>Mr. W. H. Brouse, Toronto, "Eminent Canadian Philatelist" also possessed a copy of this stamp, which later adorned the Ayer collection.

In addition to this, Mr. Howes shows a record of two copies, having been sold at the "Mirabaud Sale" in Paris, in 1890.

The late John N. Luff, (Canada Stamp Sheet IV.—142,) said: "It is my opinion that both the wove and laid papers are genuine and I think that both varieties might occur though there was only one lot sent out by the printers. It does not, of course, follow that the entire batch was printed on the same day [*Which we have proven*] or that two varieties of paper might not have been used. The early printers were not always very particular about their paper,

---
21. Philatelic Record, Vol. X, P. 124.

Fig. 7. 6d on laid. Note Exchange Markings of Montreal (Ib) and Rouses Point (IIb).

Fig. 8. 3d. Very fine bottom sheet margin copy on thin laid from "St. Thomas Jun 1 1851" to New York. A rare example of short payment passing through.

provided it was somewhat alike in a general way. **Some collectors claim that laid paper is often of such nature that the lines do not show in some parts of the sheet, and I believe there is evidence to support this theory."**

That there is considerable difficulty in seeing the laid lines in the paper is demonstrated by the fact that many copies of the Six Pence offered by dealers or auctioneers as "thin wove" are in reality on the laid paper.

Copies of the Twelve Pence on thin wove paper are also well known, and we therefore list this stamp on three different papers.

A. Thin laid semi-transparent.
B. Thin wove paper semi-transparent.
C. Medium thick wove paper.

The stamps are printed in greyish black to (intense) deep black on paper A and B and in greyish black on the medium thick wove, paper C.

The plate shows a large number of re-entries and minor varieties; in fact, more so than any of the other values of this issue, and it is particularly strange when it is considered that of the Six Pence value, there are only slight minor varieties in the entire plate of two hundred subjects. It can therefore be taken for granted that the plate was certainly laid down by a different siderographer than the one who made the Six Pence plate.

The Plate

The alignment of the plate was made from the right hand side and there is a peculiar thing noticeable, namely, almost without exception the left hand corners of the stamp are higher than the right hand ones of the stamp to the left. It looks as if the transfer roll reliefs had not come out quite straight from the hardening process. The stamps are spaced fairly regularly—about 1½ to 1¾ mm. vertically and 1¼ to 1½ mm. horizontally. Guide lines show at the left of the outer margin on many stamps and the position dot is in the middle of the left outer frame line just above the center of the cross on the left hand crown in the legend band. As usual it does not show on the left hand vertical row of stamps.

The principal plate varieties are as follows:

All Are Re-Entries

LEFT PANE

#11—Transfer roll set too far to left.
  (a) Outer frame double at upper right and lower left corner, also lower right corner doubled.
  (b) Both figures in all four corners affected.
  (c) Outer ovals show extra lines below "L V E," inner to left of "T A ENCE."
  (d) Nearly all letters affected.
  (e) Line through middle of period after "PENCE."

#38—Transfer roll set too high and too far to right.
  (a) Frame shows doubling in all four corners.
  (b) Figures in upper left corner, double line through bottom of "1", "2", also affected.
  (c) Outer oval at top and right, and inner oval at left and lower left shows parts of extra lines.
  (d) Letter "C" of "Canada" is affected.

#54—Transfer roll set too low and too far to right.
- (a) Outer line double at right and bottom right corner.
- (b) "2" of "12" in lower right corner double on top.
- (c) Extra line in outer oval to right of crown.
- (d) Double frame at left of back-ground of medallion.
- (e) Lower left "12" looks smaller due to partial obliteration by second entry.

#61—Transfer roll set too low, and too far to left.
- (a) Outer frame shows traces at right and left side, clear double lines in design, bottom line double across frame, connecting lower frame lines.
- (b) "2" of "12" in lower left, lower right and upper right corner doubled.
- (c) Double line to right of outer oval, double frame to medallion at right.
- (d) "TAGE" affected.

#72—Transfer roll set too high and too far to left.
- (a) Outer frame at top and at left double and cuts into design at lower right.
- (b) Figures in upper left and lower right corner affected.
- (c) Top of medallion extending into design, clear double line.
- (d) Scrolls extend into right margin.

#74—Transfer roll set too high and too far to right.
- (a) Margins at right and upper right show double line.
- (b) Figures slightly affected.
- (c) Outer oval double line over right of "POSTAGE" and "ENCE."
- (d) "C A - ADA - GE - ELVE - PENCE" affected.

RIGHT PANE

#56—Transfer roll set too high and too far to right.
- (a) Double outer frame at upper left and inner frame at upper right, lower right and lower frames doubled. At lower left corner frame line connects.
- (b) Figures in lower left corner double.
- (c) Inner and outer ovals double in middle of left side.
- (d) "TAGE" of Postage affected.

#61—Transfer roll set too low to left.
- (a) Frame double at left and right bottom.
- (b) Double inner oval lower left.
- (c) "WELVE - P" affected.

#73—Transfer roll set too high and too far to left.
- (a) Outer frame traces of doubling at top and left and right.
- (b) "2" of upper right "12" affected.
- (c) Outer oval over "N A" inner oval over "E - PEN."
- (d) All letters of "TWELVE PENCE" affected.
- (e) Short transfer at top.

All these varieties occur of course on the plate proofs.

The stamp did not prove popular and distribution was very limited. As reference to Appendix O #1 will show there was even some doubt as to whether the stamp was ever issued!

We quote from the *Metropolitan Philatelist* (Vol. XVII, P. 83, 1902) the well known list showing the Post Offices which received the Twelve Pence.

CANADA ONE SHILLING POSTAGE STAMP.

Total number rec'd. from Contractors..51,000
Total number issued to postmasters.. 1,510

Balance (destroyed May 1, 1857)..49,490

NOTE—On May 4, 1851[21b], the first and only consignment of the Canada 1 shilling postage stamp, to the number of 51,000 (value £2,550), was received by the Post Office Department, Canada, from the Contractors, Messrs. Rawdon, Wright Hatch & Edson, New York.

The issue of this stamp began on June 14, 1851, and concluded on December 4, 1854, when the stamp was discontinued. During its issue 1,510 stamps of that denomination were sent out to postmasters, leaving a balance on hand of 49,490, which, on May 1st, 1857, were, in accordance with the practice of the Department in cases of the discontinuance of stamps, destroyed. As has already been observed, there was only the lot of this stamp received from the contractors.

DETAILS OF ISSUE

Date of Issue.	Name of Office.	Name of P. M.	No.
June 14, 1851	Hamilton	E. Ritchie	300
Oct. 17, 1851	Chippewa	W. Hepburn	100
Nov. 13, 1851	Thorold	J. Keefer	20
Nov. 25, 1851	Toronto	C. Berczy	200
Mar. 8, 1852	Montreal	J. Porteous	200
Sept. 14, 1852	Ingersoll	D. Phelan	100
Apr. 5, 1853	*Bytown	G. W. Baker	100
Oct. 20, 1853	Sherbrooke	Wm. Brooks	15
Jan. 13, 1854	Smith's Falls	Jas. Shaw	50
Jan. 20, 1854	Bytown	G. W. Baker	100
Feb. 8, 1854	L' Islet	Ballantyne	15
Feb. 27, 1854	Ingersoll	Chadwick	20
Mar. 22, 1854	Sault S. Marie	Jos. Wilson	25
May 15, 1854	Port. du Fort	McLaren	15
Oct. 21, 1854	Rowan Mills	de Blaquiere	50
Oct. 26, 1854	Melbourne	Thos. Tait	50
Oct. 27, 1854	Montreal	A. La Rocque	100
Dec. 4, 1854	Smith's Falls	Jas. Shaw	50
		Total no. issued	1,510

* Now Ottawa, Capital of the Dominion of Canada.

Actually only 1450 were issued to postmasters,[21a] **as Ingersoll returned sixty copies.**

Further copies were used by the Department in franking letters outside of Canada, notably to the Engravers (Fig. 9). This was the proof sheet on thick wove and this instance creates a peculiar situation in which a proof becomes what might be termed an "official stamp". All copies on thick wove are used, and we illustrate the only copy known on cover, addressed to the Engravers!

The plate of the Twelve Pence was cancelled and forwarded to Toronto March 26, 1857[22]. The die, however, became the basis for the new 7½d stamp[23]. A laydown die was made, and only the medallion was used for the new stamp.

21a. Appendix C #28.
21b. This date is not quite correct as the 12d stamps were not sent until May 14 from New York.
22. Appendix H #53, #54.
23. Appendix H #52.

(This illustration is of a faked cover—*Publisher.*)

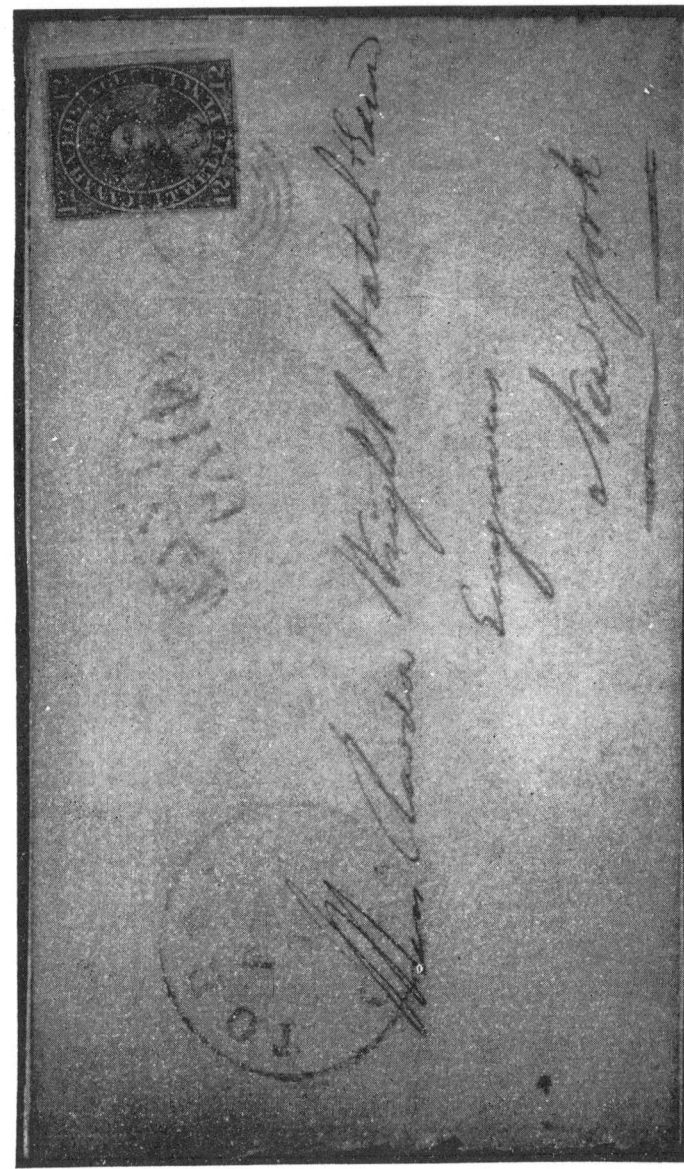

Fig. 9. A cover of great historic interest, and a philatelic gem. 12d on THICK WOVE from "Toronto C. W. Feb 1" to the contractors "Messrs Rawdon, Wright, Hatch & Edson, Engravers, New York." Note "Canada," exchange marking and New York. "Paid" both in red. Stamp is lightly tied by black cancellation, and the town mark is also in black. The addressees engraved and printed the stamp and also supplied the exchange marking. This is believed to be the only known copy on cover of the THICK WOVE PAPER.

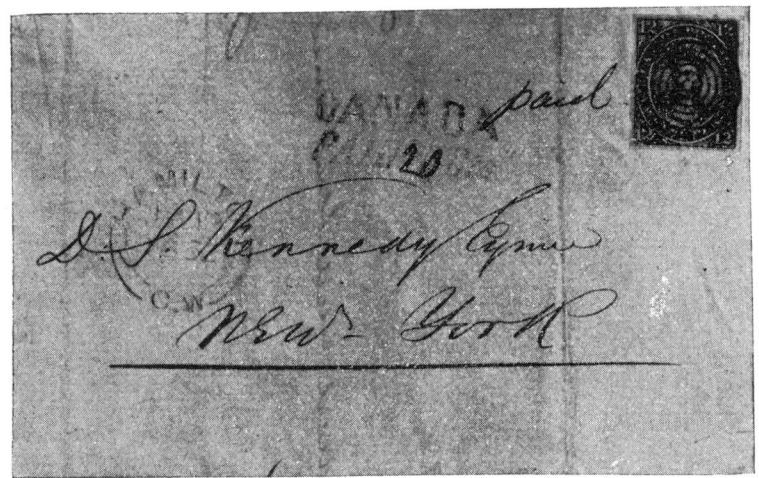

Fig. 10.
12p on thin laid, paying the double rate to the United States from "Hamilton J(ul)y 19 1852". Note Exchange Marking with "10" changed to "20" by manuscript.

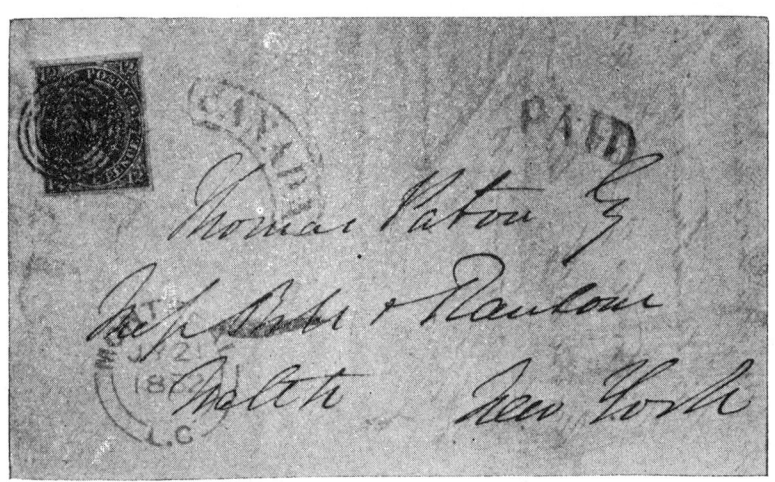

Fig. 11.
12p on thin laid, also paying the double rate to New York. Red "Montreal L. C. JY 21 1852". Note "Canada" Exchange marking and the New York "PAID" in red. Black concentric ring cancellation on stamp.

Fig. 12.
12d on thin laid, paying double rate to New York. Red Toronto, C. W. and red "Canada" exchange marking. Right sheet margin copy with concentric ring cancel in black.

Fig. 13.
3d. Very fine copy on the rare thin brittle wove from "City of Ottawa De 6 1855".

1851 Pence Issue
HANDMADE LAID PAPER

Thin to Medium semi-transparent 3d Horizontally laid; 6d, 12d Vertically laid

#	Denomination & Color	Value Factors Unused	Value Factors Used	Date Issued	Quantity	1944 Scott	1944 S.G.
1	3d Red 1851	N	N	Apr. 23, 1851	500,000	1	1a
	Orange red	1¼	7		Pane A, #47		
a	Major re-entry	3	4				
b	Strong re-entry	2½	2½				
c	Minor re-entry	2	3				
d	Short transfer	2	10				
e	Stitch wmk.		3				
	Pair	4	15				
	Strip of four	30	40				
	Block of four	80	2				
	Cover	—					
2	6d Violet 1851-4	N	N	May (6?) 1851	100,000	2	2
a	Stitch wmk.	10	10				
	Pair		8				
	Strip of three		x				
	Cover		2				
3	12d Black 1851	N	N	May 1851	50,000	3	4
	Pair	x	x				
	Cover		x		1,450 issued		
3A	12d Black, Thin wove paper 1851			May 1851	1,000	6	9a
	Pair	3					
	Cover	x					
3B	12d Black, Thick wove paper 1851	—	N	May 1851	200	6	14a
	Cover		x				

139

3p. Vertical Pair on Ribbed Paper, Lower Stamp Showing Flaws at Lower Right (#21, 31 Pane A), and Upper Stamp Showing Portion of Left Imprint. Early State of Flaw.

SECTION B. THE THREE PENCE AND SIX PENCE ON WOVE PAPER
1852

The early printings of these denominations were on laid paper, a paper that was unsatisfactory for at least two reasons, namely: impressions were not as good as desired, and the stamps did not adhere well enough to the letters. The complaint of the Post Office Department concerning the paper used was answered by letter in November, 1851[1], by the contractors in which they said that future printings would be on a more suitable paper than heretofore.

On March 20, 1852, the contractors received an order for 250,000 Three Pence stamps[2]. About a month later this order was forwarded to Toronto[3]. *These were the first wove paper stamps.* In the case of the Six Pence, however, no further supplies were ordered until February, 1855[4]. This order for 50,000 stamps was sent to Toronto on March 14, 1855[5].

From this data it can be seen that **the earliest possible date for a Three Pence on wove would be the beginning of April, 1852, and for the Six Pence on wove, the end of March, 1855.**

Fig. 14.
3d. Two blocks of four on same piece. Left block wove, right block ribbed paper. Hamilton, U. C. Jan 22. 1858.

The Wove Paper

Beginning with the orders early in 1852 and until 1857, inclusive, the stamps were printed on a wove *handmade* rag stock bank note paper, made by the same Ivy Mills, of Chester, Pa., that made the earlier laid paper[6].

Late in 1857, however, the paper became much more uniform in thickness, substance, and texture. It is wove *machine* made rag stock paper, which we believe to be the product of the Crane Paper Mill of Dalton, Mass.[7] This firm in 1857 had perfected a method of making bank note paper by machine[8]. Because of its uniformity, better surface and printing qualities, the stamps on this paper show much clearer and more uniform impressions[9].

---
1. Appendix H, #18.
2. Appendix H, #21.
3. Appendix H, #22.
4. Appendix H, #42.
5. Appendix H, #44.
6. Appendix P #2, #6.
7. Appendix P #10, #14.
8. Paper Making by Dard Hunter; 1943.
9. Appendix P #3.

Three Pence Wove Paper

Orange Red. 1851.
Hand Made Peper.
#47, 57 Pane A.
(Major Re-entry).

Orange Red. Thin Hand Made Paper.

Brown Red. 1858. Machine Made Paper.

Brown Red. 1858. #33, 34, Pane A. Both Show Re-entries.

Brown Red. 1858. #47, 48, Pane A. Major Re-entry.

Brown Red. 1858.
Machine Made Paper.
#20, 30, 40, Pane A.
Showing Right Imprint.

Ribbed Paper. #10, 20 Pane A.

Brown Red. 1858. Machine Made Paper.

The various wove papers have been extensively studied, and are the source of much perplexity to collectors. One student claimed ten distinct varieties[10]. However, since we know that until 1857 at least, the paper was handmade, allowance must be made for considerable variation in thickness, tone, and substance of such paper[11].

It will be noted that the 6d does not appear on THIN WOVE. Copies of this denomination on semi-transparent paper or less than .00275″ thick must be considered as on LAID PAPER. (See particularly Page 131 letter of May 23, 1851 from R. W. H. & E., and comment by John Luff).

While the specialist will of course wish to include such varieties that can be distinguished by careful study, we are of the opinion that for practical purposes the wove papers should be listed as follows:

HAND MADE PAPER

(Arranged in order of appearance)

Paper	Date	Characteristics	Three Pence	Six Pence
A.	1852-4	Thin to medium (.00225 to .00300″)	x	—
B.	1853-4	Hard, crisp "thin oily" (.00225 to .00300″)	x	—
C.	1855-7	Hard stout opaque (.00300 to .00450″)	x	x

MACHINE MADE PAPER

Paper	Date	Characteristics	Three Pence	Six Pence
D.	1857-9	1. Soft ribbed (Late 1857) (.00300″)	x	—
		2. Hard, medium to thick (.00275 to .00450″)	x	x
		3. Very thick, soft (1857) (.00475″)	—	x
		Number of varieties	5	3

Approximate quantities on each paper:

Paper A —3d— 500,000
Paper B —3d— 250,000
Paper C —3d— 1,200,000; 6d—150,000
Paper D1—3d— 300,000
Paper D2—3d— 600,000

Paper D2, D3—6d—100,000

Ratio of occurence of paper
3d-C-1, A-3, D1-5, D2-5, B-6.
6d-C-1, D2-4, D3-20.

Notes on the papers listed above.

Paper A. This is sometimes so thin and crisp as to be almost pelure, it lacks, however, the "glassy" effect of true pelure. The rare very thin brittle paper occurs in this group.

Paper B. A semi-transparent paper used for some of the Three Pence stamps in 1853-4, and also for part of the first order of the Ten Pence (q. v.). Delivery of June 23, 1854. (Appendix H #33).

Paper C. A comparatively white paper which takes a much better impression than the thinner papers.

Paper D1. This is a very fragile paper. The ribbing, always horizontal[12] on the Three Pence, is sometimes clearly visible when the back of the stamp is examined, but can always be seen distinctly when viewed by reflected light. Care

---
10. Stanley Gibbons Monthly Journal, Vol. VII, p. 9, 1896-7.
11. Appendix P #3.
12. The only copy with vertical ribbing we have examined was in our opinion a fake.

should be taken not to confuse it with the *LAID* paper which shows much broader alternate lines (vergeures), also visible by reflected light, or in a benzine cup. The ribbed paper is remarkably uniform in thickness, over 80% of the copies examined being .00300". We have seen a copy used December 1857. Delivery of Oct. 12, 1857. (Appendix H #60, 60A).

Paper D². This might be called "ordinary" wove paper.

Paper D³. This paper is peculiar to the Six Pence. It resembles a thin blotting paper, and stamps on it are characteristic in shade, and impression. All we have examined vary little in thickness. Delivery of Dec. 19, 1857, partly on this paper. (Appendix H #61, 62).

The only confusion possible is in distinguishing papers C, and D². D² is more even texture and the mesh of the paper more visible.

The STITCH WATERMARK variety occurs on both the handmade and machine made papers, although it is much rarer on the handmade papers. On the handmade papers it may occur horizontally or vertically, but on the machine-made paper it occurs only parallel to the long dimension of the design[13].

The Plates

The same two steel plates were used for the printings on wove paper that had been used for the laid paper printings. The size of the sheets, however, was inconvenient (200 to the impression), and on March 1, 1856[14], the contractors asked permission of the Post Office Department to cut the sheets in half, which was granted a few days later[15]. In the order for 300,000 Three Pence stamps sent on October 9, 1856, it was specifically requested that they be in *single* sheets of *one hundred stamps each*[16]. Finally the invoice of October 12, 1857, covering stamps ordered September 19, 1857, reads "Printing 300,000 Three Pence stamps in Red, 3,000 impressions (½ plate) at 20c per M $60.00[17].

This would indicate that the plate was actually cut in two, and from the fact that the major re-entry (Pane A #47) occurs in all printings, it would seem that the upper pane was the one used for most of the later orders, although the varieties from Pane B are also known in the later printings. At the time the plate was divided the IMPRINT (Type I) was added[18]. The Six Pence plate received the same treatment in filling the order for 50,000 stamps sent on December 19, 1857[19].

It was probably while the plate was being divided and the imprint added that the diagonal scratches which occur on the upper pane (Pane A) #31. All the copies we have seen of this variety are on the machine made paper of late 1857-8.

PANE A. (UPPER PANE)

No. 31. Flaws at Lower Right. (1857).

---
13. Appendix P #8.
14. Appednix H #48.
15. Appendix H #49.
16. Appendix H #51.
17. Appendix H #60A.
18. We have seen a 3d with imprint on cover dated Dec. 22, 1857.
19. Appendix H #62.

The Imprint

TYPE I FULL IMPRINT

Right Imprint Reading Down

Bottom Imprint Inverted

The imprint (Type I) consists of the name of the contractors "RAWDON, WRIGHT, HATCH & EDSON, NEW—YORK" (Page 145) 29 mm. long in upper and lower case letters, the capitals being 1 mm. high, and the other letters ½ mm. high. It is located 1 mm. from the stamps, and placed twice in each sheet margin[20], that is eight times on the sheet, viz.:

	At—TOP Over	—LEFT Opposite	—RIGHT Opposite	—BOTTOM Below
On Both				
Three Pence	#2, 3, 4	#11, 21, 31	#20, 30, 40	#92, 93, 94
Six Pence	#7, 8, 9	#61, 71, 81	#70, 80, 90	#97, 98, 99
	Normal	Reading Up	Reading Down	Inverted

The comparative scarcity of stamps showing traces of the imprint is further evidence that it was added to the plates during the last years of their use, as after the imprint had been added twenty-four stamps out of each sheet of one hundred (24%) had the imprint adjacent! Furthermore the plates of the Half-Penny and Seven-and-a-Half-Pence which were made in July and May, 1857, respectively, had the imprint rocked in when made, while the plate of the Ten Pence, made in December, 1854, never had an imprint. The evidence seems to indicate that when the Three Pence and Six Pence plates were cut in half (October-December, 1857) the imprints were added, and in the case of the Three Pence plate some subjects were re-entered and/or retouched, which may account for the theory of a third plate for this denomination.

Fig. 15.
Imprint, Type I

Shades

During the period of the printing on wove paper there were ten orders, and eleven deliveries of the Three Pence, and five orders and five deliveries of the Six Pence. These factors, coupled with the paper variations gives a wide range of shades. The quality of the press work also influences the impression[21]. Generally speaking, however, the shades may be classified as shown herewith:

		Three Pence		*Paper*	*Notes*
U	1852	Orange red		A	No imprint
V	1852-3	Red		A, B	No imprint
W	1853, 1857	Brown red		B, C	⎫ ⎧ Without and
Y	1854, 1858	Indian red		B, D1, D2	⎬ ⎨ With imprint
Z	1855-6	Rose red		C	No imprint

20. Appendix Q, #2.
21. See Information for Collectors, Page xxiv, also Appendix II #47.

		Six Pence	Paper	Notes
U	1855	Deep purple	C	No imprint
V	1855-57	Gray violet	C, D2	No imprint
W	1855-58	Gray, brownish, slate, or greenish	C, D2	Without and With imprint
Y	1857-8	Brown violet	C, D2	
Z	1858	Pale violet	D2, D3	With imprint

The delicacy of the tints used in violet and purple results in many tones of the various groups listed, and this fugitive property should be carefully considered in classifying the Six Pence colors, particularly when encountering one that doesn't seem to fit in any classification[22].

---

22. See Information for Collectors, page xxvff, also Appendix II #17.

Fig. 16.
3d. On medium wove. Left imprint copy lightly tied by blue "PAID" and four circle "37" numeral cancellation to cover with handstruck type H37 of Ottawa.

Three Pence and Six Pence of 1852-58. Wove Paper

#	Denomination and Color	1852-4 A. Thin to Medium		1853-4 B. Thin "Oily"		1855-7 C. Stout Opaque		1857 D. Soft Ribbed		E1. Hard Medium to Thick 1857		1857 E2. Very Thick Soft		Issued Quantity	1944 Scott #	1944 S.G. #
		Unused	Used	Unused	Used	Unused	Used	Unused	Used	Unused	Used	Unused	Used			
4	3d Orange red	2	2	3	1¼	N	N	6	5	5	4			April 1852 2,850,000	4	6
	Red	2	2	3	1¼											
	Indian red			3	1½	N	N									
	Rose red															
a	Maj. re-entry	15	12				8	40		30					
b	Minor re-entry	6	4				3	15		12					
c	Short transfer	8	6				4	20		15					
d	Plate flaw						x			x					
e	Stitch Wmk.	20	15				10	50		40					
	Pair	10	8				5	25		20					
	Strip of four	60	50				35	50		125					
	Block of four	x					65	75		x					
	Cover		5		4		2½		10		8				
	Δ½ as 1½d					—	—	—	—	—	x			Note 1.		
5	6d deep purple					N	1½				1½			Mar. 1855 250,000	5	12
	Gray violet						N									
	Gray, slate or greenish					N	N				1½					
	Brown violet					N	N				1½					
	Pale violet										3	12	5			
	Stitch wmk.										x					
	Pair					5	5				8		25			
	Block of four					x	x				x					
	Cover						2½				5		12			
	Δ½ as 3d.					—	x	—	—	—	x	—	x	Note 2		

NOTE 1—In May, 1856, a Canadian line of steamships was established with a letter rate of 7½d Cy., 6d Stg., per half-ounce to Great Britain. Since no stamp of this value was available until June, 1857, the rate was usually paid in cash. However, a pair and half of a 3d or a 6d and half a 3d were sometimes used to make up the 7½d rate. All the bisected 3d are from efforts of this kind. They are unofficial. See Page 165ff (Appendix B #25; M #4).

NOTE 2—Bisects of the 6d are not quite as rare as the corresponding 3d bisects, nor are they quite as important, since they were not due to the impossibility of making up a rate from the values available. (See Page 166, f.).

SECTION C. THE ADDITIONAL VALUES OF 1855-1857

Ten Pence, Seven and a Half Pence, and Half Penny

During the period between January, 1855, and the middle of 1857 the expansion of the postal service, and changes in rates necessitated the preparation and issue of three new denominations; namely, Ten Pence, Six Pence Sterling, (7½d) and One-Half Penny, respectively.

To anticipate, we tabulate the steps in the procurement of these stamps.

	Ordered	Proof	First Delivery	Quantity
Ten Pence	Nov. 13, 1854[1]	Dec. 11, 1854[2]	Dec. 22, 1854[3]	100,080
Six Pence Sterling	Mar. 23, 1857[4]	———	May 23, 1857[5]	100,080
One-Half Penny	Jun. 29, 1857[6]	———	July 24, 1857[7]	60,000

The earliest mention of the Ten Pence occurs in the Report of the Postmaster General for the year ending March 31, 1854[8], where he recommends the issue of a stamp of this denomination. The report for the year and a half ending September 30, 1857[9], mentions that Six Pence Sterling (7½d) and One-Half Penny stamps have been issued.

The design of the Ten Pence pictures Cartier[10] as requested by the Postmaster General[11]. The portrait on the Six Pence sterling was the same as on the discontinued Twelve Pence[12], while the design of the One-Half Penny was an adaptation of the then current Four Pence stamp of Great Britain[13].

The use of these denominations was as follows:

> TEN PENCE: For packet letter rate per ½ oz. by British Packets to Europe[14].
>
> SIX PENCE STERLING OR SEVEN PENCE HALF PENNY CURRENCY: For packet letter rate 7½d cy. per ½ oz. The inscription on the stamp specifies its use "Canada Packet Postage"[15]. Rate established in 1856.
>
> ONE HALF PENNY: For postage on transient newspapers, primarily[16], but could be used to pay any rate[17], and were used as letter stamps, also to make up other rates such as registry fees, soldier's letters, etc.

1. Appendix H, #34.
2. Appendix H, #39.
3. Appendix H, #40.
4. Appendix H, #52. The contractors always referred to this stamp as "Six Pence Sterling".
5. Appendix H, #56.
6. Appendix H, #57 et. seq.
7. Appendix H, #58 and notes.
8. Appendix M #2.
9. Appendix M #5.
10. Appendix N, #4.
11. Appendix H, #34.
12. Appendix H, #52.
13. Appendix H, #57 and notes.
14. Appendix H, #34.
15. Appendix M #4.
16. Appendix B #26, C #71.
17. Appendix C #50, #55.

Pence Issues on Wove Paper

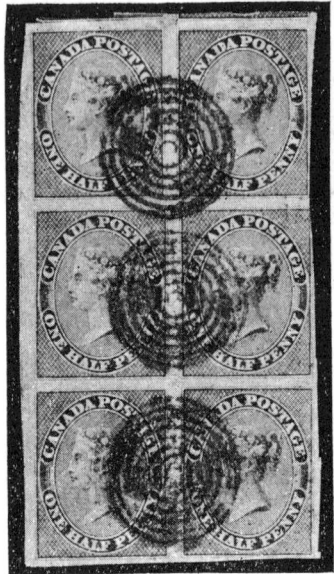

Unusually Large Block of Vertically Ribbed Paper.

Vertical Imprint Pair, #96, 108 on Sheet.

Unusual Block of ½d, Unused.

It is interesting to observe that the last two stamps were on sale in Detroit, Mich., from July, 1858[18], for the convenience of those wishing to use the Canadian Packets or to send newspapers to Canada.

Essays of 1857

Apparently the newly formed firm of Bradbury, Wilkinson & Co., of London, Eng., were aware of the desire of the Canadian Post Office Department for new stamps and submitted an essay for a 1d stamp, the portrait on which is not identifiable with any Canadian, and is presumed to be merely to show the effect of the finished design (Fig. 17).

ESSAYS BY BRADBURY, WILKINSON & CO., LONDON, 1857[19]

On Wove Paper (Very Rare)

E4Aa 1d brown.   E4Ac 1d green.
E4Ab 1d red brown.   E4Ad 1d dull ultramarine.

Fig. 17.

Fig. 18.

Two other designs, one with head of Victoria for 1d, and the other with head of helmeted and bearded warrior for 6d, are known. These are generally considered as essays for Canadian stamps, by the same firm, but we have been unable to find any definite evidence to that effect, although there is a possibility that the Victoria head was submitted in 1867 to the Dominion authorities by Bradbury, Wilkinson & Co., and the exquisite head adapted by the British American Bank Note Co. in the vignettes of the issue prepared by them.

Proofs

Engravers Progress Die Proof

Fig. 19.

This shows the outlines of the figures in the corners, but there is no background except of the medallion.

PD6a 10d black on india (Very Rare)

Contemporary Die Proof

D6a 10d blue. (This is listed for purposes of record as we know die proofs were made).

---
18. Appendix C #76.
19. These have heretofore been classified as Essays for the 1851 stamps, but as Bradbury, Wilkinson were founded in 1856 this seems improbable. The fact that the essays were in pence currency, is also evidence that they were submitted before 1859 when the currency was changed.

Contemporary Plate Proofs

On India, Sometimes Mounted on Card (Rare)

P6a 10d black P8a ½d black
 b 10d blue   b ½d deep rose
P7a 7½d black
 b 7½d green

For Post Contemporary Proofs see page 173.

"SPECIMEN" Stamps (Scarce)

Contemporary plate proofs on India, sometimes mounted on card, overprinted "Specimen" 20 x 2¾ mm. Typographed in a setting of 60 (6 x 10) applied twice to each sheet of 120, usually reading vertically, in carmine or green.

S6a 10d blue, carmine overprint, vertical
S6b 10d black, carmine overprint, diagonal[19a]
S7a 7½d black, carmine overprint, vertical
S8a ½d black, carmine overprint, vertical
S8b ½d yellow brown, carmine overprint, vertical
S8c ½d deep rose, green overprint, vertical

The Paper

As noted in discussing the Three Pence and Six Pence stamps of 1852-58 the printings previous to late 1857 are on a wove handmade rag paper, from the Ivy Mills, Chester, Pa. After that a wove machine made paper probably from the Crane Mills in Dalton, Mass., was used.

HANDMADE PAPER

Paper	Date	Characteristics	Ten Pence	Six Pence Sterling (7½d)	One Half-Penny (½d)
B	1854	Thin "oily" (.00225 to .00300")	x	—	—
C	1855-57	Hard opaque (.00300 to .00450")	—	x	x

MACHINE MADE PAPER

Paper	Date	Characteristics	Ten Pence	Six Pence Sterling (7½d)	One Half-Penny (½d)
D	1857 (Late)	1. Soft ribbed (.00300")	—	—	x
		2. Hard, medium to thick (.00275 to .00450")	x		x
Varieties of paper			2	1	3

Approximate quantities on each paper.

	10d	6d Stg. (7½d)	½d
B	100,080	—	—
C	—	82,400	920,000
D¹	—	—	600,000
D²	40,920	—	1,080,000
	141,000	82,400	2,600,000

Ratio 10d—B-1, D²-2½, ½d, D²-1, C-1 1/10, D¹-2.

NOTES—The thin paper after being dampened for printing, shrank much more in proportion than the other papers. In extreme cases the variation amounts to 1 mm. in the width of the stamp. Such "wide" and "narrow" stamps are of interest to specialists, but do not warrant special listing (Fig. 20a-d).

[19a]. This overprint is in a setting of 100, two rows repeated, and the word "SPECIMEN" 23 x 2 mm.

(a) Wide   (b) Narrow

(c) Wide   (d) Narrow   (e) Imprint at bottom

Fig. 20.

STITCH WATERMARKS: This variety occurs on all values. It has been seen by us both vertically and horizontally on the ½d and 7½d, horizontally only on the 3d, and vertically only on the 6d and 10d.

The Plates

One unhardened steel plate of one hundred and twenty subjects (12 x 10)[20] was made for each stamp. The Ten Pence never had an imprint, but the plate of the Six Pence Sterling (7½d) and the One Half Penny had the same type of imprint as the later states of the Three and Six Pence plates (Page 144). The location was 1 mm. from the stamps for both denominations as follows:

AT TOP	LEFT	RIGHT	BOTTOM
Above	Opposite	Opposite	Below
#2, 3, 4	#13, 25, 37	#24, 36, 48	#110, 111, 112
#9, 10, 11	#73, 85, 97	#84, 96, 108	#117, 118, 119
Normal	Reading Up	Reading Down	Normal

Each of these stamps can be plated, the comparative scarcity of the material being the chief obstacle to those who attempt it.

However, there are a number of plate varieties of sufficient importance to warrant listing:

The Ten Pence

RE-ENTRIES

#29 The major re-entry (Fig. 21).
#53, #90 Strong re-entry (Fig. 24, 25).
#1 Re-entry similar to #29 but not as strong, and does not show in top frame as much.

---

20. Appendix N, #2.

#70 Re-entry at left. Line in outer oval at left also shows in "AGE" of "Postage".
#52 Slight re-entry at upper left.
The left vertical row shows evidence of a guide line from top to bottom. Traces of this line may be found on #1, 13, 25, 37, 49, 61, 73, 85, 97, and 111.

Fig. 21.
#29 The Major Re-entry. Top frame line and upper left "8d Stg" strongly doubled. Line through lower part of "ANAD" of "Canada" and "ENCE" of "PENCE". Traces of doubling many other places.

Fig. 22. "CY" dot. Left Vertical Row Stamps.   Fig. 23. #1 Strong Re-entry.

Fig. 24. #53 "Ten Pence" re-entry.   Fig. 25. #90 Left Frame re-entry.

Fig. 26. Very Fine Used Block of 10d, on Thick Paper.

SHORT TRANSFERS

At top, #9, 27, 39, 51, 89, 109, 111, 117.
At bottom, #22, 43, 105, 107.
#68 Shows frame line at top double. Upper right corner is weak on #74, 99, 113.

Six Pence Sterling (7½d Cy.)
RE-ENTRIES

Fig. 26.
#7. Major Re-entry. Line through "X PEN" of "SIX PENCE" also traces in "Sterling", and "CANA" of "Canada" as well as ovals of medallion.

Fig. 27.
#60. Dots of color in "I" of "SIX", "RL" of "Sterling" and right side of medallion circle.

Fig. 28.
#66. Similar but shows line at lower left corner.

#7—a fairly strong re-entry showing line through top of letters "IX PEN" of "SIX PENCE" as well as traces of doubling in other parts of the design (Fig. 26).

#60, 66, and 81 show slight re-entries (Fig. 27, 28).

#81 shows line in arms of "K" of "Packet".

The right imprint on the bottom margin was originally entered at an angle so that it touched the lower frame lines of stamps #117 and #118 on the plate. This was corrected before the plate went to press, and it is quite obvious (Fig. 29).

Fig. 29.
Pair of 7½d with two 3d, on double registered letter to London, England. The 7½d shows bottom imprint with re-entry, and the left 3d also shows the imprint.

One Half Penny
RE-ENTRIES

Fig. 30. #120. Major Re-entry. Upper left and lower right corner doubled.

Fig. 31. Typical re-entry.

Fig. 32. #73. Bottom frame line missing.

#120—THE MAJOR RE-ENTRY. There is a strong doubling of the upper left and lower right corners, as well as doubling of other lines in the design (Fig. 30).

Four other re-entries, mostly doubling of frame lines occur, these are #62, 72, 84, 96. (Fig. 31).

SHORT TRANSFERS

Several of these are known, but #73 and #101 are particularly notable and show weak frame lines (Fig. 32), in #73 the bottom frame line is missing entirely. In addition #23, 35, 39, 44, 54, 63, 74, 89 show short transfers at top.

Shades

Since there were eight orders and nine deliveries of the One Half-Penny, it is not surprising that it varies considerably in shade. The Six Pence Sterling (7½d) was ordered only once and shows comparatively little difference, while the Ten Pence was ordered twice, and the two papers account for the variation in color.

TEN PENCE

			Paper	Notes
U	1855	Dark blue	B	⎫ Three Printings
V	1855	Dull blue	B	⎬
W	1858	Blue	D^2	⎭

SIX PENCE STERLING (7½d Cy.)

U	1857	Yellow green	C	⎫ Two Printings
V	1857	Dark green	C	⎭

ONE HALF-PENNY

U	1857	Rose	C, D^1	⎫ Several printings
V	1857	Deep rose	C, D^1	⎬
W	1858	Dull rose	C, D^2	⎭

Fig. 33.
½d block of six, from Dundas, Aug. 5, 1858.

Fig. 33a.
Two 7½d and two 3d paying the double Canadian Packet rate, and double registry rate to London. Note the Crown registered mark of the British Post Office.

Fig. 34.
6d and 10d, pair of each, paying triple rate by British Packet to London. Over payment of 2d cy!

Fig. 35.
Two ½d, 3d, and 6d making the British Packet rate. The 6d is on thick soft wove.

Fig. 36.
Superb strip of three 10d, and 7½d on Registered letter from Ottawa to London, July 1859. (Note: as this is a large cover we show only part of it).

SOLDIER'S LETTER
Fig. 57.
Horizontal pair of ½d paying the One Penny Imperial rate on Soldiers letters.
See Appendix B #34.

Fig. 58.
½d vertical Strip of six, neatly tied by four circle "41" cancellation of "Sandwich U. C. Jy 22 1858".

Fig. 39 .
3d perforated and 7½d paying the British Packet rate to England from Toronto, May 1859.
This was an overpayment of ½d cy!

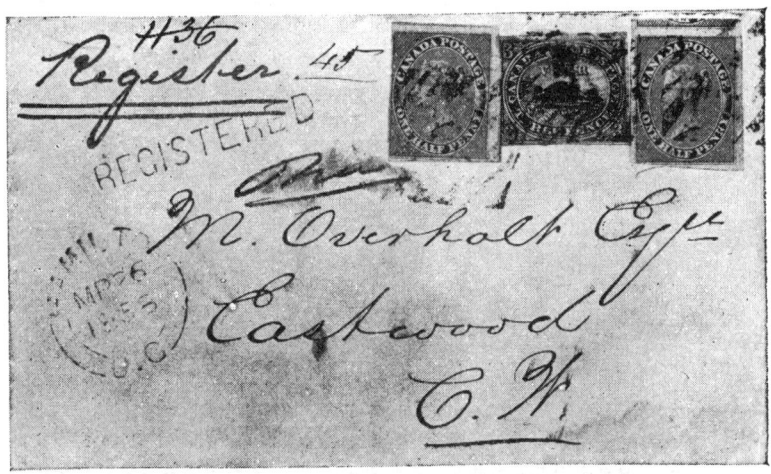

Fig. 40.
3d, and registry fee paid by two ½d from "Hamilton Mr. 26 1858".

The Additional Pence Values of 1855-57

#	Denomination and Color	B. 1854 Thin "Oily" Unused	B. 1854 Thin "Oily" Used	C. 1855-7 Stout Opaque Unused	C. 1855-7 Stout Opaque Used	D¹. 1857 Soft Ribbed[1] Unused	D¹. 1857 Soft Ribbed[1] Used	D². Hard Medium to Thick 1857-8 Unused	D². Hard Medium to Thick 1857-8 Used	Issued	Quantity	1944 Scott #	1944 S.G. #
6	10d Dark blue	2	1½					N 1¼	N 1¼	Jan. 1855	141,000	7	20
	Dull blue							2	2				
	Blue							x	15				
a	Major re-entry		15						10				
b	Minor re-entry		7						4				
c	Guide line		3						x				
	Stitch wmk.		12						15				
	Pair								R				
d	Strip of three		6						4				
	Cover	—											
7	7½d green			N	N					Jun. 2, 1857	82,410	9	22
	Dark green				1½								
a	Major re-entry				4								
b	Minor re-entry				2								
c	Imprint re-entry				8								
	Stitch wmk.				x								
	Pair				6								
d	Cover	—			2½			—					
8	½d Rose			1½	1¼					Aug. 1, 1857	2,600,000	8	23
	Deep rose					6	5	N	N				
	Dull rose					25	10	4	3				
a	Major re-entry			5	4	9	5	3	2				
b	Minor re-entry			3	2	7	4	1½	1½				
c	Short transfer			3	2			2½	2½				
	Stitch wmk.				x				3				
	Pair			5	4	25	10	7	8				
d	Strip of four								12				
	Block of four								2				
	Cover	—		—	2½	—	10	—					
	Military Cover												

1. NOTE: The ribbing may be horizontal or vertical on the ½d; the horizontal ribbing is about 25% rarer than the vertical ribbing.

THE BISECT PROVISIONALS OF 1856

Although, according to the regulations, part of a stamp could not be used in payment of postage, nevertheless examples of the 3d and 6d are known bisected and used for the proportionate fraction of the value. The introduction of the 7½d rate for letters by Canadian Packet posed the problem of making of such a rate when no stamp or combination of stamps would. A strip of three 3d one cut diagonally to make the 7½d rate or a 6d with a 3d cut diagonally was sometimes used. Such examples must be on piece or entire cover, and must be dated before June 1857, when the new 7½d (6d Stg) was ready.

The new 7½d rate was established in May 1856 for letters to England by Canadian Packets, the first voyage being at that time.[23] This rate was not provided for among the stamps then in use, a fact noted by the department and remedied a year later.

In the meantime the rate was sometimes made up by bisecting the 3d, and accepting it as 1½d, either in combination with the 6d, or with two other 3d.

The rarity of these bisections indicates that the practice was discouraged, as against the regulations, and liable to abuse.

---

23. Appendix B #25; M #4.

Bisects of the Three Pence

Fig. 41.
3d, diagonal half (U.L. to L.R.) with 6d, used June or August 1856.

Fig. 42.
3d horizontal strip of three, left stamp cut diagonally (U.L. to L.R.).

Fig. 43.
3d, vertical strip of three, lower stamp cut diagonally (U.L. to L.R.) from Montreal, July 17, 1856.

We have also seen a 3d bisected U. R. to L. L. tied by "21" in four circles.

Bisects of the Six Pence

Bisects of the 6d are in no sense to be considered as provisionals made to meet a rate for which there was no stamp or combination of stamps.

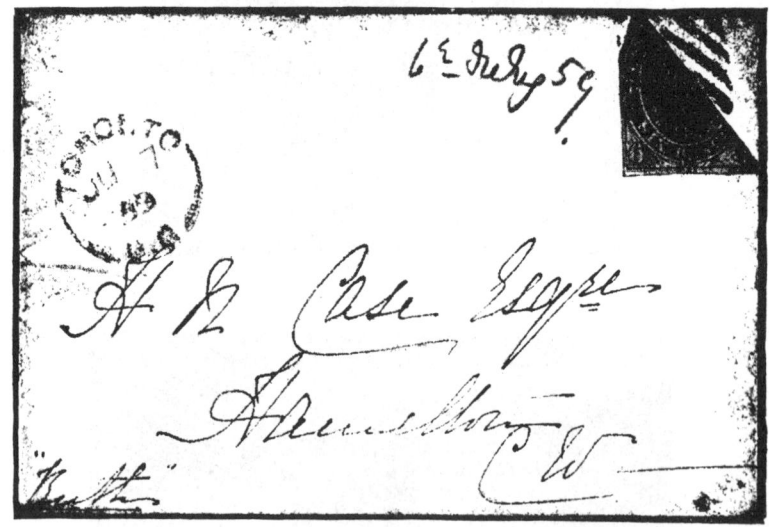

Fig. 44.
6d, diagonal half, (U.L. to L.R.) used from Toronto, June 7, 1859. The notation "July" is either in error, having mistaken "Ju" for "July" when it means "June", or the date being early in the month, the clerk had not changed the month letters. (Courtesy Godden's Gazette).

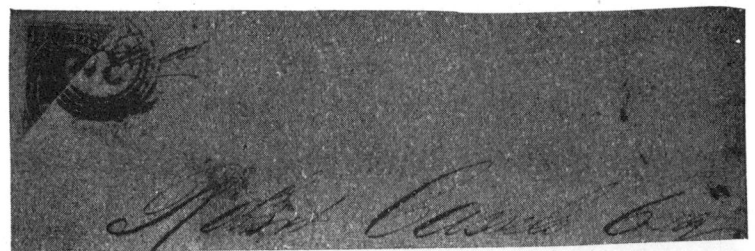

Fig. 45.
Two Bisected 6d. Upper Cover Shows Diagonal Half (U.R. to L.L.), of 6d on Thick Soft Wove, Used from Quebec. Other has One Cut (U.L. to L.R.), and Perforated, Used from Toronto, May 6, 1859.

The 6d bisects are examples of thrift. A Canadian of those days, (and many even today) would be apalled at spending five cents more than necessary, no matter how important the letter. We are indebted to such thrifty souls for the bisects of the 6d.

We have also seen a diagonal half (U. R. to L. L.) used from Quebec to Montreal Jan. 5, 1859.

SECTION D. PERFORATED "PENCE" STAMPS
(a). Experimental Perforations

3 Pence 1852-58

Fig. 46.

(a) Hyphen-hole perf. Thin paper. Probably done as early as 1855.

(b) Sewing Machine perf. About 1857.

(c) Sawtooth roulette vertically. About 1857.

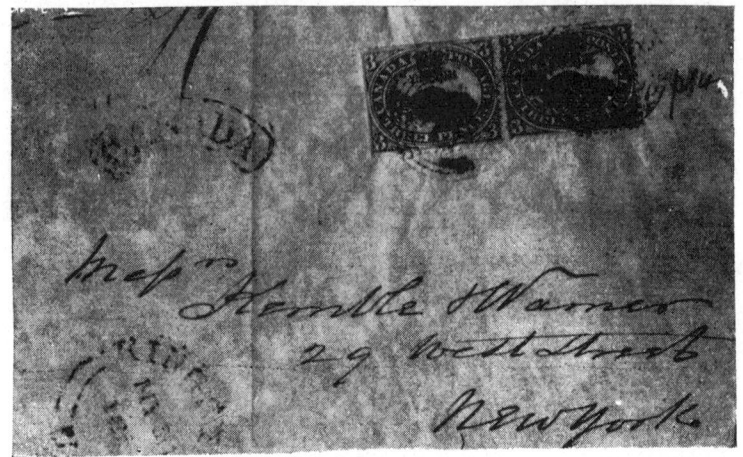

Fig. 47.
THE KINGSTON PERFORATION
The perf 14. Pair on cover dated "Kingston My 30 185(7)". From Ontario Foundry Co., Machinists, and probably makers of the perforating machine. The illustration in Howes book is from the same correspondence.

Fig. 48
Enlargements of the Hyphen-hole and Sawtooth experimental roulettes.

(b). Regular Perforation
1858-1859

The detaching of one stamp from another in the sheet rapidly and with little trouble was a problem that everyone from office boy to inventor attempted to solve almost from the day the first stamps were issued[1]. Finally in 1854 Great Britain began the regular issue of perforated stamps.

This improvement was noticed by the Canadian Postal Officials and in a letter to the contractors November 13, 1854[2], they expressed a desire to have the stamps perforated. In reply Rawdon, Wright, Hatch & Edson said that they could not "undertake to puncture around the stamps"[3].

In his report for the year ending September 30, 1857, the Postmaster General mentions that measures had been taken "for obtaining ..... stamps on sheets perforated in the dividing lines"[4].

Fig. 49.
Perforating and gumming stamps at the American Bank Note Co. in 1861.

Some sheets of Three Pence were undoubtedly taken by the Post Office Officials and experimented with as at least three forms of roulette, and a perforation 14 are known (Fig. 46). It is also possible that some bank or insurance company may have had some sheets perforated or rouletted for their own convenience.

Such efforts were unsatisfactory and in December, 1857[5], in reply to what appears to have been a telegram, the contractors state that they will enquire into "the cost of machinery for perforating stamps." In April, 1858, they state that a perforating machine can only be had from England, and that they will obtain one[6].

On May 1, 1858, the contractors were one of the firms forming the newly incorporated American Bank Note Co. (See Page 101ff) and in July the American Bank Note Co. informed the Canada Post Office Department that a perforating machine could be obtained in the United States[7]. Futhermore they offered to

---
1. Perforations and Roulettes by Winthrop S. Boggs, Chambers Stamp Journal, March 16, 1942, Vol. XV, pp. 348-49. A Roulette of July 1840.
2. Appendix H, #34.
3. Appendix H, #35.
4. Appendix M #5.
5. Appendix H, #63.
6. Appendix H, #64.
7. Appendix H, #65.

Fig. 50.
3d pencancelled vertical strip of five, perforated, showing bottom imprint.

Fig. 51.
6d perforated. Vertical pair paying the double rate to Ohio, from Hamilton C. W. Mr 24 1859. Note Canada Exchange Marking with "10" changed to "20" in ms.

"perforate your stamps at the rate of five cents per 1000 stamps,"[8] this of course being in addition to the twenty cents per 1000 stamps as called for by the contract[9]. This additional charge was agreed to late in July, 1858[10].

The first order for perforated stamps was sent October 12, 1858[11], when 600,000 Half Penny, and 300,000 Three Pence were ordered. Actual perforating was begun November 23, 1858[12], and 1000 sheets (100,000 stamps) were forwarded a few days later. The perforated Half Penny stamps could have been placed on sale about December 1, 1858[13].

An order for 50,000 Six Pence was sent December 10[14], and on December 30, 1858, 300,000 Three Pence and 50,000 Six Pence stamps were sent by express[15]. From this it would appear that January 1, 1859, is the earliest possible date for the issue of these stamps *perforated by the contractors*[16].

8. Appendix H, #65.
9. Appendix H, #16.
10. Appendix H, #66, 67.
11. Appendix H, #69.
12. Appendix H, #72.
13. Appendix H, #73.
14. Appendix H, #75.
15. Appendix H, #76.
16. Stamps or covers bearing earlier dates were probably not perforated by the contractors, or perhaps the clerk was careless in omitting to change the date logos. Such copies should only be accepted after expert examination.

The Perforations

The perforating was done by a treadle operated machine with rotary punches, the sheets of stamps being hand fed through it (Fig. 49). Each sheet received eleven rows of perforations at a time so that a sheet had only to be passed through the machine twice to be completely perforated. After a number of sheets had been perforated in one direction the machine was adjusted and the sheets were perforated in the other direction. The perforation gauges 11¾, commonly called 12. Whether the machine was of English or American make is not definitely known, but as can be seen by the illustration it operated on principles similar to that patented by William Bemrose and his son Henry, of Derby, England, on December 11, 1854[16a].

The Plates

By this time the plate of the Three Pence and Six Pence had been cut in half and the sheets contained one hundred stamps (10 x 10). The Half Penny stamp, however, being printed from a plate of one hundred and twenty stamps, (12 x 10) presented a problem. In July, 1857[17], at the time of discussing the additional charge for perforating the contractors pointed out that the Half Penny sheet was of inconvenient size to perforate, and were informed that they could "alter such as require it, to one hundred on a sheet"[18]. The perforated Half Penny stamps therefore came from a plate of one hundred subjects (10 x 10), the two left vertical rows being removed. Entire proof sheets from both states of the plate are known, the sheet from the cut down plate showing no imprints at the left, and parts of the upper left and lower left imprints missing.

Since no orders for any of the two highest denominations were placed after July 20, 1858[19] there was no occasion to perforate them, or cut the plates down to one hundred subjects.

The Paper

The paper is comparatively uniform, being a machine made wove of rag stock, probably from the Crane Paper Co.[20]

16a. See "The 3c Stamp of the United States 1851-57 Issue, Revised Edition" by Dr. Carroll Chase., pp. 169-173.
17. Appendix H, #65.
18. Appendix H, #67, 68.
19. Appendix J #1.
20. See Page 141.

Perforated Pence Issues—1858-59

#	Denomination and Color	Perforated $11¾ \times 11¾$		Experimental Roulettes		Unofficial Perforation 14×14		Issued	Quantity Perf. $11¾$	1944 Scott #	1944 S.G. #
		Unused	Used	Unused	Used	Unused	Used				
9	½d Deep rose							Dec. 1858	789,340	11	25
	Dull rose	N									
a	Major re-entry		N								
			3								
b	Minor re-entry		1½								
c	Short transfer		1½								
	Stitch wmk.		x								
d	Pair		3								
	Block of four		x								
	Cover	—	2								
10	3d Indian red							Jan. 1859	428,300	12	26
		N									
a	Major re-entry		N								
			8								
b	Minor re-entry		4								
c	Short transfer		4			x^1					
d	Plate flaw		x			x^2					
	Stitch wmk.		x								
e	Pair		2½								
			2								
	Cover	—					R				
11	6d Gray violet							Jan. 1859	50,000	13	27
	Brown purple	N									
		1¼									
	Stitch wmk.		x								
a	Pair		x								
			3								
	Cover	—	x								
	Δ½ as 3d										

NOTE 1—The experimental roulettes occur on two papers. A thin wove (paper A), and the machine made thick wove (paper D2). NOTE 2—The perforated 14 are on hard crisp "oily" paper (paper B). In a brown red shade. Genuine examples are very rare, and on cover exceedingly so. The pair illustrated was used from Kingston in May 1857 by the Ontario Foundry Co. A similar pair was in the Pack collection from the same correspondence, also used in May 1857.

SECTION E. THE POST CONTEMPORARY PROOFS AND OTHER IMPRESSIONS[1]

The existence of the pence designs, and the succeeding provincial issue of 1859 in various colors and on various papers is well known, but their exact status is somewhat of a mystery to many collectors.

The report of Tracy Edson in 1858 concerning the affairs of the newly formed American Bank Note Company mentions that proofs of all the dies and plates in possession of the new organization were taken for purposes of record.

Another consolidation took place in 1878, and there is some reason to believe that a similar procedure took place at that time also. Another re-organization took place in 1905 and the records show that the dies, rolls and plates of the 1851-58 and the 1859 issues still in existence were cancelled on January 4; 1902, and returned to the Post Office Department of Canada on February 19, 1902.

The existence of Post Contemporary die proofs is easily accounted for by the fact that a secondary die could be laid down by the transfer roll whenever necessary, and in fact was done in the case of many vignettes for bank notes as noted in the Chapter on Engravers and Printers. (See also Chapter XI).

DIE PROOFS

Vignette of 7½d on india, die sunk on card. (Rare).

P7d   black
P7e   green

Fig. 53.
The Compound Secondary Die 12d + 10c 1859.

---

1. Many of these impressions are the miscalled "Mandel" proofs. Henry Mandel was an employee of the American Bank Note Co. who formed a very fine collection of essays and proofs, particularly of those produced by the American Bank Note Co. Mr. Mandel, however, did not produce or cause to have produced the proofs attributed to him. In fact many of these impressions were made when Mr. Mandel was a young boy, long before he was with the Bank Note Co.

A small secondary die was laid down by the transfer roll, containing a 12d, and a 10c, 1859. This we believe was made about 1864. (These are rare).

	D^1 India	D^2 Thin Wove
P3b+P15a 12d+10c (1859) black	x	x
b vermilion	x	x
c chocolate	x	x
d blue	x	x
e green	x	x
f purple	x	x

The 12d is cancelled die, by fine lines on "CE" of "PENCE".

PLATE PROOFS

At the time the 1859 proofs were made (1864) pence proofs on India were also struck off in orange yellow. (Not common).

P8c ½d orange-yellow   P7c 7½d orange-yellow
P1d 3d orange-yellow   P6c 10d orange-yellow
P2d 6d orange-yellow

In 1879 the National Bank Note Co., the Continental Bank Note Co., and the American Bank Note Co., all of New York, merged to become an enlarged American Bank Note Co. At that time or shortly after proof impressions were taken from various plates, among them the 6p Canada. These proofs were overprinted "SPECIMEN" in sans serif capitals 11 mm. long by 2½ mm. high.

Fig. 54.

1879 OVERPRINTED **SPECIMEN.** IN RED. (RARE)

S2f 6p blue gray (Fig. 54).

The Trade Sample Sheets

Besides the proofs listed previously there are a number of other items frequently offered as proofs, but which are actually impressions cut from advertising sheets sent out by the American Bank Note Company, or given to salesmen to show the class of work done by the company. Entire sheets in any color are rare. They were made about 1868.

Fig. 55.
Sample sheet of 1868.

Trade Samples

SM 1-½d   SM 2-10d

Each in the following colors:[2]

(a) lilac.
(b) pink.
(c) gray.
(d) gray blue.
(e) blue.
(f) green.
(g) pale green.
(h) lemon yellow.
(i) rose.
(j) red.
(k) scarlet.
(l) dark brown.
(m) lake.
(n) slate purple.

On the following papers:
(1) Thin to medium machine made bank note paper. (All above colors, imperforate; also perforated 11¾ in gray, blue, green, pale green, and dark brown.
(2) Thick stout white paper. (Noted in black, green, red, and slate purple).

Singles cut from these sheets are sometimes offered as rare color trials or die proofs which they are not. The colors and impression are characteristic and should decieve no one after a little practice. Notice also that the 10d and ½d adjoin each other, and pairs cut from these advertising sheets are sometimes offered as rare "compound" die proofs.

---
2. Dr. Clarence W. Brazer is of the opinion that these sheets in numerous colors were used as a color chart by the Bank Note Company's salesmen.

Some of these sheets were also lithographed and the ½d and 10d may be found thus. The ½d is easily recognized by a spot of color in the frame below the "LF" of "HALF". Futhermore the impression has all the characteristics of a lithograph, being flat, slightly blurred, and "greasy" to the touch. (Noted in rose, imperforate and perforated 11¾.

Counterfeits, Fakes, etc.

Although we have examined thousands of the Pence stamps, we have seen few counterfeits, and with the exception of those *engraved* by Panelli, none of them are at all deceptive, except an *engraved* Ten Pence which is also deceptive but can readily be recognized by those familiar with these stamps.

We illustrate the Panelli counterfeits herewith:

Fig. 56.
PANELLI COUNTERFEITS
On wove paper, medium thickness. The cancellations are obviously bogus.

Fig. 57.
An Engraved Counterfeit Not by Panelli. Rather Deceptive.

A "perforated 3 pence" is occasionally found. This is engraved, and printed on thin wove paper.

Fig. 58.
Engraved Counterfeit Not by Panelli. This is apt to deceive the tyro.

In the case of fakes we are on more dangerous ground. The 3d on vertically ribbed is faked as has been noted before. Faking of the horizontal ribs is sometimes done, but the fakers usually try it on a stamp that is the wrong shade or paper. When done on the right stamp it is exceedingly deceptive and in case of doubt the stamp should be submitted to an expert.

Imperforate stamps with faked perforations are occaisionally seen. If the stamp is on the wrong paper or in the wrong shade such faking is easily detected. However as mentioned under ribbed paper expert opinion is desirable in case of doubt.

The commonest type of faking however is the removal of the word "Specimen" from proofs of the 12d. Such efforts are usually readily detectable by careful examination. The use of ultra violet light, and quartz lamps is almost infallible in showing up the work of the faker. Other proofs altered to resembled the issued stamps can usually be told by the paper differences, in the case of the 12d, however, expert opinion is advisable.

Cover Fakes

We have seen a number of covers, originally stampless, to which stamps have been added. Generally speaking such efforts to "make things look like what they ain't" are crude, but here again a through familiarity with shades, paper, perforations, cancellations, dates of use, rates, and regulations are essential in weeding out the more cleverly done works of this class.

Fake Essays and Proofs

The rapidly increasing interest in this class of material is beginning to attract the "altruistic" gentry. Sample sheets cut up, and offered as die proofs, is one example of this type of misrepresentation. In case of doubt reference to those thoroughly familiar with this field is advisable.

The Engraved Similitudes of the 7½d, 10d, and 10c 1859

A counterfeit, strictly speaking, is an imitation made to deceive the Post Office or collectors. The similitudes, however, were engraved by a reputable firm to be used on a philatelic letterhead or visiting card. We discuss and list them in order that collectors will not be deceived as to their true status, and so that there can be no thought that they are government work, or due to a desire to mulct collectors.

SIMILITUDE DIE PROOFS

(a)   (b)

Fig. 59.

7½d black on thick white card.
7½d black on manila paper.
10d black on manila paper.

Impressions Cut Down to Stamp Size

10d blue on thin yellowish paper.
10d blue on thin crisp white paper watermarked "Superfine" in Old English letters.

Overprinted "Specimen" Diagonally in Bright Red

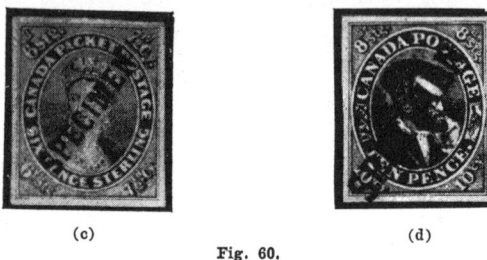

(c)   (d)

Fig. 60.

7½d green on thin yellowish paper, overprint 17½ x 3 mm.
10d dark blue on thin yellowish paper, overprint 22½ x 4 mm.

Other papers and colors may exist, we list only those we have seen.

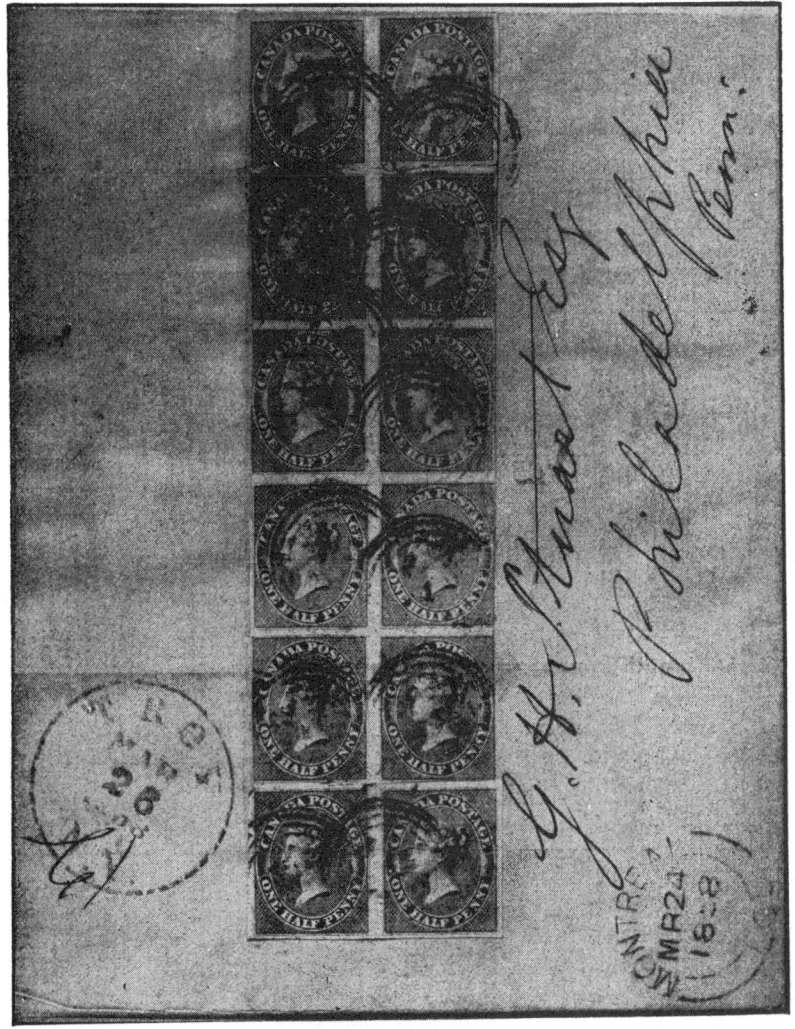

½d on Thick Wove. Block of 10 and a Pair Paying the 6d Rate to the United States.

Chapter IX

THE DECIMAL CURRENCY ISSUE OF 1859

The cumbersome system of pounds, shillings and pence, figured at different rates; sterling, and that of currency; plus the common use of decimal values by the commercial community particularly those firms having extensive dealings across the border, had long been a source of irksome confusion to all concerned.

Finally, as a result of much agitation, a statute was enacted in 1853[1] which legally established the relationships of the three monetary values as follows:

English Sterling (STG.)	Halifax Currency (Cy.)	United States Decimal (Cts.)	In Practice
£1.0.0	£1.4.4	4.86 2/3	4.87
1s	1.2½d	.24 1/3	.24
1d	1¼d	.02	.02

While this act was of some help the increasing volume of business soon made it clear that only a uniform monetary system would really solve the difficulties. The legislative bodies therefore passed an Act[2] effective July 1, 1859, placing the Canadian monetary system on a decimal currency basis. This necessitated the postage stamps being changed to express the values in "cents" instead of "pence" as heretofore.

The Post Office Department, well aware of the pending change, on March 16, 1859, notified the contractors that they were desirous of having the stamps altered and ordered a first supply of 1,000,000 each of the One Cent, and Five Cents, 100,000 each of the Ten Cents and Twelve and a Half Cents, and 50,000 of the Seventeen Cents[3].

The first delivery of the new stamps was made on May 28, 1859[4], consisting of 100,000 each of the Ten Cents and Twelve and One Half Cents.

Postmasters were notified of the forthcoming new stamps in a circular dated June 12, 1859[5]. They were also requested to return the unsold pence stamps on July 1st[6], although pence stamps remaining in the hands of the public were still available for postage[7].

The basis for the new stamps was the Pence Issue. With the exception of the 12½c the respective Pence dies were modified (and thereby cancelled), and new transfer rolls containing two reliefs were made to lay down the plates. Only one relief at a time, however, was used in rocking in the plates.

The small line projecting into the white oval above and between the "O" and "S" of "Postage" on the 10d and 17c has been cited as evidence that the dies were altered. This however, does not necessarily follow, as the transfer roll of the pence denomination could have been used to lay down a secondary die, which duly worked over would become the original die for the "cents" value. As shown on page 218, however, the documentary evidence indicates that the Pence dies were altered, except the 7½d. In this case the 7½d roll *was* used to lay down a secondary die, which was worked over to make the new 12½c die. There are certain markings common to both the 7½d and 12½c stamps, showing a common origin at some point during production, but there are also certain other markings peculiar to each die. Furthermore the characteristics of the 12d die are not found on either the 7½d or the 12½c stamps, thus effectively

---
1. Appendix A #8.
2. Appendix A #9.
3. Appendix H #77.
4. Appendix H #82.
5. Appendix B #31.
6. Appendix B #31.
7. Appendix B #31 and L #9, 11, 12.

disposing of the possibility of the 12d die or roll being used as the basis for either of these stamps.

In August, 1864, a Two Cents value was added to make up various rates. The design was adapted from the One Cent[8]. This stamp was ordered in June, 1864, and the first supply sent amounted to 100,000 stamps[9]. The 1c roll was used to lay down a secondary die which was worked over to make the new 2c die. A two relief roll was made, although only one relief was used at a time.

The use of the other denominations is clearly set forth in the circular of June 12, 1859, referred to above.

It can thus be seen that no essays were necessary.

We have never seen any contemporary die proofs. Post contemporary die proofs will be found listed on page 174, and 215.

Contemporary Plate Proofs

As in the Pence Issue contemporary plate proofs are known in black and colors of issue. Furthermore, at the time various post contemporary Pence proofs were made, proofs of the decimal issue were also made in various colors.

REFERENCE LIST

PLATE PROOFS ON INDIA (SCARCE)

(Sometimes Mounted on Card.)

P12a 1c black
  b 1c deep rose
  c 1c orange yellow
P13a 2c dull rose
  b 2c green
P14a 5c black
  b 5c vermilion
  c 5c orange yellow

P15a 10c black
  b 10c dark brown
  c 10c dull lilac
  d 10c red violet
  e 10c orange yellow
P16a 12½c black
  b 12½c blue green
  c 12½c dark blue
  d 12½c orange yellow

P17a 17c black
  b 17c deep blue
  c 17c bright blue
  d 17c orange yellow

"SPECIMEN" STAMPS

Contemporary plate proofs were also overprinted "SPECIMEN" in black or carmine, vertically or diagonally, similar to the Pence stamps.

1st Setting. 100 subjects reading vertically, (V); reading diagonally, (D), in serifed capitals (scarce).

	Black	Carmine
S12a 1c deep rose	V,D	
S14a 5c vermilion	H	D
S15a 10c dull violet		V,D
b 10c black		D
S16a 12½c blue green	V,D	V
b 12½c black		V
c 12½c blue		V
S17a 17c blue		V,D

[8] Appendix H #104.
[9] Appendix H #106.

Fig. 1. The Sans Serif "Specimen" Overprint.

2nd setting occurs only on the 12½c. "Specimen" is in sans-serif block capitals in carmine, reading vertically. This setting was also of 100 subjects, but has three varieties of overprint, viz: (Fig. 1.)

"Specimen" 20 mm. long, thin letters, 1st to 4th vertical rows............(40)
"Specimen" 21½ mm. long, medium letters, 5th vertical row............(10)
"Specimen" 20 mm. long, thick letters, 6th to 10th vertical rows........(50)

(100)

(Scarce to Rare)

S16d 12½c black, overprint 20 mm. long, thin letters
S16d-y 12½c black, overprint 21½ mm. long, thick letters
S16d-z 12½c black, overprint 20 mm. long, thick letters
S16e 12½c blue, overprint 20 mm. long, thin letters
S16e-y 12½c blue, overprint 21½ mm. long, thin letters
S16e-z 12½c blue, overprint 20 mm. long, thick letters

See post contemporary compound die proofs for listing of 10c die proof with 12d of 1851 (Page 174).

The Paper

The paper of this issue being a machine made rag wove does not show the great variations that occur in the early Pence stamps. Nevertheless the separate "runs" do show some differences and the specialist may note six or seven varieties. For practical purposes, however, three varieties are all that are necessary, viz.:

	Thickness
A. Thin semi-transparent sometimes very soft	(.00275" to .00350")
B. Thick, opaque, sometimes soft or with distinct mesh	(.00325" to .00425")
C. Stout crisp	(.00375" to .00450")

Stitch watermark can occur on any value—horizontal on all but 5c on which it is vertical.

The Perforations

All of these stamps were normally issued perforated. The researches of Dr. Lewis L. Reford of Montreal demonstrate that two perforating machines were used, one gauging 12, while the other gauges slightly less, which we conveniently call 11¾. These perforations occur as follows[10]:

---

10. See Appendix J #2, for detailed analysis of orders, quantities, and perforations.

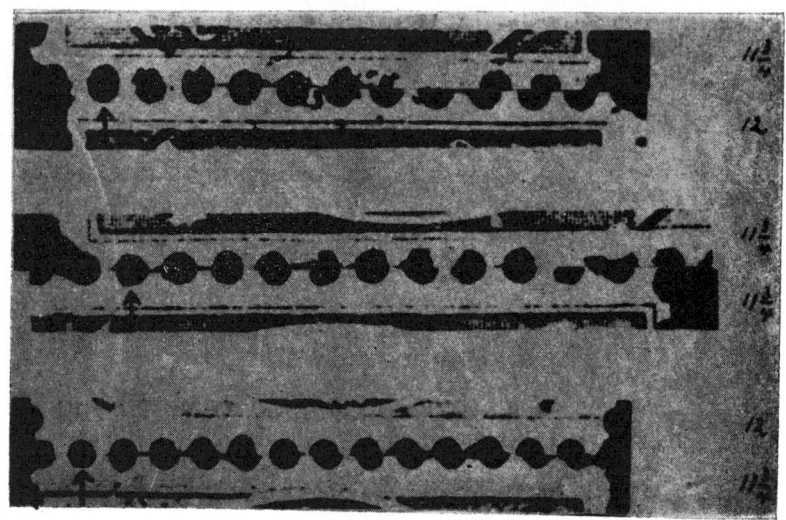

Fig. 2.
Enlargement to show the differences between the two perforations occurring in this issue.

	11¾ x 11¾ *Issued*	11¾x12 *(all except 5c)* 12 x 11¾ *(5c only)* *Ordered*	12 x 12 *Ordered*
1c	July 1, 1859	Sept. 2, 1862	Nov. 28, 1864
2c	—	June 14, 1864	Nov. 28, 1864
5c	July 1, 1859	Sept. 2, 1862	Nov. 28, 1864
10c	July 1, 1859	Sept. 2, 1862	Nov. 28, 1864
12½c	July 1, 1859	Oct. 29, 1862	Nov. 28, 1864
17c	July 1, 1859	Oct. 29, 1862	Nov. 28, 1864

Imperforates

Mint blocks of all values imperforate are known, in correct colors and gum. They probably were made about 1864 (late) or 1865 (early) as they include the Two Cents which was not ordered until June, 1864. They may have been sample sheets for the postal officials, or for purposes of record, as no satisfactory used copies have been noted.

The Plates

The plates of this issue have been the subject of intensive study by many students, but particularly by Senator James A. Calder[11], F.R.P.S.L., of Ottawa, whose articles are outstanding contributions to philatelic literature[12]. Work is still progressing, but it is believed that the number of plates was as follows:

One Cent: Probably two plates.

Five Cents: At least two and possibly three plates (see note about 5c varieties.)

Other Denominations: One plate each.

Each plate, of unhardened steel as usual, consisted of 100 subjects (10x10[13]) rocked in with a roll bearing two reliefs although only one relief was used at a time. Apparently no imprints were entered on the plates until late 1864[14], as the earliest dated copies showing traces of imprint are dated 1865. Since all values were ordered on November 28, 1864, the imprints were probably added at that time. The new plates of the 1c and 5c also were made. We might also observe that all imprint copies we have examined are perforated 12 x 12.

Each plate had a printing area 198½-199½x239-244½ mm., not including the imprints, which as noted above were added later.

The Imprint

Fig. 3. Type II Imprint.

---
11. Some Phases of The Canada '59 Issue, London Philatelist, 1939, also bound separately.
12. Stamp Specialist, Red Book, 1942, and Brown Book, 1943. Both these are examples of philatelic writing of the highest standard. They are models of thoroughness and accuracy.
13. See Appendix Q #3 for plate arrangement.
14. See Appendix J #2. Order of Nov. 28, 1864.

IMPRINT TYPE II (Fig. 3).

This reads "American Bank Note Co., New York," in type similar to the imprint of the Pence plates. Its total length is 28 mm. and it is placed about 1mm. from the stamps, eight times on the plates as follows:

	Top Above	Left Opposite	Right Opposite	Bottom Below
1c	#2, 3, 4 #7, 8, 9 Normal	#11, 21, 31 #61, 71, 81 Reading up	#20, 30, 40 #70, 80, 90 Reading down	#92, 93, 94 #97, 98, 99 Inverted
2c	Ditto	Ditto	Ditto	#92, 93, 94 #97, 98, 99 Normal
5c	Ditto	Ditto	#20, 30, 40 #70, 80, 90 Reading up	#92, 93, 94 #97, 98, 99 Inverted
12½c	Ditto	Ditto	#20, 30, 40 #70, 80, 90 Reading down	#92, 93, 94 #97, 98, 99 Normal
10c	#2, 3 #8, 9 Normal	#11, 21 #71, 81 Reading up	#20, 30 #80, 90 Reading down	#92, 93 #98, 99 Normal

The 17c plate apparently never had the imprint rocked in.

In laying out the plates the method similar to that for the Pence stamps was used, namely a series of position dots and lines. There is usually a series of ten position dots in the right sheet margin some 3 to 4mm. from the stamps. In the case of the Five Cents because of its horizontal format these dots are located in the top sheet margin. A number of lines were drawn from these dots across the plate, as a guide for the transfer press operator (the siderographer) in rocking the subjects on the plate. These dots and lines are of importance to students re-constructing the plates.

Fig. 4. Bottom margin strip of five showing no trace of imprint. After the imprints were added it would be impossible to get a strip of this length without at least one stamp showing part of the imprint.

Plate Varieties

The comparatively long period of use (ten years) and the fact that some eight or more plates were required resulted in quite a number of varieties aside from the guide lines and dots mentioned above. Many of these varieties are minute, and of interest only to the advanced specialist.

We mention some and illustrate the more important varieties herewith.

ONE CENT

Re-Entries

#51 shows a fairly strong re-entry at upper left and top-doubling of inner and outer frame lines.

#49 and 58 show slight doubling of top outer frame line, probably due to recutting.

Flaws

Two small flaws are known, one of which is quite rare. In the Reford collection there is a series of six stamps showing its development. It is similar to the "burr" variety on the 17c.

Short Transfers

#48 and 82 on the sheet show short transfer at top.

TWO CENTS

Frame Lines

Frame lines doubled. There is a faint doubling of part of one or more of the frame lines in positions Nos. 1, 2, 4, 19, 21, 23, 27, 31, 32, 35, 78, 82, 87 of the sheet.

Extended frame lines. The outer frame lines are projected slightly in the following position on the sheet.

    (a) Left outer frame line extends downward—Nos. 12, 19, 27, 38, 40, 48, 52, 53, 63, 66, 67, 69, 70, 96.
    (b) Right outer frame line extends downward—Nos. 11, 13, 16.
    (c) Left outer frame line extends upward—Nos. 24, 57, 64.

#77 Neck-Cheek Scratches.

(d) Bottom outer frame line extends to left—No. 90.
(e) Right outer frame line extends both upward and downward—No. 61.
(f) Both side frame lines extend downward—Nos. 4, 21.
(g) Left and bottom outer frame lines extend downward and left respectively—Nos. 30, 80.

From the characteristics of the above varieties it would seem that the frame lines were re-cut and/or retouched by hand.

Flaws

The cheek-neck scratches. No. 77 shows two parallel scratches running N. W. and S. E. across the cheek and neck of head—approximately 4½ millimeters in length. (See page 187.)

There are a number of other minute marks of color on various stamps; notably #41, dot in "C" of "Cents"; #71, dash over "D" of "Canada", etc.

Traces of *short transfers* are evident on several positions but they are too slight to warrant notice except by those plating this stamp.

FIVE CENTS

The plates of the 5c Beaver are prolific in re-entries and flaws. The most important of the re-entries being the well known major re-entry. (Scott #15c).

NOTE ON PLATES

Plate I Perf. 11¾ x 11¾—1859-62. No imprint.
Plate II Perf. 11¾ x 11¾ and 12 x 11¾—1859-64. No imprint.
Plate III (?) Perf. 12 x 12—1864-68. Imprint.
Plate III is quite probably, a re-entered state of plate I or II, most likely plate I.

The Major Re-entry. No. 47 on Sheet. 1865-68. Perf. 12 only. Plate III. (This may be Plate I re-entered). See also Page 204, Fig. 7.

The minor re-entries are numerous, and Senator J. A. Calder has tabulated some fifty-seven varieties, many of which are very minute. We illustrate herewith nineteen of these minor re-entries which in our opinion are of sufficient importance to warrant attention by most collectors of Canada.

It is interesting to observe that of these 57 re-entries 31 are perf. 12 only, 4 are perf. 11¾ only, while 22 are perf. both 12 x 11¾ or 12 x 12.

The arrangement shows the top and then the bottom of the stamp. Only such portion as is necessary to show the re-entry is illustrated.

Unless given the plate position is not known for certain.

No. 1. 1865-68. From Bottom Row of Sheet. Perf. 12 only. Plate III.

No. 2. 1865-68. Perf. 12 only. Plate III.

No. 3. 1865-68. Perf. 12 only. Plate III

No. 4. 1863-68. Number 40 on Sheet. Perf 12 x 11¾, 12. Plate I.

No. 5. 1865-68. From Bottom Row of Sheet. Perf. 12 x 11¾, 12.

No. 6. 1863-68. From Bottom Row of Sheet. Perf. 12 x 11¾, 12. Plate I.

No. 7. 1865-68. From Ninth Horizontal Row of Sheet. Perf. 12 only. Plate III.

No. 8. 1862-64. From Bottom Row of Sheet. Perf. 12 x 11¾ only. Plate I.

No. 9. 1863-69. Number 9 on Sheet. Perf. 12 x 11¾, 12. Plate I.

No. 10. 1865-68. From Bottom Row of Sheet. Perf. 12 only. Plate III.

No. 11. 1865-68. From Bottom Row of Sheet. Shows Imprint. Perf. 12 only. Plate III.

No. 12. 1865-68. From Left Vertical Row of Sheet.

No. 13. 1859-65. Plate I.

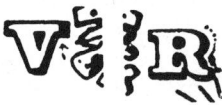

No. 14. 1865-68.

No. 15. 1865-68.

No. 16. 1865-68.

No. 17. 1865-68.

Plate Flaws on the 5c Beaver

These flaws are also numerous. We illustrate twenty-five of the more **obvious varieties.** Unless noted the plate positions have not been definitely ascertained.

Flaw #6. "Rock in Waterfalls"

Flaw #1. "Log in Waterfall". This exists in Two Stages, Single Line (See "No. 1" Below) and Two Lines as Illustrated Above.

No. 1. 1863-68. "Log in Waterfalls." Plate I.

No. 2. 1865-63. "Comet."

No. 3. 1863-65. "Shaded Tree." Plate I.

No. 4. 1865-68. "Crown Line." Shows Imprint at Right.

No. 5. 1863-65. "Split Beaver." Plate I.

No. 6. 1865-68. "Rock in Waterfalls."

No. 7. 1865-68. "Leaping Fish."

No. 8. 1863-65. "PO" Stroke." Plate I.

No. 9. 1863-65.
"Sunbeam" Flaw.
Plate I.

No. 10. 1863-65.
"Radio Aerial."
Plate I.

No. 11. 1863-68.
"Broken Aerial."
Plate I.

No. 12. 1859-62.
"Cross POS"
Stroke.
Plate I.

No. 13. 1865-68.
"DA" Stroke.

No. 14. 1865-68.
"E-C" Stroke.

No. 15. 1865-68.
"T" Strokes.

No. 16. 1863-65.
"R. R. Junction."
Plate I.

No. 17. 1865-68.
Curl Under "T."

No. 18. 1865-68.
"Low Moon"
Flaw.

No. 19. 1865-68.
"High Moon"
Flaw.

No. 20. 1863-65.
"E" Break.
Plate I.

No. 21. 1863-65.
"Crossed Corner."
Plate I.

No. 22. 1865-68.
"Comma" Variety.
Shows Imprint at Bottom.

No. 23. 1865-68. "The Blot."

No. 24. 1865-68. "E" Stroke. From Right Vertical Row of Sheet.

No. 25. 1865-68. "5-S" Stroke.

NOTE: The figures prefixed by "#" are sheet positions.

TEN CENTS

Re-Entries

#29. Left ornament doubled. Known from July, 1862.

#51. Lower Right X doubled at bottom. Known as early as July, 1862.

Flaws

3.
#3. "String of pearls." This is known on the proofs and has been seen on nearly all printings.

4.
#9. Large dot on upper left stroke of lower right "X". Normally the dot is small and clear, but in this case it is larger and less distinct.

Short Transfers

#22, 45, 50 and 78 show short transfers at top.

TWELVE AND A HALF CENTS

Re-Entries

#94. Line at top of "STERLING" and bottom of "AGE". Traces of doubling also show in other portions of the stamp.

Flaws

There are a number of minute flaws but none prominent enough to warrant listing.

Short Transfers

#56 and 98 show short transfers at top.

SEVENTEEN CENTS

Re-Entries

1. #100. The Major Re-Entry.

2. #5 Shows Thoughhout the Life of the Plate.

3. #41. This Shows in Early Impressions, but Later Impressions May Show No Trace of this Re-Entry.

4. #80 Shows Throughout the Life of the Plate.

The Last Vertical Row.

5. #10.

6. #20.

7. #30.

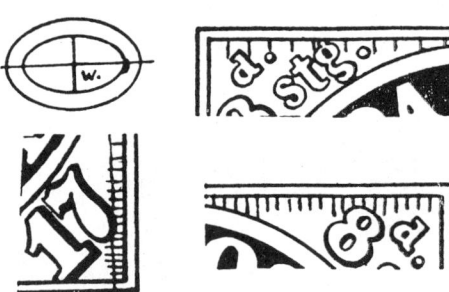

8. #40.

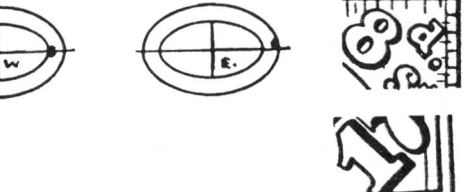

9. #50.

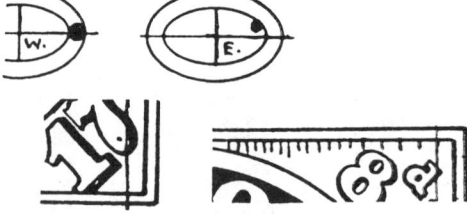

10. #60.

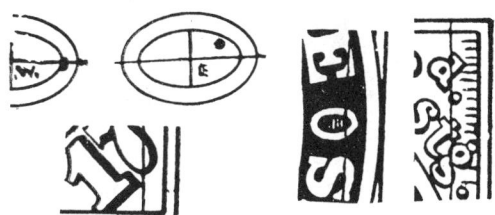

11. #70.

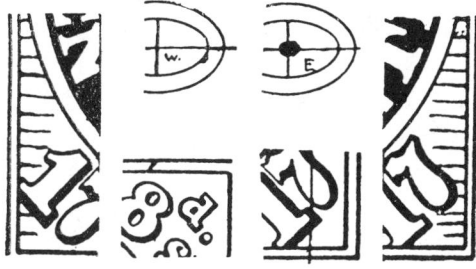

12. #90.

The last vertical row, positions 10, 20, etc., to 100 are characteristic. This row should be as popular with Canadian students as the three vertical rows of the Plate III of the 3c 1851 are with U. S. collectors. (See re-entries for #80 and #100).

"Burr on Shoulder" variety. Late state of plate, #7 on sheet.

Flaws

1. #7. First State. Early Impressions Show These Characteristics.

2. #7. Second State. The last Two Orders, However, Show the Burr Flaw Over the Shoulder on This Position. It Is a Very Rare Variety as It Did Not Become Fully Developed Until the Last Printing, perforated 12 x 12 only.

3. #6. Dashes on Second "E" of "Seventeen."

4. #42. Line in Right "7" Traces of Short Transfer at Upper Right.

5. #46. Line from "G" and Short Tranfer at Top.

6. #73. Line from "g" to "G."

7. #75. Pitted "E." The Plate Evidently Became Pitted in This Area and the Ink Filled Cavities Show on the Stamp.

8. #87. Dot in "D" of "Canada" and Upper Right Frame.

9. #88 Line Through Left "7".

In addition to those noted on the previous varieties the following show short transfers:

AT TOP: #11, 14, 15, 19, 24, 38, 45, 53, 57, 89, 96, 98.
AT BOTTOM: #57, 63, 82, 83.

In the case of #76 the transfer is weak at right, as though the roll was not correctly rocked on the plate.

Fig. 6.
Pair of ½d with 17c paying 19c rate to Germany from Ottawa July 14, 1859. London July 27, and exchanged at Aachen (Aix la Chappelle) on July 28.

Fig. 7.
Single and block of four on piece, the U. R. stamp showing major re-entry.
(See Page 188)

Fig. 8.
3d perforated with 5c making 10c rate to the United States. The 3d has the Major re-entry.
(See Page 127)

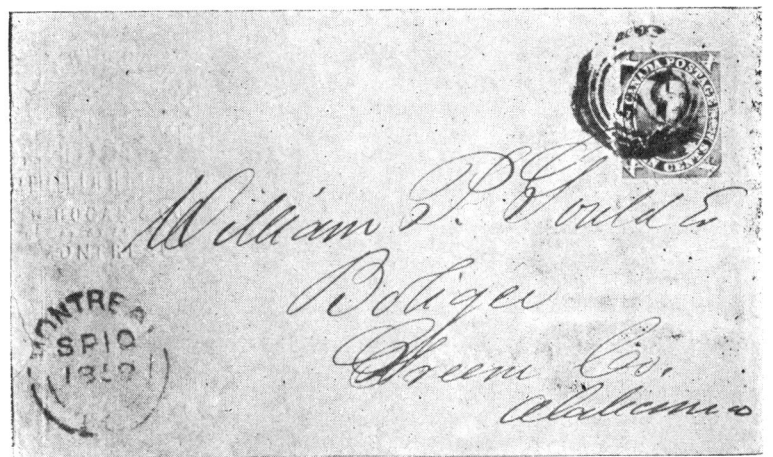

Fig. 9.
10c black brown. Montreal September 10, 1859. Corner card of St. Lawrence Hall, a popular hotel of the time.

Fig. 10. Vertical block of Eight of 17c.

Soldier's Letters

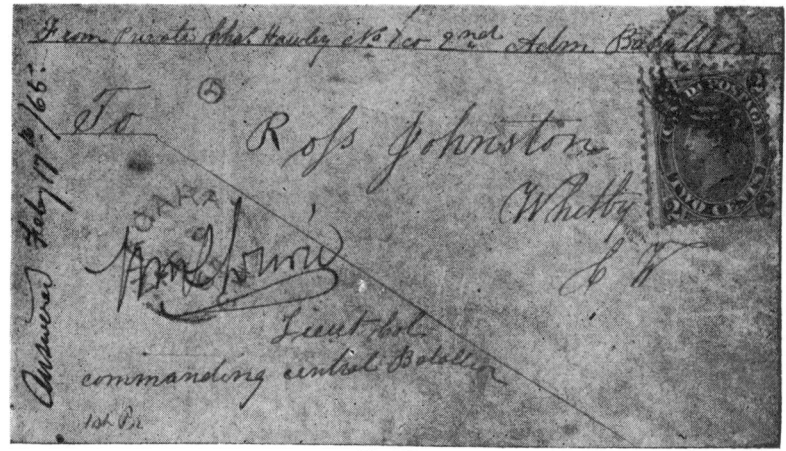

Fig. 11.

2c rose of 1864. Feb. 9, 1865, from Niagara, C. W. to Whitby, C. W. The normal rate would have been 5c. This is a Volunteer Militia Letter. See Appendix B #4.

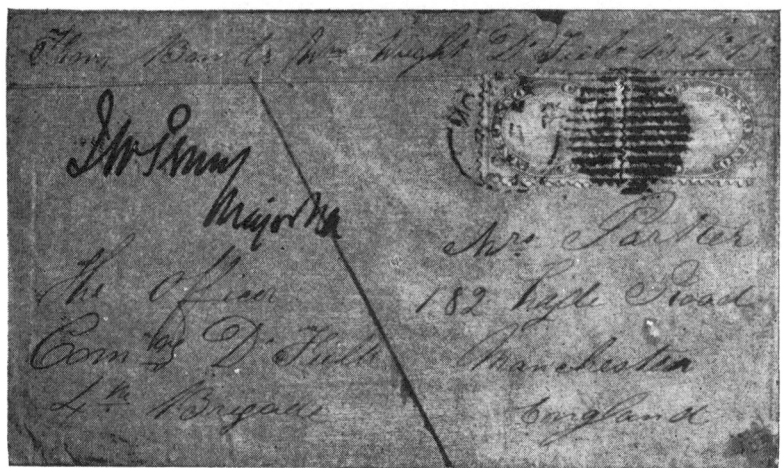

Fig. 12.

Two singles of the 1c on a soldier's letter to Manchester, Eng. From Montreal March, 1863, arriving in Manchester May 14, 1863. Normal rate would have been at least 12½ cents. This is an Imperial Military Rate Letter. See Appendix B #18, Paragraph 88.

Bisects

In this issue the 1c, 5c, and 10c are known bisected. The 1c and 5c were so treated to make up the necessary ½c on the 12½c rate. The 10c, however, was merely to make a 5c rate.

We list such bisections we have seen or have been reliably reported. All diagonal halves unless otherwise stated.

1c. Horizontal half with 12½c and three 1c to make 17c rate to Ireland. Nov. 18, 1863. (Fig. 13).

5c. U. L. to L. R. with pair of 5c to make 12½c rate to the United Kingdom. (Fig. 14).

5c. U. L. to L. R. with 10c from Montreal, Jan. 20, 1860, making 12½c rate to the United Kingdom. (Fig. 15).

10c U. R. to L. L. as 5c, from Bowmanville to Whitby, Feb. 14, 1860. (Fig. 18).

10c. U. R. to L. L. as 5c from Lennoxville.

10c U. R. to L. L. as 5c, from Barrie, Nov. 5, 1860. (Fig. 16).

10c U. R. to L. L. as 5c, from Carleton Place, Oct. 9, 1860. (Fig. 17).

10c U. L. to L. R. as 5c, from Quebec, July 9, 1869. (Fig. 19).

10c U. L. to L. R. as 5c, tied by "Kings & Toronto GD. TR'K. R. Way, "Nov. 28, 1859." The probably unique example of a bisect tied by a Railway Cancellation. (Fig. 20).

Fig. 13. Horizontal half of 1c with four 1c and 12½c making 17c rate.

Fig. 14. Pair and diagonal half of 5c making 12½c rate.

Fig. 15. Diagonal half of 5c with 10c making 12½c rate to United Kingdom.

Fig. 16. Diagonal half of 10c from Barrie, 1860.

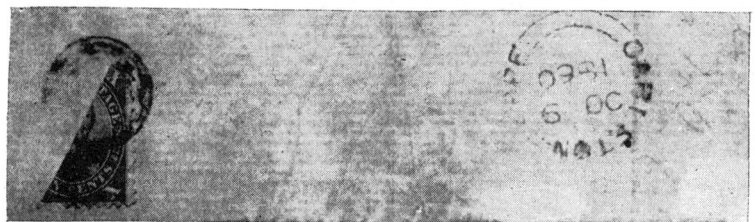

Fig. 17. Diagonal half of 10c from Carleton Place, 1860

Fig. 18. Diagonal half of 10c from Bowmanville, 1860.

Fig. 19. Diagonal half of 10c from Quebec, 1860.

Fig. 20. Diagonal half of 10c tied by a Railway Cancellation.

Counterfeits, Etc.

Engraved Counterfeits by Panelli.

Engraved Similitude, Made at Same Time the 7½d and 10d [Illustrated in Pence Chapter. (Pages 177-8)

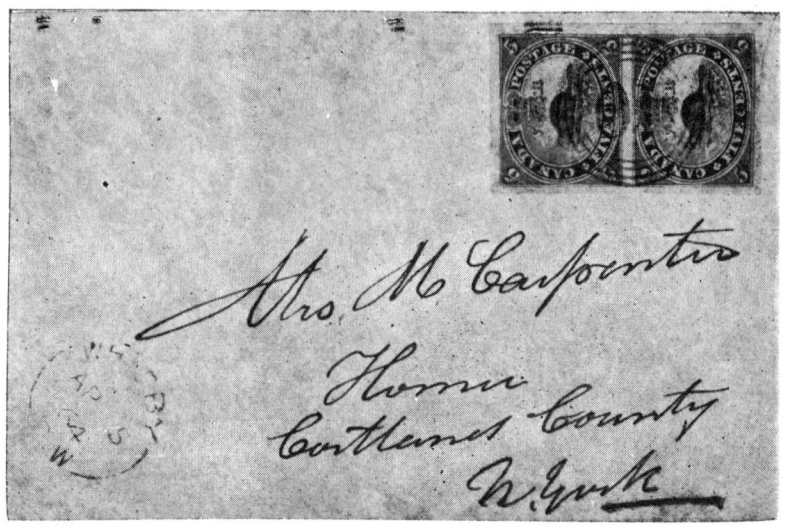

Fig. 21.
An excellent faking job. The apparently fine IMPERFORATE pair was neither imperforate nor a pair. Furthermore the four ring numeral cancellation in blue was also bogus.

We have seen few counterfeits of this issue, and those we have seen are crude. Illustrated are typical examples of the 1c and 10c, engraved by Panelli. They are imperforate, on poor quality wove paper, and usually with cancellations unlike any normally found on Canadian stamps.

FAKES: The chief danger is the so-called imperforates, made from proofs, carefully backed, sometimes mounted on covers and neatly (too neatly) cancelled. None of these, however, should deceive any one familiar with these stamps.

Decimal Issue of 1859-68

All issued July 1, 1859, except 2c, Aug. (1?), 1864.

#	Denomination and Color		Perforations	Thin Semi-transparent Unused	Thin Semi-transparent Used	Thick Opaque Unused	Thick Opaque Used	Hard, crisp Unused	Hard, crisp Used	Quantity Issued	1944 Scott #	1944 S.G. #
12	1c Rose	1859-62	11¾	2	6	4	5	1¼	1½	27,500,000		
	Dull red	1860-65	11¾, 12 x 11¾, 12	4	4	6	7	2	2			
	Rose red	1860-68	11¾, 12 x 11¾, 12	1½	2	3	4	N	N		14	29
a	Re-entry			15	8	25	20	8	5			
b	Double frame line			8	6	15	12	4	3			
c	Imperforate							12	—			
	Pair								2½			
	Block of four							15	35			
	Cover			—	4	—	8	—	3			
	Two or pair on military cover (2c rate)[2]								100			
	½ used as ½c[1]								x			
13	2c Rose red	1864-67	12 x 11¾, 12	1½	1½	—	—	N	N	865,000	20	44
	Claret red	1865-67	12	1¾	1½	—	—	N	N			
a	Double frame line			7	5	—	—	1¼	4			
b	Line on cheek & neck			6	4	—	—	5	3			
c	Imperforate							4	—			
	Pair				12	—	—	5	8			
	Block of four							70	x			
	Cover				10				2½			
	Military cover[2]			—	x	—	—		100			

1. Horizontal ½. See Illustration page 207.
2. Imperial Military rate covers are rarer than those of the Volunteer Militia. Factor 150.

Decimal Issue of 1859-68 (Cont.)

#		Denomination and Color	Perforations.	Thin Semi-transparent.		Thick Opaque		Hard, crisp		Quantity Issued.	1944 Scott #	1944 S.G. #
				Unused	Used	Unused	Used	Unused	Used			
14	5c	Brick red 1859-60	11¾	7	3	4	9	1½	1½	39,800,000	15	31
		Dark red 1860	11¾	7	3	4	9	1½	1½			
		Brown red 1861-67	11¾, 11¾ x 12, 12	5	2	2	6	N	N			
		Vermilion 1862-67	11¾, 11¾ x 12, 12	8	4	5	10	2	2			
		Salmon red 1864-66	11¾ x 12, 12	5	2	2	6	x	N			
a		Major re-entry			200		300	20	100			
b		Minor re-entry			20		40		10			
c		"Log" in waterfalls							x			
d		Plate flaw		8	5	15	10	5	3			
e		Imperforate						25				
		Pair		15	12		50	7	6			
		Block		60	300			25	160			
		Cover			5		10		2			
		4½ used as 2½c							x			
15	10c	Black brown 1859	11¾	4	4			15	10	The black brown is on a medium opaque crisp paper. 5,700,000	17	37
		Choc. purple 1859	11¾	1¾	2			2	2			
		Purple (red to gray) 1859-64	11¾, 12 x 11¾	1¾	2	5	3	N	N			
		Violet (dark to slate) 1864-66	12 x 11¾, 12	1¾	2	5	3	N	N			
		Red lilac 1866-68	12 x 12	15	10	17	10	8	5			
a		Re-entry		14	8			7	4			
b		"String of pearls"		15	8			6				
c		Imperforate				15	7		2½			
		Pair							60			
		Block of four			5		8		3			
		Cover			6				450			
		4½ used as 5c										

212

Decimal Issue of 1859-68 (Cont.)

#	Denomination and Color	Perforations.	Thin Semi-transparent. Unused	Thin Semi-transparent. Used	Thick Opaque Unused	Thick Opaque Used	Hard, crisp Unused	Hard, crisp Used	Quantity Issued.	1944 Scott #	1944 S.G. #
16	12½c Olive gr'n 1859-60	11¾	3	2¾	6	4	2	1¾	3,200,000		
	Yellow gr'n 1859-64	11¾	1¾	1¾	—	—	1¼	1¼			
	Green 1860-65	11¾, 12 x 11¾, 12	1½	1½	—	—	N	N		18	40
	Blue gr'n 1865-68	12	1¾	1¾	—	—	1¼	1¼			
a	Re-entry		10	7	12	9	7	5			
b	Imperforate						10	—			
	Pair						3	4			
	Block of four						10	8			
	Cover		—	12		16	—	8			
17	17c Blue 1859-64	11¾, 12 x 11¾	1¼	1½	—	—	N	N	600,000	19	42
	Deep blue 1863-65, 1867	12 x 11¾, 12	1¾	2¼	—	—	1½	2			
	Dull Blue 1860-61, 1864	11¾, 12 x 11¾	1½	1¾	—	—	1¼	1½			
a	Major re-entry		12	7	—	—	8	5			
b	Minor re-entry		5	3	—	—	3	2			
c	"Burr over shoulder"				—	—	—	x			
d	Plate flaw						2	1½			
e	Imperforate		3	2	—	—	7	—			
	Pair			6	—	—		4			
	Block of four			100	—	—		60			
	Cover		—	12	—	—		8			

TRADE SAMPLE SHEET OF 1864.

We have starred the British North American items, which account for eleven out of twenty stamps. Note that the 1c New Brunswick is duplicated. It is interesting to observe that three of the Canadian and the New York Postmaster's designs originated with R. W. H. & E., and that the two U. S. Essays are attributed to Gavit & Co., and Bald, Cousland & Co., respectively. See "Essays for U. S. Adhesive Postage Stamps," by Clarence W. Brazer. (American Philatelic Society 1941).

B. Post Contemporary Impressions

DIE PROOFS

The following die proofs were made after the stamps were current, in 1875 and 1879 respectively.

1875

On large piece of india paper mounted on card. No cross hatching. (Rare.)

D17a 17c bright yellow green.

1879

The so called "Goodall" proofs which were made when Albert G. Goodall was president of the company, and shortly after the merger of the National Bank Note Co., and the Continental Bank Note Co., with the American Bank Note Co. The United States issues were printed in five colors, but we have seen the Canadian "Goodalls" only as noted.
See Note on page 173 concerning Henry Mandel.
On small pieces of india paper mounted on card. (Very rare.)

	(U) black	(V) deep green	(W) dull gray blue	(Y) deep brown	(Z) dull red
D12a 1c			x	x	x
D13a 2c			x	x	x
D14a 5c			x	x	x
D15a 10c			x	x	x
D16a 12½c			x	x	x
D17b 17c			x	x	x

Note: The 1c shows cross hatching around the design.

Proofs

We have seen the 2c in issued color overprinted "PROOF" horizontally in green, in sans serif letters similar to S2f. (Page 174, Fig. 54). Probably made about 1879.

P13c 2c dull rose (green overprint).

Trade Sample Sheet

In 1864 a sample sheet of twenty items was made. This simply consists of various plate proofs firmly pasted in the spaces provided. All the B. N. A. proofs were in the colors of issue. (See page 214).

EPILOGUE TO THE PROVINCIAL ISSUES

The conclusion of the history of the 1851-59 issues took place when the plates, rolls, and dies were actually destroyed.

As we have noted the plate of the 12p was cancelled and sent to Canada March 26, 1857.[1] The contractors, however, retained the die and transfer roll. The roll was used for a lay down die of the 7½d stamp.[1] The roll was also used to lay down dies fom which various post contemporary proofs were made.

When the decimal currency issue was ordered the dies were altered and new rolls made to lay down the plates. The one cent roll was also used to make a lay down die for the 2c in 1864.

Thus the 12c plate was destroyed in 1857. The dies of the ½p, 3d, 6d, and 10p were destroyed in making them into the dies for the decimal stamps of 1c, 5c, 10c, and 17c respectively. However, none of the transfer rolls were destroyed then, and all the plates were in existence with the exception of the 12p, although the die was still extant, and the transfer roll. A new die was made for the 12½c.

The importance of the disposition of the plates of the Provincial stamps is such as to warrant the quotation in full of certain significant correspondence. These letters show that the dies, plates and rolls were cancelled January 4, 1902, and on February 19, 1902, said items were shipped to Canada. The various dies and plates were cut apart and thrown into a river some miles from Ottawa, after having been laying in the vaults of the Department for years!

Correspondence relating to the disposition of the dies, rolls and plates of the stamps of the various Canadian Provinces, made by Rawdon Wright, Hatch & Edson, and The American Bank Note Co., prior to 1867.

February 19, 1902.

R. M. Coulter, Esq.,
    Deputy Postmaster General,
        Ottawa, Canada.

Dear Sir—

Referring to your letters of October 4th and November 8th, 1901, I have now to advise that we have shipped to your address this day, by National Express, three (3) boxes containing:

Box No. 1	11	cancelled	Plates of Postage Stamps of Province of Canada
Box No. 2	6	".	Plates of Postage Stamps of Nova Scotia
	7	"	Plates of Postage Stamps of New Brunswick
Box No. 3	12	"	Rolls of Postage Stamps of Canada
	6	"	Rolls of Postage Stamps of Nova Scotia
	7	"	Rolls of Postage Stamps of New Brunswick
	8	"	Dies of Postage Stamps of Canada
	5	"	Dies of Postage Stamps of Nova Scotia
	7	"	Dies of Postage Stamps of New Brunswick

as per detailed list enclosed herewith. We also hand you duplicate Certified Invoice as passed to the Express Company. Kindly attend to the despatch at your Custom House, and acknowledge receipt at your convenience,

Yours respectfully,

(signed) T. H. FREELAND,
Vice President
(A.B.N.Co.)

---

[1] Appendix H #52

PROVINCE OF CANADA
POST OFFICE DEPARTMENT

Box No. 1

Cancelled Plate	—	100 stamps	½ penny[3]
"	"	100 "	1c
"	"	100 "	2c
"	"	100 "	5c
"	"	200 "	3 pence[4]
"	"	200 "	6 pence[4]
"	"	120 "	8 pence sterling[5]
"	"	120 "	6 pence sterling[6]
"	"	100 "	10c
"	"	100 "	12½c
"	"	100 "	17c

The 12 pence plate was cancelled and returned to the Department on March 26, 1854. See Appendix H #52.

Box No. 2

NOVA SCOTIA
POST OFFICE DEPARTMENT

Cancelled Plate	—	100 stamps	1c
"	"	100 "	2c
"	"	100 "	5c
"	"	100 "	8½c
"	"	100 "	10c
"	"	100 "	12½c

NEW BRUNSWICK
POST OFFICE DEPARTMENT

Cancelled Plate	—	100 stamps	1c
"	"	100 "	2c
"	"	100 "	5c Victoria Head
"	"	100 "	5c McConnell Head (*Sic*)
"	"	100 "	10c
"	"	100 "	12½c
"	"	100 "	17c

Box No. 3

PROVINCE OF CANADA—POST OFFICE DEPARTMENT

[It will be observed that the Bank Note Co. uses the word "subjects", whereas we term them "reliefs".]

Roll	—	2 subjects	½ penny stamp
"		2 subjects	1 cent stamp
"		2 subjects	2 cent stamp
"		2 subjects	5 cent stamp
"		1 subject	3 pence stamp
"		1 subject	6 pence stamp
"		1 subject	8 pence stg stamp[5]
"		2 subjects	6 pence stg stamp[6]
"		2 subjects	10 cent stamp

3. Note that the plate had only 100 subjects when cancelled, as compared with the original 120 subjects when first made.
4. Both sections of the plate.
5. 10d currency.
6. 7½d curency.

"	2 subjects	12½ cent stamp
"	1 subject	12 pence stamp
"	2 subjects	17 cent stamp

See Note 9 below.

NOVA SCOTIA—POST OFFICE DEPARTMENT

Roll —	1 subject	1 cent stamp
"	1 subject	2 cent stamp
"	2 subjects	5 cent stamp
"	1 subject	8½ cent stamp
"	1 subject	10 cent stamp
"	2 subjects	12½ cent stamp

NEW BRUNSWICK—POST OFFICE DEPARTMENT

Roll —	2 subjects	1 cent stamp
"	1 subject	2 cent stamp
"	1 subject	5 cent stamp (Victoria)
"	1 subject	5 cent stamp (McConnell) (*Sic*)
"	2 on one	10 cent stamp[10]
"	2 subjects	12½ cent stamp
"	1 subject	17 cent stamp

PROVINCE OF CANADA—POST OFFICE DEPARTMENT

Die 1c   (altered from ½ penny)
Die 2c
Die 5c   (altered from 3 pence)
Die 6 pence sterling[11]
Die 10c   (altered from 6 pence)
Die 12 pence
Die 12½c and 6 pence stg.[12]
Die 17c   (altered from 8 pence stg. 10 pence cy)

NOVA SCOTIA—POST OFFICE DEPARTMENT

Die 1c
Die 2c
Die 5c
Die 8½c
Die 12½c (altered from 10c)

NEW BRUNSWICK—POST OFFICE DEPARTMENT

Die 1c Essay (never used)
Die 1c
Die 2c
Die 5c (Victoria Head)
Die 5c (McConnell Head) (Sic)
Die 10c (two on one die)[13]
Die 12½c
Die 17c

---

9. Note that the first two-subject roll was made for the 7½d stamp.
10. This refers to the fact that two subjects were taken up on one rocking of the roll. (See below).
11. 7½d currency.
12. Note that the 12½ was the only one of the 1859 issue that was not from an altered die.
13. The die had two engravings on it, hence in rocking the roll two subjects would be taken up at a time, two reliefs, but each slightly different.

INVOICE

(Original filled in by longhand)

National Express
Ottawa, Canada

3 boxes Nos. 1, 2, 3,
containing cancelled
steel plates, dies and rolls
for the Govt. of Canada
} no commercial value.

(signed) T. H. FREELAND, V. Pt.

T. H. Freeland, V. Prest.
N.Y.
19 Feb'y 1902

---

19 Feb'y, 02
Deputy Postmaster General,
Ottawa, Canada

3 boxes per National Express
Nos. 1, 2, & 3. containing cancelled
Postage stamp plates
" " dies
" " rolls
} no value

(signed) T. H. FREELAND, V. Pt.

N.Y. - 19 Feb'y '02

THE DOMINION OF CANADA

THE DOMINION SEAL*

On July 1, 1867, the provinces of Ontario, Quebec, (then known as Canada West, and Canada East, respectively), New Brunswick and Nova Scotia united to become the "Dominion of Canada". Provision was made for the admission of the other provinces and Newfoundland. In 1869 the Dominion purchased the Hudson Bay Co's. territories for £300,000. From this vast area the Red River and Portage LaPrairie settlements and a large surrounding area was admitted as the Province of Manitoba July 15, 1870. A year later, July 20, 1871, British Columbia and Vancouver Island became part of the Dominion, which now stretched from ocean to ocean. On July 1, 1873, Prince Edward Island was admitted, so that the territorial area was much as it is today.

On May 8, 1882, the Province of Manitoba was enlarged and out of the remaining Northwest Territory the districts of Alberta, Assiniboia, Athabasca, Keewatin, and Saskatchewan were created, with a vast area being left in what was still designated as the Northwest Territory[1].

In 1905, however, the districts of Assiniboia, Saskatchewan, Alberta, and Athabasca, were formed into the Provinces of Saskatchewan and Alberta respectively. The remaining area is now divided into the Yukon Territory, and the districts of Mackenzie, Keewatin, and Franklin.

On March 1, 1927, the Judicial Committee of the Privy Council of Great Britain awarded the whole of the Atlantic watershed of the Labrador Peninsular to Newfoundland. This resulted in an area of some 110,000 square miles (almost twice the area of New York State) being transferred from Quebec to Newfoundland. None of the changes after 1873 affected the stamp issues.

---

*From a die proof in black on India, by the British American Bank Note Co., Die number 169.

1. The Postal History of the Northwest Territory and Manitoba is discussed in the chapter on the Northwest Territory cancellations, and also Appendix K, and B #49.

Chapter X

INTRODUCTION TO THE QUEEN'S HEAD ISSUES OF 1868-97

This beautiful and complicated group of stamps, bearing the exquisite vignette of "Victoria's Head to Right" was issued in two sizes, the large size first in 1868, commonly called the "Large Queens," or "Large Cents," and in 1870 the small size began to appear, which is commonly referred to as the "Small Queens" or "Small Cents" stamps.

Much patient study has been done on these stamps by many notable students, particularly Dr. Lewis L. Reford, Dr. Kenneth Day, Mr. L. D. Shoemaker, Mr. A. K. Grimmer, the late Mr. Charles L. Pack, and a host of others. Careful

Charles Henry Jeens
1827 — 1879

Self portrait of the famous English engraver made when he was 47 years of age. He engraved the original Queen's head adapted for the Large and Small Queen designs, as well as the original Seal and Codfish used `r the 1865 issue of Newfoundland by the American Bank Note Co.`

study of their conclusions, as well as the available literature, reams of correspondence, plus examination of many thousands of these stamps, and last but not least the study of official records never before examined by philatelists, leads us to venture the conclusions presented herewith, confident that much remains to be done, and certain that many years will elapse before a reasonably complete and accurate story of these difficult issues will be known.

All of these stamps are of similar design, differing only in the ornamentation surrounding the vignette. The portrait of the Queen was engraved by Alfred Jones[1], from a similar work by the famous English engraver Charles Henry Jeens[2]. The lettering was done by Henry Earle, Sr., and although William C. Smillie was primarily a script letter engraver it is possible he did the ornamental work[3].

The original issue of 1868 began to be replaced by the new small design in January, 1870, when the 3c was issued in the reduced size.

They were all produced by The British American Bank Note Co.

---
1 See Chapter VII, Page 110.
2 Jeens was born in 1827 and died in 1879.
3 W. C. Smillie was president of the British American Bank Note Co.

of Montreal & Ottawa[4]. This firm was founded in 1866, and its work was of the highest quality, comparing favorably with the greatest firms in the United States and Great Britain. As shown in Chapter VII the officers were former American Bank Note Co. men.

The overlapping of the large design and the small design stamps, as well as changes in colors, denominations, perforations, papers, etc., have made it necessary for us to group the large designs together, although the large 5c and later printings of the half cent and fifteen cents belong to the small design issues.

All of these stamps were printed from *unhardened steel plates,* either at Ottawa or Montreal, but never at both places simultaneously.

The division of the study of these stamps is as follows:

1. April 1, 1868. Large design ½c to 15c[5].
2. January, 1870. Small design.
    (a) First Ottawa Printings 1870-74—1c, 2c, 3c, 6c.
    (b) Montreal Printings 1874-87—½c, 5c, 10c added.
    (c) Second Ottawa Printings 1888-97—8c, 20c, 50c added in 1893.

During the Montreal Printings the registered letter stamps and Official Seal were introduced. (See chapter on Registration stamps.)

Details of plate arrangement, imprints, perforation, gum, shades, etc., are taken up in their respective groups.

One of the chief obstacles to a solution of many of the problems concerning these stamps has been the regrettable lack of official records of this period. Investigation was further hindered by two factors having to do with the manufacture of the plates: First, none of the plates were numbered as was the practice in the United States, and second, the excellence of the work done makes it almost impossible to allocate varieties to any particular plate.

However, with the discovery by us of some records concerning the relations between the British American Bank Note Co., and the Government a great deal of what was hitherto dim and obscure has been cleared up.

At the risk of being tedious we venture to outline the steps which have resulted in the conclusions presented in this and the succeeding chapters concerning these stamps.

For sometime previous to undertaking this book we were not convinced that the Large Queen plates were made in Montreal. This doubt was based on a number of minor points relating to paper money as well as stamps. None of these points were conclusive in themselves but cumulatively they seemed to indicate that for several years, from 1868, to say 1875, the stamps were printed in Ottawa. Both the Post Office Department and the British American Bank Note Co., were quite certain that no stamps were printed in Ottawa until 1888. In view of such opinion we had to suspend judgement until more evidence one way or another was forthcoming.

The first bit of evidence was the study of the composite proof sheet (Fig. 1) with the imprint reading "Montreal & Ottawa," while the script letter specifically read "Specimens Engraved by British American Bank Note Comp Ottawa, Canada." The fact that only the 1c Small Queen is shown, while all the Large Queens are in evidence indicated that this proof was made late in 1869.

Upon studying the letter in Appendix H #117 we were still further convinced that stamps were at first engraved and printed in Ottawa.

Discovery of the letter from Alfred Jones, as quoted in Appendix O #5 clinched the matter in our opinion. However, careful study of the stamps revealed certain peculiar facts, among which was the lack of the 10c with anything but a "Montreal" imprint. This stamp appeared late in 1874. Furthermore, why was the word "Ottawa" dropped from the imprint if the firm did not at least formerly have an office there as indicated by the old "Montreal and Ottawa" imprint?

---

4 Although the concern had offices in both cities the stamps were printed only in Ottawa until late in 1874.
5. The entire set is chronicled in "The Stamp Collectors Magazine", for May 1, 1868.

Fig. 1. Proof sheet of "Specimens engraved by the British American Bank Note Comp., OTTAWA, CANADA." (Note "OTTAWA, Canada). Imprint type III at bottom. The row of 1c stamps immediately below the vignette is in the Small Queen design. This fact coupled with the imprint type indicates latter part of 1869 as the date this plate was made. It was this sheet that gave us the first evidence that the stamps were printed in Ottawa from 1867, which led to further search and conclusive evidence for the classification of printings we have adopted. This sheet is known on cardboard in Black, Dull Red, and Green.

We continued our search for definite data, and fortunately, as we will show, succeeded in finding important information concerning these complicated issues; information which we feel marks a milestone in the history of the study of these stamps

Examination of the records, dated 1886, shows the following important data.

Small Queen Plates

Re-entering of 7 one cent plates.
Re-entering of 1 two cent plate.
Re-entering of 12 three cent plates.
Re-entering of 1 two cent registered letter plate.

Manufacture of the following NEW plates:

7 one cent plates.
1 two cent plate.
11 three cent plates.
1 five cent plate.
1 two cent registered letter plate
1 five cent registered letter plate.

From this it will be seen that there were at least

14 one cent plates,
2 two cent plates,
23 three cent plates,
2 five cent plates,
2 two cent registered letter plates,
2 five cent registered letter plates,

By the End of 1886

At least two six cent plates were made as we have seen two imprints for this stamp.

Each of these six cent plates was re-entered, and we are of the opinion that only two plates were necessary.

In other words, prior to the "Ottawa" plates we believe the Small Queens were produced from the following number of plates:

½c— 1 ("Montreal"), 200 subjects.
1c—14 (1 "Montreal & Ottawa", 13 "Montreal"), all 200 subjects.
2c— 2 (1 "Montreal & Ottawa", 1 "Montreal"), both 200 subjects.
3c—25 (2 "Montreal & Ottawa", 23 "Montreal"), all 200 subjects.
5c— 2 (1 "Montreal", 1 No imprint (?)), both 200 subjects.
6c— 2 (1 "Montreal & Ottawa", 1 "Montreal"), both 200 subjects.
10c— 1 ("Montreal"), 100 subjects.
Official Seal—1 ("Montreal"), 50 subjects.

The question of the registered letter plates is discussed in the chapter on those stamps (q.v.).

As far as the Ottawa plates of 1888 onwards we believe the following were made, bearing the "Ottawa" imprint.

1c—4 "Ottawa". Made in 1892. 200 subjects.
2c—1 "Ottawa". Large imprint made 1889. 200 subjects.
    1 "Ottawa". Small imprint made 1892. 200 subjects.
3c—8 "Ottawa". Made 1892. 200 subjects.
5c—1 "Ottawa" Large imprint made 1889. 200 subjects.

Fig. 2. Advertising Sheet of the British American Bank Note Co., about 1873. Note 3c Large Queen in upper left corner, and $3.00 Bill Stamp in upper right corner. Also the octette of small queen vignettes as used on the 8c of 1893. Vignettes and lettering in black, remainder in yellow. Proof on india paper. (About half actual size).

The new values of 1893: 8c—two plates, 200 subjects, no imprint; 20c and 50c, one plate each, 100 subjects with a new type of "Ottawa" imprint.

This is an average of approximately 200,000 impressions per plate[5a] for the 1c, 2c, and 3c plates. This may seem high, but there is ample evidence that plates under careful handling would give 200,000 impressions when unhardened[6]. It should be kept in mind that the plates could be re-entered, and were re-entered at least once, if not several times. The guarantee of 25,000 impressions before "retouching" and 15,000 impressions after "retouching" was very conservative, for several reasons. First, the Bank Note companies are as a matter of course conservative as befits their responsible work; second, even though most plates would give many more impressions than warranted, it sometimes happened that a plate would wear or become defective in a comparatively short while. Since the Bank Note company had to replace, at its own expense, any plate failing to deliver the warranted number of impressions the expected life of a plate was always figured most conservatively; and is so even today.

To sum up, we believe that the number of plates used to produce the Small Queens issues was as follows:

	"Montreal" & "Ottawa" 1870-74	*"Montreal"* 1874-87	*"Ottawa"* 1888-97	Totals
½c issued 1882	—	1	—	1
1c issued 1870	1	13	4	18
2c issued 1872	1	1	2	4
3c issued 1870	2	23	8	33
5c issued 1876	—	2[7]	1	3
6c issued 1872	1	1	—	2
8c issued 1893	—	—	2[8]	2
10c issued 1874	—	1	—	1
Totals of	5 4 Denoms.	42 7 Denoms.	17 5 Denoms.	64 8 Denoms.

It may be questioned "aside from the record given, what evidence for re-entering have we for the six cents, and the later plates?"

In answer to that we would point out that we have examined thousands of these stamps, as well as a very fine collection of the plate varieties of the 2c, 3c, 5c, and 6c stamps. From this study we concluded, independently of the official records that the plates were re-entered in 1875, 1887 and 1895 at least.

It is rather curious that where the re-entry is visible, (and we are referring to definite re-entries, and not slight blurrings, "kisses", etc., such re-entries being checked by examination of at least *three* examples of each) and a dated copy available, no re-entries of any significance occur until 1875. As would be expected in 1887 a new crop of re-entries may be noted. Later re-entries, that is between 1892 and 1897 are noted and 71% of them are dated 1895, or later. These re-entries, we have reason to believe are on the "Montreal,, plates which were kept in service after the new 1892 "Ottawa" plates of the 1c, 2c, 3c, and possibly 5c were made.

The data given above is by no means to be considered the last word on the

---

5a. See Appendix J #5 for quantities issued.
6 The 3c 1861 plates of the United States averaged 402,000 impressions. .Perkins, Bacon in 1854 stated that their experience in printing from "soft" steel plates was that the plates would hardly give half the number of impressions that a hardened plate would. (They frequently got 700,000 impresions from a hardened plate, and in one instance a plate gave over 1,000,000 impressions!). See Essay Proof Journal, January 1944. "Four Re-entered Plates of the U. S. 1861-66 Issue" by Karl Burroughs, also "The Line Engraved Stamps of Great Britain" by E. D. Bacon, Appendix C #182, 248, 209. It should also be noted that the U. S. 3c Green and 3c vermilion of 1870-90 averaged over 200,000 impressions per plate, the National Bank Note Co. averaging almost 225,000 impressions per plate. In addition we have been assured by Bank Note Officials that in 1870, an unhardened steel plate would, under certain conditions, give over 200,000 impressions. (See also footnote 10a, page 228).
7 It is possible that the second 5c plate went to press without an imprint which, when the plate was re-entered in 1889, may have had the "Ottawa" imprint added. In other words the 5c could have been produced from two plates.
8. The 8c plates had no imprint.

subject. Rather it is merely a suggestion to other students to continue their studies, which we are confident will result in the solution of many of the problems surrounding this fascinateing group of stamps.

In concluding this discussion of the production of the Large and Small Queen Issues we quote from *Official Records* (which we found) where necessary.

Two firms, Matthews & Smillie, and Burland & L'Africain early in 1866 made tenders to supply stamps under conditions briefly as follows:

Matthews & Smillie

Charge 20% less than the American Bank Note Co., i. e. *20c per 1,000 stamps*. Guaranteed 25,000 impressions per plate before retouching and 15,000 afterwards. The machinery to be admitted duty free.

Burland & L'Africain

Charge 25% less than the American Bank Note Co.—i.e. *$18\frac{3}{4}c$ per thousand stamps*. Machinery to be admitted duty free. Materials also to be admitted duty free.

The two firms consolidated, upon the express wish of the government, August 7, 1866, and notified the said government that they had made application for "Letters Patent" under the name of the British American Bank Note Company. The amalgamated firm submitted proposals to engrave and print stamps for a term of ten years from the date of contract.

The British American Bank Note Co.'s Proposal

The terms of this proposal were as follows:

"*First*: They are prepared to execute the work in Canada, either at Montreal or at Ottawa as the Government may determine.

"*Second*: If desirable the work may be under the supervision of such Government officer or officers, as may from time to time be appointed for that purpose.

"*Third*: Whenever it is desired dies of vignettes or lathework, may be reserved for the exclusive use of the Government, subject to any extra cost which may be incurred in production.

"*Fourth*: The work done to be fully equal in every respect, to anything heretofore supplied to the Government and at rates corresponding to those heretofore charged or as low as the price of material or compensation of artistic skill will justify.

"*Fifth*: To that end they propose to use the patent colours, for the use of which in Canada and the other British North American Provinces, Messrs. Burland, L'Africain & Co. have the exclusive right reserved by Letters Patent, this being the only absolute protection against counterfeiting and altering postage stamps.

"We also guarantee to introduce from time to time any improvement in the arts of engraving and printing, which experience may hereafter develop.

"*Sixth*: Should the Government require the work to be done in Ottawa, the undersigned would propose that a suitable building, free of cost be provided by the Government, and furnished with the necessary safeguards for the due execution and protection of the same.

"*Seventh*: As this project is entirely new and hazardous in Canada, and the enterprise a very expensive one, it is respectfully requested that the machinery, paper, and material of all descriptions used in the business be admitted free of duty.

"W. C. SMILLIE
"For self and associates.
"B. CHAMBERLAIN
"For self and associates."

A schedule of prices accompanied this tender and we quote:

ENGRAVING

	$ cts.
1 stamp plate, postage, single plate[9]	100.00

All original vignettes, dies or lathework charged according to size and quality of work[10].

PRINTING

Postage stamps, per 1000 stamps	.25
Other stamps, per 1000 impressions	50.00
Bank note paper, per 1000 sheets of 16 lbs. weight	22.50

All other paper according to size and quality.

The Government's Counter Proposal

The government made a counter proposal on August 17, 1866. This we quote as follows:

"*1st*: The Company shall execute all Government work in Canada, at Ottawa, employing a staff of skillful artists in all their various branches.

"*2nd*: The work shall be under the supervision of such Government Officer or Officers as may from time to time be appointed for that purpose.

"*3rd*: The Government shall have the right to reserve to itself the exclusive use of any die or plate upon paying for it.

4th: The work shall be in every respect fully equal to that heretofore supplied from other sources and charged for upon a schedule of prices to be agreed upon, the basis of which shall be that the total cost of the work shall not exceed that heretofore charged by the present current rates of the American Bank Note Company.

"*5th*: The Company shall guarantee that each plate shall give 25,000 (twenty-five thousand) impressions, before retouching and 15,000 (fifteen thousand) afterwards, excepting where the patent green is used, when the number of impressions guaranteed shall be only 10,000 (ten thousand).[10a]

"*6th*: The Government shall have the right to use for cancelling stamps and for all other purposes required, the patent colours for which Messrs. Burland, L'Africain & Co., have the exclusive right.

"*7th*: The Company shall introduce from time to time any improvements in the arts of engraving and printing which experience may show to be of value.

"*8th*: The Government will admit all the necessary machinery duty free.

"*9th*: The contract to be terminated at the option of either party by giving the other six months' notice.

"*10th*: The dies and plates to be in the possession and under control of the Government, and when used, to be under supervision of a Government Officer, who shall keep a record of all work done."

These terms were immediately agreed to by Messrs. Smillie and Chamberlain for the British American Bank Note Co., which prepared to commence work.

Certain rules and regulations were drawn up, and an officer was sent to New York and Washington, "to make himself acquainted with all the checks and safeguards in use there for similar work."

The government provided the necessary space for the production of stamps and on December 20, 1866, began to draw up the contract. On January 23, 1867,

---

[9] This means a plate of 100, not a double plate of 200.

[10] Dies generally cost $100.00 each. See also Appendix M #13, Appendix J #5, and Appendix H #117.

[10a] To show how conservative this guarantee was, if the usual life of a plate was little more than the guarantee it would have required sixty to seventy plates for the Large Queens alone! The 3c Small Queen would have required over 100 plates of 200 subjects! In the case of the 3c green of the United States 1870-90 we know that 297 plates were required some of which were little used. Assuming 40,000 impressions per plate, 25,000 originally, and 15,000 after re-entering, it would have required at least 832 plates; almost thrice the number actually used; and this for a green stamp, green being notoriously hard on the plates.

Fig. 3.
$5.00 note of "The Province of Canada", originally engraved and printed by the "American Bank Note Co., New York" as can be seen at lower center of frame. Later issues were by the "British American Bank Note Co., Montreal & Ottawa", whose imprint is just above the Signature of the "Deputy Receiver General". The counters are in green, rest of the note in black on white paper. Note just above the A.B.N.C. imprint the "Canada Bank Note Printing Tint", protecting Mathews patent (See Chapter VII, page 107).

Mr. Smillie as president of the British American Bank Note Co., requested that the contract be for a term of ten years, terminable on six months notice by either party.

From this data we know that the first contract was from October 1867 to 1877, and that it was renewed in 1877 for a further period of ten years, that is until 1887. The 1877 contract provided for the manufacture of stamped envelopes.

In 1887 a new contract was made, again for ten years, due to run until 1897.

We also know that the American Bank Note Co., in 1866-7, supplied the British American Bank Note Co. with a number of transfer rolls bearing various vignettes pending new vignettes engraved by the B. A. B. N. Co.

However, W. C. Smillie had left the British American Bank Note Co. in 1882 to become vice-president of the Canada Bank Note Co. of Montreal. This concern succeeded in securing the contract in 1891, offering equal if not finer work at a reduction of 35% in cost or thirteen cents per thousand for ordinary stamps!

They prepared a most attractive stamp and proceeded to lay down plates. The British American Bank Note Co., however, bought the Canada Bank Note Co., and assumed the contract, but continued to supply stamps of the same design as previously. The Canada Bank Note Co.'s new design was used for the Universal Postal Union Card of 1896.

Further details will be discussed under the respective issues, but we tabulate herewith the four stages of the contractual relations between the British American Bank Note Co. and the Government.

	Original Contract 1867-77	First Renewal 1877-87	Second Renewal 1887-92	Assumption of Canada Bank Note Contract 1891-97	Notes
	(Prices per 1000)				
Regular Postage	.25	.25	.20	.13	See Appendix M #12, 21, 27
Registered Letter Stamps	.50	.50	.40	.28	
Envelopes					
1c & 3c	—	3.00	3.00	2.50	
3c Large	—	3.50	3.50	3.00	
3c 2nd qual.	—	—	3.25	—	
Post Cards Engraved					
1c	1.25	1.25	—	—	
2c	3.50	3.50	3.50	2.75	
1c+1c	3.25	3.25	3.25	2.75	
Typographed					
1c	—	1.25	1.25	.90	1.25 to 1890
			1.00		1.00 from 1890.
Large 1c	—	—	—	1.30	
Medium 1c	—	—	—	1.75	1892-3
				1.05	1893 on
Letter Cards	—	—	—	1.75	

The data given above throws considerable light on these issues, and taking all the available information into consideration we are able to offer the following conclusions: *First*, as to why the Large Queen design was dropped, and the Small Queen design substituted: *secondly*, and as a correlative fact, the conclusion that all the Small Queen plates except the 10c, were 200 subjects, in two panes of 100; the 10c in 100 subject plates.

Various explanations have been offered for the reduction in size of the stamps but none have seemed to us to be convincing. The saving of paper would be insufficient to warrant the expense of new dies and plates. However, within a year the contractors were having difficulty in supplying the demand for stamps[11]. The problem faced by the Post Office and the contractors was one of increasing the output of stamps with the labor and machinery available, and at as little extra cost as possible.

The difficulty was met by the decision to produce smaller stamps in sheets of two hundred, two panes of 100, the smaller plate of two hundred being only a little larger that the old Large Queen plates of 100. Note that the *height* of a Small Queen stamp is only slightly greater than the *width* of a Large Queen. Furthermore the *width* of a 200 subject Small Queen plate is only a little greater than the *height* of a Large Queen plate. To put it another way a 200 subject Small Queen plate would, if placed sidewise, fit on the press as readily as a Large Queen plate placed normally.

The decision to reduce the size of the stamps was made by July 1869[12], if not sooner, and an entire set of dies of 1c, 2c, 3c, 6c, 12½c, and 15c were engraved. Plates of the 1c and 3c were laid down between August 1869 and December 1869 when printing of the Small Queens began[13]

The reasons for the irregularly spaced issuing of the various Small Queen values is easily explained. The 1c and 3c plates were the most used, and when it was necessary to re-enter or make a new plate, a new Small Queen plate would be laid down. Both the 1c and 3c Large Queen plates had given over 100,000 impressions, and needed re-entering; consequently Small Queen plates were laid down instead. The 2c plate, after some 80,000 impressions, was replaced in 1872 by the 2c Small Queen, the same procedure being followed for the 6c[14]. The ½c plate lasted until 1882, and when a new plate was needed the well known midget stamp was issued. The 12½c and 15c plates never needed re-entering and therefore were never issued in the Small Queen design, although a plate was apparently made for the 12½c, as finished proofs are known, but there is some question as to these being plate proofs.

Reference to the proposal of the British American Bank Note Co. shows that single plates were to cost $100.00, and Bank Note paper $22.50 per 1,000 sheets, and "all other paper according to size and quality". The new 200 subject plates would fit on a sheet of bank note paper, with less wastage, and an adjustment in the cost of plates was made of $150.00 per plate[15], the charge for re-entering being $75.00 per plate. The rate of 25 cents per 1,000 was continued until 1887, as the 200 subject sheets required extra handling, cutting into panes of 100, meaning twice as much perforating, etc.

Printing Varieties. 1868-97.

There are a number of interesting printing varieties of these issues. The commonest of course being the well known "off sets", or impressions *in reverse* on the back of the stamp. Exceptionally clear examples are of interest to specialists. They occur on all denominations.

The true *printed on both sides,* however, is extremely rare, and unused examples of the 1c Small Queen are usually from the strip of twenty appearing on the back of a normal sheet. Probably caused by two sheets of paper, one extending below the other so that the bottom row of one impression appeared on the second sheet. This was turned over and used, the sheet with only 190 impressions probably being destroyed. That other "printed on both sides" sheets occurred can be concluded from the existence of used examples of this variety. *It should be observed that the true "printed on both sides" shows the design reading normally on both impressions, and not in reverse as the case with "offsets"*[16].

11. Appendix H #119, 120; J #5.
12. American Journal of Philately Aug. 20, 1869.
13. Appendix J #5.
14. See Chapter XI Page 245 for details of the two 6c Large Queen plates.
15. Records dated 1886.
16. "Double offsets" are known which are sometimes confused with "printed on both sides," but they lack the characteristics of the actual variety under discussion.

Fig. 4. 1c Yellow. Printed on Both Sides. This Is the Back Impression. Note That It Is the Bottom Row of the Sheet.

Double Prints, "Kisses", Etc.

These varieties, while interesting are not of the same significance as the "printed on both sides." A true double print is one which has passed through the press twice. We are doubtful that any such variety actually exists, as they should be more frequent than they really are. "Kisses" are those impressions, apparently double prints, which are caused by the sheet falling back on the plate when being removed, or by similar causes.

We illustrate two exceptionally fine examples of these "kisses." (Fig. 5). While very rare when showing so clearly, they are freaks, and do not contribute much to our knowledge of the plate and its characteristics. The 6c Large Queen is also known showing fine examples of "kisses".

Slight doublings usually blurred, caused by inexpert removal of the printed sheet from the plate, or creep of the paper under pressure, vagaries of ink, and paper damping should not be confused with re-entries which are constant, and in proper impressions clearly defined.

Shades

While there are distinct shades of these stamps, some quite characteristic, the attempt to differentiate slight differences as "printings", etc., is likely to cause more confusion than to help solve the various problems surrounding these issues.

Perusal of Section II-A, on Printing in "Fundamental Information for Collectors of Canada", (Page xxiv) should be sufficient to convince collectors that variations in shades are bound to occur with comparative ease and frequency, and furthermore that the variations may be due to trivial causes. The illustration of the pages from the color mixers book giving the recipe for various colors is still further evidence of the complexity of the inks involved. The chances of variations in the ingredients was prevalent, and these variations would affect the final result in printing. In addition the passing years are bound to change the shades of stamps to some extent.

Perforation Varieties

As noted, three guages of perforation are well known, 12x12, 11½x12, 12½ x 12½. The only other varieties are errors, such as imperforate rows, resulting in imperforate between pairs, and double perforations. The latter are freaks and of minor interest. We have seen the following:

Fig. 5. Two Excellent Examples of a "Kiss" or Slip print. NOT a Double Print or Re-entry

½c, 1c, 2c, 5c, and 6c double vertically and the 3c double horizontally, all Small Queens. Other varieties undoubtedly exist.

In the Ottawa printings of 1888-97 a 12 x 12¼ perforation is well known. Since they only occur on the second Ottawa printings no confusion can exist between these and the rare 12½ x 12½ perforation of 1870.

Other Varieties Which Frequently Are the Causes of Erroneous Classification

"Ribbed" Printing Caused by Worn Blankets. NOT Ribbed Paper, or Laid Paper.

Dry Printing NOT a Worn Plate.

Similar Variety to Dry Paper, and/or Poor Mixing of Ink. NOT Worn Plate, or a Faded Stamp.

Partial Impressions Caused by Scraps of Paper Accidentially Left, on Plate, or By Sheet Corner Folding Over.

Chapter XI

THE LARGE QUEEN DESIGNS
Issued April 1, 1868

(Commonly called the "Large Queens" or "Large Cents")

As announced in "Department Order No. 2" of March 1, 1868, the long expected new series of seven denominations was placed on sale at all post offices in the Dominion April 1, 1868[1]. From that date onward no other stamps were to be sold by the postmasters[2], although provincial issues remaining in the hands of the public were to be accepted in payment of postage[3].

Provincial stamps still on hand in the post offices, however, were turned in to be destroyed[4].

The commencement of the operation of the Dominion Post Office (April 1, 1868) was also the date for the general reduction of postage rates, as enacted by Parliament in the Post Office Act of 1867[5]. The reduction applied particularly to letters which were now three cents per half ounce if *paid,* and five cents if *unpaid.*

---

[1] Though copies of these stamps dated in March, 1868, are known, they are merely examples sold prior to the official date of issue through carelessness or ignorance on the part of some postmasters, or failure to change the date stamp.
[2] Appendix B #30.
[3] Appendix B #40.
[4] Appendix B #40—Page 201.
[5] Appendix A #11—Paragraph 19.

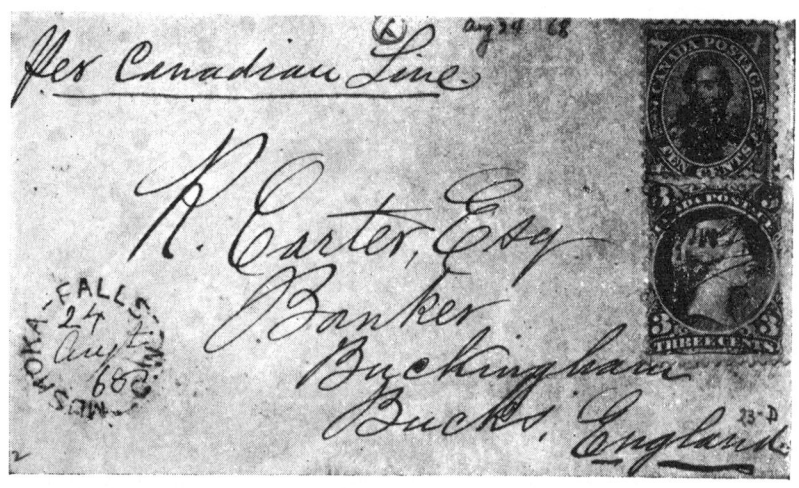

Fig. 1. 10c 1859 (perf. 12x12) with 3c Large Queen, from "Muskoka Falls, C.W." August 24, 1868, to England. A rare combination.

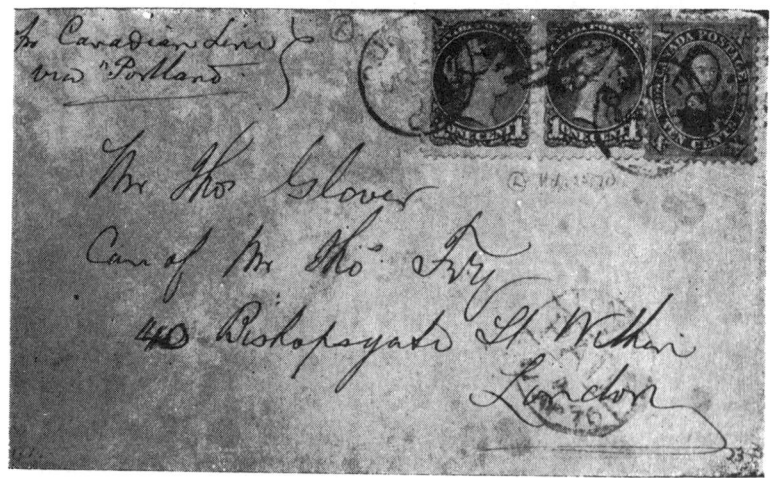

Fig. 2. 10c 1859 (perf. 12x12) with a pair of 1c Small Queens, used from Quebec to London, Eng., March 25, 1870. A rare combination.

Fig. 3.
Nova Scotia 5c, 1860, with 1c and 2c Large Queen paying rate to California, Dec. 14, 1868. (Overpayment of 2c).

We tabulate below the chief rates and the denominations of the stamps for such rates:

Postage Rates of 1868

Denomination	Class	To ——
Half Cent	Periodicals weighing less than 1 oz. per number.	Any place in the Dominion, P. E. I., Newfoundland, or the United States.
One Cent	Circulars, pamphlets, books, etc., per oz.	
Two Cents	Transient newspapers[6].	
Three Cents	Letters, per ½ oz.	Any place in the Dominion or P. E. I.
Six Cents	Letters, per ½ oz.	Any place in the United States or Red River.
Twelve & One Half Cents	Letters by Canadian Packets per ½ oz. Parcel post per 8 oz.	The United Kingdom or Newfoundland. In the Dominion.
Fifteen Cents	Letters by British Packets, via New York per ½ oz. (until 1875).	The United Kingdom.
Five Cents	Letters by any packet per ½ oz. (from 1875).	The United Kingdom.

A FIVE CENTS was engraved in 1867[7], but no plate was laid down until 1875 when the reduced rate to the United Kingdom made it necessary to hastily prepare and issue this denomination pending the engraving and printing of a new small size stamp conforming with those in use at that time.

---

6 A transient newspaper is one that is mailed by one person to another, and not mailed by a publisher to a subscriber.
7 A. J. of P. Vol. I. June 1, 1868, describes design of die proof.

Essays

Fig. 4 Essay for 1868 issue by National Bank Note Co. Frame by Douglas S. Ronaldson. Vignette by Alfred Jones. Note similarity of vignette to 8c Small Queen. Also note Liberty Head design essayed for United States.

The only essay which we can definitely attribute to this issue was submitted by the National Bank Note Co., New York, in 1867.

Typographed on Thin Card (Fig. 4)

E22a 3c pale rose pink.
b 3c dark rose pink. } Scarce
c 3c yellow green.
d 3c blue green.

Designed by Joseph C. Lindsley, vignette engraved by Alfred Jones, lettering by D. S. Ronaldson[10]. See Page 300 for the large "head to left" essays formerly attributed to this issue.

We also list herewith the Bradbury, Wilkinson Essays, heretofore believed to be essays for the 1851 issue. They are attributed to Canada, but there is no indication of country, although the head is similar to that on the Large Queens. We incline to the belief that the design was submitted by Bradbury, Wilkinson & Co. in 1867 shortly after the formation of the Dominion, and while the design was pleasing it was the desire and intention of the government to have the stamps made in Canada. It is quite possible that the British American Bank Note Co. was requested to adapt this design, which they did, with modifications.

---

[10] See page 60 #85 E-Gc in "Essays for U. S. Adhesive Postage Stamps," by Clarence W. Brazer, Handbook Committee American Philatelic Society, 1941.

Essay E18a-c.

TENTATIVE LISTING

1867(?) Essays by Bradbury, Wilkinson & Co., London.

PLATE PROOFS (Rare)

E18a 1d black on card. (.008" thick).
    b 1d brown on stout wove. (.004 thick).
    c 1d red violet on stout wove.
    d 1d red on stout wove.
    e 1d green on stout wove.

Proofs

Fig. 5. Die Proof of ½c Black.

REFERENCE LIST
DIE AND PLATE PROOFS. 1868 (Large Queen Issue)

		DIE D. On India	P. On Card	PLATE G. Glazed Wove*	F. Perf'd & Gummed	N. India	Notes
P18	(a) ½c black	30.00	15.00				
	(b) green	30.00	15.00	x			
	(c) dull red		15.00			x	
P19	(a) 1c black		15.00				
	(b) dull red		15.00				
	(c) brown		15.00				
	(d) blue		15.00				
	(e) green		15.00		x	x	
P21	(a) 2c black		15.00			x	
	(b) green		15.00				
	(c) dull red		15.00				
P22	(a) 3c black		15.00				
	(b) green		15.00	x			
	(c) dull red		15.00	x			
	(d) lilac		15.00			x	
P23	(a) 5c black		15.00				
	(b) green		15.00				
	(c) olive green		15.00				
	(d) dull red	30.00	15.00	x			
	(e) rose		15.00			x	
	(f) blue		15.00			x	
	(g) dull or'n red		15.00				
P24	(a) 6c black		15.00				
	(b) black brown		15.00				Pl. I.
	(c) green		15.00				
	(d) dull red		15.00				
	(e) vermilion		15.00				
P26	(a) 12½c black		15.00				
	(b) green		15.00				
	(c) dull red	x	15.00	x		x	
	(d) blue		15.00				
	(e) rose		15.00				
P27	(a) 15c black	30.00	15.00				
	(b) green		15.00				
	(c) dull red		15.00				
	(d) deep lilac		15.00			x	

NOTES

*The glazed wove has a yellowish coating on the surface of the paper. They are very scarce.

The die proofs are usually cut down but when they have full margins there is a two line imprint, "British American Bank Note Co.—Montreal & Ottawa" below the design.

We are of the opinion that plate proofs on card of any of the above in other than color of issue are cut from the large advertising sheet shown on page 223 Multiples of any of the proofs are rare and blocks exceedingly so.

Beware of bicolor proofs of the 3c cut from advertising sheets. Page 225. They are of minor interest, and worth only a fraction of the prices that regluar proofs are.

The Plates

The plates were of unhardened steel and consisted of one hundred subjects $(10 \times 10)^8$, with the imprint centrally located on each margin. In addition the half cent, one plate at least of the three cents, the five cents, Plate I of the six cents and the twelve and one-half cents has the denomination in serifed captials four millimeters high above the first and second stamps of the sheet (Fig. 9, 15).

---
8 Appendix Q #4.

Fig. 6. 1c Showing Type III Imprint.   Fig. 7. 3c Showing Type III Imprint.

Fig. 8. 15c Top Block Showing Type IV Imprint.

Fig. 9. Plate I. Top Marginal Copy Showing Traces of Denomination in Words Above, Known as "Counters".

Fig. 14. 5c Mint Block of Eight Showing Imprint Type V.

Fig. 12. Plate I. Position Dot at Extreme Lower Left Corner.   Fig. 13. Plate II. Position Dot Below "S" of "SIX"

There are two types of imprint, both of which read "British American Bank Note Co., Montreal & Ottawa."

Imprint Type III: British American BANK NOTE Co., Montreal & Ottawa[8]. 50 x 1¾mm. (Fig. 6, 7). Known on 1c, 2c, 3c, and 6c.

Imprint Type IV: "British American Bank Note Co., Montreal & Ottawa. 53 x 1¼mm. (Fig. 8). ½c, 3c, 6c, 12½c, 15c.

The imprints are located on all values as follows:—

Above	Opposite	Opposite	Below
#4, #5, #6, #7	#51, #61	#50, #60	#94, #95, #96, #97
Normal	Reading Up	Reading Down	Normal

No positive evidence has been shown to indicate more than one plate was made for each denomination, except the three cents, and six cents. Single copies of the six cents may be identified as follows:

PLATE I. Position dot at extreme lower left, below foliate ornament (Fig. 12). Imprint III.
PLATE II. Position dot below "S" of "SIX" (Fig. 13). (Imprint IV[9].)

The two three-cent plates can be identified only by the imprints.

The FIVE CENTS plate made in 1875 has the imprint type V located as shown. (Fig. 14).

The HALF CENT is 17 x 21mm., while the other denominations are 20 x 24mm. Slight variations due to contraction and expansion of the paper are known. The workmanship on the plates is of the highest standard, and as with previous issues the method of guide lines and dots was used in laying them down. The guide dot is usually quite visible at the lower left corner of the stamp, but does not occur on the left vertical row.

The horizontal and vertical guide lines were usually burnished off, but evidences are particularly strong on the two cents plate, and traces may be found on the other denominations, notably the twelve and one-half cents.

---

[8] Although the imprint reads "Montreal & Ottawa" the Large Queens were printed only in Ottawa, until 1875. We have a similar instance in the 1851-57 issue of United States where the imprint reads "Toppan, Carpenter, Casilear & Co. (or without Casilear after 1854), Bank Note Engravers, Phila., New York, Boston & Cincinnati." but the stamps were produced only in Philadelphia.

[9] Plate II has been noted in May 1869, and the first plate may have been damaged, a second plate being made, to supply the demand for this value until the damaged plate was repaired.

Fig. 15. Top Marginal Copy Showing Portion of Denomination in Large Shaded Letters, Known as "Counters."

Fine Mint Block.

Fig. 16. Imperforate Pair.

Re-Entries

Fig. 17. Re-entry on the 2c. Note Doubling in "ANADA POS."

These are singularly absent, the only one warranting listing being on the two cents (Fig. 9). This shows strongly in the word "CANADA"[8a], and occurs in all printings.

Other Varieties

Late printings of the 15c show three small dots at the upper right of the right "15", on #10 of the plate. (Fig. 19).

8a We have seen this re-entry as the fourth stamp in a block of ten (5 x 2). It therefore is not in the first three vertical, the right vertical or the bottom horizontal row of the sheet.

Fig. 18. 12½c Blue. Very Fine Used Block of Eight.

Fig. 19. 15c. #10 on Plate Showing Variety—Three Dots at Right by "15". This Also Occurs on the Imperforates, and the Damage Probably Took Place About 1892.

Fig. 20. Mint Block of Twenty (5x4) of the 1c Red on Thick Paper (Paper B).

Fig. 21. 2c 1868. Mint Block on Thin Semi-Transparent Paper. (Paper A).

The Paper

This phase of the Large Queens has been the subject of much study, and we are fully aware that our conclusions may run somewhat counter to those of other students. We are of the opinion that the matter of paper varieties has been overdone, as was the case with the wove papers of the Pence stamps.

Examination of several thousand specimens of this issue, including several hundred with watermarks, and some half dozen copies of the fifteen cents, script watermark, as well as a careful study of all available literature has led us to make the following classification of papers (arranged in order of earliest occurrence):

Date	Type	Characteristics	Values	Other Students.
A. 1868-69	Wove	Thin to medium (.0031" to .0038") crisp porous, semi-transparent, showing faint horizontal or vertical mesh. (Fig. 22).	All except 1c yellow and 5c	Pack's A Studd's A, A^1, A^2
B. 1868-80	Wove	Medium to thick[9] (.0032" to .0040") white or yellowish sometimes soft, faint to distinct horizontal mesh. (Fig. 23).	All	Pack's B, C, D, E, F, I. Studd's B, C, E, F, H, X
C. 1868-69	Wove	Medium to thick (.0032" to .0041") with a distinct vertical mesh, and WATERMARKED "E & G BOTHWELL CLUTHA MILLS" in two lines of sans-serif letters (Fig. 24, 28).	All except 1c yellow or orange and 5c (½c?)	Pack's J, W, P.W. Studd's J, W, P.W.

NOTE: The vertical mesh, and opaqueness of this paper are characteristic. The mesh is sometimes so strong as to impart a vertical "ribbing" to the paper.

Date	Type	Characteristics	Values	Other Students.
D. 1868	Laid	Thin to medium horizontally laid (.0025" to .003"). (Fig. 25).	1c red 3c. (2c?)	Pack's K, L
E. 1873-97	Wove	Medium to thick (.0033" to .0038") poor quality grayish, faint to strong horizontal mesh, or sometimes showing distinct quadrille ribbing.	½c 5c 15c	Pack's G Studd's G, Y, Z, Z^1
F. 1876-77	Wove	Medium (.0035") white with horizontal mesh, WATERMARKED "Alexr. Pirie & Sons" in one line of script letters (Fig. 26, 27, 29).	15c	
G. 1880 (?)	Wove	Very thick (.0040") white with a pebbly grain. Commonly called "carton paper."	15c	Pack's H Studd's H, H^1

All of these papers are machine made of rag stock. See Appendix P #15, 16.

We are of the opinion that most of the paper was made by E. & C. Bothwell, or Alexander Pirie & Sons.

---

[9] The so-called "ordinary" wove paper.

PAPER A.
Fig. 22. The Thin Semi-Transparent Paper.

PAPER B.
Fig. 23. The Medium to Thick Ordinary Paper.

PAPER D.
Fig. 25. The Laid Paper.

PAPER C.
Fig. 24. "The E. & G. Bothwell, Clutha Mills" Paper.
NOTE " G E " of Watermark and Vertical Mesh).

Fig. 26. Two copies of the 15c, Each with Script Watermark. One Perforated 12, the Other 11½ x 12

Fig. 27. The "Alexander Pirie & Co." Script Watermark Paper.

Fig. 28. Magnificent Unused Block of Twenty (10x2) of the 2c Showing the "E. & G. Bothwell, Clutha Mills" Watermark. Courtesy of Godden's Gazette.

Fig. 29. The Script Watermark in Full (Actual Size). Courtesy of the London Philatelist.

The Perforations

Generally speaking these stamps were perforated on machines similar to those used for the 1859 issue, the wheels giving a perforation gauging between 11¾ and 12. The 1c, 2c, 3c, 6c and 12½c were only perforated thus. The later printings of the ½c and 15c, and all the 5c, however, were perforated on two machines, one gauging 11½, the other 12 (11¼-11½ x 11¾-12). It is always 11½ x 12, never 12 x 11½.
    Perforation 1—12 x 12. 1868-97. All except 5c.
    Perforation 2—11½ x 12. 1873-78, ½c, 5c, 15c only.
    NOTE: Only the ½c and 15c exist with both perforations.

Fig. 30. 12½c. Pair Watermarked "MILL" (Paper C). Right Stamp Showing Left Frame Line of "12½" missing, Indicating that the Variety is #67 on the Sheet.

Fig. 31. Shows Typical Position Dots at U.L., U.R. and L.L. on Clearly Printed Copies.

The Gum

Four types of gum are known, as follows:

Type	Date	Characteristics	Values
V	1868 to Middle 1873	Thin, smooth, white to yellowish.	All but 5c
W	Middle 1873 to 1878	Streaky, brownish.	½c, 5c, 15c
Y	1878-1888	Very smooth, shiny yellowish.	½c, 15c
Z	1888-1897	Smooth, thick brownish.	15c

Gum W gives the appearance of a typically hand gummed operation; done with a brush. Gum W usually indicates perforation No. 2 (11½x12).

See Small Queen section for Gums Y and Z.

Fig. 32. The Smooth Gum. Gum V.

Fig. 33. The Streaky Brownish Gum. Gum W.

Table of 1868 Issue Arranged by Paper, Perforation and Gum

Date	Paper	Perforation	Gum	Values
1868-69	A	12 x 12	V	All but 1c yellow, and 5c.
1868-80	B	12 x 12	V	All but 5c.
	B	11½ x 12	V	½c, 5c, 15c
1868-69	C	12 x 12	V	All except 1c yellow or orange, or 5c. (½c ?).
1868	D	12 x 12	V	1c red, 3c.
1873-97	E	12 x 12	W	½c, 15c.
	E	11½ x 12	W	½c, 5c, 15c.
	E	12 x 12	Y	½c, 15c.
	E	12 x 12	Z	15c
1876-77	F	12 x 12	W	15c
	F	11½ x 12	W	15c
1880	G	12 x 12	Y	15c

Table of 1868 Issue Arranged by Denominations

	Papers	Perfs	Gums
½c black	A, B, E	1, 2	V, W, Y
1c red	A, B, C, D	1	V
1c yellow	B	1	V
2c green	A, B, C	1	V
3c red	A, B, C, D	1	V
6c brown	A, B, C	1	V
12½c blue	A, B, C	1	V
15c violet to gray	A, B, C, E, F, G	1, 2	V, W, Y, Z
5c Green	B, E	2	W

Sets To Make Complete Showing of This Issue

SET 1. ½c, 1c red, 2c, 3c, 6c, 12½c, 15c—paper A, perf. 1, gum V.
SET 2. ½c, 1c red, 1c yellow, 2c, 3c, 6c, 12½c, 15c—paper B, perf. 1, gum V.
SET 3. 1c red, 2c, 3c, 6c, 12½c, 15c—paper C, perf. 1, gum V.
SET 4. 1c red, 3c red—paper D, perf. 1, gum V.
SET 5. ½c, 15c—paper E, perf. 1, gum V.
SET 6. ½c, 5c, 15c—paper E, perf. 2, gum W.
SET 7. ½c, 15c—paper E, perf. 1, gum Y.

Single stamps:—
    5c—paper B, perf. 2, gum W.
    15c—paper F, perf. 1, gum W.
    15c—paper F, perf. 2, gum W.
    15c—paper G, perf. 1, gum Y.

A complete showing of the above will require considerable hunting, and a deep purse.

The change in the color of the 1c was to avoid confusion with the 3c, especially under artificial light; candle, oil lamp or gas.

Bisects

Although it was against the regulations to bisect stamps the practice persisted especially in the provinces of New Brunswick and Nova Scotia where it had been the habit to divide stamps and use them for a proportionate fraction of their value.

Of the Large Queens the 2c and 6c are well known bisected. The 2c cut diagonally in pair with 2c making 3c rate, and the 6c cut in half diagonally or vertically for the 3c rate are the usual bisections. All of these items shou'd be accepted only from reliable sources as there are some rather well done fakes in existence.

We have noted the following bisects of this issue:
(All diagonal unless noted otherwise)

2c. Left half cut U.R. to L.L. Annapolis, N. S. to Plainfield, N. S., Aug. 1, 1870.

2c. Left half U.L. to L.R. Bridgetown, N. S. to Lower Granville, N. S., Aug. 16, 1872.

Both with another 2c to make 3c rate.

6c. Right half, cut U.L. to L.R. Annapolis to Yarmouth, Apr. 7, 1869.

6c. Right half cut U.R. to L.L. Annapolis, N. S. to Bridgetown, N. S., July 1, 1869.

6c. Left half cut U.R. to L.L. Clementsport, N. S. to Bridgeport, N. S., Dec 8, 1870.

6c. Right half cut U.L. to L.R. Wilmot, N. S. to Clementsport, N. S., Mar. 17, 1870.

6c. Right half cut U.R. to L.L. Annapolis, N. S. to Clementsport, N. S. July 5, 1869.

6c. Left half cut L.R. to L.L. Eglington, U. C., Fe. 1, 1869 to Toronto, C. W. (Plate I). (Fig. 34).

6c. Right *vertical half*. Annapolis, N. S. to Bridgetown, N. S., Aug. 17, 1870.

6c. Left *vertical* half tied by Halifax & Annapolis Railway Cancellation to cover, September 3, 1870. (Fig. 35).

Fig. 34. 6c Plate I From Eglington, U. C. Fe 1, 1869 to Toronto.

Fig. 35. Left Vertical Half Tied by Halifax & Annapolis Ry. Cancellation, Sept. 3, 1870.
(Lot 165, Pack Sale, Dec. 6, 1944)

Counterfeits

We have seen only one counterfeit of these stamps. This is a crudely lithographed label with perforations in no way resembling the genuine. Produced in Germany in the 1880's, by Spiro Bros.

Fig. 36. Lithographed Counterfeit of the 2c 1868, with Bogus Cancellation, by Spiro Bros., of Hamburg, Germany.

1868 Large Queen Issue of April 1, 1868

#	Denom. & Color	A. Thin Semi-Transparent		B. Ordinary wove				C. Block Watermark		D. Laid		Quantity	1944 S. #	1944 S.G. #
				Perf. 12 x 12		Perf. 11½ x 12								
		unused	used	unused	used	unused	used	unused	used	unused	used			
18	½c Black	2½	2	½	½				?			6,500,000	21	54
	Gray black			N	N									
a	Horiz. pair imperf. between.													
	Strip of four	10	15	x	10	2	12							
	Block of four	15		5		2	1½							
	Cover	—	4	7	3		1½							
				—										
19	1c Brick red			N	N			8	4	70	40	Appendix J #5.	22	55
	Red brown	2	1½	4	3½									
	Pair	5	5	6	8				R					
	Strip of three	10	12	10	25									
	Block of four	25		—	3					—	60			
	Cover	—	5											
20	1c Orange	Jan 1869		2	1½							Appendix J #5.	32	76
	Yellow orange	Apr. '69		1½	1¼									
	Yellow			N	N									
a	Imperforate													
	Pair	—		3	3									
	Strip of three	—		8	7									
	Block of four	—		RR	60									
	Cover	—		—	5									
21	2c Deep green	1½	1½	N	N							10,500,000	23	56
	Blue green	May '68		1½	1¼			7	7		?			
	Pale green	Oct. '68		1¼	1¼									
	Emerald green	187-		4	2									
a	Re-entry 1868			x	x									
	Pair	5	4	4	3									
	Strip of three	10	8	9	7									
	Block of four	x	x	14	15			RR	30					
	Cover	—	8	—	5			—						

Note: Stamps on paper C, not showing watermark are worth 33 1/3% of the factors given.

1868 Large Queen Issue of April 1, 1868 (Continued)

#	Denom. & Color	A. Thin Semi-Transparent		B. Ordinary wove				C. Block Watermark		D. Laid		Quantity	1944 S.#	1944 S.G. #
				Perf. 12 x 12		Perf. 11½ x 12								
		unused	used	unused	used	unused	used	unused	used	unused	used			
22	3c Brown red Rose red · 1868 Dull red · 1869 Pair Block of four Cover	1½ — —	3 8 —	2 2 N —	2 2 N 5 35 5	— — — —	— — — —	x — —	10 35 —	30 — —	25 100 100 —	29,300,000	24	58
23 a	5c Olive green Imperforate Block of four Cover	— — —	— — —	— — —	— — —	N R R —	N — — 6	— — —	— — —	— — —	— — —	Issued Oct. 1, '75 1,000,000	42	70
24	5c Deep brown Chocolate Sepia Pair Block of four 4½ as 3c Cover	1¾ — — — — —	2 — — — — 5	2 1½ 5 10 — —	2 2 1½ 4 x x 4	— — — — — —	— — — — — —	x — — — — —	35 — — — — —	— — — — — —	— — — — — —	Plate I Plate I, II Plate I, II	25	59
25	6c Yellow brown Light brown Pair Block of four 4½ as 3c Cover	—	—	N 1½ 3 8 — —	N 1½ 4 x x 4	—	—	—	—	—	—	Plate I, II Plate II Total 10,000,000	25	59
26 a	12½c Bright blue Blue Dull blue Value tablet frame missing Pair Block of four Cover	1½ — 1¼ — —	1¼ — — — 9	N N 1¼ x —	N N N 5 3½ x 7	—	—	11 — —	8 — x	—	—	1,900,000	26	61

Note: Stamps on paper C, not showing the watermark are worth approximately 33 1/3% of the factors given.

The 15c Large Queen. 1868-97.

#	Denomination	A.Thin 1868-69	B. Ordinary 1868-80 P 12x12	B. Ordinary 1868-80 11½x12	C.Block Wmk. 1868-69	E. Grayish woove 1875-97 12 x 12	E. Grayish woove 1875-97 11½x12	F. Script Wmk. 1876-77 12x12	F. Script Wmk. 1876-77 11½x12	G.¹ 1880	Date	Notes	1944 S.#	1944 S.G.#
27a	15c Purple	20 4	4 2	3 1½							1868	Gum V	27	63
b	Reddish pur.		3 1½								1868	V		
											1874			
c	Gray purple		3 1½	x	xR 20		x				Jun. 1868	V		
											Aug. 1874	W		
d	Lilac purple		N N			x					Jan. 1869	V		
e	Slate purple						x				1888-90	Z		
	Pair	8	3	6	4½									
	Strip of three	15	6											
	Block of four	60	15											
	Cover	8	4		x		x							
28a	15c Violet													
b	Gray violet		4	3	6 4	x	xx	30 50	R		Dec. 1874	W		
											Jan. 1880	Y		
c	Deep violet		x x			x	x				1880. '81	Y		
d	Slate violet					x	x					Z		
	Pair		8	6							1888-1890			
	Strip of three		16	12										
	Block of four		60	45										
	Cover			10	x		x		x					

¹ "Carton" paper.
Note: Stamps on Paper C, not showing the watermark are worth approximately 25% of the factor given.
Factors for multiples and covers are for normal shade.
First figure for unused second for used, in each column.

264

The 15c Large Queen. 1868-97.

#	Denomination	A. Thin 1868-69	B. Ordinary 1868-80 P 12x12	B. Ordinary 1868-80 11½x12	C.Block Wmk. 1868-69	E. Grayish wove 1875-97 12x12	E. Grayish wove 1875-97 11½x12	F. Script Wmk. 1876-77 12x12	F. Script Wmk. 1876-77 11½x12	G.¹ 1880	Date	Notes	1944 S.#	1944 S.G.#
29a	15c Gray	—	x	x	—	N	N	—	2	—	Jan. 1876	Gum	28	67
b	Olive gray	—	x	x	—	N	N	—	3	—	Aug. 1877	W		
c	Br'wnish gray	—	x	x	—	N	N	—	1¼	—		W		
d	Gr'nish gray	—	x	x	—	N	N	—	1½	—	Jul 1878	W		
e	Lilac gray	—	x	9	—	N	N	—	2	—		Y		
f	Slate gray	—	x	4	—	N	N	—	—	—	1880-1888	Y		
	Pair	—	x	—	—	3	3	—	5	—		Z		
	Strip of three	—	—	—	—	6	6	—	10	—				
	Block of four	—	—	—	—	15	15	—	16	—				
	Cover	—	—	—	—	—	—	—	6	—				
30a	15c Blue slate	—	—	—	—	3	2	—	—	10 x	1880-90	Y		
	Pair	—	—	—	—	7	4	—	—	—		Z		
	Strip of three	—	—	—	—	5	9	—	—	—				
	Block of four	—	—	—	—	40	22	—	—	—				
	Cover	—	—	—	—	—	4	—	—	—				
31a	15c Deep brown purple	Imperforate	—	—	—	6	—	—	—	—	1893			
	Pair		—	—	—	15	—	—	—	—				
	Block of four		—	—	—	35	—	—	—	—				

¹ "Carton" paper.

Total number issued 2,546,900, which can be divided approximately as follows: Paper A—100,000; Paper B, C—500,000; Paper E, F, G—1,946,900, of which over 90% are on Paper E. Stitch watermark has been noted on the gray violet.

Fig. 1.
The Earl of Dufferin, Governor General of Canada 1872-78. Vignette Engraved About 1877 by B. A. B. N. Co. From Die Proof in Black on India.

Chapter XII

THE SMALL QUEEN DESIGNS OF 1870-93

(Commonly called the "Small Queens" or "Small Cents")

The handsome designs of the Large Queen's head began to be superseded by similar but smaller designs in January, 1870. There was no official notification of the new design, but it was decided upon about a year after the issue of the 1868 series as is evident from the fact that the stamp magazines of the day were anticipating the change in August, 1869[1], and we quote: "Canada is shortly to have a new set of stamps. It seems they are about to alter their stamps to make them smaller, so as to save paper. The head will still remain exactly the same as now, but the frame and margin around the head will be considerably less."[2]

This forecast proved to be substantially correct, although the head is also reduced in size and the reason for the change was not correctly divined.

As shown in Chapter X the reason for the reduction in size was primarily the practical problem of more stamps, more quickly, and at little extra expense.

We know that orders for the small 1c and 3c were made on December 17, 1869[3], and the reputed date of issue of the 3c is January 12, 1870[4].

The new designs were all of the same size, that is 17 x 21mm. the same as the half cent of 1868. In 1882 the diminutive half cent appeared which measures 15 x 18¼mm. The supplementary values of 1893 were somewhat larger, being adapted from the Bill stamps of 1868.

These small designs were in use for a period of over twenty-five years, during which time there were many changes of shades, plates, and papers. We have therefore divided these issues as follows:

A. FIRST OTTAWA PRINTINGS. 1870-1874.

    1c, 2c, 3c, 6c. Four denominations.
    Also the 1c Post Card.

B. MONTREAL PRINTINGS. 1874-87.

    ½c, 1c, 2c, 3c, 5c, 6c, 10c. Seven denominations.
    Also 2c, 5c, 8c Registered Letter Stamps, Official Seal, 1c and 3c Envelopes, 1c Wrappers, 1c and 2c U. K. and 2c U.P.U. Cards.

C. SECOND OTTAWA PRINTINGS. 1888-97.

    ½c, 1c, 2c, 3c, 5c, 6c, 8c, 10c, 20c and 50c. Ten denominations. Also 2c and 5c Registered Letter Stamps, 1c,, 2c, 3c Envelopes, 1c Postal Bands, 1c, 2c Post Cards.[5]

---

1. American Journal of Philately, Vol. II, August 20, 1869.
2. See Chapter VII, page 110. Alfred Jones, secretary of the British American Bank Note Co., was also a stockholder and engraver for the National Bank Note Co., at that time, which firm produced the 1869 issue, of the United States.
3. Appendix J #5.
4. We have examined a 3c dated Jan. 15, 1870, another Jan. 18, 1870, and a pair on cover dated Jan. 25, 1870.
5. The Officially Sealed label was also probably printed during the period 1888-97, but from the Montreal plate.

Fig. 2.
Enlarged Engravers Progress Proof of Vignette for Small Queens Head Issue Showing Traces of Upper Panel in Which "CANADA POSTAGE" Will be Engraved, and Ruled Lines Bounding Proposed Stamp. (#Ea28a).

Essays

Essays are known for the ½c, 1c, 12½c, and 15c, and plates were made for the 1c at least, (Figs. 3-6), but no stamps of 12½c or 15c were ever issued in the small designs.

Fig. 3. Die Proof of Essay for ½c, #E38.

Fig. 4. Finished Proof of 1c Essay E28

Fig. 5. Die Proof of Small 12½c, Essay #E26.

Fig. 6. Die Proof of Small 15c, Essay #E27.

1870-97. Essays for Small Queen Designs

(All are rare)

			D Die Proof On India	P P'ate Proof on India	F Finished Proof*
Ea28a		black, vignette only (Fig. 1).	x	Progress die proof (unique?)	
E38	(a)	½c light brown	x		
E28	(a)	1c yellow	x		x
E26	(a)	12½c dull rose	x		
	(c)	bright blue		x	x
E27	(a)	15c black	x		
	(b)	blue	x		

*Gummed and perforated.

Proofs of Issued Designs. 1870-97.

		Die D. India	Plate Proof P Card	C Thin Wove	Notes
P38	(a) ½c black		60.00		"Montreal" plate.
P28	(a) 1c black	x	60.00		"Montreal" plate.
	(b) yellow		60.00		
	(c) orange		60.00		
	(d) green		60.00		
	(e) dull red		60.00		
	(f) blue		60.00	x	
P29	(a) 2c green		60.00		
P30	(a) 3c vermilion		60.00		
	(b) blue green			x	
P35	(a) 5c olive		60.00		"Montreal" Plate
	(b) blue			x	
P31	(a) 6c yellow brown	x	60.00		
	(b) blue			x	
P47	(a) 8c blue gray	x	60.00		
	(b) smoky yellow	x			
P37	(a) 10c pale lilac		60.00		
P48	(a) 20c vermilion		60.00		
P49	(a) 50c blue black	x	60.00		

NOTE: We believe the 1c card plate proofs in black, green and dull red are from the advertising sheet illustrated on page 223. Blocks of any of these proofs except the 20c, and 50c are very scarce. There are no doubt proofs in other colors, etc., which should be recorded.

Fig. 7. Enlargement of 1c Die Proof in Black.

A. THE FIRST OTTAWA PRINTINGS—1870-74

The stamps of this group appeared as follows:

1c March 1870	3c January 1870
2c February 1872	6c January 1872[6]

The Plates

Fig. 8. Type III Imprint. 1870.   Fig. 8. Type IV Imprint. 1870-74.

The plates were of *unhardened* steel and consisted of two hundred subjects (10 x 10 + 10 x 10) arranged in two panes of 100, separated by a vertical gutter 15-17 mm. wide between the panes. The imprints were type III and IV on the 3c, and type IV only on the 1c, 2c, and 6c. The denomination was also expressed in words over the 1st, 2nd, and 3rd stamps of the left pane, and the 8th, 9th, and 10th stamps of the right pane. These indications of denomination are known as "counters".

The usual method of guide lines and position dots was used, and the position dot is usually discernable at the lower left corner of all stamps except those from the extreme left vertical row of the sheet. The production of these plates was so excellent that there are few if any plate varieties worthy of listing. We are also of the opinion that only one plate was necessary for the 1c, 2c, and 6c, while for the 3c we know that at least two plates were made[7].

Re-Entries

The only notable re-entry on these plates occurs on the 6c, which shows evidence of re-entry throughout the entire design, but particularly in "Canada Postage" and below the lower edge (Fig. 11).

This re-entry probably occured during the making of the plate; there is evidence that it was burnished out and a fresh entry made late in 1874. This variety has been noted only in yellow brown.

---
6. We have been unable to find any definite evidence that the 10c was printed in Ottawa previous to 1888.
7. The 3c exists with two imprints. Appendix J #5 shows approximate quantities printed. See notes also to that table.

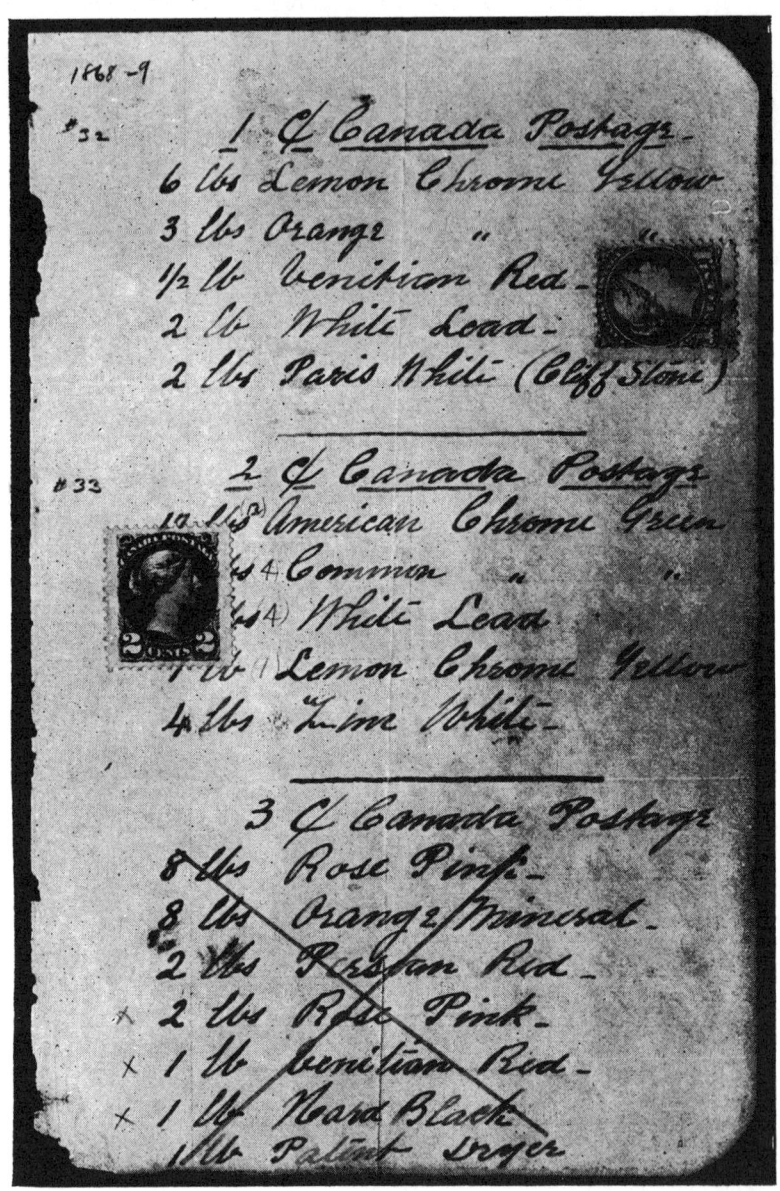

Fig. 10a.

Page from the recipe book for mixing the inks used for printing the Large and Small Queens. Since there is no 5c or 10c recipe given it must be before 1875, and the last 12½c deliveries were made in 1871. The stamps may have been affixed later, so they are not reliable aids in dating these pages. Since the 1c yellow recipe is given, and a revised 3c recipe shows, we are of the opinion that these pages were used about 1869.

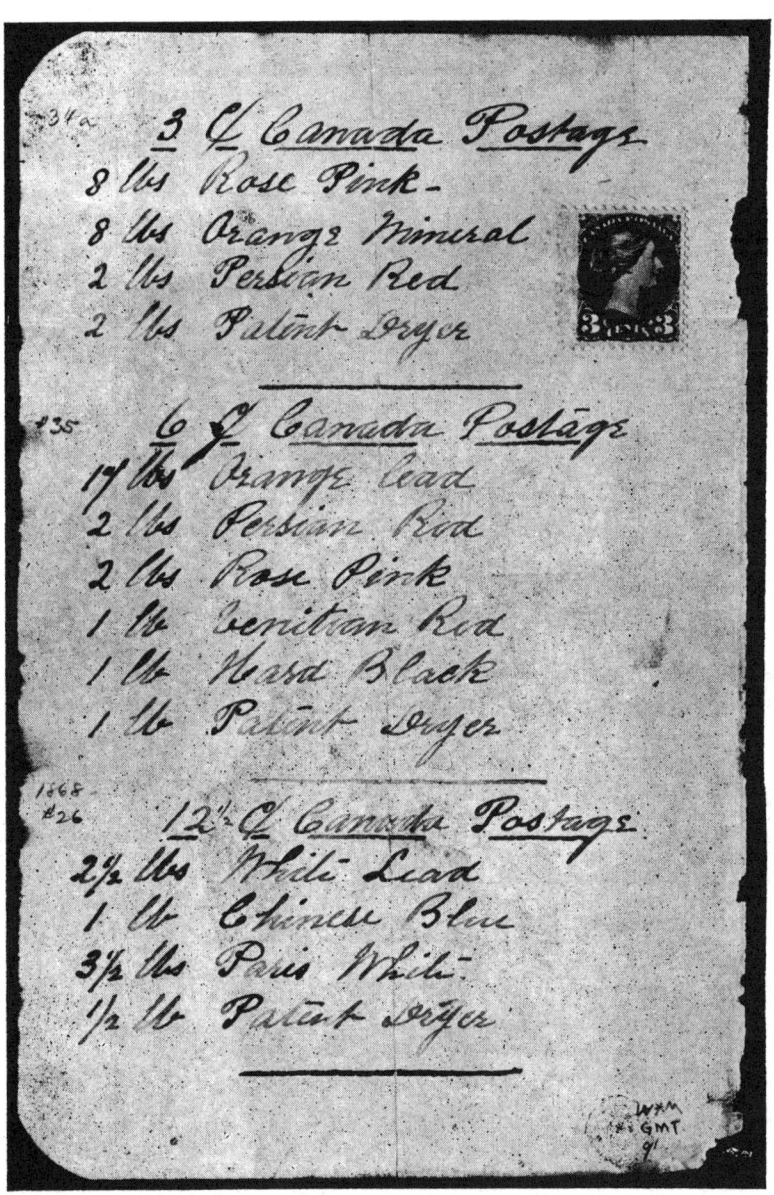

3 ¢ Canada Postage
8 lbs Rose Pink
8 lbs Orange Mineral
2 lbs Persian Red
2 lbs Patent Dryer

6 ¢ Canada Postage
14 lbs Orange Lead
2 lbs Persian Red
2 lbs Rose Pink
1 lb Venitian Red
1 lb Hard Black
1 lb Patent Dryer

12½ ¢ Canada Postage
2½ lbs White Lead
1 lb Chinese Blue
3½ lbs Paris White
½ lb Patent Dryer

Fig. 10b. Other side of Page from recipe book for mixing inks.

Fig. 11.

6c Major Re-entry. Note Line Through "Canada Postage" and Extra Line Below Design. Location Undertermined, but Not From Top or Left Vertical Row of Either Pane. A Similar Re-entry is Known Which shows Only in "Cents" and Below Edge of Design. Has Been Noted Early in 1873.

The question of other plate varieties is difficult to answer, since we are of the opinion that such re-entries that are noticeable were made in 1875 after the Ottawa plant was closed, and all the work was done in Montreal. Until, or unless, large blocks and sheets showing imprints are examined in an attempt to locate the position of these re-entries it will be difficult to definitely allocate them to the first Ottawa, or Montreal plates.

The Perforations

Three perforation varieties occur as follows:

1. 12 x 12 (11¾-12 x 11¾-12). This is the usual perforation, and occurs throughout the issue.
2. 11½ x 12 (11¼-11½ x 11¾-12). This begins in 1873 and continues through the Montreal printings until 1879.
3. 12½ x 12½. This is a full 12½ x 12½, and occurs on the 3c copper red, the first order, and possibly on the 1c. All copies we have examined were used in Nova Scotia or New Brunswick. It is quite rare, but copies are found occasionally, and a more careful search of collections and stocks will undoubtedly result in a number of other specimens being found[8]. The first order for the 1c was placed at the same time as the 3c, and it is quite possible that it also exists perforated 12½.

---

8. At the time of writing we know of sixty copies of the 3c perf. 12½ x 12½, ten of which are on covers (Figs. 12-17).

The 12½ Perforation

Fig. 12.
Left and Right Stamps Are Perforated 12½. Middle Stamp Is Normal 12 Perforation.

Fig. 13.
3c Dull Red, perf 12½x12½. On Cover from St. John, N. B., February 7, 1870. This Is the Earliest Date We Have Noted for this Perforation.

Fig. 14.
"H & P R, N. S , EAST, FE 26, 70" (Halifax & Pictou Ry.), Perf 12½x12½.

Fig. 15.
"H & P R, N. S. EAST AP 25 70". Perf 12½x12½.

Fig. 17.
2c Large Queen, with 3c Small Queen, Perforated 12½x12½ on Registered Cover from Truro, N. S., to Arcadia Mines, N. S. March 8, 1870. A Rare Cover.

Fig. 16.
"ST. JOHN, N. B. Au 27, 1870" Double Circle "7". Perf 12½x12½.

The 11½ x 12 Perforation

Fig. 18.
Upper Stamp Perforated 11½x12, Lower Stamp Normal Perforation 12x12. This Came into Use in 1873 and Continued Until 1879.

The Paper

Papers B, and E, as described for the 1868 issue occur on these stamps. Also two other varieties of paper sufficiently distinct to warrant listing are known.

    B. 1870-74—Smooth medium to thick stout (.0032" to .0040"); white or yellowish wove; sometimes very soft but usually crisp; faint to distinct mesh.

    B^1. Crisp, white or yellowish, 1870-73.

    B^2. Very soft, white, 1871.

    E. 1873-74—Medium to thick (.0033" to .0038"); poor quality; faint to strong mesh; sometimes showing distinct quadrille ribbing.

We have reason to believe that these were all Bothwell, or Pirie papers.

Small Queens. First Ottawa Printing 1870-74.

#	Denom. & Color	Paper = Perf. = Date	B 12x12 Unused	B 12x12 Used	B¹ 12x12 Unused	B¹ 12x12 Used	B¹ 12½x12½ Unused	B¹ 12½x12½ Used	B² 12x12 Unused	B² 12x12 Used	E (a) 12x12 Unused	E (a) 12x12 Used	E (b) 11½x12	1944 S.#	1944 S.G.#
28	1c Orange	Mar. 1870	10	60	x	x	?	?	x	100	12	60	x	33	80
	Orange yellow	Mar. 1872	3	15	2	12	—	—	—	—	10	50	x		
	Dull yellow	Sept. 1872	2	4	3	6	—	—	—	—	12	60			
29	2c Deep green	Feb. 1872	3	5	x	x	—	—	—	—	N	N	x	34	81
	Yellow green	1872	N	N	4	3	—	—	—	—			65		
a	4½ as 1c	1873		x											
30	3c Copper red	Jan. 1870	10	14	8	12	x	275	10	10	2	2	—	36	86
	Rose red	Sept. 1870	6	6	5	5	—	—	—	—			—		
	Red (note¹)	1872	N	N	N	N	—	—	—	—	2	2	5	4	
31	6c Yellow brown	Jan. 1872	N	N	2	1½	—	—	—	—	7	5	x	7	38	88
a	Major re-entry	1872	x	20		20	—	—	—	—	x	12		15		
b	4½ as 3c			x											

Factors: Blocks—Five times above factors; Covers—Double above factors.

Note 1. Includes carmine red, dull red and orange.
Note 2. See Section F Page 301 for discussion of Bisects.

The Gum

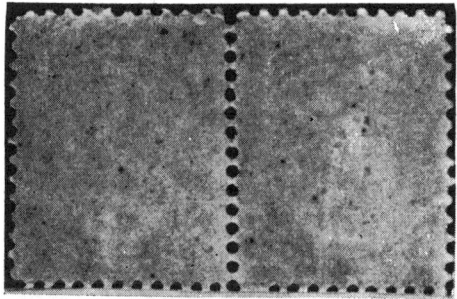

Fig. 19.
Gum V. Dull, Smooth, with Particles of Foreign Matter.

Fig. 20.
Gum W. Thin, Streaky, with Bubbles.

Two gums, V and W as described for the 1868 issue occur on these stamps:
V. 1870-73—Thin, smooth white to yellowish (Fig. 19).
W. 1873-74—Streaky, brownish (Fig. 20).
Gum W usually indicates an 11½ x 12 perforation.

1870-74 Issue Arranged by Paper, Perforation, and Gum.

	Paper	Perforation	Gum	
1870-74	B	1	V	1, 2c, 3c, 6c
1870-73	B¹	1	V	1c, 2c, 3c, 6c
1870-	B¹	3	V	3c
1871	B²	1	V	1c, 3c
1873-74	E	1	V	1c, 2c, 3c, 6c
1873-74	E	1	W	1c, 2c, 3c, 6c
1873-74	E	2	W	1c, 2c, 3c, 6c

1870-74. Issue Arranged by Denominations

	Papers	Perfs.	Gums
1c	B, B¹, B², E	1, 2	V, W
2c	B, B¹, E	1, 2	V, W
3c	B, B¹, B², E	1, 2, 3	V, W
6c	B, B¹, E	1, 2	V, W

1870-74 Issue Arranged by Sets

SET 1—1c, 2c, 3c, 6c.....	Paper B	Perf. 1	Gum V
SET 2—1c, 2c, 3c, 6c.....	" B1	" 1	" V
SET 3—1c, 3c................	" B2	" 1	" V
SET 4—1c, 2c, 3c, 6c.....	" E	" 1	" W
SET 6—1c, 2c, 3c, 6c.....	" E	" 2	" W
Single Stamp 3c.............	" B1	" 3	" V
Also possible 1c.............	" B1	" 3	" V

B. THE MONTREAL PRINTINGS—1874-87

New Values of 1874-82.

The British-American Bank Note Co. in the latter part of 1874 (Sept. or Oct.) moved all their Ottawa establishment to Montreal, and from that date until the end of 1887 did all their work at the latter city. The stamps printed between 1874 and 1887 are somewhat different in shade and plates made after 1874 bear a new imprint, "British American Bank Note Co., Montreal," Type V, (Fig. 21). They are located as described for the Large Queen plates. (Page 245).

The plates used at Ottawa were re-entered, and as the volume of stamps required increased due to the compulsory prepayment of postage from Oct. 1, 1875[9], new plates were laid down from time to time. The position dot is usually discernable at the lower left corner of all stamps except those from the extreme left vertical row of the sheet. On the plates made after 1885 the position dot is not discernable in most instances.

Three new denominations, ½c, 5c, and 10c, were introduced, as well as a new class, Registered Letter Stamps, and the Officially Sealed Label also made their appearance during this period.

These stamps were produced under the terms of the original 1867 contract, that is at 25c per thousand.

9. Appendix B #43.

Fig. 21. Type V Imprint.

Plate Varieties

Since the plates were of *unhardened steel*, they could be and were re-entered. As a result the chief varieties in this group are re-entries; and we are of the opinion that if enough examples could be found with the imprint we would find that most of them occur on the "Montreal & Ottawa" plates.

The color of the 1c is such that re-entries are difficult to discern and to our knowledge only one or two of minor interest have been reported. In the case of the 10c no re-entries have been noted, and this is not surprising considering that only one plate was necessary to produce *all* the small queens of this denomination.

The remaining denominations, ½c, 2c, 3c, 5c, and 6c, show a number of re-entries; all minor.

In 1886 many of the old plates were re-entered, and the consequent deepening of the lines results in richer shades. The effect of re-entering was so evident that the Halifax Philatelist of January 1888 noted that "The plate of the 2c stamp has been re-engraved. Color is now dark green." We also note that the astute Mr. Moens in "Le Timbre Poste" 1888, Vol. XXVI: p. 61, remarks "Nous avons egalement recu ce timbre qui parait lithographie, par suite d'usure de la planchen croyons nous, car la feuille entiere que nous avons annonce que l'impression a ete faite, comme anteriurement, par la British American Bank Note Co. de Montreal et Ottawa, qui ne s'occupe pas d'impression lithographique que nous sachions.", appropos of the reported 2c lithographed. Moens merely calls attention to the fact that the so called lithograph was from a late state of the Montreal & Ottawa plate, which had been in use for over fifteen years, and had given about 185,000 impressions before re-entering, as the new 2c Montreal plate was not made until 1886. In other words the one two-cent plate turned out all the stamps of this denomination until late 1885 or early 1886!

This fact should serve to caution students from drawing conclusions from the quantity printed as to the number of plates used. Reference to the Large Queens of 1868 shows that two plates were used for the 3c and 6c values, although more 1c and 2c were produced than 6c! The explanation lies in the volume of stamps required at a given time; or a plate may be laid up and not carefully protected in which case corrosion may necessitate the making of a new plate[1].

In 1886, a new series of plates were put into service, all bearing the "Montreal" imprint, and of these the 2c was the first of that denomination to bear the Type V imprint (Fig. 21).

The new plates apparently were produced in a manner somewhat different than the previous plates. A faint line was ruled across the plate indicating horizontal rows, but instead of these lines marking the base of the design, they indicated the exact bisection of the design horizontally. These lines terminated in a position dot at the left end, and sometimes visible at the left edge of the medallion of the first vertical row of the plate. They were so faintly drawn that they are rarely visible in the finished stamp, although clearly printed copies of the 2c, and 3c will sometimes show traces of them.

The plates therefore were as follows:

	M. & O.	Montreal 1874-85	Montreal 1886-87	Notes on Montreal Plates
½c	—	1	—	Plate made in 1882.
1c	1	6	7	6 made 1874-5, 7 made 1885-6
2c	1	—	1	1 made 1886
3c	2	12	11	The M. & O. plates were discontinued shortly after 1874.
5c	—	1	1	One made in 1875, one 1886.
6c	1	1	—	Made about 1875.
10c	—	1	—	Made late 1874.

1. The subject of plates, impressions, volume needed etc., requires careful consideration See Essay Proof Journal, January 1944, "Four Re-entered Plates of the U. S. 1861-66 Issue", by Karl Burroughs.

Fig. 22. 3c. Top Strip of Ten Right Pane Showing Type V Imprint and Counters at Upper Right. Second Montreal Plate, 1866.

Fig. 23. 10c. Top Strip of Eight, Showing Type V Imprint, and Counters Above 2nd and 9th Stamps of the Sheet. This Was the Only 10c Plate and We Believe Had Only 100 Subjects.

Fig. 24. Top Strip From Right Pane of the 2c "Montreal" Plate, After Re-entering. Note Counters at Upper Right.

Fig. 25.

5c. Block of Twenty-One (7 x 3) With Top Margin, Showing "FIVE CENTS", but No Trace of Imprint Which Should Appear Over the Fourth to Seventh Stamps. Early State of First 5c Plate. When Re-entered About 1889 the Type VI Imprint Was Added.

The first Montreal plates show a small position dot at the lower left of the stamp on all positions except the left vertical row of the sheet. The plates made 1885 or later do not show this mark. Specialists therefore can divide this group into two parts:

E—Montreal plates 1874-85—1c, 3c, 5c (Early plates).
L—Montreal plates 1886-87—1c, 2c, 3c, 5c (Late plates).

A position dot at lower left indicates:

1c—M & O, or Early Montreal plate.
2c—M & O plate.
3c—M & O, or Early Montreal plate.
5c—Early Montreal plate.
6c—M & O plate.

The absence of a position dot at the lower left indicates (for 90% of the stamps)—

1c—Late Montreal, or an Ottawa plate.
2c—Late Montreal, or one of the Ottawa plates.
3c—Late Montreal, or an Ottawa plate.
5c—The Ottawa plate.
6c—The Montreal plate.

As noted before the left vertical row of the Montreal & Ottawa, and early Montreal plates show no position dot.

Stamps showing a position dot at left side of medallion indicates a late Montreal plate or Ottawa plate made previous to 1892.

When the position dot shows at the right side of the medallion it indicates an Ottawa plate made in 1892 or later.

The above is a general guide to the position dots on the various plates. The exceptions are the few instances where the position dot has been covered by the design or burnished off in finishing the plate.

It was during the latter part of this period (1886-88) that the practice of lettering the panes began—although the lettering does not necessarily indicate the order in which the plate was made, but rather the order of lettering.

We have noted the following letters and plates:

A 2c M & O. Left pane.
   6c M & O. Left pane.
   1c Ottawa (1892).
B 2c Montreal. Right pane.
   1c Ottawa.
C 3c Montreal & Ottawa.
   6c Montreal. Right pane.
   2c Ottawa. (large Imprint).
   1c Ottawa (1892).
D 1c Ottawa (1892).
E 3c Ottawa (1892).
F 3c Ottawa (1892).
G 3c Ottawa (1892).
H 1c Montreal. Left pane.
   3c Montreal.
I 1c Montreal. Right pane.
S 1c Montreal (with "3" struck over "1").
   2c Ottawa (large imprint).

In addition we have seen the following numerals:

1, 2 on left and right panes of ½c, also on 2c large "Ottawa," and small "Ottawa" imprints.
3c "Montreal" with "3".

Perforations

Two perforations occur on these printings.

1. 12 x 12 (11¾-12 x 11¾-12). The usual perforation occurring throughout the issue.
2. 11½ x 12 (11¼-11½ x 11¾-12). In use until 1879.

Papers

As noted under the Large Queen designs Paper B and E ordinarily occur.
- B. 1874-80. Smooth, medium to thick stout (.0032" to .0040"), white or yellowish wove, sometimes soft, but usually crisp, faint to strong mesh occaisionally showing distinct quadrille ribbing.
- E. 1874-97. Medium to thick (.0033" to .0038"), poor quality white or grayish wove, faint to strong mesh, sometimes showing distinct quadrille ribbing.

The Gum

Two types of gum occur on these printings; viz:
Gum W. 1874-78 Streaky, Brownish. (Fig. 20).
Gum Y. 1878-87 Smooth, shiny yellowish. (Fig. 26).

Gum W. usually indicates an 11½ x 12 perforation.

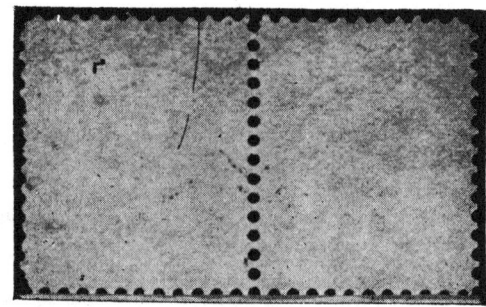

Fig. 26.
Gum Y. Thin Smooth Shiny Gum. Z is similar but Brownish and More Thickly Applied.

1874-87 Issue Arranged by Paper, Perforation and Gum

	Paper	Perforation	Gum	
1874-80	B	1	W	1c, 2c, 3c, 5c, 6c, 10c
	B	2	Y	1c, 2c, 3c, 5c, 6c, 10c
1874-79	E	1	W	½c,1c,2c,3c,5c,6c,10c
1874-87	E	2	Y	1c, 2c, 3c, 5c, 6c, 10c

1874-87 Issue Arranged by Denomination

	Paper	Perforations	Gums
½c	E	1	W
1c	B, E	1, 2	W, Y
2c	B, E	1, 2	W, Y
3c	B, E	1, 2	W, Y
5c	B, E	1, 2	W, Y
6c	B, E	1, 2	W, Y
10c	B, E	1, 2	W, Y

SET 1—1c, 2c, 3c, 5c, 6c, 10c....Paper B   Perf 1   Gum W
SET 2—1c, 2c, 3c, 5c, 6c, 10c.... "   B   "   2   "   Y
SET 3—1c, 2c, 3c, 5c, 6c, 10c.... "   E   "   2   "   Y
SET 4—½c, 1c, 2c, 3c, 5c, 6c,
       10c .... "   E   "   1   "   W
SET 5—1c, 2c, 3c, 5c................. "   E   "   1   "   W

It is interesting to note that during the currency of this issue a 3c stamp was issued by Liberia which, with the exception of the vignette, and the substitution of the word "INLAND" for "Canada Postage" is the same design as the 3c Small Queen. The Liberia stamp, however is lithographed in black. (Scott Type A2).

Small Queens—Montreal Printing. 1875-87.

#	Denom. & Color	Paper— Perf.	c B 11½x12 unused	c B 11½x12 used	d 12x12 unused	d 12x12 used	e E 11½x12 unused	e E 11½x12 used	f E 12x12 unused	f E 12x12 used	Notes	1944 Scott #	1944 S.G. #
32	1c Orange yellow	1874-87	5	14	4	4	5	14	4	4		33	79
	Yellow	1874-82	8	10	2	2	8	10	2	2			
	Lemon	1886-87	—	—	N	N	—	—	N	N			
	Ochre	1879-80	—	—	7	5	—	—	7	5			
33	2c Yellow green	1874-80	5	4	2	2	5	4	2	2		34	82
	Blue green	1880-87	—	—	N	N	—	—	N	N			
	Deep green	1874-76	10	7	3	3	10	7	3	3			
a	7½ as 1c		—	—	x	x	—	—					
34	3c Brown red	1875-6, 1885-7	6	5	1½	1½	6	5	1½	1½	⎫ Numerous	36	86
	Orange red	1876-9, 1886	4	3	1¼	1¼	4	3	1¼	1¼	⎬ Shades		
	Vermilion	1880-85	—	—	N	N	—	—	N	N	⎭ A number		
a	Re-entry												
35	5c Bronze green	Feb. 1876	5	4	3	3	5	4	3	3		43	87
	Olive gray		—	—	N	N	—	—	N	N			
36	6c Dark yellow brown	1875-87	3	2	N	N	3	2	N	N		38	88
a	Re-entry		—	x	6	15	—	x	6	15			
b	4½ as 3c												
37	10c Dim magenta[1]	1874	6	6	2	2	2	2	4	4		40	90
	Dull magenta	1875-78	4	4	N	N	3	3	N	N			
	Lilac	1876-87	3	3	N	N	—	—	N	N			
	Rose lilac	1883-87	—	—	N	N	—	—	N	N			
38	½c Black	Jul. 1882	—	—	N	N	—	—	N	N		45	101
a	Re-entry		—	—	2	2	—	—	2	2			

Other Factors: Covers—Double the factors. Blocks—Six times the factors for mint blocks, and eight times for used blocks, except the ½c—no premium. 1. Heretofore referred to as "faded" magenta. This is a misnomer as it implies that the ink has lost its original intensity of color, whereas the first printing was in this weak color, probably due to a disproportion of white.

Fig. 27.
Type VI Imprint.
The First or Large "Ottawa" Imprint which Occurs Only on the 2c, and 5c Plates Made in 1888-89. The 2c from this Plate Occurs Imperforate.

C. THE SECOND OTTAWA PRINTINGS 1887-97, AND ADDITIONAL VALUES OF 1893

The British American Bank Note Co., Ottawa.

The revised contract of 1887 required that the British American Bank Note Co,. do all the government work at Ottawa, as had been done in the 1868-74 period. Accordingly, the company after the completion of its own building, transferred its stamp printing to Ottawa. We believe, also, that the contract provided that the plates were to be kept in repair at no expense to the government.

Imprints

The old "Montreal" plates were continued in use, many of them being re-entered, and when new plates were needed a 200 subject plate of one pane was laid down bearing an new imprint "British American Bank Note Co., Ottawa" (Type VII.) This was located once at the top above the 10.h and 11th stamps and twice at bottom, below the 185th and 186th stamps, and again below the 195th and

Fig. 28.
Imprint Type VII. 40 x 1 mm.
Used for the 200 Subject (20 x 10) Plates of 1892 and Later—1c, 2c, 3c Only.

291

Fig. 29.
Strips of ½c showing incorrect spacing of perforation wheels resulting in alternate "wide" and "narrow" stamps. The second and fourth stamps if separated are potential "Imperforates." The reason why two "wide" stamps are not found as pairs is explained by the illustration. The lower strip shows result of perforation wheels being loose and resulting in imperforate between pairs.

196th stamps of the sheet in two panes (10 x 10). In the case of the two-cent and five-cent at least, one plate, each of 200 subjects (in two panes of 10x10) was laid down. This had the imprint (Type VI) once at the top, above the 5th and 6th stamps, and once at the bottom, below the 95th and 96th stamps of each pane.

The plate of the 1c and 3c also had the denomination in large sans-serif capitals above the 2nd and 3rd, and 18th and 19th stamps of the sheet.

The new plates were not introduced until 1892, after the assumption of the contract of the Canada Bank Note Co. That contract, as far as we can determine, provided that the plates should be kept in repair and new plates for the then current denominations be made at no cost to the government.

The second Ottawa Printings are of great interest to the advanced student of plate varieties, as it is on these printings that most of the plate varieties and re-entries occur, including the most remarkable of all Canadian plate varieties.

Before discussing the plates we give the following brief notes on the perforations, paper, and gum.

Perforations

As before, the perforation is 11 x 12 (11¾-12 x 11¾-12, or 11¾-12 x 12-¼). We know of no varieties except the ½c part perforates, and the imperforates.

The Paper

Paper E, a medium to thick (.0033" to .0038") poor quality paper showing a faint to strong horizontal mesh or ribbing was used.

From 1893 the paper is somewhat better in texture and substance. Specialists may classify this as E[1]. It is usually whiter than the original paper E.

Watermarked Paper

We have examined several copies of the 1c and 3c, from the "Ottawa" plates, imprint type VII, watermarked in old English capitals. All the stamps seen were left marginal copies, and in the case of the 3c were imperforate. Not enough of the watermark had been noted to definitely establish the words, etc., but search through existing collections and stocks will probably result in a solution of this problem[1].

The Gum

Comparatively little variation in gum may be noted. Gum Z, a smooth thick, brownish substance was consistently used throughout this period.

This table shows how the various characteristics overlap. The early Ottawa printings occur on four papers, three perforations and two gums. The Montreal printings come on two papers, three gums, two of which are new, the first of these disappearing by the time the new plates appear, so that by the time of the 2nd Ottawa printings there is one paper and one gum.

1893 Specimen Stamps

We have noted examples of the second Ottawa printings overprinted diagonally "Specimen" in serifed capitals in violet. They are rare.

---

1. We venture the opinion that the watermark is a form of Alexander Pirie & Sons, as we have seen some of their paper with the watermark in tall old English capitals.

Fig. 30.
A Potential "Imperforate." No Stamp of the Dominion Issue Should be Accepted as Imperforate Unless in a Pair or Block.

Fig. 31. "Specimen" Overprint.

REFERENCE LIST
"SPECIMEN"

S39 ½c Black
S40 1c Yellow
S41 2c Green
S42 3c Vermilion
S43 5c Gray
S44 6c Red brown

S47 8c Blue gray
S46 10c Brown red
S29 15c Slate gray
S48 20c Vermilion
S49 50c Blue

The Plates

The same plates as used for the Montreal printings were continued in these issues. In the period of 1888-92 a 2c, and 5c plate was made, each of 200 subjects, in two panes of 100 (10 x 10), and with a new imprint, type VI, known as the Large Ottawa imprint. All of *unhardened* steel.

In 1892 upon assumption of the contract of the Canada Bank Note Engraving and Printing Co. new plates were laid down of the 1c, 2c, and 3c, consisting of solid blocks of 200 (20 x 10) with the imprint once at the top, over #10 and #11, and twice at bottom below #185, 186, and #195, 196.

The number of plates used during the period on the basis of available evidence was:

	"Montreal"	"Ottawa"	Total	Notes
1c	3	4	7	
2c	—	2	2	One with Large "Ottawa" imprint.
3c	4	8	12	
5c	—	1	1	
6c	2	—	2	One M & O.
10c	1	—	1	(Not re-entered)
Total	10	15	25	

The plates were extensively re-entered as follows:
    1c—Several plates—1895.
    2c—Montreal plate—1891.
    3c—Several plates—1890, again 1894.
    5c—One plate—1892.
    6c—"Montreal Plate"—1892.
    6c—M & O plate—1895.
    10c—This plate was not re-entered.

Re-Entries

Generally speaking the work was so excellently done that only great familiarity with these stamps can detect evidence of re-entry—there are a few exceptions however as follows:

2c. "CENTS" strongly doubled, also traces in left and right "2" Position and pane not known to us.

The Major Re-entry of the 2c (Fig. 33).

This remarkable re-entry is really a badly misplaced entry. The re-entry occurs in the margin below the right bottom corner of the design, where there is a duplication of a small section of the background of the medallion with a section of the curved outline at the right. Most re-entries show as duplications of parts of a design close together,—rarely more than 1 mm. apart, but in this case the original entry is half the length of the stamp too low down. There are also three short, slightly sloping lines on the upright stroke of the "E" of "CENTS". In view of the extraordinary position of these remains of an original design it seems fairly clear that this variety is not due to the usual cause.

It will be remembered that the early Montreal plates had a position dot placed to indicate the bottom margin of the design. The later plates had guide lines ruled horizontally indicating the exact bisection of the design. We are of the opinion that the transfer press operator erroneously began entering the design using the guide line below to place the lower edge of the design. Having discovered the error the misplaced entry was either burnished out or since so little had been entered the placing of the tranfer roll was corrected and the stamp properly re-entered. This re-entry occurs on the Montreal plate, pane as yet not ascertained, and position still uncertain, although not in the first three, or last vertical rows.

Fig. 32. Re-entry, No. 7 Right Pane, Montreal Plate.

Fig. 33. Enlargement of strip of 3 showing major re-entry of the 2c (center stamp). Note also traces of horizontal guide line through middle of stamps. A Similar Example of a Misplaced Entry is Found on the 3p. New Zealand 1862-73 (Type A1).

The 6c Plate

The *Montreal* plate was entirely re-entered, so that practically every stamp on the plate shows evidence of such work. Two subjects, however, show such strong doubling as to warrant attention. Both are from the right pane.

#7. Very strong doubling of lower half of design, particularly in "CENTS" and lines on face of vignette. (Fig. 32).

#81. Similar but not so strong, especially on face of vignette.

Having described the re-entries of the same design we now discuss

THE MOST REMARKABLE VARIETY OF CANADIAN STAMPS

The Double Entry on the 6c Montreal Plate, Ottawa Printings

Fig. 34.
Enlarged Illustration of the Remarkable Double Entry Occuring on the Late State of the 6c Montreal Plate 2nd Ottawa Printings. The Horizontal Lines and Many of the Vertical Lines Are Traces of a 5c Entry.

This unusual variety, the only one so far known in Canada, and rarely occurring elsewhere[1], apparently occurs only in the last printings of the 6c stamp.

As we have noted the plates were of unhardened steel, and when through wear or damage it was necessary to strengthen or deepen any subject on the plate, it was only necessary to rock the transfer roll over the subject needing attention. If accurately done no trace is discernable. If, however, slight in-

---

1. Other similar examples are in U. S. 1908 where a 1c subject is known showing traces of a 2c entry. Also in Second Issue of U. S. Revenue stamps there are traces of a 70c entry on the 60c stamps. In this case it is known that the roll had reliefs of both values on it. the U.S. 5c error of 1917 is the classic example of the wrong entry due to using the wrong roll because of a similarity of the designs. Similar examples are known in the 1874-80 issue of Mexico.

accuracies occur such inaccurracies will show up as a "re-entry" or "double transfer".

It is obvious therefore that in a series with similar designs such as the Small Queens it is possible that in re-entering the plate, or subject the siderographer used the wrong roll, the one with reliefs of the 5c stamp and began his re-entry with it. Discovering his mistake, he picked the roll bearing 6c reliefs and proceeded to enter the correct design. There is also the possibilty that the roll was mixed relief roller, that is it contained the designs of two or more stamps. In rocking in the stamp above the roll may have rocked to far down and the upper part of the 5c relief was entered on the plate[2]. Careful study, however, leads us to the theory of use of the wrong roll.

We believe this to be a variety on a very late state of the Montreal plate as it was done about 1895. In our opinion only about 5,000 copies of this could have been issued, and we know of no unused copies, and only three or four used specimens. (Figs. 34, 35).

In any event we consider it no exaggeration to call this *the most remarkable variety in Canada.*

---

2. Mixed relief rolls are known to have been used as early as 1855 by Perkins, Bacon. We also know that the American Bank Note Co. was using mixed relief rolls both in New York and Ottawa as early as 1896.

Fig. 35. Illustration to Show Relative Position of the Two Entries.

D. THE ADDITIONAL VALUES OF 1893

British American Bank Note Co. Vignette Die No. 11.
Similar to the Die for 20c, 50c. 1893, and the Bill Stamps
of 1868-82.

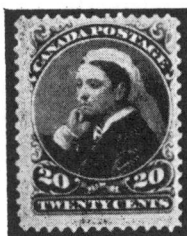  

In 1893 three new denominations were added. The 8c for postage plus registration, and the 20c, and 50c for parcels, etc. The 8c was similar to the other low denominations except the profile of Queen Victoria faces to the left. This stamp was printed from two plates of two hundred subjects (20 x 10) without any marginal marks, imprints, etc.

The 20c and 50c were each from one plate of one hundred (10 x 10) with a new form of imprint (Type VIII) located above the 5th and 6th stamps, and below the 95th and 96th stamps of the sheet. As casual inspection will show they were adapted from the Bill Stamps of 1868, and the similarily is so great that Bill Stamps of these denominations have been seen used for postage.

On all of these plates the position dot is usually placed so that it falls in a colored area of the stamp and is therefore not discernable. Sometimes it may be seen at the right of the medallion midway between the top and bottom of the stamp.

Perforations

All of the printings of this group were perforated 12 x 12 (11¾-12 x 11¾-12, 11¾-12 x 12-12¼), and we know of no important varieties.

Fig. 36. Type VIII Imprint.

E. THE CANADA BANK NOTE ENGRAVING & PRINTING CO. ESSAYS OF 1891.

The Canada Bank Note Engraving and Printing Co. secured the contract for printing stamps in 1891, at the rate of 13 cents per thousand. The official records show that one cent, two cent, and three cent (1891) stamps were engraved and proved by the Canada Bank Note and Engraving Company but were never issued. Before the company was instructed to print the stamps it was purchased by the B. A. B. N. which took over its contract and continued supplying stamps according to the design then in use. (See history of postal cards for further discussion of this design).

Plate of 100, with imprint at top, bottom (inverted), right (reading down) and left? (reading up?).

REFERENCE LIST

Line Engraved

DIE PROOF
Vignette Only. (Very rare).

E40a Dull rose on India.

PLATE PROOFS

On India (Rare)

E40b	1c Orange yellow.	E41c	2c Green.
E41a	2c Blue.	E41d	Orange.
E41b	2c Yellow green.	E42a	3c Orange red.

On Thin Bond Paper (Onion Skin) (Scarce)

E41e 2c Green.   E41f 2c Orange red.

Fig. 57. The C. B. N. E. & P. Essay of 1891.
Note the portion of a running horse at right across block vertically. We have seen other blocks showing this design also.

Lithographed

Lithographed On Smooth Coated White Wove Paper. (Scarce)

E40c	1c Orange yellow.	E41j	2c Red brown.
E40d	1c Lemon yellow.	E42b	3c Black.
E41g	2c Olive green.	E42c	3c Carmine.
E41h	2c Yellow green.	E42d	3c Red orange.

On Bluish Wove (Rare)

E41k 2c Blue.

F. Small Queen Bisects

The bisects of these issues should be divided into two distinct groups, viz: those actually made to meet a temporary shortage, or because the sender was thrifty enough to endeavor to get full value; and those made for Philatelic purposes.

All bisects were against the regulations, but the habit persisted, particularly in the Maritime Provinces.

We list such bisects we have seen, but others undoubtedly exist. All diagonal, *unless otherwise noted.*

2c—U.R. half, cut U.L. to L.R. with whole 2c to make 3c rate—Wilmot, N. S., to Bridgetown, N. S., Sep. 5, 1873. (Fig. 38).

2c—R. *Vertical* half with another 2c making 3c rate from Westville, N. S. Dec. 16, 1885. (Fig. 39).

6c—L.R. half, cut U.R. to L.L. as 3c rate, from ——ville Ferry, N. S., to Bridgetown, N. S., April 3, 1875.

6c—L.L. half, cut U.L. to L.R., as 3c rate from Niely Point, N. S. to Bridgetown, N. S., Jan. 6, 1874.

1c—U.R. or L.R. on "Railway News," a Newspaper, from "Frederiston, N. B.", Nov. 5, 6, or 7, 1897. Newspaper rate was ½c. (Fig. 42).

6c—L.L. half, cut U.L. to L.R. as 3c from Windsor, N.S., Dec. 17, 1888 (on small piece). (Fig. 40).

Bisects from St. John, N. B., and Halifax, N. S., in 1884, and 1896 are of philatelic origin. This applies particularly to vertical halves of the 2c on Bank Notices in September and October 1884, and cancelled "Halifax, Canada". Due to the efforts of a certain Hechler, who was a dealer at the time.

Fig. 38.
One and Diagonal Half of 2c Used to Make 3c Rate from "Wilmot, N. S., Sp. 5, 1873" to "Bridgetown, N. S."

Fig. 39
2c Right Vertical Half and Single making 3c rate from Westville, N. S., Dec. 16, 1885.

Fig. 40.
6c Yellow Brown Diagonal Half as 3c from "Windsor, N. S., DE. 17, 88".

Fig. 41.
6c Red Brown Diagonal Half as 3c from "St. Johns, N. B., JA. 3, 93". A "Hechler" Bisect.

Fig. 42.
Diagonal Half of 1c Yellow Used on "The Railway News" from "Fredericton, N. B., No. 5, 97", and No. 7, 98" Respectively.

Two Examples of "Hechler" Bisects.

Fig. 43.
2c Left Vertical Half as 1c on a Bank Notice, "SP. 18, 84", Halifax, N. S.

Fig. 44.
Right Vertical Half As 1c. Also on Bank Notice, "OC. 24, 84", Halifax, N. S.

G. THE IMPERFORATES

According to Dr. Lewis L. Reford[1] "the first imperforates were given to Mr. Lauchlan Gibb, of Montreal as a compliment, by the Post Office Authorities in Ottawa, in recognition of his services to the Department in advising them about new issues, designs, etc. He was allowed to use them as "franks," but got only one sheet of each denomination. I have several covers addressed to himself for his friends. He was a very generous man, and gave away a great many to his friends and young collectors. His specimens were gummed."

"Furthermore, there was a great boost given to stamp collecting, about 1896 to 1900, by the Jubilee set, and change from the 1870 design. About 100 sheets of each denomination "got out," mostly gummed, but also some ungummed—printer's waste. The New England Stamp Co., of Boston, obtained most of these, but could not sell them. They tried to do so to Scott and Gibbons, but both firms refused to catalogue them. Then Howes's book on Canada came out, and it was stated that these stamps were really on sale at Montreal and other G.P.O.'s, and someone showed some of Mr. Gibb's covers at a meeting of the Royal Philatelic Society in London. Mr. Gibb did not challenge any statement or take part in this discussion, however, as he had sold some of his copies and did not want to influence their value. Then they began to filter out into auctions, and finally Scott and Gibbons bought out the New England Stamp Co. and sold most of their stock at a very high price. Then, and then only, did Gibbons catologue them."

"Howes' illustration of a pair of 2c imperfs. on a registered cover, dated "Como, Que, Mar. 20-95," is probably one of Mr. Gibb's covers, as it is known that he lived at Como, Que., a very small village. Mr. Gibb died in 1926."

After careful study of the available evidence we believe the information given above as substantially correct, and doubt that any of these stamps were regularly on sale at any Post Office.

As far as the plates used; we have noted the following:

½c—"Montreal" imprint type V.
1c—"Ottawa" imprint type VII.
2c—"Ottawa" imprint type VI.
3c—"Ottawa" imprint type VII.
5c—"Montreal" imprint type V.
6c—"Montreal & Ottawa" imprint type IV.
8c—No imprint.
10c—"Montreal" imprint type V.
15c—"Montreal & Ottawa" imprint type IV.
20c—"Ottawa" imprint type VIII.
50c—"Ottawa" imprint type VIII.

The 15c and 50c are in distinctive shades unlike those on the perforated stamps. There are several shades of the other values, but similar to the regular stamps. We have noted three gums—one thick, smooth and yellowish; another thin yellowish and slightly streaky; and the last white, thin and smooth. The latter is unlike any gum on the regularly issued stamps, and is possibly an ungummed item privately treated.

These were, unfortunately the beginning of a long series of "favor" or "backstairs" items, none of which were regularly issued, and collectively are the only unsavory items marring Canada's clean record.

---

1. Stamp Collecting; Aug. 28, 1926, page 591.

Fig. 45. 3c Imperforate Pair. "Montreal My. 24, 00".

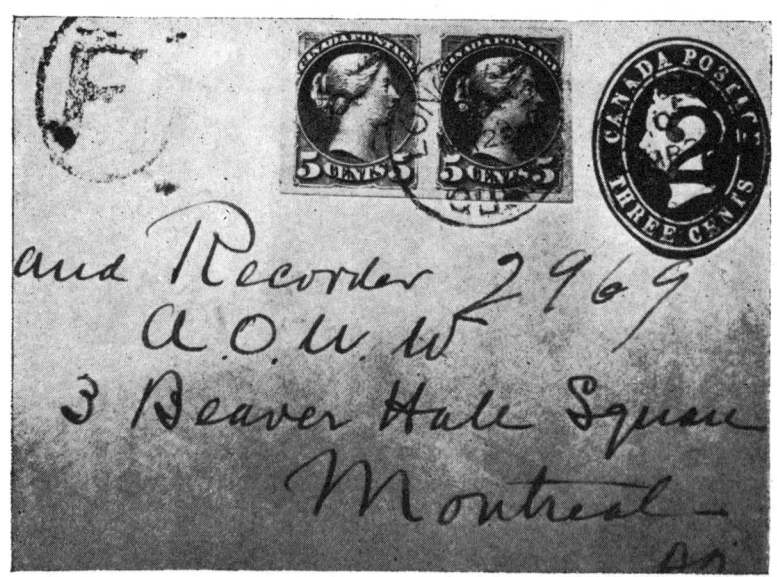

Fig. 46.
Imperforate Pair on 2c on 3c Red Envelope "Longueil, Que., Mr. 22, 00".

Small Queen Set of Imperforate Pairs

F. CONCLUDING NOTES

After thirty years of consistently fine work a new administration saw fit to let the contract to another firm, the American Bank Note Co. Accordingly in April, 1897, the British American Bank Note Co. ceased printing postage stamps for the Dominion Government. The plates, dies and rolls were cancelled and destroyed. We have seen impressions from the cancelled plates as follows:

    1c Black. Left and Right Panes, "Montreal" Plate cancelled by vertical cuts.
    2c Pale green. Left pane. "Montreal & Ottawa" Plate, cancelled by a series of short dashes.
    2c Black. Left pane, "Montreal & Ottawa" Plate, similarly cancelled.

All on thick soft porous white wove paper. In addition the sample sheet illustrated on page 223, in black on card, cancelled by heavy horizontal cuts.

There is no doubt that all the dies, transfer rolls, and plates were cancelled, and in all probability destroyed.

The following table is an estimate of the quantities of the various stamps produced by the plates of the Small Queen stamps.

Table of Approximate Production of the Various Small Queen Plates.

(Quantities are in Millions of Stamps).

Group	Denomination →	½c	1c	2c	3c	5c	6c	10c
I	1870-73 Montreal & Ottawa Plates only. Perf. 12.	—	17.25	4.75	59.25	—	5.25	—
II	1873-75 Montreal & Ottawa Plates only. Perf. 11½x12.	—	18.50	8.00	45.50	—	7.25	—
III	1876-79 Montreal & Ottawa and first Montreal Plates. Perf. 11½x12.	—	59.50	10.75	125.00	5.25	4.75	.60
IV	1880-85 Montreal & Ottawa Plates and 1st Montreal. Perf. 12.	1.50	141.00	13.75	276.75	11.25	4.25	1.00
V	1886-92 Montreal & Ottawa 1st and 2nd Montreal. Perf. 12.	4.00	250.50	12.50	449.25	9.00	5.00	1.50
Va	1890-92 Montreal & Ottawa, Montreal, & 1st Ottawa. Perf. 12.	—	—	31.75	—	8.25	—	—
VI	1893-97 2nd Ottawa Plates in addition to certain of the above.	3.50	214.25	62.50	396.25	15.00	1.75	1.00
	Totals	9.00	701.00	144.00	1,352.00	48.75	28.25	4.10

NOTES ON THE TABLE ON PAGE 309

The ½c and 10c were produced from only one plate each—"Montreal" plate.
½c plate—45,000 impressions.
10c plate—41,000 impressions (plate of 100).
The other denominations as follows:
  6c Two plates—One "Montreal & Ottawa".
             One "Montreal".
Approximately 141,250 impressions per plate.
  2c Four plates—Approximately 180,000 impressions per plate.
             One "Montreal & Ottawa".
             One "Montreal".
             One "Ottawa" 20 x 10.
             One "Large Ottawa".
  5c Three plates—Two "Montreal".
             One "Large Ottawa" Approximately 152,000 impressions per plate.
  1c Eighteen plates—Approximately 194,750 impressions per plate.
  3c Thirty-four plates—Approximately 198,800 impressions per plate.

See page 226 for detailed analysis of number of plates for each denomination.
tion.

Note Concerning Shoemaker's Classification of 3c.

In "Stamps" magazine for March 8, 1941, there was an article by Mr. L. D. Shoemaker on "The Three Cent Small Queen Issue of Canada." This was the most ambitious attempt to solve the complexities of these stamps that had appeared in any American Philatelic publication. To those having access to this excellent article we append the following table showing the relationship between our classification and the classification given in Mr. Shoemaker's article.

#	Shade	12x12	Perforation 12½x12½	11½x12	Shoemaker's Classification Printing
30	Copper red	x	x	—	1
	Rose, rose red	x	—	—	2A, 2B
	Carmine red	x	—	x	3, 4, 5, 6, 7, 8
	Dull red	x	—	x	9
	Orange	—	—	x	10
34	Brown red	x	—	x	11, 13, 25, 26
	Orange red	x	—	x	12, 14, 15, 16, 17, 24
	Vermilion	x	—	—	18, 19, 20, 21, 22, 23
42	Dull orange	x	—	—	27, 28
	Rose carmine	x	—	—	29, 30, 33a
	Bright Vermilion	x	—	—	
	Aniline Vermilion	x	—	—	31,32,63,34,35,36,37
	Pale Vermilion	x	—	—	

Schematic Summary of Small Queen Printings

Group	Position Dot	Perforations	Denominations	Papers	Gum	Plates of	Imprints	Counters	Notes
First Ottawa 1870-74	Lower Left Corner	12x12 11½x12 12½x12½	1, 2, 3, 6 1, 2, 3, 6 3	B, B¹, B² E B¹	V W	200 (10x10+ 10x10)	III, IV	1c, 2c, 3c 6c Above #2 & 3 or 8 & 9 on Sheet	Ottawa Plates Carried Over into Montreal Printings
Montreal 1874-87	Lower Left Corner on Early plates At Right of Medallion from 1885	11½x12 12x12 12x12	1,2,3,5,6,10 ½, 1, 2, 3, 5, 6, 10 1c, 2c, 3c, 5c	B E E	W Y Z Y Z	200 (10x10+ 10x10) Except 10c Plate of 100 (10x10)	V on New Plates	1c, 6c Above #2, 3, 8, 9 3c—above #1, 2, 3, 4 & 7, 8, 9, 10 5c above #1, 2, 3 only, on the sheet	Counters on New Plates
Second Ottawa 1888-97	Not usually visible, but if so at right of Medallion	12x12	½c, 1, 2, 3, 5, 6, 8, 10, 20, 50	E, E¹	Z	New plates 200 (20x10) made in 1892 for 1c, 2c, 3c	VI or VII on New Plates None on 8c	Above 1, 2, 3, & 18, 19, 20 on 1c, 2c, & 3c plates made after 1892	M & O, Montreal Plates Used Until 1892. All from 1892 to 1897

Second Ottawa Printings 1888-97.

Papers E¹—1890-93, E²—1893-97

1888-97 Perf. 12 x 12, 12 x 12¼.

#	Imprint	V 1888-92 Unused	V 1888-92 Used	VI 1890-97 Unused	VI 1890-97 Used	VII 1892-97 Unused	VII 1892-97 Used	Notes	1944 Scott #	1944 S.G. #
39	½c black	N 525 80	N x	— —	— —	— —	— —		45	101
a	Horiz. pr. imperf. between									
b	Imperforate pair									
40	1c yellow 1888-93	N	N	—	—	N	N		33	80
	Orange yellow 1893-97	—	—	—	—	40	x 80			
a	Imperforate pair	—	—			—	—			
b	4½ as ½c									
	(On "Railway News")									
41	2c deep sea green 1888-90	N	N	—	—	—	—		34	103
	Deep blue green 1889-92	3	2	N 20	N	N 15	N x 25	Fig. 33		
	Yellow green 1891-97	N	N	—	—	50				
a	Imperforate pair	—	—							
b	Major re-entry		150							
c	Strong re-entry	7	25							
d	Minor re-entry	2								
42	3c dull orange 1888	30	10	—	—	—	—		37	106
	Rose carmine 1888	100	35	—	—	N	N			
	Bright vermilion 1889	N	N	—	—	N	N			
	Aniline vermilion	N	N	—	—	75	x 50			
	Pale vermilion 1897	—	N	—	—	10				
a	Imperforate pair	—	—			—	—			
b	Re-entry	10	50							
43	5c gray 1888-94	N	N	N	N	—	—		44	107
	Brownish gray 1894-7	—	—	N	N	—	—			
a	Imperforate pair	25	x							

See next page for other factors.

Second Ottawa Printings 1888-97 (Cont.)

#	Denom. & Color	Imprint	V 1888-92 Unused	V 1888-92 Used	VI 1892-97 Unused	VI 1892-97 Used	VII 1892-97 Unused	VII 1892-97 Used	Notes	1944 Scott #	1944 S.G. #
44	6c red brown Deep red brown Deep Chestnut (Re-entered "Montreal" plate)	1890-92 1893-7 1893-7	N N 2	N N 2	— — —	— — —	— — —	— — —	6c has Imprints IV or V.	39	108
a	Imperforate pair		25	—					The Imperforates have Imprint IV		
b	Major re-entry		20	15							
c	Minor re-entry (numerous)		2	3	—	—	—	—			
45	6c (with Entry of 5c) deep chestnut	1895		x	—	—	—	—	"Montreal" plate (Fig. 34).		
46	10c carmine pink Red (shades) Brown (shades)	1889-93 1894-97 1894-97	2 2 N	1½ 1½ N	— — —	— — —	— — —	— — —		41	112
a	Imperforate pair		10	x	—	—	—	—			
47	8c gray (shades) Purple (shades)	1896-8 1893-8	N N	N N	— —	— —	— —	— —	No imprint	48	119
a											
b	Imperforate pair (Bluish gray)		10	x	—	—	—	—			
48	20c vermilion		N	N	—	—	—	—	Imprint Type VIII.	46	115
a	Imperforate pair		10								
49	50c blue		N	N	—	—	—	—	Imprint Type VIII.	47	116
a	Imperforate pair (Prussian blue)		10								

Large blocks of ½c, 1c, and 3c are common enough. Blocks af 2c, 5c, 6c, 10c—6 times factor. Blocks of 8c, 20c, 50c—5 times factor Exceptions are 3c Dull Orange or Rose Carmine—7 times factor. Covers—2 times factor. Imprints, except of the 2nd Ottawa plates of the 1c, 2c, and 3c, are very scarce.

Chapter XIII

INTRODUCTION TO THE ISSUES PRODUCED BY THE AMERICAN BANK NOTE CO., AND ITS SUBSIDIARY, THE CANADIAN BANK NOTE CO.
1897-1929.

When the American Bank Note Co. secured the postage stamp printing contract in 1897 a new era began in the history of Canadian philately. For a continuous period of more than thirty years this concern, which in 1923 became the Canadian Bank Note Co. (wholly owned subsidiary of the American Bank Note Co.), supplied the postage stamps, post cards and wrappers to the Post Office Department of Canada. Beginning with the handsome Jubilee issue of 1897 the artistic standards were well maintained during the years this firm held the contract, and the workmanship is of the highest quality.

We give herewith a brief analysis of the conditions and terms of the various agreements between the company and the Canadian officials, which we believe are of interest to collectors. Further details will undoubtedly be revealed as study progresses.

As mentioned in the chapter, on engravers and printers, one of the conditions of the contract was that the company erect a plant at Ottawa. This was done, and the original plant has been enlarged from time to time. As in the case of the British American Bank Note contracts, "improvements in the art of practical use" were to be adopted, and we know that such was the case, as for instance the hardening of the printing plates in 1904-05 and thereafter, the adoption of chrome plating the printing surfaces in 1927, as well as other improvements of various kinds.

Some of these various improvements are reflected in the stamps, sometimes obviously, and in instances only slightly, or not at all.

The assertion that the Jubilee issue of 1897 at least was produced in New York has some basis in fact, but the contract provided that the dies could be engraved at Ottawa, or elsewhere, *provided* that they were not *hardened* until they were in Ottawa. In other words the transfer rolls and plates were to be made in Ottawa only, and as a corollary, the printing was to be done at Ottawa only.

The table below gives the contract price (per thousand stamps, unless noted otherwise) of the various issues from 1897 to 1922.

Regular Postage Issues

	1897 to 1907	*1908-12*	*1913-22*	*Notes*
1c—2c	.10	.09	.087	In 1916—1c and
3c to 50c	.10	.09	.09	2c were .087
Special Del.	.20	.20	.20	1920—3c—.097
Postage Dues	.20	.20	.18	
Official Seals	.20	.20	.20	
Booklets* 1c	—	—	.009 Each	1917—French
2c	.0075	.0075	.0075 Each	Booklets
3c	—	—	.009 to .012 ea.	1c—.01 to .012 ea.
War Tax	—	—	.10 to .107	2c—.0085 to .0105 ea.
Coils*	—	—	.05 to .06	

* The price for booklets is for covers and binding only, coils for winding only, stamps at regular contract rate per M.

315

The Commemorative Issues.

Jubilee 1897	.20
Imperial Penny Postage	.45
Quebec Tercentenary	.27
50th Anniversary of Confederation	.21

In 1923 a sliding scale was adopted. The price depending on the volume of stamps and the cost of plates. The rates were as shown herewith:

	1922-25	*1925-29*	*Notes*
Regular stamps—1c, 2c, 3c	.127 to .12	.127 to .12	
Regular 4c to 10c	.13	.13	
Regular stamps 20c	.14	.14	
Regular stamps 50c	.20	.20	First 500 M @ .65, each additional M @ .30
Regular stamps $1.00	.65 to .30	.30	
Special Del. 10c	.75	.35	
Special Delivery 20c		1.25	
Postage Dues 1c, 2c, 5c	.18	.18	
Booklets—Regular	.01 each	1c— .015 Ea.	
Booklets—Combination	.0125 each	2c, 3c— .01 Ea. Comb. .0125 Ea.	
Coils	.10 per roll	.10 per Roll	
Pre ncelled		.115 per Roll	
Air Mail		.39	

Special Issues, Commemoratives.

2c on 3c (Two line surcharge) 808 sheets—$50.00

Confederation Issue, 1927.
    1c — .12
    2c — .255
    3c — .415 & .28 — (10,000,000 @ .415; 2,900,000 @ .28)
    5c — .205 & .13 — (20,000,000 @ .205; 4,500,000 @ .13)
    12c — .415

Historical Issue, 1927.
    5c — .205 & .13 — (10,000,000,00 at each rate)
    12c — .47
    20c — .415

Scroll Issue—1928-30.

1c — .127	10c — .39 to .28 to .20
2c — .269 to .127	12c — .38 to .28
3c — .127	20c — .39 to .28
4c — .23 to .13	50c —1.45
5c — .17 to .13	$1.00 —2.55
8c — .23 to .13	

Chapter XIV

THE DIAMOND JUBILEE ISSUE
1897

The year 1897 marked not only the sixtieth year of Queen Victoria's reign, but also the thirtieth year of Confederation. Canada, therefore, had a double reason to celebrate and for the stamp collector the celebration took the form of a long and handsome set of commemorative stamps.

This series was not only the first Canadian commemorative set, but also the first to be supplied by the new contractors, the American Bank Note Co., Ottawa, which had secured the contract by bidding lower than the British American Bank Note Co., and also agreeing to build a plant in Ottawa[1].

The design was by Mr. Lyndwoode Pereira of the Department of the Interior, assisted by F. Brownell and the portraits of the Queen, chosen personally by her, were the well known Chalon vignette and the famous likeness, painted by Prof. Von Angeli of Vienna, in 1862.[2]

In the course of a debate in Parliament on the 20th of May, 1897, the Postmaster General (Mr. Mulock) announced the intention of the Government to issue a set of jubilee stamps, and giving the quantity and denominations to be issued as follows:—

"It is the intention of the Government to issue a set of Jubilee postage stamps. Such stamps will be put into public use by being delivered to Postmasters throughout Canada for sale to the public in the same manner as ordinary postage stamps are sold. There will be a limit to the quantity to be issued. The denominations of Jubilee stamps, and the total number of such Jubilee stamps to be issued, are set forth in the following schedule:—

Schedule showing the Denominations and Total Number of Jubilee Stamps to be issued:

Number to be issued.	Denomination.
150,000	½c. stamps
8,000,000	1c. "
2,500,000	2c. "
20,000,000	3c. "
750,000	5c. "
75,000	6c. "
200,000	8c. "
150,000	10c. "
100,000	15c. "
100,000	20c. "
100,000	50c. "
25,000	$1.00 "
25,000	$2.00 "

---
1. Chapter VII, Page 107, XIII, Page 315.
2. Appendix N #6.

25,000	. .	$3.00 "
25,000	. .	$4.00 "
25,000	. .	$5.00 "
7,000,000	. .	1c. post cards.

Total value of one stamp of each kind, $16.21½.

As soon as the total number of stamps mentioned in said schedule is issued the plates from which they will have been engraved will be destroyed in the presence of the head and two officers of the department. On the 10th June the Post Office Department will proceed to supply Jubilee postage stamps to the principal post offices in Canada, and through them the minor post offices will obtain their supply until the issue is exhausted. If this Jubilee issue were to wholly displace the ordinary postage stamps it would supply the ordinary wants of the country for between two and three months, but as the use of the ordinary postage stamps will proceed concurrently with that of the Jubilee stamps, it is expected that the Jubilee stamp will last beyond the three months. Inasmuch as the department is already receiving applications for the purchase of Jubilee stamps, it may be stated that the department will adhere to the established practice of supplying them only to postmasters, and through them to the public, who may purchase them on and after the 19th of June, 1897.

The distribution of the stamps began on June 10, 1897, and the official date of issue was June 19, 1897 as noted above.[3]

These stamps were printed from steel plates, the ½c to 5c, and 8c in sheets of one hundred (10 x 10), and the 6c, and 10c to $5.00 in sheets of 50 (5 x 10). The imprint (Type IX) "OTTAWA No. —" appears in the top margin only, above the fifth and sixth stamps, of the sheets of 100, and above the second, third and fourth stamps of the sheet of 50.[4] This is the first appearance of plate numbers on plates of Canadian stamps. It is also interesting to observe the omission of the manufacturers name.

Not including the post card sixteen dies and transfer rolls were made, of which at least nine were used to lay down the plates. The work was so carefully done that the plate varieties are few and minute, not warranting separate listing. The transfer rolls contained from five to seven reliefs, although only one relief at a time was resorted to when rolling in a plate. Most of the rolls contained reliefs of several stamps, one indeed contained five reliefs each of a different stamp! The dies, plates, and transfer rolls were destroyed September 10, 1897.

Plate Varieties

RE-ENTRIES: 10c—#6 fairly strong, and #16 faint.
Faint horizontal guide line just below fifth horizontal row of sheet.

LINES AND DOTS: 8c—Top row may be plated by variations in the position dots between the words "Eight" and "Cents."

10c—#1, #7, vertical line between "CE" of "Cents."
15c—#4, vertical line through "N" of "Fifteen."
20c—Constant dot above jewel of crown.
"WE" of "Twenty" joined by line of color. Pos. ?.

Bisects

The 1c was bisected diagonally and used for ½c on the *"Railway NEWS,"* published at New Glasgow, N. S. Such specimens must be on a large part of the original newspaper, which also must be dated Nov. 5, 6, or 8, 1897.

3. Appendix B #51.
4. Appendix Q #5.

Proofs and Specimens

Plate proofs in trial colors and in issued colors are known on thin card, and on medium soft wove paper.

"Specimen" overprint in purple serifed capitals 2½mm. high on all values, and in sans-serif capitals 2mm. high on the 20c, 50c, and $5.00.

REFERENCE LIST
TRIAL COLOR PLATE PROOFS
On white card (Rare)

TC53a	3c lake (Note)	TC53c	3c purple
TC53b	3c indigo	TC53d	3c green

NOTE: TC53a has the imprint "American Bank Note Co., Ottawa" just below the design.

	PLATE PROOFS		"SPECIMEN"	
	A	B	C	D
			Serifed	*Sans*
	On Card	*On soft wove*	*Caps*	*Serif Caps*
P50 ½c Black	15.00	15.00	20.00	————
P51 1c Orange	15.00	15.00	20.00	————
P52 2c Green	15.00	15.00	20.00	————
P53 3c Rose	15.00	15.00	20.00	————
P54 5c Deep blue	15.00	15.00	20.00	————
P55 6c Brown	15.00	15.00	20.00	————
P56 8c Violet	15.00	15.00	20.00	————
P57 10c Purple	15.00	15.00	20.00	————
P58 15c Slate	15.00	15.00	20.00	————
P59 20c Vermilion	15.00	15.00	20.00	25.00
P60 50c Ultramarine	15.00	15.00	20.00	25.00
P61 $1.00 Lake	15.00	15.00	20.00	————
P62 $2.00 Violet	15.00	15.00	20.00	————
P63 $3.00 Brown	15.00	15.00	20.00	————
P64 $4.00 Violet	15.00	15.00	20.00	————
P65 $5.00 Olive green	15.00	15.00	20.00	25.00
SET	225.00	225.00	300.00	————

Counterfeits

Deceptive counterfeits, photo engraved, exist of the $1.00, $3.00, $4.00 and $5.00 denominations. The cancellations appear to be genuine, so that they were either made to defraud the Post Office, or a few were passed through the post to still further deceive collectors. They are slightly different in shades and paper, and not being line engraved will not mislead careful collectors.

An engraved counterfeit of the one dollar value is also known, made in Italy. It is rather deceptive but the lettering is noticeably thinner than in the genuine stamps.

Diamond Jubilee Issue—1897

REFERENCE LIST

#	Denom. & Color	Die #	Plates	Value Factor Unused	Used	Quantity	1944 S.#	1944 S.G. #
50	½c Black	F51	9	N	N	150,000	50	121
	Block of four			6	10			
51	1c Orange	F10	5, 6, 15, 16	N	N	8,000,000	51	122
a	⊿ as ½c on news'p			—	100			
	Block of four			5	8			
52	2c Green	F11	7, 8	N	N	2,500,000	52	124
	Block of four			5	20			
53	3c Bright rose	F12	1-4, 11-14, 28, 29	N	N	20,000,000	53	126
a	Pale rose			3	2			
	Block of four			5	25			
54	5c Dark blue	F13	10	N	N	750,000	54	128
	Block of four			5	8			
55	6c Brown	F14	17	N	N	75,000	55	129
	Block of four			8	12			
56	8c Slate violet	F15	20	N	N	200,000	56	130
	Block of four			5	6			
57	10c Purple	F16	19	N	N	150,000	57	131
	Block of four			5	7			
58	15c Blue slate	F17	18	N	N	100,000	58	132
	Block of four			6	12			
59	20c Vermilion	F18	21	N	N	100,000	59	133
	Block of four			6	15			
60	50c Ultramarine	F19	23	N	N	100,000	60	134
a	Sky blue			4				
	Block of four			8	10			
61	$1.00 Carmine lake	F20	27	N	N	26,700*	61	136
	Block of four			8	12			
62	$2.00 Violet	F21	26	N	N	27,052*	62	137
	Block of four			8	20			
63	$3.00 Yellow br'n	F22	24	N	N	9,515*	63	138
	Block of four			8	25			
64	$4.00 Bright violet	F23	22	N	N	9,937*	64	139
	Block of four			8	40			
65	$5.00 Olive green	F24	25	N	N	12,660*	65	140
	Block of four			8	35			

* Actual issue. It will be noted that the actual number issued of the $1.00 and $2.00 exceeded the intended number by 3,752 stamps. Only 12,500 each of the Dollar values were delivered by June 10, 1897, but deliveries of the high values continued until 1901.

The factor for covers is 2.

Chapter XV

THE MAPLE LEAF ISSUE
1897

The first regular series of stamps prepared by the American Bank Note Co. was the well known "Maple Leaf" issue, so called because of the maple leaves in the four corners of the design. The vignette is a portrait of Queen Victoria adapted from the photo by W. & D. Downey (Fig. 1), taken at the time of the Jubilee celebration in London. The maple leaves were from leaves taken from maples on Parliament Hill, Ottawa. The design was approved on or before September 29, 1897.

A master die was engraved of the vignette and "Canada Postage," from which a secondary die for each denomination was laid down, and the frame and denomination added. These became the working dies from which transfer rolls were made to lay down the plates. The minor differences in the shape and placing of the maple leaves on each value are ample evidence of the method used in preparing these stamps. The vignette was engraved by Charles Skinner.[1]

As usual, unhardened steel plates were laid down, consisting of 200 subjects, in two panes of 100 each (10x10) separated by a gutter 12-13 mm wide. The imprint (Type IX) appears in the top margin of each pane, above the 4th, 5th and 6th, or 5th, 6th, and 7th stamps.

Printed on a soft unwatermarked, white wove paper, perforated 12, except the 5c which is on a bluish wove paper. The intensity of the tint varies greatly, some being almost white.

The new stamps were announced by the following circular to the postmasters:

"Circular to Postmaster.

NEW ISSUE OF POSTAGE STAMPS, ETC.

The Postmaster-General has made arrangements for a new issue of postage stamps, letter cards, stamped envelopes, post cards and post bands. These will be supplied to postmasters in the usual way.

Postmasters are, however, instructed not to sell the stamps of any denomination of the present issue are disposed of. The filling of requisitions by the Postage Stamp Branch will be regulated by the same principle—that is to say, no item of the proposed issue will be sent out until the corresponding item of the present issue has been exhausted.

To conform to the requirements of the International Postal Union, the color of the new 1c. stamp will be green and that of the 5c. stamp a deep blue.

R. M. COULTER,
Deputy Postmaster-General."

"Post-Office Department, Canada
Ottawa, 25th October, 1897."

---

1. Charles Skinner (1845-1907) was an engraver for the American Bank Note Co.

Fig. 1. The Jubilee Portrait of Queen Victoria by W. & D. Downey, Ebury St., London. The head was the basis for the vignette on the Maple Leaf and Numeral issue.

The ½c was the first to appear, being issued November 9, 1897.

The plates were well made, and prominent varieties are few. The ½c being printed in black shows a number of small re-entries, etc., the most prominent being #69 of the left pane, which shows the outer frame line doubled on both sides, as well as the words "Half" and "Postage" duplicated strongly. There are over fifty of these minor re-entries, 75% of which are in the left pane.

There is some evidence that a plate for the ½c was made, consisting of 200 subjects (20x10), and after some 500 impressions were printed, the plate was removed and a new plate arranged in two panes of 100 was made. This may account for the numerous re-entries on the ½c, as the plate of two panes was probably hastily made. Furthermore there is evidence that the second plate was put to press without the imprint, which was added later after the first supply, urgently needed, was printed.

The 3c shows a fairly strong re-entry in #40, plate 6, we believe left pane.

In the 6c there is a strong engravers slip at the bottom frame of one stamp, #91, pane not ascertained. Owing to the fact that only 2,500 impressions were taken from the plate this variety is difficult to find.

Fig. 2

Enlargement of Engravers progress proof in purple of Half Cent Maple Leaf. Frame line, and outlines of Maple Leaves have been added. but the horizontal lines of the back ground have not been ruled in. Note that the vignette is complete. (#E66a).

As noted previously the method of production was rather unusual. The master die consisted only of the vignette and top label "Canada Postage". The transfer roll was used to lay down a secondary die for each denomination. On the secondary die the frame, maple leaves, and denomination were individually engraved.

After the die was completed it was hardened and transfer rolls were then made, which were used to lay down the plates.

Fig. 3. Engravers progress proof showing secondary die ready for engraving the denomination.

REFERENCE LIST

Engravers Progress Die Proofs (Rare)

Ea66   purple on card (Fig. 3)
E66a ½c purple on white card (Fig. 2)

A. Complete design but with white space between upper and lower labels. (Scarce)

E69a 3c violet on pale greenish blue wove
E69b 3c purple on pale greenish blue wove
E69c 3c dull red violet on white card
E69d 3c carmine on white card

B. Space filled with horizontal lines of shading (Scarce)

E69e 3c purple on india
E69f 3c purple on white card
E69g 3c lilac on white card

C. Vertical lines added but not completely covering the horizontal lines. (Scarce)

E69h 3c violet on pale greenish blue wove
E69j 3c purple on pale greenish blue wove
E69k 3c dull red violet on white card
E69m 3c scarlet on white card
E69n 3c green on white card

Finished DIE PROOFS and Plate Proofs

Die proofs are on white cards, 5"x7", and show Die No. and Imprint at bottom "AMERICAN BANK NOTE CO., OTTAWA."

Plate Proofs Are on White Card, or India Paper

		A. Die Proof on India	B. Plate Proof 1. India	2. Card	Notes
P66	½c black	50.00	25.00	10.00	
	a gray black	25.00	—	—	
P67	1c black	50.00	—	—	
	a green	25.00	25.00	10.00	Plate 4
P68	2c black	50.00	—	—	
	a purple	25.00	25.00	10.00	Plates 1, 4
P69	3c black	50.00	—	—	
	a carmine	25.00	25.00	10.00	Plate 6
P70	5c black	50.00	—	—	
	a blue	25.00	—	10.00	
P71	6c black	50.00	—	—	
	a brown	25.00	—	10.00	
P72	8c black	50.00	—	—	4. Thick Wove
	a orange	25.00	—	10.00	15.00
P73	10c black	50.00	—	—	
	a brown violet	25.00	—	10.00	—

DIE PROOFS ON CARD cut close (Rare)

D66 ½c black   D70 5c black
D67 1c black   D71 6c black
D68 2c black   D72 8c black
D69 3c black   D73 10c black

Trial Color Die Proofs, with Imprint (Rare)

70TCa 5c blue on white
    b 5c blue on bluish
    c 5c blue on pale blue
    d 5c blue on dark blue
    e 5c purple on green card
73TC 10c violet

Trial Color Plate Proofs (Very Scarce)

		A. white wove	B. white card	C. blue wove (purplish to greenish)
66TCa	½c purple		x	
68TCa	2c gray black	x		
69TCa	3c pale gray		x	
b	3c dull gray		x	
c	3c slate		x	
d	3c apple green		x	
e	3c green	x	x	
f	3c ochre		x	
g	3c orange		x	
h	3c scarlet		x	
j	3c red violet	x	x	
k	3c brown violet		x	
m	3c violet blue		x	x
70TCa	5c carmine		x	
b	5c blue gray			x
c	5c brown violet			x (Perforated)
72TCa	8c carmine	x	x	(Perforated)
b	8c dark brown		x	
E73TCa	15c purple			x
b	15c dark brown		x	
c	15c scarlet		x	

Fig. 4. Typical Recut.

Fig. 5. Typical Re-entry. Note doubling of maple leaf.

Bogus Surcharge on 3c Numeral. See Page 343.

1897-98 "Maple Leaf Issue"

#	Denom. & Color	Date Issued	Quantity Issued	Plates	Value Factor Mint	Value Factor Used	Notes	1944 S.#	1944 S.G.#
66	½c black Block of four	Nov. 9, 1897	2,000,000	1	N 5	N 10	Numerous re-entries	66	142
67	1c green Block of four	Dec. 1897	37,200,000	1, 2, 3, 4	N 5	N 10		67	143
68	2c purple Block of four	Dec. 1897	13,350,000	1, 2, 3, 4	N 5	N 12		68	144
69	3c carmine Block of four	Jan. 1898	51,750,000	1,2,3,4,5,6	N 5	N 8	Pl. 6, #40 L. Pane (?) Shows fair re-entry	69	145
70	5c blue on bluish Block of four	Dec. 1897	3,500,000	1	N 6	N 15		70	146
71 a	6c brown Gravers slip, bottom frame Block of four	Dec. 1897	500,000 (2,500)	1	N 50 10	N 50 25	#91 Pane (?)	71	147
72	8c orange Block of four	Dec. 1897	1,400,000	1	N 6	N 20		72	148
73	10c brown violet Block of four	Jan. 1898	300,000	1	N 8	N 22		73	149

All values exist imperforate, but were not regularly issued. Value about $50.00 per pair. All Plate 1, except 2c, plate 3, 3c plate 6, 1c plates 2, and 4.

Covers Factor 2, except 6c and 10c, factor 4.

Chapter XVI

THE "NUMERAL" ISSUE OF 1898

The "Maple Leaf" issue had been in use but a few months when it was decided to prepare a new series bearing numerals of value as well as words. Rumors of the impending change were noted as early as April 1898, and the 1c and 2c of the new design were chronicled in the Metropolitan Philatelist for July 2, 1898. The same publication in its August 20, 1898 number listed the new series as containing ½c, 1c, 2c, 3c, 5c, 6c, 8c, 10c, 15c, 20c, and 50c denominations. It will be observed that the 15c and 50c never appeared.

The chief objection to the "Maple Leaf" series was made by the French speaking population who found it difficult to read the values, and the postal clerks working with a large volume of mail under adverse conditions also complained of the difficulty in distinguishing the denominations. Two other factors no doubt influenced the Department, viz; the desire to improve the design artistically by enlarging the oval containing the Queen's portrait, and the increasing emphasis by the Universal Postal Union of the necessity of stamps used in the International Mails having the denomination in Arabic Numerals, a practice made mandatory at the Rome Postal Congress in 1907. In passing we might call attention to the fact that beginning with the Maple Leaf Issue the 1c stamps are green, the 3c, or 2c (whichever is the domestic rate), carmine, and the 5c, (the international rate), blue. Also, as if to emphasize the international rate, blue paper was used until 1913. Vignette engraved by Charles Skinner.

The reduction of the rate of postage to 2c per oz. in 1898 resulted in a tremendous demand for this value. As a result new plates were laid down by rolls from a new retouched die, which had a frame line consisting of a heavy line between two fine lines (Type 2). This is DIE Ib of this denomination.

Imperfs: 5c, 6c, 7c, 8c, 10c, all plate 1.

Before further discussion of the problems surrounding the 2c we list the Essays and Proofs.

REFERENCE LIST

DIE PROOFS

On Thin Card Cut Close (Rare)

D74 ½c black	D78 5c black	D82a 15c black (Fig. 1)
D75 1c black	D79 6c black	D83 20c black
D76 2c black Die Ia	D80 7c black	D83a 50c black (Fig. 1)
D77 3c black	D81 8c black	
D77a 4c black (Fig. 1)	D82 10c black	

DIE—ESSAY (Very scarce)

D82b 15c gray on card
D82c 15c green on card

DIE PROOFS

On India mounted on card 5"x7", with die number and imprint "American Bank Note Co. Ottawa" in serifed capitals 2½ mm. high, except on 4c and 7c which are in caps and lower case. (Rare).

D74a ½c black, Die F114
D75a 1c green, Die F115
D76a 2c purple, Die F116 (Die Ia).
D76b 2c black, F116 (Die Ib).
D77b 3c carmine, Die F113
D77c 4c black, Die O9
D78a 5c blue, Die F117
D79a 6c purple brown, Die F118
D70a 7c olive yellow, Die O10
D81a 8c orange, Die F119
D82d 10c brown, Die F120
D82e 15c black, Die F121
D83b 20c olive green, Die F122
D83c 50c black, Die F123

D77a, c, D82a, e, and D83a, c; are, strictly speaking, Essays, as no plates were made or stamps issued.

Without Die Number or Imprint

D77d 3c carmine on white wove

Plate Proofs on Cardboard (scarce)

P76a 2c green
P77a 3c carmine
P83a 20c green

On White Wove Perforated and Gummed (scarce)

P76b 2c gray black
P77b 3c green
P82b 10c carmine

The listing of the issued stamps will be found in the table on pages 332-3.

The Two States of the 2c Die.

As noted previously the reduction of the domestic postage resulted in an enormous increase in the demand for the 2c denomination, necessitating the use of twice as many plates, in spite of the 2c Imperial Penny Postage, and the surcharging the old 3c carmine "2 Cents".

In preparing this issue a master die consisting of the vignette and the band around it with the words "Canada Postage" was prepared. Eight secondary dies were laid down, one for each denomination, and on these secondary dies the Maple leaves, numerals and frame were engraved individually. The occurence of a small dot of color in the white oval just below the "ST" of "Postage" on all denominations is conclusive, while slight variations in the position and shape of the Maple leaves shows that the frame was added to each value.

Of the dies made in 1898, all had a frame consisting of four fine lines, except the 8c, which consisted of two fine lines between two heavy ones.

The 20c, which appeared in 1900, had a frame of two heavy lines, while the unissued 15c and 50c prepared about the same time, had frames of one thick line and two fine lines inside of one thick line, respectively.

The 7c, of 1902 has a frame of three thick lines, as had also the unissued 4c prepared at that time.

```
½c Type I frame 1898  ⎤
1c Type I frame 1898  ⎥
2c Type I frame 1898  ⎥  —2c Die Ia.
3c Type I frame 1898  ⎬  Four thin lines.
5c Type I frame 1898  ⎥
6c Type I frame 1898  ⎥
10c Type I frame 1898 ⎦
```
8c Type II frame 1898—Two thin between two thick lines.
2c carmine (Die Ib) Type III frame 1899—One thick line between two thin lines.

15c unissued Type IV frame 1900—One thick line.
20c Type V frame 1900—Two thick lines.
50c unissued Type VI frame 1900—Two thin lines and a thick line.
4c unissued Type VII frame 1902 } Three thick lines.
7c Type VII frame 1902

The 2c violet was printed from plates 1 to 12 inclusive. At the time of the change in rates, plate 1 and 2 had been discarded, and the 2c carmine first appeared from plates 3 to 10 inclusive. Plates 11 and 12 were withdrawn, and in instead reserve plates 13 and 14 were placed in use.

The withdrawn plates were re-cut with frame lines similar to Die Ib which accounts for the numerous varieties occuring on these plates.

The re-cut die Ib was used to lay down plates 15 to 20. They have Type III frames. We have seen die proofs of both states of the die. (D76a, D76b).

Later all the plates were re-entered, some quite extensively, and numerous re-entry varieties can be found, some of them showing very strong doubling over the entire stamp, but particularly at the bottom, as the stamps were re-entered by rolling the transfer roll in from top to bottom. The plates of the 1c were also extensively re-entered. (See Fig. 2 for typical re-entry).

Careful study of the purple and carmine stamps from the same plates should establish the sequence of the re-touches and re-entries of the various plates.

The only other variety worthy of note is the thick opaque paper on the 2c purple. This occurred during the later printings after dealers and collectors had stocked up, which accounts for it comparative scarcity in unused condition.

We have seen imprint strips from plates 1 and 2 on this paper.

Fig. 1. Die Proofs of the Unissued 4c, 15c, and 50c Numeral. The 15c and 50c Were Prepared in 1898, the 4c in 1902. (D77a, 82a, 83a).

Fig. 2. Typical Re-entry.

1898-1900 Numeral Issue.

Unhardened Steel Plates of 200, in two panes of 100 (10x10) Imprint Type IX

#	Denom. & Color	Die #	Date Issued	Quantity	Plates	Factor of Value Unused	Factor of Value Used	Notes	Scott # 1944	S.G. # 1944
74	½c black	F114	Sept. 1898	9,180,000	1	N 500	N		74	150
a	Imperf. pair									
75	1c green	F115	June 1898	283,500,000	1-8	N	N		75	151
a	Imperf. pair					175				
b	Re-entry					5	3	Many		
c	Re-touch					4	2	Several		
76	2c purple, Die Ia	F116	Sept. 1898	67,000,000	1-12	N 20	N 10	Pl. 11, 12 First State Base line doubled. Pl. 1, #5, Pane ?.	76	153
a	Major re-entry									
b	Minor re-entry				1, 2	3	2			
c	Thick paper					25	3	Later printings.		
77	2c carmine, Die Ia	F116	Aug.20, 1898	150,000,000	3-10, 13, 14	N 150	N		77	155
a	Imperf. pair					3	2	Many		
b	Re-entry									
c	2c Type II (Similar to Die Ib)				11, 12	12	8	Retouched Plates.		
78	2c carmine, Die Ib	F116	1900	400,000,000	15-20	N	N	Recut Die, New Plates.	—	155
a	Re-entry					3	2	Numerous.		
79	3c carmine	F113	June 1898	43,537,600	1-6	N	N		78	156
a	Re-entry					10	5	Plate 3. "3's" strongly doubled. Pos. ?.		

1898-1900 Numeral Issue.

#	Denom. & Color	Die #	Date Issued	Quantity	Plates	Factor of Value Unused	Factor of Value Used	Notes	Scott # 1944	S.G. # 1944
80	5c blue on bluish	F117	Jul. 1898	19,450,000	1-3	N	N	Plates #2, and #3 show the number reversed.	79	157
a	Imperf. pair					20				
b	Re-touch					8	12	Left frame line extends downward. Pl. ?.		
81	6c purple brown	F118	Sept. 14, 1899	460,000	1	N	N		80	159
a	Imperf. pair					15				
82	7c olive yellow	O10	Dec. 23, 1902	1,250,000	1	N	N	No gum.	81	160
a	Imperf. pair					45				
83	8c orange	F119	Oct. 1898	768,800	1	N	N		82	161
	Brown orange		Feb. 1899			2	2			
a	Imperf. pair					12				
b										
84	10c brown	F120	Nov. 29, 1900	2,250,000	1	N	N		83	164
a	Imperf. pair					15				
85	20c olive green	F122	Dec. 29, 1900	540,000	1	N	N		84	165
a	Imperf. pair					12		No gum.		

Blocks—½c to 8c Factor 5; 10c Factor 7; 20c Factor 10.

Covers—1c to 8c Factor 2½; ½c in blocks on cover is common, but a single on commercial cover is very scarce, Factor 150.

333 *

Chapter XVII

THE PORT HOOD PROVISIONALS

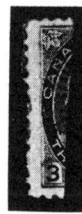 

The reduction of the postage rate from 3c to 2c for domestic letters (proclaimed December 29, 1898, and effective January 1, 1899), had the immediate effect of vastly increasing the demand for two cent stamps, while rendering 3c stamps of comparatively little use. The short notice of such a change in the rates resulted in a number of post offices running short of 2c stamps, and having an over supply of 3c stamps.

Some offices bisected 3c stamps and used them without further ado but the postmaster at Port Hood apparently felt that it would be wise to apply some distinguishing mark to the bisected portions of the stamps used on letters going outside of the county.

The explanation given by the postmaster in reply to a query on these bisects is concise and clear, and we quote it herewith:

> "When the change in Canadian postage was made—of which we got notice by wire—I had only a very few two cent stamps in stock so that before I got my supply from Ottawa I ran completely out of them, and, to keep my account straight, I was compelled to cut threes. This was for one day only, and not over 300 stamps were cut. I would say about 200 "2" and 100 "1" were used. Those stamps I put on letters for delivery within the county as much as possible. About 100 "2" and probably nearly as many "1" were marked with the figures 2 and 1 as you describe and were placed on letters for delivery in towns throughout the Dominion. Those were the only provisional stamps used by this office."

The postmaster endeavored to do the best he could under the circumstances. We should observe that only 300 stamps at most were cut, and of these only about 100 were surcharged "1" or "2" respectively.

For reasons unknown these particular bisects have been singled out for attack, and have been decried as not worthy of notice by serious philatelists, favors, etc.

We will limit our discussion to pointing out the facts which in our opinion entitle them to high consideration, in fact equal to that of any other Canadian bisect.

The argument that they were irregular and against the regulations can have little weight, as *all* Canadian bisects were against the regulations, yet bisects of the 3p., 6p., of 1851-57; the 1c, 5c, 10c, 1859; as well as those of the Large and Small Queens are held in high esteem. The stamps were bisected to meet a rate and were in use for only one day. Had speculation been the motive the period of use would have been longer, and more would have been surcharged. Instead only about 100 were surcharged. From this must be deducted those confiscated by the authorities, and others which were lost.

The reason given for bisecting is logical, and the surcharging was done by the postmaster. These are the only surcharged bisects. Furthermore bisection was an old habit in Nova Scotia.

The fact that Stanley Gibbons secured a few is not, per se, any thing against them. We are indebted to the foresight and activity of many of the great dealers for some of our choicest items, particularly in the 19th Century[1].

The postmaster's explanation of the supply of 2c stamps from Ottawa failing to arrive before his stock of this value was exhausted is consonant with the facts. Port Hood is, 221 miles from Halifax, and over 1000 miles from Ottawa. (Even today Port Hood is some 10 hours from Halifax, and over 36 hours from Ottawa by rail). The possibility of getting all the 2c stamps needed in a matter of a few hours is therefore doubtful.

From a study of singles and pairs we believe the bisections were as shown by the diagram herewith:

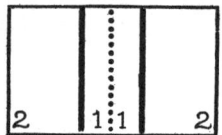

Fig. 1. Diagram of Bisection of the Port Hood Provisional.

From this it will be seen that each strip of ten would yield five pairs of 1c, and four pairs of 2c, the end of the strip being single 2c bisects.

The surcharges consisting only of the numeral "1" or "2" were handstamped on each portion, the "1" in greenish blue, and the "2" in voilet ink.

REFERENCE LIST

Prepared and issued by the Postmaster at Port Hood, N. S., Jan. 5, 1899.

			1944 S#	1944 S.G. #
#86I 2/3 of 3c carmine used as 2c (unsurcharged)				
#86II 2-1/3rds of 3c carmine used as 2c (unsurcharged)				
#86 1/3 of 3c carmine surcharged '1' in greenish blue	N	N	88C	169
#87 2/3 of 3c carmine surcharged "2" in violet	N	N	88B	170

Used copies must be on covers dated Jan 5, 1899, and there must be two 1/3rds of the 1c on genuine covers.

The 2c is known with double surcharge, but as the "2" was handstamped this is of little significance.

---
1. Notably Moens, W. S. Lincoln, Trifet, etc.

Fig. 2. 2 1/3rds Surcharged "1" Paying 2c Rate. This Piece Shows Both Left and Right Portions.

Fig. 3. 2c on 2/3rds of 3c. Right Portion.

Fig. 4. 2c on 2/3rds of 3c, "Port Hood Jan 5 99". Left Portion.

Chapter XVIII

SPECIAL ISSUES OF 1898-99

A. IMPERIAL PENNY POSTAGE ISSUE
1898

In 1898 an Imperial Postal Conference was held in London and while Imperial Penny Postage was not adopted, the first step towards that ideal was taken at the instance of the Hon. (afterwards Sir) William Mulock, Postmaster General of Canada, when a number of the British Dominions and possessions agreed to a uniform rate of 1d (2c) per ½ ounce for letters[1]. The new rate became effective Christmas Day, 1898.

The introduction of the new rate was the occasion for issuing a two-cent stamp, which the versatile Mr. Mulock had designed by R. Weir Crouch, Gustave Hahn, A. H. Howard and R. Holmes, showing a map of the world on Mercator's projection, with the British possessions indicated in red. At the foot of the design is the motto "We hold a vaster Empire than has been!" which is from "A Song of Empire" by Sir Lewis Morris composed June 20, 1887, in honor of the fiftieth anniversary of Queen Victoria's reign. We quote the stanza:—

> *We hold a vaster Empire than has been!*
> *Nigh half the race of man is subject to our Queen!*
> *Nigh half the wide, wide earth is ours in fee!*
> *And where her rule comes, all are free.*
> *And therefore 'tis, oh Queen, that we,*
> *Knit fast in bonds of temperate liberty,*
> *Rejoice to-day, and make our solemn jubilee!!*

The stamp was placed on sale December 7, 1898, although the new rate did not become effective until Christmas Day, 1898.

The American Bank Note Co., Ottawa, printed this remarkable stamp; remarkable for several reasons, among them being that it was printed in three colors, by two processes; the black line engraved, the carmine and the lavender being typographed! It also had the distinction of being the most expensive stamp to produce that Canada had ever issued, the rate being .45 cents per thousand!

Each plate consisted of one hundred subjects (10 x 10). The plate number appears at the top above the fifth and sixth stamps. The imprint, Type X, (Fig. 1) is above stamps #3, and #8 and below #93, and #98 on the sheet. Only the line engraved plate had markings, there being no markings on the typographic plates.

Four line engraved, plates were made, with plate numbers 1, 2, 3, and 5. Apparently there was no plate #4.

---
1. Appendix O # 7, #8.

Fig. 1. Imprint Type X.

Fig. 2. Plate No. "2".

Fig. 3. Imperforate Block of Four.

The numerous re-entries on plate 5 indicate that the plate was probably entirely re-entered. In addition the 46th stamp on the sheet occurs showing the two most northerly Pacific Islands side by side and again with one above the other. This was probably a repair, but our knowledge of the production of the typographic plates is not great enough to be able to state whether the two varieties of this 46th stamp are due to a new plate or a minor repair to the old plate. The variety showing the islands one above the other has been noted only in conjunction with plate 5.

It is doubtful if more than one typographic plate was used for the lavender.[2]

REFERENCE LIST

Proofs

ENGRAVED DIE PROOF (Rare)

D88   2c black on white CARD DIE # "F189½"

ENGRAVED PLATE PROOF (Scarce)

P88   2c black on white wove

TYPOGRAPHIC "RED" PLATE (Scarce)

Pa88   (2c) carmine only on white wove

TYPOGRAPHIC "OCEAN" PLATE (Scarce)

Pb88   (2c) lavender only on white wove

COMBINATION PROOFS ON WHITE WOVE (Scarce)

P88a   2c black, lavender and carmine (line and typo)
    b   2c black and lavender (line and typo)
    c   2c black and carmine (line and typo)
    d   (2c) carmine and lavender (typo)

Apparently the black portion, was first printed and then the "ocean" portion of the map was added, and finally the red was printed. Many copies show the colored portions indented, more particularly the red parts evidence that a typographic plate was employed as lithography would never show such indentation. The theory that the colored portion were lithographed probably arose from the fact that the term "surface printing" was used by earlier writers, a term meaning "typography" to Britishers, but frequently meaning "lithography" to Americans and Germans. The British generally specifically say lithography when speaking of that method of printing.

---

[2]. Dr. Dard Hunter of the Massachusetts Institute of Technology is also of the opinion that the colored portions are from typographic plates.

REFERENCE LIST

Dec. 7, 1898. White Wove Paper, Perforated 12.

#		Unused	Used	1944 Scott #	1944 S.G. #
88	2c black, lavender & carmine	N	N	85	166
a	Imperforate (pair)	70			
b	Re-entry (numerous)	2	3		
c	Re-touch (Pl. 2, 3 or 5)	4	5		
	Block of four	6	75		
	Plate block of four	10			
	Imprint single	3	10		
	Cover	—	7		
89	2c black, green blue, & carmine	N	N	86	168
a	Imperforate (pair)	65			
b	Re-entry (numerous)	2	3		
c	Re-touch (Pl. 2, 3 or 5)	4	5		
	Block of four	5	65		
	Plate block of four	8			
	Imprint single	3	8		
	Cover	—	5		
	Cover cancelled Dec. 25, 1898	—	30		

19,927,500 delivered to the Post Office Department.

(NOTE: The color differences were unintentional).

Plate Varieties

The *re-entries* are usually slight and most occur on plates 2 and 5. They show in the cable bordering the design. We have noted only two slight ones on Plates 1 and 3.

Re-Touches

PLATE 1. We have noted none definite enough to list.

PLATE 2. Number 80, and bottom row #91 to 100 show retouches to twists of cable or lines bordering cable, particularly at the bottom, left, and right sides. Sometimes the recutting shows the lines extending beyond the design.

PLATE 3. The right vertical row (#10 to #100) shows extensive re-touching of the cable. Several other subjects on this plate also show re-touches.

PLATE 5. Number 96 to 100 show slight re-touches. As noted above this plate was extensively re-entered.

Tabulation of Re-entries and Retouches.

Plate	#1	#2	#3	#5
Re-entries	2	8	2	19
Re-touches	?	12	19	6

A lithographic forgery is known, all copies we have seen being neatly cancelled "Montreal 24.12.98" in black, also forged.

Specialists will find this stamp of considerable interest, and further study should settle a number of the problems concerning this issue.

B. THE "TWO CENTS" ON "THREE CENTS" PROVISIONALS
1899

Fig. 1. Block of Four, Inverted Surcharge.

The reduction of the letter rate from three cents to two cents, effective January 1, 1899, resulted in a great increase in the demand for two cent stamps, and a corresponding decrease in the demand for three cent stamps. This was equally true of the postal stationery (see Chapter on Postal Stationery). Instructions were sent out on July 1, 1899,[1] requesting Postmasters to turn in the three cent stamps, envelopes, and letter cards.

The stock of three cent stamps still in the Department vaults was surcharged "2 Cents" in black. The surcharging was done by an electrotype plate of one-hundred subjects, and there are no varieties of importance, some broken letters, etc., being due to inking, and presswork. Overprinting was done by the Public Printing Office.

REFERENCE LIST

#		Plates	Unused	Used	1944 S.G.	1944 Scott
90	2c on 3c Carmine (Maple Leaf) July 28, 1899	5, 6	N	N	87	17J
a	Inverted surcharge		150			
	Block of four		6	8		
	Cover			21		
91	2c on 3c Carmine (numerals) Aug. 8, 1899	1, 3, 5, 6	N	N	88	172
a	Inverted surcharge		200			
	Block of four		5	6		
	Cover			2		

Care should be taken in purchasing the inverted surcharge varieties, as there are a number of forgeries in existence, some extremely well executed.

4,120,000 were surcharged divided approximately 1,375,000 Maple Leaf and 2,745,000 Numerals.

Copies of the 3c surcharged with a large "2c" similar to the surcharge on the stationery are bogus. (See page 326).

---

1. Appendix M #56.

Chapter XIX

THE KING EDWARD VII ISSUE

The death of Queen Victoria on January 29, 1901, brought to an end a great and glorious reign, and of course meant many changes in the stamp issues of the British Empire.

The contract with the American Bank Note Company still having two years to run new designs were not placed in use until 1903. On June 10 of that year, however, the following circular was sent to all the Dominion Postmasters:

"Postmasters are hereby informed that a new issue of postage stamps, bearing the portrait of His Majesty King Edward VII, and comprising five denominations (1c., 2c., 5c., 7c., and 10c), is about to be supplied to Postmasters for sale in the usual way, but none of these stamps are to be sold until the first of July, 1903.

The colours of the forthcoming series will be the same respectively as those now used for the denominations specified, except that the shade of the 7c. will be slightly deeper.

Postmasters will please bear in mind that, notwithstanding the new issue, they are not to return to the Department any of the old stamps on hand, but will sell them in the ordinary way. At first, the public may prefer getting new stamps, and if so, there is no objection to this wish being acceded to, but it is also desirable to work off in due course all remnants of old stamps.

A change in the design of the stamp of the present series of post-cards, post-bands and stamped envelopes to correspond with that above referred to, will be made as soon as the present stock of these items shall have been exhausted."

In accordance with the notification the denominations given were placed on sale Dominion Day, 1903 (July 1).

The design was similar to the numeral issue of Queen Victoria, but with the substitution of Tudor crowns in the upper corners for maple leaves. The maple leaf motif is retained, however, by placing two leaves by the numerals of value. The portrait of King Edward in Robes of State is from a photograph taken shortly before Coronation. The design was the work of the Prince of Wales, later King George V, and Mr. J. A. Tilleard of the Royal Philatelic Society.

A steel die was engraved by J. A. C. Harrison of Perkins, Bacon & Co., London. The original die shows white numerals of value on a colored ground. The American Bank Note Co., however, found it necessary to alter the design and have colored numerals on a white ground. They made one master die and five secondary dies, to which was added the denomination in words and numerals one for each value, and also electrotypes for postal stationery (q. v.). Later two further denominations were added, namely the 20c and 50c.

Fig. 1. The Perkins, Bacon Essay. Pair of Plate Proofs.

The vignette of the American Bank Note Die was engraved by Charles Skinner.

The plates were of steel and consisted of 200 subjects (20 x 10) divided by a gutter 10-11 mm. wide into two panes of 100 (10 x 10), with the imprint in the top margin above the 5th and 6th stamps of each pane. Some 1c and 2c plates were of 400 subjects (see below).

The early plates were of *unhardened steel* as usual, but around 1905 it became the practice to harden the plates. Re-entries, while well known on the 1c, and 2c, do not occur nearly as often as they do on the Maple Leaf and Numeral Issues.

Furthermore, some plates of the 1c and 2c were of four hundred subjects arranged in four panes of 100 (10 x 10), separated by a vertical gutter 10-11 mm. wide, and a horizontal gutter 25-26 mm. wide.

The block of four panes was so nearly square that as an aid to the pressman fitting the plates the word "TOP" was engraved in the upper margin of the upper right or left panes. (Fig. 2, 4, 5). In the case of two 2c plates (#73, 74) the imprint was entered *inverted!* (Fig. 6).

We have seen the following "TOP" numbers:

1c—Plates 29, 50, 51, 52, 55, 71, 72.
2c—Plate 17, 29, 64, 69, 70, 71, 73 (inverted), 74 (inverted), 84, 85.

The plate numbers at first were cut individually, but later punched in before the plate was hardened. The early numerals are thin serifed, while the punched numerals are thick curved and smaller.

We have noted the numbers as follows:

1c—1 to 4 thin; 5 and up thick.
2c—1 to 5 thin; 6 and up thick.
5c—1, 2 thin; 3 and up thick.
7c—1 thin; 2 thick.
10c—1 thin; 2 thick.
20c—1 thin.
50c—1 thin.

We believe that the thick numerals were used when additional plates were made after the first group. In other words 15 plates were made in preparing the issue, and as other plates were needed they were numbered with thick numerals. Plate 2 of the 7c did not appear until early 1910.

The occurence of "¶O" followed by various numbers refers to the "Printing Order" in filling of which the particular plate was used.

Imprint Strips from a 400 Subject Plate

Fig. 2. Imprint Strip from Upper Right Pane of Plate 71 Showing "TOP".

Fig. 3. Imprint Strip from Lower Right Pane of Plate "71" Without "TOP".

Fig. 4. Imprint Strip from Upper Left Pane of Plate 70. Note "70" Plate Number Added by Hand Punch, and Reversed.

Fig. 5. Plate 64 with "TOP". Block from One of the Upper Panes.

Fig. 6. Plate "73 TOP" Inverted. This We Believe Was An Error and Was Intended to Be on the Upper Right Pane Instead of the Lower Left Inverted. We Have Seen Plate "74 Top" also Inverted.

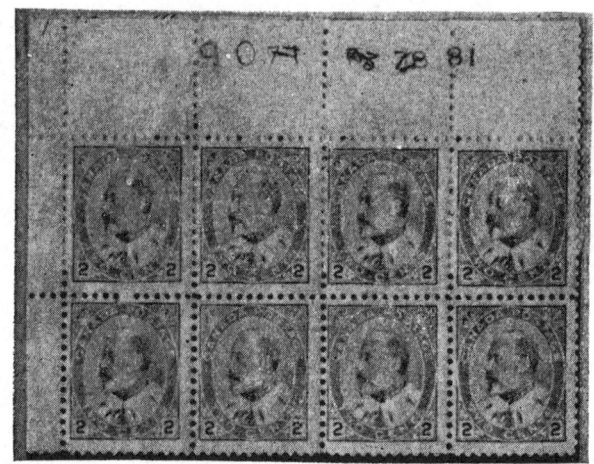

Fig. 7. Block from Right Pane Showing that the Plate Was Used in Filling Printing Orders 71, 73, 78, and 81.

Fig. 8. Block from the Rare Plate 3 of the 5c.

Fig. 9. Enlargements of 1c and 2c Stamps Showing "Hairlines" Due to Curving the Plate for Fitting on the Press.

Fig. 10. Typical Re-entries on the 1c and 2c. The Re-entries Generally Show in the Lower Part of the Design Because the Re-entering is Made from Top to Bottom and Differences in Registering Show More at the End of a "Pass" than at the Beginning. There are Many Exceptions as the 2c Illustrated Herewith Shows Evidences of Re-entry at the Top.

(a)

(b)

Fig. 11.
The 5c is Frequently Found With the Background of "Canada Postage" Showing Horizontal Lines of Shading (a) Instead of Solid Color (b). Probably Due to Wear or Cleaning of the Plate as Blue Has a Particularly Deleterious Effect on the Steel. We Have Seen Large Blocks All Stamps Showing this Characteristic.

REFERENCE LIST

ESSAYS. 1903

The American Bank Note Company apparently made a plate from the Perkins, Bacon die as large blocks of this essay are known. They are scarce, however, especially in blocks.

DIE PROOF

Ea92 1c dark green on white glazed paper (very scarce)

PLATE PROOFS

E92a 1c gray black, thin white wove, gummed.
E92b 1c pale rose, thin white wove, gummed.

ISSUED DESIGN, DIE PROOFS (Very rare)

On White Card, Cut Close

D92a	1c black	D96a	10c black
D93a	2c black	D97a	20c black
D94a	5c black	D98a	50c black
D95a	7c black		

On India. Die sunk on card (rare)

D92b 1c black. Die #F166.	D96b 10c black. Die #F170.
c 1c green. Die #F166.	c 10c plum. Die #F170.
D93b 2c black. Die #F167.	D97b 20c black. Die #F178.
c 2c carmine. Die #F167.	c 20c olive. Die #F178.
D94b 5c black. Die #F168.	D98b 50c black. Die #O-25.
c 5c blue. Die #F168.	c 50c violet. Die #O-25.
D95b 7c black. Die #F169.	
c 7c yellow bistre. Die #F169.	

SPECIMEN

Overprinted "Specimen" horizontally in serifed capitals, in violet.
S97 20c olive green.

Provisional Coils

In August, 1913, the postmaster at Quebec having a supply of King Edward 1c and 2c stamps, which had been superseded by the new King George V issue, decided to have coils made up rather than return the old stamps to Ottawa. This was done, the stamps being cancelled with the Ottawa "1" obliterator, and placed in stamp vending machines for experimental purposes. They should be collected in paste-up pairs or strips with full gum.

See particularly Pages 355-60 for detailed discussion of the experimental coils of 1910-12.

The Imperforates

The only imperforate of this issue regularly available was the 2c from plates 13 and 14, a supply of which was on sale for a number of years at Ottawa. (Further discussion of these will be found on page 359).

The other imperforates were never regularly available but have come on the market at various times, and from various sources, one being the effects of a late official in the Post Office Department.

King Edward VII Issue—1903-08

#	Denom. & Color	Date Issued	Die #	Plates	Quantity Issued or delivered	Value unused	Factor used	1944 Scott #	1944 S.G. #
92	1c. Green	July 1, 1903	F166	1-66, 70-72	1,470,000,000	N	N	89	175
a	Imperf.	May 6, 1903		2	200	100			—
b	Hair lines								
93	2c. Carmine	July 1, 1903	F167	1-30, 32, 33, 35-50, 53-64, 67-86	2,160,000,000	N	N	90	177
a	Imperf.	Sept. 1908		1, 2, 13, 14	Pl. 1, 2—200 Pl. 13, 14—100,-000	N	N	90a	177a
94	5c. Blue	July 1, 1903	F168	1-6	66,210,000	N	N	91	178
a	Imperf.	May 6, 1903		1	200	50			
b	Background of panel around head worn.			Pl. ?		4	4		
95	7c. Yellow bistre	July 1, 1903	F169	1, 2	25,305,000	N	N	92	180
a	Imperf.	June 1, 1903		1	200	20			
96	10c. Plum	July 1, 1903	F170	1, 2	15,080,000	N	N	93	184
a	Imperf.	June 1, 1903		1	230	15			
97	20c. Olive green	Sept. 27, 1904	F178	1	3,150,000	N	N	94	186
98	50c. Violet	Nov. 19, 1908	O-25	1	600,000 (Two printings)	N	N	95	187

Imprint strips of four with plate number only factor 5. Other factors: Strips of six showing number and "TOP", factor 10. Blocks of four 1c to 20c factor 6, 50c factor 8.

The following Imperforate plate numbers have been seen by us:
1c—Plate 2.
2c—Plate 1, 2.
5c—Plate 1.
7c—Plate 1.
10c—Plate 1.

SHADES

As would be expected the large quantity of stamps needed for this issue resulted in quite a wide range of shades, particularly in the 1c to 10c values, as there were a number of printings of each. In the case of the 50c, however, there were only two printings, which differ slightly in shades. These were in printing orders #72 and #74 respectively.

THE FIRST CANADIAN COILS

Fig. 12. Paste-up Strip of EX-C1.

The period of 1910 to 1913 saw the first experimentation in this form of stamp. We illustrate a paste up strip of four, of the precancel coil made up from ordinary sheet torn in strips of ten and pasted together. This was an experiment prepared by the American Bank Note Co. about 1910, for the new vending machines secured from London, England. All specimens were either precancelled as illustrated, or cancelled with the ordinary Ottawa parcel roller. Apparently only about 150 copies of this coil survived, of which there could be only some 15 paste ups, part of which would be precancelled, so that the rarity of this item can readily be realized.

Experimental Coil (1910)
Very Rare

Ex-C1 2c carmine, precancelled.
  (a) Paste up.
Ex-C2 2c carmine, Ottawa parcel cancel.
  (a) Paste up.

There is no doubt that the Canadian Post Office was somewhat interested in the various experiments to devise machines to vend or affix stamps. Inventors in this field had been particularly active in the United States (witness the numerous varieties of coils occurring in United States stamps).

Of the various companies the most familiar is

The United States Automatic Vending Co.,

whose distinctive form of separation, on the 2c King Edward has been the source of some controversy.

We give herewith a brief summary of the history[1] of the company together with other data which we believe should be of some help in deciding the status of these varieties.

The U. S. Auto-Vending Co. was formed by Mrs. Sara L. W. Coe of New York City (president) and her sister-in-law, Mrs. Henrietta T. Werden of Mt. Vernon, N. Y. From 1907 to 1912 the company had its offices in the Tower of the Metropolitan Life Building at 1 Madison Avenue, New York. Then they moved to 185 Madison Avenue, and later to 1476 Broadway. The vending mechanisms were made in their shop at 28 Liberty Street, while the cases for the machines were cast in bronze by the Tiffany Studios of New York.

At the time this company was incorporated it was the intention of the Post Office Department to purchase stamp-vending machines and maintain them in post offices lobbies, stations, hotels, etc., as a public convenience.

First Machines Tested

The machines of the United States Automatic Vending Company were, as the name of the company suggests, entirely automatic—no handles, knobs, levers or buttons to operate. *They were manufactured under American patent rights purchased from Katrine E. Fawns and Georgine Kermode of Ross, Tasmania, Australia.[2] While traveling in England in 1906 Mrs. Coe and Mrs. Werden had seen these machines in operation. Letters in Mrs. Werden's possession show that the machine was accepted for trial by the British Post Office Department in September 1906. Eighteen British post offices tested the machine and reported very favorably on it.*

Evolution of the Type I Roulette

It happened that in 1908 the U. S. Auto-Vending Co. was also making a ticket-vending machine which operated in the same manner as the stamp vendor. There being no perforations on a strip of tickets, these were fed over the rotating drum by means of notches in the side edges of the ticket strip cut to receive pairs of lugs spaced on the outer edges of the drum. It was decided to try this same scheme for advancing the stamp strip in the stamp machine. With the pins removed it was then possible to place a "shoe" over the surface of the drum to press down on the stamps and prevent their curling. A few two-cent coils were notched by hand and tested in machines in New York, one of which was reported to have been in the Plaza Hotel.[3]

---

1. Through the courtesy of Mr. George P. Howard, the well known authority on vending machine stamps.
2. Patent #878787:—Application filed Oct. 4, 1907; granted Feb. 11, 1908. Madams Fawns and Kermode had an Agency in London, which supplied the British Post Office. The original patentees were R. J. Dickie and J. H. Brown of New Zealand.
3. Mekeel's News and Trade Circular, No. 25.

The new form of feeding the stamp strip prevented curling, but introduced an unforeseen difficulty. The "shoe" pressing on the stamps created a tension which the fine 12-gauge perforation, considerably weakened by the notches, was not always able to stand. Particularly was the coil strip liable to break apart when the double paper of a paste-up pressed under the "shoe." *So the company ordered imperforate stamps and made similar coils, cut by hand with scissors.* These fed perfectly from the machine, but since there were no perforations the stamps would not readily tear off the coil strip and a slit between the notches was found advisable. Thus the Type I roulette came into existence, and was immediately patented.[4]

The first Type I coil were made entirely by hand. Later the U. S. Auto-Vending Co. acquired a Stacy Stripper whose electrically operated rotary knives cut a sheet of stamps into 20 strips in one operation. These 20 strips were then joined to form an imperforate coil of 400 stamps,—the usual length of the coils of this company. The imperforate coil was then run through a perforating machine, patented by Mrs. Werden,[5] which had "an automatic means for feeding the strip intermittently under the cutters, whereby said strip will be notched in its two edges and slit transversely a limited distance between said notches." This machine also wound the strip on a core of the proper size to fit the vending machine.

Type II Roulette

The U. S. Auto-Vending roulette on sidewise coils, called Type II, is similar in design to Type I. the notches of both perforations forming a 60° angle at the point. On the sidewise coils the points of these notches are 19.7mm apart and the slit between the notches measure 14.5mm. Type II coils saw but little service and correctly used copies are quite rare. However, there exists a sufficiently large supply in unused condition, obviously made up for the benefit of collectors.

We have already mentioned a ticket machine which was manufactured by the U. S. Auto-Vending Co. in 1908. These were made for, and tested by, the Subway Division of the Interborough Rapid Transit Company in New York. In all working parts they were similar to the stamp-vending machines, operating automatically on the insertion of a five-cent piece. The bronze cases were somewhat larger than those of the stamp-vending unit as they were made to accommodate a coil of 500 tickets, which required considerably more room than a coil of 400 stamps. The rotating drum for feeding the tickets from the machine was arranged with lugs opposite each other on the outer edges. These pairs of lugs around the drum were separated from each other by a space equal to the length of one ticket. The ticket strips were notched by hand on both sides to receive these lugs. Several of these machines were tested in ticket windows in the subway, and one was installed by the rear door of Wanamaker's Store, near the subway entrance at Astor Place.

When the Subway Company decided *not* to adopt these machines the U. S. Auto-Vending Co. was stuck with several manufactured machines and, of course, the dies and machinery for making other units of the same size.

Selling Stamps at a Profit

The same machine which was made to vend subway tickets, was remodeled to sell coil stamps at a profit.

In the interior of the machine the lugs on the rotating drum were shifted so that they would advance two stamps at each operation of the machine. The drums were, of course, the width of a subway ticket, which happened to be approximately the height of a normal stamp. Therefore the coils for these ma-

---
4. Patent #943653:—Perforation of a Coil Strip; application filed Nov. 8, 1908; granted Dec. 21, 1909.
5. Patent #964614:—Application filed May 15, 1909; granted July 19, 1910.

chines were wound sidewise and had the Type II roulette. They contained 1000 stamps, which fitted easily into the space originally provided for 500 tickets. The vending company offered the machines for sale, or gratis on a "share the profits" scheme. Instead of operating a chain of these machines throughout New York City the company turned this lucrative field over to two men by the names of Heiman and Zorke.

Type III Perforation

The business arrangement made between Mrs. Coe, president of the U. S. Auto-Vending Co., and Messers. Heiman and Zorke is somewhat obscure, but apparently the deal did not include the use of the patented perforation of two notches with a slit between. This interesting bit of information was learned a few years ago in an interview with Mrs. Werden, the only living official of the company. It explains the reason for the existence of the Type III perforation which, although different from the Type II roulette, is so nearly the same that the U. S. Auto-Vending Co. would have had no cause to produce it. Mrs. Werden disclaimed the Type III perforation as a product of her company and later wrote as follows :[6]

> "I can't find stamps with seven perforations and two notches that were ever vended from United States Automatic Vending Co. machines. We made a small machine for the counter in which the stamps came out sidewise. That is the machine Heiman and Zorke were interested in. I have been told they made hundreds of the small machines and put them in stores selling two 2c stamps for five cents. I am sure they are the machines that vended the 7 hole and notches. They could not use the two notches and cut because that was my patent."

The story is further borne out by the fact that the Type III perforation went through certain experimental steps which the U. S. Auto-Vending Co. had already been through and would not have repeated. The Lincoln commemorative stamp exists in sidewise coil form, obviously made from imperforate sheets which had been perforated 12-gauge vertically to simulate the Bureau perforation. The horizontal strips show scissor-cut edges and hand-cut notches. These were illustrated by Mekeel and Gibbons,[7] with the note that the perforation was experimental, the adopted type having fewer holes. The U. S. Auto-Vending Co. would not have gone through this experimental step as they had already learned that the 12-gauge perforation was not suited to their machine.[8]

The adopted Type III perforation shows seven holes of an 8½-gauge perforation between the notches. This private 8½-gauge perforation must have preceded the Bureau 8½-gauge by several months, and its successful use in U. S. Auto-Vending machines may have influenced the Bureau to make the change. The notches on the Type III perforation are exactly the same as on Type II,— 19.7mm. apart and opening at approximately a 60° angle. The Type III perforator was, therefore, an almost exact copy of the Type II rouletter, which suggests a closer connection between the U. S. Auto-Vending Co. and Messrs. Heinman and Zorke than the tone of Mrs. Werden's letter would lead one to believe. It is even probable that all types were perforated in the same office as "request" pairs exist partly perforated in Type II and partly in Type III. Certain values with the Type III perforation exist in block form (also some with Type I) likewise made by "request". In every case these blocks will be found to have a crease down the center where they were folded to the width of a single strip when run through the perforator.

So much for the U. S. Auto-Vending Co. Investigation into the status of the King Edward 2c with U. S. Auto-Vending separation has resulted in the following enlightening information.

6. Letter to Mr. Howard, March 16, 1938.
7. Stanley Gibbons, Inc., New York, Monthly Bulletin.
8. See previous discussion of Evolution of Type I.

In the latter part of 1910 the Post Office Department of Canada ordered from Miss Katrine E. Fawns, and Mrs. Georgine Kermode, London Eng., thirty automatic stamp delivery machines with two delivery openings, and twenty with one delivery opening, a total of fifty automatic vending machines. These were the type of machine that attracted Mrs. Coe and Mrs Werden when visiting England in 1906.[9]

The machines were for handling rolls made up from ordinary stamps perforated all around. Canadian stamps being somewhat larger, and of different perforation guage did not work as well as expected. Accordingly twenty-four of the two opening machines, and fifteen of the one opening machines had the necessary minor alterations made. That the result was satisfactory is evidenced by the fact that in the latter part of 1912 twenty more one opening machines were purchased from Madames Fawns and Kermode.

The 2c King Edward Imperforates

The generally accepted story that these were placed on sale to prevent speculation in the find of a portion of a sheet (about 230 stamps) which had blown out of a window[10] must be viewed with some reserve. That the sheet was found is reasonable enough, but other irregular varieties are well known and the Department had never placed them on sale to the general public. Also the theory that new plates numbered 13 and 14 were made to make a special supply of these stamps to agree with the found sheet is too fantastic to be worthy of serious consideration.

It should be remembered that the U. S. Auto-Vending Co. was very active in 1908, and there is no doubt that the Canadian Postal Officials were well aware of the various vending machines for stamps available in both the United States and Great Britain.

In order therefore to accomodate users of stamp affixers and also for vending machines some 100,000 stamps (1,000 sheets of 100) were placed on sale in Ottawa, July 1909, after announcement in April of that year as follows:

> "In view of the representations which have been made to the Department, it has been decided to permit the sale of the 2-cent denomination of Canadian postage stamps of the current issue, in sheets of 100, without the usual perforation."[11]

The representations mentioned could have come from the Vending Machine Companies or business houses, or both. Furthermore the sheets could have been drawn from reserve stocks, or plates 13 and 14 were merely put to press again to print the required supply as suggested by the remark that "the department intends to make a separate printing of these stamps, to supply whatever demand may occur."

In view of the above data we are of the opinion that the 2c King Edward with U. S. Auto-Vending separation should be classed as experimental coils.

REFERENCE LIST

Ex-C3 2c carmine, Type I (Roulette).
Ex-C4 2c carmine, Type II (Roulette).
Ex-C5 2c carmine, Type III (Perf. 8½).

It is a regrettable fact that the U. S. Auto-Vending, and Heiman and Zorke would apply their distinctive roulette or perforation to any imperforate sheet of United States or Canadian stamps upon payment of the small fee for preparing the coil, making it impossible, with our present knowledge to be more definite concerning the status of these varieties.

---

9. See page 356.
10. See "Canada" by Howes, Page 194.
11. It will be noted that this is all the Postal Guide stated. The rest of the quotation in Howes' book is merely that of the reporter to Mekeel's Weekly.

U. S. Automatic Vending Separations (1910)

Type I Roulette: This is the scarcest of the three varieties, and we believe some at least were made for the Canada Post Office for the vending machines which they purchased in England and had altered.

Fig. 14. Type II Roulette.

Type II Roulette: It is possible and probable that some of these were also made for the Canada Post Office. Quite scarce.

Fig. 15. Type III Perforation.

Type III Perforation: It is possible but doubtful that any of these were made for the Canada Post Office. This is known as the Heiman and Zorke perforation. The commonest of the three varieties.

(Students interested in the field of Vending and Affixing Machines are referred to "The Stamp Machines and Coiled Stamps" by George P. Howard, and published by H. L. Lindquist Publications. The Vending and Affixing Machines Perforations, Unit of the Bureau Issues Association, also is the source of much data to those interested in these stamps).

Chapter XX

THE KING GEORGE V ISSUES OF 1911-28

The "Admiral" Type

This complicated and interesting series of stamps has been the subject of much study by many students, and the last word will probably never be written.

It is therefore with considerable trepidation that we offer these notes, in the hope that they will enable students to continue their studies to fill in the gaps and revise of our knowledge of these stamps.

The death of King Edward VII on May 6, 1910, made it necessary to prepare a new issue of stamps, bearing the portrait of the new monarch King George V. Canada, however, did not move hastily, and it was not until late in 1911 that the new stamps were actually issued. The chief reason being that the contract expired early in 1912 and a new contract was made at more favorable rates. (See Chapter XIII).

There was much discussion at the time about the so-called objection to the Monarch's portrait on the stamps, but the Postmaster General was careful to point out that the objection was not to the portrait of the King, but to the mediocre likenesses that were to be seen on the various Georgian stamps of the other British possessions.

The issued design, showing a portrait of King George to the left in the uniform of Admiral of the Fleet, was made from two photographs, and met with universal approbation as it continued the high standards of dignity and beauty set by the previous issues.

The stamps were engraved and printed from hardened steel plates by the American Bank Note Co., Ottawa, on unwatermarked white wove paper.

The long life of this design, some sixteen years, including the years of the first World War, gave rise to a number of variations in die, color, perforation, etc., which makes this series so interesting to the serious philatelist.

We propose to take up each phase of this issue separately. Before doing so, however, we would call attention to the fact that during its currency the first stamp of 4c denomination was issued, also the first coils or roll stamps, and the first booklets other than 2c were placed on sale.

I. The Dies

The question of the dies used has been a matter for discussion in the philatelic press for a number of years. We propose to discuss this rather fully in an endeavor to clarify the subject.

A master die was engraved, complete except for the numerals and words of value (Fig. 1.). From this seven working dies were laid down and the necessary figures and letters added. Later additional working dies were made for new denominations, or new working dies of others. All the dies are of steel, and transfer rolls were made containing, we believe, five reliefs, for laying down the plates. The various die proofs are tabulated on Page 368.

1911 DIE I. Green, and Yellow. Note Slight Serifs on Figures of Value.

1924 DIE II. Yellow only. Note Strong Serifs on the Figures of Value.

1918 DIE I. Brown, and Carmine. "THREE" Well Clear of Medallion.

1924 DIE II.   Carmine only.   "THREE" Very Close to Medallion.

The use of a master die is easily proven by the fact that on all stamps of this design (regular issues, and war tax, any denomination) the left crown over the "NA" of "CANADA" almost touches the left vertical line of the spandrel, while the right crown, over the "ST" of "POSTAGE" is well clear of the right vertical line of the spandrel. In fact several short horizontal lines may be seen in this space.

Fig. 1. Schematic Sketch of Master Die for "Admiral" Type.
Vignette Engraved by Robert Savage.1

In the case of the 1c and 3c two working dies were made. The first 1c in 1911, and the first 3c in 1918. The new dies for each denomination were made on September 23, 1924.

In making the new dies the transfer roll containing reliefs from the master die was used to lay down the design complete but for figures and words of value, as was done in 1911. The figures and words of value were then added, as had been done with all the previous working dies.

We show enlarged illustrations of both dies of each denomination. These enlargements were made from DIE PROOFS ON INDIA, printed in BLACK.

Die Differences of the 1c and 3c George V "Admiral" Type.

DIE I, 1911	DIE II, 1924
"CENT" or "CENTS" rests on second line above foot of design.	"CENT" or "CENTS" rests on first line above foot of design.
"1"'s have straight upper serifs, and practically no serifs at foot.	"1"'s have concave upper serifs. Strong serifs at foot, and bottom of right "1" slants upwards from left to right.
"ONE" or "THREE" is well clear of the medallion.	"ONE" or "THREE" is separated from the medallion only by a thin line.
The lettering is neat and smaller than DIE II.	The lettering is larger than in DIE I.
1912—1c in green, and yellow.	1924—1c Only in yellow.
1918—3c in brown, and carmine.	1924—3c Only in carmine.

1. Robert Savage was an historical and vignette engraver for the A. B. N. Co. He was one of the greatest engravers of his time. He died in Florida in 1943.
2. The Chromium plating was introduced in 1927. The deposit is so slight (.0003" in thickness) that it has no apparent effect on the design. The coating has a tendency to crack and flake off causing various minute varieties of comparatively little interest.

The differences can be clearly seen, and are not due to *wearing of the plate, chromium plating*[2] *wet or dry paper or any of the reasons for slight variations of the printed stamps.*

There are a number of other differences but these are enough to readily distinguish the two dies.

The dies of the 2c and 20c were re-worked, and new rolls were made from the reworked dies, which when used in laying down plates will show slight variations. We illustrate herewith the original and reworked 2c dies.

Fig. 2. Enlargement Showing Differences Between 2c DIE 1a, 1b.

The original state we term Die Ia. Lower right corner slightly rounded. Occurs in carmine and green. (Plates 1 to A191, A193, A194). The reworked state we term Die Ib. There is a tiny position dot to left of left frame opposite the "2". The lower right corner is distinctly sharp angled, and the bottom frame line shows a slight projection to the right. "TWO CENTS" is slightly larger and the figures "2" are slightly different in form.

Fig. 3.
Enlarged pairs of 1c yellow (imperf x perf 8) coil showing DIE I and DIE II. Note that in Die II the numerals "1" are better formed and the "One Cent" is thicker and also well formed. These are distinct and constant differences, not due to inking, wear, or chromium plating.

Lightly printed copies may not show a dot at lower left.
This die occurs in green only. Plates A192, A195 and higher.

In regard to the 20c, the strongly recut vertical border lines of the upper spandrels occuring on plate 9 are sufficient to identfy the reworked die of this denomination.

REFERENCE LIST
Die Proofs King George V "Admiral Type"
1911-28

All on India Die Sunk on White Card (Rare)

#	Denom.	Die #	Imprint[1]	Date	Notes
D100a	1c Black	F212	Yes	1911	"DIE I" (p362)
b	1c Green	F212	Yes	1911	"DIE I"
c	1c Green	None	Yes	1915(?)	
d	1c Green	None	No	1915(?)	
D101a	2c Black	F211	Yes	1911	"DIE Ia" (Fig. 2)
b	2c Carmine	F211	Yes	1911	"Die Ia"
c	2c Carmine	None	Yes	1915(?)	"Die Ia"
d	2c Carmine	None	No	1915(?)	"Die Ia"
D103a	5c Black	F213	Yes	1911	
b	5c Dark blue	F213	Yes	1911	
c	5c Dark blue	None	Yes	1915(?)	
D104a	7c Black	F214	Yes	1911	
b	7c Olive yellow	F214	Yes	1911	
c	7c Olive yellow	None	Yes	1915(?)	
d	7c Olive yellow	None	No	1915(?)	
D105a	10c Black	F218	Yes	1911	
b	10c Purple brown	None	Yes	1915(?)	
c	10c Plum	None	No	1915(?)	
D106a	20c Black	F217	Yes	1911	
b	20c Olive green	None	Yes	1915(?)	
c	20c Olive	None	No	1915(?)	
D107a	50c Black	F219	Yes	1911	
b	50c Brownish black	None	Yes	1915(?)	
c	50c Brownish black	None	No	1915(?)	
D102a	3c Black	O-G266	No	1918	"DIE I" (p170)
D103d	6c Black	O-G421[2]	No	1918	
D100d	1c Black	X-G86[3]	No	1924	"DIE II" (p363)
D102b	3c Black	X-G87[3]	No	1924	"DIE II" (p364)
D123a	4c Black	X-G426	No	1924	
D128a	8c Black	X-G91	No	1925	
D131a	$1.00 Black	X-G8	No	1923	

1. The imprint is "AMERICAN BANK NOTE CO., OTTAWA" in serifed caps, ½ mm. high.
2. Never issued (strictly speaking this is an essay).
3. "Duplicate". "O-G" is "Original Georgian", "X-G" is "Extra Georgian".

DIE PROOFS ON WHITE CARD. Cut close (Rare)

D100e 1c Black (Die II)	D103e 5c Black	D105d 10c Black
D101e 2c Black	D103f 6c Black	D106d 20c Black
D102c 3c Black (Die II)	D104e 7c Black	D107d 50c Black
D123b 4c Black	D128b 8c Black	D131b $1.00 Black

All of these die proofs are rare, as only some seven or eight of each were made.

The Plates

The plates were of *hardened* steel, and were in a number of arrangements of 100, 200, and 400 subjects for all except booklet stamps. The booklets were from special plates of 120 subjects (6 x 20) (See booklet chapter for details).

The regular 400, and 200 subject sheets were divided into post office sheets of 100 (10x10).[3a]

In 1917 a new arrangement of a 400 subject plate was made, consisting of two panes of 200 (20x10) separated by a horizontal gutter 22½ mm. wide.

In one margin opposite the 5th and 6th horizontal rows of each pane are six graduated lines of color, while the other margin has "R-Gauge"[4] reading down. We have also seen panes of 100 with "R-Gauge" opposite the 10th, 20th and 30th stamps of the pane. This plate arrangement was used only for the 1c, 2c, and 3c denomination, and possibly the 5c.

Imprints, Plate Markings, Etc.

This is a virgin field and our notes are merely suggestive. Originally the imprint "OTTAWA—No.—" (Type IX, Fig. 4-11) was located in the upper and lower margins of the plate midway between the left and right pane margins. Later the position varied as can be seen in Fig. 6 which shows an upper right imprint over #2, 3, and 4 of the pane. The plate number in the early plates was in thick heavy figures (Fig. 4,5,8-11), but later, beginning with the "A" plates, (1915) the entire imprint was in the same thin serifed type (Fig. 6,7). The bottom imprint is inverted on the 1c plates 1, 2, 3, and 4, on the 2c plate 2, and on the 5c plate 6. It may exist inverted on other plates but if so we have not seen them.

The "A" was hand drawn on 1c plates A99 to A102, and 2c plate A80 (Fig. 6). For the later "A" plates a new imprint roll was made.

The other letters and numerals are private marks of the manufacturers, and plate handlers, and of little significance to the collector.

3a. Appendix Q #9a.
4. We venture the opinion that "R-Gauge" refers to a method of guaging the register of the press during printing.

Fig. 4. Thick No. 65. Die 1.

Fig. 5. Plate "1" 1c green. Die I, Printing order '83.

Fig. 6. Hand-drawn "A". Plate "A80".

Fig. 7. Top Imprint, from an "A" Plate. Thin Numbers. Die I.

Fig. 8. Bottom Imprint Inverted. Thick Plate Number. Die I.

Fig. 9. Shows Bottom Imprint Normal. Die I.

Fig. 10. Thick Plate Number "2". Printing Order 83.

Fig. 11. Thick Plate Number "12". Bottom Imprint Normal.

The plates were curved slightly in the vertical direction, and at the lower edge of many plates a band of lathework was entered, to aid in the detection of wear of the plate. We note five distinct patterns of this lathework band, and illustrate them herewith. The earliest date of the use of this lathework border we believe was January 1917, and it was discontinued in December 1924.

PATTERN I. January to March 1917.

PATTERN II. March 1917 to Oct. 1920. PATTERN III. March 1920 to Jan. 1921.

PATTERN V
Nov. 1920 to Dec. 1924.

PATTERN IV. Nov. 1920 to Dec. 1924.

PATTERN V, Inverted.

Table of Border Lathework of 1911-28 Issues

Pattern	1c green	1c yellow	2c carmine	2c green	3c brown	3c carmine	4c olive	5c blue	5c violet
I									
II	x	x	x	x	x		x		
III	x		x						
IV		x	x		x	x	x		
V									x

Pattern	7c olive	7c r. brown	10c plum	10c blue	20c green	50c black	$1.00 orange		WT 2c+1c brown
I									
II					20c green	50c black	$1.00 orange		
III				x	x				
IV	x	x	x						x
V	x		x						x

NOTES. Pattern V exists normal and inverted. The 8c blue and 10c brown were not issued until after the discontinuance of the lathework.

Fig. 12. Unissued 6c. Die Proof.

The later plate, made after 1924 and also after chrome-plating was introduced (Late 1927) do not have this lathework, as the wearing of the chromium surface was sufficient indication of wear and the necessity for re-coating the plate.

Plate Varieties

The plates of these stamps are remarkably free of important varieties; when one considers the number of plates used and the huge quantity of stamps printed.

Such varieties which we note are as follows:

Hair Lines

These are fine lines of color, always horizontal, that is, at right angles to the direction of curving, and occur on the 1c, and 2c, sheet and booklet stamps. The cause of these lines has been the subject of some discussion, but it appears to be due to stresses put on the plate during hardening and curving for fitting in the press.

Re-Entries

Fig. 13. Strong re-entry L. L. stamp of block of four. 1c green, Die 1, Plate 12, L. R. #35.

These are notable for their absence. A strong example is known on the 1c green (Die I) showing doubling of lower part of the stamp. (Plate 12, L.R. #35). (Fig. 13).

Since the plates were of *hardened* steel such re-entries that occur took place during the original manufacture of the plate, as it was impractical to soften, straighten, burnish, re-enter, harden and recurve a plate. (See also page xxi).

The 3c carmine, Die I, exists with a horizontal dash of color, in the right numeral tablet.

The Recuts in the Spandrels

Aside from the re-worked dies (2c and 20c) the vertical lines bounding the horizontal lines in the upper spandrels may have been recut on the die before a new transfer roll was made, resulting in slight differences in the reliefs.

Two values are worth noting:

5c blue and violet. Several positions on the plate show strengthening of one or both of the vertical lines. Probably a relief variety. (Pl. A24 shows strong vertical lines). Plates A19, and A20 show extensive re-touching of the plate.

7c olive bistre. Plate 6, positions #31, 41, 51, 61, 71, 81, 91 of one pane (probably the upper left) show these vertical lines much more distinctly than the other subjects. This is the left vertical row of the pane and the evidence seems to show that it is a relief variety. We note these in the listings as Types A and B, as distinguished from definitely known die differences.

Etching

The practice of hardening and curving the plates made the feasibility of softening and re-entering worn subjects a difficult, if not almost impossible, procedure. It was easier to make a new plate than go through such a tedious process, the results which might be unsatisfactory. Some of the differences noted on the 5c, and 7c may be due to etching the plate, but more probably are the results of the use of two different transfer reliefs in rocking in the plate. It will be noted that the two *types* of the 7c occur on the last of the plates for the bistre stamps.

Perforations

The usual perforation gauges 12, and occurs on the sheet stamps, coils, and booklets. Perforation 8 was used on coil stamps for affixing machines.

In 1924 the 1c yellow, 2c green, and 3c carmine, IMPERFORATE were placed on sale at the Philatelic Section of the Financial Branch of the Post Office Department in Ottawa. Later (1925?) imperforate specimens of the 4c, 5c violet,, 7c red brown, 8c blue, 10c bistre, 20c. 50c and $1.00 came on the market. Imperforate tete-beche blocks of twelve of the booklet stamps are also known. None of these 1925 imperforates were regularly issued.

Printing

The early printings were from flat plates (slightly curved, but not in any sense to be considered rotary press plates) on dampened paper. Late in December, 1922, the 3c brown (Die I) was printed on dry pre-gummed paper, and other denominations were gradually shifted to the new process until January, 1926, when the 5c violet was printed in this manner, marking the complete disuse of the wet paper method. The use of damp paper resulted in the stamps shrinking when dry. This accounts for the variation in size so frequently found, especially when the early and late printings are compared. Occasionally the paper was cut and/or fed into the press so that the grain caused the stamps to shrink vertically instead of the usual narrowing. Such examples are of interest to specialists.

The long period this issue was in use, coupled with the difficulties arising during the war period of 1914-18, as well as changes in method of production resulted in a wide range of shades.

Printings on damp paper are usually sharp and have an intensity of color lacking on the printings on dry pre-gummed paper.

The chief confusion arises over the three distinct shades of the 50c denomination. Officially the color is black, and the shades are unintentional. The early printing were in dark gray black and black, while the later printings have a distinct brownish cast.

The Paper

This is usually white wove, machine made, and of medium thickness (.0038" to .0045").

In 1924 the 2c green, and 5c violet appeared on a thinner, looser weave, more translucent paper (.0025"). Its use appears to have been an experiment by the paper manufacturer, and not an intention of the Post Office Department. It is a constant and distinct variety.

The rolls of paper are made up in certain weights, and it occasionally happens that when a roll is being made up the run of paper ends, and another begins, the joint made by overlapping the two runs. Normally the overlap is cut out before the stamps are printed, but the 3c carmine is known with this overlap, this being the so-called "double paper" variety.

Gum

Until late 1922 all the stamps were gummed *after* being printed on a dampened paper. Beginning that year a *dry pre-gummed* paper was used. By 1926 the damp paper method had been completely abandoned.

Previous to the use of pre-gummed paper the gum varies considerably in color and texture, but in any event it is not in itself a reliable guide to the various plates and printings.

The pre-gummed paper is much more uniform in texture, and the gum is smooth, even yellowish color, and owing to the greater pressure required in dry printing shows the impression of the stamp quite strongly.

We might say that the devising of a method of dry printing line engraved stamps was a direct result of research on the part of the American Bank Note Co., in order to compete with the Stickney Rotary Presses devised by the United States Bureau of Engraving and Printing.[5]

Fig. 14. 3c Carmine, Imperforate Pair. Die I.

Booklets

The first 1c booklets occur in this issue, and later a 3c booklet was issued as well as a combination booklet. These are discussed in detail in the chapter on booklets. (q.v.).

---

[5]. See U. S. Stamp Catalogue, #459 2c carmine issued June 30, 1914 (Scott Publications). This was the first stamp issued printed on the Stickney Rotary Press.

Fig. 15. Tete-Beche (Die I). Booket.

Fig. 16. Tete-Beche (Die I). Booklet.

Coils

Stamps in coils or rolls of 500[6] were supplied at .06 over face value to cover cost of winding. In addition to the regularly issued coils an experimental coil was made from 2c ordinary sheet *torn* in strips of 10 and pasted endwise together. Since they were perforated all around they can only be distinguished in paste up strips on the back of which is a rectangu'ar handstamp in violet "Postage Stamp Branch—May 11, 1915—P. O. D.". Other types of handstamps are known but these might be called "re-issues".

Fig. 17. "Re-issue" of 1915 Coil.

The first regularly issued coils of 1912 were made from ordinary sheets, perforated 8 vertically and cut into horizontal strips of 20 which were pasted together to make rolls of 500. In 1915 coils were made from ordinary sheets perforated 12 horizontally, and cut into vertical strips of ten, and pasted together to make rolls of 500. The available evidence indicates that the 400 subject

---

6. Although the P. O. may have intended to offer coils of 500 and 1000, we have found no evidence of anything except coils of 500 being issued.

plates (of 1917) in two panes of 200 (20 x 10) were so arranged that they could be cut into panes of 100, or strips of 20 for coils, whichever was needed at the time.

The Vending Machine Perforation—1918
(The "Toronto" perf.)

Fig. 18. Vending Machine Perf of 1918.

In July 1918 the 1c green (Die I) in coils perforated 12 x imperf. with two additional holes 3.5mm. in diameter, 5.75mm. apart, was issued. The measurements may vary slightly as the various lugs making the large holes were not uniform in size or spacing.

The endwise or vertical coils were for stamp vending machines, while the sidewise or horizontal coils were for stamp affixing machines.

The 1931 Provisional

The use of some 3c carmine coil sheets in 1931 to provide for a temporary shortage of the 3c denomination due to an increase in the postage rate, led to the issue of the compound perforation of 12 x 8. They were placed on sale June 24, 1931.

The Color Changes of 1922-25.

During the years 1922-25 a number of color changes were necessitated by adjustments in rates. The domestic rate of 3c necessitated the 3c becoming carmine, while the 1c and 2c became yellow and green respectively. The rate to Great Britain and Newfoundland being 4c, resulted in the issue of that value and the change later of the 7c to red brown. The new U. P. U. rate of 10c resulted in changing the stamp to blue, and the 5c was therefore printed in violet.

On October 1, 1925, the U. P. U. rate was reduced to 8c and the color became blue, the 10c again being changed this time to bistre brown.

A $1.00 was added in 1923 to meet the demand for a high value.

King George V "Admiral" Type 1911-28

A. 1911-21 Group.

#	Denom. & Color	Date Issued	Quantity Issued	Plates[1]	Value unused	Factor used	Notes	1944 Scott #	1944 S.G. #
100	1c green, Die I.	Dec. 22, 1911	3,218,400,000	1-96, A97-A182, A186, A187	N	N	All on damp paper	104	196
a	hair lines			1, 2, 57	20	40			
b	re-entry			Pl 12, L.R.35	50	30			
101	2c carmine, Die Ia.	Dec. 22, 1911	3,043,450,000	1-78, A79-A160	N	N	All on damp paper	106	200
a	hair lines			4, 52	25	50			
102	3c brown, Die I.	Aug. 6, 1918	2,044,000,000	A1-A120	N	N	All on damp paper	108	204
103	5c blue	Jan. 17, 1912	198,000,000	1-14	N	N		111	206
104	7c olive bistre (Type A)	Dec. 27, 1911	103,200,000	1-4, A5, A6	N	N	7 positions on plate	113	209
a	retouched spandrels (Type B)			A6					
105	10c plum	Jan. 12, 1912	148,700,000	1-12	N	N	All on damp paper	116	210
106	20c olive green	Jan. 23, 1912	96,966,000	1-4, A5-A8	N	N		119	212
a	Imperf. pair								
b	retouched die			A9	3	2			
107	50c black	Jan. 26, 1912	11,070,000	1-3, A4	N	N		120	215
a	Imperf. pair (brown black)				25				

Unused Block of Four, Factor 6.
Unused Plate Blocks of 8, Factor 15.
1. The plates were numbered continuously, but we have given, where possible the earliest number which is prefixed "A".

379 *

A. COILS 1911-21 Group.

#	Denom. & Color	Perf.	Date Issued	No. in Roll	Quantity Issued	Value unused	Factor used	Notes	1944 Scott #	1944 S.G. #
108	1c green, Die I. Paste-up Pair Hidden Plate No.	12 x imperf	Sept. 1915	500	18,050,000	N 3 x	N		131	216
109	2c carmine Paste-up Pair Hidden Plate No.	12 x imperf	Sept. 1915	500	14,290,000	N 3 x	N		132	218
110	3c brown, Die I. Paste-up Pair Hidden Plate No.	12 x imperf	Jan. 1921	500		N 3 x	N		134	218a
111	1c green, Die I. Paste-up Pair	8 x imperf	Sept. 1912	500	3,330,000	N 3	N		123	224a
112	1c green, Die I. Paste-up Pair	imperf x 8	1912	500	180,005,000	N 3	N		125	219
113	2c carmine Paste-up Pair	8 x imperf	1912	500	4,005,000	N 3	N	The 1st Regularly Issued Coils. (See Appendix B #61).	124	224b
114	2c carmine Paste-up Pair	imperf x 8	1912	500	171,742,500	N 3	N		127	221
115	3c brown, Die I. Paste-up Pair	imperf x 8	Nov. 1918	500	126,300,000	N 3	N		129	224
116	1c green, Die I. Hidden Plate No. Paste-up Pair Cover	12 x imperf +2 large holes	July 1918	500		150 x 200	300	Trial perf. in Vending Machine, Toronto P. O.	131	216
EX-C6	2c carm., paste-up pair Hidden Plate No.	12 x 12	May 11, 1915	500	18,000	100 x		These pairs are stamped in purple or black "May 11, 1915" (Fig. 17).	106	200

King George V. "Admiral" Type. 1922-28 Group.

#	Denom. & Color	Date Issued	Quantity Issued	Plates	Value unused	Value used	Factor unused	Factor used	NOTES	1944 Scott #	1944 S.G. #
117	1c yellow, DIE I Block of four Plate block of eight	June 7, 1922	1,278,760,000	A169-A182, A186, A187	1½ 8	1½ 16			Quantity Issued Includes Both Dies.	105	246
118	1c yellow, DIE II	Oct. 1924		A183, A185, A188 - A199	N	N				105	246
119	2c green, DIE Ia	June 6, 1922	See Note 1	A159-A195 A185, A186	N	N				107	247
a	Thin paper				4	8					
120	2c green, DIE Ib Block of four	1924		A196-A229	2 10	2 20			Plate A224 et seq. Chrome plated in Oct. 1927.	107	247
121	3c carmine, DIE I	Dec.14, 1923	See Note 2	A115-A131	N	N				109	249
122	3c carmine, DIE II	Oct. 1924		A132-A164	N	N			All on Dry Paper	109	249
123	4c olive	Jul. 3, 1922	75,900,000	A1-A7	N	N				110	251
a	Imperf pair				400						
124	5c violet	Feb. 2, 1922	See Note 3	A15-A25	N	N				112	252
a	Imperf pair				250						
b	Thin paper	Oct. 19 1924		A21, A22	2	6					
125	7c red brown	Dec. 12. 1924	15,780,000	A7-A8	N	N				114	254
a	Imperf pair				200						
126	8c blue	Sept. 1, 1925	24,200,000	A1-A3	N	N				115	254a
a	Imperf pair				125						
127	10c blue	Feb. 20, 1922		A21-A25	N	N				117	255
128	10c bistre	Aug. 1, 1925	85,895,000	A13-A25	N	N				118	255a
a	Imperf pair				125						
129	$1.00 orange	Jul. 2, 1923	1,865,000	A-1	N	N				122	256
a	Imperf pair				12						

1. Total was about 1,200,000,000 of both Dies Ia, Ib.
2. Total was about 1,250,000,000. Total for both Dies I, II.
3. Total was about 1,000,000,00.

Other Factors   Blocks of four unless otherwise noted. Unused factor 5, used factor 10 to 20.
Plate blocks of eight unless otherwise noted. Factor 15.

"Admiral" Type Coils. 1922-28 Group.

#	Denom. & Color	Perf.	Date Issued	No. in Roll	Quantity Issued	Value Factor Unused	Value Factor Used	Notes	1944 S#	1944 S.G. #
130	1c Yellow, Die I Paste up pair	Imperf. x 8	1923	500	25,700,000	2 6 N 3	2 6 N 3		126	257
131	1c Yellow, Die II Paste up pair	Imperf. x 8	1924	500					126	257
132	2c Green, Die Ia Paste up pair	Imperf. x 8	Aug. 1922	500	158,197,500	N	N		128	258
133	2c Green, Die Ib Paste up pair	Imperf. x 8	1924	500		x	x			
134	2c Green, Die Ia Paste up pair Hidden Plate No.	12 x Imperf.	Sept. 1924	500	250,000	N	N		133	259
135	3c Carmine, Die I Paste up pair	Imperf. x 8	Dec. 1924	500	47,585,000	N	N		133	263
136	c Carmine, Die II Paste up pair	Imperf. x 8	1924	500		x	x			

"Admiral" Type Imperforate, Part Perforate Sheet, and Compound Perforate—1922-31.

Coil Sheets of 100—Imperforate x Perf. 8

#	Denom. & Color	Date Issued	Plates	Quantity Issued	Value Factor	Notes	1944 S#	1944 S.G. #
137	1c Yellow, Die I	1923	A179-80	2200	20	Pat. II lathework, Damp ptg.	126a	257b
138	1c Yellow, Die II	1926		100,000	N	Re-issue, dry ptg no lathework	126a	257a
139	2c Green, Die Ia	1923	A188, 189	2200	20	Pat. IV lathework Damp ptg.	128a	258b
140	2c Green, Die Ib	1926		100,000	N	Re-issue, dry ptg no lathework	128a	258a
141	3c Carmine, Die I	1923	A126,128	2200	N	Pat. IV lathework Damp ptg.	130a	259a

Imperforate Sheets of 100

#	Denom. & Color	Date Issued	Plates	Quantity Issued	Value Factor	Notes	1944 S#	1944 S.G. #
142	1c Yellow, Die I	Oct. 7, 1924	A179, A180	50,000	N	Pattern II lathework	136	260
143	2c Green, Die Ia	Oct. 7, 1924	A188, A189	50,000	N	Pattern IV lathework	137	261
144	3c Carmine, Die I	Oct. 7, 1924	A126-A131	100,000	N	Pattern V lathework	138	262

Perforated 12x8

#	Denom. & Color	Date Issued	Plates	Quantity Issued	Value Factor	Notes	1944 S#	1944 S.G. #
145	3c Carmine, Die II	June 24, 1931	A13, A14, A15		N	Printed in 1924	184	263a

C. The 1923-26 Part Perforates.

In 1923 two sheets of the 1c, 2c, and 3c stamps, perforated 8 vertically and imperforate horizontally were issued as a favor to a gentlemen of considerable influence in Ottawa. At the same time some twenty sheets of each were set aside. These were later sold as a lot to another collector. Considerable interest was aroused and the collector who held the large lot sold most of them through a Montreal dealer.

When the demand for these varieties became insistent enough the Post Office Department "re-issued' the 1c and 2c in order to fill the demand. The 3c was not "re-issued" as it would have been necessary to prepare a new plate to print only 100,000 stamps.

Considerable controversy has developed over methods of distinguishing the first and second printings. We give a brief chart below showing the distinguishing differences.

	Die	*Color*	*Paper*	*Gum*	*Printing*
1c Original	I	Dark yellow	White Medium	Pebbly	Damp
Re-issue	II	Yellow	Thin Creamy	Smooth	Dry
2c Original	Ia	Dark green	White Medium	Pebbly	Damp
Re-issue	Ib	Green	Thin Creamy	Smooth	Dry
3c Original	I	Dark carmine	White Medium	Pebbly	Damp

WARNING! Be careful of imperforates faked to resemble the part perforate.

D. The 1926 Provisionals.

On July 1, 1926, the domestic postage rate was reduced from 3c to 2c per ounce or fraction thereof. When the reduction was made there were almost 130,000,000 3c carmine stamps in stock at Ottawa, costing approximately $16,000. The post offices throughout the Dominion would have difficulty in disposing of their own stocks without trying to unload the 130,000,000 held by Ottawa. The authorities therefore tried surcharging the 3c stamp "2 cents."

Accordingly 140,000 Post Office sheets of 100 were turned over to the King's Printer to be surcharged "2 cents" in one line. The King's Printer essayed three types of surcharge—viz:

"2 cents"—Sans-serif caps. 5 mm. high, black.
"2 cents"—Sans-serif caps. 3 mm. high, black.
Both black, occurring in alternate rows.
"2 cents"—Sans-serif caps. 3 mm. high, orange.

Essays for "2 Cents" Surcharge.

By the King's Printer. (Rare).

E146a {"2 cents" 5 mm. high in black } Double surcharge, one in orange.
{"2 cents" 3 mm. high in orange }
E146b {"2 cents" 3 mm. high in black } Double surcharge, one in orange.
{"2 cents" 3 mm. high in orange }
E146c "2 cents" 5 mm. high in black.
E146d "2 cents" 3 mm. high in black.
E146a, E146b exist in vertical pairs se-tenant.
E146c, E146d exist in vertical pairs se-tenant.

Vertical Pair of E146a, E146b Setenant.

The issued surcharge "2 cents" is 16 mm. long, the "2" 3 mm. high, and "cents" 2½ mm. high in sans-serif capitals, in a setting of 100. No varieties of any importance. The work was unsatisfactory, and all were destroyed; exsept 500 picked sheets which were placed on sale at the Philatelic Agency in Ottawa.

The plate numbers of the surcharged sheets placed on sale were A115, A116, A117, (Die I), and A162, A163 (Die II), upper right and upper left panes.

A second attempt was made by the Canadian Bank Note Co., and 1000 sheets of 100 were turned over to them. They requested that they be allowed to place the "2" over "Cents" in order to distinguish their work from that of the King's

Printer. These were not satisfactory, but 808 of these sheets were placed on sale at the Philatelic Agency. Upper right and upper left panes, plate A115, A116, A117 were used.

From a setting of 100. "2" shifted slightly to left on #12, 32, 70, 80, 81, 82, 83, 84, 85, 86.

The sheets being already gummed and perforated were difficult to handle for surcharging, slipping and buckling, with the result that the wastage was out of proportion to the work done.

1926 Surcharges.

REFERENCE LIST

#	Description	Value Factors Unused / Used		1944 S#	1944 S.G. #
	Placed on sale Oct. 16, 1926				
146	"2 Cents", on 3c carmine. Die I (49,800)	N	N	139	264
	Pair, one without surcharge.	50			
147	"2 Cents", on 3c carmine. Die II (200)	x			
	Placed on sale Oct. 26, 1926				
148	"2 Cents", on 3c carmine. Die I (80,800)	N	N	140	265
	Double surcharge.	25			
	Triple surcharge.	100			

Chapter XXI

SCROLL ISSUE. 1928-29.

The "Admiral" type of regular issue stamps was replaced in the latter part of 1928, and early in 1929 by a new series, the values of 1c to 8c bearing a portrait of King George V, and the higher values of large format with pictorial designs. It will be noted that they are bi-lingual, the first regular issue to be such, and all bear the word "Canada" in a scroll across the top, hence the name "Scroll Issue."

The pictorial designs of the values of 10c and up mark a new policy in the designing of Canadian Issues.[1]

The plates were of hardened steel chromium plated, which accounts for the comparatively small number of plates required. The 1c to 8c denominations were printed in sheets of 400, divided into four panes of 100 (10 x 10). The 10c to $1.00 were printed in sheets of 200 (10 x 20) divided into four panes of 50 each (5 x 10). Imprint at top (Type IX). Coils of 500 of the 1c, and 2c, as well as booklets were also available. There are no varieties of importance.

1c to 8c vignette by Robert Savage.

---
[1]. For details as to the designs see Appendix N #22, 23, 24.

REFERENCE LIST

DIE PROOFS

India Mounted On Card.

			Approved			*Approved*
D150	1c Orange		Nov. 4, 1928	D156	10c Green	Oct. 5, 1928
D151	2c Green		No. 4, 1928	D157	12c Gray	Oct. 5, 1928
D152	3c Carmine		Oct. 5, 1928	D158	20c Carmine	Sept. 15, 1928
D153	4c Bistre		Oct. 5, 1928	D159	50c Blue	Oct. 4, 1928
D154	5c Violet		Oct. 20, 1928	D160	$1.00 Olive green	Sept. 7, 1928
D155	8c Dark blue		Oct. 28, 1928			

1928-29 "Scroll Issue"

#	Denom. & Color	Issued	Plates	Value Factor Unused	Value Factor Used	Quantity Issued	Notes	1944 S.#	1944 S.G. #
150	1c Orange	Oct. 25, 1928	1-6	N	N			149	275
151	2c Green	Oct. 16, 1928	1-11	N	N			150	276
152	3c Dark Carmine	Dec. 12, 1928	1, 2, 3	N	N	10,500,000		151	277
153	4c Bistre	Aug. 16, 1928	1	N	N	6,520,000		152	278
154	5c Dark violet	Dec. 12, 1928	1, 2, 3	N	N	31,921,000		153	279
155	8c Dark blue	Dec. 21, 1928	1, 2, 3	N	N	7,750,000		154	280
156	10c Green	Jan. 6, 1929	1, 2	N	N	18,287,000		155	281
157	12c Gray	Jan. 6, 1929	1, 2, 3	N	N	3,603,000		156	282
158	20c Dark carmine	Jan. 6, 1929	1, 2, 3	N	N	6,140,000		157	283
159	50c Dark blue	Jan. 6, 1929	1, 2, 3	N	N	844,900		158	284
160	$1.00 Olive green	Nov. 5 1928	1, 2, 3	N	N	300,000		159	285

Other Factors: Blocks of four—unused factor 5, used factor 5 to 10. Plate blocks of eight—unused factor 15. This set is known imperf., in perf. vert. or imperf. horiz. These were not regularly issued. Factor for a set of any of these varieties 60.

Scroll Issue Coils—Imperf. x Perf. 8.

#	Denom. & Color	Date Issued	Rolls of	Quantity Issued	Value Unused	Factors Used	1944 Scott #	1944 S.G. #
161	1c. Orange Paste up pair	1928	500	20,000 rolls = (10,000,000)	N 3	N* 5	160	286
162	2c. Green Paste up pair	Nov. 5, 1928	500	166,518 rolls = (83,259,000)	N 5	N 15	161	287

The paste-up occurs 24 to 26 times in each roll.

The majority of these stamps were precancelled, such copies being worth about 1/3 N.

BOOKLETS—See Chapter on these issues.

390

Chapter XXII

THE ISSUES ENGRAVED AND PRINTED BY THE BRITISH AMERICAN BANK NOTE CO. 1930-35.

A. The Arch and Maple Leaf Issue. 1930-31

In 1929 the British American Bank Note Co., were successful in obtaining the contract for the production of the postage stamps of the Dominion. This was the same firm that had produced the issues of 1867-97 (see chapter X).

The new contractor's agreement ran for five years[1] at the following rates:

1c, 2c, 3c	10.4 to 11 cents
4c, 5c, 8c	12c
10c	25c
12c, 13c	65c
20c	30c
50c	75c
$1.00	1.50
Special Delivery	1.50
Air Mail	30c
Postage Due 2c	30c
1c, 4c	65c

} Per thousand stamps.

Coils $95.00 per 1000 rolls, including cost of stamps.
Precancelled, $109.25 per 1000 rolls, including cost of stamps.

---
1. From April 1, 1930 to **March 31, 1935**.

Fig. 1. Essay for 1930 Issue. Note "Post" instead of "Postage" at right (E171a).

The preparation of this issue began early in 1929, and the original design showed the word "Post" at the right instead of "Postage" (Fig. 1). Futhermore the pearl before and after "Canada" is completely colorless.

REFERENCE LIST

Die Essays of 1929 (Very Rare).

DIE PROOFS

(On India, Die sunk on white card)

Also known mounted on thick card, not die sunk.

		Approved			Approved
E163a	1c Orange	June 28, 1929	E176a	8c Blue	Aug. 3, 1929
E166a	2c Green	June 15, 1929	E178b	10c Blue	June 21, 1929
E171a	3c Carmine	June 15, 1929	E179a	12c Black	July 25, 1929
E172a	4c Olive green	Aug. 2, 1929	E180a	20c Carmine	July 25, 1929
E173a	5c Purple	Aug. 3, 1929	E181a	50c Blue	July 25, 1929
E173b	7c Red brown	Aug. 2, 1929	E182a	$1.00 Green	July 17, 1929

Aside from the lack of balance the use of the word "Post" is rather questionable, "Canada Post" being less appropriate than "Canada Postage" on a stamp indicating prepayment of the fees required on mail matter. Whatever the reason for the change some $2,450.00 was spent in preparing new dies of the accepted design.

DIE PROOFS OF ISSUED DESIGN

On India, die sunk on white card. (Rare)

D163a	1c Orange		D178a	10c Green
D166a	2c Green		D179a	12c Black
D171a	3c Carmine		D180a	20c Carmine
D172a	4c Ochre		D181a	50c Blue
D173a	5c Violet		D182a	$1.00 Green
D177a	8c Orange			

We have also seen the 2c, 3c, and 4c cut close, mounted on heavy white card.

It will be noted that the 7c was dropped.

The policy of having the values over 8c in pictorial designs was continued.[2]

The plates were of hardened steel, and for the first time Stickney rotary presses were used to print the 1c, 2c, 3c, and 5c denominations.

The 4c to $1.00 were printed from flat plates. Note that the 5c was the only denomination printed both on rotary and flat plate presses.

Three plate arrangements were used, viz:

1. 1c to 10c in sheet form. 400 subjects (20 x 20), no imprints, but with the marginal inscription "PLATE No. —" in sans-serif capitals 2¾ mm. high, and 26 to 30 mm. long (depending on the plate number), reading up at the upper left and lower left corners, and reading down at the upper right and lower right corners (we have seen examples from plates 5 and 6 of the 2c where it is at the sides midway between the top and bottom of the pane). Imprint Type XI.

2. The 12c to $1.00 denominations were printed in sheets of 200, (10 x 20) divided into panes of 50 (5 x 10). The marginal inscriptions are similar, but we have seen the 50c with it located at each side, midway between the top and bottom of the pane.

3. The coil stamps were printed from plates of 384 subjects (24 x 16), on rotary presses. This eliminated "paste up" pairs. During the coiling process

---
2. For discussion of some of the designs see Appendix N #25, 36.

Fig. 2
Micro-Photograph of re-entry on 1c orange and 1c green.

Fig. 3.

The upper stamp shows the re-entry. Lower stamp shows re-entry after being re-touched. There is a prong in the lower left of right value tablet, and there is a dot of color in the top of "E" of "CENT". Other minute traces are also discernable. The re-entry occurs in orange and green, the re-touch only in green.

the stamps sometimes snap apart and they are matched together by a piece of thin white paper which is perforated with the stamps.

The rotary press plates are curved to form a semi-circle, two being locked together make a complete cylinder. The joint between the two plates cause a thin line of color which is found between every 24th and 25th stamp of the coils, and sheet stamps that have not been cut properly sometimes show a line of color along the deckle edge of the sheet at the top or bottom. This wavy edge is a characteristic of rotary printing.

The mechanical wiper of the plates resulted in occasional examples of badly smeared impressions. Much commoner are albino plate numbers, and "phantom" plate numbers. The latter occur along the sheet margin and may be other numbers than that of the plate from which the sheet was printed. We have seen three different "phantom" numbers on the same sheet margin. None of these varieties warrant separate listing.

During the currency of this issue new dies were made for the 1c and 2c denominations. Enlarged illustrations show the main differences between the two dies.

Die I   Die II

Varieties.

Plate 2 of the 1c is notable for an extremely fine example of a re-entry. This occurs in the 96th stamp, of the upper left pane (96UL2). This was so obvious that it was retouched, but traces of the re-entry are still visible. The retouch occurs only in green.

In the 2c coil stamps a retouch to the eye and face of the King vulgarly termed "Cockeyed King" occurs on the left hand stamp of certain line pairs. Only one roll in 16 could have this variety, which cannot occur more than eleven times in any such roll of 500 stamps.

No other re-entries of importance have been seen by us.

Color Changes.

While these stamps were current changes were made in the rates of postage necessitating the following color changes, viz:

Letter postage raised from 2c to 3c July 1, 1931.

2c changed from scarlet to brown. New 3c in scarlet.

Previously the rate for foreign letters was reduced from 8c to 5c (July 1, 1930), and in accordance with the U. P. U. regulations the colors were changed as follows:

    1c from orange to green.
    2c from green to scarlet.
    5c from violet to blue.
    8c from blue to orange.

Paper, Perforations and Gum.

The paper is a rather thick white wove. The 10c is known on double paper due to the overlap of two rolls of paper.

The sheet stamps are perforated 11, and the coils 8½. The 1c green is known imperforate. This was a favor, not regularly issued.

The gum varies considerable in color from almost colorless to a distinct brownish tint. These variations are of little significance.

On some of the Stickney press printings the "ridged" gum peculiar to this type of printing, which was due to the action of two ridged steel rollers which "broke up" the gum when the web of paper was cut into sheets of 400 stamps and perforated, in order to flatten out the rolled paper and make it stack readily into piles of sheets of 400 stamps. The ridging was reduced almost to the vanishing point as the producers had found that when the web of paper was properly seasoned and not dried out too much this process, which did not add to the appearance of the stamps, was not so essential as the manufacturers of the press had supposed. In some cases the sheets, although printed on the Stickney press, show very little sign of "ridging", and this has given rise to the theory that there were some printings of the 1c, 2c, and 3c on the flat press.

The only positive means of identifying "flat" printings, as distinct from Stickney or "rotary" printings, is the type of edge at the top and bottom of the sheet. In the case of the Stickney printings this edge is wavy, whereas on the "flat" plate printings the edge of the sheets are straight at top or bottom.

Fig. 4. Imperforate Block of the 1c Green.

1930 "Arch and Maple Leaf" Issue 1933.

#	Denom. & Color	Die	Plates	Rotary or Flat	Date Issued	Value Factor Unused	Value Factor Used	Notes	1944 S#	1944 S.G. #
163	1c Orange	I	1, 2	R	July 17, 1930	N	N		162	288
a	Major re-entry	I	2	R		75	75			
	Ditto Precancelled "Montreal Que"	I	2	R		150	150	#96UL2.		
164	1c Green	I	1, 2	R	Dec. 6, 1930	N	N	Plates 3 and 4 made but not used.	163a	300
a	Major re-entry	I	2	R		50	50	#96UL2.		
b	Re-entry retouched	I	2	R		75	75	#96 UL2 retouched.		
165	1c Green	II	5-8	R		N	N		163	300a
a	Imperforate	II	5	R				One sheet known.		
166	2c Green	I	1-6	R	July 6, 1930	N	N		164	289
167	2c Scarlet	I	3-6	R	Nov. 17, 1930	N	N		165a	301
168	2c Scarlet	II	7, 8	R		N	N	#65LR8 (so called "Waxed" moustache).	165	301a
a	Long left moustache	II	8	R						
169	2c Brown	I	5, 6	R	July 4, 1931	N	N		166a	302
170	2c Brown	II	7-10	R		N	N	Plates 11 and 12 made but not used. #65LR8.	166	302a
a	Long left moustache		8	R						
171	3c Scarlet		1, 5	R	July 13, 1931	N	N		167	303
172	4c Ochre	I	1, 2	F	Nov. 5, 1930	N	N	12,402,000 issued.	168	290
173	5c Violet	I	1, 2	R	July 7, 1930	N	N		169	291

1930 "Arch and Maple Leaf" Issue 1933. (Cont.)

#	Denom. & Color	Die	Plates	Rotary or Flat	Date Issued	Value Factor Unused	Value Factor Used	Notes	1944 S#	1944 S.G. #
174	5c Violet	I	3	F	June 18, 1930	N	N		169a	291
175	5c Blue	I	3	F	Nov. 13, 1930	N	N		170	304
176	8c Blue	I	1	F	Aug. 13, 1930	N	N	4,000,000 issued.	171	292
177 a	8c Orange Red orange	I	1, 2, 3 3	F F	Nov. 5, 1930 Aug. 1932	N	N	2,000,000 issued.	172	305
178	10c Olive green (Legislative Library Ottawa)	I	1	F	Sept. 15, 1930	N	N	502,000 issued. Replaced by Sir Georges Cartier stamp Sept. 30, 1931.	173	293
179	12c Gray black (Citadel Quebec City)		1	F	Dec. 4, 1930	N	N	6,976,000 issued.	174	294
180	20c Red (Harvesting in the West)		1	F	Dec. 4, 1930	N	N		175	295
181	50c Blue (Church at Grand Pre Nova Scotia)		1	F	Dec. 4, 1930	N	N		176	296
182	$1.00 Dark Olive (Mt. Eidth Cavell, Canadian Rockies)		1	F	Dec. 4, 1930	N	N		177	297

Arch and Maple Leaf Issue. 1930-33.

COILS. Imperf x perf 8. Rolls of 500

#	Denom. & Color	Die	Plates	Issued	Value Factor Unused	Value Factor Used	Notes	1944 S#	1944 S.G. #
183	1c Orange	I	1, 2	Sept. 18, 1930	N	N		178	298
a	Line pair				3				
b	Precancelled			July 14, 1930	—	½	See precancel chapter		
184	1c Green	I	1, 2	Feb. 4, 1931	N	N		179	306
a	Line pair				3				
b	Precancelled			April 2, 1931	—	½	See precancel chapter		
185	2c Green	I	1, 2	June 27, 1930	N	N	Vulgarly known as "cock-eyed King" variety.	180	299
a	Retouched eye				24				
b	Line pair				3				
186	2c Scarlet	I	1, 2	Nov. 19, 1930	N	N	24,880,000	181	307
a	Retouched eye				24				
b	Line pair				3				
187	2c Brown	I	1, 2	July 4, 1931	N	N		182	308
a	Retouched eye				15				
b	Line pair				3				
c	Precancelled				—	½	See precancel chapter		
188	3c Scarlet	II	3	July 13, 1931	N	N		183	309
a	Line pair				3				

B. The Georges Cartier Stamp. 1931.

It was intended to issue this stamp along with the Historical Issue, but the actual issue was delayed until September 30, 1931, when it was issued as an ordinary stamp replacing the Parliamentary Library type.

The stamp was printed from three plates of 400, divided into panes of 100 (10 x 10). Plates were numbered 1, 2, and 3, and the plate number appears as described for the regular "Arch and Maple Leaf" issue.

There are two distinct shades, olive green and light olive green. There are no other varieties of importance.

C. The 3c on 2c Surcharge of 1932.

The increase in the domestic postage rate from 2c to 3c on July 1, 1931, resulted in the issue of a 3c carmine, and the change of the 2c to brown. The stocks of the 2c carmine had to be used up and it was decided to surcharge them "3" with bars obliterating the numerals "2". An electrotype plate of 100 was made, and some 25,800,000 stamps were surcharged. They were from plates 3,

Fig. 5. Block Showing Misplaced Surcharge.

4, 5, and 6, of Die I, and plates 7 and 8, of Die II. However, Die II stamps are by far the commonest.

Aside from misplaced surcharge there are no varieties of importance, such as inverted or double.

The electrotype setting of 100 has only two minor varieties, viz:

#4—Top of "3" damaged.

#54—Left end of top bar at right bend downwards.

The various minute varieties known on the basic stamp also occur. They were issued June 21, 1932.

REFERENCE LIST

#	Denom. & Color	Value Factor Unused	Used	1944 S#	1944 S.G. #
189	10c Olive green (Sept. 30, 1931)	N	N	190	312
a	Pale olive green	N	N		
190	3c on 2c Scarlet (Die I) (Jun. 21, 1932)	4	4		
191	3c on 2c Scarlet (Die II)	N	N	191	314a

D. The Medallion Issue of 1932.

The 3c Bas relief medallion design of the Ottawa Conference issue met with such approval, that it was decided to replace the Kings Head values (1c to 8c) of the "Arch and Maple Leaf" series with this Bas relief design suitably modified.

The 1c, 2c, and 3c are from rotary press plates, while the 4c, 5c, and 8c are from the usual flat plates. The plate numbers are located upper left and right, and lower left and right of the 400 subject plate, so that each post office sheet of 100 will show the plate number in one corner, depending on which of the four panes it is.

The flat plate printings are on a dry pre-gummed paper, and most of the rotary press printings are on a slightly dampened paper that was gummed after printing. However, examples of the 1c, 2c, or 3c with smooth gum (so called "flat" printing) are from rotary presses but on dry pre-gummed paper. These show the design embossed in the gum, as can be seen on the flat plate printings.

The usual albino and phantom plate numbers occur on the rotary press printings. These are of interest to specialists but do not warrant listing.

There are no varieties of importance except on the 5c. There is a slight re-entry on #79 U. L. 2. Traces appear on the bridge of the nose, and at the lower right edge of the medallion shading. This occurred during the rocking in of the plate. It was retouched but traces may still be discerned on the nose. Another re-entry shows slight doubling in "Canada".

This value is also known imperforate vertically.

The 3c is reported to occur from two dies, distinguishable by slight variations of the right hand "3". We have examined a number of so called Die I and Die II stamps, and are of the opinion that the alleged differences are probably printing and relief variations. A new die would show several points of difference.

The usual coils and booklets were also issued. (See table for listing of coils, and chapter on booklets for these interesting varieties).

The increase in the postal rates resulted in a 13c stamp being issued. This was of the same design as the former 12c stamp. It was issued on the same date as the other medallion stamps.

Fig. 6. Block of Four Imperforate Vertically.

The Medallion Issue. 1932-33
Issued Dec. 1, 1932

#	Denom. & Color	Plates	Rotary or Flat	Value Factor Unused	Used	1944 S#	1944 S.G. #
192	1c Green	1, 6	R	N	N	195	319
193	2c Brown	1, 2, 3	R	N	N	196	320
194	3c Scarlet	1-12	R	N	N	197	321a
195	4c Bistre	3-12	F	N	N	198	322
196	5c Blue	1, 2	F	N	N	199	323
a	Imperf. vertically			400			
b	Re-entry			5	x		
c	Re-entry retouched			7			
197	8c Vermilion	1, 2	F	N	N	200	324
198	13c Bright violet	1, 2	F	N	N	201	325
COILS. Imperf x perf 8½. Rolls of 500							
199	1c Green	Nov. 3, 1933	R	N	N	205	326
a	Line pair			3			
b	Precancelled			—	½		
200	2c Brown	Aug. 15, 1933	R	N	N	206	327
a	Line pair			3			
201	3c Scarlet	Aug. 16, 1933	R	N	N	207	328
a	Line pair			3			

Chapter XXIII

THE DATED DIE ISSUES
OF 1935-43

A. The King George V Dated Die Issues.
1935

On April 1, 1935, the contract for printing the postage stamps was again understken by the Canadian Bank Note Co., which is still printing the stamps. (June 1945).

The new contractors prepared new designs and plates and for the first time began the practice of engraving on the die in minute numerals the year it was engraved. These are the so called "secret dates." In the various issues we give enlarged illustrations showing the location of the date on the dies.

The first issue under the new contract turned out, unhappily, to be the last bearing the portrait of beloved King George V. The 10c to $1.00 were pictorial as in the previous issues.[1]

All of these stamps were printed on dry-gummed paper from steel plates on presses of the company's own design.

---

1. See Appendix N #64 and 35 for discussion of 10c and 20c designs.

1c to 8c

Fig. 1.
Enlarged Portions of 1937-8 Issue Showing Location of Date on the Die.

The values from 1c to 8c were printed from plates of 400 divided into four panes of 100 (10 x 10). The 10c to $1.00 were from plates of 200 (10c—20 x 10, 13c to $1.00—10 x 20) divided into four panes of 50.

The plates were chromium plated, and a number of minute dots and scratches occur on several values. These are of minor interest.

The coils were printed from plates of 250 subjects (25 x 10) which were curved. They were printed on a continuous web of paper using the "drawback" principle. This necessitated a slight adjustment at each impression of the plate so that some variation in the spacing and/or alignment may occur every 25th stamp. Paste ups, and line pairs however, were eliminated. The variations in the width of the "1" on the 1c are also due to printing, and are not constant plate varieties.

Fig. 2.
Showing poor alignment of impression on coil stamps. The spacing between the stamps may vary from 2½ to 6mm.

We have only noted one re-entry of any importance. This occurs on the 50c denomination which shows a slight doubling in "Canada" and below "Parliament Building, Victoria." It is the 25th stamp, lower right pane, plate 1.

The occurence of some stamps showing a minute break in the diagonal lines running from the edge of the medallion to the line running from above the "N" of "Cents" to the medals on the King's shoulder has led some to assume that

Fig. 3.
The re-entry on the 50c. Note particularly line through lower part of "Canada".

two dies were used for the 3c dennomination. Careful examinaeion of these lines inclines us to believe that this variation is merely a relief break on the transfer roll. The fact that one plate is known showing the lines joining, while others are broken tends to confirm this conclussion.

The paper is a medium white wove and the gum is colorless to yellowish. The sheet stamps are perforated 12, and the coils 8.

The 5c is known imperforate vertically, from plate 1. This denomination is also known on the so called "double paper" caused by printing on the paste up joining two rolls of paper.

The 3c is known printed on the gummed side of the paper in error. This is also conclusive proof the stamps were printed on a dry pre-gummed paper.

This issue is also unusual in that the name of the firm printing stamps appears on the sheets for the first time since the Small Queens. This imprint reads "Canadian Bank Note Co. Ottawa, No. —" in small serifed capitals 1½ bb. high in the four corners of the plate. Imprint Type XII. It therefore appears once on each Post Office sheet of 100, at the upper left, upper right, lower left or lower right of the respective sheet.

Fig. 4. Block of the 5c Imperforate Vertically.

REFERENCE LIST

DIE PROOFS

On India, Die Sunk On Card (Rare)

D202a	1c Green	D207a	8c Orange
D203a	2c Brown	D208a	10c Carmine
D204a	3c Carmine "X-G-579"	D209a	13c Violet
D204b	3c Carmine (no die no.)	D210a	20c Olive green
D205a	4c Yellow	D211a	50c Dull violet
D206a	5c Blue	D212a	$1.00 Bright blue

King George V, Dated Die Issue.

Issued June 1, 1935

#	Denom. & Color	Plates	Value Factor Unused	Value Factor Used	1944 S#	1944 S.G. #
202	1c Green	1, 2, 3	N	N	217	341
203	2c Brown	1, 2²	N	N	218	342
204 a	3c Carmine Printed on gum side	1-8 2	N 400	N —	219	343
205	4c Yellow	1	N	N	220	344
206 a b	5c Blue Imperf. vertically Double paper	1, 2 1	N 400 x	N	221	345
207	8c Orange	1	N	N	222	346
208	10c Carmine	1, 2	N	N	223	347
209	13c Purple	1, 2	N	N	224	348
210	20c Olive green	1, 2	N	N	225	349
211 a	50c Violet Re-entry (25LR1)	1	N 3	N 5	226	350
212	$1.00 Blue	1	N	N	227	351

COILS. 1935

Roll of 500. Imperf x perf. 8.

#	Denom. & Color	Plates	Unused	Used	1944 S#	1944 S.G. #
213 a	1c Green, Nov. 5. Precancelled		N —	N ½	228	352
214	2c Brown, Oct. 14.		N	N	229	353
215	3c Carmine, Jul. 20.		N	N	230	354

2. 31,000,000 issued.

Plate blocks of **six, factor 9.**

See booklet chapter for listing of booklet **panes.**

B. The King George VI Dated Die Issue.
1937-38

The death of King George V, and abdication of King Edward VIII, before stamps bearing his portrait could be prepared and issued, resulted in a period of two years elaspsing before the King George V dated die issue was superseded.

The new series, with dated dies as previously, show King George VI in informal attire from a photograph by Bertram Park, of London, England. The values from 10c to $1.00 were pictorial as usual.[1]

---
1. See Appendix N #37, 38, 39, 40 for details as to designs.

1c to 8c.

Enlarged Portions of 1937-38 Issue showing Location of Date on Die.

The usual chromium coated steel plates of 400 for the 1c to 8c, and 200 for the 10c to $1.00 were used. Printing was on a medium white wove dry pregummed paper. The coils are from plates of 250 subjects as described for the 1935 issue (Page 166). The 10c has been found on the so called "double paper".

During the printing of this issue, plates of 600 subjects arranged in six panes of 100 (3 x 2 panes) were made for the 2c and 3c. These plates were numbered 9 and 10 for the 2c, and 12 and 13 for the 3c. The imprints occur over the 5th and 6th stamps of the upper middle panes, and below the 95th and 96th stamp of the lower middle pane. The other panes have the imprints in the corner as usual.

This issue was also unusual in that on the pictorial design the imprint includes the title of the design in English and French, thus:

"Entrance to Halifax Harbour"
"Entree Du Port de Halifax"

on the 13c, and similarly for the other values. (Imprint Type XIII).

The 10c was originally issued in a pale carmine, but in August a much darker shade appeared.

No minor varieties of any importance have been noted.

REFERENCE LIST

DIE PROOFS
On India, Mounted On Card (Rare)

D222a 10c Dark carmine "XG-675"   D224a 20c Red brown "XG-677"
   b 10c Rose carmine   D225a 50c Green "XG-678"
D223a 13c Dark blue "XG-676"   D226a $1.00 Dark violet "XG-679"

ISSUED STAMPS

#	Denom. & Color	Issued	Plates	Value Factor Unused	Value Factor Used	1944 S#	1944 S.G. #
216	1c Green	Apr. 1, 1937	1, 2	N	N	231	357
217	2c Brown	Apr. 1, 1937	1-13	N	N	232	358
218	3c Carmine	Apr. 1, 1937	1-19	N	N	233	359
219	4c Yellow	May 10, 1937	1	N	N	234	360
220	5c Blue	May 10, 1937	1-5	N	N	235	361
221	8c Orange	May 10, 1937	1	N	N	236	362
222 a b	10c Pale carmine dark carmine Double paper	Jun. 15, 1938 Aug. 1938	1 1	1¼ N x	2 N	241	363
223	13c Blue	Nov 15, 1938	1	N	N	242	364
224	20c Red brown	Jun. 15, 1938	1	N	N	243	365
225	50c Green	Jun. 15, 1938	1	N	N	244	366
226 a	$1.00 Violet Imperf. Horizon.	Jun. 15, 1938	1	N 100	N	245	367
	Coils. Imperf. x 8. (Rolls of 500)						
227 a	1c Green Precancelled	Jun. 15, 1937 May 10, 1937		N —	N ½	238	368
228	2c Brown	Jun. 18, 1937		N	N	239	369
229	3c Carmine	Apr. 15, 1937		N	N	240	370

C. Unissued King Edward VIII Stamps.

Preparations for an issue bearing the portrait of King Edward VIII were made, but owing to his abdication never advanced beyond the stage of die proofs. The design of the low values was to be a bas-relief medallion similar to the 1932 issue. A master die was made and a transfer roll containing three reliefs of this die was made. A secondary die of the 2c was also made. Die proofs of the 3c in red, and of the 2c in green, brown and red were also made. The various models, dies, and proofs were destroyed January 27, 1929, excepting one model which is preserved at Ottawa.

D. 1942 War Effort Issue.

In May, 1942, a circular was distributed to the Postmasters and others interested announcing that on July 1, 1942, a series of new stamps relating to World War II would replace the then current issue. The new series was unusual in that it included a 16c Airmail Special Delivery stamp thereby introducing a new denomination and a new class of stamp for Canada.

The designs are as follows:

1c and 5c. King George VI in naval uniform, from a photograph by Hugh Cecil of London.

2c. King George VI in military uniform, from a photograph by Speaight of London.

3c. King George VI in Royal Air Force uniform. Also by Hugh Cecil.

4c. A composite of photographs supplied by the Department of Agriculture. It shows a lake steamer loading at a grain elevator.

8c. Another composite of photographs supplied by the Department of Agriculture. It represents a typical small farm in Eastern Canada.

10c. A composite of photographs supplied by Lt. Col. W. K. Walker, D. S. O., and the contractors. It shows the central portion of the Parliament Buildings at Ottawa. At the top is the Union Jack, with a maple leaf in the center.

13c. "RAM" Tank. From a composite photo supplied by the Department of National Defense, Ottawa. It is named after the Rocky Mountain ram whose agility is well known.

20c. Canadian Corvette about to be launched. From a composite of photographs supplied by Director of Public Relations, and the Department of Transport, Ottawa.

50c. Experts checking two 25-pounder guns. From a photograph supplied by the Department of Public Relations.

$1.00. "Tribal" Class destroyer. From a photograph supplied by the Department of National Defense. Displacement 1870 tons, four torpedo tubes, eight 4.7" guns, and a complement of 190 men. They are named after Indian tribes.

The increase of 1c in the postal rates in 1943 resulted in new 4c and 14c stamps, and the 3c color change.

WAR EFFORT ISSUE

REFERENCE LIST
DIE PROOFS

On India, Die Sunk On Card (Rare)

All with imprint "Canadian Bank Note Company, Limited" in one line of serifed caps. ½ mm. high.[2]

#	Denom. & Color	Die..#	Date on Die
D230a	1c Green	XG-739	1942[1]
D231a	2c Dark brown	XG-740	1942[1]
D232a	3c Carmine	XG-741	1942[1]
D233a	3c Rose violet	XG-741	1942[1]
D234a	4c Greenish black	XG-742	1942
D235a	4c Carmine	XG-791	1943[1]
D236a	5c Dark blue	XG-743	1942
D237a	8c Red brown	XG-744	1942
D238a	10c Brown	XG-745	1942
D239a	13c Dark green	XG-746	1942
D240a	14c Dark green	XG-795	1943
D241a	20c Dark brown	XG-747	1942
D242a	50c Bright violet	XG-748	1942
D243a	$1.00 Bright blue	XG-749	1942

1. D232a hasn't the one line inscription "H. M. King George VI" in serifed caps, while the others with his majesty's portrait have. It can thus be seen that Die "X-G741" exists in two states.
2. We believe the set also exists on India die sunk on card but without imprint and die number.

Issued Stamps

	Denom. & Color	1944 Scott #	1944 S.G. #
230	1c Green	249	375
231	2c Brown	250	376
232	3c Carmine	251	377
233	3c Rose violet (April 1943)	251A	377a
234	4c Gray	252	378
235	4c Carmine (April 10, 1943)	252A	378a
236	5c Blue	253	379
237	8c Red brown	254	380
238	10c Dark brown	255	381
239	13c Dark green	256	382
240	14c Dark green (April 17, 1943)	256A	382a
241	20c Chocolate	257	383
242	50c Violet	258	384
243	$1.00 Dark blue	259	385

Coils. Imperf x perf 8 (Roll of 500)

244	1c Green	260	385a
245	2c Brown	261	385b
248	3c Carmine	262	385c
246	3c Rose violet	263	385d
247	4c Carmine	264	385e

See Booklet Chapter for listing of Booklet varieties.

1c, 2c, 3c, 5c—1942, 4c—1943.   4c—1942.

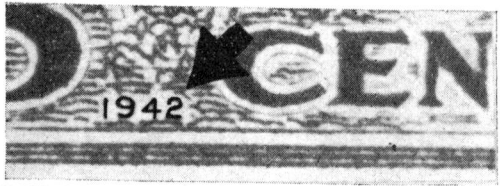

8c—1942.

10c 1942.   13c to $1.00—1942, 14c—1943.

Enlarged Portions showing Location of Dates on the War Effort Issue.

Chapter XXIV

THE 20TH CENTURY COMMEMORATIVE ISSUES.

Introductory Notes.

The commemorative issues of Canada, being comparatively straight forward and of little technical difficulty, are treated in this chapter as a group. As noted in the regular issues, the 1907-1930, and the 1935 and later commemoratives were engraved and printed by the American Bank Note Co., or its subsidiary the Canadian Bank Note Co., Ottawa. The 1932-34 commemoratives were furnished by the British American Bank Note Co., Ottawa, which held the postage stamp printing contract from 1930 to 1935, inclusive.

The plate arrangement, of course, depended on the size and format of the stamp. The plates were all of hardened steel.

We tabulate herewith the sheet and pane sizes of the various issues:

	Printed in sheets of			Issued in panes of		Notes
	100	200	400	50	100	
1908 Quebec	10x10	—	—	—	—	Issued in full sheets.
1917 Confed.	—	10x20	—	5x10	—	
1927 Historical						
5c	—	—	20x20	—	10x10	
12c, 20c	—	10x20	—	5x10	—	
1927 Confed.						
1c, 5c	—	—	20x20	—	10x10	
2c, 3c, 12c						Spec. Del sheets
10c Spec. Del.	—	10x20	—	5x10	—	20x10, panes 10x5
1932 Ottawa						3c Conference is
Conf.						only rotary press
3c, 5c	—	—	20x20	—	10x10	Commemorative.
13c	—	10x20	—	5x10	—	
1932						
U. P. U. 5c	10x10	—	—	5x10	—	
Royal William						
5c	10x10	—	—	5x10	—	
1934 Cartier 3c	—	20x10	—	—	10x10	About 50 sheets
U. E. L. 10c	10x10	—	—	5x10	—	issued undivided.
New Bruns. 2c	10x10	—	—	—	10x10	Issued in full sheets.
1935 Silver						
Jubilee						
1c, 2c, 5c	—	—	20x20	—	10x10	
3c, 10c, 13c	—	10x20	—	5x10	—	
1939 Royal						
Visit 1c, 3c	—	10x20	—	5x10	—	
2c	—	20x10	—	10x5	—	

All the issues produced by the A. B. N. Co., or the C. B. N. Co. are perforated 12, while those made by the B. A. B. N. Co. are perforated 11.

No commemorative has been issued in booklet or coil form. The 1927 Confederation Issue is unusual in that it included a Special Delivery Stamp. (See special delivery chapter).

NO COMMEMORATIVE WAS EVER REGULARLY ISSUED IMPERFORATE OR PART PERFORATE.

The Quebec Issue—1908.

I. The Quebec Tercentenary Issue.
1908

The month of July 1908 was the occasion for numerous fetes, historical pageants, etc., having to do with the three hundredth anniversary of the founding of Quebec, the first permanent settlement in Canada. The Prince and Princess of Wales (later King George V, and Queen Mary) made a visit to the celebration, being brought over by one of the most powerful battle ships of the British Navy.

The Post Office Department contributed a handsome set of seven stamps in honor of the historic event. These were designed by Machado, one of the Bank Note Co's. foremost designers. This series is also noteworthy for the fact that the French language appears on Canadian stamps for the first time. The designs are a follows:

½c Prince and Princess of Wales, Vignette engraved by Edward Gunn.
1c Cartier and Champlain, Vignette engraved by Robert Savage.
2c King Edward VII and Queen Alexandra, Vignette engraved by E. T. Loizeaux.
5c The Settlement at Quebec, Vignette engraved by E. T. Loizeaux.
7c Montcalm and Wolfe, Vignette engraved by Charles Skinner.
10c Quebec in 1700, Vignette engraved by Charles Skinner.
15c Champlain's departure for the West, Vignette engraved by E. T. Loizeaux.
20c Cartier's Arrival at Quebec in 1608, Vignette engraved by E. T. Loizeaux.

(See Appendix N #10-16 for further discussion of the designs).

REFERENCE LIST

DIE ESSAY (very rare)

DIE Sunk on India on Card.

E250a ½c Black Die F192 (Fig. 1).

On Card Cut Close

E250b ½c Black (Fig. 1).

DIE PROOFS

On India, DIE Sunk on Card (Rare)

		DIE #			DIE #
D250a	½c Black	F199	D254a	7c Black	F197
b	½c Black brown		b	7c (Olive?)	
D251a	1c Black	F191	D255a	10c (?)	F195
b	1c Green		b	10c Violet	
D252a	2c Black	F194	D256a	15c Black	F196
b	2c Carmine		b	15c (?)	
D253a	5c Black	F193	D257a	20c Black	F198
b	5c Blue		b	20c Brown	

DIE PROOFS

On Card (Cut Close) (Rare)

D250c	½c Black		D254c	7c Black
D251c	1c Black		D255c	10c Black
D252c	2c Black		D256c	15c Black
D253c	5c Black		D257c	20c Black

Plate Proof

P252a 2c carmine on white card. $50.00

Issued Stamps.

On white wove, unwatermarked paper Imprint Type IX, above #5 and 6 on all plates, and also inverted below #95 and 96 on plates 3 and 4 of the 2c. We have seen hair lines on the 1c and 2c similar to those on the King Edward VII issue (Fig. 4).

Re-entries.

In making the plates two prominent re-entries occurred, one on the ½c, and the other on the 20c. We illustrate both of these. There are also a good re-entrie⁻ on the 1c and 5c showing in the Date "1908" and the lettering at the bottom.

Fig. 1. Essay for ½c King George V in Civilian Clothes. (E250a, b)

Fig. 2. Re-entry. Line Through "CANA" and Diverging From Bottom of Design Below "NAIRE".

Fig. 3. Re-entry. Upper Right Corner.

Fig. 4 Hair Lines on 1c.

Quebec Tercentenary Issue 1908.   Issued July 16, 1908

#	Denom. & Color	Plates	Quantity Issued	Value Factor Unused	Value Factor Used	Notes	1944 Scott #	1944 S.G. #
250	½c Black brown	1	2,000,000	N	N		96	188
a	Re-entry (#44) (Fig. 2)		(20,000)	300				
b	Imperforate			5				
	Block of four							
	Plate block of 4			10				
251	1c Green	1, 2, 3, 4	22,530,000	N	N	A re-entry showing in "1908" and lettering is known.	97	189
a	Retouched (#39 Pl. ?)			10				
b	Hair Lines (Fig. 4)	3		100				
c	Imperforate			5				
	Block of four							
	Plate block of 4			10				
252	2c Carmine	1, 2, 3, 4	35,100,000	N	N		98	190
a	Hair Lines			125				
b	Imperforate			5				
	Block of four							
c	Top plate block of 4	1, 2, 3, 4		10				
	Bottom plate block of 4	3, 4		30				
253	5c Blue	1, 2	1,200,000	N	N	A re-entry showing dots through U. R. Date, and lower is known.	99	191
a	Imperforate			25				
	Block of four			5				
	Plate block of 4			12				
254	7c Olive	1	700,000	N	N	A variety showing dot in "P" of "Postage" is known	100	192
a	Imperforate			20				
	Block of four			5				
	Plate block of 4			12				

Quebec Tercentenary Issue 1908.

#	Denom. & Color	Plates	Quantity Issued	Value Factor Unused / Used		Notes	1944 S.#	1944 S.G.#
				N	N			
255	10 Violet	1	300,000	N			101	193
a	Imperforate			15				
	Block of four			6				
	Plate block of 4			15				
256	15c Orange	1	300,000	N	N		102	194
a	Imperforate			10				
	Block of four			6				
	Plate block of 4			15				
257	20c Brown	1	304,200	N	N		103	195
a	Re-entry U. R. (Fig. 3)		(3042)	5		(Pos. ?)		
b	Imperforate			10				
	Block of four			6				
	Plate block of 4			15				

421 *

II. THE UNISSUED COMMEMORATIVES OF 1914.

A. Centenary of Peace 1914

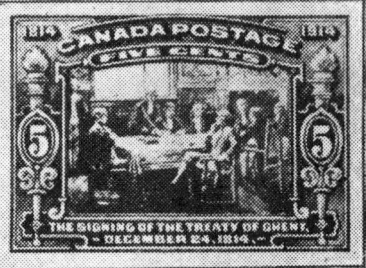

So auspicious an occaision as the anniversary of one hundred years of Peace between two great nations, Great Britain and the United States was worthy of a commemorative set of stamps. The Canadian Post Office intended to issue a handsome set of three stamps, which, owing to the outbreak of World War I, never progressed beyond the stage of Artists drawings.

> 1c. Two symbolic figures on either side of shield—one a man blowing a horn, the other a woman holding a wreath. Arms of Canada on shield. Below words "Pax Britannica et Americana". At top corners "1814-1914."
>
> 2. British and American coats of arms in circles side by side. Above a dove over a wreath in which appears the words "A Century of Peace between the British Empire and the United States." At top corners "1814-1914."
>
> 5c. Picture of signing of "Treaty of Ghent" below words "The Signing of the Treaty of Ghent, December 24, 1814." At sides torches, alight. At top corners "1814-1914."

B. MacDonald-Cartier Centenary

World War I was also the reason for not issuing another series of stamps, one that would have undoubtedly been extremely popular as the designs are handsome and striking.

This proposed issue was to celebrate the Centenary of the birth of Sir Georges Etienne Cartier, and Sir John A. MacDonald, two of Canada's great statesmen. A set of eight denominations was prepared, and in the case of the 10c two designs were made.

Die proofs of the 1c, 2c, 5c and 20c were submitted June 24, 1914, and plates of the 1c, 2c, and 5c were made. Proofs from these plates are in the Official files. Proofs of 7c and models of the 10c and 50c were submitted July 13, 1914.

All were returned to the Bank Note Co., July 22, 1914, with request that a new portrait of the Prince of Wales be prepared for the 7c.

MacDonald Monument at Ottawa.

King George V
and Queen Mary

Cartier's Monument

Cartier's Home

Prince of Wales
(Now Duke of Windsor)

Victoria Bridge,
Montreal

Western Railway and
Farming

Die Proofs MacDonald-Cartier Issue

Six sets of die proofs in private hands only one of which has the 10c "Bridge" design. None of them have an imprint. Eight dies were made, and six plates, one each for 1c, and 5c, and four for 2c. The dies and transfer rolls were destroyed November 14, 1928. Over $5000 was spent in the preparation of this series.

The vignettes of the 1c, 2c, 7c, and 20c were engraved by Robert Savage; the 10c (Bridge) by John M. Savage and E. Gunn; the 5c by Edward Gunn.

REFERENCE LIST

McDonald-Cartier Issue

DIE ESSAY. *On India Sunk On Card. (Rare)*

		DIE			DIE
D251d	1c Black	G-056	D255d	10c Brown violet (no die #)	
e	1c Green			(Mac Donald Statue)	
D252d	2c Black	G-050	D255e	10c Black (Bridge)	G-052
e	2c Carmine		D256d	20c Black	G-058
D253d	5c Black	G-051	e	20c Olive green	
e	5c Blue		D257d	50c Black (no die #)	
D254d	7c Black	G-057			
e	7c Olive green				

None of these proofs have imprints.

DIE PROOFS

On Card, Cut Close (Rare)

D251f 1c Black   D255f 10c Black (Bridge)
D252f 2c Black   D256f 20c Black
D253f 5c Black

III. THE "CONFEDERATION" AND HISTORICAL ISSUE OF 1917-27.

A. The 1917 Issue.

In spite of the great war raging at that time it was felt by the authorities that so auspicious an occasion as the completion of fifty years of confederation should not go completely unnoticed by the Post Office Department, and accordingly a modest issue of a 3c stamp commemorating the event was made.

The design is a reproduction of the painting by Robert Harris entitled "Fathers of the Confederation," and depicts the meeting held in the Parliament House in Quebec in the fall of 1864. This meeting was attended by thirty-three representatives from New Brunswick, Newfoundland, Nova Scotia, Ontario, and Quebec.

The artist was born in Wales in 1848. His family emigrated to Prince Edward Island in 1856. From 1883 to 1887 he was director of the Montreal Art School, and during the years 1893 to 1906 he was president of the Royal Canadian Academy. He died in 1926, at the age of seventy-eight.

The original painting was destroyed in the fire which swept the Parliament Buildings at Ottawa on February 3, 1916. It is interesting to observe that three of the men in this group were later pictured on stamps—John A. Mac-Donald, Thomas D'Arcy McGee, and George Etienne Cartier.

Owing to the limitations of space, and necessary artistic balance the stamp vignette omits eight figures, seven at the right and one at the left.

The American Bank Note Company prepared one die from which two transfer rolls, each bearing three reliefs, were made. The die and rolls were destroyed November 14, 1928. Engraved by Edward Gunn.

The two transfer rolls were used to lay down twelve plates of two hundred subjects. Line perforated 12 as usual. Imprint Type IX.

REFERENCE LIST

DIE PROOFS

On India, Die Sunk On Card (Rare)

D258a 3c Black. Die O-G194   D258b   Brown

On Card Cut Close (Rare)

D258c 3c Black

#	Denom. & Color	Plates	Issued	Quantity	Factor of Value Unused	Used	1944 S. #	1944 S.G. #
258 a	3c brown Imperf (no gum) Plate blk. of four	1-12	Sept. 15 1917	98,650,000	N 125 6	N — —	135	244

At least forty-eight copies of the imperforate are known.

The 2c Post Card, then current, also was issued with statistical data printed on the face in commemoration of Confederation. (See listing of Post Cards for further details.)

The stock of this stamp was exhausted at Ottawa, Jan. 1918 as per notice:

POST OFFICE DEPARTMENT, POSTAGE STAMP BRANCH.
Ottawa, Jan. 26th, 1918.
NOTICE TO POSTMASTERS.

The issue of Confederaton stamps being exhausted, Postmasters are again supplied with the regu'ar Three Cent issue. They are requested to dispose of their stock of the former stamps before resuming the sale of the latter.

E. J. LEMAIRE,
Superintendent.

B. The "Confederation" Series.

The Sixtieth year of Confederation was the occasion for issuing a handsome series of five values to commemorate this important anniversary, more especially as the Fiftieth anniversary occurred during the First World War, and was limited to a single stamp.

The dies for these stamps were approved April 20, 1927. The designs are specifically inscribed "1867 Confederation 1927" thus indicating their commemorative character, and they are also inscribed "Postes"—"Post", thereby being the first Canadian stamps, since the Quebec Tercentenary issue to have both French and English on them.

This set was also remarkable in that it included a special delivery stamp. (See chapter on Special Delivery Stamps.)
(See also Appendix N #17, 18 for biographical notes.)

Both series were issued July 1, 1927, but copies are known dated June 28, 1927. These are of no significance, merely cases of the Postmaster not obeying instructions, either in ignorance or as a favor.

C. The "Historical Series,.
1927

These were prepared in 1926, the dies being approved July 15th of that year. However the following year being the 60th anniversary of Confederation, for which another special set was to be issued the Historical Series was held over and issued concurrently with the "Confederation" Issue. The Historical series have no indication of their commemorative status, and the inscriptions are in English only. (See Appendix N #17 to 21 for biographical notes).

The "Historical" and "Confederation" Series.
Issued July 1, 1927. Perforated 12. Imprint Type IX

#	Denom. & Color	Plates	Quantity Issued	Value Factor Unused	Value Factor Used	Notes	1944 Scott #	1944 S.G. #
259	5c Violet (McGee)	1, 2	10,000,000	N	N	Historical Issue	146	271
260	12c Green (Laurier & MacDonald)	1, 2	5,000,000	N	N	Historical Issue	147	272
261	20c Carmine (Baldwin & Lafontaine)	1, 2	7,000,000	N	N	Historical Issue	148	273
262	1c Orange (MacDonald)	1-6	124,700,000	N	N	Confederation Issue	141	266
263	2c Green	1-15	278,300,000	N	N	Confederation Issue	142	267
264	3c Carmine (Parliament Bldg.)	1, 2, 3	12,900,000	N	N	Confederation Issue	143	268
265	5c Violet (Laurier)	1, 2, 3	4,500,000	N	N	Confederation Issue	144	269
266	12c Blue (Map)	1, 2	1,600,000	N	N	Confederation Issue #88, 89, 98, 99, U. R. 1 have hair lines. Factor 2.	145	270

All of the above exist, (a) Imperforate; (b) Imperforate horizontally; (c) Imperforate vertically. They were not regularly issued. A set of either variety in pairs has a factor of 125.

The Historical issue vignettes were engraved by E. T. Loizeaux, Edward Gunn, and W. Ford respectively. In the Confederation series, the 1c, 2c, and 5c vignettes were engraved by Edward Gunn.

REFERENCE LIST

DIE PROOFS.

On India, die sunk on white card (Rare)

#			DIE #	Approved
D259a	5c	Black	XG147	July 15, 1926
b		purple		
D260a	12c	Black	XG148	July 15, 1926
b		green		
D261a	20c	Black	XG149	July 15, 1926
b		carmine		
D262a	1c	Black	XG169	April 20, 1927
b		orange		
D263a	2c	Black	XG174	May 3, 1927
b		green		
D264a	3c	Black	XG176	May 12, 1927
b		carmine		
D265a	5c	Black	XG170	April 20, 1927
b		violet		
D266a	12c	Black	XG175	May 12, 1927
b		blue		

On White Card, Cut Close (Rare)

D259c	5c Black		D263c	2c Black
D260c	12c Black		D264c	3c Black
D261c	20c Black		D265c	5c Black
D262c	1c Black		D266c	12c Black

For listing of issued stamps see Table on page 427

IV. IMPERIAL CONFERENCE ISSUE.
1932

In July 1932 the representatives of Great Britain, the Dominions and Colonies met in Ottawa at the invitation of Prime Minister R. B. Bennett, then Prime Minister of Canada, for a trade conference, known as the Imperial Economic Conference.

To commemorate the important event the Post Office Department issued a series of stamps, covering the domestic, U.P.U., and registration plus domestic rates. The designs all bore the date "1932" and were inscribed "Ottawa Conference."

The 3c was printed on rotary presses while the other two values were printed on flat plate presses.

REFERENCE LIST

Issued July 12, 1932

Perforated 12, Imprint Type IX

#	Denom. & Color	Plates	Quantity Issued	Value Factor		1944 S.#	1944 S.G. #
				Unused	Used		
267	3c Carmine	1, 2	108,700,000	N	N	192	315
268	5c Blue	1	83,000,000	N	N	193	316
269	13c Green	1, 2	2,000,000	N	N	194	317

There are no varieties of importance. Plate blocks—factor 6.

The 5c air mail stamp was surcharged "6 6—Ottawa Conference—1932" and bars. (See airmail chapter).

V. THE 1933-34 COMMEMORATIVES.

These were all engraved and printed by the British American Bank Note Co., and are perforated 11. All have imprint Type XI. (Listed on page 435).

A. Universal Postal Union Issue 1933.

Issued May 18, 1933

The Executive Committee of the Universal Postal Union met in Ottawa on May 18, 1933. In honor of the event a handsome 5c stamp showing an imposing view of the Parliament buildings at Ottawa was issued. Owing to its large size the sheet margins are extremely narrow and the perforations frequently run through the plate number. There are no varieties of importance.

B. World's Grain Exhibition and Conference Issue 1933.

Issued July 24, 1933

This important conference was held at Regina, Sask., and the 20c brown red, which appropriately showed grain harvesting in the west, was overprinted in blue "World's—Grain Conference &—Exhibition—Regina 1933" in four lines of sans-serif capitals. The overprint was from an electrotype p'ate of 100 subjects. The only varieties are #19 right pane upper right bar of "x" broken, and the "XHI" of "Exhibition" is out of alignment on several subjects.

C. The Royal William Issue. 1933.

Issued August 17, 1933

This beautiful 5c stamp was issued to commemorate the crossing of the Atlantic by the steamship Royal William, thus being the first steamship to link the mother country and the colonies of the new world. She was also the first vessel to cross entirely under her own power.[1] The design obviously shows the little vessel making its crossing in August 1833. There are no varieties of importance.

D. The Cartier Quadricentenary Issue.

Issued July 1, 1934

Four hundred years previously Jacques Cartier had first set foot on Canadian soil. In commemoration of this epochal event the Post Office Department issued a large 3c stamp, unusual in that it was in blue, and of an upright format.

---

1. See Appendix N #29 for details of this historic vessel and voyage.

Vignette Made by the B. A. B. N. in the 1870's Which Was Adapted for the 1934 Cartier Issue.

The design was adapted from a vignette long used by the British American Bank Note Co. on bank notes, certificates and similar documents.[2]

The chief interest in this stamp centers around the wide spacing variety as illustrated herewith.

The official explanation of this variety is as follows:

"This pecularity is due to the fact that in transferring the die to the plate of 200, divided vertically into two panes of 100, a wide central gutter of 5mm. was left to permit of guillotining the sheets into panes, having imperforate margins in the center.

"The manufacturers had proceeded in this way with the issue of 61,850 sheets, in almost its entirety, when it was discovered that the resultant 'straight edges' were being produced contrary to an undertaking previously given to the Department that no more straight edges should occur. They accordingly made the remaining portion, consisting of about 1,000 sheets of 200, *with perforations* down the central gutter. At the time the Department had no knowledge that this gutter was wider than the others.

"The best centered of these *fully perforated* sheets were allocated for philatelic sales, in order to avoid wastage of the straight-edged stamps, which are not acceptable to the majority of philatelic clients.

"Shortly after the receipt of these sheets it was noticed by the Department that the central gutter was wider, and that philatelic oddity had occurred. Instructions were immediately given that all the remaining sheets were to be torn apart into panes of 100, and *this was done forthwith*. Meanwhile some 50 sheets had been sold intact; but so far the existence of this wide gutter had not given rise to any enquiry of the Department on the part of purchasers, and the only cases about which enquiry had been made related to the few sheets *complete,* which were sold over the counter in Ottawa. The existence of the wider inner per-

---

2. See Appendix N #4 for brief note on Cartier's life.

Block of Six Showing Both the 3½mm. and 5mm. Spacing.

forated margins *on the sheets that were torn apart seems to have passed unnoticed."*

About fifty sheets (500 pairs) were issued with this wide gutter so its scarcity is readily understandable.

Several minute plate varieties are known consisting of small spots of color, notably on plate 2, #2 and #97.

Die Proofs On India Die Sunk On Card (Very Rare)

D273a 3c Blue

(Issued stamps listed on page 435)

E. United Empire Loyalists Issue. 1934.
Issued July 1, 1934

This handsome stamp was the subject of discussion by us some time ago.[1]

Seldom if ever has another country issued a stamp so interesting to students of American history as Canada has to commemorate the settlement there of the United Empire Loyalists some one hundred and fifty years ago.

The fact that not one out of a hundred of us knows anything concerning these gallant people is a sad commentary on the lopsided ideas we have of history, and an illustration of how we know only one side of a story, our side, which in the cold light of history isn't so blameless as we would like to believe.

In school you rememger we learnt of the agitation against "Taxation without Representation," of the Boston Tea Party, of Lexington and Concord, of Washington, and Adams, of Patrick Henry and Paul Revere.

---

1. See "Within the Stamp" American Philatelist, Sept. 1934. Through the courtesy of that excellent publication we quote our remarks therein.

But what about those who remained loyal to the crown? They are either referred to in uncomplimentary terms, or merely ignored altogether, and yet the fact that so many people, (there were 35,000 active loyalists in New York alone.) were "Tories" indicated that the Patriots were not going to have everything their own way, and that a great number of sober minded and intelligent people failed to see the advantage of suddenly spurning a powerful stable government under which they had flourished for a loosely organized confederation torn with sectional jealousy and petty strife, and perhaps fall prey to some other European power.

The "State Conventions" took over the forms of law, but there was little justice for a Tory either in court or out. They were tarred and feathered, no one would buy or sell with them, they could make no legal instruments, and frequently suffered physical violence.

They felt, and not without reason, that the revolution would collapse in a short time, and consequently failed to organize as rapidly and effectively as the Patriots.

When they did get organized, however, they were zealous in their activities and certainly gave the Crown no cause to complain, and the Patriots plenty of cause for worry.

The Loyalist ladies of New York presented the "Fair American," a privateer, to the British as a New Year's gift in 1779. Numerous other loyalists performed various services, in fact most of the spies of the British Secret Service were loyalists.

Previous to the presenting of the privateer, battalions and companies had been raised. Long Island contributed 1,300 men, Connecticut and Westchester 2,000, and other sections also contributed men to fight for the Crown. In all some 15,000 were placed on the rolls of the British Army.

Money was also liberally contributed, by those whose circumstances were already reduced. Although not large amounts by today's standards, yet they loomed large in those times. In less than two weeks £2000 were given by New York City sympathizers of the King.

The hopes of the Loyalists naturally rose and fell in reverse of the Patriots. Unfortunately the Loyalist newspaper, "Rivington's Gazette," which dealt more with fancy than with fact, buoyed the Loyalists hopes too successfully, so that when the terms of the peace treaty were finally announced the blow was all the more severe. Although every effort was made by the French and British to secure reinstatement, and indeed the Loyalists themselves agreed to wholeheartedly support the new government if they were allowed to continue their lives as before, it was impossible to get more liberal terms. It is to be regretted that the new government insisted on such severe terms, as the Loyalists families were fine stock, and would have undoubtedly been a powerful steadying influence on the crude politics and economics of the new-born country.

However, it was not to be, and in New York Governor Clinton had his Confiscation Act passed. This act took all the Loyalist personal and real property from them to be divided among the Patriots.

The American representative[2] in Madrid, who, wrote an "English paper contains what they call, but I can hardly believe it to be, your Confiscation Act. If truly printed, New York is disgraced by injustice too palpable to admit even of publication. I feel for the honour of my country and therefore beg the favour of you to send me a true copy of it, that if it be false, I may by publishing yours, remove the prejudices against you occasioned by the former." Much to Jay's surprise, the copy seen by him was authentic, and his opinion of Clinton never changed.

Faced as they were by destitution, retribution, and persecution, the only thing left for them to do was to go to other parts. This they did, and their struggles were great indeed to form a new home in the wild country they were sent to.

---

2. John Jay.

The British Government appointed Sir Guy Carleton, Lord Dorchester, as leaders of the emigrants, and he performed his difficult task with amazing success considering the obstacles any nobleman faced in the new democracy.

The main streams of Loyalist migration were to Nova Scotia, and the Maritime Provinces, and Upper Canada, particularly around what is now Toronto, Hamilton, and Niagara.

In 1783 some 7000 of them left New York, half for Nova Scotia and half for New Brunswick. Later other ship-loads arrived at the struggling colony and although Governor Parr was blamed for his lack of supplies, it is hardly surprising, considering that over 35,000 people landed in a year, and that in a colony barely able to feed itself. The sufferings were great, and the ribald in the United States were soon referring to it as 'Nova Scarcity.'

The conditions, as bad as they were, were much better than that of the 20,000 or more who went to Upper Canada. Here the bitter winters caused untold suffering. Shortage of almost everything imaginable existed, and the inaccessibility of the country to trade marts made the arrival of supplies intermittent to say the least. The settlers struggled on, and when once a clearing had been made the soil was found to be wonderfully fertile. A few years and things began to get more civilized. Mills began to spring up, stores appeared, and inevitably political problems began to intrude. 1791 saw John Graves Simcoe as first governor of Upper Canada.

It may be a surprising fact but several thousand Americans, disgusted and disconcerted with the way things were going in the States, alarmed at the depreciation of currency, high taxes, and general chaos, went across the line or over Lake Ontario into equally good land and a quiet life in Southern Quebec or Upper Canada. These settlers proved to be loyal supporters of the King during the War of 1812.

The United States at that time suffered from the jitters, (it's an old custom of ours), and imagined that Great Britain was just waiting to seize us again, and that the "Canadians" were laying awake nights hoping to swoop down upon us. Just jitters, that's all. As a matter of fact England was busy with far more weighty affairs, in Europe, and the Canadians were too busy in the woods to care a whoop what happened 'south of the line.'

As the result of Southern agitation, and against the better judgment of the New England States we entered another war with England. The attempted invasion of Canada proved a failure, and our victory on Lake Erie a great success; the entire war ending in a status quo.

Since then we have gotten along with our great neighbor so amicably that the unguarded boundary of thousands of miles is held up to the World as an example of what common sense and good will could do for the tortured boundaries of other nations.

The subsequent history of the Loyalists is coincident with that of Canada, and the U. E. Loyalists contributed largely in the founding and building up of the present Dominion. How well they built and how secure are the foundations!

"The same stone which the builders refused, is become the head stone in the corner." Ps. 118:22.[3]".

There are no varieties of importance.

Die Proof On India. Die Sunk On Card (Very Rare)

D274a 10c Green

F. The New Brunswick Sesquicentenial Issue.
Issued August 16, 1934

Having commemorated the activities of one stream of Loyalists the Department hastily decided to honor the other stream that settled in the Maritime Province. The design includes a replica of the seal of the Province granted by King George III, in 1784 on its separation from Nova Scotia, and beginning as a separate colony. The United Empire Loyalists were instrumental in securing

---

3. See Also Appendix N #30 for details concerning the Monument erected at Hamilton.

The 1933-34 Commemoratives. (By B. A. B. N.)

All printed from steel plates, on white wove unwatermarked paper, perforated 11.

	Denom. & Color	Issue	Date	Plates	Quantity Issued	Value Factor Unused	Value Factor Used	1944 S.#	1944 S.G.#
270	5c Dark blue	U. P. U.	May 18, 1933	1, 2	5,100,000	N	N	202	329
271	20c Brown red	Grain Conf.	July 24, 1933	1	1,561,000	N	N	203	330
a	Right upper bar of "x" short.								
272	5c Dark blue	Royal William	Aug. 17, 1933	1, 2	4,854,000	N	N	204	331
273	3c Dark blue	Cartier	July 1, 1934	1, 2	12,370,000	N	N	208	332
a	Wide gutter (pair)			2	(500 pairs)	150			
274	10c Olive green	U. E. L.	July 1, 1934	1	3,000,000	N	N	209	333
275	2c Red brown	New Brunswick	Aug. 16, 1934	1, 2	5,050,000	N	N	210	334

Other Factors: First Day Covers—5, except U.E.L. and New Brunswick—10.

435 *

the separation. See notes on the United Empire Loyalist stamp, for further details as to the founding of New Brunswick.

The color, red brown, was intentionally light to readily distinguish it from the regular issue 2c stamps.

The only variety worth noting is the top line, which is continuous on the tenth stamp of each vertical row, while the other nine rows show this line to be broken at the left, where the white line of the panel curves upward. This is a splendid example of a relief break, and occurs on both plates. There are no other varieties of importance. (Listed on page 435).

Pair Showing Top Line Broken on the Left Stamp, While It Is Continuous on the Right Stamp.

VI THE 1935-39 COMMEMORATIVES.
A. Silver Jubilee Issue. 1935.

The sixth of May 1935 marked the twenty-fifth anniversary of the reign of King George V and Queen Mary. This event was the occasion for great celebration throughout the Empire, and commemorative stamps were issued by the various postal administrations. Canada contributed a handsome series of six stamps, the longest set since the Quebec Issue of 1908.[1] The 13c picturing the King's Yacht Brittania is considered by many to be Canada's most beautiful stamp.

These were the first stamps supplied by the Canadian Bank Note Company under its new contract. They were issued May 4, 1935.

"Weeping Princess" Variety

REFERENCE LIST
DIE PROOFS
On India, Mounted On Card.

		Approved			Approved
D276a	1c Green	Mar. 12, 1935	D279a	5c Blue	Mar. 27, 1935
D277a	2c Brown	Mar. 14, 1935	D280a	10c Green	Mar. 23, 1935
D278a	3c Carmine	Mar. 23, 1935	D281a	13c Dark blue	Mar. 13, 1935

We believe only five sets of these proofs were made.

This issue achieved wide publicity owing to a small damage to the 1c just below the right eye (left on stamp) of Princess Elizabeth, popularly known as the "weeping princess" variety. It occurs on the 21st stamp, upper right pane of plate 1 (21UR1). It was later touched out, but traces can still be seen.

Other minute varieties are known on various denominations.

The imprint is Type XII.

The 3c had three plates, while there were two plates for each of the other values.

B. The Coronation Issue.

The coronation of King George VI and his Royal Consort, Queen Elizabeth took place on May 12, 1937, and like the Silver Jubilee of King George V in 1935,

---
1. See Appendix N #31, 32, 33 for brief discussion of the designs of the 1c, 2c, and 10c.

the event was the cause of a long series of stamps being issued throughout the Empire. Canada was modest in her efforts, however, and issued a single denomination 3 cents, bearing the likenesses of King George and Queen Elizabeth.[2] It was issued on May 10, 1937. Imprint Type XII.

C. The Royal Visit Commemorative Issue. 1939.

In May and June 1939 King George VI and Queen Elizabeth visited their Dominion of Canada, and concluded with a brief visit to the United States and Newfoundland. To mark this historic occasion, the first time that a reiging monarch had visited Canada, a special set of three stamps was issued on May 15, 1939.[3]

These handsome stamps were the first bi-color stamps since the "Map" stamp of 1898, and the first bi-colors printed entirely from engraved plates. It also affords collectors the first frame and vignette combination plate numbers among Canadian Issues. Imprint Type XIII on plates.

We give a table herewith showing the combinations obtainable.

		Denomination											
		1c					*2c*			*3c*			
Frame Plate #	1	2	3	4	5	1	2	3	1	2	3	4	5
Head Plate #													
1	x	x	x	x	x	x	x	x	x	x	x	x	x[4]
2	x	x	x	x	x	x	x	x	x	x	x	x	x
3	x[4]	x[4]	x	x	—	—	—	—	x	x	x	x	x[4]
4	x[4]	x[4]	x	x	—	—	—	—	x	x	x	x	x

Total **of** 44 combinations, or if all positions are taken 176 blocks! The plate numbers **and** imprint are located at the four corners of the **plate**, or twice on each pane.

DIE PROOFS *On India, Die Sunk On Card*

D283a   1c Green and black
D284a   2c Brown and Black. Die X-G686.
D285a   3c Carmine and black

2. See Appendix N #36 for note on Queen Elizabeth.
3. See Appendix N #41, 42 for notes on designs.
4. These combinations are rare.

The 1935-1939 Commemoratives

#	Denom. & Color	Issued	Value of Factor Unused	Used	Notes	1944 S.#	1944 S.G.#
276	1c Green "Weeping Princess"	May 4, 1935	N 200	N x	31,000,000 issued	211	335
a							
277	2c Brown (31,000,000 issued)	May 4, 1935	N	N		212	336
278	3c Carmine (60,425,000 issued)	May 4, 1935	N	N	Silver Jubilee	213	337
279	5c Blue (3,000,000 issued)	May 4, 1935	N	N		214	338
280	10c Green	May 4, 1935	N	N		215	339
281	13c Dark blue (1,100,000 issued)	May 4, 1935	N	N		216	340
282	3c Carmine	May 10, 1937	N	N	Coronation	237	356
283	1c Green and black	May 15, 1939	N	N	Royal Visit	246	372
284	2c Brown and black	May 15, 1939	N	N		247	373
	3c Carmine and black	May 15, 1939	N	N		248	374

Plate number blocks of four, factor 5 to 8, except the rare combinations of the 1c, and 3c Royal Visit.

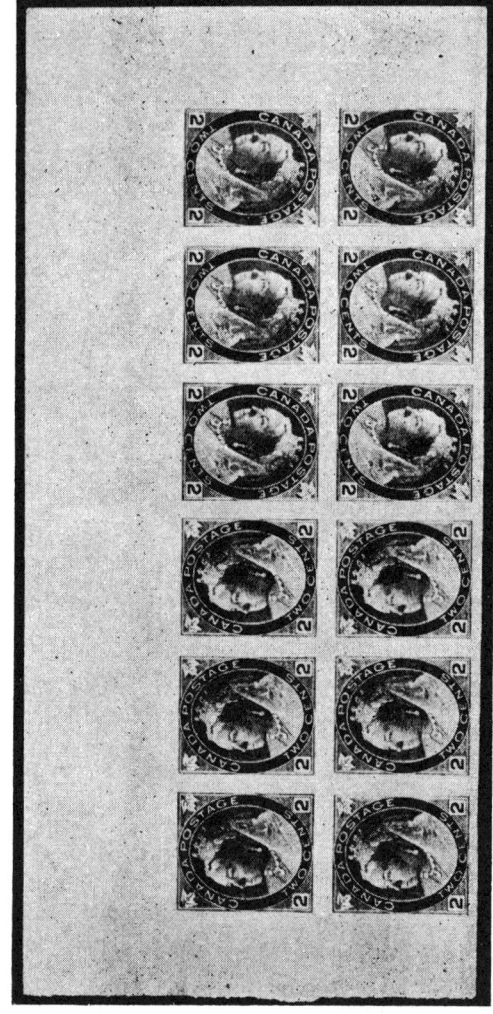

Imperforate block of 12 showing the sheet construction for booklet pane printing.

Chapter XXV

THE BOOKLET ISSUES

As noted in the chapter on the regular issues, stamps in small booklets have been provided by the Post Office Department of Canada since 1900 when the 2c Numerals was placed on sale in that form.

The various booklets form an interesting study in themselves and rather than scatter the information in the several chapters we have gathered such data in one chapter, herewith. We haven't the slightest doubt that further study will expand and revise these brief notes.

We give below a brief summary of the contract price for booklets from 1900 to 1935. (Prices are per 100 booklets), not including cost of stamps.

Denom.	1897-1912	1913-1916	1917-1922	1923
1c	—	.90	.90 in English	1.00
			1.00 in French	
2c	.75	.75	.75 in English	1.00
			.85 to 1.20 in French	
3c	—	—		1.00
Combined	—	—	1.25	1.25

	1930-1935	1925-1929
1c	.95	1.50
2c	.95	1.00
3c	.95	1.00
Combined	1.188	1.25

NOTE: All Booklets are sold at face value plus one cent.

Foremost amongst the scarce panes are the Queen Victoria Numeral of 1900 and the King Edward of 1903. Very fine panes being decidedly rare.

Of almost equal interest to the booklet pane student are the "hairline" varieties of the 1912 issue, and the PLATE and number varieties of the 1930-32 issues. The latter are due to poor cutting of the sheets as it was not intended that the plate numbers should appear on pane selvedge.

Differences in gum shades may be, and probably are, altogether fortuitous. As the gum used on stamps is a vegetable product, subject to deterioration and rancidity, the same batch will show diverse shades. But since specialists may seek these varieties, they are noted.

Under any circumstances, these gum differences cannot be looked upon as constant in all issues. The gum which may be classified as "white gum" in one issue (e.g., 1930) actually corresponds roughly to the "yellow gum" of the 1938 issue, on stamps of which the "white gum" is clear, transparent, and colorless. The specialist however, soon learns to distinguish between the gum varieties of the various issues.

Panes previous to the 1923 printing have a smooth-surfaced gum, while those of subsequent issues all show the effects of the pressure in printing, on the reverse to greater or lesser degree. Previous to 1923 a wet printing was on damp ungummed paper, but during that year the printers changed over to dry printing, on pre-gummed paper. Since damp printing uses about half the pressure on the press necessary for dry printing, the intaglio effect is not so marked; some of it disappears as the paper dries and rest is covered by the gum, which is applied later. Dry printing is on gummed paper; the heavier pressure affects the gum, which takes and retains the impression.

Panes of four previous to the 1935 Issue have long, unperforated tabs or labels at left, after that the panes are perforated as for six subjects, leaving two completely blank spaces. Sometimes these blanks spaces are heavily tinted, due to poor wiping of the plate, so called "toned paper."

General note concerning valuations: Factors are for full, O. G. panes with tabs. The rarer panes without tabs, but otherwise intact should be 40% to 50% of the factors given. Single copies from booklets are of little or no interest as they can be easily made from ordinary stamps. Factors for complete booklets are for assembled books. Deduct 10% to 20% for "exploded" booklets.

The shades vary considerably in most issues. However, only the more striking color differences are hereafter designated, as these usually indicate separate printings of the same stamp.

From the Report of Postmaster General for 1900 concerning booklets, we quote:

"In the month of June, 1900, the department commenced the issue to Postmasters, of a small book of 2 cent postage stamps, containing 12 stamps, disposed on two sheets of 6 stamps each, and interleaved with wax paper to prevent adhesion of the sheets. The size of the book is such as to make it convenient to be carried in the pocket or pocket-book. Printed on the cover is postal information calculated to be of interest to the public. The price at which the book is issued is 25 cents, one cent over the face value of the stamps being charged to cover the cost of binding, etc."

The first booklet was issued June 11, 1900, and was printed from a plate of 120 subjects (20 x 6) consisting of two vertical rows of ten panes arranged tete-beche horizontally[1]. The covers were Type I, and binding was of cloth. According to the contract these booklets cost ¾c each, plus cost of stamps.

An experimental booklet was prepared in 1899 consisting of two panes of six, perforated on all sides and enclosed in plain cardboard covers. Both front and back covers obverse and reverse, and also back of each pane, are impressed with a rubber stamp, oval in form, reading "Financial Superintendent; Official Booklet. Not for sale."

Essay for Booklet

E-BK1 2c carmine. Die 1a. (Booklet as described above). (Very Rare).

Queen Victoria Numeral Issue — June 11, 1900

Booklet Cover Type I. Coat of Arms Engraved Cloth Binding.

---
1. Appendix Q #7b.

This is the first and one of the rarest Canadian booklet panes. All copies we have seen have been Die Ib, the frameline consisting of one thick and two thin lines. At least two printings of the covers were made as the postal information on the inside shows two wordings, differing in minor details. Furthermore the binding may be over or under the covers.

Table BK I. Numeral Issue (Scott #77b)

TYPE I COVER

#	Date Issued	Den	Description	No. of panes	No. of subj.	Value pane	Factor book
BK1	June 11, 1900	2c	pale rose-carmine	2	6	N	3
BK1a	—	—	imp tetebeche block	—	12		

Covers pale rose on glazed card. Wax paper interleaving. Coat of Arms Engraved. Approximately 1,200,000 booklets were delivered to P. O. D.

King Edward Issue — July, 1903

This pane, like the Victoria, is extremely scarce. As a matter of fact, it is scarcer than its antecedent, in spite of the fact that many more were issued. The Victoria booklet being the first of this form was more frequently preserved but the King Edward booklet was used freely, and the more prominent older dealers can recall tearing these booklets apart and disposing of the stamps because they were straight edge!

Edward panes are known upon which the entire surface is scored with a network of fine vertical "hairlines". These, were probably caused by press packing, as has been discussed previously. Plate layout same as before.

Table BK II. King Edward VII Issue (Scott #90b)

TYPE I COVER

#	Date Issued	Den	Description	No. of panes	No. of subj.	Value pane	Factor book
BK2	July 1, 1903	2c	pale carmine-rose	2	6	N	3
BK2a	—	2c	vertical hairlines	2	6	1½	4
BK2b	—	2c	imp tetebeche block	—	12	—	—

Cover as before, but Postal Information varies, one being Dated "7th July 1908", and another "1 Dec 1910". Other dates possibly occur. (See p 444, 446). Approximately 11, 500,000 booklets were delivered by the manufacturers.

The rather persistent fiction concerning the existence of a 1c Edward booklet can be settled by reference to the report of the Postmaster General who specifically mentions the first booklet of the 1c denomination in 1913, discussing the new Georgian design. See also contract prices, at the beginning of this chapter.

King George V Issue — 1912-27. (Admiral Type)

The exact number of printings comprising this issue remains a problem yet to be solved. The 1c in both green and yellow apparently occurs only in Die I, indicating the use of the same plates for both colors. The 3c brown and carmine also occur only in Die I. Four plates were made for the 3c booklets, plates 1 and 2 in December 1921, and plates 3 and 4 in May 1924.

Hairlines are also found on certain panes of this Issue. The lines run horizontally, rather than vertically, as in the case of the Edward pane. These

POSTAGE RATES.

Letters and Post Cards.

On drop letters, one cent per oz. fraction thereof.

[O]n all other letters for delivery in [Ca]nada, the United Kingdom, British [Co]lonies, Egypt, United States and [M]exico, two cents per oz. or fraction [th]ereof.

Letters to all other countries, [fi]ve [ce]nts for the first ounce or fraction [th]ereof, and three cents for each [su]bsequent ounce or fraction thereof. Senders of letters to certain coun[tri]es can hereafter prepay replies, [(se]e Postal Guide, p. xliii, Sec. 16).

Post Cards for delivery in Canada, [th]e United States or Mexico, 1c. each.

Post Cards for delivery in other [co]untries, two cents each.

Newspapers and Periodicals.

When posted for delivery; (a) in [Ca]nada, the United Kingdom, the [Un]ited States, Mexico, Newfoundland, [an]d certain other British Colonies, [(ex]cept where sent from the office of a [pu]blisher) one cent per 4 oz. or frac[tio]n thereof: (Canadian publications [on]ly can go to the United Kingdom [an]d British Colonies at this rate), [(b)] addressed to all other countries, [1c.] per 2 oz.

Books, &c.

Books and printed matter generally including circulars, 1c. per 2 ozs.

Legal and Commercial Papers.

For delivery in Canada, letter rate. Addressed to United States and other countries, 1c. per 2 ozs. with minimum charge of 5c.

Commercial Samples.

For Canada, and for other countries, 1c. per 2 ozs. In the case of other countries, a minimum charge of 2c. is exacted.

4th Class Matter.
(Merchandise).

Canada and United States, 1c. per oz. or fraction thereof.

Foreign Parcel Post.

See rates and conditions in Postal Guide.

Registration.

Registration fee on all classes of matter and to all destinations, 5 cents, in addition to ordinary postage.

7th July, 1908.

Insurance of Letters.

See conditions in Postal Guide.

Special Delivery.

A 10c. Special Delivery Stamp, or Postage Stamps to that amount, in addition to postage, secure special delivery of letters at certain Canadian City Post Offices.

Money Orders and Postal Notes.

These afford a cheap, safe and convenient method for the transmission of money.

Money Orders—Commissions.

On Orders payable in Canada, the United States, Newfoundland, British Guiana, Bahamas, Barbados, Bermuda, Cuba, Hawaii, Jamaica, Porto Rico, Philippines, Leeward and Windward Islands—Limit, $100:

Up to $5			3	cents
Over 5 and up to $10			6	"
" 10	"	30	10	"
" 30	"	50	15	"
" 50	"	75	25	"
" 75	"	100	30	"

The commission on Orders issued in the Yukon is double the above rates.

Payable in the United Kingdom, [Br]itish possessions abroad, and all [ot]her countries upon which Money [Or]ders may be obtained.—Limit, $100:

[Up to $5]	$5	5c.
[Ov]er $5 and up to	10	10c.
" 10	20	20c.
" 20	30	30c.
" 30	40	40c.
" 40	50	50c.

[An]d so on up to $100.

Postal Notes.

Payable in Canada and U.S. Are issued at following rates:—

25, 30 and 40c., at - 1c. each.
60, 70, 75, 80, 90c., $1,
$1.50, $2 and $2.50, at - 2c. each.
$4, and $5, at - - 3c. each.
[$3,] at - - - - - 5c. each.

Odd cents (up to 9c.) may be added [by] affixing Postage Stamps (except to [tho]se sent to United States).

Savings Bank.

The Post Office Savings Bank [affo]rds perfect security to the deposi[to]r. The rate of interest is 3 p. c., and [de]posits can be made in even sums of [$1] and upwards, provided that not [mo]re than $1,000 is deposited during [one] fiscal year, and that the maximum [lim]it of $3,000 is not exceeded.

Postal information given in 1908 King Edward Booklet.

444

Violet Overprint Applied in 1922 to 1c Green and 2c Carmine Booklets.

are due to curvature of the plate, discussed in the chapter on this issue. There may also be found a minor hairline variety on several values, in which the colored cracks are to be seen only upon the tab, and not between the stamps themselves.

Two erroneously reported panes may here be declared nonexistent. They are the 3c brown and 3c carmine panes of 6.

This issue is noteworthy for the fact that for the first time booklets of other denominations than 2c, namely 1c, and 3c, and combination booklets were also issued. In 1922 the first panes of four appeared, and the combination booklets consist only of panes of four. Plate layout, Appendix Q #8c.

The covers up to the latter part of 1923 had the arms engraved (Type I). After that time the covers were typographed; the binding tape was omitted in the later printings of the Type I covers, we designate these as Type Ia.

The postal information also varied. The early booklets were similar to the 1910 King Edward booklets, although set differently. Later printings had the information in smaller type. About 1919 the information was in sans-serif capitals (block letters).

The change in 1923 to typographed covers also resulted in a change in the information. Until 1928 various slogans appeared in sans-serif capitals, 7½ mm. high. In 1928 similar slogans in sans-serif capitals, 3½ mm. high, enclosed in single line frames, truncated at the corners, appeared.

When the postal rates were changed in 1922 the old 1c and 2c booklets were overprinted with a handstamp advising of the new rates. This occurs in both English and French.

The Postal information therefore may be divided into five types viz:

1. Serifed upper and lower case letters. 1912.
2. Similar but smaller type.
3. Sans-serif capitals. 1922.
4. Large capitals, 7½ mm. high.
5. Small capitals, 3½ mm. high, enclosed in frame.

There are several settings of Type 1, and 2, differing in the punctuation, wording, etc.

The covers are of two types viz:

I. Engraved Arms. Information Types 1, 2, 3.
  a. Binding tape omitted. Information Type 3.
II. Typographed Arms. Information Types 4, 5.

POSTAGE RATES.

Letters and Post Cards.
On drop letters, one cent per oz.
On all other letters for delivery in Canada, United Kingdom, British Colonies, Egypt, United States and Mexico, 2c. per oz. or fraction thereof.
Letters to all other countries, 5c. for the first oz. or fraction thereof, and 3c. for each subsequent oz. or fraction thereof.
Senders of letters to certain countries can hereafter prepay replies. (See Postal Guide.)
Post Cards for delivery in Canada, the United States or Mexico, 1c. each; for other countries, 2c. each.

Newspapers and Periodicals.
For delivery; (a) in Canada, United Kingdom, United States, Mexico, Newfoundland and certain other British Colonies; (except from publisher to subscriber or newsdealer) 1c. per 4 oz. (Canadian publications only can go to United Kingdom and British Colonies at this rate) (b) to all other countries 1c. per 2 oz.

Books, &c.
Books and printed matter generally including circulars, 1c. per 2 ozs.

Legal and Commercial Papers.
For delivery in Canada, letter rate. Addressed to United States and other countries, 1c. per 2 ozs. with minimum charge of 5c.

Commercial Samples.
For Canada, and for other countries, 1c. per 2 ozs. In the case of other countries, a minimum charge of 2c. is exacted.

Merchandise.
For Canada and United States, 1c. per oz. or fraction thereof; for other countries, see rates and conditions of British and Foreign Parcel Post in Postal Guide.

Registration.
Registration fee on all classes of matter and to all destinations, 5 cents, in addition to ordinary postage.
1 Dec, 1910.

Special Delivery.
A 10c. Special Delivery Stamp, or Postage Stamps to that amount in addition to postage, will secure special delivery of letters at certain Canadian City Post Offices.

Money Orders—Commissions.
On Orders payable in Canada, the United States, Newfoundland, British Guiana, Bahamas, Barbados, Bermuda, Cuba, Hawaii, Jamaica, Porto Rico, Philippines, Leeward and Windward Islands, Guam, Panama Canal Zone, Tutuila (Samoa), Trinidad, Tobago and Virgin Islands,—Limit, $100:

Up to $5 .... 3 cents
Over 5 and up to $10 .... 6 "
" 10 " 30 ....10 "
" 30 " 50 ....15 "
" 50 " 75 ....25 "
" 75 " 100 ....30 "

The commissions on Orders issued in the Yukon are double the above rates.

Payable in the United Kingdom, British possessions, and countries not mentioned above upon which Money Orders may be obtained.—Limit, $100:
Up to - - - - - - - $ 5 - 5c.
Over $5 and up to   10 - 10c.
" 10   "   20 - 20c.
" 20   "   30 - 30c.
and so on up to $100.

Postal Notes.
Payable in Canada and U. S.
Are issued at following rates:—
20, 25, 30 and 40c., at - 1c. each.
50, 60, 70, 75, 80, 90c., $1,
$1.50, $2 and $2.50, at - 2c. each.
$3, $4, and $5, at - - 3c. each.
$10, at - - - - - 5c. each.
Odd cents (up to 9c.) may be added by affixing Postage Stamps (except to Notes sent to United States).

Savings Bank.
The Post Office Savings Bank affords perfect security. The rate of interest is 3 p. c. Deposits can be made in even sums of $1 and upwards, not to exceed $1,000 during the fiscal year, or a maximum of $3,000.

The Postal Information of 1910 King Edward Booklet.

Table Showing Cover and Postal Information.

Type of King George V 1912-28 (Admiral Type)

Date	Denom. & Color	Panes Quan.	Of	Information Type	Type	Cover Color	Arms Color	Notes
1913	1c green	4	6	1	I	pale green	green	
191(?)	1c green	4	6	2	I	pale green	green	Overprinted "Change in Postal Rates" in English or French.
1922	1c green	4	6	2	I	pale green	green	
1912	2c carmine	2	6	1	I	pale rose	carmine	
191(?)	2c carmine	2	6	2	I	pale rose	carmine	Overprinted "Change in Postal Rates" in English or French.
1922	2c carmine	2	6	2	I	pale rose	carmine	
1922	3c brown	2	4	3	I	pale brown	brown	
1922	3c brown	2	4	3	I	brown	black	Binding omitted.
1922	1c yellow	4	6	3	I	orange	black	
1922	2c green	2	6	3	I	green	green	
1922	1c, 2c, 3c comb.	1 pane of	4 of each	3	I	blue	black	
1922	1c yellow	4	6	3	Ia	orange	black	
1923	2c green	2	6	3	Ia	green	black	
1923	1c yellow	4	6	4	III	orange	black	
1923	2c green	2	6	4	III	green	black	
1923	3c carmine	2	4	4	III	red	black	
1928	1c, 2c, 3c comb.	1 pane of	4 of each	4	II	blue	black	
1928	3c carmine	2	4	5	II	red	black	

NOTE Beginning the latter part of 1916 booklets were issued with all inscriptions in French.

1912-22 (Approximate Figures).

The quantity of booklets supplied is as follows:

1c English	4,500,000
French	225,000
2c English	7,600,000
French	150,000
3c English	288,000
French	19,000

1923-28

Approximately the following quantities of booklets were supplied:

1c English	675,000
French	90,000
2c English	1,750,000
French	200,000
3c English	6,000,000
French	75,000
Combination	3,250,000

1c yellow Die 1, imperf, tete-beche booklet block.

Table BK III. King George V Issue
(Admiral Type) 1912-28 (Scott #104a, 106a, 108a, 105b, 107c, 105a, 107b, 109a).

TYPE I, Ia and II Covers, also Overprinted

#	Date Issued	Den	Description	No. of panes	No. of subj.	Value pane	Factor book
BK3	May 1913	1c	yellow green, Die 1	4	6	N	5
BK3a	May 1913	1c	hairlines bet stamps		6	5	
BK3b	May 1913	1c	hairlines in tab only		6	10	
BK4	Jan. 1912	2c	carmine red	2	6	N	3
BK4a	Jan. 1912	2c	hairlines bet stamps		6	5	
BK4b	Jan. 1912	2c	hairlines in tab only		6	3	
BK5	Oct. 1922	3c	dark brown, Die I	2	4	N	3
BK6	Dec. 1922	1c	yellow (shades) DieI	4	6	N	5
BK7	Dec. 1922	2c	green (shades)	2	6	N	3
BK6	COMB.	1c	orange-yellow, DieI	1	4	N ⎫	
BK7	BOOK #1	2c	yellow green	1	4	N ⎬	5
BK5	Dec. 1922	3c	red brown, Die I	1	4	N ⎭	
BK8	Dec. 1923	3c	rose red, Die I	2	4	N	3
BK6	COMB.	1c	chrome yellow, DieI	1	4	N ⎫	
BK7	BOOK #2	2c	green	1	4	N ⎬	4
BK8	Dec. 1923	3c	carmine red, Die I	1	4	N ⎭	

Combination Book 2 has yellow gum.

Booklets with French inscriptions are worth about five times the given factors.

The Scroll Issue 1928

This issue is distinguished by the appearance of the 5c value in booklets, the only time this denomination has been released in pane form by the Canadian Post Office.

The resulting combination booklet, consisting of three panes of the 1c, 2 panes of the 2c and a single pane of the 5c denomination was sold at post offices for 73c. There were no panes of 4 in this series.

Another distinction is the adoption of a new booklet cover; Type III. They have the new Coat of Arms, and are typographed.

The Postal Information is Type 5.

Type III Cover. No Binding. Typographed Coat of Arms. Various Slogans in Sans-Serif Caps Inside, Type 5.

The plates for these booklets were also unusual in that they consisted of 360 subjects arranged in three groups of twenty panes, tete-beche[2]. Thus each impression of the plate printed 60 panes instead of 20 panes as heretofore. We doubt that more than one plate for each value was necessary.

Table BK IV. The Scroll Issue 1928 (Scott #141a, 150a, 153a)

#	Date Issued	Den	Description	No. of panes	No. of subj.	Value pane	Factor book
BK11	Oct. 25, 1928	1c	orange	4	6	N	5
BK11a	Oct. 25, 1928	1c	imp tete beche block	—	12	400	—
BK12	Oct. 16, 1928	2c	yellow-green	2	6	N	3
BK12a	Oct. 16, 1928	2c	imp tete beche block	—	12	300	—
BK13	Jan. 6, 1929	5c	violet	1	6	N	8*
BK13a	Jan. 6, 1929	5c	imp tete beche block	—	12	75	—

* This factor is for complete combination book.

The combination booklet consists of 3 panes BK11, 2 panes BK12, 1 pane BK13. It has a blue cover. The combination booklet was also issued on March 1, 1929, bound in plain manila card covers, for the exclusive use of couriers on Rural Delivery Mail route. Approximately 16,000 of these booklets were supplied.

---
2. Appendix Q # 10.

			Factor
BK13A	1c—3 panes		
	2c—2 panes	Plain Manila Covers	20
	5c—1 pane	Complete Booklet	

NOTE: Apparently this issue was not printed in French. Of the Regular Booklets the following quantities were supplied: 1c—106,125; 2c—723,825; Comb.—26,650.

Arch Issue — 1930-31

The Arch Issue is interesting for several reasons. The new contractors, the British American Bank Note Company used Stickney Rotary Presses for all the Booklet stamps they produced. As a result of this "PLATE" and "NO.—" inscriptions occur on pane tabs for the first time. There are three shades of gum, viz: "White" ... a clear, colorless gum; "yellow" ... a somewhat deeper shade of yellow than that of the previous issues; and "brown" ... a very dark, thick, muddy gum. The panes showing the gum in ridges were made from sheets which had been passed through the gum breakers to prevent curling.

Panes of 6 occur only in Die I, while panes of 4 are Die II. See page 395

The plates were arranged differently than those previously made for booklets. The groups of six subjects were all right side up, that is there are no tetebeches.[2a] Each group of 6 was 8mm. apart horizontally, and the left edge cut. If, however, both wheels of the machine were perforators then the right edge of the panes from that vertical row of the sheet would show perforations instead of a plain edge. This accounts for the 2c perforated at right.

The numeral "2" sometimes appearing on the selvedge of the 1c green pane of 6 is *always* large, being almost double the size of that seen on other panes.

A new cover, Type IV also was used. This is similar to Type III, but the Arms are a trifle larger, the crown being decidedly different, as well as other minor changes.

Type IV Cover. 1930-35.

The postal information is in serifed capitals ¾ mm. high, enclosed in a rectangular single line frame not truncated at the corners. (Type 6). There are four of these notices in the English booklets and six in the French booklets.

The plate inscriptions (i.e. "Plate No—") are frequently poorly inked or not inked at all giving albino impressions. Some panes are scarce in this con-

---

2A. Appendix Q #10.

dition while others are common, in some instances they have been noted only as albino impressions. These variations do not warrant separate listing, nor any premium in value.

Table BK V. Arch Issue—1930-31 (Scott #164a, 163c, 165b, 166c, 167a, 163a, 166a).

TYPE IV COVER

#	Date Issued	Den	Description	No. of panes	No. of subj.	Value pane	Factor book
BK14	July 6, 1930	2c	yellow green	2	6	N	3
BK14a	July 6, 1930	2c	"PLATE"	2	6	4	
BK14b	July 6, 1930	2c	"No. 5"	2	6	4	
BK14c	July 6, 1930	2c	perf at right end	2	6	x	x
BK15	Dec. 5, 1930	1c	green	4	6	N	5
BK15a	Dec. 5, 1930	1c	"PLATE"	4	6	4	
BK15b	Dec. 5, 1930	1c	"No. 4"	4	6	4	
BK16	Aug. 1931	2c	carmine	2	6	N	3
BK16a	Aug. 1931	2c	"PLATE"	4	6	4	
BK16b	Aug. 1931	2c	"No. 4" or "5"	4	6	4	
BK17	July 13, 1931	2c	dark brown	2	6	N	3
BK17a	July 13, 1931	2c	"PLATE"	2	6	2	
BK17b	July 13, 1931	2c	"No. 4" or "5"	2	6	2	
BK18	July 13, 1931	3c	red	2	4	N	3
BK18a	July 13, 1931	3c	"PLATE"	2	4	6	
BK18b	July 13, 1931	3c	"No. 4" or "5"	2	4	6	
BK19	COMB.	1c	green	1	4	6	*
BK19a		1c	"PLATE"	1	4	6	*
BK19b	BOOK	1c	"No. 1" or "2"	1	4	N	*
BK20		2c	dark brown	1	4	6	*
BK20a	#	2c	"PLATE"	1	4	6	*
BK20b		2c	"No. 1" or "2"	1	4	N	*
BK18	4	3c	red	1	4	6	*
BK18a		3c	"PLATE"	1	4	6	*
BK18b	Aug. 1931	3c	"No. 1" or "2"	1	4	N	*

* Sum of one pane of each plus 50% for booklet of normal panes.

The combination booklet has a blue cover.

The French booklets are worth about three times the above factors.

Of BK14—2,211,000 English, and 201,000 French were supplied.

Galley THREE—Booklet

Medallion Issue — 1932

In this issue, as in the preceding, three shades of gum may be noted. These gum shades are of aid in the determination of the two panes of the 3c red. In the booklets (2 panes of 4 subjects) of 3c only this pane is relatively common, but in combination with the scarce 1c and 2c panes of 4 with dark gum it shares their scarcity.

The "PLATE" and "No.—" on the selvedge occur, as in the previous issue.

Table BK VI. Medallion Issue—1932 (Scott #195b, 196b, 197a, 195a, 196a)

TYPE IV COVER

#	Date Issued	Den	Description	No. of panes	No. of subj.	Value pane	Factor book
BK21	Dec. 1, 1932	1c	blue green	4	6	N	5
BK21a	Dec. 1, 1932	1c	"PLATE"	4	6	2	
BK21b	Dec. 1, 1932	1c	"No. 2"	4	6	2	
BK22	Dec. 1, 1932	2c	sepia	2	6	N	3
BK22a	Dec. 1, 1932	2c	"PLATE"	2	6	5	
BK22b	Dec. 1, 1932	2c	"No. 2"	2	6	5	
BK23	Dec. 1, 1932	3c	red	2	4	N	3
BK23a	Dec. 1, 1932	3c	"PLATE"	2	4	10	
BK23b	Dec. 1, 1932	3c	"No. 1" or "2"	2	4	10	
BK24	COMB.	1c	blue green	1	4	N	*
BK24a		1c	"PLATE"	1	4	2	*
BK24b	BOOK	1c	"No. 1" or "2"	1	4	2	*
BK25		2c	sepia	1	4	N	*
BK25a	#	2c	"PLATE"	1	4	2	*
BK25b		2c	"No. 1" or "2"	1	4	2	*
BK23A	5	3c	red	1	4	N	*
BK23Aa		3c	"PLATE"	1	4	2	*
BK23Ab	1932	3c	"No. 1" or "2"	1	4	2	*

* Factor for complete book of normal panes is 4.

BK23A can be distinguished from BK23 by the dark gum; BK23 has white gum. The combination booklet has a blue cover.

The plate arrangement is similar to the "Arch" Issue of 1930-31.

The "Dated Die" Issue of 1935

The new contract with the Canadian Bank Note Company necessitated a new series of stamps, and consequently new booklets. Once again special booklet plates were made, of 360 subjects for panes of six, and of 240 for the panes of four[3]. The cover was Type III, as used for the 1928 Issue.

Table BK VII. The "Dated Die" Issue of 1935 (Scott #231b, 232b, 233a, 231a, 232a)

TYPE III COVER

#	Date Issued	Den	Description	No. of panes	No. of subj.	Value pane	Factor book
BK26	June 3, 1935	1c	green	4	6	N	5
BK26a	June 3, 1935	1c	imp tete beche block	—	12	50	
BK27	June 3, 1935	2c	brown	2	6	N	3
BK27a	June 3, 1935	2c	imp tete beche block	—	12	50	—
BK28	June 3, 1935	3c	rose carmine	2	4	N	3
	COMB.	1c	green	1	4	N	*
	BOOK	2c	brown	1	4	N	*
	#6	3c	rose carmine	1	4	N	*

* Sum of normal panes +50%.

BK26, 27, and 28 exist with yellow gum, which are worth about 3 times the colorless gum panes. BK28 yellow gum are from 3c booklets of two panes,

3. Appendix Q #10.

those with colorless gum are from the 1c, 2c, and 3c combination booklets. The combination booklet has a blue cover.

French Booklets are worth about twice the above factors.

King George VI Issue.

Type V Cover. Note stippled ground.

Type VI. In French.

Type VI Cover. Price and contents on front of cover. These were the first booklets to have slogans on the outside back covers.

Beginning with this series the French Booklets are about as common as the English. Plate layout appendix Q 10.

Type VI in English.

Table BK VIII. 1937 King George VI Issue (Scott #231b, 232b, 233a, 231a, 232a)

TYPE V and VI COVERS

#	Date Issued	Den	Description	No. of panes	No. of subj.	Value pane	Factor book
BK31	May 8, 1937	1c	green	4	6	N	5
BK32	May 3, 1937	2c	brown	2	6	N	3
BK33	Apr. 15, 1937	3c	rose carmine	2	4	N	3
BK34	Apr. 15, 1937	1c	green	1	4	N	*
BK35	COMB.	2c	brown	1	4	N	*
BK33a	BOOK #7	3c	rose carmine	1	4	N	*

* Sum of normal panes +50%.

#s BK34, 35 and 33A occur on the so-called "ribbed" paper. Note under Table BK VII applies here also. The combination booklet has blue covers, the shades of which vary greatly.

Table BK IX. 1942 War Effort Issue (Scott #249b, 250b, 251a, 249a, 250a, 252Ab, 251Aa)

TYPE VI COVER

#	Date Issued	Den	Description	No. of panes	No. of subj.	Value pane	Factor book
BK36	Nov. 24, 1942	1c	green	4	6	N	5
BK37	Oct. 6, 1942	2c	brown	2	6	N	3
BK38	Aug. 20, 1942	3c	deep rose	2	4	N	3
BK39	Sept. 1, 1942	1c	green	1	4	N	*
BK40	COMB.	2c	brown	1	4	N	*
BK38a	BOOK #8	3c	deep rose	1	4	N	*
BK41	May 3, 1943	4c	deep rose	1	6	N	1 ½
BK42	Aug. 28, 1943	3c	rose violet	2	4	N	3

* Sum of normal panes +50%.

NOTE: It is impossible to differentiate between BK#s 38 and 38a except in complete booklets. The combination booklet has blue covers.

When the Airmail rates were changed the slogan referring to these rates was altered by bars crossing out the old rates, and two lines of type below giving the new rates. We have seen BK41, in French, and BK39, 40, and 38a in English so treated. Later flyleaves had the slogan in the correct rates. Plate layout as before.

Type VII Cover. Occurs in both English and French.

Table BK X. 1943 "Bantam" Booklet

This is the first radical departure in booklet make up since the first booklets were issued in 1900.

The new booklet consist of a strip of three each of the 1c, 3c, and 4c stamps. Cover in black, Type VII. Issued Sept. 1, 1943.

#	Date Issued	Den	Description	No. of panes	No. of subj.	Value pane	Factor book
BK43	COMB.	1c	green	1	3	N	*
BK44	BOOK	3c	rose violet	1	3	N	*
BK45	#9	4c	deep rose	1	3	N	*

* Sum of normal panes + 50%.

The plate arrangement is similar to the previous issues, all rows being cut apart horizontally, instead of alternate rows being cut, and perforated, as is done for the panes of four and six.

Chapter XXVI

REGISTERED LETTER STAMPS

A. Handstruck Registered Stamps. 1841-55

The system of keeping a record of letters during their transit through the mails began at an early date. As long ago as 1792 the British Post Office began the system of marking letters that contained or appeared to contain money, "MONEY LETTERS." All such letters were treated with special care and were charged as "double letters" although no compensation could be claimed for their loss. This practice was discontinued on January 1, 1840, in Great Britain, and this presumably was also true of Canada. Complaints of theft by the public led to the introduction on January 6, 1841, of a system[1] whereby a letter could be registered upon payment of a fee of one shilling, postage and registration to be paid in advance. This system was then extended to Canada, although the earlier system had been functioning in Canada as far back as 1827.

In Canada these "Money Letters" were specially entered on the Way Bills accompanying the mails. No receipt was given to the sender but the addressee had to give a receipt to the Postmaster or Carrier on delivery. They were charged as "double letters" or one rate extra, the payment being in cash, and denoted by the "Money Letter" written or stamped on them.

Stampless covers and pre-stamp covers bearing "Money Letter" or similar markings are the first *Registered Letters,* and we list below what may be considered as

Handstruck "Money Letter" Stamps

MONEY-LETTER
Type RH1

MONEY-LETTER
Type RH2

| MONEY LETTER |
Type RH3

MONEY-LETTER
Type RH4

MONEY-LETTER
Type RH5

MONEY LETTER
Type RH6

---
1. Appendix B #6.

Fig. 1. "Money Letter" (Type RH2) Struck twice in red, and tying a 6d on laid paper to cover from Coburg to Montreal, May 12, 1851.

#	Date	Red	Black	Post Office
RH1	1841-		3.00	Montreal
RH2	Oct. 1843	3.00	3.00	Montreal (Note)
RH3	May 1850	3.00		Montreal
RH4	Jan. 1853	2.00		Port Rowan
RH5	Mar. 1853	3.25	3.00	Montreal
RH6	May 1854	3.25	3.00	General use

NOTE—RH2 is known in blue from Hamilton—$5.00.

All of the above were probably furnished by Frances, London, Eng., and Types RH5 and RH6 most assuredly were (appendix F, Table B).

NOTE: Prior to 1840 money letters were sometimes marked in manuscript and these are rare.

In April, 1855, a registration system was introduced, the fee being one penny[2]. Receipts were given and taken. Furthermore, in "October, 1856, an agreement with the Post Office Department of the United States took effect for a system of registration to be applied to letters passing between the two countries. Under this arrangement a person posting a letter on either side can, by the prepayment of a fee of 3d in addition to the ordinary postage, secure a continuous record of its transmission from the place of posting to the place of destination, where a receipt will be taken and preserved of the due delivery of the letter so registered."

The Registry Rates Were As Follows:

	1855	1859	1868	1877	1889
Letters for Canada or B.N.A.	1d (2c)	2c	2c	2c	5c
Letters for the U. S.	3d (5c)	5c	5c	5c	5c
Letters for the United Kingdom	7½d	12½c	8c	5c	5c
Letters for other British Possessions, via England	——	25c	25c per letter	8c	5c
For other Foreign Countries, via England	——	*	*	(U.P.U. rate 5c)	

* "An amount equal to the postage rate."

---

2. Appendix M #3.

From early in 1858 payment of the registry fee by stamps or cash was optional, previously the fee was payable only in cash[3].

Also we note that in the Canadian Directory for 1857-8 there is the following note concerning the registry system:

> Persons transmitting letters, which they desire should pass through the post as "registered letters," must observe that no record is taken of any letter unless specially handed in for registration at the time of posting. Upon all such letters, with exception of those addressed to the United States, one penny must be prepaid, as a registration charge. If addressed to the United States, the ordinary postage rate on the letters to that country *must be prepaid,* and in addition, a registration charge of 3d. per letter. The registry thus effected in Canada will be carried on by the United States Post Office until the letter arrives at its destination.
>
> In like manner, letters addressed to Canada may be registered at the place of posting in the United States, and the registry made there will accompany the letter to the place of delivery in Canada.
>
> A certificate of registration will be given by the postmaster if required.
>
> The registration system can be applied to the letter portion of the mail only. . . .
>
> [*The Postal Department is not liable for the loss of any registered letters.*]

Upon the introduction of the registered letter system a new set of markings were introduced, as illustrated below. Reference to Appendix F, Table B shows that the first order for these handstamps was placed in May 1855 with Berri, London, Eng. Types RH7a to RH7u were supplied by this contractor, and in all probability Types RH8a to RH8d are from the same source.

The registry fee became 2 cents upon the introduction of the decimal system. **The markings shown below may be considered handstruck registered stamps where the fee is not paid by stamps** otherwise they are simply postal markings. However, prepayment of registry fee by stamp on all registered letters became compulsory on the issue of the adhesive registered letter stamps. "Registered" markings after that date are merely postal markings, and the additional types will be found in the chapter on cancellations.

3. Appendix M #6.

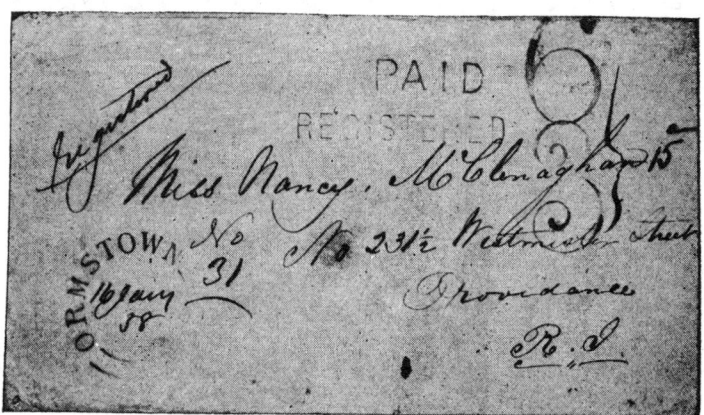

Fig. 2. Registered cover with handstruck stamps: 6d postage, 3d registry equals 15c, the correct rate ao the United States.

Handstruck Registered Stamps.
1855-68

REGISTERED — Type RH7a

REGISTERED — Type RH7b

REGISTERED — Type RH7c

REGISTERED — Type RH7d

REGISTERED — Type RH7e

REGISTERED — Type RH7f

REGISTERED — Type RH7g

REGISTERED — Type RH7h

REGISTERED — Type RH7i

REGISTERED — Type RH7j

RE GISTERED — Type RH7k

REGISTERED — Type RH7l

REGISTERED — Type RH7m

REGISTERED — Type RH7n

REGISTERED — Type RH7o

REGISTERED — Type RH7p

REGISTERED — Type RH7q

REGISTERED — Type RH7r

REGISTERED — Type RH7s

REGISTERED — Type RH7t

REGISTERED — Type RHu

RERISTERED — Type RH7ma

|REGISTERED| — Type RH8a

|REGISTERED| — Type RH8b

|REGISTERED| — Type RH8c

|REGISTERED| — Type RH8d

REGISTERED — Type RH9

REGISTERED LETTER No ___ — Type RH10

REGISTERED N° ___ — Type RH11

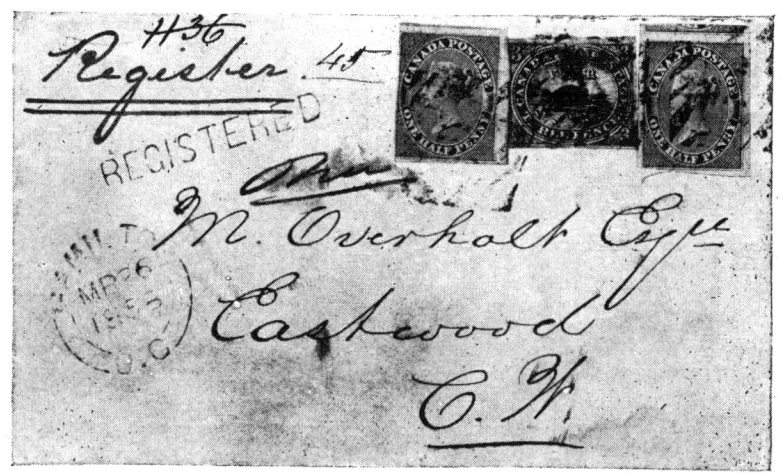

Fig. 3.
Registered letter from Hamilton, U. C., March 26, 1858, showing Registry Paid by two ½d stamps. Early example of payment of Registry fee by stamps.

#	Date	Red	Black	Blue	Post Office
RH7a-u	1855-75	1.50	.75	2.00	General use
RH7ma	1856 "Reristered" error	2.50	1.25	3.75	Brantford
RH8a-d	1856	1.00	.50	1.25	
RH9	1864	1.00	.50		
RH10	1870	.50	.50		
RH11	1872	.75	.65		

Handstruck Registered Stamps.
City Types

Type RH13　　　　　　　　Type RH12

#	Date	Black	Red	Post Office
RH12	May 1869	2.50		St. John, N. B.
RH13	Sept. 1870	2.50		Fredericton, N. B.

Any of these markings on a letter after November 15, 1875, are merely postal markings or cancellations.

The Handstruck Official Registered Stamps

These were used at the Legislative Post Office of the Canadian legislature at Ottawa.

| Type ORH1 | Type ORH2 | ORH3 |

Type	Date		Color	Value
ORH1	1859	Legislative Assembly	Red	$12.00
ORH2	1859	Legislative Council	Green	5.00
ORH3	1867	House of Commons	Red	5.00

Number ORH1, and ORH3 are usually initialed by the Member of Parliament (M.P.) sending the letter.

B. 1865 Essay for Adhesive Registered Letter Stamps.

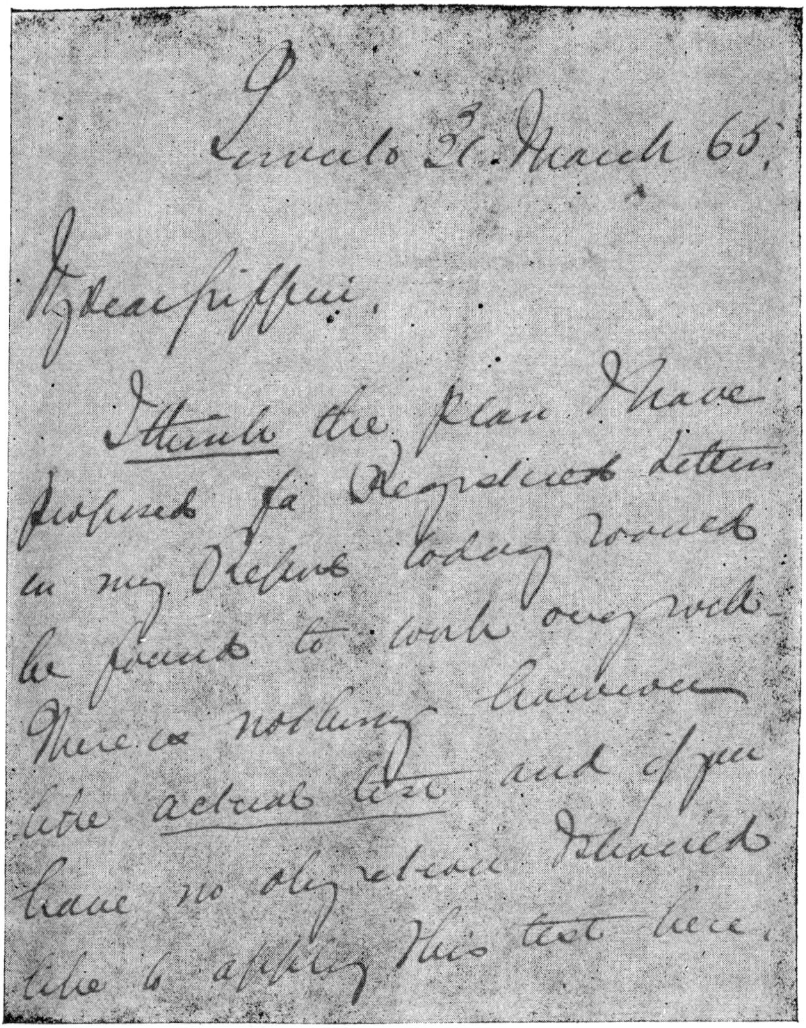

Toronto 26 March 65.

My dear Griffin,

I think the plan I have proposed for Registered Letters in my Report today would be found to work very well — however there is nothing like actual test and if you have no objection I should like to apply this test here.

Fig. 4. First page of letter from Inspector Dewe to D. P. M. G. Griffin concerning proposed Registered Letter stamps.

The report mentioned in the above letter (Fig. 4) we give herewith:

                     P. O. Inspectors Office
No. 819B,   Toronto March 31, 1865.
 Sir

  I beg respectfully to submit for your consideration the following suggestions in regard to Registered Letters which I believe would not only add to their security but be a great saving of labor in the Post Office through which they pass

1. Prepare stamps of some bright color similar to the specimen herewith sent, numbered consecutively & perforated so as to be easily divided & gummed at the back each stamp having attached to it a receipt bearing the same number as the stamp.

2. When a Registered letter is posted at an office let the postmaster tear off one of these stamps attach it to the letter and give the receipt bearing the duplicate number to the party posting the letter—see specimen enclosed.

  The figures on the stamps would show the exact number of Registered Letters posted at any office in the country and would enable you at any time satisfactorily to ascertain that every letter posted as a Registered Letter had been duly despatched to its destination.

  They would also enable you by the preservation of the original number to trace any particular Registered letter at every office through which it passed & with the aid of the receipt to identify any particular Registered letter out of three or four Registered Letters posted by different parties at the same office on the same day to the same addresses.

  They would render it compulsory on every postmaster to deliver receipts to parties posting Registered Letters. They would form an excellent check on Registered letters posted at large offices, as the wicket clerk would have to deliver to the recording clerk a Registered letter for every stamp torn from the sheet or book. They would save one entry of the address, all Registered letters posted at the city offices being now recorded twice, viz: once in a book kept in the front office and once in the despatch book kept in the back office & they would greatly facilitate the business which is sometimes very much interupted by parties waiting at the wicket for receipts for their Regd. Letters which have now to be made out in writing.

  The color of stamps would also render it almost impossible for a Registered Letter to be overlooked as is now sometimes the case.

  If you approve I could have a few stamps prepared here and test the plan (which seems to me at any rate worth a trial) and report to you at the end of a week how it succeeds.
I have the honor to be
                      Sir
                Your Obedient Servant

Hon. M. P. Howland   J Dewe
  P. M. Genl.   P. O. Inspector

Original Essay for a Registered Letter Stamp submitted by
P. O. Inspector Dewe March 31, 1855, with his report
to the P. M. G.

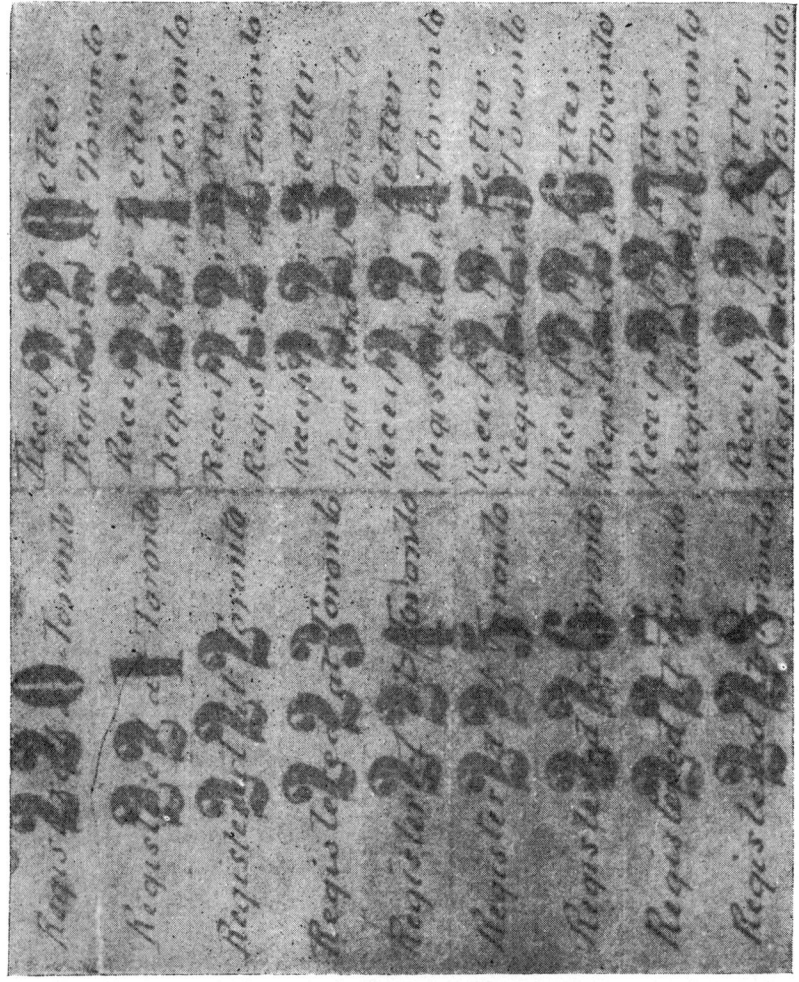

Fig. 5. Strip of 9 of first Essay for Registered Letter Stamp. Full strips were of ten (E-R1a). (Probably prepared by Ellis).

The day after the report was sent the Post Office Inspector sent the following letter to Mr. Griffin:

Toronto, 1 April 65.

Dear Griffin:

The enclosed will show you perhaps more plainly than the specimen sent yesterday how I propose the registered stamps shall be made. They would of course be on paper better adapted for the purpose.

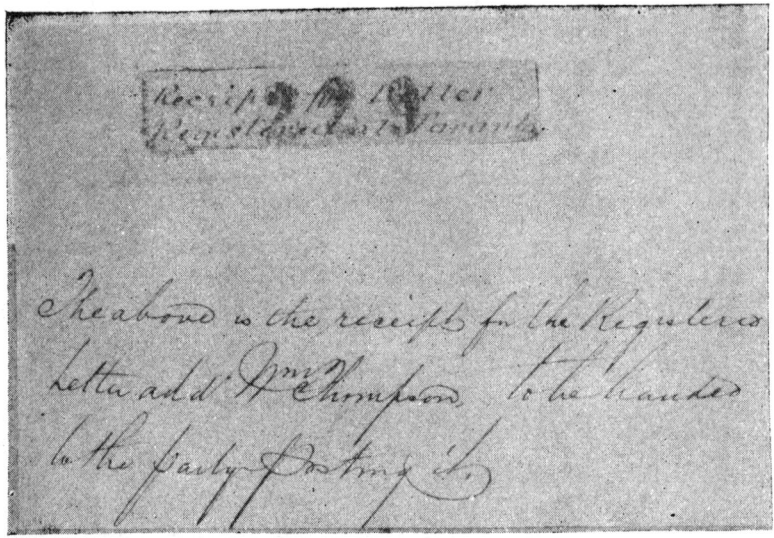

Fig. 5a. The two illustrations above are of the items enclosed in Inspector Dewe's letter of April 1, 1865.

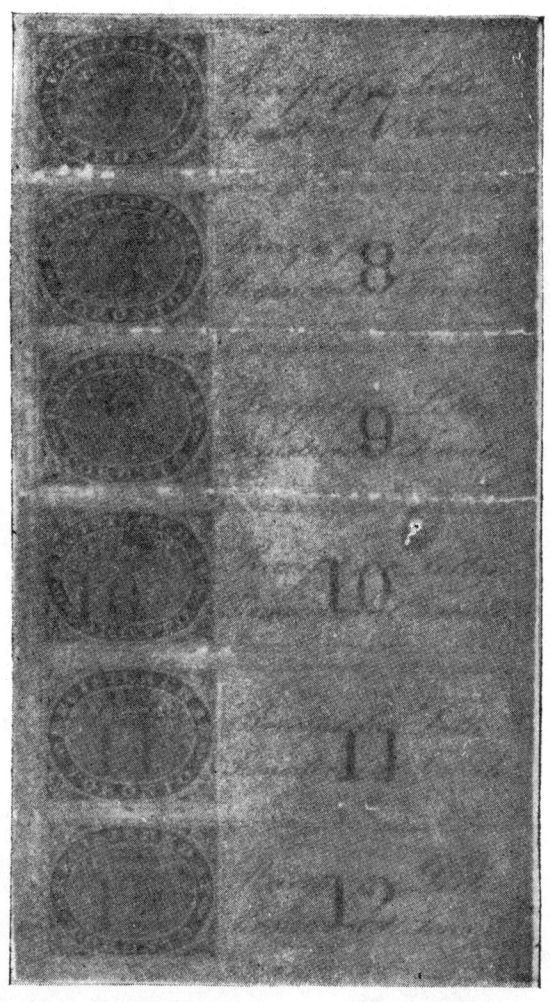

Fig. 6.
Essay by Ellis. Black on glazed Vermilion surface colored paper. Rouletted and numbered, in black. The original sheet contained 12 stamps in two vertical rows of 6. (E-R1b).

A few days later P. O. inspector Dewe submitted an "improved form of Registered Letter Stamp".

                                                                  P. O. Inspectors Office
No. 875B.   Toronto May 10, 1865
Sir:

    Referring to my letter No. 819 dated 31 March I beg to submit an improved form of Registered Letter stamp, with receipt attached and at the same time to inform you that the probable cost of these stamps with receipt attached would be $1 per thousand.

                                        I have the honor to be
                                                    Sir
                                      Your Obedient Servant
Hon W. P. Howland   J. Dewe
P. M. General   P. O. Inspector

Fig. 7.
Ellis essay on sample cover submitted by the P. O. Inspector with his letter of May 10, 1865.

REFERENCE LIST

E-R1a (2c) black on white wove. Numbered in Red. (Fig. 4). (Very rare).
E-R1b (2c) black on vermilion surface colored paper. Numbered in
                  black. Rouletted. (Fig. 6).   (Very rare)
E-R1c (2c) Unnumbered, Imperforate. (Fig. 8)   (Very rare)

Fig. 8. Essay for Registry Stamp by Ellis of Toronto. Black on vermilion surface colored paper (E-R1c).

C. The Adhesive Registered Letter Stamps
1875-1893

In 1867 the Post Office Act made the registration of letters containing valuables compulsory. The rapid increase in the volume of registered mail made it desirable for the post office department to have special stamps for registration purposes. In the P.M.G.'s report for 1872 is this comment:

"It seems expedient to adopt some distinctive postage stamp to be used only in prepayment of the Registration charge, both to make it clear that this charge has been duly paid and accounted for in every case, and to diminish the risk which is occasionally felt at points of distribution of omitting to carry on the Registration in cases where the ordinary Registration postmark is not as distinct and calculated to arrest attention as it should be.

It has always been the policy of the Canadian Post Office to admit letters to Registration at a low rate of charge for the additional security thus given, so as to leave no adequate motive, on the score of cost, for sending valuable letters through the mails unregistered: and, doubtless, the very large proportion of such letters offered for registration demonstrates a gratifying measure of success in attaining the desired object."

Fig. 9. 8c Registered letter stamp with sewing machine perforation.

The suggestion, made in the report for 1872, was finally carried out and special stamps for registration made their appearance on November 15, 1875. The report of the P.M.G. for 1875 says:

Registration

"Registration stamps have been issued, to be used by the public in prepaying the registration charges on letters passing within the Dominion, or to the United Kingdom or United States, each destination being distinguished by a different colour in the stamp, as well as by a variation in the amount of registration charge and corresponding value of the stamp.

There is a red stamp of the value of two cents for prepayment of the registration charges on letters within the Dominion.

There is a green stamp of five cents value for registered letters addressed to the United States.

There is a blue stamp of eight cents value for registered letters addressed to the United Kingdom.

These stamps are to apply exclusively to the registration charges, and the postage rates on registered letters are to be prepaid by the ordinary postage stamps.

It is believed that the use of these distinctive stamps for the registration charges, will tend to give registered letters additional security against the risk which is sometimes felt of the registration escaping observation, when such letters are dealt with hurriedly or handled at night, whilst passing through the post."

The stamps were engraved and printed by the British American Bank Note Co., from unhardened steel plates, as follows:

De-nom.	Plates	Made	Re-entered	Imprint Type	Subjects, Panes
2c	2	one 1875	1886	V	100 (5x10+5x10) Two panes
		one 1886	——	V	100 (5x10+5x10) Two panes
5c	3	one 1875	1888	V	100 (5x10+5x10) Two panes
		one 1886	——	V	100 (5x10+5x10) Two panes
		one 1888	——	VI	100 (5x20) One pane
8c	1	1875	——	V	100 (5x10+5x10) Two panes

The imprint, Type V, is located above #2, 3, 4; below #47, 48, 49; left opposite #16, 21, 26, 31 reading up; right opposite #20, 25, 30, 35 reading down on each pane of the 1875 plates. The 2c and 5c 1886 plates have the imprint at the top and bottom only of each pane, no side imprints.

The 1888 5c plate has imprint, Type VI, located above #2, 3, 4, and below #97, 98, 99 of the plate.

The plates of two panes show over the first stamp of the plate the denomination in shaded capitals while above the fifth stamp the denomination is given in numerals, viz:

Over #1	Over #5
2c "Two CENTS"	"2"
5c "FIVE"	"5"
8c "EIGHT"	"8"

Quantities from each plate approximately as follows: 2c—18,000,000 from original plate, 12,000,000 from new plates, and re-entered old plate. 5c—From

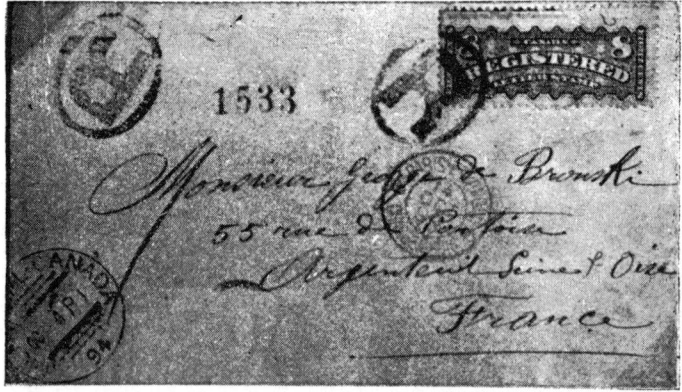

Fig. 10. An 8c Registered letter stamp paying the Registry and letter rate to France in 1894. Note traces of "Eight" above stamp, showing this to be the first stamp in sheet. Short payment of 2c which passed without being taxed.

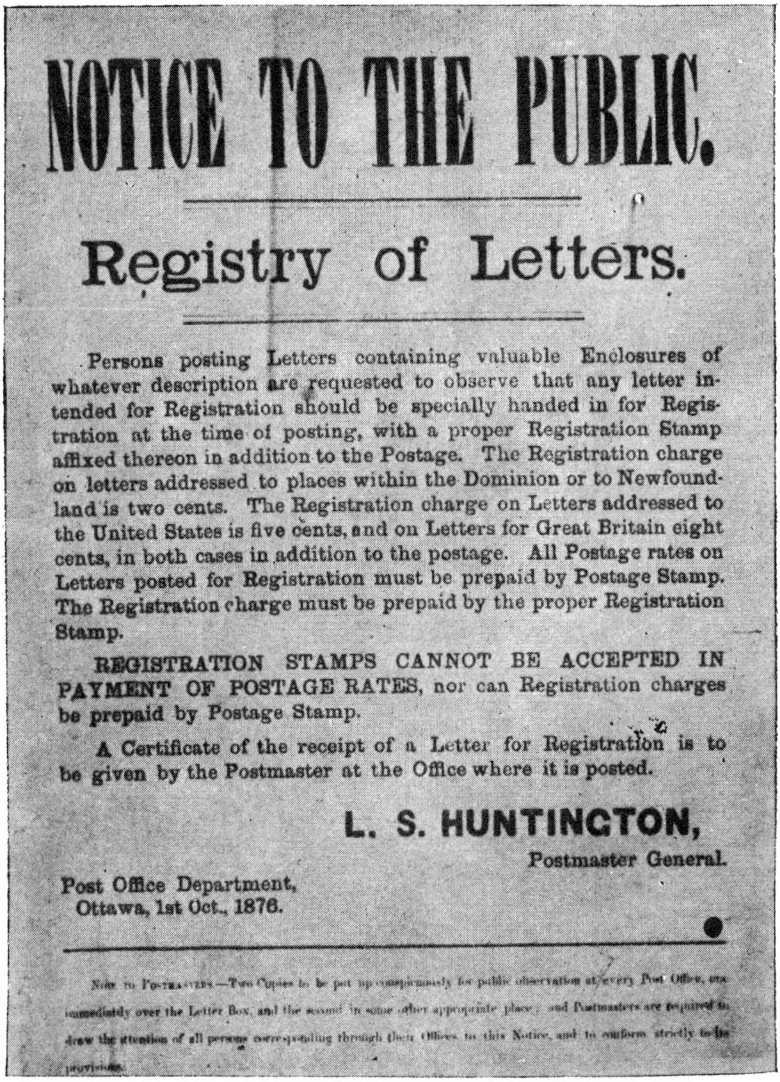

NOTICE TO THE PUBLIC.

Registry of Letters.

Persons posting Letters containing valuable Enclosures of whatever description are requested to observe that any letter intended for Registration should be specially handed in for Registration at the time of posting, with a proper Registration Stamp affixed thereon in addition to the Postage. The Registration charge on letters addressed to places within the Dominion or to Newfoundland is two cents. The Registration charge on Letters addressed to the United States is five cents, and on Letters for Great Britain eight cents, in both cases in addition to the postage. All Postage rates on Letters posted for Registration must be prepaid by Postage Stamp. The Registration charge must be prepaid by the proper Registration Stamp.

REGISTRATION STAMPS CANNOT BE ACCEPTED IN PAYMENT OF POSTAGE RATES, nor can Registration charges be prepaid by Postage Stamp.

A Certificate of the receipt of a Letter for Registration is to be given by the Postmaster at the Office where it is posted.

L. S. HUNTINGTON,
Postmaster General.

Post Office Department,
Ottawa, 1st Oct., 1876.

Note to Postmasters.—Two Copies to be put up conspicuously for public observation at every Post Office, one immediately over the Letter Box, and the second in some other appropriate place; and Postmasters are required to draw the attention of all persons corresponding through their Offices to this Notice, and to conform strictly to its provisions.

Fig. 11. Post Office Notice Concerning Registration of Letters. Note that Registration charges must be paid by Registration stamps, and that these stamps could only be used for such charges. (Later the rule was relaxed, when the rate became 5c, a 2c could be used to make up the 8c. Postage and registration rate or an 8c Registration stamp could be used to pay the whole charge.)

original plate 2,500,000, from re-entered, plus 1886 plate, 1,200,000 up to 1888, from 1888 to 1893 8,700,000 from three plates.

Proofs of the issued design are known, as follows:

REFERENCE LIST

D. Die Proof on India (Rare)	P. Plate Proof on India (Scarce)
P-R1a 2c Deep rose carmine	Scarlet
P-R2a 5c Deep green	Green
b 5c Blue	
P-R3a 8c Blue	Blue
b 8c Green	

Plate proofs are sometimes mounted on card.

Paper, Perforation and Gum

Although these stamps were in use from 1875 to 1893 only papers B and E have been noted, and Gums V, W, Y, and Z. It is rather curious that gum V should occur on these issues, as the regular stamps do not show it after the middle of 1873. Although 11½ x 12 perforations have been reported, we have not seen any examples so perforated the only perforation being 12 x 12. (See table for listing).

Concluding Note

The reduction of the Registry rate to the United Kingdom to 5c in 1878 made the use of an 8c registry stamp unnecessary. The raising of the rate to 5c for B.N.A. and U. S. mail in 1889 eliminated the 2c. Finally in 1893 it was decided to discontinue the use of special stamps to pay the Registration fee, and an 8c stamp to pay the combined postage and registration rate was issued. From 1889 it was possible to use pairs of the 2c to make up the 5c rate, the difference being made up by ordinary stamps. Prior to 1889 pairs of 2c so used were contrary to the regulations.

Fig. 12. Pair 8c paying registry and double rate to France in 1880. Overpayment of 1c.

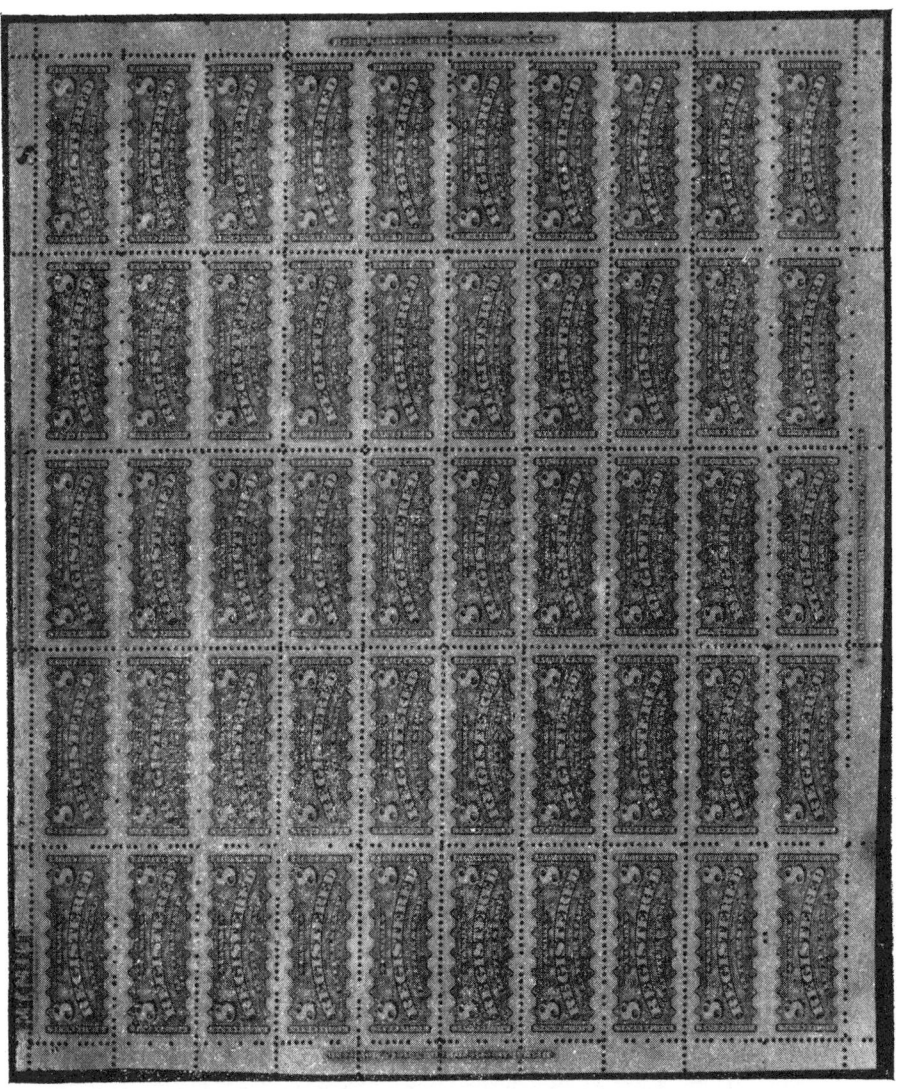

Fig. 13. Full pane of fifty (5x10) of the 8c registry stamp, showing marginal markings, imprints and plate layout.

REGISTRATION STAMPS

ISSUED NOV. 15, 1875—Perforated 12 x 12.

#	Denom. & Color		Paper B (1875-80) Unused	Paper B (1875-80) Used	Paper E (1875-93) Unused	Paper E (1875-93) Used	Notes	1944 S#	1944 S.G. #
R1	2c Orange red	1875	N	N	N	N		F1	R1
	Vermilion		2	2	2	2			
a	Deep red (scarlet) 1886		—	—	N	N	Occur with Gum V, W or Y.	F2	R2
b	Imperforate		—	.	18	x	Re-entered plate.		
							We have seen a used horizontal pair of this variety.		
	Block of four		8	8	6	8			
	On cover		—	—	—	—	Approximately 30,000,000 issued.		
	Pair on cover		—	—	—	25			
R2	5c Yellow green	1875	N	N	N	N		F3	R3
	Deep green	1886-88	—	—	2	2	Occur with Gum V, W, Y, or Z.		
	Blue green	Oct. 1888	—	—	1½	1½	Re-entered plate.		
a	Imperforate pair		—	—	18				
b	Block of four		8	10	6	10	Approximately 12,500,000 issued.		
	On cover		—		—				
R3	8c Blue		N	N	—	—		F4	R8
	Gray blue		N	N	—	—	One plate.		
	Sewing machine perf.		—	x	—	—	125,000 printed.		
a	Block of four		10		—	—	Only about 90,000 issued.		
	On cover		—	10	—	—	Gum V only.		

NOTE: See Table 7A, Appendix J, page 2 for details of quantities issued.

Chapter XXVII

THE SPECIAL DELIVERY STAMPS
1898-1942

From Die Proof in Black on India, By British American Bank Note Co., Circa 1875.

Beginning July 1, 1898, the special delivery system became operative in fourteen of the principal cities in Canada[1]. Since that time the service has been extended to other cities as conditions warranted.

The first special delivery stamp was placed on sale June 28, 1898. Printed by the American Bank Note Co., Ottawa, from a plate of fifty subjects (5 x 10) the imprint, Type IX, appears in the top margin over the second, third and fourth stamps. (See chapter XIII for details as to cost of plates, etc.)

The so-called types with or without shading under the numerals "10" are simply due to a slight wearing of the plate. There was only one die, #F126, and one transfer roll bearing two reliefs was made.

After fifteen years of use the plate was completely re-entered (December, 1913), the work being so skilfully done that no varieties of importance have been noted. Impressions from the re-entered plate are somewhat deeper in color, and this may have been the source of the theory that there were two dies.

On August 27, 1920, however, a new plate was laid down, the same transfer roll being used. The new plate consists of one-hundred subjects (10 x 10) the imprint, Type IX, as before appearing over the fifth and sixth stamps of the sheet.

The increase of the special delivery fee to 20c on September 1, 1921, made a new stamp necessary. This was not on sale until Aug. 21, 1922. The old ten green were used until the new 20c appeared, and afford the only legitimate example of multiple use of the special delivery stamp. The 20c carmine was engraved and printed by the American Bank Note Co., Ottawa, in sheets of one-hundred (10 x 10). The imprint is Type IX and appears in the top margin.

The printings were on dampened paper, but beginning in October, 1926, dry paper was used. The elimination of paper shrinkage after wetting resulted in the stamp measuring 42½-43 x 26mm., as compared with the former dimensions of 41-41½ x 26mm.

---
1. Appendix B #55.

SD1, 2

SD3

SD5, 6

SD4

SD7

SD8, 10

SD9

SD11

The Confederation commemoratives were the only commemorative set to have a special delivery stamp. This stamp is unusual in many ways, it being the only Canadian stamp picturing dogs and an ocean liner. It was the first Canadian stamp to show an airplane, a mountain, a horse, and an ecclesiastical motif. It is the only special delivery stamp of vertical format, and without the word "Delivery." Engraved and printed by the American Bank Note Co., Ottawa, from a single plate of two-hundred subjects (20 x 10), and divided into four Post Office panes of fifty (10 x 5). The imprint appears on the left or right sheet margin of the upper or lower panes, Type IX.

The change of contractors resulted in a new special delivery stamp along with the Arch and Maple Leaf issue. The design is not very distinguished. Two one-hundred subject plates (10 x 10) were made. The plate numbers, in sans serif letters and located in left hand margin. Issued September 2, 1930.

In 1932 a modification of the design, with the word "TWENTY" in the lower panel omitted, was issued; similar, in all other respects to the previous stamp. One plate of one-hundred subjects (10 x 10) was made. Both with Type XI imprint.

In 1935 the Canadian Bank Note Co. secured the contract and a handsome new stamp was issued. The design is symbolic and is known as "An Allegory of Progress." One two-hundred subject plate (10 x 20) was made, and the sheets were divided into four Post Office panes of fifty (5 x 10). The imprint appears above the 2nd, 3rd, and 4th stamps or below the corner stamps of the panes. The die was dated "1935". Type XII imprint.

In 1938 the new pictorial series was issued, and they were accompanied by a handsome new special delivery stamp bearing the Ensigns Armorial of the Dominion of Canada, granted November 21, 1921[2]. This stamp was printed from a plate of two-hundred subjects (10 x 20), divided into four panes of fifty (5 x 10). The imprint is above the third stamp of the upper left pane, and below the 48th stamp of the lower left pane, Type XII. Die dated "1937"

On March 1, 1939, the rate was reduced to ten cents. The remaining stocks of the 20c were surcharged "10" and bars obliterating the numerals "20" in the lower corners. The setting was of fifty subjects (5 x 10), and no varieties have been noted.

A month later the new ten cent appeared, printed in green. This was from a plate of one-hundred subjects (10x10) divided vertically into two panes of fifty (5x10). The imprint Type XII is located at the upper right and left, and lower right and left corners of the plate. Between the fifth and sixth horizontal rows are small colored arrows, making it possible to collect right and left arrow blocks.

The War Effort issue included a special delivery stamp, showing the Ensign's Armorial on a shield shaped device. Partially hidden on either side are two Union Jacks representing the Army, while in front at left is the Naval Ensign, and at the right is the new Royal Canadian Air Force Flag. Printed from a plate of two-hundred subjects (10 x 20), divided into four panes of fifty (5x10). Die dated "1942". Type XII imprint located as before.

Die proofs of some of these stamps are in private hands, and we list those we have seen.

REFERENCE LIST

DIE PROOFS (Rare to very rare)

On India, Die Sunk On Card

D-SD1a	1898	10c black, Die No. F126
D-SD1b		10c green, Die No. F126
D-SD3a	1920	20c black, Die No. O-G420
D-SD4a	1927	20c black, Die No. X-G177
b		20c orange, Die No. X-G177
c		20c orange, No die number.

---

2. Appendix N #44.

D-SD7a   1935 20c dark red.
D-SD8a   1938 20c scarlet.
D-SD10a 1939 10c green.
D-SD11a 1942 10c green.

On Thin Card, Cut Close (Rare)

D-SD1c   10c black.
D-SD3b   20c black.

Stamp Size, On India, Mounted On Thick Card

D-SD5a   20c brown red.

D-SD1a to D-SD4b have imprint "American Bank Note Co., Ottawa" in serifed capitals ½mm. tall.

The Bahamas Special Delivery Stamps do not fall within the scope of this work, and are therefore omitted.

1935.

1938-39. 10c and 20c.

1942. War Effort Issue.

Location of Dates on "Dated Die" Stamps

Special Delivery Issues—1898-1942

All on White Wove Paper, Perforated 12 Except SD5 and SD6, Perf. 11

#	Denom. & Color	Date Issued	Die #	Plates	Quantity Issued	Factor of Value Unused	Factor of Value Used	Notes	1944 Scott #	1944 S.G. #
SD1	10c Yellow green	Jun 28, 1898	F126	1	Total 3,666,850 all printings	N	N	The shading around the numerals "10" becomes less as the plate wore.	E1	S2
	Block of four					6	—			
	Plate block of six					16	—			
	On cover					3	1½			
a	Dark green	Dec, 1913		1 re-entered		N	N	See Note[1]	E1a	S1
SD2	10c Blue green	Aug, 1920		2		N	N	This is an entirely new plate.	E1	S3
	Block of four					6	—			
	Plate block of six					16	—			
	On cover					—	3			
	Pair on cover					—	10			
SD3	20c Carmine	Aug 21, 1922	O-G420	1	Total 875,000 all printings	N	N	41 x 25½mm. Damp paper printing.	E2	S4
	Block of four					6	—			
	Plate block					8	—			
	On cover					1½	2			
a	Carmine	Oct, 1926		1		9	1½	42½-43 x 26mm. Dry paper printing.		
	Block of four					12	—			
	Plate block					—	—			
	On cover					—	3			
SD4	20c Orange	Jun 29, 1927	X-G177	A1	600,000	N	N	Confederation Issue.	E3	S5
	Block of four					5	—			
	Plate block of six					8	—			
a	Imperf. horiz.					100	—			
b	Imperf. vert.					100	—			
	On cover					—	2			

1. The shading is strong due to re-entering of all subjects.

#	Denom. & Color	Date Issued	Die #	Plates	Quantity Issued	Factor of Value Unused	Factor of Value Used	Notes	1944 S. #	1944 S.G. #
SD5	20c Brown red Block of four Plate blk. of four On cover	Sep 2, 1930		1, 2	1,151,000	N 5 7	N — 1½	"TWENTY CENTS" Perf. 11	E4	S6
SD6	20c Brown red Block of four Plate blk. of four On cover	Dec. 24, 1932		1		N 5 6	N — 1½	"CENTS" Perf. 11	E5	S7
SD7	20c Scarlet Plate blk. of four On cover	Jun 1 1935		1		N 6	N 1½	Allegory of Progress.	E6	S8
SD8	20c Scarlet Plate block of six	Jun 15, 1938		1		N 6	N —	Coat-of-Arms.	E8	S10
SD9	10c on 20c Scarlet Plate block of six First Day Cover	Mar 1, 1939		1		N 6	N 6		E9	S11
SD10	10c Green Arrow block of 4 Plate blk. of four First Day Cover	Apr 1, 1939		1		N 8 6	N — 8	Coat-of-Arms.	E7	S9
SD11	10c Green Plate block First Day Cover	Jul 1, 1942		1		N 6	N 2	War Effort Issue.	E10	S12

NOTE—From 1935 blocks of four have no premium. From 1938 covers (except First Day) are not worth a premium.

Chapter XXVIII

THE POSTAGE DUE STAMPS

A. Handstruck Postage Dues

(See also Chapter IV)

Although Canada did not issue adhesive postage dues until 1906, markings indicating short paid postage had been applied to letters from as early as 1843. These usually were "MORE-TO-PAY" in various types, or with other wordings to indicate unpaid postage. These were commonly known as "undercharges."

MORE-TO-PAY.
H-PD1

MORE TO PAY
H-PD2

M O R E to P A Y
H-PD3

MORE-TO-PAY
H-PD4

MORE TO PAY.
H-PD5

MORE TO PAY.
H-PD6

MORE-TO-PAY
H-PD7

H-PD1 to H-PD5 supplied by Francis, the others by Berri[1].

1. "More to Pay"

			Black	
H-PD1	1843	....	$2.00	Montreal
H-PD2	1843	....	2.00	
H-PD3	1843	....	2.00	
H-PD4	1845	....	2.00	
H-PD5	1852	....	2.00	
H-PD6	1862	....	1.50	
H-PD7	1863	....	1.00	

2. Handstruck Unpaid Marks

In accordance with the Post Office Act amendments effective July 1, 1859, unpaid letters would be charged 7c per half ounce, whereas paid letters were only 5c per half ounce[2]. Accordingly a large number of hand stamps were supplied, mostly "7" but some "UNPAID 7". At least 650 of the "7" handstamps were supplied, and those types noted on covers before January, 1860, were furnished by Berri, London, England[3]. Double weight letters were struck "14", and Ottawa had a "28" for quadruple rate letters! The various handstamps varied greatly, and undoubtedly some were local productions.

---
1. See Appendix E, and F, Table B.
2. Appendix B #31.
3. Appendix F, Table A.

"7" Single Rate

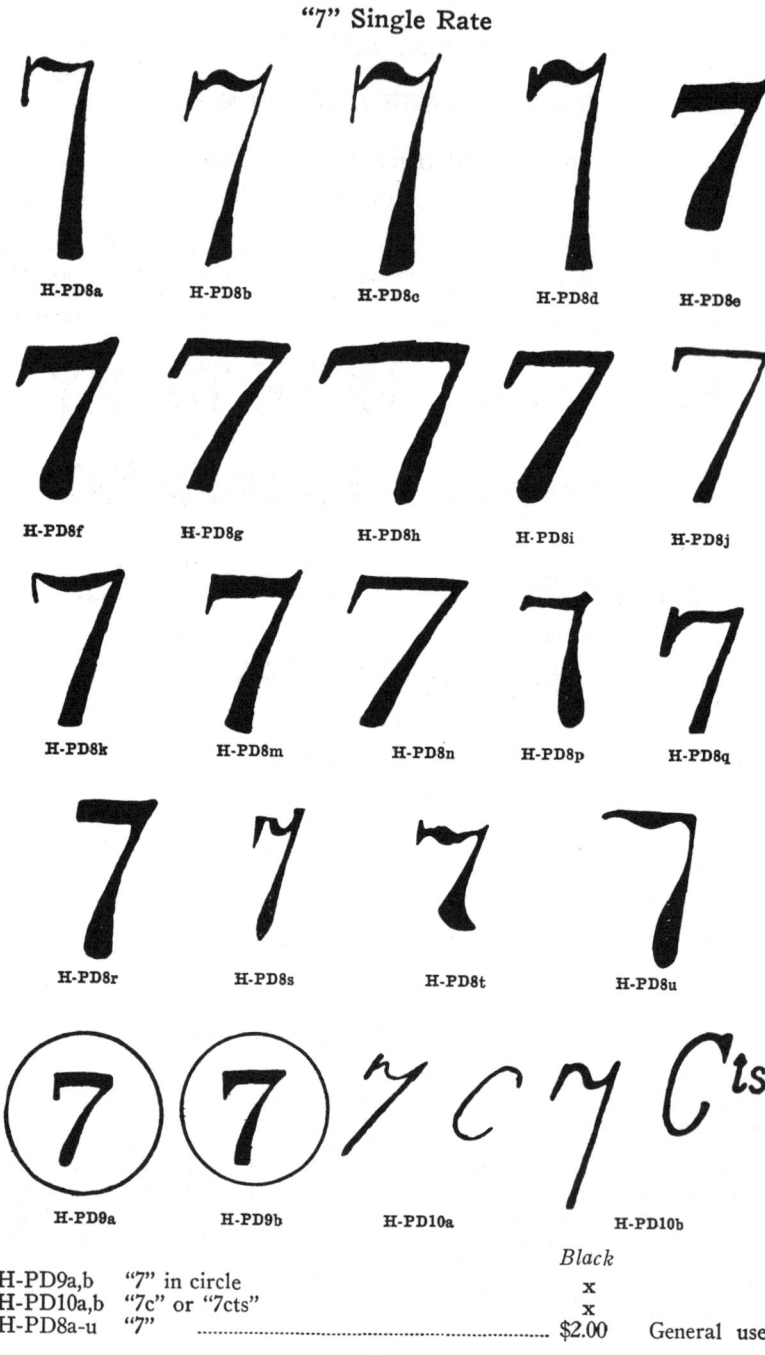

H-PD9a,b	"7" in circle		
H-PD10a,b	"7c" or "7cts"		
H-PD8a-u	"7"	$2.00	General use

Black: x, x

"14" Double Rate

14	14	**14**	*14*
H-PD11a Guelph. 1867	H-PD11b 1867	H-PD11c 1861	H-PD11d London. 1859

H-PD11a-d 1859   *Black*   x

"28" Quadruple Rate

This has been noted from Ottawa in 1865. Probably locally made.

28
H-PD12

H-PD12 1865   *Black* x   Ottawa

"Unpaid 7"

UNPAID 7	UNPAID 7
H-PD13a	H-PD14a
UNPAID 7	UNPAID 7
H-PD13b	H-PD13c
UNPAID 7	UNPAID 7
H-PD13d	H-PD13e

UNPAID 7   UNPAID 7
H-PD13f   H-PD13g

UNPAID 7
H-PD15a

We have been unable to find any record for orders of this type. It is reasonable to infer that they were locally made. They vary considerably but three classes are sufficient division of this group.

			Black	
H-PD13a-g	1860	"UNPAID" in sans-serifs letters	2.00	General use
H-PD14a	1860	"UNPAID" in serifed letters	3.00	St. Catherines
H-PD15a	1863	"UNPAID" in thick unserifed letters	2.50	Toronto

"Due" Markings

DUE   Due
H-PD16   H-PD17

The Dominion Post Office, which began operations April 1, 1868, introduced "DUE" markings on insufficiently prepaid letters. We have noted two types of these markings.

			Black
H-PD16	1868	All caps	1.00
H-PD17	1868	Caps and lower case	1.00

In 1871 "UNPAID" occurs again, similar in lettering to H-PD16.

UNPAID
H-PD18

			Black
H-PD18	1871	"UNPAID" all caps	2.50

The term "Insufficiently Prepaid" was used beginning in 1877.

INSUFFICIENTLY PREPAID
H-PD19

H-PD19 Feb.1877 .... *Black* 2.50   General use

This was struck on short paid letters, domestic or from the United States. Two hundred supplied by Pritchard & Mingard.

There is no doubt that many letters barely over weight had to be charged additional postage. The stamp "over ½oz" was used in some cases beginning in 1876.

OVER ½ OZ.
H-PD20

H-PD20   1876 "over ½oz." .... *Black* 2.00

B. Short Paid Ocean Mail Letters

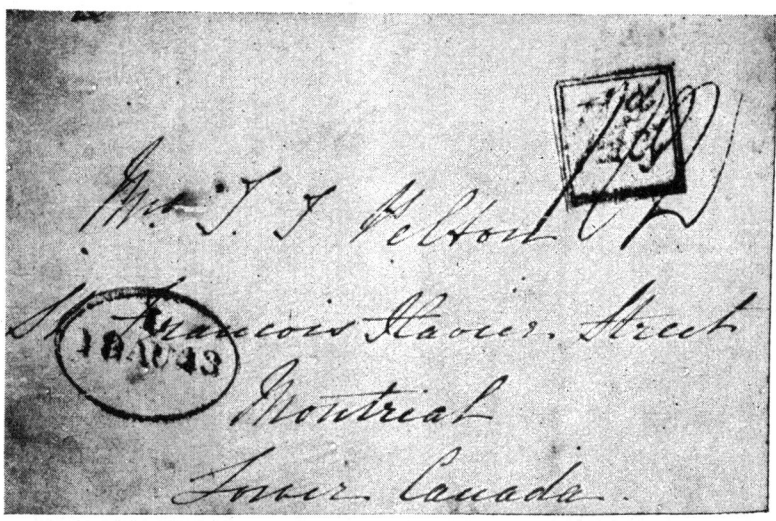

From England to Montreal. Ms. British rate of "½"—that is one shilling, two pence. Upon arrival at Quebec struck with square "¼d.cy", i.e. one shilling, four pence currency in black, as the letter was unpaid. This is Type H-PD21.

SHORT PAID__
HALF FINE__
H-PD22

		Black	
H-PD21	1843	10.00	Quebec
H-PD22	1862	x	Montreal

Eight of type H-PD22 were supplied by Berri, in 1862. They were for insufficiently paid English letters.[4]

The only example noted is struck on a cover routed by Canadian Packet on Jan. 12, 1866, from Montreal to London, England, and bearing a 12½c stamp. The regulation stamp is filled in thus: "Short Paid 6, Half Fine 3, (total) 9 (pence)." The cover is also stamped with an English rating stamp "1/-". The letter evidently was a double one and should have carried two 12½c postage stamps. Apparently half the fine was paid to the Canadian P. O. Department.

A Note on the U. P. U. Due Markings.

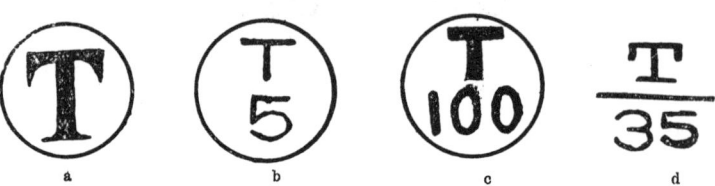

      a   b   c   d

Markings similar to the above are commonly found on covers from many countries to indicate postage is due. These are markings agreed upon by members of the Universal Postal Union, and are known as U.P.U. Due or Taxe Markings. They were agreed upon at the Third U.P.U. Congress held at Lisbon, Portugal, 1885, at which Canada was represented.

Type

(a) April 1877   Over 100 supplied between Apr. 1877 and Nov. 1893.
(b) Mar. 1890   May read 5, 10, or 25, 17½ mm. in diam.
(c) Dec. 1890   May read 5, 10, 25, 50 or 100. 19 mm. in diam. 5 of each supplied Dec. 1890.
(d)   1896   Various ratings.

---
4. Appendix E #19; Appendix F, Table B.

C. THE ADHESIVE POSTAGE DUES

1906-29
PD1-8

1930-32
PD9-13

1933-4
PD14-17

1935
PD18-21

1935 Postage Dues. Enlarged portion showing location of date on die (PD18-PD21).

In 1906 the P.M.G.'s report had the following interesting paragraphs, to wit:

A system of accounting for short paid postage collected by Postmasters, by means of special stamps known as "Postage Due" stamps, has been adopted by the Department. These stamps are to be affixed to short paid mail matter and cancelled by Postmasters when such matter is delivered to the addressee, and are not to be used for any other purpose. They cannot be used for the payment of ordinary postage, nor are they to be sold to the public.

The denominations of these stamps are 1, 2 and 5 cents.

The stamps referred to above were issued on June 1, 1906, and we give the official circular announcing the issue:

POST OFFICE DEPARTMENT, CANADA

OTTAWA, 1st June, 1906

Circular to Postmasters of Accounting Offices.

Commencing on the 1st July, 1906, the present system of collecting unpaid postage will be discontinued and thereafter the following arrangements will supersede the regulations now in force:—

(1) The Department will issue a special stamp which will be known as the "POSTAGE DUE" stamp and on delivery of any article of mail matter on which unpaid or additional postage is to be collected the Postmaster will affix and cancel as ordinary stamps are cancelled, postage due stamps to the amount of extra postage charged on such article.

(2) The short paid postage must be collected from the addressee before postage due stamps are affixed; otherwise the Postmaster is liable to lose the amount of such postage.

(3) Postmasters will obtain postage due stamps on requisition to the Department but the initial supply will be furnished without requisition, so that the new system may go into operation on the date above mentioned. When a new form is ordered "postage due" stamps will be included in the printed list, but it is proposed to use the stock on hand at present which would otherwise have to be destroyed. The denominations of the new stamps will be 1, 2 and 5 cents.

As noted under the respective regular issues the Postage Dues are all from hardened steel plates, made up as follows:

	Plate of	Panes of	Perforated
1906-29	200(10x20)	100(10x10)	12
1930-32	400(20x20)	100(10x10)	11
1933-34	400(20x20)	100(10x10)	11
1935 "Dated Dies"			12

All horizontal format until 1935, which are vertical format.

We have seen die proofs as follows:

DIE PROOFS

1906-29—On India, Die Sunk On White Card (Rare)

Die Imprint is "American Bank Note Co. Ottawa" in serifed caps ½mm. high.

D-PD1a   1c Black, Die F182 with imprint
     b   1c Violet, Die F182 with imprint
D-PD2a   2c Black, Die F181 with imprint
     b   2c Violet, Die F181 with imprint
D-PD3a   5c Black, Die F180 with imprint
     b   5c Violet, Die F180 with imprint
D-PD7a   4c Black, Die X-G188 without imprint
     b   4c Violet, Die X-G188 without imprint
D-PD8a   10c Black, Die X-G189 without imprint
     b   10c Violet, Die X-G189 without imprint

1930-32—On India, Mounted On Card (Rare)

D-PD9b   1c Violet   D-PD12b   5c Violet
D-PD10b   2c Violet   D-PD13b   10c Violet
D-PD11b   4c Violet

1933-34—On India, Die Sunk On Card (Very Rare)

D-PD14b   1c Violet

1935—On India, Die Sunk On Card

D-PD15b   1c Violet   D-DP18b   10c Violet
D-DP16b   2c Violet   D-DP13   10c Imperf horiz.
D-DP17b   4c Violet

Plate Imprints

Owing to the horizontal format of the first three issues the imprints appear to be on the sides in relation to the stamps. We have seen marginal lathework Type II. (See page 372). on the 2c violet of 1906. We have also seen the same stamp with double vertical perforations.

Adhesive Postage Dues

#	Denom. & Color	Issued	Plates	Quantity	Value Factor Unused	Value Factor Used	Notes	1944 S.#	1944 S.G.#
PD1	1c Violet	Jul. 1, 1906	1,2,A3	16,000,000	N	N	See note 1.	J1	D3
a	Imperf.		1	200	300		No gum.		
PD2	2c Violet	Jul. 1, 1906	1-4	44,178,000	N	N	See note 1.	J2	D4
a	Imperf.		2	200	100		No gum.		
PD3	5c Violet	Jul. 1, 1906	1-3	13,000,000	N	N	See note 1.	J3	D7
a	Imperf.		1	200	100		No gum.		
PD4	1c Red violet	Oct. 1924			30	40	Thin paper.		
PD5	2c Red violet	Oct. 1924			8	20	Thin paper.		
PD6	5c Red violet	Oct. 1924			4	7	Thin paper.		
PD7	4c Violet	Jul. 3, 1928	A1, A2	1,487,000	N	N		J4	D5
PD8	10c Violet	Jul. 3, 1928	A1	1,000,000	N	N		J5	D8
PD9	1c Purple	Jul. 14, 1930	1	1,070,000	N	N	No gum.	J6	D9
a	Imperf.			100	x				
PD10	2c Purple	Aug 21, 1930	1	3,078,000	N	N		J7	D10
a	Imperf.			100	x		No gum.		
PD11	4c Purple	Aug 14, 1930	1	237,000	N	N		J8	D11
PD12	5c Purple	Dec 12, 1931	1	200,000	N	N		J9	D12
a	Imperf.			100	x		No gum.		
PD13	10c Purple	Aug 24, 1932	1	300,000	N	N		J10	D13
a	Imperf. Horiz.			100	x				

Adhesive Postage Dues (Cont.)

#	Denom. & Color	Issued	Plates	Quantity	Value Factor Unused	Value Factor Used	Notes	1944 S.#	1944 S.G.#
PD14	1c Violet Plate block of 4	May 5, 1934	1		N 8	N	Bi-lingual.	J11	D14
PD15	2c Violet Plate block of 4	Dec 20, 1933	1		N 8	N	Bi-lingual.	J12	D15
PD16	4c Violet Plate block of 4	Dec 12, 1933	1		N 8	N	Bi-lingual.	J13	D16
PD17 a	10c Violet Imperf. Horiz. Plate block of 4	Dec 20, 1933	1		N x 8	N	Bi-lingual.	J14	D18
PD18 a	1c Violet Pale violet	Oct 14, 1935	1		N 15	N	"Dated die".	J15	D19
PD19	2c Violet	Sept. 9, 1935	1		N	N	"Dated die".	J16	D20
PD20	4c Violet	Jul. 2, 1935	1		N	N	"Dated die".	J17	D21
PD21	10c Violet	Sept 16, 1935	1		N	N	"Dated die".	J18	D22

Notes—PD1-8, 18-21 are Perf. 12; PD9-PD17 Perf. 11.

Other Factors: Unused blocks of four—6, unless otherwise noted. No premium on PD18-PD21.

Plate blocks of eight factor—15, unless otherwise noted, except PD18-PD21, factor 10.

Note 1.—PD1, PD2, and PD3 were printed on damp paper and then gummed until late 1924. Subsequent printings were on dry pre-gummed paper. The dry printed stamps show the design somewhat embossed on the gum. The quantities given include all printings.

Chapter XXIX

THE WAR TAX STAMPS
1915-16

The increasing financial burden of the first world war, 1914-18, was met in part by a war tax of one cent on each piece of first class matter. This tax was authorized by a "Special War Revenue Act", Bill No. 76, (Feb. 1915), in Part III of which is the following paragraph:

> "On every letter and post card for transmission by post for any distance within Canada, and on every letter and post card not intended for transmission through the mails, but for posting and delivery at the same post office, there shall be levied, a tax of one cent to be affixed thereto, at or before the time of posting the letter or post card."

The Inland Revenue Department ordered the overprinting of the 5c, 20c, and 50c postage stamps "WAR TAX" in two lines diagonally from upper left to lower right. The overprint is in black on the 5c, and 20c, and red on the 50c.

They were issued February 12, 1915, and almost immediately it was realized that confusion would result as to whether or not they could be used on mail matter, so that further issues were overprinted with "Inland Revenue" thereby definitely identifying them as revenue stamps.

At first war tax stamps were intended to pay only the war tax, but a Post Office notice of April 16, 1915, postmasters were notified that "postage stamps upon which the words 'war tax' have been printed may be accepted for prepayment of postage." As a result of this supplies of the 5c, 20c, and 50c with the original two line "War Tax" overprint were used for postage along with the other special war tax stamps. On December 30, 1915, the 5c, 20c, and 50c so overprinted were no longer available for postage.

Revenues Used for Postage

April 16 to December 30, 1915

#		Value	Factor	1944 S.G.#
RP1	5c blue (Plate 6)	N	N	225
RP2	20c deep olive green (Plates 2, 3)	N	N	226
a	sage green (Plates 2, 3)	N	N	
RP3	50c black (Plate 1)	N	N	227

We know of no varieties of overprint, which appears to be from an electrotype plate in a setting of 100.

The One and Two Cent War Tax Stamps

The 1c and 2c war tax stamps were specially prepared. The first two had the words "War Tax" outlined in sans-serif capitals on the "Admiral" type, then current.

We have seen die proofs as follows:

Die Proofs
"WAR TAX"
On India, Die Sunk on Card.

D-WT1a   1c black (Die No. "O.G.66").
       b   1c green (Die No. "O.G.66").
       c   1c green (No die number).
D-WT2a   2c black (Die No. "O.G.67").
       b   2c carmine (Die No. "O.G.67").
       c   2c carmine (No die number).

On White Card, Cut to Stamp Size

D-WT1d   1c black
D-WT2d   2c black

The details of production can be found by referring to Chapter XX, page 361 et seq.

1c had 18 plates, #A1 to A18. Plates A1 to A8 have hand drawn "A".
2c had 12 plates, #A1 to A12. Plates A1, A2 have hand drawn "A".

The 1T¢ Stamps

It was decided to prepare a new stamp which would combine the regular letter rate and the one cent war tax, and accordingly the 2c design was modified to show a large outlined "1T¢". The new design appeared in January 1916. In August the color was changed to brown. Two dies were used, and we show enlarged illustrations from die proofs in black to show the differences between them.

The chief difference is in the lines below the 'T' of "1T¢." In Die I the lines are horizontal and cross hatched, while in Die II the left portion consists only of horizontal lines, while the right portion consists of diagonal lines and dots.

The lines between the "1", "T", and "¢" respectively are decidedly different in the two dies.

Plates were as follows:
     DIE I—A1-A14
     DIE II—A15-A35

Plates A1, A2, A15, and A16 were used for both carmine and brown stamps. See table for listing of issued stamps, etc.

DIE PROOFS
On India, Die Sunk on Card (Rare)

D-WT3a   2c+1TC black, Die I.
D-WT4a   2c+1TC black, Die II.
D-WT3b   2c+1TC black, Die I. (Die "O.G.100").
       c   2c+1TC carmine, Die I.
D-WT4b   2c+1TC black, Die II. (Die "O.G.106½").
       c   2c+1TC carmine, Die II.
       d   2c+1TC brown, Die II.

On White Card, Cut to Stamp Size (Rare)

D-WT3d   2c+1TC black, Die I.
D-WT4e   2c+1TC black, Die II.

When the regular postage rate became 3c the War Tax stamps were discontinued and replaced by the regular design. (See Page 379, #102).

DIE II
Lines below 1Tc at left horizontal and cross hatched, while right position consists of diagonal lines and dots.

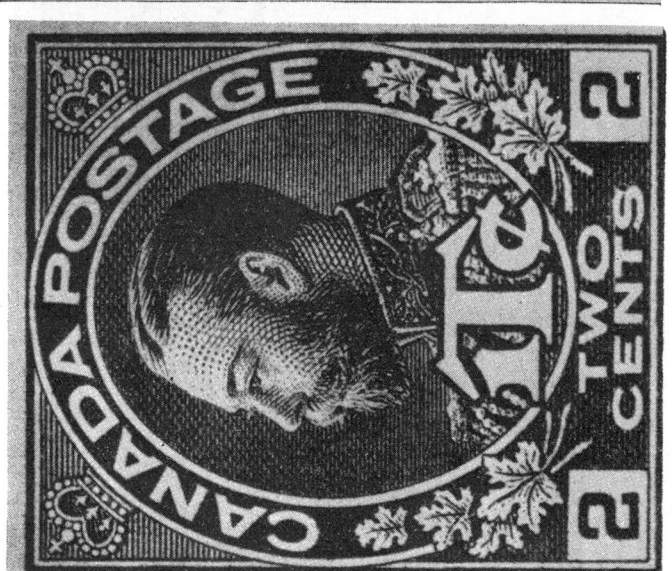

DIE I
Lines below 1Tc are horizontal, and cross hatched.

WT8. Plate "A35". Border pattern Type I. Type II pattern is also known on this stamp.

WT1. Hand Drawn "A" Plate "A8".

WT3. Plate "A1".

War Tax Stamps—1915-18.

#	Denom. & Color	Date Issued	Plates	Value unused	Factor used	Notes	1944 S. #	1944 S.G. #
WT1	1c Green	Apr. 15, 1915	A1-A18	N	N	See Note 2.	MR1	228
WT2	2c Carmine	Mar. 1915	A1-A12	N	N	See Note 2.	MR2	229
WT3	2c+1c Carmine	Jan. 1, 1916	A1-A14	N	N	Die I.	MR3	231
WT4	2c+1c Carmine	Sept. 1916	A15, A16	N	N	Die II.	MR3a	234
WT5	2c+1c Carmine		A1-A4	N	N	Perf. 12x8, Die I². See Note 3.	MR5	237
a	Arrow pair			*				
WT6	2c+1c Carmine	Aug. 2, 1916		N	N	Coil, imperf x perf 8, Die I.	MR6	235
WT7	2c+1c Brown	Sept. 16, 1916	A1, A2	N	N	Die I¹.	MR4a	238
WT8	2c+1c Brown	Aug. 28, 1916	A15-A35	N	N	Die II¹.	MR4	239
WT9	2c+1c Brown	Dec. 1916		N	N	Die I Coil, imperf x perf 8.	MR7a	241
WT10	2c+1c Brown			N	N	Die II Coil, imperf x perf 8.	MR7	243

1. These stamps are known imperforate, and part perforate vertically or horizontally. They were not regularly issued. Factor 300 for a block of four. The imperforate of WT8 is from plate A17.
2. The total sheet stamps issued was 514,000,000 divided approximately as follows: 1c and 2c (WT1, 2) 187,500,000; 3c (WT3-5, 7, 8) 327,000,000. Of the 1c and 2c, about 1/3rd of the total was 2c. The roll stamps were issued in rolls of 500, and approximately 160,000,000 stamps were issued in this form.
3. Pairs of this stamp may be obtained showing a small arrow between the stamps at top or bottom.

Chapter XXX

THE AIR MAIL STAMPS

(Including Airmail Special Delivery Stamps)

"CANADA"*

Few countries have benefited more by the development of the airplane as has Canada. The vast and remote districts, as well as the populous cities have been made easily accessible by the modern sky lines and the future will undoubtedly show Canada as one of the centers of World Aviation.

Experimental flights began as early as 1917, and by 1924 flights by private companies regularly carrying mail began, many of which issued special stamps to pay the airmail fee. These semi-official stamps are locals (in a peculiar sense), and therefore outside the scope of this work. They were, however, forerunners of the regular government issues.

In 1928 the first regular Air Mail stamp was issued, for use on the newly inaugurated Montreal-Albany (New York) route.

We give herewith brief notes concerning the designs of the various issues.

1928. 5c Brown Olive. Symbolic design "Allegory of Flight."

1930. 5c Brown Olive. Symbolic design "Air Mail Encircles the Globe."

1935. 6c Red Brown. "Daedalus in Flight" from an oil painting by A. E. Foringer, made expressly for this stamp. The background is an adaptation of the view across the Straits of Georgia from Oak Bay near Victoria, B. C.

1938. 6c Blue. Shows Air Mail Service in the North West Territories, from a picture taken at Fort Wrigley, on the Mackenzie River, by the late Richard N. Hourde. The vessel is the "Distributor" of the Hudson's Bay Company service.

Heading from die proof in black on india; by British American B. N. Co., Die No. 37 (about 1869).

1928
AM1

1930
AM2

1932
AM3

1932
AM4

1935
AM5

1938
AM6

1942
AM7-8

Date "1942" is on Bottom Leaf at Left.

The listing below shows the details of plates, panes, etc.

Date	Plate	Pane		
1928	200 (10x20)	100 (10x10).		
1930	100 (10x10)	50 (5x10).		
1935	200 (10x20)	50 (5x10)	"Dated Die".	All hardened steel plates
1938	100 (10x10)	50 (5x10)	"Dated Die".	
1942	200 (10x20)	50 (5x10)	"Dated Die".	
1943	200 (10x20)	50 (5x10)	"Dated Die".	

We have seen the following DIE PROOFS:

Die Essay (Rare)

On India, Sunk On Card. Approved Aug. 7, 1928 (Rare).

E-AM1 5c Brown Olive "POSTES-POST" approved Aug. 7, 1928.

Die Proofs (Issued Designs)

On India, Die Sunk On Card.

D-AM1p 5c Brown olive.
D-AM2b 5c Deep brown. Approved July 30, 1929.
D-AM5b 6c Red brown.
D-AM6b 6c Blue, Die X-G674.
D-AM7b 6c Blue, Die X-G750.
D-AM8b 7c Blue, Die X-G792.
D-AMSD1b 16c Blue, Die X-G751.
D-AMSD2b 17c Blue, Die X-G793.

On White Wove Cut to Stamp Size Mounted On Thick Card

D-AM2c 5c Brown olive.

The two surcharged Air Mails were overprinted from electrotype plates of 100 subjects. There are no varieties of the setting, although in the case of the 6c on 5c there are the usual inverted, double, etc., known.

The 6c on 5c was necessitated by the increase of 1c on each letter, effective July 1, 1931.

The surcharging of the 5c for the Ottawa Conference was for the purpose of expediting the official and personal correspondence of the conferees. A special air mail service inaugurated between Ottawa and Belle Isle the last landfall of vessels to Europe. This made it possible to get the mail on steamers that had left Quebec the previous day.

1935. Air Mail Enlarged Portion Showing Location of Date on Die. AM5.

Airmail Special Delivery.
1942-43

The War Effort issue of July 1, 1942, was noteworthy in that for the first time it included an airmail special delivery stamp, a class new to Canada. It was also the first stamp of sixteen cents denomination to be issued by the Dominion.

The design pictures a Trans-Canada Airway's mail plane over Drummondville, Que., and was adapted from photographs furnished by the Airways Company.

Engraved and printed by the Canadian Bank Note Co. from a plate of 200 subjects (10 x 20), divided into four panes of 50 (5 x 10). Perforated 12. White wove paper. Dated dies.

The increase of one cent in the rate effective April 1, 1943, resulted in a similar stamp of 17c denomination being issued.

AMSD1-2.

A. Air Mail Issues

#	Denom. & Color	Date	Die #	Plates	Quantity	Value Factor Unused	Value Factor Used	Notes	1944 Scott #	1944 S.G. #
AM1	5c brown olive	Sep. 21, 1928		A1, A2	10,000,030	N	N	Imprint Type IX 4 sheets } Not regularly 1 sheet } issued. 1 sheet	C1	274
a	Imperforate					600				
b	Imperf. Horiz.					1200				
c	Imperf. Vertically					1200				
	Block of four					6	7			
	First day cover						12			
	Plate block of six					12				
AM2	5c olive brown	Dec. 4, 1930		1	401,000	N	N	Imprint Type XI	C2	310
	Block of four					5	5			
	First day cover						8			
AM3	6c on 5c brown olive	Feb. 22, 1932		A1, A2	2,000,000	N	N	Rate increased to 6c July 1, 1931.	C3	313
a	Inverted surcharge					125				
b	Double surcharge					300				
c	Triple surcharge					300				
d	Pair, one without surcharge					x				
e	Diagonal surcharge					x				
f	Pair, diagonal surcharge on one, other without surcharge					x				
	Block of four					5	5			
	First day cover						4			

Air Mail Issues (Cont.)

#	Denom. & Color	Date	Die #	Plates	Quantity	Value Factor Unused	Value Factor Used	Notes	1944 Scott #	1944 S.G. #
AM4	6c on 5c olive brown Block of four First day cover	July 12, 1932		1	500,000	N 5 —	N 5 2	Ottawa Conference.	C4	318
AM5	6c Red brown Pale red brown Horizontal pair imperf between Plate block of six First day cover	June, 1, 1935		1		N 15 x 8 —	N x — — 5	Daedalus design. Imprint Type XII	C5	355
AM6	6c blue Plate block of four First day cover	June 15, 1938	X-G 674	1		N 6 —	N — 4	Stern Wheel Steamer. Imprint Type XIII	C6	371
AM7	6c blue Plate block First day cover	July 1, 1942	X-G 750	1		N 5 —	N — 4	War Effort issue. Imprint Type XIII	C7	386
AM8	7c blue First day cover	Apr. 1, 1943	X-G 792	1		N —	N 5	Rate increased to 7c Apr. 1, 1943. Imprint Type XIII	C8	387

B. Air Mail Special Delivery

	16c blue	Jul. 1, 1943[1]	X-G 750	1		N	N	Imprint Type XIII	CE1	EA1
	17c blue	Apr 1, 1943[1]	X-G 793	1		N	N	Rate increased to 17c Apr. 1, 1943. Imprint Type XIII	CE2	EA2

1. First day covers—factor 3.

Chapter XXXI

THE POSTAL STATIONERY

Introduction

This group includes stamped envelopes, post cards, wrappers and letter sheets issued by the Post Office, both Provincial and Dominion.

In common with many other Postal Administrations of the British Empire the Dominion Post Office, will under certain conditions impress the stamp on envelopes or post cards supplied by private parties. These, while of interest, are beyond the scope of this work. We do however, call attention to one or two instances of this class of material which might be confusing to collectors.

The Development of Envelopes

Envelopes to enclose letters and documents were used almost as soon as the invention of paper by the Chinese about 100 A. D.[1] Modern envelopes, however, were invented in France late in the 18th Century, but did not come into popular favor with the British and Americans until the introduction of the weight system for charging postage, that is between 1845 and 1850.

Stamped envelopes were issued by Great Britain in 1840, the now famous Mulready's, and stamped letter sheets were placed on sale at Sydney, Australia in 1838.

Mass production, however, necessitated by the lowered postage rates and tremendous increase in the volume of mail forced ingenious men to invent envelope making machinery. Among the earliest and most successful was George F. Nesbitt[2] of the famous firm of George F. Nesbitt & Co. who were active in 1840, and in 1853 secured the contract for United States envelopes, and whose machinery turned out envelopes practically the same as we know them today.

Envelope Cutting Knives

The process of die cutting envelope blanks, as it is technically called, is an old art. It was in use even before the development of envelopes, about 1845, and is still widely used in other branches of the stationery business for cutting out various odd shapes of gummed labels, such as stars, circles, airmail stickers, and even for stamp hinges. There is an infinite variety to the shapes that can be cut. Since there would be much philatelic confusion between *die* cut envelope blanks, and embossed printing *dies* with their minor varieties, it was long ago determined to call the cutting die a *knife,* see Fig. 1, and to reserve the term *die* to describe the printing form or the printed impression of the stamp on the envelope.

The forged steel envelope knife, as illustrated in Fig. 1, is properly located on a pile of paper to avoid waste, with the sharp cutting edge down against the paper. The press head forces the cutting edge of the knife through the pile of paper, and slightly into the end wood of the cutting block all as shown in Fig. 2. The cut blanks are removed from the inside of the knife, and the process repeated. The method is old, but tested by several generations of workmen, and no more efficient method has as yet been permanently adopted for the manufacture of stamped envelopes.

Some of the knife shapes were in use for many years, and successive knives were made to duplicate and replace those that wore out. In forging and tem-

---

[1]. Sir Aurel Stein in 1907 found a dozen or so letters written on paper in Sugdian and Chinese, dated about 150 A. D. and enclosed in ENVELOPES.
[2]. Appendix O #15.

pering these thick steel knives it was difficult to produce exact duplicates. The important features to maintain were the envelopes' overall size and the contour of the edges that were to be gummed. Slight variations in curves and the ends of side flaps (ungummed) were unimportant. Hence there were inevitable variations, such as occur particularly on the Dominion Envelopes of 1877-1897.

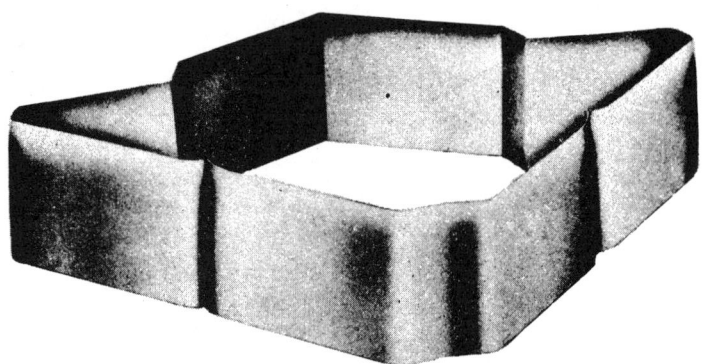

Courtesy John J. Adams
Fig. 1. Typical Envelope Cutting Knife. Cutting edge is pointed up. .Top Flap of envelope is at rear. (See footnote 3 below).

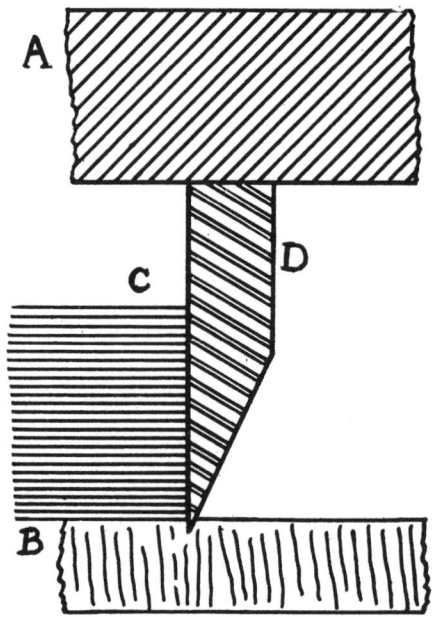

Fig. 2. Envelope Knife in Cutting Position. Section of Knife as cut is completed.
A. Above: Head of press at lowest position. B. Below: End wood cutting block. C. Left: Paper envelope blanks for printing. D.: Knife.

---

3. The various Nesbitt knives are numbered according to the system devised by the late J. M. Bartels, who was the world's greatest authority on United States envelopes.

Fig. 3.
Sub-contractor of the American Bank Note Co. for the First Canadian Envelopes.

Fig. 5.

Ten Cent Envelope With 10c 1859 Registered from Eugenia, C. W., 25 Sep 1865, to Minneapolis. Note "5" for Registry Fee, the Remaining 15c for U. S.-Canada Postage.

A. THE NESBITT ENVELOPES
1860-68

Fig. 4. Enlargements of the Nesbitt Dies.

The first mention we have been able to find concerning stamped envelopes is a letter to the Deputy Post Master General dated December 10, 1857, from Rawdon, Wright, Hatch & Edson, discussing the cost, denominations, etc.[1] In April, 1858, further mention is made in another letter quoting $1.70 per 1000 as the cost[2]. Other matters apparently caused the Post Office Department to lay aside the idea (notably the coming introduction of the decimal currency system and the new stamps necessitated by this change; perforating, etc.), but on March 22, 1859, the contractors who were then one of the constituent firms of the American Bank Note Co., wrote in great detail concerning designs, cost, quantities, etc.[3] Finally on June 15, 1859, the Deputy Postmaster General, Mr. Griffin, ordered the contractors to prepare 200,000 five cent, and 100,000 ten cent envelopes.[4]

In October, 1864, an additional 25,000 five cent envelopes were ordered.[5] These were also a different knife, known as 11. A dispute concerning the price arose[6], and when in March, 1866, another 15,000 five cent envelopes were ordered, the Bank Note Company insisting on the charge of $9.00 per thousand, coupled with the slow sales, resulted in the discontinuance of postal stationery by the Provincial government[7].

The envelopes were issued February 1, 1860[8], and in the Report of the Postmaster General dated February 20, 1860, we find the following remarks:

> "For the promotion of public convenience by facilitating the prepayment of letters, Stamped Envelopes bearing Medallion Stamps of the postage value of 5c. and 10c. respectively, have been procured and issued for sale to the public, at an advance of ½ a cent on the value of each stamp, to cover the cost of the envelope, and of engraving the stamp, &c."

Also that the sum of $1,697.95 was paid to the American Bank Note Co., "for engraving Letter and Newspaper Stamps and *Stamped Envelopes.*"

The American Bank Note Company sub-contracted with the famous firm of George F. Nesbitt & Co., of New York, who were contractors for U. S. envelopes at that time.

---
1. Appendix H #63.
2. Appendix H #64.
3. Appendix H #79.
4. Appendix H #84.
5. Appendix H #107.
6. Appendix H #113, and #114.
7. Appendix H #115, and #116.
8. Appendix B #33.

The Nesbitt plant was located at the corner of Pearl and Pine Sts., occupying an area nearly half a square block. (Fig. 10).

The envelopes produced by Nesbitt are similar to the second issue of United States envelopes which were issued late in 1860, and the Canadian envelopes may have been the model for the United States "star" dies. Owing to the comparatively small printings there are no die varieties.

REFERENCE LIST

ESSAY

The original die prepared for these envelopes was rejected as not being a good likeness of the Queen. The lettering is larger, nose more prominent and the pendant curl of the chignon much larger. [8a]
E-PS1a 5c Vermilion on buff laid. (Very rare).
The issued dies measured as follows: 5c 19.8 x 23.8mm.; 10c 19.5 x 25mm.

Proofs

#	Denomination and Color	WOVE PAPER A. White	B. Buff	LAID PAPER C. White	D. Buff	NOTES
PPSIa	5c black	20.00				
b	5c blue	20.00[1]		50.00		
c	5c green	20.00[1]		50.00		
d	5c brown	20.00				
e	5c carmine	20.00	25.00	50.00	50.00	
f	5c red	20.00	25.00	50.00	50.00	This is on a "Patent line" envelope, wmkd POD-US "SAMPLE" printed below stamp.[8b]
g	5c+5c red				60.00	
PPSIIa	10c blue	25.00[1]				
b	10c green	25.00[1]				
c	10c red	25.00				
d	10c dark brown	25.00		50.00	50.00	
e	10c pale brown	25.00				
f	10c black	25.00				

1. Ruled lines on back in blue. Prices are for cut squares.

Essay for Letter Sheet

E-PSIa 5c red on buff laid (entire) 60.00 "SAMPLE" printed below stamp.[8b]

The above varieties have generally been considered as reprints made by Nesbitt for "exhibition" purposes in 1868. The fact that all of them were chronicled by the "Stamp Collectors Magazine", Bath, Eng. in 1864-65, as well as other evidence inclines us to the opinion that they are proofs or possibly samples of the firms work for display, similar to the specimen sheets prepared by the Bank Note Companies. (See chapter VIII page 175).[8c]

The Issued Envelopes

Issued February 1, 1860-9) (Fig. 4). Embossed, on envelope made of white laid paper, with batonné lines 18 mm. apart. Watermarked "CaPOD" in two lines (Fig. 6) as requested by the Post Office Department[8d]. The first lot was knife 2, 139 x 83 mm., hand gummed. The second order for the Five Cents was knife 11, 139 x 83 mm., also hand gummed.

8a. Appendix H #90, #91.
8b. See concluding notes at end of chapter. (Page 513).
8c. Appendix H #94, #97.
8d. Appendix H #84.

The envelopes sold for 6c and 11c respectively or $5.50 and $10.50 a hundred. On October 1, 1864, the price per hundred was reduced to $5.30 and $10.30 respectively. Sales, however, did not materially increase from that date.

Fig. 6. Watermark of the Nesbitt Envelopes.

REFERENCE LIST

#	Date	Denom. Color	Knife	Entire Unused	Used	Cut Square Unused	Used	Quantity Issued
PS-I	1860	5c bright red	2	$12.50	$20.00	$3.00	$5.00	200,000
PS-II	1860	10c black brown	2	35.00	75.00	15.00	25.00	44,176
PS-III	1864	5c bright red	11	17.50	25.00	—	—	24,954

Cut-squares of this and other early issues were permitted to be used as adhesives, a practice now long forbidden. Covers bearing these should not be accepted unless the cut-square is well tied to the envelope by the cancellation, as "fakes" are not uncommon.

We might call attention to the fact that the 10c envelope unused, entire is scarce indeed, and used entires are decidedly rare.

Counterfeits

These envelopes have been counterfeited. Of the 5c at least three varieties are known—one on white wove and two on pale buff, while of the 10c two forgeries on pale buff are known.

Fig. 7.
Counterfeits of the 1860 10 cent envelope, uncancelled and cancelled. Red brown on medium buff wove. Probably by Spiro Bros. Hamburg, about 1870. The "Cancellation" is similar to that found on many of the stamps of Saxony.

---
9. Appendix B #33.
10. Appendix H #S4.

Nesbitt Knife 2. Size 3. 1853. (Canada 1860).

By laying the entire envelope on the diagram the knife can be easily identified.

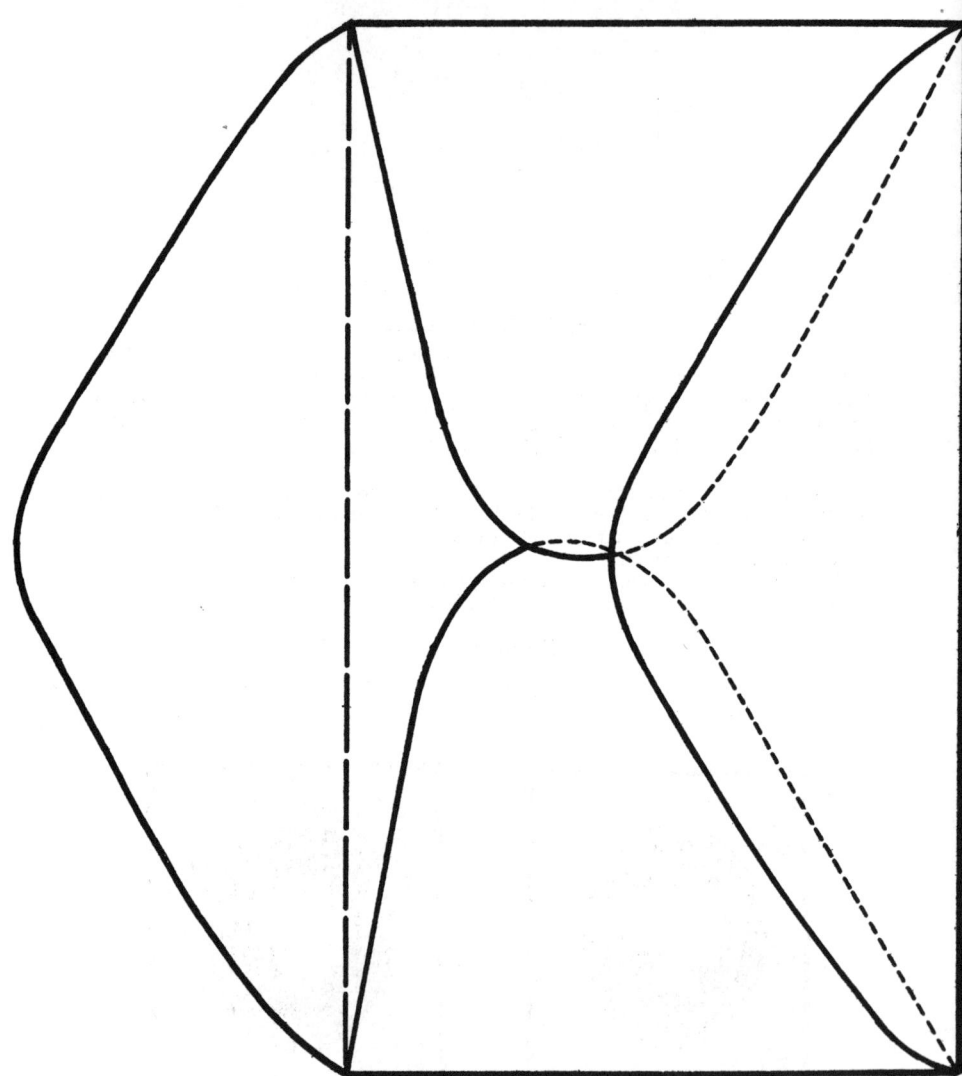

Fig. 8. Both 5c and 10c Envelopes Occur In This Knife.

Dimensions: 139 x 83 mm. 5½ x 3¼ inches.
Flaps: Top —Wide curved point. Side—usually Right over Left; occasionally Left over Right.
Note: All curves broadly rounded. Compare with Knife 11.

Nesbitt Knife 11. Size 3. 1861. (Canada 1864).

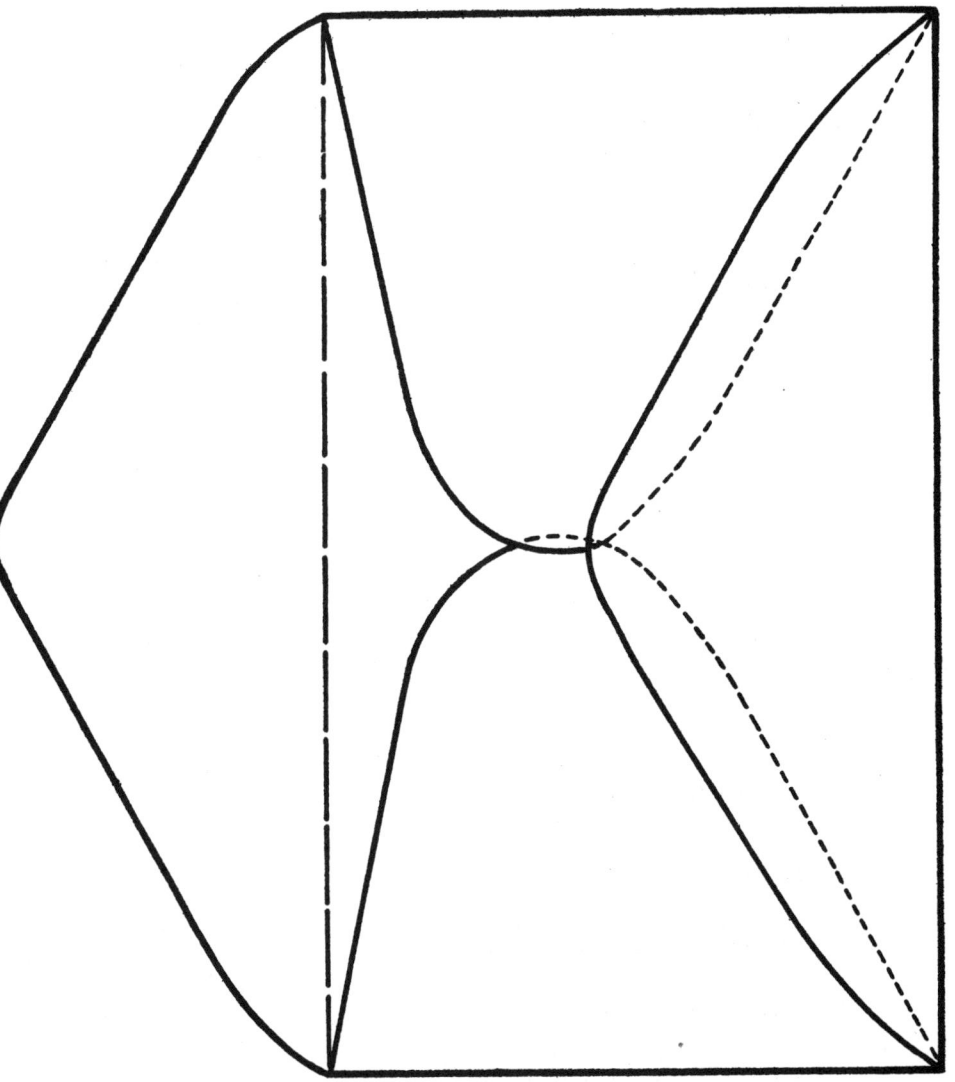

Fig. 9. Only the 5c Occurs In This Knife.

Dimensions: 139 x 83 mm. 5½ x 3¼ inches.

Flaps: Top—Small round point. Side—usually Right over Left; occaisionally Left over Right. Ends broadly rounded and overlap slightly. Bottom—Medium round point.

Note: Compare with Knife 2.

Quantities of Stamped Envelopes[11]

	5c	10c	Value
Received from manufacturers	200,000	100,000	$21,500.00
Issued for sale during 8 months to Sept. 30, 1860	136,177	45,651	12,283.09
Remaining	63,823	54,349	9,216.91

The number of stamped envelopes, actually used by the public, has been but small, as a considerable proportion of those issued remain in the hands of the Postmasters.

QUANTITIES

	5c	10c
Balance on hand Sept. 30, 1860	63,823	54,349
Returned by Postmasters, unsold	1,529	1,905
	65,352	56,254
Issued for sale during year	20,700	806
Balance on hand Sept. 30, 1861	44,652	55,448
Returned by Postmasters, unsold	251	314
	44,903	55,762
Issued for sale during year	9,595	844
Balance on hand Sept. 30, 1862	35,308	54,918
Returned by Postmasters, unsold	—	4
	35,308	54,922
Issued for sale during year	15,200	900
Balance on hand Sept. 30, 1863	20,108	54,022
Returned by Postmaster, unsold	5,000	2,997
	25,108	57,019
Issued for sale during nine months	14,800	850
Balance on hand June 30, 1864	10,308	56,169
Returned by Postmasters, unsold	6,444	5,632
Received from manufacturers	25,000	—
	41,752	61,801
Issued for sale during year	23,583	5,598
Balance on hand June 30, 1865	18,169	56,203
Returned by Postmasters, unsold	382	225
	18,551	56,428
Issued for sale during year	16,225	625
Balance on hand June 30, 1866	2,326	55,803
Returned by Postmasters, unsold	—	193
Deduct envelopes received short	10	—
	2,316	55,996
Issued for sale during year	2,270	172
Balance on hand June 30, 1867	46	55,824

---

11. This table was also printed in Howes' book, but the original figures had a number of errors which have been corrected. From the Report of the P.M.G.

VIEW OF THE NESBITT ESTABLISHMENT IN 1840.
(From an Old Wood Cut.)

Fig. 10.
Corner of Wall and Water Sts., New York.

Concluding Remarks.

There is still much to be learned concerning these envelopes. Two of the listed items E-PS1a, and P-PS1e bearing impressions of the Canadian 5c envelope stamp are quite possibly essays for the United States letter sheet and compound envelopes of 1861 respectively (Scott U36, U28, U29).

5c Nesbitt Envelope "Too Late", and Concentric Ring Obliteration. Somerset, C.E. DE 10, 1860.

Notes on the 1865 Essays by Nesbitt.

These were apparently made for Nova Scotia but may possibly have been intended for Canada.

Knife 2, 138 x 79 mm. No value expressed. Batonné lines 25 mm. apart. Unwatermarked. Handgummed.

Fig. 11. E-PSIIIa-c.

E-PSIIIa Vermilion
    b Green
    c Dark blue

These were known as early as September 1865.

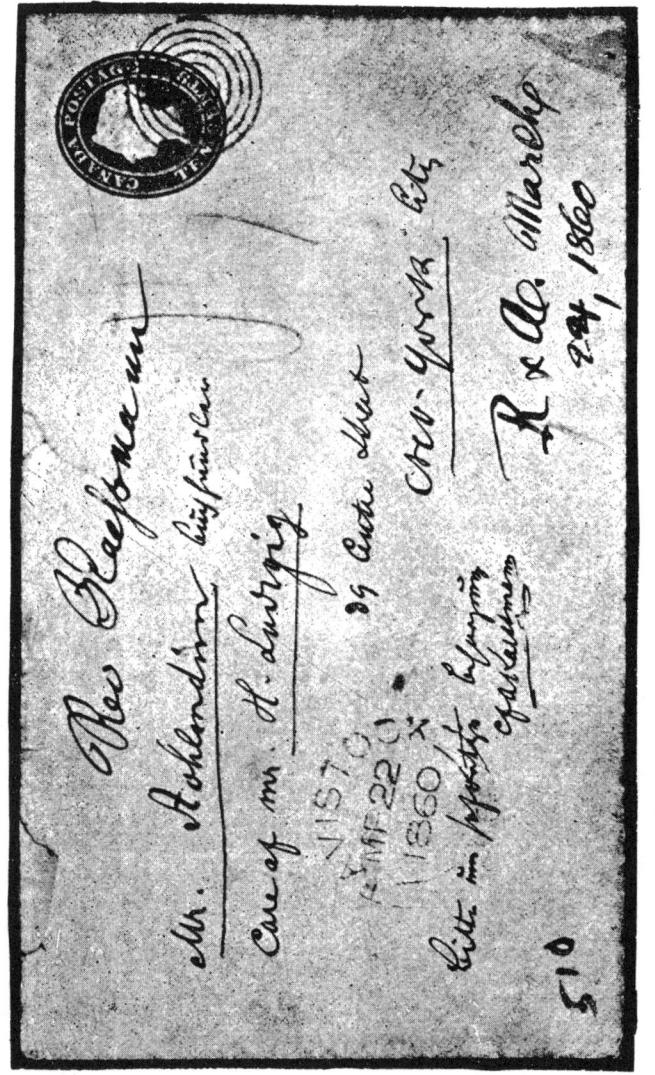

Fig. 12. 10c Nesbitt from Tavistock, Mr. 22, 1860. Early use of this rare envelope.

Chapter XXXII

THE ENVELOPES AND WRAPPERS OF THE DOMINION
1875-1944

It was ten years after Confederation in 1867 that the first Dominion stamped envelopes appeared, although wrappers were issued in 1875. Evidently the unsatisfactory experience of the Provincial period caused the autharities to hesitate before venturing to issue stamped envelopes again.

However, the decision having been made the British American Bank Note Co. contracted to furnish the envelopes at $3.00 per thousand for the small size 1c, and 3c, and $3.50 per thousand for the larger 3c.[1]

The American Bank Note Co. apparently sought to provide these envelopes as we know of essays of 1c and 3c which we illustrate herewith.

A. DOMINION ENVELOPES

Fig. 1. Enlarged Illustrations of the Designs of E-PS1a, E-PS2a.

ESSAYS FOR 1877 ENVELOPES

By the American Bank Note Co. (Rare)

E-PS1a   1c Blue on white (140 x 81 mm.)
E-PS2a   3c Pale blue on white (132½ x 79½ mm.) Manuscript "Specimen".

Late in 1876 the British American Bank Note Co. using the former Provincial envelope design as a model wrote to Henry Mitchell[2], die sinker of Boston, Mass., with instructions and a sketch of the proposed envelope. (Fig. 2).

The first knife used for these envelopes had concave sides to the top flap. These may be considered as essays. There was also a knife used, which had a similar top flap but the end of the side flaps were straight rather than rounded.

We list herewith the Essays by the British American Bank Note Co. in 1877.

---

1. See Chapter X, page 230 for further details of the contract.
2. Henry Mitchell was a noted die sinker, and engraved the dies for many United States envelopes, including the 1876 Centennial, 1887, 1899, 1903 issues, etc. He died Aug. 1, 1909.

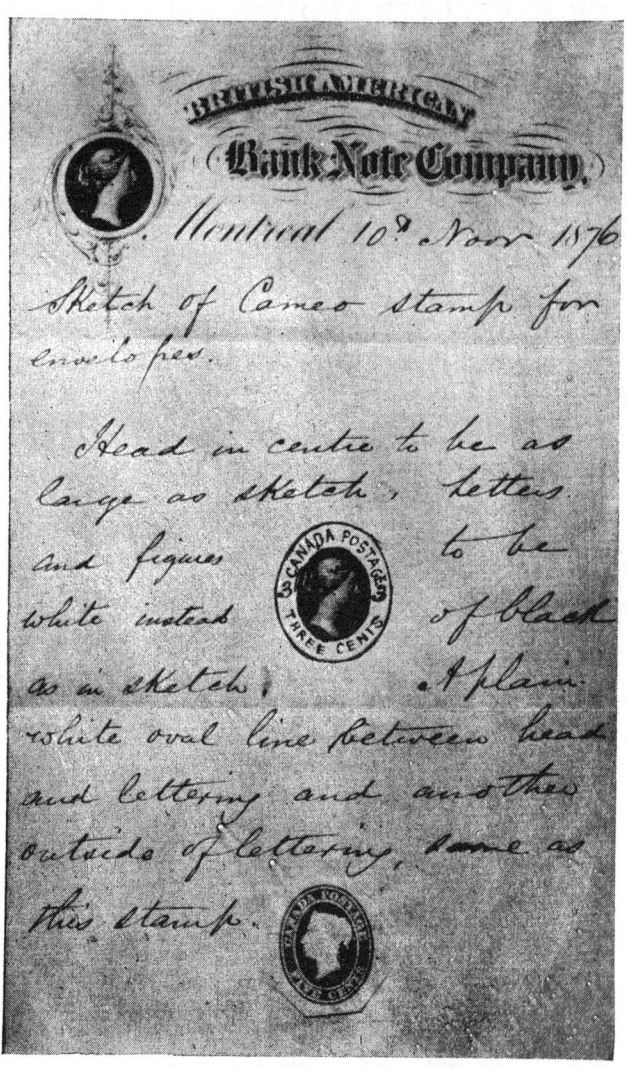

Fig. 2.
Original Sketch and Instructions from British American Bank Note Co. to Henry Mitchell Concerning the Engraving of the Die for the First Dominion Envelope.

Essays of Issued Design

Top flap slightly tongued, rounded point.

E-PS1b   1c Dark blue on white wove (138x83 mm.=5½x3¼"). Low back, side flap over left. Square gum³. (RARE).

E-PS2b   3c Pale blue on white laid (138 x 79 mm.=5½ x 3⅛"). Batonné lines spaced 18 mm. apart. Low back, right side flap over left. Side flaps with straight ends. (RARE).

E-PS2c   3c Red on white laid (138 x 79 mm.=5½ x 3⅛"). Batonné lines spaced 18 mm. apart. Low back, right side flap over left. Side flaps with straight ends. (Scarce).

       d   3c Red on white laid (1888?). Batonné lines spaced 24 mm. apart. (Uncommon).

Before further discussion of envelopes we give a brief description of the methods of producing envelopes, which, we hope, will clarify many obscure points, and permit a more accurate classification of Canadian envelopes. The lack of a clear knowledge of how envelope dies are made has resulted in considerable confusion as to die varieties, etc.

Envelope Dies

An envelope die is a form of typographic die, the white portions being more or less recessed. In making an envelope die the process is as shown in the chart below.

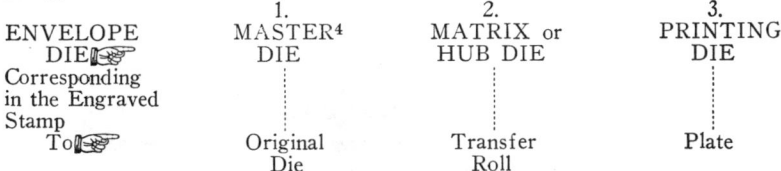

	1.	2.	3.
ENVELOPE DIE☞	MASTER⁴ DIE	MATRIX or HUB DIE	PRINTING DIE
Corresponding in the Engraved Stamp To☞	Original Die	Transfer Roll	Plate

The master die is cut by the engraver in soft steel. The colorless lines of the printed impression are cut into the surface of this die. When the engraving is completed the die is hardened and it is ready for transferring to the hub or matrix die.

The hub die is somewhat larger in diameter than the master die. The hardened master die is placed in a press, and under enormous pressure is forced into the soft steel face of the hub die, thus tranferring the design to the hub.

The pressure is applied directly and not by rocking as in the case of the transfer roll in laying down a plate. The pressure in transferring has to be applied several times, the displaced metal being removed between the applications of pressure. When satisfactorily transferred, the design is carefully examined and minor corrections made by hand if necessary.

This die is then hardened and used to make the printing dies which are of soft steel and comparatively thin. (See diagrams). The final working die is then examined, any necessary corrections made and after hardening, is ready for fitting on the printing press. (Fig. 4).

Where another denomination of similar design is needed a new hub die is made by removing the denomination. This blank value die is hardened and forced into another steel hub which becomes a secondary master die on which is engraved the desired denomination. The secondary master die is then used to produce the printing dies as previously described.

Electrotype of the master die can be made by taking a wax impression, coating it with plumbago, and then immersing the impression in an electroplat-

---

3. Square gum ends in a sharp vertical line, and indicates hand gumming.
4. The master dies became working dies and were so used until 1930 when line cut reproductions of the die were made to keep up with the increasing quantity of envelopes needed.

ing bath. Electrotypes are comparatively short lived, but have the advantage of being cheaply, quickly, and easily made while steel printing dies take considerable skill and time, and are expensive. (Fig. 3).

Late impressions from an electrotype are usually worn and defective, particularly if the design has a number of fine lines, as for instance, the King George V designs of 1912-33.

Embossed envelope stamps are printed from hardened steel dies or electrotypes which print against a resilient backing, usually leather. The envelope blank is between the die and the soft backing of the platen. The colorless portions of the design are recessed in the printing surface. The face of the die or electrotype is inked, and the pressure forces the paper into the recessed portion resulting in embossed lettering and portrait. Thin colorless lines may fill up with ink and disappear in the printing. Letters closely spaced will sometimes become joined if the narrow raised portion becomes worn. Dies for flat presses may have finer lines because of more accurate register. Two or more blanks fed into press at once result in one being albino. If no envelope blank is fed the ink is transferred to the backing, and the next blank will be printed in color on both sides. This is a form of offset. If a random printed blank is fed into the folding machine wrong side up the stamp is folded inside.

Fig. 3.
ELECTROTYPE.
Schematic Diagram of Method of Making Electrotypes of Working Dies. (See note 5.)

So much for the process of manufacture. The various issues were supplied as follows: The British American Bank Note Co., supplied only the 1c and 3c designs of 1877, and the ornate 2c of 1895. The only variations are in the sizes of the envelopes, the spacing of the batonné lines, and the accidental shades of paper.

The American Bank Note Co., did not undertake the production of stamped envelopes, and since 1897 envelopes have been supplied by the Printing and Stationery Department at Ottawa.

The 2c on 3c Provisionals of 1899.

The reduction in the postage rate, from 3c to 2c, effective January 1, 1899, made it necessary to surcharge the 3c envelopes "2c" pending the preparation of a new 2c envelope die. This was done by the Post Office Department.

Soft rubber stamps bearing the figures "2c" were provided and the surcharge was applied by these handstamps. There are two distinct types, one with

---

5. From Essay-Proof Journal. Copyright by Essay-Proof Society. Adapted by permission of Essay-Proof Society, and Frank D. Collins.

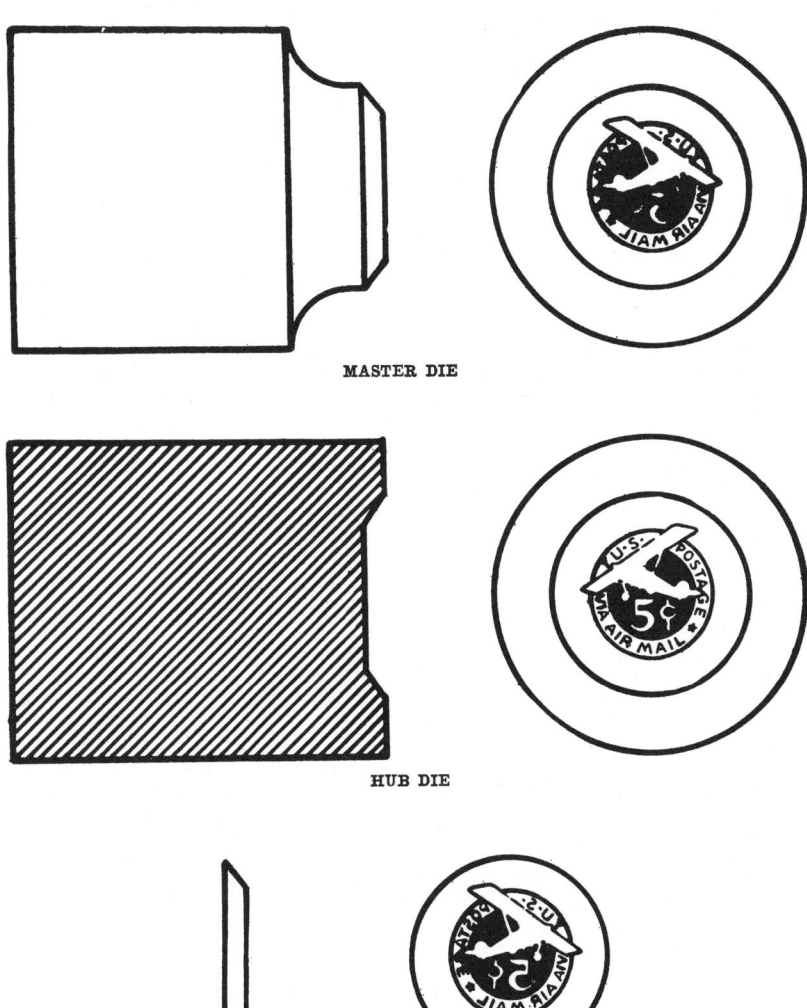

Fig. 4.
Schematic Side and Front Views of Envelope Stamp Dies, 1
1. From "Envelope Dies and the U. S. Air Mail Envelopes" by Frank D. Collins, The Essay-Proof Journal, October 1944, p183-189. Copyright by Essay-Proof Society. Reproduced by permission of The Essay-Proof Society and Frank D. Collins.

serif to "c" the other without. The serifed type is scarce, the handstamp being in use for only a few days. As usual with handstamping the position varies, and doubles and inverts are known. but are worth little more than ordinary. The quality and color of the ink varies somewhat, but none of these differences warrant separate listing.

The Envelopes Supplied by the Printing and Stationery Department. 1897-1944.

The first new design appeared in April 1898, the die being supplied by Messrs. Tho. De La Rue, London, Eng. This design did not meet with favor and was replaced in July 1898 by a new and more attractive design, of the 1c followed in January 1899 by the 2c denomination. Again, Thomas de la Rue & Co., London, Eng., supplied the master die with the value tablet left blank, and made working dies for the 1c and 2c respectively.

When a new design was needed, bearing the head of King Edward VII. Messrs. De La Rue, supplied two steel dies, one for each denomination. These two dies remained in service for a period of seven years, and produced all the Canadian envelopes from 1905 to 1912 inclusive, totaling approximately 7,000,000 1c, and 18,0000,000 2c.

The variations in the impression are due to press work, and are not die differences. Extreme variations in printing are of interest, however, to the specialist.

In 1912 the new King George V envelopes appeared, similar in design to the previous issue, and dies from De La Rue as before. In 1920 the same firm supplied the die for the 3c of this design.

Owing to the long life of this issue there are many variations in impression, some showing detailed embossing, others shallow embossing, and still others a flat impression without embossing. There also distinct variations in the total height of the impression. While of interest these variations, in our opinion, are not die varieties, but are due to printing methods, worn plates, etc, and the use of electrotypes.

Late in 1930 the impressions showing colored lines in the hair and beard were issued. These are from line cut reproductions of the Master Die. This was an economical and rapid method of duplicating the die, and furthermore in the case of the compound envelopes, was the only way in which an additional impression could be added to a completed envelope.

The new 1931 design was typographed as have been all succeeding issues. There are no "Die" varieties after this issue. We believe the dies of the 1931 and 1933 designs were engraved by the British American Bank Note Co., and the Public Printing and Stationery office made the necessary electrotypes for printing.

With the advent of the King George VI design the first of the "Dated Die" envelopes appear: The date "19-38" is in the lower corners. The die was engraved by the Canadian Bank Note Co.

The 1931-33 Surcharged Envelopes

Owing to changes in the postage rates it became necessary to surcharge some envelopes. These surcharges are from electrotypes and were made by the Public Stationery and Printing Office. The work was carefully done and there are few errors.

The Registered Envelopes. 1912-31.

During the currency of the King George V 1912-31 issue a number of envelopes of cloth lined cream, wove paper with blue cross lines and inscriptions were impressed with a 10c stamp in brown on the flap. The envelopes were made by McCorquodale & Co. Ltd., of England, and the stamp was impressed by the Public Printing and Stationery Office, at Ottawa. They were for international use.

Printed to Order Envelopes

In common with the Post Office of Great Britain, and many of the colonies, and dominions, the Canadian Post Office will impress the stamp on any private supply sent in by firms (under certain regulations), with the result that impressions may be found on numerous varieties of paper, and quite an extensive showing can be made of these. (We do not list these varieties as they do not come within the scope of this work.)

However, the 1877 designs are well known on amber manila paper, and since they are occasionally offered as essays or proofs, we wish to warn collectors that they are private envelopes stamped by the Public Stationery and Printing Office in 1899 for the firm of Frederick Burnett, Brantford, Ont. They are 10½ x 4 3/8" in size, high backed, square gum.

PVT-PS1   1c Blue on amber mania (5,000). Issued December 13, 1899.
PVT-PS2   3c Red on amber manila (3,000). Issued December 13, 1899.

In 1894 1,000 1c envelopes were stamped Hope & Co. Who and where they were we do not know, and it is possible that 3c red on wove paper which appeared late in 1894 were for this firm.

Concluding Notes.

In Chapter X, Page 230 will be found the contract prices for the envelopes supplied by the British American Bank Note Co. When the contract terminated the stamping of envelopes was taken over by the Public Stationery and Printing Office.

As noted the 1c and 3c were supplied at $2.50 per M, and the 3c larger size at $3.00 per M. We might also remark that the 2c of 1895 was also $3.00 per M.

The laid paper varies from white to cream, these variations being slight and due to accidental causes. The batonné lines[1] are known in three spacings, viz:

A   18 mm. apart   1877-87   1st contract Montreal Ptg.
B   24 mm. apart   1888-92   2nd contract Ottawa Ptg.
C   27 mm. apart   1893-97   3rd contract Ottawa Ptg.

Paper B is known with the watermark "C P Co" (Canada Paper Co.) in sans-serif letters 25 mm. tall. Reported so far only on the 3c red.

The prices for envelopes supplied by the Public Stationery and Printing Office were as follows: $1.75 per 1,000 to late 1911. 1912-13 $1.50, 1913-14 1c, 2c @ $1.60, also 2c @$1.70.

The envelopes were on laid paper until 1898-99 when wove paper was introduced and has been used consistently ever since.

---

[1]. The batonne or chain lines are the lines crossing the closely spaced laid lines which are known as vergeures.

Envelope Types 1877-1944

Type I
1877-96
Die By B. A. B. N. Co.

Type II
1895
Die By B. A. B. N. Co.

Type III
1898
Die By De La Rue

Type IV
1899-1904
Die By De La Rue

Type V
1905-1912
Die By De La Rue

Type VIa
1912-30
Die By De La Rue

Type VIb
1930-31
Line Cut Copy of Master Die

1933
Surcharge 3c on 2c #PS48

Type VII
1931-32
Die By B. A. B. N. Co.

Type VIII
1933-37
Die By B. A. B. N. Co.

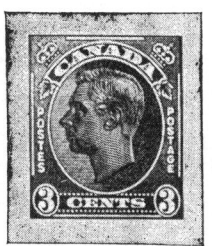

Type IX
1938 "Dated Die"
Die By C. B. N. Co.

Canadian Envelope Knives

L. B. equals Low back. Side Flaps overlap—Right over left (R/L) or left over right (L/R).
H. B. equals High back. Side tongues do not meet.

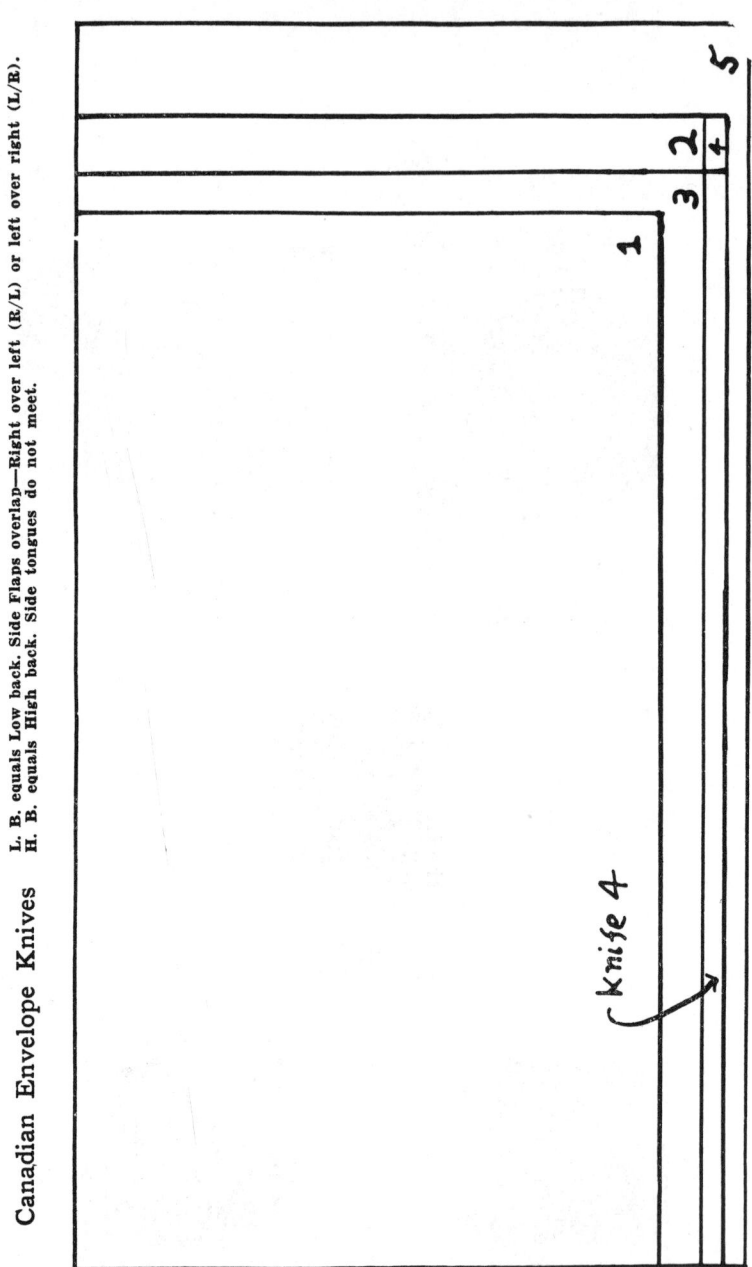

Knife 1 —5½″ x 3 1/8″ equals 138x79 mm. L. B. R/L. Pointed Flap.
Knife 2 —6″ x 3 3/8″ equals 151x86 mm.
Knife 3 —5¾″ x 3½″ equals 146x89 mm.
Knife 4 —6″ x 3½″ equals 151x89 mm. L. B. L/R Rounded Flap.
Knife 5 —6½″ x 3 5/8″ equals 167x93 mm. H. B. Rounded Flap.
Knife 5a—6½″ x 3 5/8″ equals 167x93 mm. Flap at end. Registered Envelope only.
Knife 6 —9 ½″ x 4 1/8″ equals 241x106 mm. H. B. Rounded Flap.
Knives 7, 8, 9 are the same size as knives 4, 5, and 6 respectively but are H. B. end seams on the outside, much more gum, Flap somewhat pointed.

Victorian Envelopes

October 1, 1877¹ Type I. Pointed flap. White laid paper—manufactured by the British American Bank Note Co. in Montreal, until 1888, and from that time in Ottawa, Ont. During the currency of these envelopes they appeared in numerous shades of color, and the paper varied slightly.

#	Batonné lines spaced ☞ Description	Knife 1, 1a (138 x 79 mm.)			Knife 2 (150 x 85 mm.)			Cut Square
		1877-88 A. 18mm	1888-91 B. 24mm	1891-97 C. 27mm	1877-88 D. 18mm	1888-91 E. 24mm	1891-97 F. 27mm	
PS1	1c Blue	1.00 1.00	.50 .50	.50 .50	— —	— —	— —	.05 .05
PS2	3c Red²	.50 —	.40 .40	1.00 .75	1.00 4.00	1.50 2.00	.50 2.00	.05 .05
a	Carmine	.50 —	.25 .25	1.50 1.00	1.50 4.00	1.00 2.00	.25 2.00	.03 .03

NOTES: Many defective impressions of these envelopes may be found such as albinos, partially inked or overinked, etc. None of these have more than a curiosity value as freaks. PS2a has been seen with the printed franks of the Northern Pacific Express Co. in black, or blue.

1. See Appendix B #45.
2. PS2E is known watermarked "CPCo" in letters 25 mm. tall. Probably "Canada Paper Co.", and its occurrence unintentional.

Victorian and King Edward VII Envelopes (Cont.)

#	Description	Date of Issue	Type	Knife 2 A. 150x85mm. Unused	Knife 2 A. 150x85mm. Used	Knife 3 B. 149x87mm. Unused	Knife 3 B. 149x87mm. Used	Knife 4 C. 148x87mm. Unused	Knife 4 C. 148x87mm. Used	Knife 5 D. 150x89mm. Unused	Knife 5 D. 150x89mm. Used	Cut Square Unused	Cut Square Used
PS3	2c Blue green	Jun. 14, 1895	II	.50	.50	—	—	—	—	—	—	.05	.05
PS4 a	3c Bright red With return card	Apr. 1898	III	—	—	.45	.50	—	—	—	—	.04 —	.05 —
PS5	1c Green	Jul. 22 1899	IV	—	—	.75	1.00	.20	.25	2.00	2.00	.02	.03
PS6	2c Violet	Jan. 2, 1899	IV	—	—	—	—	4.00	10.00	—	—	.50	1.50
PS7 a	2c Vermilion With return card	Jan. 8, 1899	IV	—	—	—	—	.25 1.00	.20 1.00	2.00	2.00	.03 —	.02 —
PS8	2c Carmine	1904	IV	—	—	—	—	—	—	2.00	2.00	.20	.20
PS9	1c Green	Feb. 1905	V	—	—	—	—	—	—	.10	.05	.02	.01
PS10	2c Red	Feb. 1905	V	—	—	—	—	—	—	.15	.05	.03	.01

528 *

NOTES: PS3 was engraved and printed by the British American Bank Note Co., Ottawa, on laid paper. All others were engraved by Thomas de la Rue of London, and printed by the Public Stationery and Printing Office, on wove paper. PS4a, PS7a have a two line inscription in black at the upper left corner "If not called for in ten days return to.................". Of PS6 only 10,000 were issued, as follows:

LIST OF POST OFFICES TO WHICH 2c PURPLE ENVELOPES WERE ISSUED, AND THE QUANTITY IN EACH CASE.

Belleville, Ont., 500; St. Catherine's, Ont., 500; Toronto, Ont., 2000; Corinth, Ont., 100; Haliburton, Ont., 100; Mount Albert, Ont., 100; Tamworth, Ont., 500; Hagersville, Ont., 100; Hamilton, Ont., 500; Loring, Ont., 100; Newton, Ont., 100; Ottawa, Ont., 700; St. Casimir, Que., 100; Sherbrooke, Que., 500; Montreal, Que., 1000; Rigand, Que., 100; Maitland, N. S., 100; Truro, N. S., 100; Yarmouth, N. S., 100; Andover, N. B., 200; Centerville, N. B., 100; Shoal Lake, Man., 100; Winnipeg, Man., 2000; New Westminster, B. C., 100; Greenwood, B. C., 200.

The Provisional Envelopes of 1899

#	Description	On #	Knife	Entire Unused	Entire Used	Cut Square Unused	Cut Square Used
PS11A	2c on 3c Red	PS2A	1	2.00	2.00	.25	.25
B	2c on 3c Red	PS2B	1	2.00	2.00	.25	.25
a	Carmine			2.00	2.00	.25	.25
C	2c on 3c Red	PS2C	1	2.00	2.00	.25	.25
PS12A	2c on 3c Red	PS2D	2	2.00	2.00	.25	.25
B	2c on 3c Red			2.00	2.00	.25	.25
a	Carmine	PS2E	2	2.00	2.00	.25	.25
C	2c on 3c Red	PS2F	2	1.00	1.00	.15	.15
PS13	2c on 3c "C" with Serif.	PS2B	1	10.00	10.00	2.00	2.00
PS14	2c on 3c Red	PS4	3	.50	.50	—	—
a	With return card			.50	.50	.05	.05
PS15	2c on 3c "C" with Serif.	PS4	3	10.00		2.00	—

These surcharges were made from soft rubber stamps, and since they were hand struck the impressions vary greatly. The first supply was struck with the serifed "C" stamp, which was discarded after about three days use, the normal type being substituted and used consistently thereafter.

Inverted and doubles have been reported but as with all handstamped surcharges such varieties are of minor importance.

Dominion of Canada King George V Envelopes. 1912-31.

Type VIa. Design Embossed, Early Impressions Strongly Embossed, Later Impression Practically No Embossing.

#	Description	A. Knife 4 148x87mm. Unused	A. Knife 4 Used	B. Knife 5 162x85mm. Unused	B. Knife 5 Used	C. Knife 6 237x106mm. Unused	C. Knife 6 Used	Cut Square Unused	Cut Square Used
PS16	1c Green	.10	.05	.10	.05	.25	.30	.02	.01
PS17	1c Orange	.10	.10	.05	.05	.40	.05	.02	.02
PS18	2c Red	.15	.10	.30	.40	.06	.10	.01	.02
PS19	2c Vermilion	—	—	.08	.05	.05	.10	.02	.01
PS20	2c Green	.08	.05	.10	.05	.08	.05	.02	.01
	Return card in E.	—	—	.50	.40	—	—	—	—
	Return card in F.	—	—	.70	.50	—	—	—	—
PS21	2c Brown	—	—	1.00	1.00	—	—	.25	.25
PS22	3c Brown	.30	.35	.15	.20	.10	.10	.03	.04
PS23	3c Red	—	—	.05	.10	.40	.40	.03	.02
PS24	3c Vermilion	—	—	.05	.05	.15	.12	.01	.01
	Return card in E.	—	—	.70	1.00	—	—	—	—
	Return card in F.	—	—	1.50	2.00	—	—	—	—

Type VIa. Entire Design Surface Printed. No Shading on Head. 1922-27. End Seams. Three New Knives.

#	Description	A. Knife 7 (150 x 85mm) Unused	A. Knife 7 Used	B. Knife 8 (237 x 106mm) Unused	B. Knife 8 Used	C. Knife 9 (162 x 85mm) Unused	C. Knife 9 Used	Cut Square Unused	Cut Square Used
PS25	1c Green	50	.50	.50	.50	—	—	.10	.10
PS26	1c Orange	—	—	.40	.40	.10	.10	.02	.02
PS27	2c Red	.50	.50	2.00	2.00	2.00	2.00	.50	.50
PS28	2c Green	—	—	.50	.50	2.00	2.00	.10	.10
PS29	2c Brown	—	—	.40	.40	—	—	.08	.08
PS30	3c Red	—	—	.20	.20	—	—	.05	.05
PS31	3c Brown	—	—	—	—	.10	.08	.02	.02

King Geo. V Envelopes. 1930-31

Type VIb. Head Shaded. From a Typographic Block of the Steel Die.

#	Description	A. Knife 5 162x85mm. Unused	Used	B. Knife 6 237x106mm. Unused	Used	Cut Square Unused	Used
PS32	1c Green	.10	.10	.10	.10	.02	.01
PS33	1c Orange (on manila).	—	—	.05	.10	.02	.02
PS34	2c Red	.75	.75	.75	1.00	.10	.10
PS35	2c Green	.15	.20	.20	.20	.03	.05
PS36	2c Brown	.05	.05	.05	.05	.03	.01
PS37	3c Red	.10	.10	.10	.15	.04	.02

The Compound Envelopes of 1931

These have an impression of Type VIb to the left of the original stamp which is Type VIa. The relative positions of the two impressions varies greatly.

#	Description	A. Knife 6 162x85mm. Unused	Used	B. Knife 7 150x85mm. Unused	Used	Cut Square Unused	Used
PS38	2c+1c Vermilion and green	.50	.50	.50	.50	.10	.10

The 1927-31 2c on 3c Provisionals

On Type VIa Design.

Two types of surcharge— I 23 mm. long.
II 25 mm. long.

#	Type of Surch.	Description	A. Knife 5 162x85mm. Unused	Used	B. Knife 6 237x106mm. Unused	Used	C. Knife 7 150x85mm. Unused	Used	Cut Square Unused	Used
PS39	I	2c on 3c Brown	7.50	7.50	5.00	5.00	.50	.50	.20	.20
PS40	II	2c on 3c Brown	10.00	10.00	—	—	2.00	2.00	.50	.50
PS41	I	2c on 3c Red	—	—	2.00	2.00			.50	.50
PS42	I	2c on 3c Vermilion	—	—	2.00	2.00	—	—	.20	.20
PS43	II	2c on 3c Vermilion	—	—	5.00	5.00	.50	.50	1.50	1.50

On Type VIb Design.

#	Type of Surch.	Description	A. Unused	Used	B. Unused	Used	C. Unused	Used	Cut Square Unused	Used
PS 44	I	2c on 3c Red	.50	.50	.75	.75	—	—	.15	.15

NOTE: PS42B and PS43B are known with return card in English. Worth about twice as much as normal.

King Geo. V Envelopes. 1931-32.
Type VII Design. Typographed.

#	Description	A. Knife 6 237x106mm. Unused	A. Knife 6 237x106mm. Used	B. Knife 7 150x85mm. Unused	B. Knife 7 150x85mm. Used	Cut Square Unused	Cut Square Used	Issued
PS45	1c Green	.10	.10	.05	.04	.03	.02	Feb. 2, 1932
	2c Brown	.15	.10	—	—	.04	.02	Feb. 4, 1932
PS47	3c Red	.15	.10	.10	.10	.04	.02	Dec 15, 1931

The 1933 Provisional "3 3" on 2c Vermilion.
Black Surcharge

#	Description	Unused	Used			Unused	Used	
PS48	3c on 2c Vermilion	.10	.15			.05	.10	

Regular issue. Type VIII. Typographed.

#	Description	A. Knife 5 162x85mm. Unused	A. Knife 5 162x85mm. Used	B. Knife 6 237x106mm. Unused	B. Knife 6 237x106mm. Used	Cut Square Unused	Cut Square Used	Issued
PS49	1c Green	.30	.15	.50	.15	.05	.02	May 15, 1933
PS50	2c Brown	.35	.15	.50	.15	.05	.02	Apr 29, 1933
PS51	3c Red	.50	.20	.50	.15	.08	.02	Jun 20, 1933

King George VI Issue.
Type IX. "Dated Die". Typographed.

#	Description	A. Knife 5 162x85mm. Unused	A. Knife 5 162x85mm. Used	B. Knife 6 237x106mm. Unused	B. Knife 6 237x106mm. Used	Cut Square Unused	Cut Square Used	Issued
PS52	1c Green	.05	.02	.05	.05	.02	.01	Jun 10, 1938
PS53	2c Brown	.07	.02	.07	.05	.03	.01	Jun. 2, 1938
PS54	3c Red	.10	.02	.10	.04	.04	.01	Jun. 1, 1938
PS55	3c Violet	.10	.05	.10	.05	.04	.01	1943
PS56	4c Red	.10	.05	.10	.05	.05	.01	1944

Compound Envelopes.

#	Description	Unused	Used	Unused	Used	Unused	Used	Issued
PS57	2c+1c Brown & green	.12	.06	.12	.06	.05	.02	July 2, 1943

King George V Registered Envelope.
Type Va Design Impressed on Flap.

R-PS1 10c Brown .15 .75

These are of a special size and design, and intended for foreign registered letters.

Notes on the Tables

The tables listing the various issues of envelopes have been simplified as much as is consistent with comprehensiveness and accuracy.

It will be noted that we have listed cut squares. Cut squares have always been popular in the United States, and indeed have distinct advantages over the entire, in being more compact, and enabling a collection to be easily mounted and examined. It is hoped that the recognition given by us to Cut Squares will stimulate more careful study of these items. We might say that practically all the catalogues of Postal Stationery such as Dr. Ascher's, Grosser Ganzsachen Katalog, Bartels Catalogue of the Stamped Envelopes and Wrappers of the United States and Possessions, Fifth (Thorp) Edition, list cut squares, as well as entires.

B. DOMINION POSTAL BANDS AND PUBLISHER'S WRAPPERS

Postal Bands were first issued in May 1875[1], and in July 1907 the first Publisher's Wrappers appeared. All are typographed, and were produced by the contractors for the adhesive stamps[2], and the designs correspond or closely resemble the post cards then current.

The denomination is usually one cent, but the first issue of publisher's wrappers included 2c and 3c denominations, which proved to be of so little use that the remainders were surcharged "1c" in large black letters after a short time.

All of these varieties are common, with the exception of the 2c and 3c, and the 1c on 2c or 1c on 3c, which range from scarce to decidedly rare. Reference to the Postmaster General's report shows that of the 2c 580,546 were issued to postmasters while only 63,790 of the 3c were so issued. First issued July 11, 1907, and discontinued June 18, 1908—the remainders being surcharged 1c on 2c, and 1c on 3c.

The following quantities were surcharged:

    1c on 2c   1,000
    1c on 3c 44,300

Resulting in an actual issue of unsurcharged 2c of 579,546, while of the 3c only 19,490 were issued.

---
1. See Appendix M #14.
2. See page 91.

Postal Bands. 1875-1938.

#	Denom. & Color	Date	Entire Buff				White Wove		Cut Square Buff				White Wove		Notes
			Pale		Dark				Pale		Dark				
			Unused	Used	Unused	Used	Unused	Used	Unused	Used	Unused	Used	Unused	Used	
PB1	1c Blue	May 1875	3.00	3.00	3.00	3.00			.50	.50	.50	.50			[1]
PB2	1c Blue	April 1882	1.00	1.50	1.00	1.50			.15	.25	.15	.15			
PB3	1c Blue	May 1887	1.00	1.50			.60	1.50	.15	.25			.10	.25	
	Blue violet														
PB4	1c Blue	Feb. 1892	2.00	2.00	2.00	4.00	.60	1.50	.15	.30	.30	.60	.10	.25	
PB5	1c Black	Feb. 1894	.20	.70	2.00	4.00			.05	.20	.30	.60			
PB6	1c Green	June 1898	1.50	2.00	.50	1.00			.25	.30	.08	.15			Maple Leaf
PB7	1c Green	Oct. 1903	.50	1.00	.50	.30			.08	.15	.08	.05			Edw. VII
			Laid	Kraft	Manila wove				Laid	Kraft	Manila wove				
PB8	1c Green	1912	.30	.60	.06	.10			.05	.10	.02	.03			King Geo. V
PB9	1c Orange	1922	.06	.06	.06	.10			.02	.02	.02	.03			Scroll Issue
PB10	1c Orange	1928	.06	.08					.02	.03	.03	.03			Arch & Maple
PB11	1c Orange	Aug. 7, 1930	.06	.10	.10	.10			.02	.03	.02	.03			
			Wove	Kraft					Wove	Kraft					
PB12	1c Green	Jun. 5, 1931	.06	.10	.06	.10			.02	.03	.02	.03			Arch & Maple
PB13	1c Green	May 18, 1933	.06	.10	.06	.10			.02	.03	.02	.06			Medallion Issue
PB14	1c Green	Apr. 27, 1935	.06		.06	.20			.02		.02	.03			"Dated Die"
PB15	1c Green	1938			.06	.10					.02	.03			King Geo. VI

Note Sizes: PB1, 2, and 4 are 6½" x 15" (175x382 mm). PB3 and 5 are 8" x 12" (202 x 304 mm) PB6 to PB15 are 6" x 13½" (163x341 mm). For illustrations of designs see pages 536, 537.

1. Design similar to PB3 but with faint scallops around inner oval.

Publisher's Wrappers

For Publishers to mail periodicals to subscribers in the United States.

#	Denom. & Color	Date Issued Unused	Date Issued Used	Entire Manila Unused	Entire Manila Used	Entire Kraft Unused	Entire Kraft Laid Used	Cut Square Manila Unused	Cut Square Manila Used	Cut Square Kraft Unused	Cut Square Kraft Used	Notes
PW1	1c Green	Jul. 11, 1907		.50	1.00			.10	.20			King Edward VII.
PW2	2c Carmine	July 11, 1907		2.00	2.00			.40	.40			King Edward VII.
PW3	3c Slate violet	July 11, 1907		6.00				1.25				King Edward VII.
PW4	1c on 2c Carmine	Jun. 18, 1908		15.00	x			.40	2.00			King Edward VII.
PW5	1c on 3c Slate violet	Jun. 18, 1908		10.00	10.00			3.00	3.00			King Edward VII.
PW6	1c Green	1912		.10	.10	.06	.10	.02	.02	.01	.02	King George V, Admiral Type.
PW7	1c Orange	1922		1.00	.50			.20	.10			Background of parallel lines throughout.
PW8	1c Orange			.06	.20			.01	.05			Parallel lines back of head only. Rest of shading of cross hatching
PW9	1c Orange	1928				.06	.30					Scroll Issue
PW10	1c Orange	1930		.10	.20			.02	.05	.01	.08	Arch & Maple Leaf Issue
						Wove				*Wove*		
PW11	1c Green	Jan. 8, 1931		.06	.10	.06	.20	.01	.02	.01	.05	Arch & Maple Leaf Issue
PW12	1c Green	May 29, 1933				.06	.20			.01	.05	Medallion Issue
PW13	1c Green	Aug 20, 1935				.06	.20			.01	.05	"Dated Die"
PW14	1c Green	Feb. 16, 1936				.06	.20			.01	.05	"Dated Die", Medallion
PW15	1c Green	1938				.06	.20			.01	.05	King George VI.

\# PB1 to PB4 vary in length from 9½" to 11½" (235 to 280 mm.). The later numbers are almost uniformly 10¾" long (280 mm.). The width of all is approximately 5" (127 mm.). For illustrations of designs see pages 536, 537.

Chapter XXXIII

THE POST CARDS AND LETTER CARDS.

I. The Line Engraved Cards

Canada was progressive enough to adopt the post card three years before the United States. The post card was first introduced in the posts of Austria and placed on sale the first of October, 1869, the proposition for their introduction having been made to the Administration by Prof. Emanuel Hermann of the Military Academy at Weinerneustadt. However, the first idea for them did not originate with him. The post card is an American invention. As early as 1861 John P. Charlton of Philadelphia, Pa., copyrighted a post card, and H. L. Lipman of the same city sold cards similar to Charlton's copyright, and was probably associated with Charlton[1].

In 1865 Dr. Stephan, Director of the Post of Germany, proposed correspondence cards with space for an adhesive stamp to pass at a low rate.

The project of Dr. Stephan set forth the issuing of a "Post-Blatt," post leaf, destined to pass through the mails without cover at a reduced rate of postage, and to have the address *only* on one side, the message on the other. This was indeed the idea of our present postal card.

Nevertheless the idea, for one reason or another, was not adopted in Germany at that period, and it was probably this indifference which inspired Prof. Hermann to make a proposition of the same nature to the Administration of the Austrian Posts.

These first cards, some of which are quite rare today, bore the yellow stamp of 2 kr. type of the adhesives of 1867. By June, 1871, the first Canadian card appeared, and Canada was the eleventh country to issue post cards, preceding the United States and Newfoundland by 3 years.

From report of P. M. G. for June, 1870, we abstract the following:

> The introduction of what are known as "post cards" in the United Kingdom, and the convenience which is stated to have attended their use, have induced the Department to make arrangements for the manufacture of similar post cards for the use of the public in Canada. These post cards will be sold at one cent each, and may be posted for any address within the Dominion—and will be conveyed to destination, and be delivered in like manner with letters—the one cent covering the cost both of the card and of postage.
> They may be used for any communication, which can advantageously be written and sent by such a medium; and, it would seem unquestionable, must, in Canada as in England, prove to be extremely convenient for many objects and purposes.

Canada's rate of 1 cent was only 1/3rd the letter rate, and was lower than that of any other nation, until the United States in 1873 followed Canada's practice[2].

The Postmaster General's report for 1871 mentions that Post Cards were issued in June, 1871[3] and that by the end of December 1,470,600 cards had been issued.

---

1. See Essay-Proof Journal, January 1944, Vol. I, No. 1, p. 19—"Postal Card Essays and Proofs by Clarence W. Brazer, D. Sc.".
2. In most countries the Post Card rate was ½ the letter rate, but in Austria and France it was originally 2/5th of the letter rate. Newfoundland also had the 1c rate, and preceded the United States by one month in issuing cards.
3. The actual date was May 1, 1871.

PC1, 2
PC3 is similar in design but for "TWO CENTS."

UPC1.

PC4-6, PB2.   PC7-8, PB3.   PB4, 5

PC9-14, PB4, 5.

"Dated Die"
PC117- PC126
The Date in the Lower Corners Just
Below the Medallion.

Medallion Design.
PC127-PC138.

Other cards are similar in design to the current adhesives.

A. For Domestic and United Kingdom Mails

The first card is similar in design to the current regular postage stamps with the upper inscriptions of course being on the card instead of on the impressed stamp. The portrait is the same. They were produced by the British American Bank Note Co., of Montreal and Ottawa. Printed in sheets of nine (3 x 3), at least and cut into single cards before distribution to the post offices. Late in (3 x 3), and cut into single cards before distribution to the post offices. Late in 1876 "Ottawa" was dropped from the imprint, otherwise the card shows little variation, although the border shows evidence of re-working. Some of the later printings have a bluish cast due to insufficiently wiped plates. In common with line engraved stamps these cards are known with various re-entries. These are particularly noticeable in the border, but fine examples also appear in the stamp impression. Several plates were used, (at least 2) and it would seem that Canadian students have a fertile field of investigation in the study of these and other line engraved cards.

On Nov. 1, 1872 the rate of one-cent for post cards was extended to include Newfoundland. Beginning July 1, 1872, the United States accepted Canadian post cards if franked with an additional 1c stamp. Effective January 1, 1875, the additional 1c fee was abolished.

On January 1, 1877, a new 2-cent card was issued for use to the United Kingdom. Very similar to the current 1-cent card, but the border is somewhat different, and the card is printed in yellow green.

Both these cards were produced by the British American Bank Note Co, Montreal.

They vary considerably in shade and stock. See page 230 for contract rates.

Proofs

We have seen the following proofs of the line engraved cards:

Die Proof On Card. (Rare)

D-PC2   1c yellow brown
D-PC3   2c green

B. The Universal Postal Union Cards

The admission of Canada into the Universal Postal Union on July 1, 1887, resulted in the 2c card being changed to conform with its new use.

From 1882 onwards the only line engraved cards have been the Universal Postal Union cards. The last new production of the British American Bank

Note Co. was the 2c card of 1896. This is printed in a brilliant vermilion, with no border frame. There is a scarce shade of this card in a carmine vermilion. The removal of the border, and arrangement of the inscriptions was made in order to conform with the regulations of the Universal Postal Union.

A slight re-entry showing doubling at the left is known.

With the assumption of the contract by the American Bank Note Co., in 1897 the remaining U. P. U. cards are the product of that company. The 2c maple leaf design appeared first in orange, and later in blue. The King Edward VII and King George V designs are also in blue. When the rate was raised to six cents in 1922 the 2c cards were surcharged "6 CENTS" in brownish red.

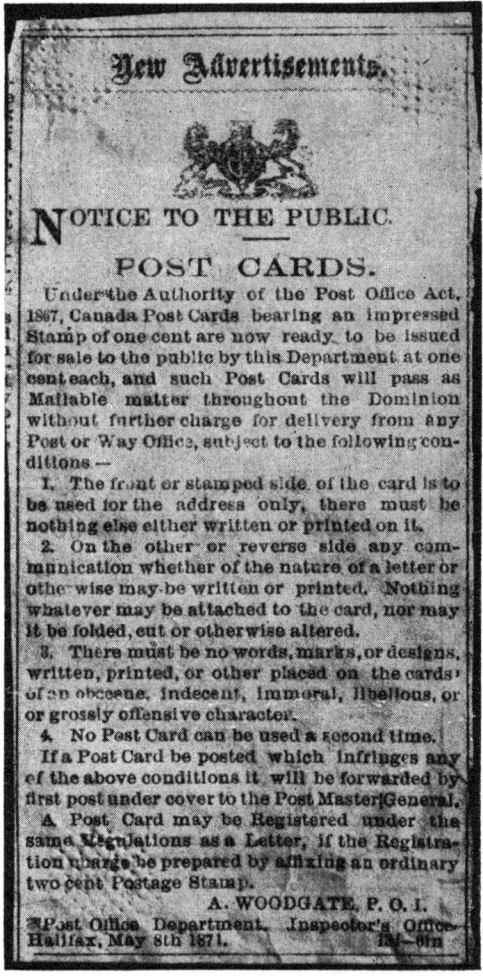

Advertisement of May 1871 in a Halifax Newspaper Announcing the Issue of Post Cards.

Size 2. 5" × 3" = 125 × 75 mm.
Size 5. 5¼" × 3⅛" = 135 × 80 mm.
Size 6. 5⅛" × 3³⁄₁₆" = 131 × 83 mm.

4¾" × 3" = 118 × 75 mm.

5½" × 3⅜" = 140 × 86 mm.
6" × 3⅝" = 152 × 92 mm.

DIAGRAM SHOWING POST CARD SIZES
By laying the card on the diagram the size may be readily determined.

Line Engraved Post Cards

A. For Domestic and United Kingdom Mails

All are 118 x 75 mm. (4 5/8" x 3"). Size 1. Engraved and Printed by the British American Bank Note Co.

#	Denom. & Color	Entire unused	used	Notes
PC1	1c Blue	.15	.10	Imprint reads "British American Bank Note Co. Montreal & Ottawa" Issued May 1871.
a	Re-entry.	.75	.25	
PC2	1c Blue	.20	.10	Imprint reads "British American Bank Note Co. Montreal" Issued June 1876
a	Re-entry.	.75	.25	
PC3	2c Green	.75	1.50	Issued Jan. 1, 1877. "To United Kingdom"

PC1 was printed in Ottawa only until late 1874, then in Montreal until early 1876. PC2 and 3 were printed in Montreal only. PC3 118,070 were issued.

NOTE: There are many distinct shades of the above cards. The number of printings, and variations in the stock used to print on, in addition to other factors such as press work, wetting of card, etc. make it practically impossible to classify the shades in any logical order.

540

B. The Universal Postal Union Cards. 1877-1922.
All Of These Cards Are Line Engraved

#	Denom. & Color	Date	Entire Unused	Entire Used	Notes
UPC1	2c Green	Jan. 1, 1877	.60	3.00	Printed by the B.A.B.N.Co. in Montreal until 1888, then in Ottawa[1].
UPC2 a b	2c Scarlet Bright scarlet Re-entry	Sept. 1896 Aug. 1897	1.00 3.00 6.00	5.00 15.00 30.00	Printed by the B.A.B.N. CO. in Ottawa. @$2.75 per M[2]. Entire left side of stamp doubled.
UPC3	2c Orange red	Dec. 1, 1897	1.25	5.00	Queen Victoria, Maple Leaf. By American Bank Note Co., Ottawa.
UPC4	2c Blue	June 1898	1.00	4.00	Queen Victoria, Maple Leaf. By American Bank Note Co., Ottawa.
UPC5	2c Blue	Dec. (?) 1903	.75	2.00	King Edward VII. By American Bank Note Co., Ottawa.
UPC6	2c Blue	Feb. 1912	.50	1.50	King Geo. V, "Admiral Type" $3 per M. By American Bank Note Co., Ottawa.
UPC7	6c on 2c Blue (on UPC6)	Sept. 1922	.25	2.00	Surcharge is typographed in brownish red. 72,000 surcharged at $1.51 per M.

1. At $3.50 per M until 1892—then $2.75 per M.
2. UPC2 is undoubtedly the handsomest post card ever issued by Canada. This design was intended for a regular series of adhesives by the Canada Bank Note Engraving & Printing Co. (See chapter VII, page 115 and chapter XII page 301.) The plate cost $100.00
3. UPC3-5 were supplied at $2.26 per M.

II. The Typographed Post Cards

Beginning in 1882 a cheaper and more rapid method of manufacturing post cards was introduced, namely typography. The appearance of cards printed by this method was so different than that of the line engraved cards heretofore issued, that the Postmaster General explained the new card in a detailed circular dated April 1, 1882[1].

With the exception of the U. P. U. cards, all Canadian post cards have since been typographed. Up to the time of writing (1944) no lithographed cards have been issued.

The various varieties occurring on these cards are mostly electro flaws, and are therefore of comparatively little significance.

A constant electro flaw, consisting of a large, white oval between the base of the neck and the "ON" of "One", is found on both PC6 and PC6a.

In 1897 the American Bank Note Company began printing the post cards. The rates were as follows:

PER 1000 CARDS

Year	Post Cards	Reply Cards	Business Cards
1897-1912	.80	2.00	—
1912-1922	.70[2]	1.50	—
1923-1928	1.25	2.50	5.00

In December of 1897 the advertisement cards were announced[3]. These cards were issued singly in packages of 100; in sheets of 8 (2 x 4) in packages of 125 sheets (1000 cards), or in sheets of 16 (4 x 4) in packages of 125 sheets (2000 cards). Large quantities were used by the three leading railway systems of Canada to advertise the various attractions along their lines. These are not official view cards and they are outside the scope of this work.

The stock on which the various cards have been printed varies considerably in color and texture. Only the thick soft white card designated "mimeo" warrants separate listing. The use of "mimeo" stock began about 1915.

Two dies are known on the 1912-28 issue, as follows:

Die I —Features fine, regular; horizontal lines in crowns: four braids on epaulet to right of stamp.

Die II—Features coarse, irregular; vertical lines in crowns; five braids on epaulet to right of stamp.

NOTE: There are a number of other differences between the two Dies, being plainly distinguishable to the naked eye, but the above will suffice for the purpose of identification.

The Arch and Maple Leaf design, supplied by the British American Bank Note Co. in 1930, is noted in two dies, viz:

Die I —Vignette has diagonally lined background.

Die II—Vignette has horizontal lined background.

Various varieties, other than those listed are known, many being private orders which were supplied to various concerns by the Post Office Department. Among these may be noted the menu cards of the Hamilton Philatelic Society, and the "Centenary of the Postage Stamp" by the same organization. Another variety that is frequently seen is PC72 on pale blue mimeo stock with the inscription "This is the first Coloured Post Card issued by the Canadian Post Office. Keep it as a Souvenir .", which was issued by a clothing firm.

---

1. Appendix B #48.
2. The Confederation Commemorative Card (PC62, PC63) were .75 per 1,000, 11,000,000 being supplied.
3. Appendix B #54.

The Typographed Post Cards. 1882-1894.

#	Denom. & Color	Date	Entire Unused	Entire Used	Notes
PC4	1c Blue gray	Apr. 11, 1882	.20	.05	The colors listed are merely groups. The shades are numerous and they merge into one another. All size 2.
a	Blue	May 1883	.30	.10	
b	Ultramarine	Feb. 1884	.20	.05	
c	Lilac	Mar. 1885	.30	.20	
PC5	1c Sage green	Nov. 1886	.60	.40	Size 2.
a	Bistre gray		.60	.40	
PC6	1c+1c Slate	Dec. 1887	.60	3.25	Size 2.
a	Stamp at left	Sept. 1884	6.00	25.00	This is not an error of cutting.
PC7	1c Olive bistre	Mar. 1887	1.00	.75	Size 2.
a	Blue	Feb. 1889	.15	.10	
b	Green		.60	.40	
PC8	1c+1c Slate green	1887	.50	1.00	Size 2. Reply portion has design of PC5.
a	Olive green		.75	1.50	
b	Reply on back of message card		15.00		
PC9	1c Blue	Dec. 1891	.10	.05	Size 2.
PC10	1c Black	1892	.20	.10	125 x 75 mm. (Size 2).
PC11	1c Black	Feb. 17, 1893	.30	.20	152 x 92 mm. (Size 4). Large.
PC12	1c Black	Feb. 1894	.40	.10	140 x 86 mm. (Size 3). Medium.
PC13	1c+1c Slate green	Dec. 1892	.75	1.50	125 x 75 mm. (Size 2).
a	Olive green		1.00	2.00	
b	Reply on back of message card		15.00		
PC14	1c+1c Olive black	Nov. 1894	2.00	4.00	
a	Black		.50	1.00	

All printed by the British American Bank Note Co., in sheets of 40 (5 x 8). See page 230 for contract prices.

543 *

The Typographed Post Cards. 1897-1904.

Jubilee Issue

#	Denom. & Color	Date	Entire Unused	Entire Used	Notes
PC 15	1c Black	June 19, 1897	.06	.05	140 x 86 mm. (Size 3)[1].

Maple Leaf Issue (Size 2)

#	Denom. & Color	Date	Entire Unused	Entire Used	Notes
PC16	1c Green	Dec. 1897	.20	.05	
PC17	1c Rose carmine	(June ?) 1898	.50	.40	
PC18	1c+1c Black Reply on back of message card	(Aug.,) 1898	.10 15.00	1.00	

King Edward VII Issue.

#	Denom. & Color	Date	Entire Unused	Entire Used	Notes
PC19	1cGreen	Aug. 1903	.20	.05	
PC20	1c Rose carmine	Dec. 1903	.50	.40	
PC21	1c+1c Black Reply on back of message card	Jan. 1904	.10 15.00	1.00	

All printed by the American Bank Note Co., Ottawa.

1. Although it was intended to issue 7,000,000 of these cards only 4,240,000 were delivered by the manufacturers.

After 1898 the varieties of inscriptions on post and reply cards of these issues are so numerous as to render it impractical to list their many variations individually.

Punctuation has been faithfully followed, as it represents the only method of distinction between certain forms. Forms Ja, Jb and Jc etc. are identical except for the placement of periods.

It has not been considered necessary to differentiate between Gothic and Roman lettering, as no duplication of lettering is known.

Inscription *Code*

Blank card, no inscription ....None
Horizontal line ....A
Vertical line ....B
BUSINESS REPLY CARD C
CANADA ....Da
CANADA. ....Db
CANADA POST CARD ....E
CARTE RÉPONSE D'AFFAIRES ....F
CÔTE RÉSERVE À L'ADRESSE. ....Ga
CÔTE RESERVÉ À L'ADRESSE. ....Gb
CÔTE RÉSERVE À L'ADRESSE IMPRIMEE SEULEMENT..........Ha
CÔTE RESERVÉ À L'ADRESSE IMPRIMEE SEULEMENT..........Hb
CÔTE RESERVE À L'ADRESSE IMPRIMÉE SEULEMENT..........Hc
L'ESPACE CI-DESSOUS EST RÉSERVE À L'ADRESSE....................I
L'ESPACE CI-DESSOUS EST RESERVÉ À L'ADRESSE....................I
POST CARD — CARTE POSTALE ....Ja
POST CARD. — CARTE POSTALE ....Jb
POST CARD. — CARTE POSTALE. ....Jc
(REPLY) ....K
REPLY POST CARD. — CARTE POSTALE REPONSE. L
THE ADDRESS ONLY TO BE PRINTED ON THIS SIDE............M
THE ADDRESS ONLY TO BE WRITTEN ON THIS SIDE. ....N
THE ADDRESS TO BE WRITTEN ON THIS SIDE ....O
THE SPACE BELOW IS RESERVED FOR ADDRESS ONLY. ....P

Use of Code: Each of the following code letters determines the inscription in *only one line* of a card. It is thus easy to determine at a glance the total number of lines in any inscription, and, by reading the various code-lines as listed above, determine the complete inscription. For example, the code for bilingual inscription type "DJNG" translates thus:

D=CANADA
J=POST CARD—CARTE POSTALE
N=THE ADDRESS ONLY TO BE WRITTEN ON THIS SIDE
G=CÔTE RESERVE À L'ADDRESSE

Post Cards. King George V "Admiral Type", 1912-28[1].
(ENTIRE)

	Denom. & Color	Inscription	Die I A. Regular Stock		B. Mimeo. Stock		C. Die II		Notes
			Unused	Used	Unused	Used	Unused	Used	
PC25	1c Red	None	.50	.30	—	—	1.00	1.00	1912
PC26	1c Red	A	.50	.50	—	—	—	—	
PC27	1c Red	AB	—	—	—	—	1.50	1.50	
PC28	1c Red	PI	1.50	1.75	—	—	1.00	1.00	
PC29	1c Green	None	.50	.50	—	—	—	—	1915
PC30	1c Green	A	.10	.25	.40	.40	—	—	
PC31	1c Green	AB (in green)	.50	.50	—	—	—	—	
PC32	1c Green	AB (in black)	.75	1.00	—	—	—	—	
PC33	1c Green	AE	1.50	1.50	—	—	—	—	
PC34	1c Green	EO	.10	.10	.50	.50	—	—	
PC35	1c Green	PI	1.00	1.00	—	—	—	—	
PC36	1c Green	DJNG	.10	.05	.25	.25	—	—	
PC37	1c Orange	None	1.00	.70	—	—	—	—	1922
PC38	1c Orange	A	.50	.30	—	—	—	—	
PC39	1c Orange	E	.08	.04	.70	.50	—	—	
PC40	1c Orange	DJ	.10	.05	.25	.25	—	—	
PC41	1c Orange	EO	1.00	.75	.25	.25	—	—	
PC42	1c Orange	EO	.15	.10	—	—	—	—	Inscription with serifs
PC43	1c Orange	DJNG	.10	.05	—	—	—	—	Sans-serif inscription
PC44	1c+1c Black	EO+EKO	.10	1.00	.40	.40	—	—	
PC45	1c+1c Black	Djng+DJng	.75	1.50	1.00	2.00	—	—	
PC46	1c+1c Orange	E+EK	.06	.75	—	—	—	—	
PC47	1c+1c Orange	DJ+DL	1.00	2.00	—	—	—	—	
PC48	1c+1c Orange	EO+EKO	.60	1.25	—	—	—	—	
PC49	1c+1c Orange	Djng+DJng	.50	1.00	—	—	—	—	

1. For differences between Die I and Die II, see page 542.

King George V "Admiral Type". 1912-28.
(ENTIRE)

#	Denom. & Color	Inscription	Die I				Die II		Notes
			A. Regular Stock		B. Mimeo. Stock		C. Regular Stock		
			Unused	Used	Unused	Used	Unused	Used	
PC50	2c Green	None	1.00	.70	—	—	.20	.15	Sept. 1922
a	Background partly cross hatched.	None	1.00	.70	—	—	—	—	
PC51	2c Green	A	.20	.20	—	—	—	—	
PC52	2c Green	D	.05	.05	.50	.50	—	—	
PC53	2c Green	DJ	.25	.20	.30	.30	—	—	
PC54	2c Green	EO	.20	.10	—	—	—	—	
PC55	2c Green	DJNG	.05	.05	.40	.40	—	—	
PC56	2c Red	None	.70	.70	—	—	—	—	1915
PC57	2c Red	A	.50	.50	—	—	3.00	3.00	
PC58	2c Red	AB	1.00	1.00	.75	.75	2.00	2.00	
PC59	2c Red	EO	.35	.20	—	—	1.50	1.50	
PC60	2c Red	PI	1.00	1.00	.50	.40	—	—	
PC61	2c Red	DJNG	.30	.20	—	—	2.50	2.50	
PC62	2c Red	EO	1.00	1.00	.75	.75	—	—	
PC63	2c Red	DJNG	1.50	2.00	—	—	—	—	See note 1.
PC64	½c Violet	DC	.50	.45	—	—	—	—	
PC65	½c Violet	DCE	.50	.45	—	—	—	—	
PC66	½c Violet	DCM	.05	.45	—	—	—	—	
PC67	½c Violet	DCFMH	.50	.65	—	—	—	—	
PC68	1c+½c Orange & violet	E+DC	.30	.50	—	—	—	—	
PC69	1c+½c Orange & violet	EO+DCM	.50	1.00	—	—	—	—	
PC70	1c+½c Orange & violet	Djng + Dcemh	.50	1.00	—	—	—	—	See note 2.

1. July 1917 with statistical table at left. Commemorating 50th Anniversary of Confederation.
2. A variety of PC70 is known in which the inscription on the 1c card is in sans-serif letters. This card has been erroneously listed as lithographed (See page 542).

547 *

Post Cards. King George V "Scroll" Issue. 1928.
(ENTIRE)

#	Denom. & Color	Inscription	A. Regular Unused	A. Regular Used	B. Mimeo.	Notes
PC71	½c Violet	DC	.05	.20		
PC72	½c Violet	DCF	.35	.25		
PC73	1c Orange	None	.60	.40		
PC74	1c Orange	E	.30	.20		
PC75	2c Green	None	1.00	.75		
PC76	2c Green	EO	1.50	1.50		
a	Stamp inverted at lower left	EO	6.00			
PC77	1c+½c Orange & violet	E+DC	.20	.40		
PC78	1c+½c Orange & violet	DJ+DCE	.30	.60		This has erroneously been reported as lithographed (See page 542).
PC79	1c+1c Orange	E+DJ	.50	1.00		

Post Cards. King George V "Arch and Maple Leaf" Issue. 1930[1].

(ENTIRE)

#	Denom. & Color	Inscription	Die I A. Regular Stock		B. Mineo. Stock		C. Die II		Notes
			Unused	Used	Unused	Used	Unused	Used	
PC80	½c Violet	DC	.15	.08	—	—	.40	.40	Oct. 25, 1930
PC81	½c Violet	DCF	.05	.10	—	—	.40	.40	Oct. 25, 1930
PC82	1c Orange	None	.80	.40	—	—	2.00	2.00	Oct. 25, 1930
PC83	1c Orange	E	.20	.10	—	—	1.00	1.00	Oct. 4, 1930
PC84	1c Orange	DJ	.30	.20	—	—	.75	.75	June 24, 1930
PC85	1c Green	None	.15	.08					
PC86	1c Green	E	.06	.04	.10	.10			Dec. 18, 1930
PC87	1c Green	DJ	.06	.04					Dec. 17, 1830
PC88	2c Green	None	1.00	.70			1.00	1.00	July 4, 1930
PC89	2c Green	E	.06	.35					
PC90	2c Green	DJ	.20	.15					
PC91	2c Red	None	.40	.20					
PC92	2c Red	E	.15	.10					Feb. 4, 1931
PC93	2c Red	DJ	.20	.15					Dec. 11, 1931
PC94	2c Brown	None	.25	.20					
PC95	2c Brown	E	.25	.10					
PC96	2c Brown	DJ	.06	.15					

1. For differences between Die I and Die II, see page 542.

"Arch and Maple Leaf" (Cont.)
(ENTIRE)

	Denom. & Color	Inscription	Die I A. Regular Stock		B. Mineo. Stock		Die II C		Notes
			Unused	Used	Unused	Used	Unused	Used	
PC97	2c Brown	ER	.06	.10					Pictorial Cards issued by the Post Office Dept. For list of views see page 551
PC98	2c Brown	DJB	.06	.10					
PC99	1c+½c Orange & violet	EDaC	1.00	2.00					Feb. 5, 1931
PC100	1c+½c Green & Violet	EDaC	.20	.40					Feb. 5, 1931
PC101	1c+1c Orange	E+EK	.50	1.00					June 14, 1930
PC102	1c+1c Orange	Daj+DbL	.50	1.00					June 14, 1930
PC103	1c+1c Green	E+EK	.40	.80			.06	1.00	April 13, 1931
PC104	1c+1c Green	Daj+DbL	.10	.80					April 13, 1931

List of Official View Cards on PC97 and PC98.

In 1930 the Canadian Post Office Department issued a series of official view cards.

Title of View	Dept. Order
Legislative Building, Edmonton, Alta.	451
Bird's Eye View, Edmonton, Alta.	542
Bird's Eye View, Calgary, Alta.	543
Banff, Bow River Valley, Alta.	455
Kicking Horse Canyon, Yoho Park, Alta.	454
Lake Louise, Alta.	456
Guide at Lake Agnes, Lake Louise, Alta.	457
Birdseye View, Vancouver, B. C.	501
Vancouver Harbour, B. C.	503
Granville Street, Vancouver, B. C.	504
Lumberman's Arch, Vancouver, B. C.	505
Okanagan Valley, B. C.	506
Sinclair's Canyon, Kootenay National Park, B. C.	507
Wapta Falls, Yoho National Park, B. C.	508
Legislative Buildings, Victoria, B. C.	509
Harbour, Victoria, B. C.	510
Clear Lake Golf Course, Riding Mountain National Park, Man.	351
Legislative Buildings, Winnipeg, Man.	352
Old Fort Garry Gate, Winnipeg, Man.	353
Street Scene, Winnipeg, Man.	354
Legislative Buildings, Fredericton, N. B.	151
King's Square, Saint John, N. B.	152
Saint John Harbour and Commercial Metropolis, N. B.	153
Harbour Saint John, N. B.	154
Reversing Falls, Saint John, N. B.	155
Beausejour, N. B.	156
Citadel Hill, Halifax, N. S.	101
Legislative Buildings, Halifax, N. S.	102
Northwest Arm Looking South, Halifax, N. S.	103
Light House, Lunenburg, N. S.	104
Hantsport, N. S.	105
Fishermen's Race, Halifax, N. S.	106
Block House, Annapolis Royal, N. S.	107
Hut Pool, Margaree Valley, N. S.	108
Parliament Hill, Ottawa, Ont.	51
Parliament Hill from Ottawa River, Ottawa, Ont.	52
Memorial Chamber, Parliament Buildings, Ottawa, Ont.	53
Panorama, Parliament Buildings, Ottawa, Ont.	54
Rideau Canal Along Driveway, Ottawa, Ont.	55
Toronto and Harbour, Ont.	301
Toronto and Harbour from Royal Canadian Yacht Club, Ont.	302
Niagara Falls, Ont.	303
Chippewa Falls Hydro-electric Station, Queenston, Ont.	304
Welland Ship Canal, Looking North, Ont.	305
Cruising, Muskoka Lakes, Ont.	306
Lake Rousseau, Muskoka Lakes, Ont.	307
Sleeping Giant Rock, Thunder Cape, Lake Superior, Ont.	308
High Falls, Near Bracebridge, Ont.	309
Sunnyside Beach, Toronto, Ont.	311
Legislative Buildings, Charlottetown, P. E. I.	201
Great George St., Charlottetown, P. E. I.	202
Churchill, Charlottetown, P. E. I.	203
Skyline, Montreal, Que.	251
View from Mount Royal Looking South, Montreal Que.	252
Interior of Notre Dame Church, Montreal, Que.	253
St. James' Cathedral, Montreal, Que.	254
Chateau de Ramezay, Montreal, Que.	255

Title	Number
Citadel and Heights from Harbour, Quebec, Que.	256
Montmorency Falls, Que.	257
Cape Trinity from Cape Eternity, Saguenay River, Que.	258
Quebec Bridge Over the St. Lawrence River, Que.	259
Legislative Buildings, Regina, Sask.	401
Saskatoon, Sask.	402
Sunset, Waskesiu Lake, Prince Albert National Park, Sask.	403
Shipping on the Great Lakes	310
Harvesting, Western Canada	404
Mount Robson	458
Oat Field, Western Canada	459
Ranch Scene, Western Canada	460
Buffalo, Western Canada	461

These were apparently printed in groups of four as we have seen a complete set of 22 uncut sheets of four, in the following arrangement:

Sheet Order Numbers

I	II	III	IV	V	VI	VII
105, 108	104, 101	152, 151	154, 156	259, 201	257, 255	252, 251
107, 103	106, 102	106, 101	153, 155	258, 202	256, 203	252, 251

VIII	IX	X	XI	XII	XIII	XIV
253, 254	310, 54	53, 308	301, 302	301, 311	305, 307	354, 351
252, 251	52, 54	51, 55	303, 309	303, 309	306, 304	353, 404

XV	XVI	XVII	XVIII	XIX
352, 401	460. 457	453, 454	456. 456	455, 456
403, 402	459, 451	455. 452	458, 458	455, 458

XX	XXI	XXII
503, 508	505, 507	501, 501
506, 461	504, 510	509, 509

From this it can be seen that several designs occur more than once as follows:

Design	Once in Sheets	Twice in Sheet	Total
54	—	IX	2
101	II, III		2
106	II, III		2
251	VIII	VII	3
252	VIII	VII	3
301	X, XII	—	2
303	XI, XII	—	2
309	XI, XII	—	2
455	XVII	XIX	3
456	XIX	XVIII	3
458	XIX	XVIII	3
501	—	XXII	2
509	—	XXII	2

71 designs— 5 occur three times
7 occur twice
59 occur once

} 88 cards=4 to a sheet. 22 sheets.

Post Cards. King George V Medallion Issue. 1933-34.
(ENTIRE)

#	Denom. & Color	Inscription	A. Regular Stock		B. Mimeo. Stock		Notes
			Unused	Used	Unused	Used	
PC105	½c Violet	DC	.05	.10			May 26, 1933
PC106	½c Violet	DCF	.30	.10			May 29, 1933
PC107	1c Green	None	.05	.10			Feb. 5, 1934
PC108	1c Green	E	.06	.10	.25	.25	April 25, 1933
PC109	1c Green	DJ	.20	.10			May 15, 1933
PC110	2c Brown	None	.40	.20			
PC111	2c Brown	E	.06	.05			April 15, 1933
PC112	2c Brown	DJ	.30	.20			July 11, 1933
PC113	1c+½c Green & Violet	E+DC	.06	.40			June 20, 1933
PC114	1c+½c Green & Violet	DJ+DCF	.30	.60			April 17, 1934
PC115	1c+1c Green	E+EK	.06	.40			May 26, 1933
PC116	1c+1c Green	Daj+DbL	.30	.60			May, 15, 1933

Post Cards. King George V "Dated Die" Issue. 1935.
(ENTIRE)

#	Denom. & Color	Inscription	A. Regular Stock		B. Mimeo.		C. Die II Regular Stock		Notes
			Unused	Used	Unused	Used	Unused	Used	
PC117	½c Violet	DC	.04	.10					July 26, 1935
PC118	1c Green	None					.40	.30	June 13, 1935
PC119	1c Green	E	.06	.08	.30	.30			May 21, 1935
PC120	1c Green	DJ	.06	.08					May 9, 1935
PC121	2c Brown	None					.06	.08	Sept. 3, 1935
PC122	2c Brown	E	.40	.20					June 4, 1935
PC123	2c Brown	DJ	.20	.10					Aug. 29, 1935
PC124	1c + ½c Green & violet	E+Dc					.20	.40	Oct. 1, 1935
PC125	1c + 1c Green	E+EK					.06	.60	July 13, 1935
PC126	1c + 1c Green	DJc+DJb					.30	.60	Sept. 1, 1935

Post Cards. King George V Dated Die Issue—Medallion Type. 1935.
(ENTIRE)

#	Denom. & Color	Inscription	A. Regular Stock Unused	A. Regular Stock Used	B. Mimeo. Stock Unused	B. Mimeo. Stock Used	Notes
PC127	½c Violet	DC	.12	.06			Oct. 7, 1935
PC128	½c Violet	DCF	.06	.04			Oct. 1, 1935
PC129	1c Green	None	.06	.04			
PC130	1c Green	E	.06	.04	.06	.06	Aug. 26, 1935
PC131	1c Green	DJ	.06	.04			Aug. 20, 1935
PC132	2c Brown	None	.06	.04			
PC133	2c Brown	E	.06	.04			Oct. 26, 1935
PC134	2c Brown	DJ	.06	.04			Nov. 5, 1935
PC135	1c+½c Green & violet	E+DC	.06	.12			Feb. 28, 1936
PC136	1c+½c Green & violet	DJ+DCF	.06	.12			Oct. 9, 1935
PC137	1c+1c Green	E+EK	.40	.80			
PC138	1c+1c Green	DJ+DL	.06	.12			June 2, 1936

Post Cards. King George VI Issue. 1938.
(ENTIRE)

#	Denom. & Color	Inscription	Stock A. Regular		Stock B. Mimeo.		Notes
			Unused	Used	Unused	Used	
PC139	1c Green	None	.04	.02	.04	.02	
PC140	1c Green	E	.04	.02			May 28, 1938
PC141	1c Green	DJ	.04	.02			May 11, 1938
PC142	2c Brown	None	.20	.10			
PC143	2c Brown	E	.06	.02			May 14, 1938
PC144	2c Brown	DJ	.06	.02			June 2, 1938
PC145	3c Brown	E+EK	.06	.06			
PC146	3c Brown	DJc+DJb	.06	.06			1943—Due to increase in Postal Rates.
PC147	3c Brown	None	.10	.05			
PC148	3c Rose violet	E	.10	.05			1944—Color changed to conform with adhesive of same denomination.
PC149	3c Rose violet	None	.30	.30			
PC150	3c Rose violet	DJ	.10	.02			
PC151	1c+1c Green	E	.10	.02			May 28, 1938
PC152	1c+1c Green	DJ	.10	.10			Nov. 1, 1938

D. The Letter Cards.

LC4 to LC8 Maple Leaf Type.

LC1-LC3

LC9.

LC9a.

Showing Both Types of Surcharges.

Letter cards, similar to those issued by various European countries[1] were issued by Canada in February 1893. The 3c card was followed in 1895 by 1c, and 2c card[2]. They were used primarily by banks, and other institutions to send statements and notices to their customers and stock holders.

The first three (LC1 to LC3) were printed by the British American Bank Note Co. The design is a crude imitation of the 1879 U.P.U. card of Great Britain.

The remaining cards (except the 2c surcharges) were the work of the American Bank Note Co., which used the same design as on the adhesive stamps.

Certain banks also had letter cards specially printed for their use, amounting to about 500,000. The Canadian Pacific Railway had 48,000 1c statement forms printed for monthly reports, in 1892-3.

---
1. Appendix M #23, 24.
2. Appendix M #25, 26.

Letter Cards.
(ENTIRE)

#	Denom. & Color	Date	A. $12\frac{1}{4} \times 12\frac{1}{4}$ Unused	Used	B.[1] $12\frac{1}{4} \times 11\frac{1}{2}$ Unused	Used	Notes
LC1	1c Black	Oct. 1895	1.00	1.00	30.00	30.00	
LC2	2c Green	Oct. 1895	2.00	2.00	60.00	60.00	
LC3	3c Red	Feb. 17, 1893	.50	.70	25.00	25.00	
LC4	1c Black	Jan. 1898	Rough Paper Perf. 12 1.00	1.50	Glazed Paper Perf. 12		
LC5	1c Green	Mar. 1898	2.00	3.00	3.40	4.00	"Maple Leaf"
LC6	2c Green	Dec. 1897	1.50	2.50			
LC7	2c Carmine	Mar. 1898	1.00	1.50	1.50	2.50	
LC8	3c Carmine	Jan. 1898	1.50	2.50			
	Provisionals of 1899. 2c on 3c. Surcharge in violet black.						
LC9 a	2c on 3c Red (LC3) "C" with serif	Feb. 1898	.75 20.00	1.50 20.00	30.00	30.00	"Maple Leaf"
LC10 a	2c on 3c Carmine (LC8) "C" with serif	Feb. 1898	1.00	1.00			"Maple Leaf"

NOTE: We do not consider the shades of the 2c on 3c surcharge worthy of separate listing. When it is considered that it was hand-stamped, on cards varying considerably in shade of stock and impression the distinction heretofore made loses its force.

1. In this card the horizontal perforations do not cross the vertical line of perforations, used copies can be distinguished by the vertical perforations guaging $11\frac{1}{2}$ instead of $12\frac{1}{4}$.
LC1 to LC3 were supplied to the department at $1.75 per M by the B. A. B. N. Co. LC4 to LC8 were by the A. B. N. Co. and were furnished at the rate of $3.66 per M. (See page 230).

Chapter XXXIV

THE OBLITERATIONS AND CANCELLATIONS

Introductory

In recent years collectors in all countries have been giving a great deal of attention and study to obliterations and postal markings of all kinds, with the result that there has developed a vast field, we might almost say a distinct hobby within philately, with its own organizations, periodicals, catalogues, etc.

It is now pretty generally admitted that no specialized collection is worthy of such recognition unless there are a number of pages devoted to postmarks, cancellations, etc. An accurate knowledge of the various markings, their period of use, and the regulations governing such use are all particularly valuable in determining the genuineness of certain stamps, more so when on piece or entire cover. Indeed the postmarks, rating stamps, and other Post Office marking devices in many instances have an historical interest that far exceeds the postage stamps themselves.

The increasing interest in the historical phase of the hobby bids fair to elevate philately to one of the specialized fields of history and historical research.

We have, therefore, included a fairly extensive study of the various postal markings found on Canadian stamps and covers, knowing full well that there are many gaps in our knowledge, gaps which we hope will be a challenge to other students to do research work and endeavor to fill in the picture more completely. Further study is certain to bring to light more accurate information as to the earliest dates of use of many markings, as well as much other data.

The Division of the Field of Postal Markings

Generally speaking the various markings struck on mail matter are divisible into two broad groups, with a third group combining the characteristics of both as shown, viz.:

1. The official obliterations, postmarks, etc., furnished by the Post Office administration for the purpose of aiding the personnel in the handling of the mail, keeping accounts, etc.

2. Various fancy markings, fashioned at the whim of a local postmaster, or clerk, which, aside from obliterating the stamp are of no assistance to the functioning of the postal service.

3. In this group are markings of local significance, but which also combine information of significance to the Post Office Administration. In this class are the fancy Toronto "2" leaf cancellations, made locally but carrying the office number, and as a modern instance, the slogan cancellation, advertising some event, charity, or duty, combined with the town mark.

Our study also requires that divisions of these groups be made as follows:

CLASS 1. POSTMARKS: These are generally circular in design, although straight line and even triangular marks are known. They show the name of the Post Office, when the piece of mail was posted, and when it was received at its destination. Some postmarks indicate the offices where the letter was handled *en route*, such postmarks being known as *transit* marks. These postmarks were supplied with or without moveable type for the date. If type was not supplied, the postmaster was required to write in the date with pen and ink[1].

---
1. Appendix C ≠5B, and B #21.

CLASS 2. RAILWAY POSTMARKS: Circular or straight line in form. Used by the railway mail clerks to mark mail delivered to or handled on the train. As a rule they indicate the name of the railway, branch, or Railway Post Office route, the date, the direction of train movement, and frequently the identity of the mail clerk by a letter or number.

CLASS 3. STEAMBOAT POSTMARKS: Similar to railway postmarks, but a much smaller class, and used by the clerks to mark mail carried by inland river and lake boats.

CLASS 4. REGULATION MARKS: Made of brass or steel, and set in wooden handles. These marks were used to indicate that the regulations of the Department governing the handling of the mail were carried out. They include "Too Late," "Advertised," etc. Many of these we classify with the HANDSTRUCK STAMPS (q.v.).

CLASS 5. OBLITERATORS: Popularly called "killers." Supplied at first only to larger and more important offices[1] for the cancellation of postage stamps. When not supplied postmasters were required to cancel stamps by marking them with a cross in pen and ink[2].

These markings, as well as others, referred to in the discussion of the HANDSTRUCK STAMPS (q.v.) were supplied chiefly by five manufacturers, viz.: Rawdon, Wright, Hatch & Edson,[3] John Francis, D. G. Berri, John Ellis, and Pritchard & Maynard and their successors Pritchard & Mingard.

Historically the marks fall into three groups:

1. The Imperial Markings 1765 to 1851.
2. The Provincial Markings 1851 to 1868.
3. The Dominion Markings 1868 to date.

Group I.

Class 1. Postmarks.

These were the marks supplied by the Post Office Department to practically all but a few of the smaller offices where the postmaster would write the name of the post office on the letter.

As noted in Chapter II straight line marks were introduced by Hugh Finlay in 1765, and circular marks shortly thereafter. By the beginning of the Nineteenth Century, however, the number of Post Offices and volume of mail was so great that these marks are comparatively common, and at the time stamps were introduced there were about six hundred offices[4], most of them being supplied with postmarks. When the Dominion took over the unified service there were over 2300 offices in the former provinces of Upper and Lower Canada alone, and another 1300 offices in the former provinces of Nova Scotia and New Brunswick. Compulsory use of stamps to prepay postage became effective in 1875, and at that time there were almost 5,000 Post Offices in the Dominion.

A complete list of all these Offices, the postmarks of which, theoretically could be found on stampless covers, either as a handstamp or in manuscript would involve much research, and serve little practical purpose.

The Postmarks may be divided into main groups, and a representation of these groups is comparatively easy to obtain. We would, however, warn collectors against too fine a division of the types, etc. All of the early postmarks were hand cut in steel or brass, and as several orders were placed for these postmarks they will all vary to some extent, and in some cases the diameter may differ by a millimeter or two. Minor differences in the letters are also frequent. In addition the normal wear and tear, and the care taken in striking may produce differences which may lead the tyro to "discover a New Type".

---

1. Appendix C #5B.
2. Appendix C #5B; B. #21.
3. Appendix H #2, E, and F.
4. Appendix R #1.

With these thoughts in mind we proceed to a brief analysis of the postmarks commonly found on the covers used during the Imperial and Provincial Administrations. Just as many of the Imperial markings were carried over to the Provincial administration, so also were many of the Provincial marks carried over to the Dominion Post Office. In the case of the obiterations some of the Provincial types were still in use in the opening years of this Century!

THE MONTH ABBREVIATIONS

Before listing and discussing the various postal markings we give below the abbreviations for months in Canadian Post Marks. These are of two kinds,

(a) The British two letter abbreviation.
(b) The American three letter abbreviation.

Month	(a) British	(b) American
JANUARY	JA	JAN
FEBRUARY	FE	FEB
MARCH	MA	MAR
APRIL	AP	APR or APL
MAY	MY	MAY
JUNE	JU	JUN
JULY	JY	JUL
AUGUST	AU	AUG
SEPTEMBER	SE or SP	SEP
OCTOBER	OC	OCT
NOVEMBER	NO	NOV
DECEMBER	DE	DEC

Care should be taken not to confuse the British abbreviations, misreading "Ju" as July for instance.

Before discussing the various types of town marks known we list herewith the Post Offices of Canada together with date of establishment, from an official list by D.P.M.G. Stayner, dated Jan. 1, 1841, showing "the Names and situations of all the Post Offices in the provinces of Upper and Lower Canada, and of that part of New Brunswick[1] under my immediate charge, stating when each was Established."

OFFICIAL LIST OF POST OFFICES, 1840

Figures Given After Post Office and Province
Is Distance in Miles from Quebec

Post Office and Province When Established
Abbotsford, L. C. (219)........Previous to 1828
Adelaide, U. C. (723)................6th July, 1833
Adolphustown, U. C. (411)...Previous to 1828
Albion, U. C. (609)....................6th Oct., 1832
Aldboro', U. C. (740)................6th Oct., 1831
Alexandria, U. C. (263)......Previous to 1828
Allen's Mills, U. C. (421)...6th August, 1836
Ameliasburg, U. C. (453).........6th Oct., 1832
Amherstburg, U. C. (825).......Oldest record,
 23rd July, 1810
Amiens, U. C. (730) ....6th Feb., 1837
Ancaster, U. C. (611).........Previous to 1828
Asphodel, U. C. (498)..............6th Jan., 1836
Aylmer, U. C. (684)..................6th Oct., 1836
Aylmer, L. C. (310)..................6th Jan., 1832
Ayr, U. C. (637) ....6th May, 1840
Babyville, U. C. (210)..............6th Oct., 1831
Barnston, U. C. (235)..............6th Oct., 1832
Barrie, U. C. (608)...................6th Oct., 1835
Bath, U. C. (397)................Previous to 1828
Batiscan, L. C. (69)..................6th Jan., 1837
Bayham, U. C. (685).................6th Jan., 1830
Beachville, U. C. (673)............6th July, 1836

Post Office and Province When Established
Beamsville, U. C. (627)........... 6th Oct., 1832
Beauharnois, L. C. (205)........6th April, 1829
Beaverton, U. C. (629).............6th Jan., 1836
Besancour, L. C. (85)..............6th April, 1832
Bedford, L. C. (225)........ ....6th Jan., 1830
Belleville, U. C. (438)....Previous to 1828 (2)
Berthier, L. C. (135)................Oldest record,
 7th April, 1800
Beverly, U. C. (349)...........Previous to 1828
Bloomfield, U. C. (423)............6th April, 1831
Bolton, L. C. (244)...................6th April, 1831
Bond Head, U. C. (600)............6th Aug., 1837
Boucherville, L. C. (187)...Previous to 1828
Bradford, U. C. (595)..............5th July, 1840
Brantford, U. C. (629).......Previous to 1828
Brighton, U. C. (454)...............6th July, 1831
Brockville, U. C. (323)...Oldest record, (3)
 July, 1810
Brome, L. C. (250)...................6th April, 1831
Brock, U. C. (556)....................6th Aug., 1836
Brompton, L. C. (173).............6th July, 1831
Brougham, U. C. (541).............6th Aug., 1836
Buckingham, L. C. (285).........6th Jan., 1832

561*

Post Office and Province	When Established
Burford, U. C. (639)	Previous to 1828
Burritt's Rapids, U. C. (347)	6th Oct., 1839
Bytown, U. C. (303)	6th April, 1829
Cacona, L. C. (120)	6th Jan., 1832
Caledon, U. C. (605)	6th Oct., 1839
Caledonia, U. C. (257)	6th May, 1837
Camden East, U. C. (411)	6th Oct., 1832
Campbelltown, N. B. (303)	6th July, 1837
Canboro, U. C. (639)	6th April, 1836
Cape Cove, L. C. (441)	6th Jan., 1837
Cap Sante, L. C. (30)	Previous to 1828
Carleton, L. C. (330)	6th Jan., 1830
Carleton Place, U. C. (350)	6th Oct., 1830
Castleford, U. C. (352)	6th Jan., 1832
Cavan, U. C. (514)	6th Jan., 1830
Cedars, L .C. (217)	6th April, 1837
Chambly, L. C. (195)	Previous to 1828
Champlain, L. C. (75)	6th April, 1837
Chateauguay, L. C. (196)	6th April, 1829
Chateau Richer, L. C. (15)	6th April, 1832
Chatham, L. C. (228)	1st May, 1829
Chelsea, L. C. (313)	6th Feb., 1837
Chinguacousy, U. C. (590)	6th Oct., 1832
Chippawa, U. C. (666)	Oldest record, 23rd July, 1801
Churchville, U. C. (584)	6th Oct., 1831
Churchville, L. C. (242)	6th April, 1831
Clarenceville, L. C. (227)	6th April, 1832
Clarendon, U. C. (355)	6th Nov., 1837
Clarke, U. C. (502)	6th April, 1835
Clearville, U. C. (745)	6th Oct., 1831
Cobourg, U. C. (484)	Previous to 1828 (4)
Colborne, U. C. (468)	Previous to 1828
Colchester, U. C. (815)	6th Oct., 1831
Coldwater, U. C. (657)	6th Oct., 1835
Compton, L. C. (200)	6th July, 1829
Consecon, U. C. (438)	6th Jan., 1836
Cooksville, U. C. (572)	6th Jan., 1829
Cornwall, U. C. (262)	Oldest record, 24th August, 1803
Coteau du Lac, L. C. (223)	Previous to 1828
Credit, U. C. (574)	6th Oct., 1831
Daillebout, L. C. (153)	6th Nov., 1836
Danville, L. C. (171)	6th Jan., 1832
Darlington, U. C. (513)	Previous to 1828
Dawn Mills, U. C. (773)	6th Feb., 1837
Delaware, U. C. (705)	Previous to 1828
Demorestville, U. C. (428)	5th April, 1829
Deschambault, L. C. (42)	6th Jan., 1837
Dewittville, L. C. (232)	6th Oct., 1832
Drummondville, U. C. (663)	6th April, 1830
Drummondville, L. C. (136)	Previous to 1828
Dundas, U. C. (608)	Previous to 1828
Dundee, L. C. (255)	6th July, 1830
Dunham, U. C. (234)	Previous to 1828
Dunville, U. C. (676)	6th July, 1830
Durham, U. C. (150)	6th July, 1836
East Farnham, L. C. (247)	6th Feb., 1837
Eaton, L. C. (204)	5th July, 1830
Edwardsburg, U. C. (382)	6th April, 1837
Ekfried, U. C. (719)	6th Feb., 1837
Eldon, U. C. (619)	6th Nov., 1837
Elora, U. C. (657)	6th Oct., 1839
Emboro, U. C. (681)	6th July, 1836
Emily, U. C. (542)	6th Aug., 1836
Eramosa, U. C. (650)	6th Oct., 1839
Erieus, U. C. (770)	6th Oct., 1831
Erin, U. C. (603)	6th Oct., 1839
Errol, U. C. (751)	6th Feb., 1837
Esquesing, U. C. (589)	6th Oct., 1832
Etobicoke, U. C. (565)	6th April, 1832
Farmersville, U. C. (339)	6th July, 1836
Fenelon Falls, U. C. (566)	6th July, 1838
Fergus, U. C. (658)	6th April, 1836
Fitzroy Harbour, U. C. (334)	6th Jan., 1832
Flos, U. C. (636)	6th Aug., 1837
Fort Erie, U. C. (679)	Oldest record, 23rd July, 1801
Frampton, L. C. (44)	6th Oct., 1836
Frankford, U. C. (454)	6th July, 1838
Franktown, U. C. (341)	6th Oct., 1832
Fredericksburg, U. C. (406)	Previous to 1828
Frelighsburg, L. C. (243)	Previous to 1828
Frost Village, L. C. (242)	Previous to 1828
Galt, U. C. (627)	Previous to 1828 (5)
Gananoque, U. C. (355)	Previous to 1828
Gaspe Basin, L. C. (487)	6th Jan., 1837
Gentilly, L. C. (76)	6th Jan., 1831
Georgeville, L. C. (284)	Previous to 1828
Georgina, U. C. (609)	6th Oct., 1831
Goderich, U. C. (711)	6th Oct., 1835
Gosfield, U. C. (802)	6th Oct., 1831
Granby, L. C. (228)	Previous to 1828
Grand Falls, N. B. (227)	6th Jan., 1837
Grenville, L. C. (240)	Previous to 1828
Grimsby, U. C. (624)	Previous to 1828
Grondines, L. C. (48)	6th Jan., 1836
Guelph, U. C. (642)	6th July, 1828
Haldimand, U. C. (475)	6th April, 1832
Hamilton, U. C. (604)	Previous to 1828
Hatley, L. C. (207)	Previous to 1828
Hawkesbury, U. C. (242)	Previous to 1828
Henryville, L. C. (221)	Previous to 1828
Hemmingford, L. C. (218)	6th Oct., 1831
Hereford, L. C. (221)	6th Oct., 1831
Hillier, U. C. (434)	Previous to 1828
Holland Landing, U. C. (590)	6th Oct., 1831
Howard, U. C. (753)	6th Oct., 1831
Hull, L. C. (304)	6th April, 1833
Huntingdon, L. C. (238)	6th July, 1830
Huntley, U. C. (409)	6th April, 1837
Industry, L. C. (176)	6th July, 1833
Inverness, L. C. (57)	6th Jan., 1832
Isle aux Noix, L. C. (220)	Previous to 1828
Isle Verte, L. C. (132)	6th Oct., 1831
Jordan, U. C. (637)	6th April, 1840
Kamouraska, L. C. (90)	Previous to 1828
Katesville, U. C. (720)	6th Feb., 1837
Kemptville, U. C. (338)	6th April, 1831
Keithburn, L. C. (228)	6th May, 1837
Keswick, U. C. (603)	6th Jan., 1836
Kilmarnock, U. C. (366)	6th Aug., 1829
Kingsey, L. C. (169)	6th April, 1836
Kingston, U. C. (379)	Oldest record, 22nd Oct., 1801
Kitley, U. C. (345)	6th Jan., 1832
La Baie, L. C. (114)	6th April, 1829
La Beauce, L. C. (31)	6th Oct., 1831
L'Acadie, L. C. (202)	6th Oct., 1835
Lachine, L. C. (189)	6th April, 1829
Lachute, L. C. (232)	6th Oct., 1835
Lacolle, L. C. (216)	6th April, 1832
Lanark, U. C. (378)	Previous to 1828
Lancaster, U. C. (246)	Previous to 1828
Laprairie, L. C. (189)	Previous to 1828
L'Assomption, L. C. (159)	Oldest record 4th Sept., 1809
Leeds, L. C. (46)	6th Jan., 1833
Lennoxville, L. C. (191)	6th April, 1831
Les Eboulemens, L. C. (69)	6th April, 1832
Lindsay, U. C. (556)	6th Aug., 1836
L'Islet, L. C. (48)	6th July, 1833
Lloydtown, U. C. (599)	6th Oct., 1831
Lochaber, L. C. (280)	6th Jan., 1833
Lochiel, U. C. (257)	Previous to 1828
London, U. C. (694)	Previous to 1828
Longueuil, L. C. (183)	6th Feb., 1837
L'Orignal, U. C. (248)	6th April, 1829
Lotbiniere, L. C. (46)	6th July, 1833
Loughboro', U. C. (395)	6th July, 1836
McGillivray, U. C. (714)	6th Oct., 1836
McKillop, U. C. (688)	6th Oct., 1836
McNab, U. C. (360)	6th May, 1839
Madawaska, N. B. (192)	6th July, 1837
Madoc, U. C. (480)	6th July, 1836
Maitland, U. C. (320)	5th July, 1830
Manningville, L. C. (234)	6th Oct., 1831
March, U. C. (316)	Previous to 1828
Markham, U. C. (576)	6th Jan., 1829
Mariposa, U. C. (566)	6th Aug., 1836
Marmora, U. C. (468)	Previous to 1828
Marshville, U. C. (662)	6th April, 1836
Martintown, U. C. (275)	Previous to 1828
Maskinonge, L. C. (118)	6th Oct., 1839
Matilda, U. C. (296)	Previous to 1828 (5a)
Melbourne, L. C. (159)	5th July, 1835

Post Office and Province	When Established
Merrickville, U. C. (372)	6th July, 1829
Mersea, U. C. (793)	6th Oct., 1835
Metis, L. C. (207)	6th April, 1836
Middleton, U. C. (666)	6th July, 1831
Milford, U. C. (426)	6th Oct., 1832
Mill Creek, U. C. (391)	6th Jan., 1839
Milton, U. C. (600)	6th April, 1836
Mohawk, U. C. (634)	6th April, 1836
Montreal, L. C. (180)	Oldest record, 7th April, 1800 (But date not known, supposed to have been at the time of the Conquest.)
Mono Mills, U. C. (618)	6th Oct., 1839
Moore, U. C. (775)	6th Feb., 1837
Mosa, U. C. (729)	6th April, 1832
Moulinette, U. C. (269)	6th Oct., 1835
Murray, U. C. (444)	Previous to 1828
Murray Bay, L. C. (90)	6th April, 1832
Nanticoke, U. C. (667)	6th Aug., 1839
Napanee, U .C. (409)	Previous to 1828
Napierville, L. C. (207)	6th April, 1832
Nassagiweya, U. C. (611)	6th Jan., 1840
Nelson, U. C. (591)	Previous to 1828
Newborough, U. C. (364)	6th Jan., 1836
New Carlisle, L. C. (380)	6th Jan., 1837
New Glasgow, L. C. (216)	6th April, 1833
New Ireland, U. C. (67)	6th Jan., 1837
Newmarket, L. C. (586)	Previous to 1828
Niagara, U. C. (660)	Oldest record, 22nd Nov., 1802
Nicolet, L. C. (102)	Previous to 1828
North Augusta, U. C. (332)	5th July, 1840
North Georgetown, L.C. (218)	6th July, 1830
North Port, U. C. (432)	6th Aug., 1836
Norton Creek, L. C. (214)	6th Oct., 1831
Norval, U. C. (584)	6th Oct., 1836
Norwich, U. C. (651)	6th Jan., 1830
Oakville, U. C. (594)	6th Oct., 1835
Oakland, U. C. (639)	6th April, 1840
Orillia, U. C. (693)	6th Oct., 1835
Ormstown, L. C. (225)	6th Oct., 1836
Oro, U. C. (630)	6th Oct., 1835
Osgoode, U. C. (329)	6th July, 1838
Osnabruck, U. C. (275)	6th Jan., 1829
Otonabee, U .C. (502)	6th April, 1832
Otterville, U. C. (657)	6th Aug., 1837
Oxford, U. C. (665)	Previous to 1828
Pakenham, U. C. (346)	6th April, 1832
Palermo, U. C. (586)	6th April, 1837
Paris, U. C. (632)	6th Jan., 1832
Penetanguishene, U. C. (661)	6th Jan., 1830
Percy, U. C. (471)	6th Jan., 1836
Perth, U. C. (365)	Previous to 1828
Perce, L. C. (450)	6th Jan., 1837
Peterboro, U. C. (527)	5th Jan., 1830
Petite Nation, L. C. (270)	Previous to 1838
Philipsburg, L. C. (231)	Previous to 1838
Pickering, U. C. (534)	6th Jan., 1829
Picton, U. C. (418)	Previous to 1828
Plantagenet, U. C. (267)	6th July, 1838
Point Abino, U. C. (690)	6th July, 1838
Point St. Peter, U. C. (465)	6th Jan., 1837
Pointe Claire, L. C. (199)	6th Oct., 1835
Port Burwell, U. C. (693)	6th Jan., 1830
Port Colborne, U. C. (662)	6th April, 1836
Port Dalhousie, U. C. (643)	6th July, 1831
Port Dover, U. C. (660)	6th July, 1831
Port Hope, U. C. (491)	Previous to 1828
Port Neuf, L. C. (35)	Previous to 1828
Port Robinson, U. C. (650)	6th April, 1836
Port St. Francis, L. C. (99)	6th July, 1836
Port Sarnia, U. C. (765)	6th Feb., 1837
Port Stanley, U. C. (713)	6th Jan., 1830
Port Talbot, U. C. (721)	Previous to 1828
Port Trent, U .C. (449)	Previous to 1828
Prescott, U. C. (311)	Previous to 1828 (6) (Supposed to have been in 1800.)
Preston, U. C. (630)	6th Feb., 1837
Princeton, U. C. (642)	6th May, 1836
Quebec, L. C.	(Date not known, supposed to have been at the time of the Conquest.)

Post Office and Province	When Established
Queenston, U. C. (653)	Oldest record, 23rd July, 1801
Raleigh, U. C. (757)	Previous to 1828 (6a)
Ramsay, U. C. (358)	6th April, 1837
Rawdon, U. C. (453)	6th April, 1832
Rawdon, L. C. (180)	6th Oct., 1831
Repentigny, L. C. (165)	6th Feb., 1837
Richmond, U. C. (397)	Previous to 1828
Richmond, L .C. (160)	Previous to 1828
Richmond Hill, U. C. (626)	6th Jan., 1836
Rigaud, L. C. (225)	6th Oct., 1835
Rimouski, L. C. (180)	6th Jan., 1832
Riviere du Loup, L.C. (119)	Previous to 1828
Riviere du Loup en bas, L. C. (114)	6th Jan., 1832
Riviere Ouelle, L. C. (78)	Previous to 1828
Robinson, L. C. (215)	6th Jan., 1839
Romney, U. C. (784)	6th Oct., 1831
Russelltown, L. C. (225)	6th Oct., 1831
St. Andre, L. C. (109)	6th Jan., 1832
St. Andrews, U. C. (269)	6th April, 1830
St. Andrews, L. C. (225)	Previous to 1828
Ste. Anne de la Perade, L. C. (60)	Previous to 1828
Ste. Anne la Pocatiere, L. C. (74)	6th July, 1831
Ste. Anne bout de l'Isle, L. C. (207)	6th Oct., 1835
St. Antoine, L. C. (25)	6th July, 1831
St. Catherines, U. C. (638)	Previous to 1828
St Cesaire, L. C. (213)	Previous to 1828
St. Charles, L. C. (165)	Previous to 1828
St. Croix, L. C. (34)	6th July, 1831
St. Denis, L. C. (159)	Previous to 1828
Ste. Elizabeth, L. C. (144)	6th Nov., 1836
St. Eustache, L. C. (201)	Previous to 1828
St. Francis, L. C. (123)	5th July, 1831
St. George, U. C. (625)	6th October, 1835
St. Hilaire, L. C. (172)	Previous to 1828
St. Hyacinthe, L. C. (179)	6th Oct., 1828
St. Jacques, L. C. (171)	6th Oct., 1835
St. Jean Port Joli, L.C.(54)	Previous to 1828
St. Johns, U. C. (648)	6th Oct., 1831
St. Johns, L. C. (207)	Previous to 1828
St. Laurent, L. C. (187)	6th July, 1836
St. Luc, L. C. (201)	6th July, 1836
Ste. Luce, L. C. (194)	6th Oct., 1836
Ste. Marie de Monnoir, L. C. (190)	6th July, 1831
St. Martin, L. C. (192)	6th July, 1836
Ste. Martine, L. C. (208)	6th April, 1833
St. Nicholas, L. C. (16)	6th July, 1831
St. Ours, L. C. (152)	Previous to 1828
St. Paul's Bay, L. C. (60)	6th April, 1832
St. Pie, L. C. (224)	6th Jan., 1837
St. Pierre les Becquets, L. C. (66)	6th July, 1831
St. Roch des Aulnois, L. C. (69)	Previous to 1828
St. Roch l'Achigan, L. C. (170)	6th Jan., 1832
St. Stanislaus, L. C. (76)	6th Jan., 1837
St. Sylvester, L. C. (38)	6th Jan., 1837
St. Theres de Blainville, L. C. (209)	6th Jan., 1837
St. Thomas, U. C. (705)	Previous to 1828
St. Thomas, L. C. (34)	Previous to 1828
St. Vincent de Paul, L. C. (192)	5th July, 1836
Sandwich, U. C. (809)	Oldest record, 20th March, 1802
Scarboro, U. C. (568)	6th April, 1832
Seneca, U. C. (618)	6th Jan., 1839
Seymour East, U. C. (462)	6th April, 1837
Seymour West, U. C. (470)	Previous to 1828
Shannonville, U. C. (429)	6th July, 1833
Sheffield, U. C. (621)	6th April, 1837
Sherbrooke, L. C. (187)	Previous to 1828 (7)
Simcoe, U. C. (653)	6th July, 1829
Smith's Falls, U. C. (359)	6th July, 1830
Smithville, U. C. (634)	5th July, 1831
South Potton, L. C. (260)	6th Feb., 1837

Post Office and Province	When Established
South Gower, U. C. (331)	6th Oct., 1836
Stanbridge East, L. C. (229)	6th July, 1836
Stanley's Mills, U. C. (598)	6th Oct., 1832
Stanstead, L. C. (221)	Previous to 1828
Stoney Creek, U. C. (611)	Previous to 1828
Stratford, U. C. (665)	6th Oct., 1835
Streetsville, U. C. (579)	6th Jan., 1829
Stukely, L. C. (247)	6th Oct., 1832
Sutton, L. C. (257)	6th Feb., 1837
Terrebonne, L. C. (201)	Previous to 1828
Thamesville, U. C. (744)	6th Jan., 1840
Thornhill, U .C. (568)	6th Jan., 1829
Thorold, U. C. (642)	Previous to 1828
Three Rivers, L. C. (90)	Oldest record, 7th April, 1800
Temiscouata, L. C. (144)	23rd Nov., 1839
Toronto, U. C. (556)	Oldest record, 23rd July, 1801
Trafalgar, U. C. (579)	Previous to 1828
Trois Pistoles, L. C. (146)	6th Jan., 1832
Tyrconnel, U. C. (729)	6th Feb., 1837
Uxbridge, U. C. (541)	6th Aug., 1836
Vankleehill, U. C. (248)	6th July, 1831
Varennes, L. C. (182)	Previous to 1828
Vaudreuil, L. C. (210)	6th Oct., 1835
Vaughan, U. C. (569)	6th Nov., 1837
Vercheres, L. C. (175)	Previous to 1828
Victoria, L. C. (226)	6th Jan., 1839
Vienna, U. C. (690)	6th April, 1836
Vittoria, U. C. (667)	Previous to 1828
Wallaceburgh, U. C. (782)	6th Feb., 1837
Walpole, U. C. (677)	6th April, 1836
Walsingham, U. C. (680)	6th July, 1831
Warwick, U. C. (737)	6th Feb., 1837
Waterloo, L. C. (239)	6th April, 1836
Waterloo, U. C. (641)	6th Oct., 1831
Wellington, U. C. (429)	6th April, 1830
Wellington Square, U. C. (597)	Previous to 1828
West Flamboro', U. C. (611)	6th April, 1840
Westmeath, U. C. (382)	6th May, 1837
Westminster, U. C. (701)	6th Jan., 1840
West Shefford, L. C. (252)	6th Feb., 1837
Whitby, U. C. (525)	Previous to 1828
Whitehall, U. C. (769)	6th Feb., 1837
Williamsburg East, U. C. (284)	6th Oct., 1835
Williamsburg West, U. C. (228)	6th July, 1830
William Henry, L.C.(140)	Previous to 1828(8)
Williamstown, U. C. (252)	6th April, 1833
Wilmot, U. C. (647)	6th May, 1837
Wilton, U. C. (405)	6th Oct., 1832
Woodstock, N. B. (300)	6th July, 1838
Woodstock, U. C. (655)	6th Oct., 1835
Woolwich, U. C. (643)	6th May, 1837
Yamachiche, L. C. (108)	6th Jan., 1833
Yamaska, L. C. (127)	Previous to 1828
Yonge, U. C. (333)	6th Jan., 1833
York, U. C. (623)	6th April, 1836
York Mills, U. C. (562)	6th Jan., 1836
Zone Mills, U. C. (764)	6th Jan., 1840

GENERAL POST OFFICE, Quebec, Jan. 1841

1. These offices may therefore be considered as Canadian Offices until April 5, 1851 inclusive.
2. Formerly Bay of Quinte.
3. Formerly Elizabethtown.
4. Formerly Hamilton.
5. Formerly Shade's Mill.
5a. Later named Iroquois.
6. Formerly Augusta.
6a. Later Chatham.
7. Formerly Ascott.
8. Later known as Sorel.

(It is interesting to observe that Stayner would not be responsible for dates earlier than his records showed, although we know some Offices were in existence in the 18th Century, and indeed he qualifiedly admitted as much).

To this was added a list of offices established Jan. 1, to July 6, 1841; viz: Beach, Waterdown, Dereham, Innisfil, Sharon, Williamsburg North, Adjala, Arnprior, King, Moria, Halmer, Nottawasaga, Sandy Hill, St. Vincent, Sunnidale, Sparta, Pointe a Cavagnol, St. Michel.

Small offices were also constantly being closed and others merged or changed in name. The following offices were closed in 1838:
Hope, Portland, St. Benoit, St. Genevieve, St. Giles, St. Gregoire, St. Mathias, Sidney and Waterford. In 1839 these offices were also Closed: Camden West, Cascades, Eastville, Lyndhurst, Maidstone, and Potton. Eastville grossed only 7s 11d for the year, or less than $2.00!

Stayner also explained the method of establishing new post offices as follows: —"The inhabitants of the place where the Post Office is needed, address me by Memorial or Letter, stating their wants, and recommending a person as Post Master; the merits of the application are then enquired into by the Surveyor, who visits the place indicated for the Offce, ascertains the fitness of the individual nominated as Post Master, and reports the results of his investigation to me. By this report I am in most cases governed ; but I beg to observe that the question of creating a new Post Office, or changing a Post route, or increasing the travel of the Mail upon a line of post, frequently involves a necessity for much research and correspondence, and that there is no branch of my duty which calls more foricbly for the exercise of the best judgment I can commond than this."

As a matter of interest we show how the various applications were handled, from a report dated 1841:

A Return of the applications for New Offices which have been Refused during the three years ended the 5th July, 1840, with the grounds for such Refusal.

Name of Person applying for New Post Office, and date of Application.	Place	The Reasons for not granting the Application.
James Read Esq., and other Inhabitants of the settlement. 1st. Jan. 1839.	South West River Bridge, Ste. Marie de Monnoir, District of Montreal, Lower Canada.	Refused until the projected improvements on the Road leading from St. Cesaire through this settlement to St. Johns are completed:— the correspondence of the place could not be expected to defray more than a fourth of the expense of serving it as an independent bye-Route.
Hiram Cotton, Esq., and other Inhabitants of the Township. Date not known.	Litchfield, On the Ottawa, District of Montreal, Lower Canada.	Because in the present state of the Litchfield Road, the expense of supplying an Office in this Township would exceed, in an unreasonable proportion, the correspondence to be accommodated.
Mr. Thomas Quilliam. 12th March, 1839.	St. Remi, District of Montreal, Lower Canada.	In consequence of the paucity of correspondence, and the impossibility of finding any one who would correctly discharge the duty of Post Master—it having for the latter reason chiefly, been already found necessary twice to close the Office.
J. B. Aylesworth, Esq., 20th May, 1839	Newburg, Camden East, Midland District, Upper Canada.	Because this location is in too close proximity to an established Office, being only distant two and a half miles from Camden East, without possessing any of the peculiar claims to consideration which have in some instances induced me to waive objections of a somewhat similar character.
Stephen Payment, Esq. September, 1839.	Ste. Genevieve, District of Montreal, Lower Canada.	An Office was in operation in this place in the years 1836 and 1837, but during that time the correspondence was so insignificant, not averaging more than 8s, a quarter, that I declined to accede to this application for its re-establishment, and with less hesitation, as the village is distant but five miles from the Pointe Claire Office.
Adiel Sherwood, Esq. 16th March, 1840.	Easton's Corner, Township of Wolford, Johnstown District, Upper Canada.	This settlement was not deemed to be sufficiently advanced to require a separate Post Office, having already the advantage of Post accommodation in tolerable proximity, viz.—at Kilmarnock, distant five miles, and Merrickville, seven miles.

It may be proper to mention that besides the above, about Twenty-four other Applications for New Offices from both Provinces, have been received by me, some of which will be acceded to as soon as the Post Office Surveyor can be spared from other important duties to superintend their erection. The remainder are under consideration.

T. A. STAYNER, D. P. M. G.

General Post Office,
Montreal, 26th July, 1841.

From the above it would appear that pre-stamp covers from St. Remi, and St. Genevieve should be scarce. For the year ending July 5, 1838, St. Genevieve grossed £1-4-1½! See particularly pages 9 to 11.

Former Canadian OFFICES now in the UNITED STATES

From sometime before 1787 there were two offices in Upper Canada, viz: Michilimackinac and Detroit which were Canadian offices until 1797, when they became United States offices. A straight line DETROIT marking of 1792 is known.

The following offices have been listed on several unofficial lists we have seen. They were either discontinued or the name of the office was changed, and we have not as yet been able to definitely identify them. Other students can, no doubt, supply this information, as well as additional names to this list:

Augusta, L. C.
Bastard, U. C.
Caldwell Manor, L. C.
Charlottenburg, U. C.
Hallowell, U. C.
Long Point, U. C.
Monahan, U. C.
Mount Pleasant, U. C.

Newark, U. C.
Newcastle, U. C.
New Johnston, U. C.
Pointe Olivier, L. C.
Shefford, L. C.
Shipton, L. C.
Yarmouth, U. C.

Chapter XXXV

IMPERIAL AND PROVINCIAL MARKINGS

Groups 1 and 2.

The Townmarks are divisible into three main divisions, viz.:
(a) Straight line.
(b) Circular.
(c) Oval, triangular, etc.

Division a. Straight Line Town Marks.

In Chapter II we gave a brief survey of the early Postal markings, many of which were carried over into the 19th Century. We list herewith, however, such straight line markings first used after 1800, but before Confederation in 1867.

EUGENIA   **Harwich**

Type A. One Line.

North Douro   **North Douro**

Ma 24 64   **Dec 3rd**

Original. Worn.
Type B. Two Lines—With Month and Day, Sometimes With Year Also.

Post Office	Type	Date	Red	Black	Notes
Brockville	A	1824		5.00	
Cornwall	A	1821			
Dundas	B	1802		5.00	
Eugenia	A	1865			
Fredericton	A	1817			N. Bruns.
Harwich	A	1859			
Kingston	B	1814			
L'Assomption	B	1826			
LaPrairie	A	1821			
Niagara	A	1805			
North Duoro	B	1863		5.00	
Perth	A	1827			
Queenston	B	1817			
Sandwich	B	1810		15.00	
Windsor, C.W.	B	1844	10.00	7.50	

Division b. Circular Town Post Marks.

Type I—Single Outer Circle—a-j Large Circle Type
(over 25 mm. in diameter)

Type Ia

Type Ib

Type Ic

567

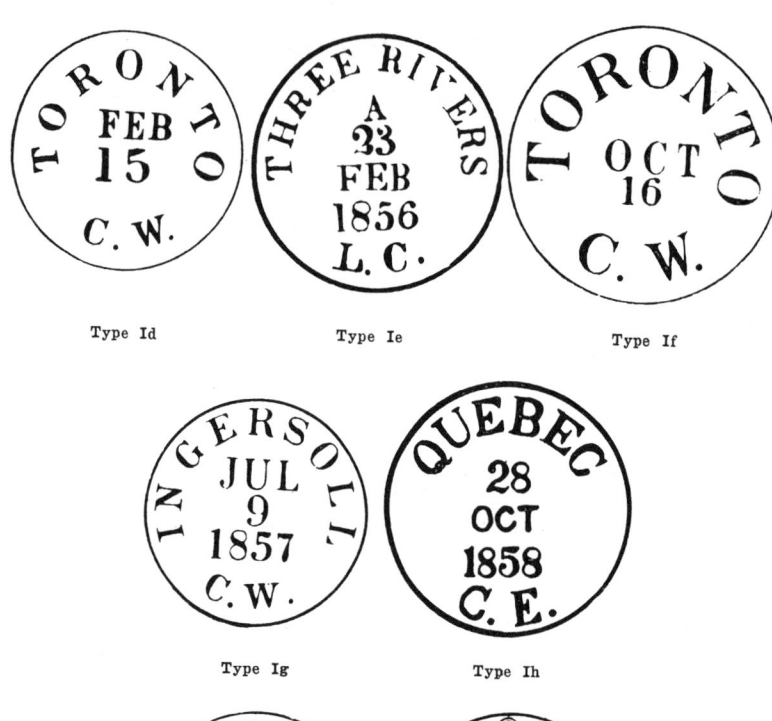

Type Id   Type Ie   Type If

Type Ig   Type Ih

Type Ij
Date in Outline   Type Ij
Date Solid

Type I—k-l—Small Circle Type (25 mm. or less in diameter)

Type Il   Type Ik

Type	Diameter in mm.	Letters	Year Date	Known used in	Notes
Ia	26	serifed solid	No	1798	Medium circle
Ib	31	”	No	1802	Thick circle
Ic	27	”	No	1821	Thick circle
Id	32	”	No	1855	Thick circle
Ie	34	”	Yes	1856	Thick circle
If	37	”	No	1856	Thin circle
Ig	30	”	Yes	1857	Thin circle
Ih	34	”	Yes	1858	Thick circle
Ij	32	serifed outline	Yes	1859	Thin circle
Ik	20	sans-serif thin	Yes	1864	Thick circle
Il	23	”	Yes	1864	Medium circle

Type II. Double Outer Circle

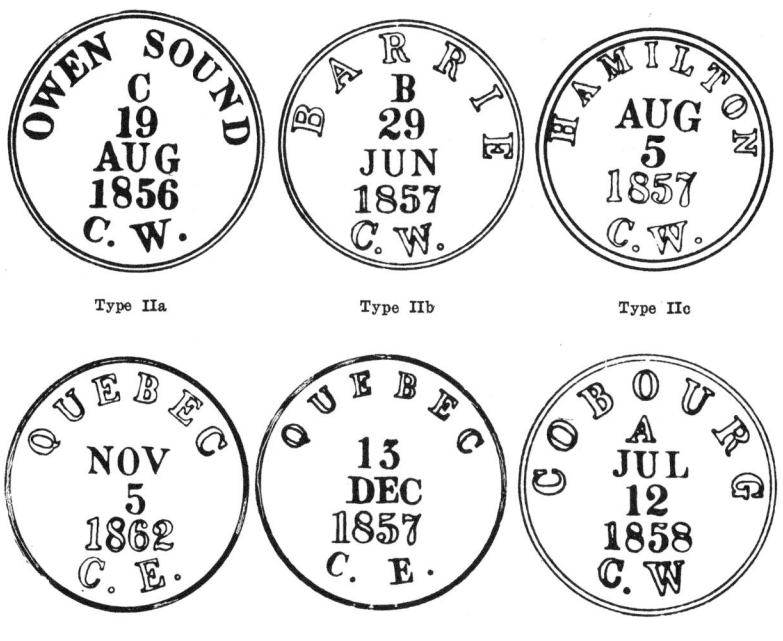

Type IIa

Type IIb

Type IIc

"CE" or "CW" in Outline

Type IId

"CE" or "CW" Solid

Type IIe

Type	Diameter in mm.	Letters	Year Date	Known used in	Notes
IIa	35	serifed solid	Yes	1856	
IIb	33	serifed outline	Yes	1857	
IIc	32	”	Yes	1857	Circles wide apart
IId	34	”	Yes	1857	Circles very close together
IIe	35	”	Yes	1858	Circles similar to IIb

Type III. Double Circle With Post Office Name Between

Type IIIa   Type IIIb (Toronto)   Type IIIc

Type IIId (York became Toronto in 1834)   Type IIIe

Type	Diameter in mm.	Letters	Year Date	Known used in	
IIIa	30	serifed solid	Yes	1832	
IIIb	30	”	No	1833	
IIIc	30	”	—	1835	Date in manuscript
IIId	35	”	Yes	1837	
IIIe	33	”	Yes	1861	

Type IV. No Outer Circle—a-e Serifed Letters 3-3½ mm Tall

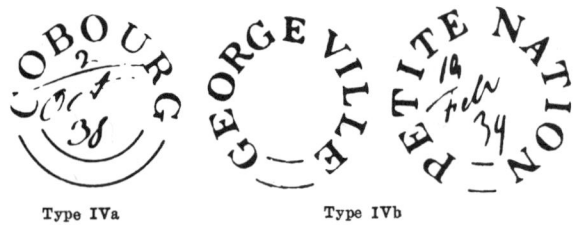

Type IVa   Type IVb

Type IVc   Type IVd

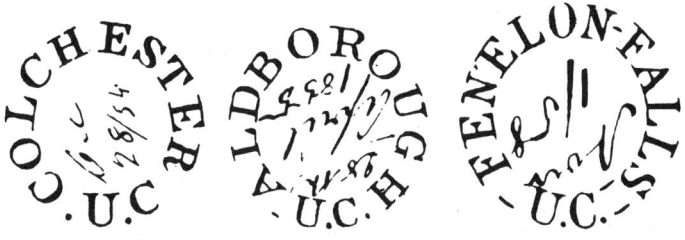

Type IVe   Type IVf

The examples illustrated show how the length of the Post Office name made it necessary to adjust the curved lines.

Type	Diameter in mm.	Letters	Year Date	Known used in	Notes
IVa	23	serifed solid	—	1830	Date in manuscript
IVb	25	”	—	1839	Date in manuscript
IVc	30	”	Yes	1839	Date in ms. is some instances
IVd	30	”	—	1843	Date in manuscript
IVe	27	”	—	1854	Date in manuscript Must be fully 27 mm. in diameter
IVf	30	serifed solid	—	1858	Letters 5 mm. high

The Sans-serif Letter Group.

The sans-serif letter group. Types IVg to m have the lettering in thin sans-serif type.

Type IVg
Date may be in full,
or abbreviated.

Type IVh

571 *

Type IVj   Type IVl

Type	Diameter in mm.	Letters	Known used in
IVg	23-24	Type set date	1845
IVh	23-24	Manuscript date	1847
IVj	25-26	Type set date	1848
IVk	25-26	Manuscript date	1856
IVl	20-22	Type set date	1859
IVm	20-22	Manuscript date	1861

Division c. Special Types.

We have noted some unusual types which we illustrate herewith. They are either locally made or types that were used exclusively by one office.

1851 Red; Black    1859    1859 Red

1856    1867

Type IIIa
Also Dunnville

Type IIIb

Type IIIc
Noted also from Bayham
U. C. 1835

572*

Type IIId
Clearville '53
Canboro '59
York '53

This does not appear to be a copy of any type. It is possible that the Postmaster had this made pending the receipt of the postmark from the Department. This office was not in existence in 1851.

The examples illustrated herewith are undoubtedly attempts to replace stamps lost or damaged, and were made in the town served by the particular Post Office named thereon.

Division d. The Duplex Markings.

These were introduced in May 1860, being supplied by Berri[1]. They are usually 21 mm. in diameter, and the obliterator has 13 bars. However the town mark varies from 20 to 22 mm. and the obliterators vary from 12 to 14 bars.

Type a.
Without
"AM" or "PM"

Type b.
With
"AM" or "PM"

These have been noted from nineteen offces viz.:

Type			Type		
b	Barrie	'60	a	Hamilton	'62
b	Belleville	'60	a	Kingston	'61
b	Brantford	'65	a	London	'61
b	Brockville	'60	a	Montreal	'60
b	Chatham	'62	b	Ottawa	'60
b	Cobourg	'60	b	Peterboro	'60
b	Dundas	'61	b	Port Hope	'60
b	Galt	'65	b	St. Catherines	'60
b	Goderich	'64	b	Simcoe	'61
b	Guelph	'60	b	Three Rivers	'63

The dates are the earliest noted from the respective office. We have not seen Brockville, but it apparently was ordered, and we therefore list it.

Slightly different types were used in Quebec and Toronto.

---

1. See Appendix C #98, and Appendix E #14.

	Diameter	Bars	Notes
Toronto	20 mm.	10 broken	
Quebec	20 mm.	8	With outer circle.

The illustrations show the earliest noted dates.

PROVINCIAL POST OFFICE CANCELLATIONS

We give herewith a list of the Provincial Post Offices we know to have had Postmarks together with the Type noted, and date, where possible. The figures in brackets give the population in 1851. (See also pages 563-567).

The figures "30", "59", "67" etc. indicate the year 1830, 1859, or 1867 etc. in which the particular type of cancellation has been noted. "X" indicates this town and type has been seen but date not noted, or not clear enough to be certain.

Types I, II, and III

Ashton Station, Q. Type Ij, '67
Belleville (4000) Type Ia, X IIc, '57.
Barrie (750) Type IIb, '57
Berlin (750) Type Ic, X
Bentinck Type Ig, '59
Boynton, Q. Type Il, '67
Blairton, O. Type Il, '67
Brantford Type Ie, '57
Caledon (800) Type IIId, '44
Chambly Basin Type Id, '64
Chatham (3200) Type Ic, X (Formerly Raleigh)
Clarenceville Type IIId, '61
Clifton Type Ig, '59
Cobourg (4000) Type Ie, '59; Type Ij, '58; Type IIe, '58
Coldwater (120) Type IIId, '39
Green Bay Type Il, '67
Grantley, Q. Type Il, '67
Haldimand Types IIIc, IIId, '47
Hamilton (10312) Types Ib, '35;
Ingersoll Type Ig, '57
Kingston (1300) Type Il, '67
La Chute Type IIId, '40
Leith, Ont. Type Il, '67
Lloydtown (400) Type IIId, '47
Lobo, Ont. Type Il, '67
London (6000) Types Ig, '57; IIb, '58; IIc, '58
Montreal (50,000) Types Ia, '32; Ie, '57; Il, '64; IIIa, ?; IIId, '41
North Station Mills, Q. Type Il '67
Oro Type IIId, '59
Ottawa (Formerly By Town) (8000) Type Ie, '58
Owen Sound (800) (Formerly

Sydenham—1856) Types Ie, '56; Ig, '62; IIa, '56
Port Hope (2500) Types Ie, '57; IId, '59
Port Robinson (400) Type IIId, '46
Prescott (2400) Type IIId, '42
Quebec (40,000) Types Ie, '56; Ig, '59; Ih, '58; Ik, 64; Il, '57; IIc, '62; IId, '57
Repentigny (900) Type IIId, '60
Riviere du Loup En Bas (2500) Type IIId, '48
St. George (150) Type IIId, '44
St. Hyacinthe (3000) Type Ie, '57
St. John's (2500) Type Ic, '42
St. Leonard, Q. Type Il, '67
St. Thomas (1050) Type Ie, X
St. Wenceslas Type Il, '67
Simcoe (1600) Type Ig, X
Stanley Mills Type IIId, '46
Stouffeville Types IIId, '46
Stottville Type IIIe, '61
Stratford (300) Type Ig, '57
Stukely Type IIId, '61
Thorold (1000) Type IIe, X
Three Rivers (4000) Types Ic, '56; IIb, '59; IId, '59
Toronto (30,000) Types Id, '55; Ie, '58; If, '56; IIc, '58; IIId, '37
Vienna (800) Type IIId, '45
Wardsville Types Ie, X; Ig, '58
Wellington (500) Type IIId, '46
Whitby (1100) Types Ie, X; Ig, '58; IIc, '61; IIe, X
Windsor Types Ig, '58; IIc, X
Yonge Type IIId, '47
York (Became Toronto 1834) Type Ic, '33; IIIb, '33

Type IV

Adolphus Town Type IVa, '39
Aldborough Type IVd, '55
Alnwick Type IVg-h, X
Amherstburg (1300) Type IVc, '39
Amiens Type IVc, '39
Assomption (See St. Assomption)
Aylmer-Ottawa[1] (1000) Type IVj-k, '58
Barrie (750) Type IVc, '39
Belleville (4000) Types IVc, '39; IVg-h, X.
Bells Corners Nepean[2] Type IVj-k, '64
Berlin (750) Type IVg-h, '59
Birmingham Type IVg-h, X
Bobcaygeon Types IVg-h, X; IVl-m, '64
Botany Type IVl-m, '67
Bowmanville (1500) Type IVg-h, '56.
Bradford (600) Types IVc, '39; IVj-k, '52
Brantford (4000) Types IVc, '39; IVl-m, '59
Bridgeworth Type IVg-h, X
Brighton (700) Type IVg-h, '51
Brock Type IVc, '39
Brockville (300) Type IVg-h, '55
Burlington Type IVc, '39
By Town (8000)[3] Type IVc, '30
Carillon Type IVj-k, '52
Chatham (2700) (Formerly Raleigh) Type IVg-h, X
Chippewa (1200) Type IVc, '39
Clifton[4] Type IVj-k, '52
Clinton Type IVl-m, X
Cobden Type IVg-h, '62
Coburg (4000) Types IVa, '38; IVc, '39
Colchester Type IVd, '54
Comber Type IVg-h, X
Cornwall (1500) Types IVa, '38; IVc, '39
Darlington Type IVc, '39
Delaware Type IVc, '39
Douglas Type IVg-h, '59
Dundas (2500) Types IVc, 39; IVg-h, X
Dunham Type IVj-k, '64
Embrun Type IVl-m, '64
Eugenia Type IVl-m, X
Euphrasia Type IVg-h, '50
Farmersville (220) Type IVg-h, '62
Farnham East Type IVc, '39
Fenelon Falls Types IVd, '58; IVf, '58
Fitzroy Harbor Type IVj-k, '64

Fort Williams, Lake Superior, Type IVg-h, X
Frankford (450) (Later Manchester) Type IVg-h, P51
Franktown (100) Type IVj-k, '64
Galt (2000)[5] Type IVg-h, '54
Gananoque (800) Types IVa, '41; IVc, '39; IVg-h, '64
Georgina Type IVg-h, X
Georgeville Type IVa, '45
Goderich (1200) Type IVc, '39
Granby (1300) Type IVj-k, '61
Greenock Type IVg-h, X
Grenville (250) Type IVc, '39
Griffith Type IVl-m, '61
Guelph (1800) Type IVc, '39
Hamilton (10312) Types IVg-h, X; IVj-k, '47
Hatley Type IVa, '48
Holland Landing (350) Type IVc, '39
Howard Type IVc, '39
Hull Type IVj-k, '63
Ingersoll Types IVg-h, '56; IVl-m, X
Kemptville (1000) Type IVg-h, '52
Kincardine Type IVy-r, X
King Type IVg-h, '61
Kingston (13000) Types IVc, '39; IVl-m, '58
Knowlton Type IVl-m, '67
Lanark (300) Type IVo, '40
La Prairie (1684) Type IVc, '39
Lindsay (550) Type IVl-m, '65
London (6000) Types IVc, '39; IVg-h, '60; IVl-m, '59
Longueil (4500) Type IVg-h, X
L'Original (650) Type IVc, '39
Mallorytown Type IVl-m, '62
Manitowaning Lake Huron Type IVg-h, '64
Manotick Type IVl-m, '65
Marmora (200) Type IVc, '39
Maxwell Type IVl-m, '66
McDonald's Corners Type IVl-m, '69
Merritsville (250) Type IVj-k, '58
Mill Creek (250) Type IVg-h, X
Mill Pond Type IVg-h, X
Minden Type IVl-m, '64
Montebello Type IVg-h, X
Montreal (50,000) Types IVc, '39; IVg-h, '51; IVl-m, '61
Morrisburg Type IVg-h, '56
Napanee (1000) Type IVc, '39
Newboro (300) Type IVg-h, '60
New Hamburg Type IVg-h, '59
Newmarket Type IVc, '39

Niagara (3000) Types IVc, '39;
IVg-h, '61; IVj-k, '47
Norwich (450) Type IVj-k, '60
Norwood Type IVg-h, '51
Oakville (700) Type IVj-k, '56
Odessa Type IVg-h, X
Ottawa (Formerly By Town q.v.)
Types IVe, X; IVg-h, '61; IVl-m, '58
Oxford[7] Type IVa, '37
Pakenham (250) Type IVj-k, '57
Paris D.P.O. (1800) Type IVl-m, '60
Paris Station (1800) Type IVl-m, '63
Pembroke Type IVg-h, '68
Pepperlaw Type IVg-h, X
Penetanguishene Type IVd, '65 ;
Percy (350) Type IVg-h, '51
Perth (2000) Types IVc, '39; IVg-h, '59; IVl-m, '58
Peterboro (2000) Types IVc, '39; IVg-h, X
Petite Nation Types IVb, '39; IVg-h, X; IVj-k, '53
Picton (1600) Types IVc, '39; IVg-h, X
Port Hope Type IVc, '39
Portland (150) Type IVg-h, X
Port Neuf Type IVc, '39
Port Robinson (400) Type IVl-m, '67
Port Sarnia (800) Type IVc, '39
Port Stanley Type IVg-h, X
Prescott (2400) Types IVg-h, '59; IVl-m, X
Quebec (40,000) Types IVc, '39; IVl-m, '59
Queenston (400) Type IVc, '39
Raleigh[8] Type IVc, '39
Renfrew Types IVg-h, '65; IVj-k, '53
Richmond Hill Types IVg-h, '59; IVj-k, '64
Rondeau Type IVg-h, '64
River Trent (1000) Type IVa, '42
Russell Type IVl-m, '64
St. Assomption[9] Types IVa, '30; IVg-h, X
St. Agathe Type IVg-h, X

St. Angelique Type IVg-h, X
St. Catharines (4000) Types IVc, '39; IVl-m, '67
St. Denis-Richeleu[10] Type IVj-k, '53
St. Hilaire (1000) Type IVg-h, X
St. Hyacinthe (3000) Type IVg-h, '51
St. Thomas (1050) Type IVc, '39
St. Vincent (2900) Type IVc, '39
Sandwich Type IVc, '39
Sarnia Type IVl-m, '62
Saugeen Type IVg-h, '54
Seymour East (150) Type IVg-h, X
Shannonville (300) Type IVg-h, X
Sterling Type IVg-h, 55
Stoney Creek Type IVj-k, '65
Stratford (300) Type IVl-m, '65
Strathroy (100) Type IVg-h, X
Streetsville (1000) Type IVj-k, '62
Suspension Bridge (Formerly Clifton) Types IVg-h, '54; IVj-k, X
Tamworth (125) Type IVg-h, X
Three Rivers (4,000) Type IVc, '39
Toronto (30,000) (Formerly York) Types IVc, '39; IVg-h, X; IVj-k, '50; IVl-m, '58
Trenton Type IVg-h, '57
Verchères (2800) Type IVc, '39
Victoria (300) Type IVa, '48
Warsaw (100) Types IVg-h, '61; IVj-k, '61
Waterdown Type IVg-h, '58
Waterloo (2500) Types IVg-h, '66; IVj-k, '48
West Arran Type IVl-m, '58
West Flamborough Type IVd, '43
White Lake Type IVg-h, X
Whittington Type IVl-m, '62
Williamstown (400) Type IVj-k, '61
Windsor Type IVg-h, X
Woodstock Types IVc, '39; IVg-h, X; IVl-m, '64
Woolwich Type IVc, '39

NOTES

1. Or Aylmer, East, as distinguished from Aylmer, Middlesex, or Aylmer, West.
2. Carleton County, as distinguished from Bell's Corners, Huron County.
3. Became Ottawa in 1854, q.v.
4. Became Suspension Bridge in 1854, q.v.
5. Was known as Shade's Mill until 1827.
6. Became Welland in 1858.
7. Became Woodstock in 1851, q.v.
8. Became Chatham in 1851 or earlier, q.v.
9. Error for L'Assomption. P. M. cut "St." out so that later impressions read simply "Assomption".
10. As distinguished from St. Denis de la Bouteillerie.

Valuations

The determination of the valuations of the various types is rather difficult and depends on a number of factors such as the volume of mail likely from a post office, (usually closely connected with the population), the length of time a particular type was in use, etc. For instance the Type II markings are generally scarce, (and we believe proved impractical), and were soon replaced by the other types, particularly Type IV. Otherwise the smaller post offices are usually scarcer than the cities. If Montreal, Quebec, and Toronto be considered as having a factor of 1, then Cobourg and Belleville should have a factor of 10, Port Robinson 100, and Coldwater 350.

Notes on Colored Postmarks.

Reference to Appendix B #3, 4, shows that Paid letters were to have rate marked in red, while unpaid were to be rated in black. However, as far as we have observed there was no specific ruling concerning the color used for the postmarks or obliterators. Black is used but red, blue, and green are quite frequent.

The one regulation insisted upon was that postmarks and other cancelling stamps should be frequently cleaned with soap and water so as to give a clear impression. The use of ordinary ink for postmarks and obliterators was never permitted, and many postmasters were reprimanded for infringing this rule. This, of course, did not apply to the authorized pen and ink obliteration of postage stamps.

Specifically the following colors have been noted:

Black, blue black, red, brown red, brick red, orange red, carmine, pink, brown, red brown, black brown, gray brown, bronze brown, orange brown, chocolate, blue, gray blue, ultramarine, green, blue green, gray green, orange, brown orange, purple, magenta.

We are of the opinion that this is much too lengthy. The ink of the period of stampless covers (That is up to 1875) was not chemically as stable as the modern inks. Furthermore postmasters were not very careful as to cleaning their cancelling devices. The ink itself may have became foul, etc. These as well as others factors would tend to affect the color of the postmark as it appears on various covers. One of the commonest errors is the classification of a cancellation as "green" when it is merely blue struck on a yellow envelope!

We therefore limit our colors as follows: (Listed in order of scarcity).

BLACK—Including blue black, black brown, gray brown, chocolate, gray green.
RED—Including brown red, brick red, orange red, red brown, orange brown, brown, carmine, pink, orange, brown orange. *(R)*
BLUE—Including gray blue, ultramarine. *(B)*
GREEN—Including blue green, bronze brown. *(G)*
PURPLE—Including magenta. *(P)*

Post Offices Known to Have Used Colored Postmarks Between 1800 and 1870, Other Than Black. (Numerals 55, 62 etc. Indicate Year 1855, 1862, etc.)

	R	B	G	P		R	B	G	P
Adelaide	52				Brockton	60			
Amherstburg C. W.		63			Brougham			67	
Beaverton C. W.	68			55	Claremont		62		
Belleville C. W.		53			Conway			59	
Belmont	61				Dereham		65		
Berlin C. W.		54			Drummondville				55
Brantford				53	Fingel	52			

577

	R	B	G	P		R	B	G	P
Fort William		65			Pepperlaw				54
Glen Allan		66			Picton C. W.			62	
Hamilton C. W.		43			Port Hope C. W.		62	64	
Hemmingford		62			Quebec C. E.	61			
Kingston C. W.	31				Ruthven			63	
Lake Superior					St. Catherines C. W.	60			
Lindsay C. W.			55		Sandwich C. W.				54
Lucknow		66			Sarnia		42		
Madoc		64	66		Sault Ste Marie			65	
Markham		61			Sharon			62	
Manchester		59			Seaforth				66
Minden	65				South Monaghan		62		
Montreal C. E.	35				Straffordville				65
Marmora, C. W.	66				Streetsville C. W.			67	
Montebello		62			Tamworth	55			
Niagara C. W.	30				Vankleekhill			63	
Norwich C. W.			60		Wellington C. W.		46		
Norwood C. W.		67			Whitby C. W.		57		
Oakland		66			Whitfield			60	
Orangeville		64			Wroxeter				62
Oxbridge		60			Yorkville C. W.			63	65
Pembroke C. W.		52	63						

Class 2—Railway Postmarks.

This extensive group is treated in chapter XXXVII.

Class 3—Steamboat Postmarks.

A smaller group but neverless important. See chapter XXXVIII.

Class 4—Regulation Marks

Division a. Late Fee or Supplementary Mail.

A very careful search has failed to reveal any reference in the Post Office Department records to this regulation stamp. As, however, it has been seen only on the 6d. postage stamp, the current rate to the United States, the explanation for its use is probably as follows:—

The mail bags for the United States were made up, closed and sealed at a certain hour in the Montreal, Toronto, Quebec and other offices. If letters were received for despatch after the time so fixed a "Late Fee" was charged and a supplementary bag was arranged for to be sent forward with the regular mail of the day.

The illustration shows the only type that has been located. It is from a cover dated March, 1854. *"Late Fee" well centered on a 6d. stamp is a rarity.*

Type	Date		Black
			Black
I	1854	6d Laid	Very rare.
I	1855	6d Wove	Rare.

Division b. Too Late[1].

TOO LATE   TOO LATE   *TooLate*
  Type 1   Type 2   Type 3

Too Late   TOO LATE   TOO LATE
  Type 4   Type 5   Type 6

TOO-LATE
Type 7

Type	Date		Color	Post Office
1	May 1839	2.00	black	Toronto
		3.00	red	Toronto
2	Nov. 1840	R	black	Niagara
		2.50	blue	Toronto
3	May 1841	1.00	red	Toronto
		2.00	black	Toronto
4	Mar. 1853	3.00	black	Berlin, now Kitchener
5	Nov. 1859	1.00	red	?
		2.00	black	?
6	Sept. 1864	3.00	black	Beaverton
7	Apr. 1868	.50	black	General use.

    Types 3 and 5 are common, and Type 7 very common but any struck on a postage stamp is rare. 2c and 3c Small Queen have been noted with type 3, in black and blue respectively.
    These continued in use for many years, and in May 1892 Pritchard and Andrews the contractors supplied an additional 50 markings of Type 7.

Division c. Way or Way Letter[2].

There were two kinds of way letters:
    (a). Those handed to a mail courier on his route to a post office, and
    (b). Those delivered by the courier at the request of the postmaster to individuals along the route from one post office to another[3].
The system was particularly prevalent in the Maritime Provinces.

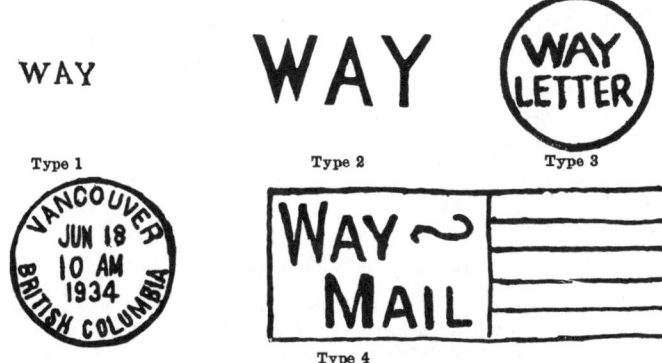

1. Appendix B #7, 12 and 23, P. 21 for definition of "Too Late" letters.
2. Appendix B #1.
3. Appendix B #23, R #85.

Type	Date		Color		
1	1797 May	....	black	Vercheres	V. Rare
2	1859 May	....	black		5.00
3	1868	....	black		2.00
4		....	black	Vancouver	

Division d.

"Not Called For", "Advertised", "Advertised and Not Called For".

The correspondence and regulations of the Department contain many references to the advertising of letters not called for. The advertisements appeared either in the post office lobby, or in the local or nearest newspaper. Prior to the handstamps the Postmaster would write "Advertised and Not Called For" and name of Post Office. All these regulation stamps are quite rare.

ADVERTISED & NOT CALLED FOR

Type 1. Toronto 1853   Type 2. Montreal 1860   Type 3. Montreal 1860

ADV.   ADVERTISED

Type 4. Quebec 1862   Type 5. 1867

ADV.⁼ NOT CALLED FOR

Type 6. 1864

ADVERTISED &

NOT CALLED FOR   NOT CALLED FOR

Type 7. Picton 1864   Type 8. Windsor 1867

1 — Toronto, ..., 1853.
2 — Montreal, Sept. 15, 1860.
3 — Montreal, Sept. 15, 1860.
4 — Quebec, Sept. 3, 1862.
5 — Montreal, June 8, 1864.
6 — Picton, Oct. 1, 1864.
7 — Montreal, Mar. 6, 1867.
8 — Windsor, March 9, 1867.

Division e. Forwarded.

Nine types of these are illustrated. The P. O. Department records respecting their use, shows they were furnished to the various Post Offices[1]. These stamps were used when a letter addressed to a certain office was sent or forwarded to another office that was known or surmised to be the present address of the person to whom the letter was directed. All in black unless otherwise noted.

---
1. Appendix B #7.

FORWARDED
Type 1. April 1843

FORWARDED
Type 2. Frankford 1848
(Green)

FORWARDED
Type 3. Peterboro 1865

[FORWARDED]
Type 4. 1837

FORWARDED
Type 5. Toronto 1857

FORWARDED
Type 6.

FORWARDED
Type 7.

FORWARDED
Type 8. Sandwich 1856

FORWARDED
Type 9. Prescott 1842

1 Used April 15, 1843.
2 Frankford, June 15, 1848 (green)
3 Peterboro, June 26, 1865.
4 Used Sept. 1837.
5 Toronto, Sept. 2, 1859.
6 Used March, 1857.
7 Used March, 1867.
8 Sandwich, Sept. 3, 1856.
9 Prescott, March 30, 1842.

Very few covers have been noted carrying this regulation stamp.

Division f. "Missent" and "Missent To".

MISSENT
1859

MISSENT-TO
London 1857

MISSENT-TO
1863

The following is an extract from a letter sent by the P. O. Department to the postmaster at Huntingdon L. C., May 21, 1830:

"When letters arrive at your office missent by accident as sometimes happens. You will mark them "MISSENT TO" (here insert the name of your office) and you will have them put in a mail and addressed to the office where they should have been sent originally."[1]

Some of the larger offices were supplied with hand stamps for this purpose but ordinarily the words "Missent To" were written on the envelope.

1. See Appendix B #2, R5; #7, #10, P4, etc.

Three types are illustrated. The earliest dates of these are:
1 Used in 1859.
2 London, Aug. 25, 1857.
3 Ontario U. C., Nov. 17, 1865.

They are all quite rare.

Class 5—Obliterations

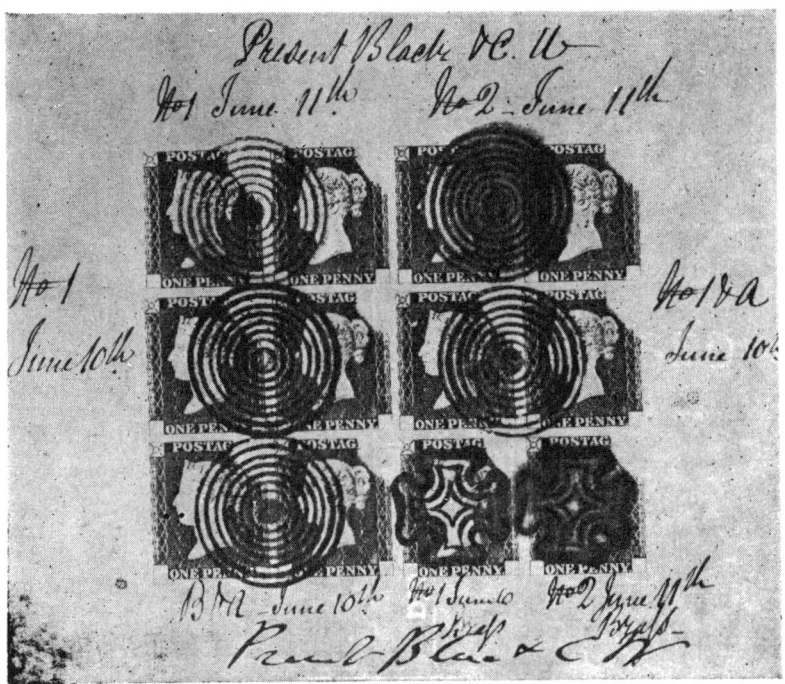

This is a proof impression of 1d stamps of Great Britain with various obliterations tried by the authorities. There is a distinct family resemblance between the concentric rings on this proof and those made in London in 1850-51 for the Canada Post Office.

A. The Concentric Ring Obliterations

This type was the first obliteration introduced for use by the authority of the Post Office Department. First used in April 1851, they show great variations, as they were cut individually, and later orders for these types did not correspond with the originals.

The seven types illustrated below are characteristic. They were usually struck in black (B), but are also known in blue (Bl), red (R) green (G), carmine or pink (C), and purple or violet (V).

We are doubtful of brown, which may be faded black, or due to some other cause; ultramarine, which may be a faded blue; orange, which may be a faded or oxidized red, etc.

TYPE 1—SEVEN RINGS

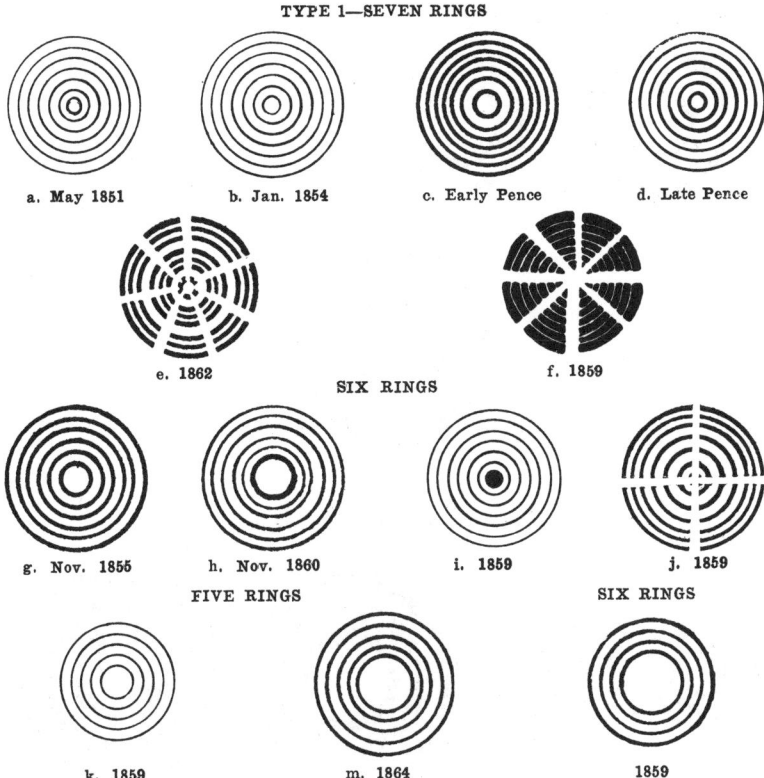

These types of obliterations continued in use in a number of small offices for many years and may be found as late as 1930. Generally speaking, however, their use was pretty well discontinued by the early years of the 20th century. Type 1f may be found cut into four, six, seven or eight segments.

The order of rarity is as follows, beginning with the commonest: 1a, b, c, d, 2b, c, a, 3a, 1f, 2d, 1e, 4, 3b.

Types 1a, b, c, and 2a are probably by Francis.
Types 1d, 2b, c, 3a, by Berri.
Types 3b, and 4 by Ellis.
Types 1e, f, and 2d are variations of their groups, and were probably made by the local office.

THE LATER RING OBLITERATORS

Type 2. Obliterators Consisting of a Single Ring

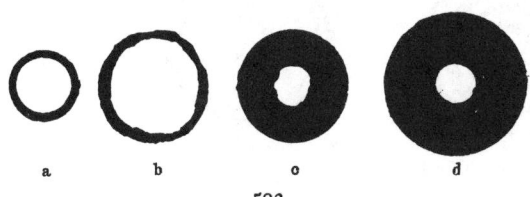

Type 3. Two Ring Obliterators

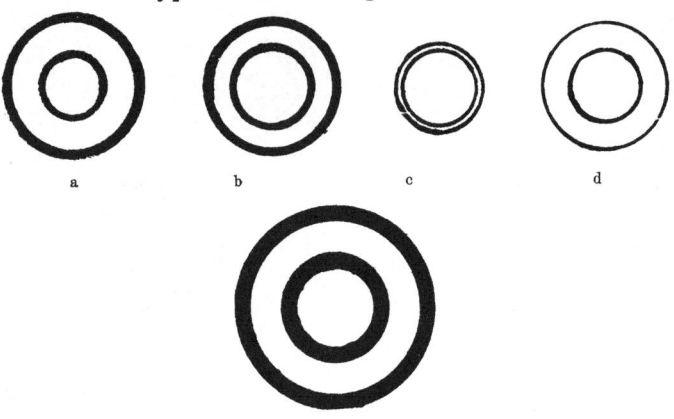

Type 4. Three Ring Obliterators

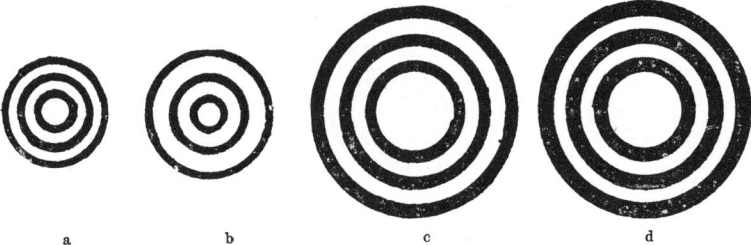

Type 5. Four Ring Obliterators

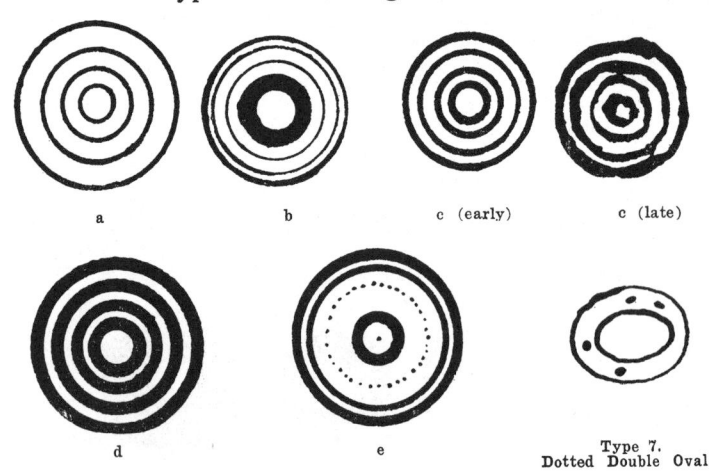

Type 7.
Dotted Double Oval

Types 5Ca and 5Cb are two states of practically the same cancel although noted from different offices.

Type 5E has all the earmarks of a patent scarifying cancel, the dotted circle being the edges of knives which were supposed to cut into the stamp.

Small
Type 2a

Medium
Type 2b

Large
Type 2b

Type 4b

Type 7. Six Rings

Various Markings.

Type 3.
(Page 579)

Type 5.
(Page 579)

A Halifax "Killer".

Some Miscellaneous Markings

Used in Offices which have been damaged by fire, flood, etc.

Used on letters which have been paid through to destination. A U. S. Marking.

Table of Factors   Concentric Ring Cancellations—1851-1900.

Type	COLOR	PENCE ISSUES ½d	3d	6d	7½d	10d	1859 ISSUES 1c	2c	5c	10c	12½c	17c	Large Cents Issue—1868 ½c	1c Red	1c Yellow
1a	Black	1	1	1	1	1	1	1	1	1	1	1	1	1¼	1½
to	Red		2	x			2		4	2¼	3	1½	2		
1c	Blue	1¼	1½	x	x	x	1½	x	1½	1¾	2		1¼		
	Green	1½	3	x	x		2½		1¼	3¼			2		2
2a	Blue								3						
2b	Black														
2c	Black														
2d	Black														
3a	Violet														
3b	Black														
3c	Black, Violet														
3d	Black														
3e	Black														

Table of Factors — Concentric Ring Cancellations—1851-1900. (Cont.)

Type	LARGE CENTS ISSUE—1868 (Cont.)						SMALL CENTS ISSUE—1870-97							NOTES
	2c	3c	5c	6c	12½c	15c	½c	1c	2c	3c	5c	6c	10c	2c Reg.	
1a	1	1	1	1¼			1½	2	1½	1	1		1	1½	
to		2						3	4	9					Known on nearly all the later issues up to 1830.
1e		1¼	1¼	1½	1			5	3	3	1½				
		2¼		2		2		10		25	2				

The Later Types

Type	2c	3c	5c	6c	12½c	15c	½c	1c	2c	3c	5c	6c	10c	2c Reg.	NOTES
2a															
2b								4		7					Used in P. E. I.
2c								4	3	5					Coburg
2d									3½	6					Nanaimo 1886
3a								5	5	7					
3b										5					May 1880.
3c										12/V20					
3d								6		8					
3e															Varies somewhat in diameter.

Table of Factors — Concentric Ring Cancellations—1851-1900. Later Types. (Cont).

Type	Color	PENCE ISSUES 3d	1859 ISSUES 5c	LARGE CENTS ISSUE—1868 2c	LARGE CENTS ISSUE—1868 3c	SMALL CENTS ISSUE—1870-97 ½c	1c	2c	3c	5c	6c	10c	NOTES
4a	Blue		1½										
4b	Black						7		9				
4c	Black				2*								
4d	Black				2								
5a	Black								12				
5b	Black						8		18				
5c	Black								18				
5d	Black						12						
5e	Black						14		22				Scarifying Cancel
6a	Black						8		14				Appeared in 1877.
7	Black			2			4				Blx Rx		Dotted Double Oval

B. Target Cancellations.

Target cancellations are concentric ring cancellations characterized by a center of solid color.

TYPE 1. BULL'S EYE AND ONE CIRCLE.

A   B

TYPE 2. BULL'S EYE AND TWO CIRCLES.

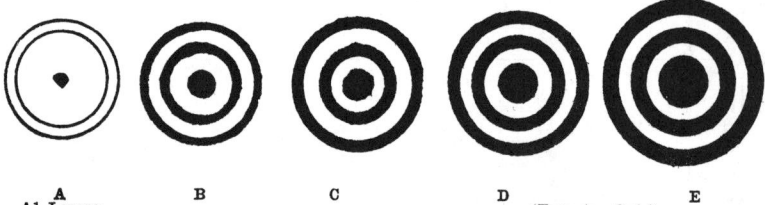

A
A1 Larger Bull's Eye

B   C   D (Toronto, Ont.)   E

Types 2b to e are comparatively common.

TYPE 3. BULL'S EYE AND THREE CIRCLES.

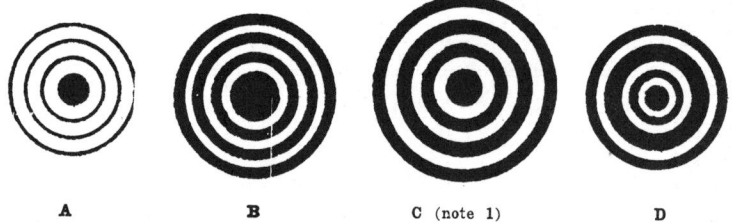

A   B   C (note 1)   D

TYPE 4. BULL'S EYE AND SIX CIRCLES.

TYPE 5. BULL'S EYE AND EIGHT CIRCLES

---

1. Note: Two of these were supplied by Pritchard and Mingard in April 1876.

Table of Factors

Target Cancellations—1868-97.

Type	COLOR	½d	PENCE ISSUES 3d	6d	7½d	10d	1859 ISSUES 1c	2c	5c	10c	12½c	17c	Large Cents Issue—1868 ½c	1c Red	1c Yellow
1a	Black														
1b	Black														
2a	Black														
2b	Black														
2c	Black, Violet														
2d	Black, Violet														
2e	Black, Violet, Carmine or Green								2						
3a	Black														
3b	Black														
3c	Black														
3d	Black							x							
4	Black						1½		1¼	1½	1½	x			
5	Black														

Table of Factors — Target Cancellations—1868-97. (Cont.)

Type	LARGE CENTS ISSUE—1868						SMALL CENTS ISSUE—1870-97								NOTES
	2c	3c	5c	10c	12½c	15c	½c	1c	2c	3c	5c	6c	10c	2c Reg.	
1a		2													
1b								5							
2a		x					5			6					
2b					1½			5	8	6	4	6			Known on many later stamps.
2c		x				3		6	6	8 V12					
2d		x				3		6	6	7 V11	6	5			
2e						2		7		10 V20 C20 G30	5 V10	B1 1½ G3	3	10	Known also on 8c 1893—B1 2, V4
3a								2		10					
3b					1½			1½	1½	5					
3c															2c 1898—7
3d															
4		2													
5															2c 1898—15

C1. Four Ring Numeral Obliterators.
1857-70

On March 1, 1857, a cancelling device consisting of a numeral in four concentric rings was furnished to a number of offices, in alphabetical order. As there were over 1200 offices in Canada in 1857, these numbers were only given to certain money order offices. Toronto being the headquarters at that time was not assigned a number.

The normal cancellation of this type is illustrated herewith. (Probably supplied by Berri).

Some offices had variations which we illustrate. These are listed on the tables as 1a, 10a, etc. These were no doubt locally cut, due to loss or damage of the original canceller.

40a

The last two #516 and #627 were the only ones of their type used, the normal type never having been issued for these numerals. (Probably supplied by Berri).

NOTES: #9 was not issued in order to avoid confusion with #6.

#21 exists in three varieties, viz:
    I—1857—"2" Very thin with straight foot.
    II—December 1857—"2" With curved foot.
    III—December 1859—"2" Thicker than variety I. Straight foot.

#27 exists in two varieties, viz:
    I—"7" is rounded at base.
    II—"7" is square at base.

Table of Factors

Four-Ring Numeral Cancellations—1868-97. #1-17.

#	POST OFFICE	PENCE ISSUES					1859 ISSUES						Large Cents Issue—1868		
		½d	3d	6d	7½d	10d	1c	2c	5c	10c	12½c	17c	½c	1c Red	1c Yellow
1	Barrie, U. C. (a) another type	x	1½	x	x	x	3	1¼	4	1½	x	x			
2	Belleville, U. C.	B	B1½	B			2	B	B2	B1½	B1¾			B	B
3	Berlin, U. C. (Now Kitchener)	x	1½	x	x	x	2½	1¼	3	1½	2	2			
4	Bowmanville, U. C.	x	2	x	x	x	x	x	4	x	x	x		x	x
5	Brantford, U. C.	x Bx	1¼ B1¾	x			2 B2½	x	3 B4½	1½	2				B
6	Brighton, U. C.	x	1½	x	x	x			10			x			
7	Collingwood Harbor	x	2	x	x	x	3		3	2	2½				
8	Chatham, U. C.	x	1½	x	x	x	2½	x	3	2	x	x		x	x
10	Coburg, C. W. (a) another type	x	1¼	x	x		1½	x	1½	1½	2	x		x	x
11	Cornwall, U. C.	x	1¾	x	x	x	2	x	2½	2	x	x			
12	Dundas, U. C.	x	1½	x	x	x	2½	1½	3	2	x	x		3	
13	Galt, U. C. (a) another type	x	1½	x	x	x	2		3	2	x	x			x
14	Goderich, U. C.	x	1¾	x	x	x			3						
15	Guelph, U. C.	x	1¼	x	x	x	2	1¼	2½	1½	2½	x			x
16	Hamilton, U. C.	x	1¼	x	x	x	2	x	2½	1½	1½	x			
17	Ingersoll, U. C. (a) another type	x	1½ R	x	x	x R	2½	x	2½	2	2¼	x			x

Table of Factors   Four-Ring Numeral Cancellations—1868-97. #1-17. (Cont.)

#	LARGE CENTS ISSUE—1868 (Cont.)						SMALL CENTS ISSUE—1870-97							2c Reg.	NOTES
	2c	3c	5c	6c	12½c	15c	½c (1870)	1c	2c	3c	5c	6c	10c		
1		3													
2	B	B3	B		B	B				B2					Also noted for Norwood, U. C.
3															
4	×	3			×			×		×					
5	B	B3													
6															
7		3	×		×										
8	×	6 3	×	×	×										
10															
11							×	×							
12	×	6 2	×	×	×		×	×							
13															
14	×	3	×	×	×					×	×				
15															
16											×				
17	×	3 2½			×						×				

Table of Factors Four-Ring Numeral Cancellations—1855-70. #18-28.

#	POST OFFICE	PENCE ISSUES ½d	3d	6d	7½d	10d	1859 ISSUES 1c	2c	5c	10c	12½c	17c	Large Cents Issue—1868 ½c	1c Red	1c Yellow
18	Kingston, U.C.	x	1¼	x	x	x	2	1¼	4	1¾	x	.1½			
19	London, U.C.	x	1¼	x	x	x	2		6 B12	x B	1¾ B3	1½ B4			x D
20	Melbourne, U.C.	x	1½	x	x	x	3½		7	1¼	2	x		x	x
21	Montreal, L.C.	x	1½	x	x	x	3	x	1¼	1½	x	1¼	x	x	x
	a Another type													x	
22	Napanee, U.C.	x	1¾	x	x	x	4		2	1¼	1¾	1½		x	x
	a Another type														
23	Niagara, U.C.	x	1½	x	x	x	6		7	1¾	2	1½		x	x
24	Oakville, U.C.	x	1½	x	x	x	x		14	1¾	2	x		x	x
	a Another type														
25	Oshawa, U.C.	x	1¾	x	x	x	x		8 R16	1½	2	x		x	
26	Owen Sound, U.C.	x	1½	x	x	x	3		3	1¼	2	1½		x	x
	a Another type														
27	Ottawa, U.C.	x	1¼	x	x	x	3	1¼	7	1	1	x		x	
28	Paris, U.C.					x	6		6	1½	1¾	1½			x

Table of Factors Four-Ring Numeral Cancellations—1855-70. #18-28. (Cont.)

#	LARGE CENTS ISSUE—1868 (Cont.)						SMALL CENTS ISSUE—1870-97							2c Reg.	NOTES
	2c	3c	5c	6c	12½c	15c	½c	1c	2c	3c	5c	6c	10c		
18															
19	x	3 / B4			x										
a		2½													
20		4	x	x			x				x				
21	x	2	x		x						x				Three types.
a		5													
22	x	3			x		x	15		10	x				
a		3													
23	x	3			x										
24	x	3			x										
a		4													
25	x	3					x	10		15					
26		3½				x									Later impressions show wearing of ink pad and appear to be struck through cloth.
a		3													
27	x	3			x			15		15				10	Two types.
28		3½													

Four-Ring Numeral Cancellations—1855-70. #29-40.

#	POST OFFICE	PENCE ISSUES					1859 ISSUES						Large Cents Issue—1868		
		½d	3d	6d	7½d	10d	1c	2c	5c	10c	12½c	17c	½c	1c Red	1c Yellow
29	Perth, U.C.	x	1½	x	x	x	4		2	1¼	1½	1¼			
30	Peterboro, U.C.	x	1¼	x	x,	x	5		2	1	1¾	2		x	
31	Picton, U.C.	x	1½	x	x	x	5		4	2	2	1¼		x	
	a Another type														
32	Port Dover, U.C.	x	1¾	x	x	x	3		10	2¼	2	x		x	
33	Port Hope, U.C.	x	1½	x	x	x	x		4					x	x
34	Port Sarnia, U.C.	x	1½	x	x	x	7		4	1½	2	x			
	a Another type														
35	Prescott, U.C.	x	1½	x	x	x	5		8	1¼	2	x		x	x
36	(Preston, U.C.) ?	x	1¾	x	x	x	x		4	1½	2	1¼		x	x
37	Quebec, L.C.	x	1¼	x	x	x	1¼	1½	2	1¼	1¼	1¼		x	x
38	St. Catherines, U.C.	x	1½	x	x	x	3½	x	14	2	2	2		x	
39	St. Hyacinthe, L.C.	x	1½	x			5		8	2	1¾	x			
	a Another type														
40	St. Thomas, U.C.	x	1½	x			5		14	2½	3	1½			
	a Another type														

Table of Factors   Four-Ring Numeral Cancellations—1855-70. #29-40. (Cont.)

#	LARGE CENTS ISSUE—1868 (Cont.)							SMALL CENTS ISSUE—1870-97						2c Reg.	NOTES
	2c	3c	5c	6c	12½c	15c	½c	1c	2c	3c	5c	6c	10c		
29		3½													
30	x	3			x		x	15		15					Also known on 5c Env. after 1868. The impression is much worn.
31		3½			x										
a		7													
32	x	3					x	15							
33	x	3			x										
34		3													
a						x									
35	x	3		x											
36	x	3	x		x										
37	x	2½			x		x	15		15					
38		3													
39					x										
a		3													
40															
a		3													

Table of Factors   Four-Ring Numeral Cancellations—1855-70. #41-627.

#	POST OFFICE	PENCE ISSUES ½d	3d	6d	7½d	10d	1859 ISSUES 1c	2c	5c	10c	12½c	17c	Large Cents Issue—1868 ½c	1c Red	1c Yellow
41	Sandwich, U.C.	x	1¾	x	x	x	3		14						
42	Sherbrooke, L.C.	x	1½	x	x		5		5	2					
43	Simcoe, U.C.	x	1½	x	x		2½		8	2¼					
44	Smith's Falls, U.C.	x	1¾	x	x	x	5		16	3	3	2		x	x
45	Stanstead, L.C.	x	1¾ B-2				5		10 B	3	2				
46	Stratford, U.C.	x	1½	x	x		3		14	2½	2½	2			
47	Three Rivers, L.C.	x	1½ B	x	x	x	3		2 B4	2	2	2			
48	Thorold, U.C.	x	1¾				3		4	2½	3				
49	Whitby, U.C.	x	1¾	x	x	x	6 B9	1¼ B3	6 B12	2 B3	2 B2½	x B			
50	Windsor, U.C.	x	1½	x	x		3	10	5						
51	Brockville, U.C.	x	1½	x			2½		4	1¾	2	1½			
52	Clifton, U.C.	x	1½	x			4½		10						
516	Montreal, L.C.						x		4					x	x
627	Senate, Ottawa.														x

601 ★

Table of Factors   Four-Ring Numeral Cancellations—1855-70. #41-627. (Cont.)

#	LARGE CENTS ISSUE—1868 (Cont.)						SMALL CENTS ISSUE—1870-97								NOTES
	2c	3c	5c	6c	12½c	15c	½c	1c	2c	3c	5c	6c	10c	2c Reg.	
41										17		×			
42															
43	×	2½													
44				×	×	×		15		15					Also known on 3c 1897-4 leaf.
45		3 B					×	×		15 B		× B			Late 1864 to middle 1865 canc. was in Blue.
46		3		×											
47		3													
48	×	4		×											
49		3						15		15					
50	×	4		×	×										
51	×	6		×	×		×								
52	×	6		×	×					30					
516															
627															

C2. Other Numeral Obliterators of the 1857 Series.

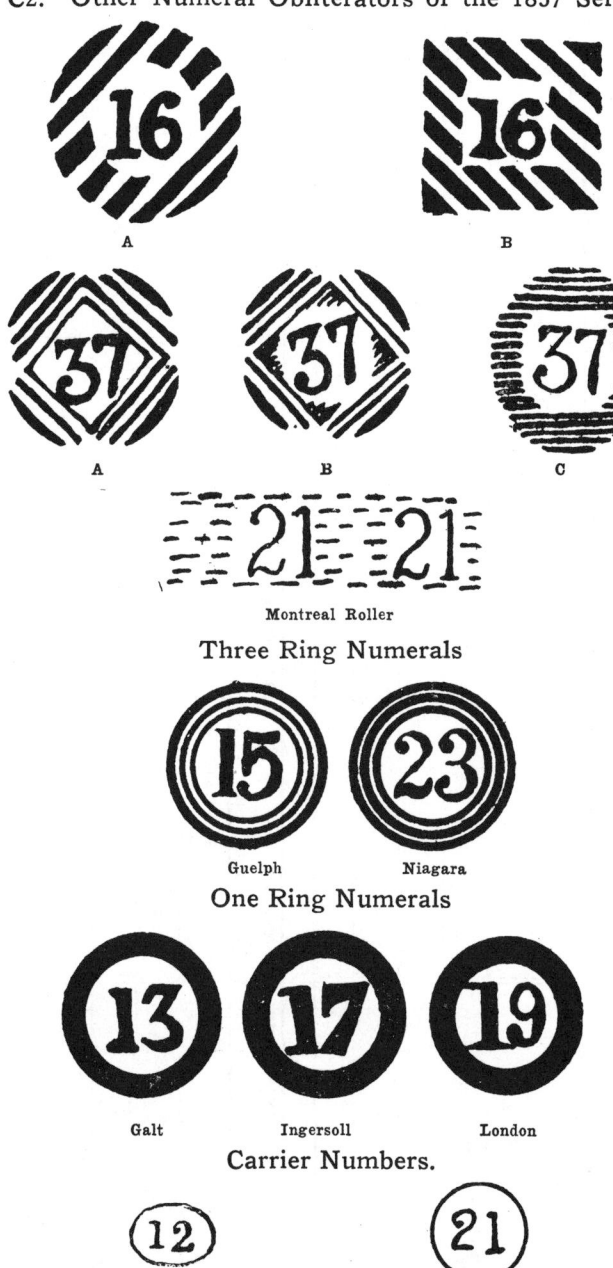

Montreal Roller

Three Ring Numerals

Guelph   Niagara

One Ring Numerals

Galt   Ingersoll   London

Carrier Numbers.

Numerals of this type are carrier's numbers, struck on packets of letters made up for the carriers.

Table of Factors. Other Numeral Cancellations of the 1857 Series.

#	POST OFFICE	PENCE ISSUES ½d	3d	6d	7½d	10d	1859 ISSUES 1c	2c	5c	10c	12½c	17c	Large Cents Issue—1868 ½c	1c Red	1c Yellow
16A	Hamilton	x	2	x			x		4	x					
16B		x	2	x			x		3	x					
21	Montreal (Roller)	x	5	x	x	x	x		5		3				
37A	Quebec						x		3		x			x	
37B							x		3						
37C							x	x	2	x	1½	x			

#	LARGE CENTS ISSUE—1868 (Cont.) 2c	3c	5c	6c	12½c	15c	SMALL CENTS ISSUE—1870-97 ½c	1c	2c	3c	5c	6c	10c	2c Reg.	NOTES
16A															
16B															
21		3						125	30	75		8			
37A	x	3			x										
37B		3													
37C															

Table of Factors   Three Ring Numerals—1868-97.

#	POST OFFICE	½c	1c Red	1c Yellow	2c	3c	5c	6c	12½c	15c	1c	2c	3c	NOTES
					LARGE CENTS ISSUE—1868						SMALL CENTS ISSUE 1870-97			
15	Guelph												8	
23	Niagara				x	3								

One Ring Numeral—1868-97.

13	Galt					2½								
17	Ingersoll			x		3								
19	London		x			3								

D1. Toronto Obliterators.

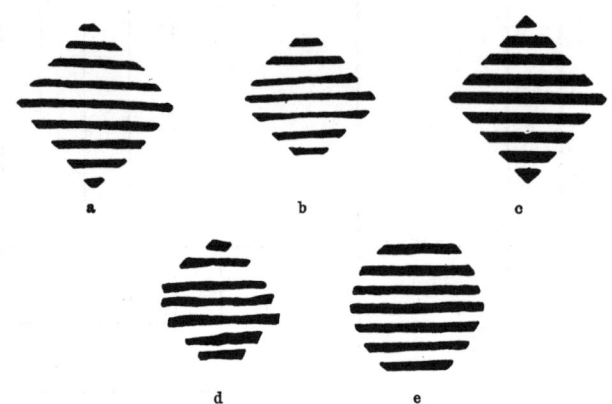

Type	Date	
a	June 1857	On Pence Issue
b	March 1858	,,
c	August 1858	,,
d	August 1858	,,
e	November 1858	,,

Types a and b are scarce, the other types are comparatively rare.

D2. The Toronto Scarifying Obliterators. 1867.

The following types were so constructed that the dots slightly cut or punctured the stamps. They were undoubtedly intended as "SCARIFYING OBLITERATORS"[1]. All are scarce.

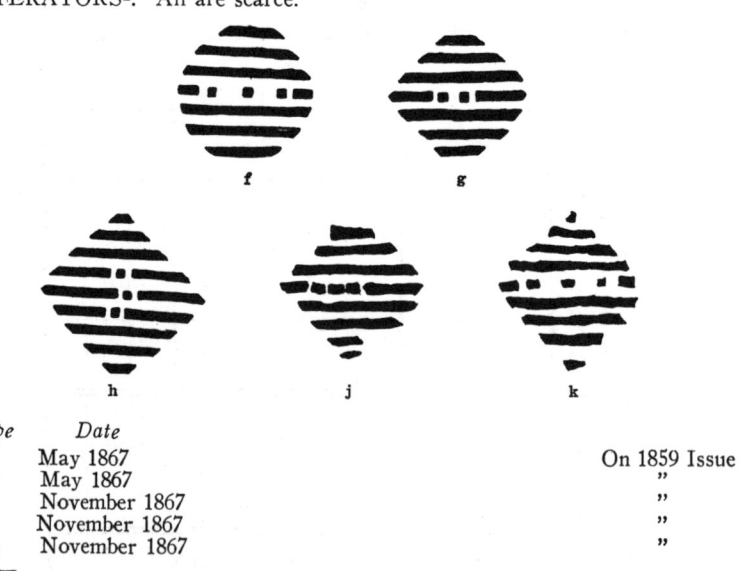

Type	Date	
f	May 1867	On 1859 Issue
g	May 1867	,,
h	November 1867	,,
j	November 1867	,,
k	November 1867	,,

1. Appendix L #42.

E. Seal Obliterators.

ype 1.   Type 2.   Type 3.

All Post Offices were supplied with brass seals which were used to seal mail bags, bundles of letters, reports to the P. O. Department. They were usually impressed in wax. Occasionally however one would be used to cancel stamps. In black.

Type 1. Kingston, U. C. 1860 (?) Very Rare.
Type 2. Niagara, Aug. 1861. Extremely rare.

The "1857" seal however occurs only on postage stamps, and was evidently the expression of a patriotic P. M.'s loyalty to the Queen. 1857 was the 20th anniversary of Queen Victoria's Reign.

Type 3. Black — 1857 — on ½p and 3p.

Most impressions are so blurred as to be indistinguishable. Clear impressions are extremely rare. The Post Office at which this was used is not definitely known to us.

Chapter XXXVI

THE POSTMARKS AND CANCELLATIONS OF THE DOMINION.
1868-1900

Introduction

When the Dominion Post Office began operations, combining into one system the former Provincial Post Offices of Canada, New Brunswick, and Nova Scotia there were more than 3600 post offices in operation. At first the various postmarks and cancelling devices of the former administrations were continued in use, but as new Post Offices were opened and the older markings had to be replaced they were supplied from Headquarters at Ottawa. It would serve no purpose to attempt to list all the various Post Offices supplied, as the type was comparatively uniform[1]. In late nineteenth century the use of cancelling machines began, and advertising and slogan cancellations were introduced. The Flag Types are of interest as well as the various Philatelic Exhibition Cancels, but the slogans are far to numerous to list. As evidence, however, of the volume of markings required we show the quantity of devices supplied in certain years:

	Town Marks			Obliterators	
	(a) without outer circle	(b) with outer circle	(c) with "Killer"	(a) Rubber	(b) Roller
1888	452	111	20	250	—
1893	444	202	45	34	—
1898	515	74	36	2829	32
1903	666	784	—	500	61

By 1905 the volume was sufficient to require several suppliers. In 1909 the various contractors furnished over three thousand five hundred marking devices to the Post Office Department!

Of the various special markings not noted in their respective sections the following quantities were ordered:

Marking	Quantity and Date
Closed Against Inspection	100 in 1880
Forwarded	100 in 1877. Similar to E-Type 2. (Page 583)
Free	25 in 1877
Missent To	375 from 1877 to 1893 in six orders. Similar to F, Type 2, (Page 583).
Not Called For	2250 from 1877 to 1894 in nine orders.
Returned for Better Direction	100 in 1877
Refused	125 - 100 in 1877, and 25 more in 1895.
Return To	500 from 1878 to 1895 in five orders.

---

1. See, however, Chapter XXXIX on the Northwest Territories Post Offices.

Class 5

(See Note Below)

A. The Two-Ring Numeral Obliterators

On April 1, 1868, a new series of numeral obliterators was introduced in accordance with the new arrangements made by the Dominion Post Office Department. These consist of two heavy circles with a numeral in the center and were distributed according to the financial importance of the office, Montreal being 1, Toronto 2, etc. Some of these numerals continued in use until the early years of the 20th century. Probably furnished by Berri.

Note Cuts to Distinguish from #9 Late State of This Number

The occurence of the same numeral from two different post offices is known in several instances. Possibly due to the discontinuance of one as a money order office and the opening of another to which the number was transferred.

NOTE: Chapter heading from a proof of a Bank Note counter by the British American Bank Note Co.

Table of Factors Two-Ring Numeral Cancellations—1868-97. #1-16

#	POST OFFICE	PENCE ISSUES ½d	3d	6d	7½d	10d	1869 ISSUES 1c	2c	5c	10c	12½c	17c	Large Cents Issue—1868 ½c	1c Red	1c Yellow
1	Montreal												x	2	2
2	Toronto												4	2	2
3	Quebec												4	2	1½
4	Halifax												2	2	1½
5	Hamilton												3 V4	1½	1¼
6	London													2½	2½
7	St. John, N.B.												1½	1¾	1¼
8	Ottawa												x		
9	Kingston												x	x	2
10	Sydney, N.S.												x	2½	1¾
11	Fredericton, N.B.												x	2	1¼
12	St. Catharines, W.												x	x	2
13	Belleville, Ont.												x	1¾	1¼
14	Guelph													x	1¼
15	Brantford												x	1¾	1¼
16	Brockville														x

Table of Factors — Two-Ring Numeral Cancellations—1868-97. #1-16 (Cont)

#	LARGE CENTS ISSUE—1868 (Cont.)						SMALL CENTS ISSUE—1870-97								NOTES
	2c	3c	5c	6c	12½c	15c	½c	1c	2c	3c	5c	6c	10c	2c Reg.	
1	1½	2	1½	1½	1½	1¼		3		1½					
2	1½	3½	1½	2	1½	2		1½		1¾					Late state shows circles cut into four segments.
3	1½	3	1½	2	1½	x		1½	x	2					
4	2	4	x	2½	1½	x		1¾		1½					See end of list.
5	1¼ R2½	3		1½	1½			1½	x	2	x				
6	2	3	x	2	1½	x		x		x					Rings broken at base to distinguish from "9."
7	1½	3		1½	1¼	1½		1½		2	3	1½			
8		4		2½	2	2									
9	x	5	x	2	2½			x		x					
10	2½	3		x	2	x		x	5 B6	5 B5		2 B3			
11	1½	2½		1½	1½	1¾		2		1½	1¼	1¼			This has thicker numerals in some cases.
12	2½	2½		3	2¼	1½		5	6	1½					
13	2	2½		2	x	x				5					
14	x	2½						5							
15	2	2½		2½	2	x		x	x	x					
16															

Table of Factors   Two-Ring Numeral Cancellations—1868-97. #17-32.

#	POST OFFICE	PENCE ISSUES ½d	3d	6d	10d	7½d	1859 ISSUES 1c	2c	5c	10c	12½c	17c	Large Cents Issue—1868 ½c	1c Red	1c Yellow
17	St. Hyacinthe												x	x	x
18	Yarmouth, N.S.												x	2	x
19	Peterboro												x	1¾	x
20	Galt may be #20, or #22.														3
21	Goderich												x	x	x
22	Galt may be #20, or #22.														
23	Woodstock												x	x	2
24	Stratford, C.W.												x	x	1½
25	New Glasgow, N.S.												x	2	x
26	Windsor, C.W.												3½	x	x
27	Ingersoll												x	2	x
28	Sarnia												x	x	x
29	Coburg												x	x	x
30	Pictou, N.S.												x	x	2
31	Still remains to be identified														
32	Barrie												x	x	2

Table of Factors — Two-Ring Numeral Cancellations—1868-97. #17-32. (Cont.)

	LARGE CENTS ISSUE—1868 (Cont.)						SMALL CENTS ISSUE—1870-97							2c Reg.	NOTES
#	2c	3c	5c	6c	12½c	15c	½c	1c	2c	3c	5c	6c	10c		
17	x	8		x				x		x					Shelburne is also known with this #.
18	x	3	x	2	1¾			x							Known on 3c Four Leaf of 1897.
19	x	3	x	2½		3½							x		
20	5	7													
21	2	3		2½	x	x			x						Impressions on 3c 1870 are in thicker numerals.
22		3		3				x		x					
23	x	3		2½				x		3	x				
24		3		x				x		x			x		
25		3													
26	x	3		2½		x		x		3					Leamington is known with this # also.
27	2	3		x	x	2½				6					
28	2¼	3	1½	x	x	2½				3					
29	x	3		3	x	x				2½					
30	2¼	3		x	2½	3½				2½		x			Known on 3c Jubilee.
31		9													
32	3	G4		3	x					2½					

Table of Factors   Two-Ring Numeral Cancellations—1868-97.   #33-48.

#	POST OFFICE	PENCE ISSUES ½d	3d	6d	10d	7½d	1859 ISSUES 1c	2c	5c	10c	12½c	17c	Large Cents Issue—1868 ½c	1c Red	1c Yellow
33	Sherbrooke												x	x	2
34	Branchton, U.C.												x	x	
35	Lindsay, C.W.												4	x	
36	St. John's, C.E.												x	x	x
37	Amherst												x	2½	
38	Bowmanville												x	x	x
39	Still remains to be identified.												x	x	2
40	Cornwall												x	x	1½
41	St. Mary's, C.W.													x	1¾
42	Acton Vale														
43	Windsor, N.S.													x	x
44	Owen Sound													x	x
45	Perth													2	1½
46	Dundas													x	x
47	Napanee													x	
48	Simcoe												x	x	1½

Table of Factors. Two-Ring Numeral Cancellations—1868-97. #33-48. (Cont.)

#	LARGE CENTS ISSUE—1868 (Cont.)						SMALL CENTS ISSUE—1870-97							2c Reg.	NOTES
	2c	3c	5c	6c	12½c	15c	½c	1c	2c	3c	5c	6c	10c		
33	2¾	2½		x	x			x		2		x			Known also from Eaton, C.E.
34		7													
35	3	3½		x	2½	x		x		5			x		
36	2½	3	1¾	x	x	x		x		4			x		
37	3	3		x						3½					
38	x	3	x					x		4					
39	3	3		x		x		10		5	x	x	x	x	Known on 3c 1897—Four leaf Also with thinner circles in use in 1897.
40	3	3	x	3		x		x	4	5	x				
41	x	3		2½				x		x					In use in 1897.
42		8													
43	x	4		x				x		6					
44		3½	x	3				x	x	8					
45		3		x				x		3					Known on 3c Four leaf and 3c Numeral; 1897.
46		3		3				x		2½					
47	x	3		2¾	2½			x		3					
48		3						x		2½					

Table of Factors. Two-Ring Numeral Cancellations—1868-97. #49-60, 4.

#	POST OFFICE	PENCE ISSUES ½d	3d	6d	7½d	10d	1859 ISSUES 1c	2c	5c	10c	12½c	17c	Large Cents Issue—1868 ½c	1c Red	1c Yellow
49	Prescott														x
50	St. Andrews, N. B.													x	x
51	Picton													x	x
52	Caledon, U. C.												x	2	1½
53	Three Rivers												x	x	1½
54	Truro, N. S.												x	x	x
55	Berlin, C. W.												x		1¾
56	Brampton, Ont.												x		
57	St. Thomas												x	x	x
58	Aylmer, U. C.												x	x	x
59	Clinton, U. C.														
60	Newmarket												x	x	x
4	Watson's Corners, U. C.														

Table of Factors. Two-Ring Numeral Cancellations—1868-97. #49-60, 4. (Cont.)

#	LARGE CENTS ISSUE—1868					(Cont.)	SMALL CENTS ISSUE—1870-97								NOTES
	2c	3c	5c	6c	12½c	15c	½c	1c	2c	3c	5c	6c	10c	2c Reg.	
49	2½	3								2½					
50	2½	3						x		3					Known on 1, 2, 3c Jubilee and 5c Four leaf.
51		6													
52	x	3		x	2¾			x		2¾					
53	x	3		x				x		3					
54	2½	3		x		x				3¼					
55	x	3		x				x		3					Now known at Kitchener.
56	x	7		x		x		x		3½					
57	3	8		3						4		x			Exists in a very worn state.
58	x	2½						x		3					Also noted for St. Thomas, U. C.
59		5								4					
60	x	6½		x	x			x		6				x	
4								4½	8	5					Numeral is tall and thin.

B1. The Hamilton, London, and Ottawa Obliterators Numerals Five, Six and Eight

Hamilton "5"

Type 1a

Type 1b
After Late 1876

London "6"

Type 1

Type 2

Ottawa "8"

Type 1   Type 2   Type 3   Type 4

Type 5

Type 6 of Ottawa is Similar to Kingston Type 1 but with an "8" in Lozenges.

B2. The Kingston, Fredericton, and Guelph Cancellations—1868-90

Kingston "9"

Type 1  Type 2  Type 3  Type 4

Type 5  Type 6  Type 7  Type 8

Type 9  Type 10  Type 11

Type 12  Type 13

Fredericton "11"

Type 1a—7 Bars
Type 1b—8 Bars

Guelph "14"

Type 1

Table of Factors. The Hamilton Duplex "5" Cancellations—1868-97.

| Type | ½c | 1c Red | 1c Yellow | LARGE CENTS ISSUE—1868 ||||||| ½c | SMALL CENTS ISSUE—1870-97 |||||| 2c Reg. |
				2c	3c	5c	6c	12½c	15c			1c	2c	3c	5c	6c	10c	
1a				x	x		x	x				x		5 B7				
1b (Nov., 1876)												6	4	8	2	8	x	

The London Duplex "6" Cancellations—1868-97.

	½c	1c Red	1c Yellow	2c	3c	5c	6c	12½c	15c		1c	2c	3c	5c	6c	10c	2c Reg.
1			x	x	2		x	x	x		x	x	4	x	x	x	
2			x	x	2		x	x	x		x		5				

The Ottawa "8" Cancellations.

	½c	1c Red	1c Yellow	2c	3c	5c	6c	12½c	15c		1c	2c	3c	5c	6c	10c	2c Reg.
1			x		3		1¾										
2			x	x	3		2						2				
3			x	x	3		2	x	x				2				
4		x	x		3		2	x	x				2				
5		x			3												
6					x												

Guelph "14" Cancellations

	½c	1c Red	1c Yellow	2c	3c	5c	6c	12½c	15c		1c	2c	3c	5c	6c	10c	2c Reg.
1			2		3								3				

Table of Factors.   The Kingston "9" Cancellations—1868-97.

Type	LARGE CENTS ISSUE—1868									SMALL CENTS ISSUE—1870-97							
	½c	1c Red	1c Yellow	2c	3c	5c	6c	12½c	15c	½c	1c	2c	3c	5c	6c	10c	2c Reg.
1																	
2			x		3												
3			x		3												
4			4		3		x										
5			x		3												
6		x		x	3												
7		x	x	x	3		x	x	x		x	x	x				
8		x	x		3		x	x	x		4		4				
9			x	x	3		x	x	x		x		x				
10		x	x		3						x		x				
11					•								4				
12												x	3½				
13		x			3								4				

Fredericton, N. B. "11" Cancellations—1868-97.

		½c	1c Red	1c Yellow	2c	3c	5c	6c	12½c	15c	½c	1c	2c	3c	5c	6c	10c	2c Reg.
1a	7 bars			x		2		x	x	x		x						
1b	8 bars					2½		x	x			2		4			3	

C. THE TORONTO "2" CANCELLATIONS—1868-90

These were locally made but include the "2" numeral assigned by the P. O. Department. See Page 611.

Table of Factors.   The Toronto "2" Cancellations—1868-97.   All in Black.

Type	½c	1c Red	1c Yellow	2c	LARGE CENTS ISSUE—1868 3c	5c	6c	12½c	15c	SMALL CENTS ISSUE 1870-97 ½c	1c	2c	3c	5c	6c	10c	2c Reg.
1		x	x		3				1¼								
2		x	x		3												
3					3												
4		x	x		3												
5			x		3												
6		x	x		3												
7			x		3												
8			x		3												
9			x		3												
10			x		3												
11			x		3												
12		x	x		3												
13											5		3				
14											3		2				
15					8												
16					8												

D. The Duplex (or "Killer") Cancellations

The problem of cancelling the stamp and postmarking the letter clearly was one constantly engaging the attention of the Postal Officials. In the beginning it was easy enough to strike the town mark twice, once on the stamp and once on the cover. Frequently the town mark was struck on the cover, and a separate obliterator was used to cancel the stamp.

The increasing volume of mail, and the necessity for speeding up the handling of this volume resulted in the introduction of the Duplex marking. This included a town mark, and along side of it an obliterator, thus making it possible to postmark the letter and cancel the stamp at one strike.

These duplex marks assumed a number of forms, the obliterator usually being oval or circular and composed of a varying number of lines or bars. Some had a numeral either in a circle or lozenge in the center of the obliterator. For other than first class mail, obliterators only were frequently used, and these often had the city name on them.

By 1891 it was decided to issue combined obliterators and postmarks. These first appeared in the middle of January 1892, and were single markings that were introduced for use in eight of the larger post offices. As follows: Halifax, Hamilton, London, Montreal, Ottawa, St. John, Toronto, and Winnipeg.

Late in April 1893 a similar form but square—the circle being filled out by thin lines was tried. Twenty-five post offices used these as follows:

The 1893 Duplex Cancellation

Post Office	1893	Post Office	1893
Aldergrove, B.C.	May 16	Mount Forest, Ont.	May 16
Beaverton, Ont.	April 26	New Germany, Ont.	May 20
Beeton, Ont.	May 18	Ottawa, Canada.	May 5
Brockville, Ont.	April 26	Point St. Charles, Que.	May 3
Byng Inlet North, Ont.	May 6	Rat Portage, Ont.	April 28
Coleman, Ont.	April 26	St. Ann's, Ont.	May 31
Cumberland, Ont.	April 26	St. Hilarion, Que.	April 26
Dutton, Ont.	April 26	Shannonville, Ont.	May 31
Grimsby, Ont.	May 18	Spring Hill Mines, N. S.	April 26
London, Ont.	April 28	Terrebonne, Que.	April 26
London East, Ont.	May 31	Three Rivers, Que.	May 18
Mansonville, Que.	June 9	Westville, N. S.	April 26
Montreal, Canada.	May 19		

The lines were too thin, and in June of the same year this type was superseded by a similar type but with heavy bars. This proved satisfactory and was widely distributed until about 1903 or 1904. We have seen this from over two hundred and fifty post offices, as well as four Railway routes.

E. Crown Obliterators.

Introduced in 1868, there are several types of these cancellations, two being used at the legislative post office at Ottawa, and one in general use at the Victoria, B. C., post office. We have not as yet definitely allocated the remaining types.

Type 1
(Feb. 1880)
Ottawa
At the Legislative P.O.

Type 2
(Apr. 1880)

Type 3
(Sept. 1880)
Victoria, B. C.
General Use

Type 4

Type 5

Type 6

Type 7

Type 8

Fig. 1. The "Victoria B. C." crown cancel. First used in September 1880, when two were furnished to the Victoria P. O.

Fig. 2. Second Type of Ottawa Crown, which was placed in use April 1880. Note that the crown is more in outline, not obliterating the stamp so heavily.

Available information shows that only Types 1, 2, and 3 were officially supplied by the P. O. Department. The remaining types are probably local products produced by or for Postmasters for various reasons.

A Few Obliterators.

  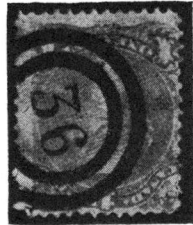

Table of Factors.   The Crown Cancellations—First Used in 1868.

| Type | POST OFFICE | Large Cents Issue—1868 | | | SMALL CENTS ISSUE—1870-97 | | | | | | | 2c Reg. | NOTES |
		½c	12½c	15c	½c	1c	2c	3c	5c	6c	10c		
1	Ottawa							10					
2	Ottawa	x	x	2½	60	50	25	35			3	15	8c-10, 20c-5, 50c-5
3	Victoria, B. C.			3½		50		15		x	x	25	50c-10
4								25					
5								30					
6								25				30	
7								25					
8								25					

628*

F. THE REGISTERED MARKINGS.

(Other Than Those Covered In Chapter XXVI)

Many of the handstruck registered stamps were carried over into the adhesive registered stamp period beginning in 1875. However a few new types of registered markings were introduced after that date.

Type 1. Oval 35x25 mm.   Type 2. Octagonal 27 mm. side to side.   Type 3. Small Circular. 20 mm. in diameter.

Type 4. For Packets. 45x30 mm.

With the discontinuance of special registered letter adhesives the well known "R" in oval or circle markings so commonly used throughout the British Empire were introduced for use on registered letters.

A. 21x25 mm.   B. 22 mm. in diameter.

None of these markings are particularly scarce.

These crown registered markings are British markings struck on registered letters from overseas by the registry division of the Post Office in Great Britain. Usually in red.

G. THE NON-OFFICIAL OBLITERATORS.

a. The Letter Cancellations.

These are fancy cancels made at the whim of various postmasters or clerks. We illustrate a few of those we have examined. They are interesting but their value is problematical, but $1.00 to $5.00 each when on 3c S. Q., and three times that when on cover.

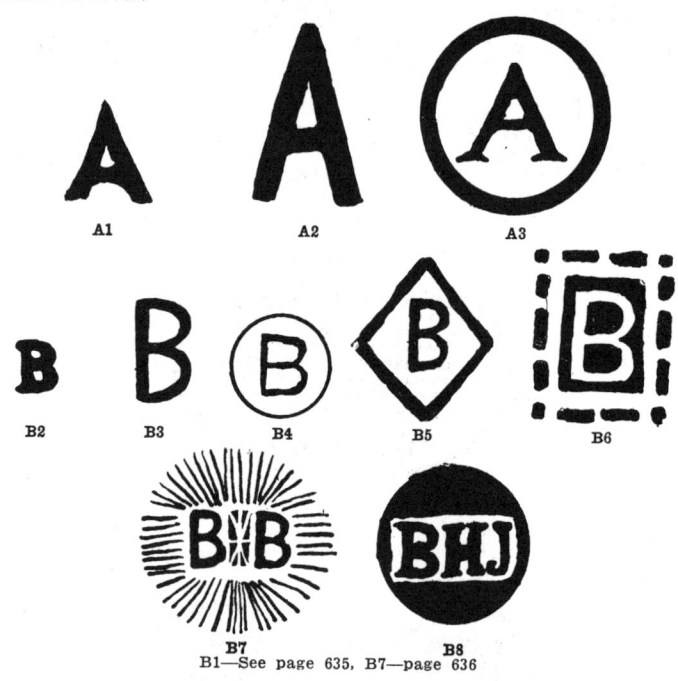

B1—See page 635, B7—page 636

Napanee "B" 1876.
Type 9.

C2   C3   C4   C5

C1—See page 635.

C6   C7

D1   D2   E1   E2

E3—See page 635

E4

G1   G2   H2

H1—See page 635

H3　　　H4　　　H5

H6　　　H7　　　H9
　　H8—See page 635

J1　　　J2　　　J3

K1　　K2　　K3　　K4
L1, L2—See page 635, L4—See page 633

L3

M1　　M2　　M3　　M4

M5　　　　　　M6　　　　　　M7

N1　　　　N2　　　　N3　　　　N4

N5　　　　N6　　　　N7　　　　N8

Port Carling, Ont. "L" 1877. Type 4

O2 O3 O4
O1—See page 635

O5 P1 P2 P3

P4 R1 R2 S1

S2 S3 T2
T1—See page 635

V1 V2 V3

W1 W2 Y1

635 *

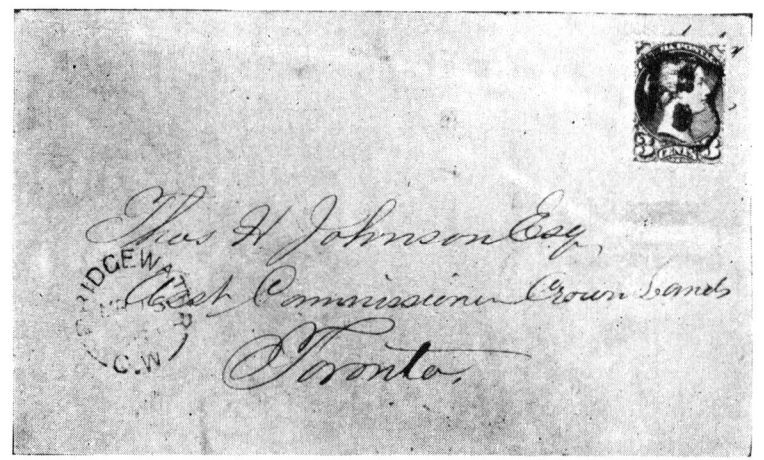

Bridgewater, C. W. "B" 1876.
B—Type 7.

b. The Star Cancellations.

We illustrate herewith some of the various star cancellations we have seen. These are also the product, for the most part, of a postmasters or clerks artistic desires. Probobly cut in wood, or ordered fom a firm supplying rubber or metal stamps.

Type 7.

Type 14.

Type 8b

Type 11

Type 10b.

Type 10a.

Type 12.

Six or More Points on Star.

Type 5.

Type 6.

Type 8.

Type 10.

Type 7—See page 636, Type 11—See page 636

Four Pointed Stars.

Type 1.

Type 2.

Type 3.

Type 4.

Five Pointed Stars.

Type 1.
(See footnote 1).

Type 2.

Type 3.
(See footnote 1).

Type 4.

1. These was made by the Contractors in April 1880.

Type 5.   Type 6.   Type 7.   Type 8a. Two Types

Type 8b.   Type 9a. 3c S. Q. Three Types Black, Purple.   Type 9b.   Type 9c.

Types 10 and 12 see page 637.

Type 11.

c. The Fancy and So-Called Cork Cancellations.

This large group of markings, while attractive are of comparatively little value to the historian of the Postal Service. Nevertreless since collectors seem interested in them we append herewith a brief note regarding them.

The most attractive are the "Leaf" cancels, of which at least fifteen types are known, mostly from Toronto, but also from Montreal, and several small cities.

Usually in black, but also known in other colors, such as purple. Value from $2.00 for the simpler types on the "Leaf" and "Numeral" issues, to $10.00 for an elaborate design on an 1859 or Large Queen stamp.

"Leaf" Cancels.

A Masonic Cancel.

New Liverpool, U. C. Honey Comb Cancel. 1872

Another large group is the pinwheels, propellers, and similar designs. We have seen at least twenty distinct types. Mostly in black but some in purple. We would value at from $1.00 to $5.00 depending on how elaborate the design and the desirability of the stamp.

So-Called "Cork" Cancellations.

The so called "Cork" cancellations consisting of a circular or rectangular mark cut into segments, or with fancy designs of no particular significance constitute a vast group, of which at least 150 types have been seen by us. The great majority are in black, but blue, violet, purple, and green are also known.

The value is purely a matter of agreement between the parties concerned, but the more attractive ones should be worth an additional $1.00 over the value of the stamp on which it occurs.

Although commonly known as "Cork" cancellations, we doubt that any of them were actually made of Cork[1]. The simpler ones were probably made of brass, while the more elaborate ones of wood, carved by the postmasters. Some may have been made of rubber, as that was a popular material for cancelling devices in the 1880's and 1890's.

---

[1]. Cork does not carve readily, and the cancelling ink was made primarily for metal devices.

H. MILITARY MARKINGS OF THE DOMINION.[1]

Campe

I. Circular 20-22 mm. in diameter. No outer circle. Similar to Type IV1. of Postmarks. (q.v.)

June 16, 1886, July 23, 1886   Nov. 14, 1930, June 27, 1940

II. Circular 27-29 mm. in diameter, with outer circle.

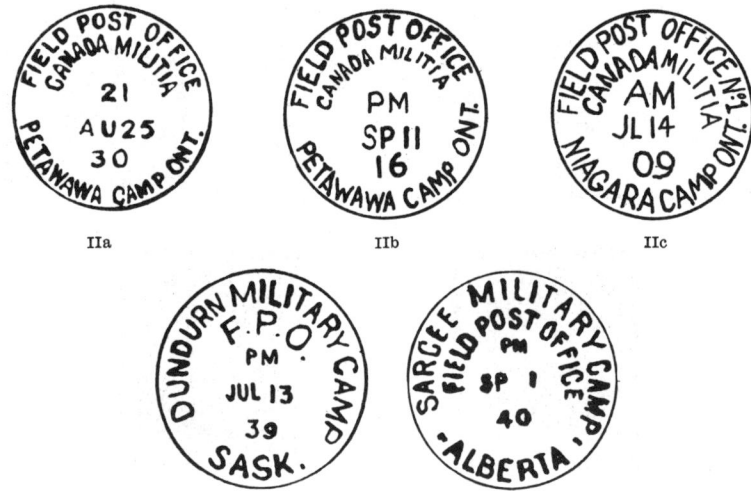

IIa   IIb   IIc

IId   IIe

III. Circular 23-24 mm. in diameter. Outer circle.

IIIa   IIIc   IIIb

1. When dates are given it indicates the earliest and latest dates known to us.

IV. Circular 22 mm. in diameter, with killer.

V. Straight Line.

ROYAL REVIEW,
EXHIBITION PARK CAMP

OCT 11 1901
TORONTO
ARMY POST OFFICE.

(a) Five Lines. Only date we know of.

(b) Two Lines and Ten Bars.

"M.P.O." or "A.P.O."

I. Circular 23-34 mm. in diameter. With outer circle.

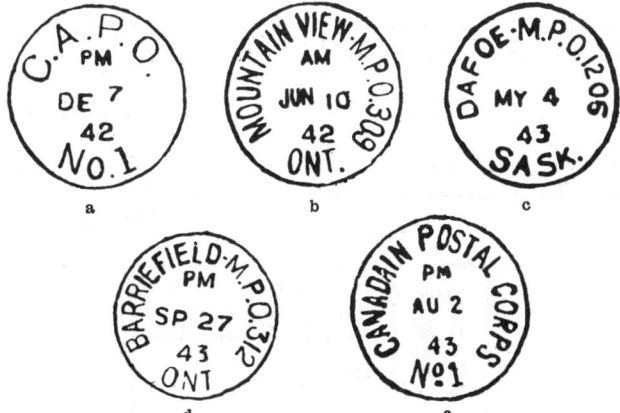

Type VI simply reads Military Post Office and number.

643

II. Circular 22 mm. in diameter, with outer circle and wavy line "killer".

III. Circular 33 mm. in diameter, with outer circle.

Oval.

Rectangular.

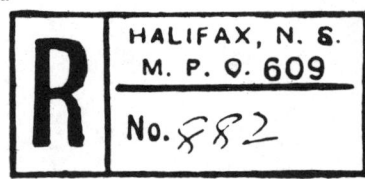

a   b

c. Registered Letter Marking.

Overseas Units.

I. South African War 1899-1901.

April 11, 1900. Dec. 24, 1900.

This was used by the Canadian South African Postal Corps consisting of five men, who left for South Africa early in 1900, arriving there Feb. 17, 1900.

II. World War I, 1914-18.

A special postmark, used by the Canadian troops on Board R. M. S. *Megantic*.

The Canadian Expeditionary Force postmark was only for use *outside* of Great Britain, as letters posted from the Canadian Camp in England have to be franked with British stamps.

Sep. 30, 1914. Jan 29, 1915.

III. Siberian Expeditionary Force, 1918-19.

IV. World War II, 1939-45.

a

b

c

J. THE EXPRESS COMPANY CANCELLATIONS.
a. Barnard's Express Ranch.[1]

Barnard's Express was a British Columbia company, known also as Barnard's Cariboo Express. The company had a large ranch at the north end of Lake Okanagan primarily for breeding horses for its express lines. Both types occur on the 3c Small Queen, and type 2 is known on the 3c Large Queen, always in black. They are quite rare, and should be worth $8.00 to $10.00 each.

b. Wells, Fargo & Co's. Express.

A Wells, Fargo Cancel.   Red Wells, Fargo Cancellation on 1c Yellow. We have seen only one example of this cancellation.

This colossus of Express Companies operated in British Columbia and occasional copies of Large or Small Queens are seen with the oval cancel of this company usually reading "Wells, Fargo & Co's Express Victoria", or with the word 'Express" omitted. Struck in black, blue, or violet. **On 3c and 6c Small** Queens, and 15c Large Queen. Stamps off cover with Wells, Fargo markings should be worth $5.00, on cover $10.00 and up, depending on the combination.

c. Vickers Express.

We have seen a number of 3c vermilion, Small Queens, with a violet cancellation, two of which are illustrated. None of the strikes are very clear, but we have identified them as the marking of Vickers Express. This was organized by John J. Vickers in 1854 who secured a contract over the Northern Railway opened at that time. He expanded steadily and did a good business on various Ontario Railways including part of the Canadian Pacific. In 1888 he sold out to the American Express Co. The cancellations are decidedly scarce.

---

1. The History of Barnard's Express is fully discussed in, "Barnard's Cariboo Express" by Messrs. Hitt and Wellburn, in The Stamp Specialist Black Book.

Chapter XXXVII

THE RAILWAY POST MARKS OF CANADA
1853-1943

The first railway in Canada was the Champlain & St. Lawrence, which was opened for traffic in 1836. It ran from La Prairie to St. John's, P.Q., a distance of sixteen miles. Other short lines were built, but it was not until the control of the Post Office was in provincial hands that the use of the railway as a means of mail transportation was taken up in earnest[1], and in 1852 the mileage of railway mail routes amounted to 213 miles[2].

Canadian postal officials were quite aware of the possibility of sorting the mail in transit, (as had been done in England since 1838) and in 1853 an order

Fig. 1. Type 9a on Small Cover to Montreal with 3d Wove Paper.

Fig. 2. Type 15b Struck on Cover to United States with a 6d on Laid "Grand Trunk Railway" Struck in Red by the Sender, "Y. J. & Co. Drawer 14", whose Cachet is also in Red.

---
1. Appendix G. 8 et seq.
2. Appendix G #33.

for railway markings was sent to John Francis, two each for the St. Lawrence and Atlantic, and the Ontario, Simcoe, and Huron Railroads[3].

Each succeeding year saw an increase in the mileage, number of clerks and volume of mail matter sorted by the Railway Post Office, until today it is a vast and vital part of Canada's efficient postal service.

Fig. 3. Same Red Markings as in Fig. 2 on Cover With Two 3d, Laid. No Railway Cancellation.

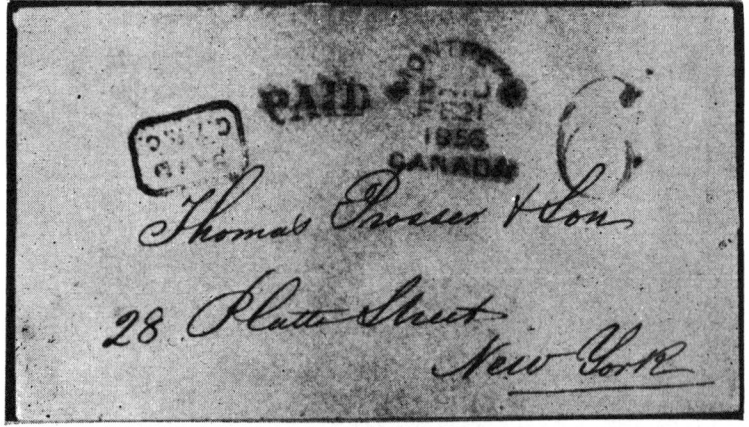

Fig. 4. "PAID GTRC" Type 23, Struck in Black on a Stampless Cover to New York, Also Struck With Red H32a and H103, Besides Red "PAID" of New York.

---

3. Appendix G #1.

A. THE RAILWAY CANCELLATIONS OF THE PROVINCIAL POST OFFICE
1853-1867

1. Railroad Cancellations.

Buffalo & Lake Huron   **Great Western**   **Hamilton & Toronto**

Type 1.   Type 2.   Type 3.   Type 4.
The order was for a "stamp" reading "GW.R.H.&T." (Appendix G #2)

Montreal, Shefford & Chambly   **Ontario, Simcoe & Huron**

Type 5.   Type 6a.   Type 6b.

Ottawa & Prescott

Type 7.
(Bytown became Ottawa in 1856).

Type 8a.   Type 8b.

Type 8c.   Type 8d.   Type 8e.

St. Lawrence & Atlantic

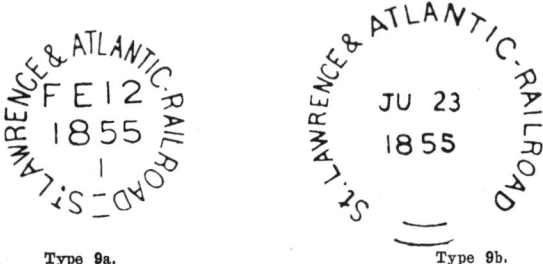

Type 9a.   Type 9b.

Stanstead, Shefford & Chambly   **Welland**

Type 10.   Type 11.

2. Railroad Route Cancellations.

Brockville & Montreal   **Brockville & Ottawa**
G.T.R.

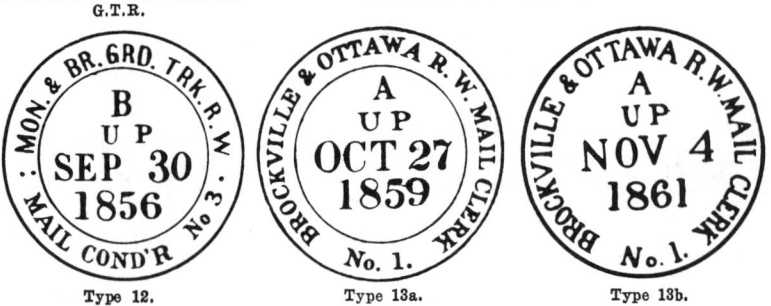

Type 12.   Type 13a.   Type 13b.

Grenville & Ottawa

Island Pond & Montreal (G. T. R.)

Kingston & Toronto (G. T. R.)

Montreal & Kingston (G. T. R.)

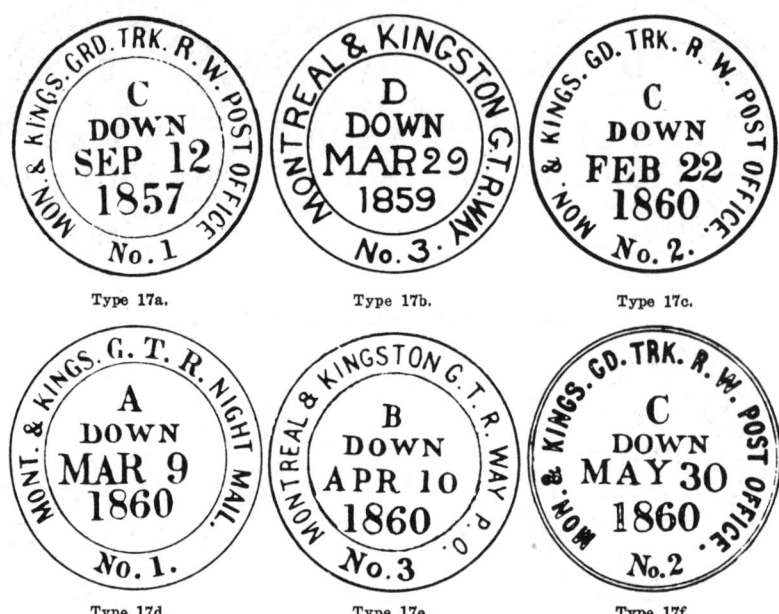

Type 17a.   Type 17b.   Type 17c.

Type 17d.   Type 17e.   Type 17f.

Montreal & Quebec (G. T. R.)   Montreal & Toronto (G. T. R.)

Type 18.   Type 19.

Quebec & Richmond (G. T. R.)

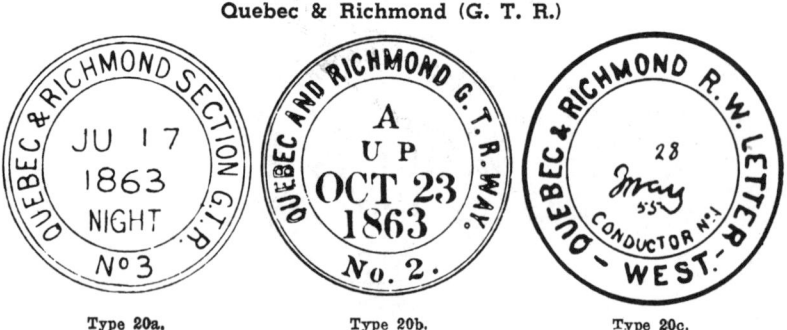

Type 20a.   Type 20b.   Type 20c.

Quebec & Riviere Du Loup (G. T. R.)

Type 21a. Type 21b.

Toronto & Sarnia

Type 22.

3. Miscellaneous Provincial Railway Markings.

Type 23. Type 24.

We have seen covers bearing the above markings, (See page 650 for Type 23 illustration), dated in the early provincial period. These are possibly forerunners of the markings issued by the post office department.

Type	Date	Black
23	1856	15.00
24	1855	15.00

Provincial Railway Cancellations—1853-1867.
1. Cancellations or Markings Consisting of Railroad Name, Date, Etc

Railroad	Type	Date	Miles	Status in 1944	Value Factor	Notes
Buffalo & Lake Huron	1	1853	162	CN	15	
Great Western	2	1859	275	CN	15	
Great Western, Sarnia Branch	3	1860	51	CN	20	
Hamilton & Toronto	4	1861	38	CN	15	
Montreal, Shefford & Chambly	5	1864	16	CN	35	
Ontario, Simcoe & Huron[1]	6a	1860	95		30	
"	6b				25	
Bytown & Prescott	7	1855	59	CP	40	
Ottawa & Prescott	8a	1859	59	CP	40	
"	8b	1864			60	
"	8c	1865			40	
"	8d	1866			25	
"	8e	1867			25	
St. Lawrence & Atlantic	9a	1855	147	CN	30	
"	9b	1855			35	
Stanstead, Shefford & Chambly	10	1864	43		30	
Welland	11	1865	14	CN	25	

CN—Canadian National; CP—Canadian Pacific.
1. Chartered as the Toronto, Sarnia, & Lake Huron in 1849. Took the name of Ontario, Simcoe, & Huron Ry. in 1857, and that of the Northern in 1858.

2. Provincial Railway Route Cancellations 1855-67.

Route	R. R.	Type	Date	Miles	Status in 1944	Value Factor	Notes
Brockville & Montreal	G. T.	12	1856	126	CN	40	
Brockville & Ottawa		13a	1859	76	CP	25	Single circle.
		13b	1861			25	
Grenville & Ottawa		14a	1859	62	CP	25	Single circle.
,,		14b	1860			25	
,,		14c	1861			25	
Island Pond & Montreal	G. T.	15a	1855	147	CN	25	Formerly St. Lawrence & Atlantic
,,		15b	1855			20	
,,		15c	1858			20	
,,		15d	1861			20	
,,		15e	1861			15	
Kingston & Toronto	G. T.	16	1857	161	CN	25	Single circle.
Montreal & Kingston	G. T.	17a	1857	173	CN	40	Single circle.
,,		17b	1859			40	
,,		17c	1860			35	
,,		17d	1860			35	
,,		17e	1860			30	
,,		17f	1860			30	
Montreal & Quebec	G. T.	18	1855	177	CN	25	
Montreal & Toronto	G. T.	19	1859	334	CN	25	
Quebec & Richmond	G. T.	20a	1863	103	CN	25	
,,		20b	1863			20	
,,		20c	1855			20	
Quebec & Riviere DuLoup	G. T.	21a	1867	115	CN	25	Ms. date.
		21b	1863			25	
Toronto & Sarnia	G. W.	22	1857	179	CN	25	Single circle.

NOTE ON THE STRAIGHT LINE.
"Wm. Cuppage" Cancel on 3d 1851.

We have examined a 3d wove, with a black straight line cancellation reading "WM. CUPPAGE". It was probably struck by him on a letter bearing an adhesive stamp which had escaped cancellation, and he used his facing slip stamp to do it.

Mr. Cuppage was a first class mail clerk of the railway mail service, and received a salary of about $800.00 per annum—which was a good salary in the 1850's.

WM. CUPPAG....

B. THE RAILWAY CANCELLATIONS OF THE DOMINION POST OFFICE 1869-1943.

As noted in the Provincial Railway Cancellations the direction the train was running is given in the cancellation. The common designations are:

East or E.
North or No, N.
South or So, S.
West or W.

D. E. i.e. Day East
D. W. i.e. Day West.
N. E. i.e. Night East.
N. W. i.e. Night West.
Sp. i.e. Special.

Up or Down

The indication of direction is usually placed over the date in the circular cancellations. It may however occur transposed with the year. Reversed letters such as oN instead of No, or inverted E, are sometimes seen. These errors indicate that the direction as well as the date logos are hand set by the clerk.

More recent practice merely gives the train number assigned by the railroad company to the particular train. It should be remembered that:

WEST OR SOUTHBOUND TRAINS are ODD numbered
EAST OR NORTHBOUND TRAINS are EVEN numbered

It can thus be seen that the train number indicates the direction the train is running.

In the lists following the arrangement of the routes is STRICTLY ALPHABETICAL by route termini only.

As examples:

"Montreal and Toronto" will be found only under "Montreal & Toronto"—irrespective of any other arrangement of spelling or names for that route. In other words if the cancellation were to read Toronto and Montreal—it would still be found under the Montreal and Toronto listing. Where only one route designation is known, for example—Winnipeg and Edmonton, the listing will be found under Edmonton and Winnipeg. That is, no matter what arrangement or abbreviations occur, the termini are in alphabetical order. This eliminates unnecessary duplication of the same route, and only advanced specialists are interested in every variation of spelling, number, etc.

The cancellations are divided into four main types—described at the head of the listing.

When the date is given thus 6/9/87, 8/23/93, etc., such dates are the date of delivery by the contractor of the cancellation. Where the date is in year only, thus—1902, 1942, etc., in italics, indicates approximate year when the cancellation was in use. Such dates may be found too late by other students upon further investigation.

IT IS NOT CLAIMED THAT THIS LIST IS IN ANY WAY FINAL, AND WE ARE CONFIDENT THAT OTHER ROUTES, TYPES, DATES, ETC., WILL BE FOUND.

"CANADIAN PACIFIC"[1]

THE ABBREVIATIONS USED TO INDICATE THE RAILWAY OPERATING A GIVEN ROUTE.

1. D.A.—Dominion Atlantic.
2. E. & N.—Esquimault & Nanaimo.
3. G. T.—Grand Trunk.
4. I. C.—Intercolonial.
5. M. C.—Michigan Central.
6. N.—Canadian National.
7. N. A.—Northern Alberta.
8. N. B.—New Brunswick.
9. N. B. & C.—New Brunswick & Canada.
10. N. Y. C.—New York Central.
11. P.—Canadian Pacific.
12. P. E. I.—Prince Edward Island.
13. P. G. E.—Pacific Great Eastern.
14. P. M.—Pere Marquette.
15. Q. C.—Quebec Central.
16. Q. & L. St. J.—Quebec & Lake St. John.
17. Q. M. O. & O.—Quebec, Montreal, Ottawa & Occidental.
18. T. & N. O.—Temiskaming & Northern Ontario.
19. W. & A.—Windsor & Annapolis (Nova Scotia).
20. W. C.—Western Counties (Nova Scotia).

The types of railway cancellations in the following list:
Type I 21-23 mm. in diameter, circular but no outer circle.[2]
Type II 22-25 mm. in diameter, circular with outer circle..[3]
Type III Straight Line.
   a One Line.
   b Two Lines.
Type IV Square barred with route in circle.[4] Bars very thick, June 1893.

The arrangement of listing is as follows: Route, Length in Miles (to nearest mile) Railroad at time of Establishment of Route, Railroad it is now a part of, the Types, and Notes.

---
1. From a die proof in black on India, Die No. 112, by the British American Bank Note Co., about 1874.
2. See page 574, Type IV1 for illustration.
3. See page 570, Type Il for illustration.
4. See page 625 for illustration.

I. Railway Route Markings, Having Names of Termini Only.

Route	Miles	R. R. At Time of Est.	Now Part of	Type I	Type II	Type III a 5/10/90	Type III b	Notes
Agnes & Sherbrooke	130	P	P		1903	5/10/90		
Alameda & Brandon	45		N		1914			
Albert & Salisbury	25		N		5/26/90	5/10/90		
Allandale & Beeton	91		N		1890			
Allandale & Hamilton	52		N		1942			
Allandale & Meaford	39		N					
Alliston & Penetguishene	73		N			5/10/90		
Allo & Midland					1890			
Amherst & Halifax	141	I. C.	N	8/3/74	1932			
Amherst & St. John	137	I. C.	N	7/4/76	3/6/82	5/10/90		
Amherst & Truro	77	I. C.	N		3/16/92	5/10/90		
Amulet & Cardross	102	N. B.	P		1892			
Andover & McAdam[1]	108	N. B.	P	2/25/81	10/3/87	5/10/90		Est. 10/3/87
Andover & Vanceboro[2]	131	W.&A.	P	2/25/81				
Annapolis & Halifax[3]	92		P		3/2/83	5/10/90	11/3/79	I-IIIa 5/10/90
Annapolis & Middleton	28		D. A		1918			
Annapolis & Yarmouth[3]	86	W.C.	P		3/6/82	5/10/90		
Arden & Ottawa[4]	100		P	11/3/79	1942	5/10/90		
Armstrong Sta. & Capreol	540		N		1942			
Armstrong Sta. & Winnipeg	391	N	N		1941			
Arrowhead & Robson[5]	127	P	P		6/9/83	5/10/90		
Arthabaska & Three Rivers	35	G. T.	P		1942			
Assiniboia & Weyburn	111	P	P		1900			
Bancroft & Trenton	100		C. N.		5/19/94	5/10/90		
Barrie & Meaford	53	G. T.	C. N.		**1908**			
Beauce Jct. & St. George	8	Q. C.	Q. C.		1919			
Beauce Jct. & St. Sabine		Q. C.	Q. C.		**1935**			
Beebe Jct. & Stanstead	4	C. P.	C. P.					
Beechers Falls & Dudswell Jct.					1908			
Beechers Fall & Lime Ridge[6]					1909			
Beeton & Collingwood	41		C. N.		11/15/92			

Route	Miles	R. R. At Time of Est.	Now Part of	Type I	Type II	Type III a	Type III b	Notes
Belleville & Madoc	27		N.		1/5/83	5/10/90		
Belleville & Peterboro[7]	63	G. T.	N.		10/31/92	5/10/90		
					12/9/98			
Biggar & Loverna	104		P.		*1920*			
Binscarth & Saskatoon	269		P.		*1936*			
Binscarth & Winnipeg	201		P.		*1910*			
Blackwater Jct. & Hamilton					*1916*			
Blackwater Jct. & Midland	74				*1899*			
Blackwater Jct. & Orillia	42		N.		8/26/89	5/10/90		
Blaine & Vancouver[8]	36	G. N.	G. N.		11/29/07			
Blenheim & Leamington					1897			
Blenheim & Midland					*1934*			
Blenheim & Sarnia					7/9/87			
B. Bay & Ottawa					*1938*			
Blyth & Kincardine					*1928*			
Bolton & Hamilton					*1928*			
Boundary Line & Winnipeg[9]	165		P.		*1915*			
Brandon & Bulyea	264		P.		*1914*			
Brandon & Estevan	164		P.		*1905*			
Brandon & Lanigan	322		P.		*1922*			
Brandon & Regina	221	P.	N.		*1904*			
Brandon & Saskatoon	343	N.	N.		*1904*			
Brandon & Winnipeg	135	N. P.	N. P.		11/9/91			
Brantford & Bridgeburg[10]	76				*1903*	7/9/94		
Brantford & Ft. Erie	76		N.		7/9/94			Now B. & Ft. Erie No.
Brantford & Ft. Erie North[11]	76		N.		*1936*			
Brantford & Goderich	92	G. T.	N.		7/9/94	7/9/94		
Brantford & Sarnia	114		N.		*1897*			
Bridgeburg & Courtright					*1918*			
Bridgeburg & Goderich	161				*1908*			
Bridgeburg & St. Thomas[12]	130				*1903*			
Bridgewater & Middleton	55		N.		*1928*			

Route	Miles	R. R. At Time of Est.	Now Part of	Type I	Type II	Type III a	b	Notes
Brockville & Carleton Place[13]	45	P.	P.		1900			
Brockville & Montreal	126	G. T.	N.		11/3/86 1855			
Brockville & Ottawa	76	**P.**	P.		6/9/90	5/10/90		
Brockville & Westport	45		N.		1897			
Calgary & Camrose	211	N.	N.		1942			
Calgary & Edmonton	194	P.	P.		4/9/94			
Calgary & McLeod	109		P.		1942			
Calgary & Medicine Hat	176		N.		1935			
Calgary & Moosejaw	438	P.	P.		1900	5/10/90		
Calgary & Saskatoon	400	N.	N.		1923			
Calgary & Winnipeg	832	P.	P.		1910			
Calgary & Vancouver	642	P.	P.		1942			
Calumet & Montreal	60		P.			5/10/90		
Calumet & Ottawa	215	P.	P.		9/29/94 1937	2/2/92		
Campbellton & Gaspe	376	N.	N.		10/29/07			
Campbellton & Halifax	304	I. C.	N.		10/19/07			
Campbellton & Levis	187	GT+IC	N.	7/20/76	5/3/88	5/10/90		
Campbellton & Moncton	466	I. C.	N.		11/23/93			
Campbellton & Montreal		GT+IC	N.		3/16/93 12/23/93			{IV 4/6/94, IV "local" 9/9/94. Type II may read Express or local.
Campbellton & Quebec	200	I. C.	N.		5/2/92 7/9/87	5/10/90		
Campbellton & Riviere du Loup[17]	189	I. C.	N.	6/23/79				
Camrose & Munson	20				1918			
Canfield & Jarvis	84				1916			
Canfield Jct. & London	77		N.		6/9/87	5/10/90		
Canfield Jct. & St. Thomas	153		N.		1900			
Canora & Regina	176		N.		1923			
Chambord & Quebec[14]	158		N.		x	5/10/90		
Charlottetown & Georgetown		P.E.I.	**N.**		4/26/93	8/23/93		

Route	Miles	R.R. At Time of Est.	Now Part of	Type I	Type II	Type III a	Type III b	Notes
Charlottetown & Murray Harbor	56	P.E.I.	N.		1942			
Charlottetown & Sackville	89	P.E.I.	N.		1919			
Chatham & Elora					1912			
Charlottetown & Souris (East)	60	P.E.I.	N.		4/26/93	4/26/93	5/10/90	Ry. "Through Express" 10/17/89 II.
Charlottetown & Tignish	115	P.E.I.	N.		x	x		
Chatham & London	64	N.	N.		1920			
Chatham & Walkerville	86	N.	P.M.		1902			
Chicoutimi & Quebec	227	N.	N.		1940			
Clifton & London	50	N.	N.		1890			
Clifton & Windsor					1918			
Cochrane & North Bay	254	T&NO	T&NO		1934			
Cochrane & Quebec	575	N.	N.		1934			
Coe Hill & Trenton	74		N.		10/26/88	5/10/90		
Collingwood & Hamilton	108		N.		1928			
Colonsay & Regina	134		P.		1942			
Columbia & Kootenay[16]	113		I.		1928			
Connor & Riviere du Loup	56	N.Y.C.	N.Y.C.		1942			
Cornwall & Ottawa	107	P.	P.		1908			
Coronation & Lacombe	140	E.&N.	E.&N.		1931			
Courtenay & Victoria					1942	5/10/90		
Courtright & St. Thomas	116				6/9/87			
Dauphin & Swan River[18]	39		N.		1935			
Dauphin & Winnipegosis					1903			River Steamer.
Dawson (Y.T.) & Nenana	505	N.A.	N.A.		1929			
Dawson Creek & Edmonton[19]					1942			
De Lisle & Three Rivers	19		P.		1908			
Deloraine & Napinka	203	P.	P.		1942	5/10/90		
Deloraine & Winnipeg					1/9/87			
Depot Harbor & Ottawa	57		N.		1912			
Deschaillons & Levis					1942			
Deschaillons & Lyster Sta					1912			

Route	Miles	R.R. At Time of Est.	Now Part of	Type I	Type II	Type III a	b	Notes
Drumheller & Saskatoon	315	N.	N.		1936			
Drummondville & Sutton	62	P.	P.		1942	5/10/90		
Dundee & Montreal								
Edmonton & Edson	66		N.		1920			
Edmonton & Elk Point	146	N.	N.		1935			
Edmonton & Humboldt			N.		1912			
Edmonton & Lloydminster	177	P.	P.		1938			
Edmonton & North Battleford	254		N.		1942			
Edmonton & Prince George	489	N.	N.		1935			
Edmonton & St. Paul De Metis	127		N.		1930			
Edmonton & Saskatoon	331		N.		1922			
Edmonton & Spirit River	362		N.		1920			
Edmonton & Vegreville	73		N.		1921			
Edmonton & Wembley[20]	422	N. A.	N.A.		1932			
Edmonton & Winnipeg	802		N.		1910			
Edmundston & McAdam	162		P.		1903			
Edmundston & St. John	246	P.	P.		1942			
Edmundston & St. Stephen	196	P.	P.		1931			
Esquimalt & Nanaimo	69		E.&N.		1890			
Esquimaux Pt. & Quebec					1927			
Elmira & Galt	25		N.		4/20/93	4/20/93		
Elora & Streetsville	56		P.		5/26/90	5/10/90		
Elora & Toronto	66		N.		1902			
Emerson & Winnipeg	66		P.		1910			
Empress & Swift Current	118	P.	P.		1942			
Englehart & North Bay	140		P.		1909			
Estevan & Moosejaw	144		P.		1930			
Estevan & Winnipeg	165		P.		1910			
Eston & Saskatoon	161	N.	N.		1942	5/10/90		
Fergus & Harrisburg	45	G. T.	N.			5/10/90		
Ft. Coulonge & Ottawa	69		P.		4/29/93			

Route	Miles	R. R. At Time of Est.	Now Part of	Type I	Type II	Type III a	Type III b	Notes
Ft. Covington & Montreal	73		N.		1930	5/10/90		
Ft. Erie & Goderich					5/9/87			
Ft. Erie & Hamilton	76		N.		1928			
Ft. Erie & Midland					1903			
Ft. Erie & St. Thomas	118		M. C.		5/9/87	5/10/90		
Ft. Erie, North & St. Thomas[21]					1937			1, 2, 3.
Ft. Francis & Winnipeg	208	N.	N.		11/9/07			
Ft. William & North Bay	630		P.		1942			
Ft. William & Ottawa	875		P.		1910			
Ft. William & Toronto	811	P.	P.		1933			
Ft. William & Winnipeg	419		P.		11/19/07			
Galt & Waterloo	15		N.		2/9/92	2/9/92		
Garneau Jct. & Riviere a Pierre	40		N.		1910			
Gaspe & Matapedia	202		N.		1942			
Glenboro & Winnipeg	105	P.	P.		1/9/87	5/10/90		
Goderich & Harrisburg	112		N.		1910			
Goderich & Guelph	95		P.		1930			
Goderich & Stratford	50	G. T.	P.		1895			
Goderich & Toronto	135	G. T.	N.		1918			
Grand Mere & Three Rivers	27	P.	P.		1924			
Grandes Piles & Three Rivers	30		P.		1910			
Gravenhurst & North Bay	116		N.		8/23/94	5/10/90		
Gravenhurst & Toronto	112	G. T.	N.		4/16/91	5/10/90		G. T. R.
Gretna & Winnipeg	108		P.		4/12/92			
Gronlid & Lanigan	102		P.		12/7/88	5/10/90		
Gronlid & Regina	207		P.		1940			
Guelph & Harrisburg	28	P.			1942			
Guelph & Owen Sound	115				1935			
Guelph & Palmerston	43	N.	N.		1936			
					1935			

Route	Miles	R. R. At Time of Est.	Now Part of	Type I	Type II	Type III a	Type III b	Notes
Guelph & Southampton	102		N.		*1890*			
Haliburton & Lindsay	56		N.		12/28/94	5/10/90		
Halifax & Moncton	189	I. C.	N.		8/16/82		5/10/90	
Halifax & Moncton		P.	P.		12/6/89		5/10/90	
Halifax & Sackville	151		N.		*1890*			
Halifax & St. John	278		N.		*1890*			
Halifax & Sydney	288		N.		*1890*			
Halifax & Truro	64		N.		*1942*			
Halifax & Yarmouth	250		N.		*1880*			
Hamilton & Kincardine	161		N.		*1920*			
Hamilton & Lindsay	110		N.		*1929*			
Hamilton & London	81		N.		*1890*			
Hamilton & Meaford	144		N.		*1922*			
Hamilton & Niagara Falls	44		N.		*1942*			
Hamilton & Owen Sound	166	N.	N.		*1942*			
Hamilton & Palmerston	95	G. T.	N.		*1916*			
Hamilton & Port Dover	54		N.		6/9/87	5/10/90		
Hamilton & Port Rowan[22]	78,63	N.	N.		*1931*	5/10/90		
Hamilton & Toronto	39		N.		10/21/89	5/10/90		
Hamilton & Windsor	191		N.		*1942*			{Type II reads "P O Car".
Harrisburg & Palmerston	72	G. T.	N.		9/19/93			
Harrisburg & Southampton	131		N. A.		*1890*			
Hartney & Virden	88		P.		*1918*			
Hartney & Winnipeg	174		P.		*1920*			
Herveyville & La Tuque	50		N.		*1913*			
Hines Creek & McLennon	115		N. A.		*1942*			
Hope & Vancouver	90		P.		*1917*	5/10/90		
H. Bank & Salisbury								
Hardesty & Wetaskiwin	95		P.		*1910*			
Harvey & Salisbury					*1890*			
Humboldt & Winnipeg	489		P.		*1910*			
Hunt & Vancouver					*1904*			
Inverness & Point Tupper	62	N.	N.		*1931*			

Route	Miles	R.R. At Time of Est.	Now Part of	Type I	Type II	Type III a	Type III b	Notes
Island Pond & Levis	172		N.		1942		5/10/90	"Day West"
Island Pond & Montreal	147	G. T.	N.				5/10/90	"Night East" or "West", or "Day East".
Island Pond & Richmond[23]	71		N.		8/1/89			
Kamsack & North Battleford	225		N.		1918			
Kamsack & Saskatoon	278	N.	P.		1942			
Kamsack & Winnipeg	80		N.		1942			
Kelowna & Sicamous	137	P.	P.		1942			Lake Steamer.
Kincardine & London	66		N.		6/9/87	5/10/90		
Kincardine & Palmerston		G. T.			1/19/95			
Kindersley & Saskatoon	126	N.	N.		1942			Connects with Kingsgate & Spokane R.P.O. U. S.
Kingsgate & Yahk	10½	S. I.			1942			
Kingston & Pembroke	139		P.		1890			
Kingston & Montreal	173	G. T.	P.		8/1/89		5/10/90	
Kingston & Renfrew	104		N.		1934			
Kingston & Sharbot Lake	47		P.		10/26/88	5/10/90	5/10/90	"Day East" or "West" "Night East or West" See notes.
Kingston & Toronto[24]	161	G. T.	N.		4/20/80	4/26/82		
Kingston & Tweed	88		P.		12/9/89	5/10/90		
Kirkella & Strassburg	204		P.		1902			
Lac Frontiere & Vallee Jct.	79	Q. C.	Q. C.		1931			
Lac Megantic & Levis	215	Q. C.	Q. C.		1903			
Lac Megantic & Sherbrooke	68	Q. C.	Q. C.		11/9/91			
Lac Megantic & Tring Jct.	60	Q. C.	Q. C.		5/2/91			
Lake St. John & Quebec					8/12/93	6/2/90		
La Tuque & Quebec	131		N.		6/2/90			
Leamington & Walkerville					1910			
Lacombe & Stettler					1890			
Lethbridge & Weyburn	411	P.	P.		1918			
Levis & Montreal	163		N.		1916			
Levis & Richmond					10/19/07			
Levis & Riviere du Loup	115		N.		1898			
					1890			

667

Route	Miles	R. R. At Now Time of Part of Est.	Type I	Type II	Type III a	Type III b	Notes
Levis & St. Francois Beauce	63			1890	5/10/90		
Levis & Sherbrooke	147	Q. C.					
Lindsay & Midland				1890			
London & Midton		N.		1910			
London & Niagara Falls	126	N.		6/9/87		5/10/90	"Express" or "Accom
London & Owen Sound		N.		1920			
London & Sarnia	59	N.		5/9/87			
London & Southampton	129	P.		1942			1, 2, 3.
London & Toronto	115	P.		9/29/94			
London & Windsor	112	P.		5/9/87	5/10/90	5/10/90	"No. 2" or "No. 1"
London & Wingham	108	N.					
London & Wiarton				1918			
London & Walkerville				1910			
Lorne & Toronto				6/2/90			
Labelle & Montreal				1902			
Lanigan & Regina	106	Q. C.		1931			
Lunenburg & Middleton	55	N.		1910			
Macklin & Moose Jaw	271	P.		1914			
Macklin & Outlook	119	P.		1918			
Madawaska & Ottawa	130	N.		1942			
Malone & Montreal	66	N.Y.C.		1942			
Maniwaki & Ottawa	82	O&OV		5/16/93	5/16/93		
Manilla & Whitby		P.			5/10/90		
Mansonville & Montreal				1/28/93	5/10/90		
Maryfield & Moose Jaw	228	N.		1918			
Maryfield & Radville	140	N.		1918			
Massena & Montreal	95			1890			
Matane & Quebec				1931			
Matane & St. Flavie				1910			
Matapedia & Gaspe	202	N.		1902			
Matapedia & Paspebiac	102	N.		1890			
Matapedia & Port Daniel	121	N.		1902			
Maynooth & Trenton	116			1923			

Route	Miles	R. R. At Time of Est.	Now Part of	Type I	Type II	Type III a	Type III b	Notes
Meaford & Sault Ste. Marie					1902			
Meaford & Owen Sound					1918			
Meaford & Toronto	115		N		1933			
Meaford & Wiarton					1890			
Medicine Hat & Nelson	450		P		1942			
Megantic & Montreal	175		P		1918			
Melville & Regina	397		N		1910			
Merriton & Port Colborne					1918			
Midland & Port Hope			P		8/23/94	8/23/94		
Midland & Toronto					1890			
Midway & Nelson	130	P			1942			
Midway & Saskatoon					1918			
Moncton & Quebec	492				1890			
Moncton & Sackville	38	N			1942			
Moncton & St. John	89		N		11/6/82			
Montebello & Ottawa	44		P		3/21/91	5/10/90		
Mont Laurier & Montreal	158		P		1942			
Montreal & Nicolet	82		N		1898			
Montreal & Newport	108		P		1932			
Montreal & North Bay	359		P		1934			
Montreal & Ottawa	111	P	P.		11/6/91	1/10/93		
Montreal & Perth	140		P.		4/28/93	5/3/93		
Montreal & Picton	265		N		1890			
Montreal & Pierreville	67		N		1902			
Montreal & Quebec	178		P.		1942			
Montreal & Richmond	76		N		8/1/89			
Montreal & Riviere a Pierre	138		N		1935			
Montreal & Rouses Point			D.&H.		1931		5/10/90	{"Night East" or "West".
Montreal & St. Agathe des Monts	64		P.		**1900**		5/10/90	
Montreal & St. Albans	64	N	N		1929		5/10/90	
Montreal & St. Armand	50		N					

Route	Miles	R. R. At Time of Est.	Now Part of	Type I	Type II	Type III a	Type III b	Notes
Montreal & St. Jerome	33		P		1898			
Montreal & St. John	482		P		10/3/92			
					9/7/91			
Montreal & Sherbrooke	106	P	P		2/19/89	5/10/90		
Montreal & Smiths Falls	129	P	P		1/9/93	1/9/93		
Montreal & Three Rivers	101	P	P		10/6/94	5/10/90		
Montreal & Toronto	334	G. T.	N		12/9/90			
Montreal & Waterloo (Que)	341	P	P		9/6/90			
Montreal & Victoriaville	74		N		10/29/91			
Moose Jaw & Outlook	129		P		1931	5/10/90		
Moose Jaw & North Portal	119	P	P		1914			
Moose Jaw & Shaunavon	167	P	P		1938			
Moose Jaw & Winnipeg	186	P	P		1942			
Moose Jaw & Virden	398	P	P		1942			
Munson & Saskatoon	305		N		1929	5/10/90		
Napanee & Tamworth					1935			
Napanee & Tweedsdale					1910			
Napinka & Winnipeg	222		P		1890			
Natashquan & Quebec								
New Glasgow & Port Hawkesbury	82		N		1929	5/10/90		
New Glasgow & Point Tupper	80		N		5/18/93			
New Glasgow & Truro	43		N		5/3/93			
Newport & Sherbrooke	20		P		1931			
Niagara Falls & Toronto	83		N		4/23/93			
Nicolet & Ste. Hyacinthe	68				12/21/94	12/21/94		IV 1/16/94.
Nipissing & Toronto	223		N		4/26/82			
Nordegg & Red Deer					1935			
North Battleford & Prince Albert	131		N		1938			
North Battleford & Regina	259		N		1898			

670

Route	Miles	R. R. At Time of Est.	Now Part of	Type I	Type II	Type III a	b	Notes
North Bay & New Liskeard	114		P		7/13/86			
North Bay & Ottawa	248	P	P		1910			
North Bay & Sault Ste. Marie	258		P		1935			3.
North Bay & Timmins	258		T. & N.O.		3/16/95			
North Bay & Toronto	228		N		1923			
Okanagan Landing & Penticton								Lake Steamer CPR
Okanagan Landing & Sicamous	46		P		1902			
Orangeville & Teeswater	83		P		6/9/94			
Orillia & Toronto	92		N		1918			
Ottawa & Parry Sound	258		N		2/2/94	5/10/90		
Ottawa & Pembroke	118	P.	P		6/20/82	2/2/94		
Ottawa & Port Arthur	874		P		3/26/98	5/10/90		
Ottawa & Prescott	53		P		10/8/89	5/10/90		
Ottawa & Sault Ste. Marie	406		P		11/5/92	2/2/92		
Ottawa & Sudbury	327		P		2/2/92	5/10/90		
Ottawa & Toronto	263		N		1/26/93	5/10/90		
Ottawa & Toronto	247	G. T.	P		1898			
Ottawa & Waltham	80		P		1942			
Owen Sound & Toronto	129		P		1942	6/16/94		
Oxford Jct. & Pictou	78		N		11/24/91			
Palmerston & Southampton	59		N		1935			
Palmerston & Stratford	37		N		1920			
Pasqua & Swift Current	117		P		1928			
Pembina & Winnipeg	69		N.P.		1942			
Pembroke & Renfrew	51		N		1928			
Picton & Trenton	31		N		10/26/88	5/10/90		
Pictou & Truro	59		N					
Point Tupper & Sydney	102		N		11/24/91	5/10/90		
Point Tupper & Truro	123		N		1890			

Route	Miles	R. R. At Time of Est.	Now Part of	Type I	Type II	Type III a	b	Notes
Portage La Prairie & Winnipeg	56		P		1900	5/10/90		
Port Arthur & Winnipeg	424	P.	P		11/5/86	5/10/90		
Port Colborne & Port Dalhousie			N			1/23/92		
Port Dover & Stratford	92		N		6/9/87	5/10/90		
Port Du Chene & Southside			N			5/10/90		
Port Hawkesbury & Truro	125		N		?/13/81	3/2/83		
Port Hope & Toronto	70		P		8/26/89	5/10/90		
Prince Albert & Regina	249		N		1911			
Prince Albert & Saskatoon	87		N		1942			
Prince Albert & Spirit River					1940			
Prince Albert & Swan Creek	262		N		1916			
Prince Albert & Winnipeg	546		N		2/15/80			Now Charlotteville & Sackville.
Prince Edward Island Boat	9		N		1913-19			
Prince George & Prince Rupert	467		N		1942			
Prince Rupert & Winnipeg	1758		N		1910			
Quebec & Richmond	103	G. T.	N		10/17/89			
Quebec & Riviere Du Loup	125	G. T.	P	6/23/79	12/9/89			"Express" may read "Through", "Local", or "Mixed".
Quebec & Roberval	188	Q.&L.St.J.	N		1890	5/10/90	5/10/90	
Quebec & Sherbrooke	147	Q. C.	Q. C.		1920			
Quebec & St. John	581	I. C.	Q. C.	6/23/79	1942			
Quebec & Three Rivers	78	Q.M.O. & O.	N		1928	5/10/90		
Quebec & Tourville	118	N	P		1942			
Quesnel & Squamish	347	P.G.E.	P.G.E.		1911			
Regina & Souris	215		P		1942			
Regina & Swan River	242		N		1939			
Regina & Winnipeg	357		P		1942			
Regina & Yorkton	122		N		1942			

Route	Miles	R. R. At Time of Est.	Now Part of	Type I	Type II	Type III a	Type III b	Notes
Renfrew & Sharbot Lake	57		P		1942			
Reston & Wolesley	122		P		1942			
Richmond & T. Pond					8/1/89			{Error should be I. Pond. (q.v.)
Ridgetown & Sarnia					1899			
Rimouski & St. Angele	328		N		1937			
Rivers & Saskatoon	533		N		1935			
Rivers & Wainwright	267		N		1910			
Rivers & Watrous	143		N		1920			
Rivers & Winnipeg	81		P		1942			
Ruby & Vancouver	214		N		11/9/07	1/16/82		
St. Frances & Winnipeg	90		N		10/3/92			
St. John & Vanceboro	44(?)		N		1942			
St. John & Waterloo	90		P		1900			
St. John & Truro	100		N		1898			
St. Mary's & Toronto					1927			
St. Thomas & Stratford						5/10/90	5/10/90	Night or Day.
St. Thomas & Toronto	110		M. C.		1928			
St. Thomas & Vanceboro	82		N		5/9/87	5/10/90		
St. Thomas & Windsor	170	G. T.	N		8/5/83	1/12/82		
St. Vincent & Winnipeg	324		N		8/12/93	5/10/90		
Sarnia & Stratford	183		P		1919			
Sarnia & Toronto	38		Q. C.		5/2/89	5/10/90		
Saskatoon & Yorkton	22		N			5/10/90		
Sault Ste. Marie & Sudbury	82		N		1935			
Sherbrooke & Stanstead	212		P		1933	5/10/90		
Sifton & Winnipegosis					4/30/95	5/10/90		
Simcoe & Stratford	151		P		1942			
Smiths Falls & Toronto	115	P.E.I.	N		1910			IV 1/16/94.

Route	Miles	R. R. At Time of Est.	Now	Type I	Type II	Type III a	b	Notes
Stratford & Toronto	87		N		1918			
Stratford & Wiarton	106		N		2/20/03	5/10/90		
Swan River & Swift Current			N		1935			
Swan River & Wembley		N			1942			
Swan River & Winnipeg	293		N		1942			
Swan River & Yorkton	120		N		*1942*			
Sydney & Truro	225		N		*1920*			
Teeswater & Toronto	139		P		1910			Steamer
Vancouver & Victoria			P			5/10/90		
Victoria & Wellington	77		E.&N.		1942	5/10/90		
Virden & Winnipeg	223		N		1917			
Wainwright & Watrous	266		N		10/26/07			
Winnipeg & Yorkton	301		N					

1. Now included in Andover & Vanceboro.
2. Includes the former Andover and McAdam.
3. See Halifax, Digby & Yarmouth.
4. Arden is now Ardendale.
5. Steamboat on Arrowhead Lake.
6. Now obsolete.
7. See Belleville, Peterboro, & Toronto.
8. Connects at Blaine with U. S. R. P. O.—Blaine & Seattle.
9. In the U. S. this is Minneapolis & Winnipeg R.P.O.
10. Formerly Brantford & Ft. Erie, q.v.
11. Formerly Brantford & Bridgeburg, q.v.
12. Now Fort Erie & St. Thomas, q.v.
13. The original cancellation read "Brookville" in error. A corrected one was furnished a few days later. We have not seen the error in actual use, and it may not have ever been used.
14. In 1940 became part of Chicoutimi & Quebec, q.v.
15. Includes former Chambord & Quebec, q.v.
16. Lake Steamer.
17. Dec. 9, 1889 new cancel reading Riviere du Loup & Campbellton was furnished.
18. Now included in Swan River & Wembley, q.v.
19. Includes former Edmonton & Wembley, q.v.
20. Now included in Dawson Creek & Edmonton, q.v.
21. Formerly Bridgeburg & St. Thomas, q.v.
22. 78 miles via Fort Dover, 63 miles Direct.
23. Original cancel read "Richmond & T. Pond" in error. We have never seen this in actual use.
24. Aug. 9, '83 five cancels reading "R.P.O. #1" (to 5") were furnished. On July 9, 1890 another reading "G. T. Ry T & K No 1" was furnished.

2. Railway Markings With an Intermediate Point Given in the Designation.

Route	Mileage	Railway	II	Type of Marking III a	III b	IV
Allandale, Orillia & Midland	56		N	1935		
Belleville, Peterboro & Toronto	156		N	1935		
Canfield Dundas & St. Thomas			N	1897		
Chicoutimi, Lake St. John & Quebec	227		N	1918		
Chicoutimi, Roberval & Quebec	230		N	1903		
Edmundston, Hardesty&Saskatoon	368		P	1900		
Edmundston, Wainwright & Saskatoon	330		N	1916		
Fort William, Sudbury & Toronto				1935		
Goderich, Stratford & Toronto	134		N	1918		
Halifax, Bridgewater & Yarmouth	250		N	1935		
Halifax, Digby & Yarmouth	217	D.A.	P	1930		
Kingston, Sharbot Lake & Renfrew	104		P	1935		
Lac Frontiere, Vallee Jct. & Levis	123	Q.C.	Q. C.	1942		
Levis, Vallee Jct. & St. Sabine	99	Q.C.	Q. C.	1930		
London, Blenheim & Sarnia			N	1918		
London, Hamilton & Toronto	120			May 31, 1893	June 22, '93	
London, Paris & Toronto		G.T.	N	1890		
London, Port Hope & Midland			N	1928		
London, St. Mary's & Toronto			N	1918		
London, St. Thomas & Simcoe				1932		
London, St. Thomas & Windsor				1935		
London, Stratford & Toronto	121		N	Jan. 28 1893	June 22, '93	
London, Wiarton & Owen Sound				1935		
Matane, Joli & Montreal	397		N	1902		
Montreal, Calumet & Ottawa	125		P	1918		
Montreal, Coteau & Ottawa	116	C.A.	N	1890		
Montreal, Drummondville & Quebec			N	1918		May 10, '90
Montreal, Garneau Jct. & Quebec	177		N	1935		
Montreal, Island Pond & Portland	295		N,MeC	1918		
Montreal, Richmond & Sherbrooke	101	G.T.	N	1930		
Montreal, Rigaud & Ottawa	111		P	1918		
Montreal, Smiths Falls & Toronto	339	P	P	Nov. 19 1890		
Montreal, Sorel & Nicolet				1918		
North Bay, Gravenhurst & Toronto	228		N	1935		
North Bay, Sudbury & Sault Ste. Marie	262		P	1935		
Ottawa, Port Arthur & Winnipeg	1297	P	P	1903		
Port Hope, Peterboro & Toronto	124		N	1918		
Toronto, London & Windsor	227			1932		
Toronto, Palmerston & Wiarton			N	1930		

3. Railway Markings Giving the Name of Railway Only.

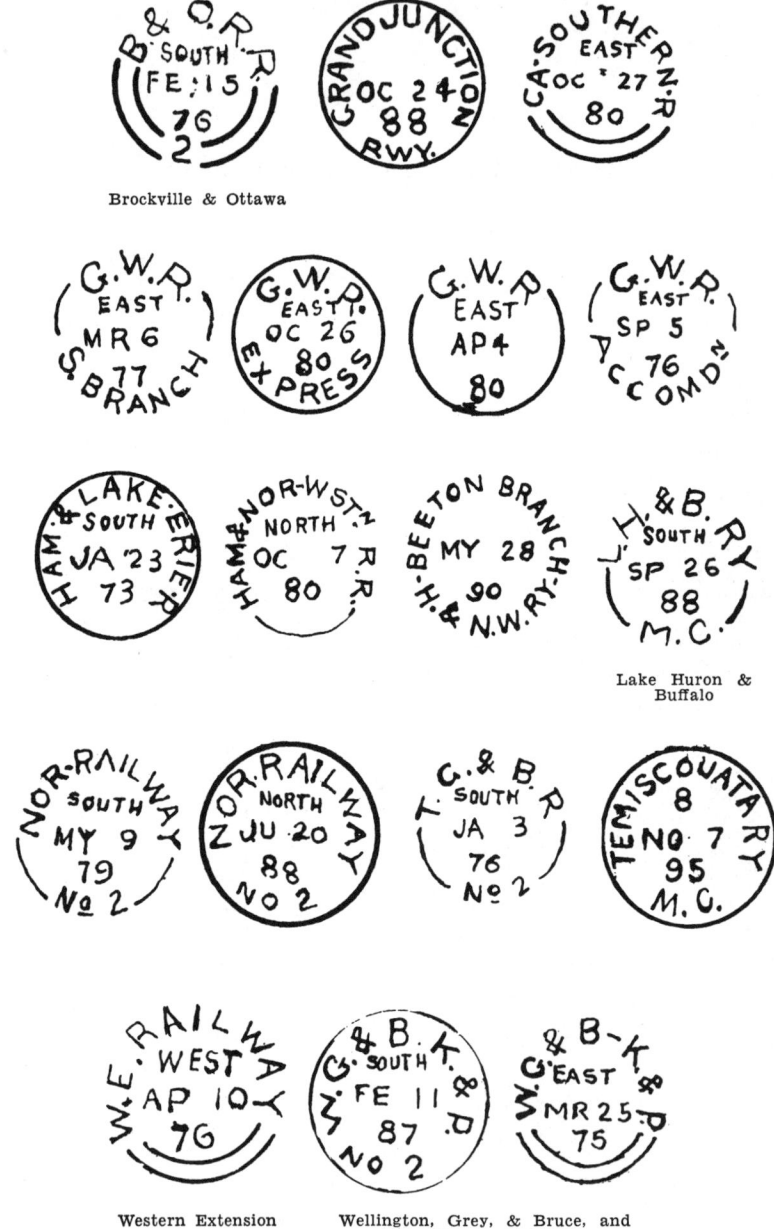

Brockville & Ottawa

Lake Huron & Buffalo

Western Extension   Wellington, Grey, & Bruce, and Kingston & Pembroke

Name of Railway	Approx. Mileage	Abbreviation	Type of Marking I	Type of Marking II	Type of Marking III
Brockville & Ottawa	(58)		Feb. 1876		1
Buffalo & Lake Huron (See also Lake Huron & Buffalo)		B.&L.H.R.	Apr. 6, 1879		
Canada Atlantic	(165)	C. A. R.	Jan. 2, 1882	Sep. 28, 1887	Feb. 2, 1892
Canada Central 1.	(210)	Can. Centl.	Nov. 14, 1876		
Canada Southern 2.	(360)	CA So.	1879	Jun. 9, 1886	Apr. 6, 1879
St. Clair Branch	(62)		Oct. 25, 1878	Oct. 1878	
Canada Northern			1903		
Canadian Pacific		C. P. Ry.			
British Columbia	(650)	B. C.	Mar. 20, 1890	Jan. 6, 1893	
Souris Section			Aug. 15, 1892	Jan. 2, 1882	
West of Winnipeg	(1,550)			Jun. 2, 1893	
West of Winnipeg, Local (#1, 2, or 3)				June. 2, 1893	
New Brunswick Div.		N. B. DIV.		Mar. 2, 1891	
Brockville & Ottawa Div.			Nov. 25, 1880		
Central Ontario	(105)	C. O.		Aug. 2, 1886	
Credit Valley—Elora Branch	(128)		Aug. 5, 1882		
Main Line	(175)		Aug. 5, 1882		
Esquimault & Nanaimo	(75)	E. & N.		Sept. 9, 1886	
European & North American 8.	(210)	E. & N.A.		Sept. 9, 1886	
G. B. & L. E.			Jul. 12, 1882	Nov. 25, 1890	
Great Western	(650)	G. W. R.	Apr. 6, 1879		
Accom					
Express			Apr. 6, 1879	Nov. 25, 1890	
Sarnia Branch	(51)		Mar. 1877		
MAINLINE			1876	Oct. 1880	
			Apr. 1880		
Grand Junction	(90)	G. Jct.	Oct. 1888		
Green Bay & Lake Erie			Jul. 12, 1882		
Hamilton & Lake Erie	(33)	G.B.&L.E.	Jan. 23, 1873		
Hamilton & North Western	(140)	H. & N. W.	Mar. 26, 1879	Nov. 25, 1890	
Beeton Branch	(25)		Aug. 20, 1881		
Collingwood Branch	(20)		Oct. 13, 1879		
Halifax & Southwestern		H. & S. W.		1913	
Kennebec & Levis		K.&L.	6/23/79		
Kingston & Pembroke, Northern Div.	(105)	K.&P.Nor.		1885	
Lake Huron & Buffalo (See also Buffalo & Lake Huron)		L. H. & B.	Mar. 5, 1881		
Levis & Kennebec 6.	(45)	L. & K.	Jun. 23, 1879		
London & Port Stanley	(26)	L. & P. S.	1877		
Massawippi Valley	(38)	M. V.		Aug. 2. 1886	
Manitoba & Northwestern	(235)	M.&N.W.			May. 10, 1890
Midland	(445)	Mid.	Jan. 25, 1883	Apr. 9, 1883	
Northern 5.	(250)	Nor.	May 1879	May 15, 1882	
Nor & P Jct.				Jan. 9, 1887	
Ontario & Western		O. & W.	Apr. 12, 1876		
Port Dover & Lake Huron 3.	(63)	P.D.&L.H.	Apr. 12, 1876		
Prince Edward County Ry	(32)	P. E. C.			
Prince Edward Island	(210)	P. E. I.		May 1, 1880	
Pontiac & Pacific Jct.	(71)	P. & P. Jc.		Feb. 16, 1889	
Quebec Central	(213)	Q. C.	Nov. 2, 1882	Aug. 9, 1888	
Quebec & Lake St. John	(287)	Q.&L.St.J.	May 2, 1891	Dec. 9, 1889	
Quebec, Montreal, & Ottawa		Q. M. & O.		Apr. 30, 1886	
Quebec, Montreal, Ottawa & Occidental	(330)	Q.M.O.&O.	May 2, 1878		
St. Lawrence & Ottawa 7.	(54)	St.L.&O.	Feb. 25, 1881	Sept. 15, 1887	
Shefford Ry.	(66)			Aug. 1, 1889	
Toronto, Grey & Bruce 9.	(192)	T. G. & B.	Jan. 1876		
Temiscouata	(113)	T.		Sept. 2, 1892	
Victoria	(56)	Vic.	Jun. 25, 1879	Aug. 9, 1883	
Wellington, Grey & Bruce 4.	(185)	W.G.&B.	May 1875	Feb. 1887	
Welland	(25)	W.	Feb. 25, 1881		
Western Extension		W. E.	Apr. 1876		
Whitby, Port Perry, Lindsay & Victoria	(70)	W.Pt.P.L. & V. Rys.		Nov. 25, 1878	

1. Consolidated with the Canada Central in 1877, which became "Canadian Pacific Railway, Eastern Division" in 1881.
2. Now part of the Michigan Central.
3. Became part of the Grand Trunk about 1880.
4. Leased 1878 to Great Western.
5. Formerly the Ontario, Simcoe & Huron.
6. Became part of Quebec Central 1881.
7. Formerly the Bytown & Prescott.
8. Corporate Title "St. John & Maine" from 1879.
9. Became part of the Grand Trunk, 1880.

4. The Registered Railway Markings.

Type I.   Type II.   Type III. Octagonal.
20 mm. in diam.   31 mm. in diam.   30 mm. wide.

REGISTERED G.W.R.	REGISTERED G.W.R. ACCOM.
REGISTERED G.W.R. EXPR.	REGISTERED P. D. & L. H
REGISTERED WELLAND-R.	REGISTERED WEST. EXT

Type IVa.   Rectangular 40-42x11-13 mm.

Type IVb.   Similar, but with pointed ends.

| REGISTERED C. S. R. | REGISTERED H & L.E R. |

Type V.   Rectangular 50-51x20-21 mm.

List of Registered Railway Markings.

All have the word "Registered" above the name of the Railway

Railway	Abbreviation	Type	Date	Notes
Buffalo & Lake Huron	B. & L. H.	II	July 1878	
		IVa	1881	
Canada Southern	C. S. R.	V	1878	
St. Clair Branch		IVb	Oct. 25, 1878	
		IVa		
Grand Trunk—EAST	G.T.R.E.	I	Jun. 1878	
Sarnia Branch	G.T.R.S.B.	IVa	1878	
Grand Junction	G. Jct.	IVa	Feb. 1882	
Great Western	G. W. R.	IVa	1878	
Accomodation	G.W.R. Accom.	IVa	1878	
Express	G.W.R. Expr.	IVa	1878	
Sarnia Branch	G.W.R. Sarnia Branch	Oval	Jul. 1878	
Hamilton & Lake Erie	H.&L.E.R.	V		
Hamilton & Northwestern	H.&N.W.	III	Jul. 1878	
		IVa	Mar. 1879	
Hamilton & Toronto	H.&T.R.	IVa	Oct. 1876	
Huron & Lake Erie	H.&L.E.	V	1875	
London, Hamilton & Buffalo	L.H.&B.	IVa	Mar. 1881	
Muskoka Branch		I	1876	
Port Dover & Lake Huron	P.D.&L.H.	IVa	Jul. 1878	3 varieties.
Southern Extension		IVa	Oct. 1876	
Toronto, Grey & Bruce	T.G.&B.	I	1875	
	T. & N.	I	Oct. 1876	
	T. & S.	IVa		
Welland		IVa	1875	
Western Extension	West Ext.	IVa	Oct. 1876	
Wellington, Grey & Bruce	W.G.&B.	IVa	Oct. 1876	2 varieties.
Whitby, Port Perry, Lindsay & Victoria	W. Pt. P. L. & W.	IVa	Nov. 1878	

5. Miscellaneous Notes.

When the railways were being extended into vast new areas the end of the track was the location of a temporary post office which moved forward as the line was built. We illustrate an "END OF STEEL" marking used during the building of the Grand Trunk Pacific to Prince Rupert. See also page 693.

A Note on the Travelling Letter Boxes.

Supplementing the service provided by the Railway Post Offices is the system of "Travelling Letter Boxes" or "Train Boxes."

These are steel locked boxes, with a slot for depositing letters which are carried on certain trains in which Railway Post Offices are not maintained.

These boxes are carried in the baggage car, and at the various stops en route, they are placed in the door for the purpose of enabling persons to mail any outgoing letters they may have.

At the terminals the boxes are taken to the post office or transferred at junction points to Railway Mail Clerks who open them and forward the contents in the usual manner.

At some of the larger terminals the letters taken from these boxes are each struck with a marking reading "Travelling Letter Box." It appears that they are of two main types, the machine cancel with a slogan, and a similar form which is handstruck on pieces of mail which cannot be put through the cancelling machines.

How extensive the use of these boxes is can be realized by noting that in 1942 approximately 175 routes had this service; some routes having more than one box on them. In addition at least five coastwise steamer routes (under the jurisdiction of the Railway Mail Service) also had Travelling Letter Boxes at that time.

The system was in operation as early as 1893 if not for some time previously, and is still functioning.

Chapter XXXVIII

STEAMBOAT AND STEAMSHIP MARKINGS

STEAMBOAT[1]

Almost as soon as steamboats were plying on the rivers of Canada their usefulness in mail carrying was recognized. Steamboat captains would pick up letters and deliver them to the first post office port the boat called at. For this service they were entitled to one penny per letter. Some of these boats had sufficient volume of mail to warrant the letters being stamped "Steamboat" and until 1847 all such letters are those handled by the boats as private carriers and not as contractors for the mails.

Pair of 3d on Wove with "Steamboat Letter Montreal Aug. 23, 1855" in Black

In 1846 tenders were asked for the conveyance of mail by steamboat, with the additional stipulation that a mail conductor, or an employee of the contractor in charge of the mail should have a room for the exclusive use of the Post Office.[2]

In September 1847 detailed instructions were issued to the mail contractor[3], and from these instructions we can see that on each boat carrying mail there was a letter box for the reception of mail at ports of call. On leaving a port the post office conductor on the boat was required to write on the face of each letter at the left-hand corner the name of the place at which the letter was received and stamp it with his office stamp (steamboat postmark). Mail in sealed bags delivered by postmasters to the boat was not dealt with in this way.

---
1. Chapter heading is from a die proof of the British American Bank Note Co., made about 1870.
2. Appendix S #1.
3. Appendix B #14.

Lake Ontario Steamboat Advertisements of 1835

LAKE ONTARIO.—ARRANGEMENTS FOR 1835.—The steamboats GREAT BRITAIN and UNITED STATES will run as follows until the 1st of June.

The Great Britain, Capt. J. Whitney.

Going Up.—Leaves Prescott, Tuesday evening; Brockville, do. do.; Kingston, Wednesday noon; Oswego, do. evening; Cobourg, Thursday morning; Port Hope, do. do.; Toronto, Friday morning, and arrives at Niagara same morning.

Coming down.—Leaves Niagara, Saturday, 4 P. M; Toronto, do. evening; Port Hope, Sunday morning; Cobourg, do. do; Oswego, Sunday evening; Kingston, Monday morning; Brockville, do. noon, and arrives at Prescott, Monday afternoon.

The United States, Capt. J. Van Cleve.

Going Up.—Leaves Ogdensburgh, 8, Saturday evening; Kingston, Sunday, 7, A. M; Sacket's Harbor, Sunday, 1 P. M; Oswego, Sunday, 10, P. M; Rochester, Monday, 8, A M; Toronto, do 9 in the evening, and arrives at Lewiston on Tuesday morning early.

Coming Down.—Leaves Lewiston, Tuesday, 7, A. M. Rochester, Wednesday, 8, A. M; Oswego, Wednesday, afternoon; Sacket's Harbor, Wednesday, 12 at night; Kingston, Thursday, 7 in the morning, and arrives at Ogdensburgh in the forenoon.

From 1st June to 1st September, the two boats will, in connexion, perform three trips in each week, starting from Niagara and from Ogdensburgh and Prescot, every other day, (excluding Sundays,) as follows:

The Great Britain.

Going Up.—Leaves Prescott, Tuesday evening Brockville, do. do; Kingston, Wednesday, 12 noon; Oswego, do. evening; Toronto, Thursday, at noon, and arrives at Niagara, Thursday, P. M.

Coming Down.—Leaves Niagara, Thursday, 10 in the evening; and arrives at Oswego, Friday afternoon.

Going Up.—Leaves Oswego, Friday 6 the evening; Toronto, Saturday, 12 noon, and arrives Niagara in the afternoon.

Coming Down.—Leaves Niagara, Sunday, 4, P. M; Oswego, Monday, 7 in the morning; Kingston, Monday, 2, P. M; Brockville, do. evening, and arrives at Prescott the same evening.

The United States.

Coming down.—Leaves Lewiston, Tuesday evening; Rochester, Wednesday morning; Oswego, do. evening; Sacket's Harbor, do. 12 at night; Kingston, Thursday morning, and arrives at Ogdensburgh, Thursday, P. M.

Going Up.—Leaves Ogdensburg, Thursday evening; Kingston, Friday morning; Sacket's Harbor, Friday noon, and arrives at Oswego same afternoon.

Coming down.—Leaves Oswego, Friday, at 6 P. M; Sacket's Harbor, Friday, 11, P. M; Kingston, Saturday, 7, A. M. and arrives at Ogdensburgh, Saturday afternoon.

Going Up.—Leaves Ogdensburgh, 8, Saturday evening; Kingston, Sunday morning; Sacket's Harbor, Sunday noon; Oswego, Sunday evening; Rochester, Monday morning; Toronto, Monday evening, and arrives at Lewiston early Tuesday morning.

And after the first of September, the respective boats will resume their trips as first above stated.   ap 9-C&S

THE TRANSIT, Hugh Richardson, master, and **CANADA,** Frank Bury, master, steam packets for Niagara and Toronto.

The TRANSIT, daily, leaves Toronto at 7 A. M. and Niagara at 2 P. M.

The CANADA, daily, leaves Niagara at 7 A. M. and Toronto at 1 P. M.

Passengers returning to either of the ports, in either of the Packets, within a week, will only be charged half price for the return.

Good accommodation for horses, carriages, and cattle.

☞ No luggage taken in charge, unless booked and paid for.

HUGH RICHARDSON, Managing Owner.
City of Toronto, 1835.   aug 18.C&S

Other Steamboat Advertisements of 1835

a. Private "Steamboat" Markings

STEAM BOAT
Type I. Three Rivers. 1817.

STEAM BOAT
Type II. Kingston to Toronto and vice versa. 1840.

Type III. Quebec. 1842.

b. Markings of Contract Steamboats[3a]

Double weight letter, Quebec to Philadelphia, with "Steamboat Letter" Type I, "PAID" of New York, and "Canada" exchange marking Type Ia, all in red. Two 6p stamps, on laid paper, tied by black concentric ring cancel.

Type IV   Type Va-d   Type VI

3a. Appendix L #36. Typical contract letter.

STEAMBOAT

Type VII   Type VIIIa. Strokes of letter about 1½ mm. thick.
Type VIIIb. Strokes of letters about 1mm. thick.

"Steamboat" Type VIIIa tying a 3p perforated to a cover which is also struck with "Ottawa and Grenville" Railway cancellation. Both markings in black.

c. Ship Letter Marks

Type II.

Types V, VI

Letters received at Quebec from various merchant vessels not under contract to carry mails were struck with the markings noted above. At first the shipmasters received one penny per letter (Act of 1711), and did not have to accept such mail. In 1790 the fee was two pence, and in 1814 the rate was made three pence, and the following year an act was passed making it compulsory on all shipmasters to carry such mails as should be tendered them by the Post Office. By 1840 the rate was again 2d per letter or packet. The system of "ship letters" began to decline rapidly with the opening of regular contract service by Cunard in 1840, and Hugh Allan in 1855.

d. Canadian Packet (Allen Line) Markings[4].

Hugh Allan, founder of the famous line of Canadian steamers, which had the mail contract for so many years. (See Appendix M #4, 8). Illustration is from a die proof in black on india, by the British American Bank Note Co., made about 1877, Die #39.

BY-CANADA PACKET	BY-CANADIAN PACKET	CANADIAN-PKT E JA 13 1866
Type I	Type II	Type III

Of these, three types have been noted. Letters from Canada to Great Britain were forwarded either from Quebec or Halifax by Canadian Packet or from New York or Boston by Cunard Packet. The sender of the letter, usually in writing on the face, indicated the route to be taken, and as the postage rate varied, put on the appropriate postage stamp or stamps. When letters reached Great Britain the receiving office at the port usually stamped on them if they arrived from Quebec or Halifax "By Canada Packet", or equivalent words. Those illustrated, however, were used in Canada.

REFERENCE LIST

Type	Date				Black	Red
		Private Steamboats				
I	1817	Three Rivers			12.50	
II	1840	Kingston-Toronto			10.00	15.00
III	184-	Quebec			30.00	
		Contract Steamboats				
IV	Steamboat Letter		Quebec	1851	7.50	5.00
V	Similar but smaller	(a)	Hamilton	1847	—	50.00
		(b)	Kingston	1847	x	20.00
		(c)	Toronto City	1852	7.50	25.00
		(d)	Montreal	1853	7.50	10.00
VI	Double Circle		Kingston	1854	7.50	
VII	Crown Type		Niagara	1854	—	25.00
VIIIa	Straight Line		(Lake Ontario)	1858	7.50	
VIIIb	Similar but thinner letters		?	1860	7.50	

4. Appendix M #4, 7, 8 and 9, and Appendix S #3.

Ship Letter

Type	Date		Black	Red
I	1793	"HALIFAX SHIP LRE"	35.00	
II	1800	"Ship Letter QUEBEC" Double oval	15.00	
III	1801	Halifax	15.00	
IV	1839	Circular, Date in center	50.00	
V	1840	Montreal	60.00	
VI	1840	Quebec	25.00	35.00

See also Handstruck Postage Dues—Ocean Mail Letters. Page 485.

The Allan steamer "Hibernian", 3,000 Tons, 11 knots 300 feet long. Built 1861. From a die proof in black on India, by the British American Bank Note Co., made about 1877, Die #141.

Canada Packet

			Black	Red
I	By-Canada PACKET	1855	—	x
II	By Canadian Packet	1859	7.50	
III	Canadian PKT (and date)	1866	x	

e. Marine and Sea Post Offices

Later years show a number of other markings used by the various inland and coastal steamers conveying mails. Some of these are under the jurisdiction of the Railway Mail Service, as they are run in connection with the various Railway Post Offices.

We list a few of the recent ones that have come to our attention:

1. "BURRARD INLET."—1920.
2. "Quebec & Blanc Sablon Sea Post."—1935-1937.
3. "Quebec & Lourdes Du Blanc Sablon Sea Post."—1937.
4. "S. S. DISTRIBUTOR POST OFFICE."—1937.
5. "PORT COLBORNE ONT MARINE POST OFFICE."—1939-1942.
6. "MUSKOKA LAKES STR. No 2."—1940.
7. "CORNWALL ONT MARINE POST OFFICE."—1940.
8a. "EASTERN ARCTIC PATROL-R.M.S."—1941.
8b. "EASTERN ARCTIC PATROL in oval."—1941.

Chapter XXXIX

THE POSTAL DEVELOPMENT OF THE NORTHWEST[1]

The special report of the P. O. Inspector in 1882 is the best possible discussion of the development of the Postal Service in the vast territory from Winnipeg to British Columbia and north to the Arctic that we know of and we give it herewith practically in its entirety:

Winnipeg, Manitoba,
16th December, 1882.[1a]

SIR—In compliance with your instructions, I have visited Winnipeg and made personal enquiry into the history, present condition and future requirements of the postal service in Manitoba and the territory of the North-West.

I have prepared statements to accompany this Report, showing the details of the postal organization and service throughout that region.

The history and growth of the postal service is so intimately connected with the progress of the country, that, although I may perhaps be overstepping the usual official routine, I will in the course of the following Report, narrate briefly a few facts of general interest, than which nothing can more strongly illustrate the rapid strides which have been made, especially within the last two or three years, in the development of this portion of the Dominion.

Before the year 1853 only three mails were despatched and received each year; one to and from New York Factory, connecting there with the ship that came annually from London, bringing out goods for the trade with the Indians during the ensuing season, and taking home on the return voyage the proceeds (in the shape of furs and skins) of the previous year's trade. The two others to and from Montreal, via Lake Superior and the Ottawa River.

The starting of the brigade of boats from Montreal in the spring, surrounded as it was by circumstances of a wild and picturesqque character, formed quite an interesting scene, and their arrival on the Red River about forty days afterwards was an event anticipated with anxiety by the citizens of Assiniboia, who, in the midst of their untrodden wastes, awaited the receipt of news many weeks old from the outer world.

In 1853, a mail service was organized once per month between Fort Garry and Fort Ripley, in Minnesota, then the nearest United States Post Office.

In 1857, the American Government, having established a Post Office at Pembina, on the International Boundary, with a mail service once per month and subsequently once per fortnight, a mail was carried with the same frequency from and to Fort Garry.

In 1862 the United States authorities having increased the service to Pembina to twice and subsequently to three times per week, two trips per week, instead of one, were made by the courier between Fort Garry and Pembina.

The round trip from Fort Garry to Pembina and back, for which 25 shillings sterling, or about $6.25, was paid, occupied from three to four days. The mode of conveyance was on horseback in summer and dog sledge in winter; a very moderate sized bag being sufficient to contain all the matter in transit.

From the year 1862 to the year 1871, to which date the postal service was carried on by the Hudson's Bay Company, the Red River country, so far as the mails were concerned, was entirely dependent on the United States Post Office at Pembina; letters and papers inwards being sent in the American mails to Pembina and forwarded from there to Fort Garry, and letters and papers outwards, to which it was necessary that United States stamps (which were sold in Fort Garry) should be attached, being carried to Pembina and thence despatched as if posted at the Pembina office to their respective destinations.

In all of the expense of the local service a charge was made of one penny on each letter weighing less than half an ounce, of one half penny on each paper and of two pence on each periodical and magazine.

---
1. For Postal History of the Red River District See Appendix K.
1a. See also Appendix M #17, 18.

Besides the Post Office at Fort Garry there were three or four sub-Post Offices on the Red and Assiniboine Rivers, to and from which mails were carried, though not with any great regularity, once in each week.

The Post Office in Fort Garry was kept in part of a small log house on what is now called Post Office Street; the space appropriated for Post Office business, including the public lobby, being about 12 by 14 feet. The Postmaster was Mr. A. G. B. Bannatyne, who, with the assistance of one clerk, performed all the duties.

In the year 1870 Manitoba and the North-West Territory became part of the Dominion, and in the following year, 1871, were brought within the Canadian postal service, 21 Post Offices, including the Post Office at Fort Garry, were established, with a regular weekly or semi-weekly mail service. Closed bags were exchanged between Fort Garry and Windsor, Ontario, and a contract entered into for the conveyance of the mails three times per week by an extension of the tri-weekly stage route between St. Cloud (the then nearest United States railway station) and Pembina on to Fort Garry, the journey between St. Cloud and Fort Garry, 427 miles, occupying about seven days.

The annual reports of the Postmaster-General show the growth of the postal service from July, 1871, to the 30th June, 1882, its revenue and its cost of maintenance.

Gradually, by the extension northward of the lines in Minnesota, Fort Garry was rendered more accessible by railway.

On the 15th January, 1875, the stages to Pembina being made daily, a daily mail was established from thence to Fort Garry.

On the 8th January, 1879, the line of railway communication was completed to Winnipeg, and from that time a speedy and direct communication has been had with all parts of the United States, and through the United States with all parts of the Dominion. Two mails daily are now received and despatched at Winnipeg, the time occupied in the transit of a letter either to or from

Windsor, Ont., being			2½ days
Toronto	do		3 days
Ottawa	do		3½ days
Montreal	do		3½ days

Of the 207 Post Offices now in existence,

21	were established in		1871
5	do		1872
5	do		1873
2	do		1874
3	do		1875
12	do		1876
4	do		1877
12	do		1878
50	do		1879
31	do		1880
17	do		1881
45	do		1882

207

On the 1st August, 1876, a mail was established once in every three weeks between Winnipeg and Edmonton, a distance of about 900 miles, serving five intermediate offices. The trip either way was performed in about twenty-one days. The amount paid for the service, which was contracted for by the late Hon. James McKay, was $10,000 per annum.

On the expiration of this contract, tenders were invited in the usual manner, and a new contract entered into with Mr. J. W. McLean, which took effect on 1st November, 1880, the amount paid being $24,250 per annum. It should be stated that between the period of making the first and second contracts the weight of the mails carried had very greatly increased. Under a provision made in this contract, the payment to the Contractor has been from time to time reduced in proportion to the distance over that portion of his route on which the mails have been carried by railway. The mails are now carried from Troy (Qu'Apelle station, 323 miles west of Winnepeg) to Edmonton, a distance of 584 miles, and the amount paid annually to the contractor is $15,792. The time occupied in the trip either way is about fifteen days.

The returns for the fiscal year ending 30th June, 1883, will doubtless show a much higher rate of increase, the receipts of the Winnipeg office alone being now at the rate of $63,000 per annum, or more than double the whole revenue collected not three years since, at all the offices in Manitoba and the North-West, while all the new offices recently established along the lines of railway produce large revenues. I may mention as an illustration, that the sale of postage stamps at the Post Office at Brandon, which was established on 1st August, 1881,[2] (not much more than 16 months ago) now averages $800 per month, or between $9,000 and $10,000 per annum.

In the year 1876, the Winnipeg Post Office was removed to the building in which it is now held, on Main Street, but to which last year it was found necessary to make a considerable addition.

During the present year the interior of the office was remodelled and furnished with new fittings and 1,304 lock boxes.

A free delivery by letter carriers was also established and 12 street letter boxes placed in different parts of the city from which collections are made three times daily.

DIRECT MAILS ARE EXCHANGED,

Between	And
Winnipeg	St. Vincent.
do	St. Vincent and St. Paul postal car.
do	Breckenridge and St. Paul postal car.
do	Windsor, Ontario.
do	Toronto, do
do	Toronto and Montreal postal car.
Winnipeg and St. Vincent postal car	⎰ St. Paul and St. Vincent postal car. ⎱ Windsor, Ontario.
Emerson	St. Vincent.
do	St. Vincent and St. Paul postal car.
do	Breckenridge and St. Paul postal car.
do	Windsor, Ontario.

The staff of the Inspector consists of 5 persons whose united annual salaries and provisional allowances amount to $6,740.

There are on the staff of Railway Mail Clerks, 1 Chief Clerk and 6 Clerks whose salaries amount annually to $5,656, exclusive of mileage allowance.

There are now 877 miles of railway over which mails are carried, viz:—

Route.	Railway in miles. Actual length of	No. of Postal Cars on Road daily.	No. of Mail Clerks.	Distance Travelled in miles.	Daily Service by Bags in charge of Company's Servants.
Rat Portage and Thunder Bay..	300				300
Rat Portage and Winnipeg........	136				272
Stonewall and Winnipeg............	20				40
St. Vincent and Winnipeg........	65	1	3	130	130
Verdun and Regina......................	180				352
Verdun and Winnipeg................	176	2	3	360	
Total	877	3	6	490	1,094

2. The P. M. G. Report for 1881 gives the date as Nov. 1, 1880.

The circumstances of this part of the Dominion are so constantly changing, the population is scattered over such a vast area, and the progress of the settlements so rapid, that it is difficult, if not impossible, to foresee what provision it will be desirable to make for the extension of the postal service during the coming year. Much will of course depend on the number, extent and direction of the various new settlements in regard to which even the most careful estimates may be at fault.

Population will, no doubt, be attracted principally towards the lines of railway, completed or in course of construction.

The number of miles of railway in operation, over which mails are now carried is:

By postal car	245	
By Baggage	631	
		876
In operation over which mails are *not* carried		343
Now in course of construction and to be completed by 31st Dec., inst.		91
To be completed next year		407
Total		1717

There will, therefore, be about 841 additional miles of road in operation next year, the carriage of mails over which, daily, Sundays excepted, will be demanded, and which at the rate of 4 cents per mile travelled would entail an additional outlay of $20,958.64.

To this must be added the cost of transportation between the several stations and postoffices, the cost of the establishment of new offices, and of a greater frequency of service over existing routes, all of which must involve a large outlay.

The following figures may perhaps form some basis on which to estimate the additional expenditure required, including the $20,985.64 estimated for Railway service.

Estimated cost of service of new offices for which application has been made	$11,000
Alterations in existing Post Routes under consideration	27,000
Cost of new routes which may be required	15,000
Total	$53,000

To this again must be added, a certain percentage which will doubtless, be wanted to serve new settlements, which will come into existence over the whole country, and which should be supplied with postal accommodation.

This expenditure may seem very large and out of proportion to the past and present requirements. Three facts should be borne in mind, however. The first, that where there is regular Railway communication, it is naturally enough expected that it will be used for postal purposes. The second, that the establishment of mail communication, than which nothing is perhaps more generally appreciated, is essential to the convenience and prosperity of the country; that its absence, than which nothing is more keenly felt, means hardship to the new settlements, obstruction to all kinds of business, and general dissatisfaction and complaint.

The third is that the cost of postal service in Manitoba and the North-West is much higher than the cost of similar service in the older portions of the Dominion, where not only is there greater competition for mail contracts, but where wages and cost of outfit for such work are materially lower, and the facilities for the performance of mail service more readily attainable.

In view of these considerations, and further, in view of the immigration during the coming year of a superior class of settlers, whose correspondence is large, and to whom postal facilities are a necessity, I would respectfully recommend that a liberal appropriation should be asked, not only for the establishment of new offices and mail route, but for the improvement of existing lines whereon the settlement and revenue collected may warrant a greater frequency of service.

I have made careful enquiry as regards the present and proposed arrangements for the mail service to and from Fort Walsh, Fort McLeod and Calgary.

The present arrangements for the service of these places is as follow:

Closed bags are made up at Windsor for Fort Walsh and Fort McLeod three times per week, and despatched by United States mails to the nearest frontier offices in Montana.

The bags for Fort Walsh are taken to Assiniboine, and the bags for Fort McLeod to Benton, the journey from Windsor occupying about nine days.

Couriers run once in every 10 days.

Between	Distance in Miles.	Days occupied in Journey.	Cost per annum.
			$ cts.
Assiniboine and Fort Walsh	160	5	5,000.00
Benton and Fort MacLeod	220	6	6,000.00
Fort McLeod and Calgary	100	3	2,400.00
Total	480	....	13,400.00

Leaving each terminus of the route on the 5th, 15th and 25th of each month.

One-third of the cost is paid by the Montreal Police, one-third by the North-West Government, and one-third by the Indian Department.

Though the correspondence inwards is, as already stated, made up at Windsor in closed bags, there is no provision for the making up of closed bags for Windsor in return, the bags are consequently returned to Windsor empty, and the outgoing letters and papers, on which American stamps have to be placed, are carried to Assiniboine and Benton and forwarded from thence through the ordinary United States mails. I fear that in this way losses have occurred. It was only a short time since that I was informed of the non-receipt by the Department of the Interior of a packet containing original notes of survey, which, if not recovered, will entail considerable inconvenience.

It is now proposed that the above routes be discontinued, and that the matter for and from Maple Creek, (to which point the station at Fort Walsh is, I understand, to be removed) Fort McLeod and Calgary shall be carried via Winnipeg.

That a regular post office shall be established at the western extremity of the track of the Canadian Pacific Railway, that this office shall move with the end of the track as it extends westerly, and that from it should be served, once in ten days, or once per fortnight a sub-office, to be established at Fort McLeod and a sub-office to be established at Calgary.

That the office at the end of the track should be known as the "Western Terminus" office; that it should be placed under the charge of Mr. Fauquier (son of the late Bishop Fauquier), of the Mounted Police, who, with a small detachment of the force, will be stationed at the end of the track, and that it should exchange mails with the travelling post office between Winnipeg and Verdun, either daily, or as often as the trains run over the road.

The estimated cost of the above proposed arrangement is as follows:—

Between	Distance in Miles.	Days occupied in Travel.	Cost per Annum.
			$ cts.
Regina and West Terminus (which will this winter be at Maple Creek) by railway	245	1	*6,134.80
West Terminus and Fort McLeod	190	5	3,000.00
Fort McLeod and Calgary	100	3	2,000.00
	535	....	11,134.80

*For daily service.

After the track crosses the Seven Persons River, 60 miles west of Maple Creek it is proposed that the couriers shall run.

Between	Distance in Miles.	Days occupied in Travel.	Cost per Annum.
			$ cts.
Regina and West Terminus (at Seven Persons' River) by railway	305	1	7,637.20
West Terminus and Calgary	180	5	3,000.00
Calgary and Fort McLeod	100	3	2,000.00
	585	....	12,637.20

The reasons for the change being that the route is a better one from Seven Persons River to Calgary than to Fort McLeod, and that as the track is extended westward, the distance that the mail is carried by courier will be shortened and the cost correspondingly diminished.

Under the proposed plan not only will the transit of correspondence to and from Maple Creek (to which the Fort Walsh station is to be moved) be considerably expedited, but a reduction will be effected in the present cost, as will be seen by the following comparative statements.

Time occupied in transit of correspondence:

Between		By present Route. Days	By proposed Route. Days
Ottawa and Fort Walsh		15	....
do	Maple Creek	....	7
do	Fort McLeod	20	12
do	Calgary	23	15

Total cost of present Route $13,400
   do   of proposed 11,134

         Decrease $2,266

The present services between Assiniboine and Fort Walsh, Benton and Fort MacLeod, would of course be dispensed with. The contracts do not expire until the 1st April, 1883, but I am informed the contractors would probably be willing to terminate them at an earlier date for a small compromise.

I may state that offices will no doubt, during the coming summer be required at several points on the Railway, and that a communication being established to and from the end of the track, all these offices could, without additional expense, receive and despatch their mails.

By the autumn of 1883 it is expected that the end of the track will be at Calgary which is a centre for the ranche country, and which will be the most convenient distributing point for mails going southward 100 miles to Fort McLeod and northward 220 miles to Edmonton. Calgary is 245 miles west of Maple Creek and 846 miles west of Winnipeg.

At Calgary there is a settlement numbering about 300 souls. There are also stationed at this place 60 or 70 mounted police.

About twenty-five miles west of Calgary is the Cochrane ranche, comprising within its limits 210,000 acres, and stocked with about 500 horses and 18,000 head of cattle.

At Morleyville, 17 miles beyond the Cochrane ranche, and forty-two miles west of Calgary, there is a settlement consisting of about sixty souls.

On the trail between Calgary and Fort McLeod there are two small settlements. The one at High River, thirty-five miles south of Calgary, consisting of about fifty souls; the other at Willow Creek, about twenty-five miles south of High River, and thirty miles north of Fort McLeod, consisting of twenty souls.

Fort McLeod is a centre for the settlements on the Belly and Old Man Rivers, as also for the settlement at Pincher Creek, thirty-five miles west, (probably the largest in that part of the country), which consists of about eighty souls. There are also in the neighborhood of Pincher Creek several small ranches.

Between Calgary and Edmonton there are two small settlements, the one where the trail crosses the Red Deer River, the other where the trail crosses the Battle River.

Edmonton is the centre of a large settlement and the "frontier" town for the extensive country to the north and westward drained by the Athabasca and Peace Rivers.

Though it may somewhat extend my report, I venture to lay before you a few facts which will, I trust, convey some idea of the wonderful progress which has, within a comparatively short time, been made in Manitoba and the North-West Territory.

The rapidity with which the City of Winnipeg has grown has, perhaps, rarely been equalled. In 1871 it was a small village, containing about 300 or 400 inhabitants. It was, as already stated, distant from the nearest railway station, St. Cloud, 427 miles, and the journey thither occupied seven days. It is now a city of considerable importance. A larger mercantile and banking business is done there in proportion to its size than in any city in the Dominion. Its population is about 25,000; the value of assessable property over $30,000,000. The value of imports for the year ended 30th June last was $4,936,213, and the duties collected $1,016,001. For the quarter ended 30th September the value of imports was $3,249,446, and the Duties collected $553,566, being at the rate of $2,214,264 per annum.

At only two other cities in the Dominion, viz., Montreal and Toronto, are the customs and postal receipts exceeded.

It is the centre of four great divisions of the Canadian Pacific Railway; one destined (in connection with lines already completed or in course of construction through Canadian territory) to reach the Atlantic, stretching 426 miles eastward to Thunder Bay on Lake Superior; one destined (in connection with lines in course of construction in British Columbia) to reach the Pacific, stretching 510 miles westward to Swift Current; one stretching 67 miles southward on the east side of Red River to St. Vincent, and one stretching 69 miles southward on the west side of Red River to Gretna, the roads on both sides of the river connecting at their southern termini on the International Boudary line with the American railway system.

There are also centreing at Winnipeg two smaller lines of railways.

One (the Canadian Pacific) stretching 20 miles north-westerly to Stonewall and one (the Manitoba Southwestern) stretching 53 miles south-westerly to Carman. Another branch of the Canadian Pacific is also in course of construction stretching 22 miles northeasterly on the west side of the Red River to Selkirk.

It will be seen by the above that Winnipeg is now the centre of six lines and will probably next year be the centre of seven lines of railway.

There are at the Winnipeg station of the Canadian Pacific Railway 16 miles of siding. In the nine months, ended 30th September last, there were "handled" at this station 85,714 loaded and empty freight cars, being an average of 9,524 cars per month.

In 30 days, during the present season, there arrived by train from the south 30,000 passengers, being an average of 1,000 per day. What was the total number of arrivals during the year I regret I have been unable to ascertain.

Throughout the vast extent of Manitoba and the North-West astonishing progress has been made. Thriving settlements have grown up where a very short time since there was not a solitary inhabitant, and the first pioneers isolated by great distances from their "nearest neighbor" have soon found themselves in the centre of prosperous farming communities.

Villages and towns, with their churches, their schools, their mills, stores and hotels, have sprung into existence with a rapidity almost unprecedented and many places at which but a short time since there was nothing but the desolate prairie are now centres at which a large business is transacted and in which the value of property has risen to a height which it would be difficult to exaggerate.

I cannot better illustrate this than by the following statistics, with which the Postmasters of the several places mentioned have furnished me the figures in which, though they may not be in every case critically correct, are perhaps as nearly so as it is possible for a rough estimate to make them.

Name of Place	Situation	Date of Establishment of Post Office	Population	Churches	Schools	Flour Mills	Saw Mills	Factories	Stores	Hotels	Value of Assessable Property $
Brandon	On C. P. Ry., main line	Aug. 1, 1881	3,200	6	2	1	1	2	79	16	3,690,940
Birtle	54 miles N.W. from Rapid City	Sept. 1, 1879	600	1	1	2	1	1	12	3	250,000
Emerson	On St. Vincent Branch of C. P. Ry.	Jan. 1, 1879	3,000	6	6	1	3	6	65	10	1,600,000
Gladstone	On W. & N. W. Ry.	April 1, 1872	500	3	1	1	2	....	9	4	697,000
Minnedosa	18 miles N. from Rapid City	Aug. 1, 1876	600	2	1	1	2	....	12	5	173,157
Morris	On C. P. Ry., on West side Red River	Jan. 1, 1874	400	4	1	1	1	14	4	Not stated
Portage la Prairie	On C. P. Ry., main line	July 1, 1871	3,000	7	5	1	12	12	71	18	6,500,000
Regina	do	Aug. 3, 1882	900	2	....	....	....	....	30	10	Not stated
Rapid City	20 miles N. from Brandon	Sept. 1, 1879	750	4	3	2	1	2	10	5	Not stated

Selkirk	On C. P. Ry., July 1, 1871								
	Selkirk Branch..		700	4	2	1....	1 8	2	879,519
Stonewall	On C. P. Ry., Jan. 1, 1876								
	Stonewall Br'ch		500	4	1	1....	7	2	Not stated
West Lynne	Opposite Emerson	July 1, 1878	400	2	1	1....	2 9	8	738,235
Prince Albert	Saskatchewan River	Dec. 1, 1878	1,500	4	3	2 2	2 23	6	2,500,000

The rapidity of railway construction during the present year has perhaps never been equalled. Notwithstanding the difficulties which the contractors, Messrs. Langdon & Sheppard experienced in the spring from the floods as well as from the scarcity of labour, they have during the present year built the 345 miles between Flat Creek (Oak Lake Station, 165 miles West of Winnipeg) and Swift Current, 510 miles west of Winnipeg, on which daily passenger and freight trains are now running.

Before the 31st instant they expect to have the track (a portion of which is already laid) completed 91 miles further west to Maple Creek, which will probably be the base of operations for next season's work and to which construction trains with material will probably run daily through the winter.

It will be seen from the above that during the present year there have been completed on the main line west of Winnipeg no less than 436 miles.

Some idea of the magnitude of this work may be formed when it is stated that it has given employment to between 3,000 and 4,000 men and about 1,500 teams, and that the quantity of earth "moved" each day has averaged 55,000 cubic yards.

	Miles
Besides the above work there have been constructed between Winnipeg and the International Boundary Line at Gretna	67
And between Morris Junction and Manitoba City	34
Total	101

making altogether 537 miles of road in a single season.

It will be seen that the number of miles of railway now completed and operated is as follows:—

	Miles
By Canadian Pacific Railway Company	831
By Manitoba South Western Colonization Railway Company	53
By Portage la Prairie, Westbourne & North Western Company	35
Total	919

	Miles
That by the end of the year there will be completed in addition to the above	91

Making a total distance by 31st December, 1882 of	1,010
And that by the end of next year about	707
(Including the 300 miles between Rat Portage and Thunder Bay) will have been added to the line over which there will be regular passenger and freight traffic	
Making a grand total of	1,717

Since the above was written I have been informed that it is the intention of the Portage la Prairie, Westbourne & North Western Railway Company to build 250 miles of railway during next year, west of Gladstone. This will make the number of miles in operation in 1883 1,967, or in round numbers not far from

2,000 miles. When it is remembered that the country through which these gigantic works have been and are being constructed was, a very few years ago, almost a solitary waste, roamed over by the Indian and visited at intervals only by the adventurous traveller and the officers of the Hudson Bay Company, some idea may be formed of what in a short time has been accomplished and of what may possibly be acomplished in years yet to come.

In connection with the means of internal communication provided by railways completed or in course of construction, a few facts in regard to the arrangements now being made for passenger and freight traffic by steamboat during the summer of 1883, on the Red River, the River Assiniboine, Lake Winnipeg and the River Saskatchewan may not prove uninteresting.

On the Red River two steamers will provide for one, two, or three trips per week each way, according to the business requirements, between Emerson and Winnipeg, a distance (by river) of about 100 miles, the round trip being performed in about 28 hours.

On the River Assiniboine two steamers will provide for trips about once per week between Winnipeg, Brandon and Fort Ellice, a distance of (by river) about 450 miles, and, so long as water is high enough, Fort Pelly, a distance of (by river) about 700 miles, the round trip between Winnipeg and Fort Ellice being performed in from ten to fourteen days, and between Winnipeg and Fort Pelly in about three weeks.

On Lake Winnipeg a steamer is to make regular weekly trips, with passengers and freight, between Winnipeg and Grand Rapids, where the River Saskatchewan falls into the lake, a distance of about 350 miles, the round trip being performed in about five days.

Besides this steamer there will be employed on Lake Winnipeg eight freight steamers and seventeen barges, having an aggregate carrying capacity of 4,000 tons. Several barges will also be employed in the transport of lumber.

On the River Saskatchewan, five steamers, having an aggregate carrying capacity of 1,200 tons, will provide for a trip once per week each way between Grand Rapids and Edmonton, a distance of about 1,000 miles, the round trip being performed in about 20 days.

In addition to the above, I am informed that a steamer is being built by the Hudson's Bay Company on the Athabasca, to run on that and Peace River, a navigation of over 1,000 miles.

Taken together, the distance over which steamers will run are as follows:

	Miles
On Red River	100
River Assiniboine	700
Lake Winnipeg	350
River Saskatchewan	1,000
River Athabasca and Peace River	1,000
Being a total of	3,150

In addition to the means of communication which I have endeavoured briefly to describe, it may be perhaps interesting to add that scattered over the immense area between Labrador in the east, Alaska and British Columbia in the west, the Arctic Seas in the north and the Provinces and Territories of the Dominion in the south are the Trading posts of the Hudson's Bay Company, to and from each of which there is a regular communication provided by the company, which according to the distance and situation is more or less frequent; the most distant point, however, receiving and despatching one or two mails every year. East of the Rocky Mountain Range I am informed that there are 130 of these posts. Some idea may be formed of the distance to be traversed when it is stated that the trip from the most northerly post on the Mackenzie River to Winnipeg occupies nearly the whole summer, or from four to five months.

In concluding this report I beg to say that the information it contains has been procured from the most reliable sources and that it has been my object, while sketching the history, the present condition and the future requirements of the Postal Service, to put you in possession of such facts as I trust will convey some idea of the rapid progress which has been made and which is being made in this portion of the Dominion.

Hoping for your approval.

I have the honor to be, Sir,

Your obedient servant,
J. DEWE,
Chief P. O. Inspector.

The Honorable
The Postmaster General,
Ottawa, Ontario.

The Report of the P. M. G. for the following year (1883) has addiitional data of interest concerning Manitoba and The Northwest Territories, viz:

IMPROVEMENTS IN RAILWAY MAIL SERVICE DURING THE YEAR ENDED 30TH JUNE, 1883.

On 1st July, 1882, the Mail Service by Railway, in charge of Baggagemen, between Winnipeg and the Rat Portage, was increased from 3 to 6 times per week, each way

On 1st August, 1882, the Postal Car Service, West of Winnipeg, was extended from Brandon to Oak Lake, 33 miles.

On 15th September, 1882, the Postal Car Service, West of Winnipeg, was extended from Oak Lake to Gopher Creek, 14½ miles.

On 15th September, 1872, the daily Mail Service by Railway, in charge of Baggagemen, was extended from Gopher Creek to Troy, Assiniboia, 144 miles.

On 1st October, 1882, the daily Mail Service by Railway, in charge of Baggagemen, was further extended to Regina, from Troy, 32 miles.

On 7th December, 1882, a tri-weekly Mail Service by train, in charge of Baggagemen, was established between Rat Portage, and Thunder Bay, Ontario, 300 miles.

On the 21st May, 1883, the Postal Car Service, west of Winnipeg, was extended from Gopher Creek to Moosomin, Assiniboia, 39 miles.

On 1st June, 1883, a daily Service was opened up over the Canadian Pacific Railway, South-Western Branch, between Winnipeg and Manitoba City, 103 miles, the mails being carried in charge of Baggagemen.

On 5th June, 1883, the daily mail service in charge of Baggagemen was extended from Regina to Moose Jaw, 42 miles, and on 12th June, 1883, the service was further extended from Moose Jaw to Medicine Hat, 262.

Improvements in Railway Mail Service, from 1st July, 1883 to 25th October, 1883

On 1st August, 1883, a mail service was opened up over the Gretna and Pembina Junction Branch of the Canadian Pacific Railway—14 miles—twice per week; the mails being in charge of Baggagemen.

On 20th September, 1883, the daily mail service by train between Rat Portage, Keewatin and Thunder Bay (now Port Arthur), Ontario,—300 miles—was increased from three to six times per week, each way.

On 1st October, 1883, the mail service by the Canadian Pacific Railway, west of Winnipeg, was netended from Medicine Hat to Calgary, 180 miles, and mails have since been carried daily, on this section, in charge of Baggagemen.

On 21st October, 1883, the postal service, west of Winnipeg, was extended from Moosomin to Moose Jaw—179 miles.

To facilitate the exchange of mails at certain points, the postal cars west of Winnipeg, have been supplied with mail-bag catchers, and catching posts have been erected near the McGregor and Douglas Station sidings, and at the railway track opposite the Griswold, Manitoba, Post Office.

It is proposed to place similar posts along the line of the Canadian Pacific Railway, west.

There are now 1,478½ miles of railway over which mails are carried, viz:—

Route	Actual length of Railway in miles.	Daily Service by Travelling Post Office.			Daily Service by bags in Baggage Car.	Semi-weekly Service by bags in charge of Baggagemen.
		No. of Postal Cars on road daily	No. of Mail Clerks.	Distance travelled in miles.		
					Miles per day.	Miles per week.
Winnipeg and St. Vincent	67	1	3	134	*134	
" Moose Jaw	398	3	6	796		
" Stonewall	20				40	
" Manitoba City	103				206	
" Port Arthur	435				870	
Moose Jaw and Calgary	441½				883	
Pembina Mountain Junction and Gretna	14					56
	1,478½	4	9	930	2,133	56

* The mails on this route being large and important, are in charge of a Mail Clerk, who travels in the Baggage Car.

W. W. McLeod,
Post Office Inspector.

We append herewith a list of the Post Offices in the Northwest Territories together with such data we have found concerning the Cancellations, etc.

List of Post Offices in Alberta, Assiniboia, Keewatin, Northwest Territory, and Saskatchewan, up to 1900.

Also The Pioneer Manitoba Offices

The listings of the N. W. T. markings are up to 1900, by that time development was so rapid that the cancellations from the various districts become quite common and the Small Queen stamps had become obsolete.

In the case of Manitoba we list what we consider to be the pioneer offices, viz: those established previous to the division of 1882, which took place May 8, 1882, the Post Office making the change July 1, 1882.[1]

The dates given for the various cancellations are nearly all from the official records. It will be noted in a few instances that the date of the cancellation is earlier than the date the office was established. This is due to the order for the cancellation being placed well in advance, and the date is when the contractor sent the device to the P. O. Department. Where there are several dates given for the same Type it is to be understood that a new marking of that type was furnished on the dates given. Some markings were returned to Ottawa and re-cut after being worn or damaged. Such examples are noted by "Re-cut" preceding the date. When the date is given in brackets, it indicates approximate date of establishment of the office.

The records available to us unfortunately are not as complete or accurate as we would like, but students can no doubt, by further investigations, fill the gaps in the data presented herewith.

For descriptions of types see Page 714.

---

1. See also Appendix B #49.

Alberta (up to 1900).

Post Office	Date Est.	Type I	Notes
Agricola	(1892)	Oct. 26, 1892	
Anawan	(1897)		1898 Cancel seen.
Angus Ridge	(1893)	Nov. 30, 1893	
Anthracite	Jun. 1, 1887	Jun. 2, 1887	
Banff	Jun. 1, 1886	Jul. 9, 1886	Type II Feb. 20, '92
Barnett	(1891)	Nov. 2, 1891	
Bears Hill	(1892)	Dec. 23, 1892	
Beaumont	(1895)		1896 Cancel seen.
Beaver Hills	(1894)	Jun. 30, 1894	
Beaver Lake	(1892)	Oct. 3, 1892	
Blind River	(1889)	Jan. 16, 1889	
Bowden	(1892)	Dec. 23, 1892	
Brice	(1892)	Jul. 29, 1893	
Bruderheim	(1895)		1896 Cancel seen.
Calgary	Oct. 1, 1883	Aug. 2, '83	Type III Oct. 26, '88
		Recut Nov. 8, '88	Recut Mar. 2, '92
Canmore	(1885)	Apr. 19, 1894	Type IV Sept. 16, 1893
Carberry	Apr. 19, '94		Was DeWinton, Man. until 1883 (q.v.)
Cardston	(1892)	Aug. 2, 1892	
Cash City	(1889)	Jan. 9, 1890	
Clover Bar	(1885)		
Cochrane	Jul. 1, 1887	Sept. 6, 1887	
Colles	(1893)	Oct. 2, 1893	
Coutts	(1893)	Jun. 13, 1893	
Cree Hill	(1890)	Dec. 9, 1890	
Davisburg	Jul. 1, 1888	Aug. 6, 1888	
Dewdney	(1891)	Jul. 3, 1891	
Didsbury	(1895)	Jan. 26, 1895	
Duhamel	(1893)	Nov. 29, 1893	
Dunbow	(1889)		
Edmonton	Mar. 1, 1878	Sep. 2, '83	Type III Feb. 9, '89
			Type IV Apr. 6. '94
			Formerly N.W.T.
Edna	(1894)	Jun. 30, 1894	
Edwell	(1894)	Feb. 23, 1894	
Egg Lake	(1897)		1898 Cancel seen.
Ellersbie	(1897)		1898 Cancel seen.
Fetlock	(1892)	May 2, 1892	
Fishburn	(1894)	Nov. 19, 1894	
Fort Kipp	(1885)	May 6, 1886	
Fort McLeod	Oct. 1, 1883	Oct. 6, 1883	
Fort Saskatchewan	May 1877		Formerly N. W. T.
Giroux	(1885)		
Gillingham	(1898)		
Gladys	(1890)	Feb. 3, 1890	
Gleichen	(1885)		
Greenlaw	(1892)	Jan. 23, 1892	
Harrisboro	(1890)	Jun. 27, 1890	
High River	Feb. 1, 1884		
Hollbrook	Jul. 1, 1886	Sept. 9, 1886	
Horse Hills	(1896)		1896 Cancel seen.
Innisfail	(1892)	Mar. 9, 1892	
Jumping Pond	(1892)	Aug. 2, 1892	
Kirkpatrick	(1885)		

Post Office	Date Est.	Type I	Notes
Kananaskis	Jul. 1, 1888	May 30, 1888	
Knee Hill Valley	(1894)	Jul. 26, 1894	Now Kneehill
Lac la Biche	(1893)	Jul. 31, 1893	
Lacombe	(1891)	Nov. 9, 1891	
Lamerton	(1893)	Aug. 29, 1893	
Lamoreux	(1896)		1896 Cancel seen.
Langdon	(1890)	Dec. 19, 1890	
Leduc	(1895)		
Lethbridge	Oct. 1, 1885	Jun. 13, '88	Type IV Apr. 23, '94
Lewisville	(1893)	Nov. 30, 1893	
Lineham	(1895)	Feb. 25, 1895	
Livingstone		Apr. 19, '94	See N.W.T.
Logan	(1892)	Sep. 2, 1892	
Lyndon	(1893)	Jul. 31, 1893	
Macleod	(1892)		Formerly Ft. McLeod (q.v.) Type III Sep. 19, '92 Type IV Feb. 26, '94
Marlborough	(1885)		
Manawan	(1894)	Jun. 30, 1894	
Meadow Creek	(1895)		
Milford		Feb. 16, '89	Formerly N.W.T.(q.v.)
Millarville	(1892)	Jul. 2, 1892	
Millet	(1897)		
Millward	May 1, 1885		
Midnapore	Feb. 1, 1884		
Morinville	(1892)	Jan. 26, 1893	
Morley	(1894)		
Mosquito Creek	(1889)		
Mountain View	(1894)	Sep. 29, 1894	
Moneta	(1892)	Jan. 23, 1892	
Namao	(1892)	Jun. 9, 1892	
Nanton	(1893)	Jul. 31, 1893	
New Lunnon	(1893)	Aug. 29, 1893	
New Oxley	(1889)		
Northern	(1898)		1899 cancel seen
North Fork	(1892)	Feb. 2, 1892	
Okotoks	(1885)		
Olds	(1892)	May. 2, 1892	
Oxbow	(1892)	May 2, 1892	
Pakan	Jun. 1, 1887	Jul. 9, 1887	
Panima	(1894)	Mar. 20, 1894	
Pekisko	Aug. 1, 1886	Sep. 6, 1886	
Pine Creek	Jul. 1, 1887	Jul. 6, 1887	
Pine Lake	(1896)		
Penhold	(1892)	Jan. 23, 1892	
Pincher Creek	(1885)		Now Pincher
Ponoka	(1897)		
Poplar Grove	(1891)	May 2, 1891	
Priddis	(1894)	Jun. 30, 1894	
Red Deer	(1885)		Type III Jul. 2, '92 Type IV Sep. 20, '94
Red Lodge	(1896)		
Riviere qui Barre	(1896)		
Rosebud	(1896)		
Saddle Lake	(1893)	Jul. 31, 1893	
Saint Albert	Jul. 1, 1880	Aug. 20, 1890	Formerly N.W.T. (q.v.)
Shehs Lake	(1891)	Dec. 2, 1891	

Post Office	Date Est.	Type I	Notes
South Edmonton	(1891)	Sep. 2, 1892	
Spring Bank	(1891)	Feb. 28, 1891	
Spruce Grove	(1894)	Jun. 30, 1894	
Stand Off	(1896)		
Starbuck	Aug. 1, 1887		
Strangmuir	(1889)	Dec. 2, 1889	
Tindastoll	(1892)	Jul. 2, 1892	
Tofield	(1898)		
Urquhart	(1897)		
Vegreville	(1895)		
Waghorn	(1891)	Sep. 5, 1891	
West Macleod	(1894)	Sep. 29, 1894	
Wetaskiwin	(1892)	Oct. 23, 1892	
White Fish Lake	(1894)	Sep. 29, 1894	
White Mud	(1898)		
White Sand	(1892)	May 2, 1892	
Whitford	(1897)		
Yarrow	(1895)	Apr. 26, 1895	

Assiniboia (up to 1900).

Post Office	Date Est.	Type I	Notes
Abernathy	(1885)		Now Sask
Adair	(1894)	April 19, 1894	Now Sask.
Alameda	Dec. 1, 1883		Now Sask.
Alma	(1897)		
Antler	(1885)		Now Sask.
Arcola	(1889)	Mar. 9, 1889	Now Sask.
Armstrong's Lake	(1885)		
Arrochar	Sept. 1, 1886	Oct. 5, 1886	
Balgonie	Nov. 1, 1883		Now Sask.
Bienfait	(1893)	Apr. 24, 1893	Now Sask.
Belle Prairie	(1894)		
Benbecula	(1886)	May 6, 1886	
Boscurvis	Jul. 1, 1885		
Balcarres	(1885)		Now Sask.
Broadview	Nov. 1, 1882		Type III Apr. 19, '95 Formerly N.W.T. (q.v.)
Blackwood	Jul. 1, 1887	Oct. 3, 1887	
Boharm	(1890)	Jul. 9, 1890	
Brookside	(1893)	Oct. 2, 1893	
Bredenbury	(1890)	Jul. 9, 1890	Now Sask.
Cannington Manor	Mar. 1, 1888	Apr. 12, 1888	
Carievale	(1891)	Mar. 21, 1891	Now Sask.
Carlyle	Dec. 1, 1883		Now Sask.
Carnduff	(1885)		Now Sask.
Caron	(1885)		Now Sask.
Carnoustie	(1895)		
Carsdale	Jan. 4, 1884		
Churstbridge	(1889)	May 15, 1889	
Chickney	May 1, 1887	Jul. 9, 1887	
Coalfields	(1890)	Aug. 9, 1890	
Clare	(1885)		Now Clair, Sask.
Clumber	Oct. 1, 1887	Nov. 6, 1887	
Cote	(1891)	Apr. 2, 1891	Now Sask.
Coteau	(1894)	Apr. 19, 1894	
Cotham	(1891)	Sept. 5, 1891	
Craven	Jan. 1, 1884		Now Sask.

Post Office	Date Est.	Type I	Notes
Crescent Lake	Jan. 1, 1884	Mar. 25, 1891	
Davin		May 26, 1890	Now Sask.
Dennington	Oct. 1, 1886	Nov. 9, 1886	
Domremy	(1888)		
Dongola	(1888)	Nov. 2, 1888	
Dundurn	(1894)	Sep. 29, 1894	Now Sask.
Dalesboro	(1885)		
Dunleath	1894	Sep. 29, 1894	
Dunmore Junction	Feb. 1, 1886	Apr. 8, 1886	
		Jul. 15, 1893	Now Dunmore
Earlswood	(1888)		
Edenwold	(1890)	Dec. 9, 1890	
Ebenezer	(1891)	Jul. 27, 1891	Now Sask.
Elmore	Jan. 1, 1887	Sep. 6, 1887	
Edgely Farm	(1885)		Now Edgeley, Sask.
Ellisboro	Jan. 1, 1884		
Estevan	(1892)		Type III Oct. 3, '92
			Type IV Jan 16, '95
			Now Sask.
Esterhazy	Sept. 1, 1886	Oct. 5, 1886	Now Sask.
Fairlight	(1893)	Jul. 8, 1893	
Fairmeade	(1885)		
Ferndale	Oct. 1, 1887	Nov. 6, 1887	
Fishing Lake	1894	Jun. 30, 1894	Now Sask.
Fitzmaurice	1895	Apr. 26, 1895	Now Sask.
Fleming	(1885)		Now Sask.
Forrest Farm	(1885)		(Now Forrest, Man?)
Fletwode	(1895)	Apr. 26, 1895	
Fort Pelly	(1889)	Aug. 26, 1889	Now Pelly, Sask.
Gainesborough	(1895)		(1895 cancel seen) Now Sask.
Glen Adelaide	(1885)		
Gordon	(1897)		Now Man.
Glen Ewen	(1890)	Dec. 9, 1890	
Grierson	(1890)	Jul. 9, 1890	
Graburn	(1897)		
Grenfell	May 1, 1883		Type IV Jan. 29, 1895
			Now Sask.
Gull Lake	(1889)	May 15, 1889	Now Sask.
Hayward	(1885)		(Hayward, Man?)
Hednesford	Jul. 1, 1887	Jul. 9, 1887	
Heron	(1896)		
Hazelcliffe	(1892)	Feb. 2, 1892	Now Sask.
High View	(1895)	Jan. 26, 1895	
Hillburn	Jan. 1, 1884		
Hillesden	(1892)	Oct. 26, 1892	
Hill Farm	Jul. 1, 1887	Sep. 23, 1887	
Hirsch	(1893)	Jan. 2, 1894	Now Sask.
Hyde	(1893)	Mar. 29, 1893	
Josephsburg	(1890)	Jun. 27, 1890	Now Alta.
Indian Head	(1882)	Mar. 12, 1892	Now Sask.
			Formerly N.W.T. (q.v.)
Kamsack	(1888)	Dec. 13, 1888	Now Sask.
Karndac	(1889)		
Katepwe	(1885)		
Kaposvar	(1891)	Sep. 5, 1891	
Kenlis	(1890)	Aug. 9, 1890	
Kennell	(1893)	Feb. 25, 1893	
Kinbrae	(1885)		
Kissina	(1897)		1898 cancel seen

Post Office	Date Est.	Type I	Notes
Kleczkowski	(1897)		1898 cancel seen
Kronan	(1896)		(Now Kronan, Sask?)
Kutawa	(1888)		
Lac Chapleau	(1896)		1896 Canc. seen
Lac Marguerite	(1895)	Feb. 25, 1895	
Langenberg	Feb. 1, 1888	Apr. 12, 1888	Now Sask.
Landestrew	(1892)	Sep. 2, 1892	
Lebret	Jan. 1, 1886		Now Sask.
Logberg	(1892)	Sep. 2, 1892	
Longlaketon	Feb. 1, 1884		
Loon Creek	(1885)		
Lorlie	Jul. 1, 1887	Jul. 9, 1887	Now Sask.
Lumsden	(1892)	Oct. 26, 1892	
Marlborough	(1885)		Now Alta.
Maple Creek	Jul. 1, 1883	Jan. 20, 1883	Type IV Aug. 23, '93 Now Sask.
Marieton	(1885)		
Maryfield	(1896)		Now Sask.
Mc Lean	(1885)	Feb. 25, 1893	Now Sask.
Medicine Hat	Jul. 1, 1883	Jul. 20, 1883	Type III Feb. 20, '91 Type IV Jul. 28, '94 Now Alta.
Moffat	(1886)	May 6, 1886	
Montmartre	1894	Sep. 29, 1894	Now Sask.
Montgomery	(1885)		
Moose Jaw	Jul. 1, 1883	Jan. 20, 1883	Now Sask. Type III Apr. 2, '91 Type IV Jul. 28, '94
Moosomin	Nov. 1, 1882	Jan. 2, 1883	Now Sask.
New Finland	(1897)	Jun. 9, 1893	
North Portal	1894	Aug. 29, 1894	Now Sask.
Oak Lake	Jul. 1, 1882		
Oakley	(1893)		
Ohlen	Nov. 1, 1887	Dec. 6, 1887	
Otthom	(1897)		Now Sask.
Oxbow	(1893)		Now Sask.
Parkbeg	(1898)		Now Sask.
Parkin	(1885)		
Pasqua	Oct. 1, 1883		Now Sask.
Parklands	Jul. 1, 1885		Now Alta.
Pense	Nov. 1, 1883	Type III Jan. 16, 1893	Now Sask.
Pengarth	Jul. 1, 1886	Sep. 9, 1886	
Percy	(1889)	Feb. 9, 1889	
Perley	Jul. 1, 1887	Oct. 27, 1887	
Pheasant Forks	Dec. 1, 1883		
Pioneer	(1894)		
Point Elmira	1891	Feb. 28, 1891	
Prosperity	1895	Mar. 21, 1895	
Qu'Appelle		Formerly NWT Type III Mar. 3, '90 Recut Apr. 18, 1889 Now Sask. Recut Mar. 29, 1890	
Qu'Appelle Station	(1885)	Type III Feb. 19, 1889 Now Sask.	
Redpath	Jan. 1, 1884		Now Sask.
Regina	Aug. 3, 1882	Dec. 19, 1882	Type III Oct. 2, 1891 Type III Jun. 6, 1890 Type IV Sep. 23, 1893 Now Sask.
Rose Plain	(1885)		
Riga	(1889)	Nov. 2, 1889	

Post Office	Date Est.	Type I	Notes
Riversdale	(1890)	Sept. 2, 1890	
Reynoldton	(1890)	Oct. 6, 1890	
Rocanville	Jan. 1, 1884		Now Sask.
Roscoe	1894	Jun. 30, 1894	Now Sask.
Rossetti	(1895)		
Rothbury	(1892)	Sep. 2, 1892	
Rouleau	1895	Apr. 26, 1895	Now Sask.
Saltoun	(1892)	Jun. 9, 1892	
Saltcoats	(1889)	Feb. 2, 1889	Now Sask.
Sancte Andrea	Sep. 1, 1887	Oct. 3, 1887 Feb. 12, 1894	
Sheho	(1892)	Oct. 3, 1892	Now Sask.
Sintaluta	Jul. 1, 1888	Aug. 15, 1888	Now Sask.
Silton	Jan. 1, 1888	Jan. 25, 1888	Now Sask.
Spy Hill	(1888)	Mar. 23, 1888	Now Sask.
Steep Creek	(1898)		
Stony Beach	(1893)	Jul. 31, 1893	
Strassburg	Jul. 1, 1886	Sep. 9, 1886	Now Sask.
Strathcarrol	(1890)	Feb. 3, 1890	Now Sask.
Summerberry	(1885)		Now Sask.
Summer	(1885)		
Sunnymeade	(1885)		
Swift Current	Aug. 1, 1883	Oct. 6, 1883	(Note) Now Sask.
Tontallon	(1897)		Now Sask.
Tetlock	(1892)	May 2, 1892	
Theodore	(1893)	Jan. 2, 1894	
Thingvalla	(1892)	Jun. 9, 1892	
Tiree	(1895)		
Touchwood Hills		(NWT Oct. 8, 1879)	Type II Feb. 20, '90 Now Sask.
Tregarva	(1885)		
Valley	(1891)	Feb. 28, 1891	
Valley View	1895	Apr. 26, 1895	
Wallace	(1885)		Now Sask.
Walsh	(1891)	Sep. 5, 1891	Now Alta.
Wapella	Nov. 1, 1883	Jan. 29, 1895	Now Sask.
Wawota	(1885)		Now Sask.
Welwyn	Jan. 1, 1884		Now Sask.
Weyburn	(1895)		Now Sask.
Wood Mountain	(1894)	Aug. 29, 1894	Now Sask.
Whitewood Station	Nov. 9, 1883		Type III Dec. 8, 1894 Became Whitewood 1894. Now Sask.
Winlaw	(1885)		Now Sask.
Wishart	Feb. 1, 1884		Now Sask.
Wolseley	Jul. 1, 1887	Jun. 9, 1887	Type IV Mar. 29, '94
Workman	(1885)		
Willow Bunch	1895	Apr. 26, 1895	Now Sask.
Yellow Grass	(1896)		Now Sask.
Yorkton	Jan. 1, 1884	Nov. 23, 1893	Now Sask.

(Note) Swiftcurrent closed between June 30, 1891 and June 30, 1897.

Keewatin (up to 1900)

Big Fork	Jul. 1, 1883	Oct. 6, 1883	Closed 1887
Cross Lake	1879	Dec. 6, '79	Became Lake Deception 1881 (q.v.)
Darlington	Oct. 1, 1878		Become Cross Lake 1879 (q.v.)

Post Office	Date Est.	Type I	Notes
Fort Francis		Apr. 9, 1877	Formerly in N.W.T.
Gimli[1]	Nov. 1, 1877	Jan. 2, 1878	
Hoosavick	Jul. 1, 1878	Sep. 20, 1878	Closed Feb. 28, '81
Keewtin	Mar. 1, 1880		Became Keewatin Mills '81
Lake Deception	1881	Jan. 26, 1881	Formerly Cross Lake
Pine Falls	Nov. 1, 1879	Dec. 6, 1879	Became Ft. Alexander 1881
Rat Portage[2]	Sep. 1, 1879	Jan. 3, 1883	Formerly in N.W.T.
Whitemouth	Aug. 1, 1880	Jan. 3, 1881	

1, 2 See same notes on next page.

Northwest Territories (up to 1900).

All Type I Markings, Unless Otherwise Noted

Post Office	Date Est.	Type I	Notes
Battleford[4]	Jul. 1, 1876	Apr. 9, 1877	
Birtle[1]	Sep. 1, 1879	Oct. 8, 1879	
Blake[1]	Oct. 1, 1879	Jan. 2, 1880	
Brandon[1]	Nov. 1, 1880	Jan. 3, 1881	Type III Feb. 18, '89
Bridge Creek[1]	Nov. 1, 1879	Dec. 6, 1879	
Broadview[3]	Nov. 1. 1882	Jan. 2, 1883	
Cadurcis[1]	Feb. 1, 1881	Feb. 5, 1881	
Carleton[4]	Aug. 1, 1876	Apr. 9, 1877	Closed Jul. 31, '85
Eden[1]	Oct. 1, 1879	Jan. 2, 1880	
Edmonton	Oct. 1, 1876	Apr. 9, '77	Became Ft. Saskatchewan May 1877 (q.v.)
		Jul. 5, '78	Recut Apr. 18, '89
Fairview[1]	Jul. 1, 1880	Aug. 5, 1880	
Fort Cudahy	1895	Apr. 26, '95	Now Forty Mile, Yuk.
Fort Edmonton[5]	Mar. 1, 1878	Feb. 12, 1879	Became Edmonton 1879 (See Alberta)
Fort Ellice[1]	Sep. 1, 1879	Oct. 8, 1879	
Fort Francis	Jan. 1, 1876	Apr. 3, 1876	Included in Keewatin 1877
Fort Saskatchewan[5]	May 1877	Feb. 12, 1879	Formerly Edmonton
		Mar. 9, 1886	
Grand Valley[1]	Oct. 1, 1879	Jan. 2, 1880	
Grandin[4]	Aug. 1, 1877	Nov. 26, 1877	
Hazeldean[1]	1879	Dec. 6, '79	Became Strathclair (q.v.) Closed 1881
Hallsford[1]	1880		
Indian Head[3]	Nov. 1, 1882	Jan. 2, 1883	
Livingstone[5]	Aug. 1, 1876	Apr. 9; '77	Closed Sep. 30, '79
Little Saskatchewan[1]	Oct. 1, '76	Apr. 9, 1877	Became Hallsford 1880 (q.v.)
McGregor[1]	Nov. 1, 1880	Jan. 3, 1881	
Milford[5]	Nov. 1, 1881	May 14, 1881	Spelt "Millford"
Minnedosa[1]	Aug. 1, 1876	Jan. 3, 1881	
Newdale[1]	Feb. 1, 1881	Feb. 5, 1881	
Oak River[1]	Nov. 1, 1879	Dec. 6, 1879	
Oberon[1]	Jul. 1, 1880	Aug. 5, 1880	
Odanah[1]	Oct. 1, 1880	Dec. 26, 1880	Closed Jun. 30, 1886
Ospray[1]	Jul. 1, 1880	Aug. 5, 1880	
Petrel[1]	Jul. 1, 1880	Aug. 5, 1880	
Prince Albert[4]	Jan. 1, 1879	Mar. 17, 1879	
Qu'Appelle[3]	Jul. 1, 1880	Aug. 5, 1880	
Rat Portage	Sep. 1, 1879	Dec. 6, 1879	Included in Keewatin 1882 (q.v.)
Rapid City[1]	Sep. 1, 1879	Oct. 8, 1879	

Post Office	Date Est.	Type I	Notes
Richmond[1]	Oct. 1, 1879	Jan. 2, 1880	
Rossburn[1]	Oct. 1, 1880	Nov. 26, 1880	
St. Albert[5]	Jul. 1, 1880	Aug. 5, 1880	
Salisbury[1]	Sep. 1, 1879	Oct. 8, 1879	
Saskatchewan Landing[4]	(1880)	(May 1885)	
Shell River[1]	Aug. 1, 1876	Jan. 3, 1881	
Shoal Lake[1]	Aug. 1, 1876	Apr. 9, '77	Became Raven Lake 1887
Souris Mouth[1]	Nov. 1, 1880	Jan. 3, '81	Became Two Rivers '84
Stobart[4]	May 1, 1879	Apr. 6, 1879	
		Jun. 23, 1888	
		Sep. 23, 1894	
Strathclair[1]	Late 1880	Nov. 26, 1880	Formerly Hazeldean
Touchwood Hills[3]	Sep. 1, 1879	Oct. 8, 1879	Closed Sep. 1, 1880
Troy	Aug. 1, 1882	Oct. 9, 1882	
Wolf Creek	Oct. 1, 1882	Dec. 9, 1882	Closed 1886

1. Included in Manitoba, 1882. (q.v.)
2. Formerly in N.W.T. Included in Keewatin in 1882.
3. In assiniboia 1882 (q.v.)
4. Included in Saskatchewan. (1882) (q.v.).
5. Included in Alberta. 1889.

Saskatchewan (up to 1900).

Post Office	Date Est.	Type I	Notes
Aldina	(1893)	Jul. 29, 1893	
Alvena	Oct. 1, 1887	Nov. 6, 1887	
Aaskana	Jan. 1, 1888	Jan. 25, 1888	
Battleford		Dec. 9, 1883, Apr. 8, 1886	Formerly NWT.
Batoche	Jan. 1, 1884		
Birch Hills	(1896)		
Baljennie	Nov. 26, 1891	Jun. 26, 1891	
Bison	(1897)		
Boucher	Feb. 1, 1888	Apr. 12, 1888	
Brancepeth	(1891)	Jun. 26, 1891	
Bresaylor	(1888)	Feb. 9, 1889	
Carleton		Mar. 3, 1890	Formerly N.W.T. (q.v.)
Cumberland House	(1891)	Jun. 2, 1891	
Coxby	(1891)	Dec. 2, 1891	
Colleston	(1891)	Dec. 2, 1891	
Domremy	(1898)		
Duck Lake	1894	Nov. 6, 1894	
Fort A La Corne	(1891)	Jun. 2, 1891	
Flett's Springs	(1895)	Apr. 26, 1895	
Fort Pitt	(1885)		
Garonne	(1898)		
Glen Mary	(1891)	Dec. 2, 1891	
Grandin			Formerly in N.W.T. (q.v.)
Hague	(1895)		
Halcro	Jun. 1, 1887	Jul. 9, 1887	
Lily Plain	1895	Mar. 21, 1895	
Kinisteno	Jan. 1, 1883	May 2, 1883	
Llewellyn	(1892)	Mar. 2, 1892	
Melfort	(1892)	Sep. 2, 1892	
Meota	(1894)	Oct. 23, 1894	
Mistawasis	(1891)	May 2, 1891	
Osler	(1891)	May 2, 1891	
Onion Lake	(1890)	Aug. 9, 1890	
Prince Albert			Type III Nov. 19, '88 Type IV Jan. 12, 1894 See N.W.T.
Puckahn	(1885)		
Ralphtown	(1885)		
Red Deer Hill	(1885)		
Rosthern	(1893)	Oct. 2, 1893	
Saskatchewan	Mar. 1885		
Saskatchewan Landing		Apr. 12, 1888	See N.W.T.
Saskatoon	(1885)		
Shell Brook	(1894)	Dec. 21, 1894	
Steep Creek	(1896)		
Stobart			Formerly N.W.T.
The Pas	(1891)	Jun. 26, 1891	
Vandale	(1893)		
Weldon	(1898)		
Willoughby	Jan. 1, 1883	May 2, 1883	
Wingard	(1889)	Jan. 16, 1889	

Manitoba Post Offices Established Between July 15, 1870 and July 15, 1882.

(These are the Pioneer Manitoba Offices)

Post Office	Date Est.	Type I	Notes
Alexandria	Jun. 1, 1878	May 13, '78	Closed 1885
Archibald	Oct. 1, 1879	Jan. 2, '80	
Argyle	Nov. 1, 1880	Jan. 3, '81	
Arnaud	Sept. 1, 1879	Oct. 8, '79	
Assiniboine	Sept. 1, 1879	Oct. 8, '79	
Baie St. Paul	Jul. 1, 1871		
Balmoral	Sept. 1, 1879	Oct. 8, '79	
Beaconsfield	Oct. 1, 1879		
Beausejour	Jun. 1, 1881	Aug. 20, '81	
Beaver Creek	Jul. 1, 1881	Jul. 2, '81	
Belmont	1881		Closed 1887?
Birds Hill	Sept. 1, 1879	Oct. 8, '79	
Blumenort	Dec. 1, 1880		
Blythfield	Oct. 1, 1879		
Boyne River	Jul. 1, 1875	May 3, '78?	
Burnside	Jul. 1, 1871		
Calf Mountain	Oct. 1, 1879	Jan. 2, '80	
Campbellville	Aug. 1, 1878	May 13, '78	
Carman	Nov. 1, 1880	Jan. 3, '81	
Clandeboye	Jun. 1, 1876		
Clear Springs	Nov. 1, 1879	Jan. 2, '80	
Clydesdale	May 1, 1881	Jul. 2, '81	Became Neepawa 1882 (q.v.)
Cook's Creek	Oct. 1, 1873		
Creeford	Mar. 1, 1882		
Crystal City	Nov. 1, 1879		
Darlingford	Jan. 1, 1882	Apr. 5, '82	Closed Sept. 30, 1887
Deloraine	Mar. 1, 1882	May 5, '82	
Delorme	Jul. 1, 1880	Aug. 5, '80	Became Naas 1883
Desford	1879	May 5, '82	
DeWinton	Oct. 1, 1881	Dec. 2, '81	Became Carberry Alta. '83
Dominion City	1880?	May 6, '80	
Dundee	Nov. 1, 1879	Dec. 6, '79	
Dynevor		Apr. 12, '76	Formerly St. Peters
Eagle's Nest	1875		
East Selkirk	Nov. 1, 1880	Jan. 3, '81	
Elton	1881	Apr. 1, '81	
Emerson	Nov. 1, 1878	Feb. 12, '79 Jun. 18, '80 Nov. 12, '80	Type III Dec. 2, '82
Fort Garry	(Note)	Nov. 29, '80	(Now Winnipeg q.v.)
Foxton	Nov. 1, 1879	1871	
Gauthier	Oct. 1, 1880	Nov. 26, '80	Formerly St. Pie
Gladstone		Oct. 15, '79	Formerly Palestine
Glenora	Jun. 1, 1881	Aug. 20, '81	
Golden Stream	1879	Jan. 2, '80	
Greenford		May 5, '82	
Greenridge	Oct. 1, 1879	Jan. 2, '80	
Greenwood	Jul. 1, 1875		
Grenfell	Oct. 1, 1881	Dec. 2, '81	Do not confuse with Grenfell, Assa.
Headingly	Jul. 1, 1871		
High Bluff	Jul. 1, 1871		

Post Office	Date Est.	Type I	Notes
Holland	Jul. 1, 1880	Aug. 5, '80	
Indian Ford	Jul. 1, 1880		
Indian Mission	Oct. 1, 1872		
Kildonan	Jul. 1, 1871		
Lake Francis	Feb. 1, 1881	Feb. 5, '81	
Lakeside	Sept. 1, 1879	Oct. 8, '79	Closed Jul. 31, 1881
Langvale	Mar. 1, 1882	May 5, '82	
Lettellier	Jun. 1, 1880	Aug. 5, '80	
Lintrathen	Jun. 1, 1881	Aug. 20, '81	
Littleton	Jun. 1, 1881	Aug. 20, '81	Became Cyprus River '87
Loretto	May 1, 1875		
Lorne	Oct. 1, 1879	Jan. 2, '80	Closed 1883?
Lower Fort Garry	Jul. 1, 1878?		
Mapleton	Jul. 1, 1871		Closed Jan. 31, 1876
Marney	Jan. 1, 1882	Mar. 6. '82	Closed Nov. 30, 1887 Re-opened Mar. 1, 1888
Marringhurst	Feb. 1, 1881	Feb. 5, '81	
Meadow Lea		Oct. 8, '79	Formerly Woodlands
Miami	Jun. 1, 1878	May 13, '78	Closed 1884?
Middle Church	1875		
Mill Brook	Nov 1, 1879	Dec. 6, '79	
Minnewashta	Nov. 1, 1879	Jan. 2, '80	Closed 1887?
Morris	Jan. 1, 1874		
Mountain City	Oct. 1, 1879	Dec. 6, '79	
Neepawa			Formerly Clydesdale
Nelsonville	1878	May 13, '78	Became Nelson 1882
Newhaven	Oct. 1, 1879	Jan. 2, '80	
Niverville	May 1, 1879	Apr. 6, '79	
Norquay	Mar. 1, 1882?	Mar. 6, '82	
Oak Bank	Nov. 1, 1880	Jan. 3, '81	
Oakland	1877		
Oak Point	Oct. 1, 1872		
Olive	Jan. 1876	Jul. 2, '81	
Ossowa	Jan. 1876	Jul. 5, '78 Mar. 18, '80	
Otterbourne	Sept. 1, 1879	Oct. 8, '79	
Palestine	Apr. 1, 1872		Became Gladstone 1879
Parker's Creek	May 1, 1872		Closed Jul. 31, 1881
Pembina	July 1, 1871		Closed 1887?
Pembina Crossing	Oct. 1, 1879	Dec. 6, '79	Closed Oct. 31, 1885
Pequis	1876	Jun. 6, '76 Dec. 20, '81	Spelled "Peguis" Spelled "Peguis"
Pigeon Lake	Jul. 1, 1871		
Pilot Mound	Nov. 1, 1880	Jan. 1, '81	
Plympton	Oct. 1, 1879	Dec. 6, '79	
Point a Grouette	Sept. 1, 1873		Closed 1875?
Pomeroy	Jan. 1, 1879	Mar. 17, '79	
Point du Chene	Jul. 1, 1879		Closed 1875?
Poplar Heights	Oct. 1, 1879	Jan. 2, '80	Became Reaburn 1884
Poplar Point	Jul. 1, 1871		
Portage La Prairie	Jul. 1, 1871	Aug. 13, 1878 Mar. 1, 1881 Nov. 2, 1882 Mar. 19, 1883 Jun. 2, 1883 Recut Dec. 22, 1883	
Prairie Grove	1876	Jun. 6, '76	
Preston	Oct. 1, 1879	Dec. 6, '79	Closed Sept. 30, '87
Prospect	Oct. 1, 1879	Dec. 6, '79	Closed Oct. 31, '81

Post Office	Date Est.	Type I	Notes
Rat River	Oct. 1, 1879	Jan. 2, '80	
Reinland	Dec. 1, 1880		
Ridgeville	Nov. 1, 1879	Dec. 6, '79	
Rockwood	Oct. 1, 1873		Became Stony Mountain 1881 (q.v.)
Rosseau Crossing	Jul. 1, 1876		Closed 1880?
Roundthwaite	May 1, 1881	Jul. 7, '81	
Ruttanville	Nov. 1, 1880		
St. Agathe	1875		
St. Andrews	1875		
St. Ann's	1875		
St. Boniface	May 1, 1872		
St. Charles	Jul. 1, 1871	Jun. 2, '83	
St. Francois Xavier	Jul. 1, 1871		
St. James	July 1, 1871	Aug. 20, '78	
St. Jean Baptiste	Sept. 1, 1877	Nov. 26, '77	
St. Laurent	1875		
St. Leon	Oct. 1, 1879	Jan. 2, '80	
St. Norbert	Jul. 1, 1871		
St. Peters	Jul. 1, 1871		Became Dynevor Apr. 1876 (q.v.)
St. Pie	Oct. 1, 1879	Jan. 2, '80	Became Gauthier Oct. '80 (q.v.)
St. Vital	Sept. 1, 1873		
Salterville	Jun. 1, 1878	May 13, '78	
Scratching River	Jan. 1, 1874		Closed 1887?
Selkirk	Jan. 1, 1876	Apr. 3, '76	
Silver Springs	Oct. 1, 1879	Dec. 6, '79	
Snowflake	Nov. 1, 1880	Jan. 3, '81	
Somerset	Jun. 1, 1881	Aug. 20, '81	
Springfield	Jan. ?, 1881		
Stodderville	Jan. 1, 1878	May 13, '78	Spelled "Sttodderville"
Stonewall	Jul. 1, 1878	Sept. 20, '78	
Stony Mountain			Formerly Rockwood
Sunnyside	Nov. 1, 1879	Dec. 6. '79	
Swan Lake	Nov. 1, 1881	Dec. 2, '81	
Tannenan	1879		Closed 1887?
Thornhill	Oct. 1, 1879	Jan. 2, '80	
Totogon	1876	Jun. 6, '76	Closed 1886?
Treherne	Jul. 1, 1880	Aug. 5, '80	
Turtle Mountain	1880		Type II May 5, '82
Victoria	July 1, 1878	Sept. 20, '78	Became Wavy Bank '82 (q.v.)
Warrington	Dec. 1, 1880		
Wavy Bank			Formerly Victoria
Wellington	Dec. 1, 1877	Jan. 2, '78	
Wellwood	July 1881	Aug. 20, '81	
Westbourne	July 1, 1874		
West Lynne	Jul. 1, 1871		
White Mud River	Jul. 1, 1871		Closed 1875?
Winnipeg (Note)		Apr. 12, '76 Type III Apr. 26, '80 Jul. 16, '79 (Canada) Jun. 2, '81	Formerly Fort Garry
Woodslands	Nov. 1, 1875		Became Meadow Lea 1879 (q.v.)
Woodside	Jul. 1, 1874	Nov. 6, '80	

Supplementary Note on the Yukon Service.

The Postmaster General's report for 1900 has the following note:

YUKON MAIL SERVICE

The following post offices have been established in the Yukon and Atlin Districts:—Atlin, Log Cabin, Lake Bennett, Tagish Lake, Dawson.

During the winter season the North-west Mounted Police performed for the Post Office Department the following services:—

Sixteen trips from Bennett to Dawson.
Thirteen trips from Dawson to Bennett.

Mails were also conveyed at about fortnightly intervals between Log Cabin and Atlin. The total value of the services so rendered has been fixed by the Comptroller of the North-west Mounted Police at $47,400. During the winter small quantities of mail matter were distributed by the police at certain of their posts between Bennett and Dawson. At Dawson several members of the force rendered assistance in receiving, sorting and delivering the mails, until November 1, 1898, when the present postmaster was installed.

On the opening of navigation in the spring of 1899, the Department wholly dispensed with the services of the North-west Mounted Police, placing the carriage of the mails under contract, first, for the season of navigation of 1899, with Mr. John Irving, and, at the close of the season of navigation of 1899, with the Canadian Development Company under a contract for four years. Under the terms of this contract the contractors are during the winter season to perform a service once a week between Bennett and Dawson, and between Dawson and Bennett and twice a week between Bennett and Atlin, and Atlin and Bennett, for $64,000 a year, and a service of at least semi-weekly frequency between Bennett and Dawson, Dawson and Bennett, Bennett and Atlin and Atlin and Bennett during the period of navigation for $11,000 a year.

The cancellations are as follows:

Yukon.

Post Office	Est.	Canc.	Type
Dawson	Nov. 1, 1898	Jun. 16, 1899	Type II
Dominion		Oct. 29, 1907	Type II
Forty Mile			Formerly Ft. Cudahy, N.W.T. (q.v.).
Tagish Lake		Nov. 25, 1899	Type I
White Horse			

The Pembina, U. S., Cancellation.

As mentioned in Inspector Dewe's report a monthly mail service between Fort Garry and Fort Ripley, Minn., a distance of almost 400 miles was organized in 1853. Four years later with the opening of the United States Post Office at Pembina, N. D., only about 70 miles from Fort Garry the Pembina office became the exchange point for the Red River and Fort Garry mails.

In 1858 the Postmaster at Fort Garry received stamps[1] and occaisional copies of the pence issues have been found bearing the Pembina postmark, showing that the letters they franked went by that Route.

We have only seen this on the 7½p, but it could exist on the ½p, 3p, and 6p as well.

Note Concerning the List of Northwest Territory and Manitoba Post Offices and Cancellations.

The cancellations are of four main types, viz:

    Type I   20 x 22 mm. in diameter, no outer circle. (Similar to Type IVl, IVm, chapter XXXV, page 572).
    Type II   20 x 24 mm. in diameter, no outer circle. (Similar to Type IVg, chapter XXXV, page 571).
    Type III   20 x 22 mm. in diameter, with outer circue, and otherwise similar to Type I.
    Type IV   Six heavy bars, circular center with name of P. O. 25 x 28 mm.

---
1. See Appendix K, #2.

Chapter XL

THE STAMPS, COVERS AND SEALS OF THE DEAD LETTER OFFICE

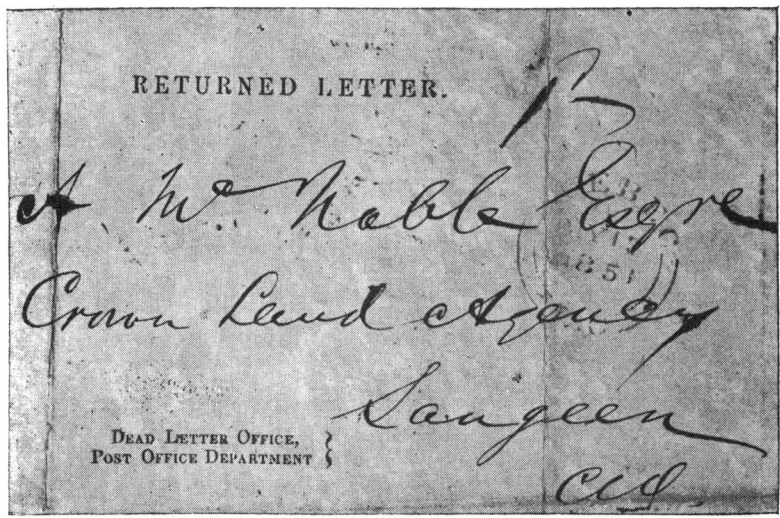

A "Returned Letter" cover from Quebec May 13, 1851.

The Dead Letter Office was established in England in the latter years of the 18th century, but it was not until the late 1820's that it can be said to have fully developed and functioned in a manner similar to the present time.

The Canada Dead Letter Office came into existence during T. A. Stayner's regime, and is known to have been functioning as early as 1830.

In that year Stayner's instructions were that all unclaimed letters which had been in a Post Office for three months, and had been advertised[1] for at least six weeks of that time, were to be considered "dead letters" and should be forwarded to the General P. O. (Quebec) along with the refused letters and the accounts. The letters from Great Britain were returned to the Dead Letter Office in London, but those mailed in British North America were opened and if possible returned to the sender for payment of postage. Letters from the United States were treated in the same manner, but if they contained money or valuables they were sent to the Post Office Department, Washington, D. C.

All such returned letters were to be marked "advertised and not called for. Post Office .... (Date)" Various forms of "Returned Letter" wrappers were used to enclose the letter being sent to the sender because of inability to deliver to the addressee. Some of the forms were carried over and used during the early days of Provincial control.

During Provincial control various other types of returned letter covers were used, as well as a number of handstamps, the date usually being in manuscript.

With the formation of the Dominion in 1867 additional handstamps were introduced similar to the regular town markings then current.

By 1875 the volume of mail handled by the Dead Letter Office became so great that the "Request Letter" or return card was introduced. This enabled

---

1. Advertisements could be in a newspaper or by hand bills displayed at the Post Office.

senders to have the inscription "Please return in .... days", etc., printed on the cover, thus enabling them to be returned to the sender without passing through the Dead Letter Office[2].

Occasionally, however, a letter with the return request would be sent to the Dead Letter Office, and even less often opened by mistake. It was to Officially Seal these erroneously opened letters that the adhesive labels were introduced. They continued in use until about 1929, three designs being used.

A. The Handstruck Stamps of the Dead Letter Office

Type HS-OS1
1851 (Reconstructed. Probably 30 mm. in diam.)

Type HS-OS2
1860 (Also reconstructed. 25 mm. in diam.)

Fig. 2. Cover with Type 2 Handstruck Stamp of D. L. O.

Type HS-OS3.
Original 1867
1st. Recut Feb. 1883
2nd Recut Mar. 1889

Type HS-OS4.
25 mm. in diam.
New Nov. 1873
1st Recut in 1876
2nd Recut in 1879
3rd Recut in 1889

Type HS-OS6.
Sept. 1883.
1st Recut Dec. 1888
2nd Recut Mar. 1889

2. See Appendix M #14.

Type HS-OS7.
New July 1881—#1, 2.
1st Recut Apr. 1883
2nd Recut Feb. 1890
Type HS-OS8.
Similar but reading
"Dead Letter Branch"
Dec. 1893.

Type HS-OS9.
Aug. 1892.

Type HS-OS10.
Dec. 1893.

Type HS-OS11.

Dead Letter Office, Clerk's Markings.

Type HS-OS-A.
#1, 2, 3 Mar. 1880

NO·TRACE·IN
D. L. O.

Type HS-OS-B.
April 1877.

D. L. O. Record,
No......................

Type HS-OS-C.

NO·MONEY·ENCLOSURE
WHEN·OPENED·IN·D.L.O.

Type HS-OS-D.

717

The Handstruck Stamps of the Dead Letter Office

Type	Date		Color	Value	Notes
HS-OS1	1851		Black	2.50	Probably 30mm. in diam.
HS-OS2	1860		Black	2.00	25mm. in diam. (Fig. 2).
HS-OS3	1867		Black	1.00	Recut in 1883, and 1889.
HS-OS4	1874		Black	1.00	Recut in 1876, 1879, 1889.
HS-OS6	1883	(Sep.)	Black	1.00	Recut in 1888, and 1889
HS-OS7	1881	(Jul.)	Black	.75	#1, 2 Recut 1890, 1893.
HS-OS8	1893	(Dec.)	Black	.50	Reads "Dead Letter Branch"
HS-OS9	1892	(Jan.)	Black	.50	
HS-OS10	1893	(Dec.)	Black	.50	
HS-OS11	1899		Black	1.00	"Ottawa Branch"
HS-OSA	1880	(Mar)	Black	.50	#1, 2, 3.
HS-OSB	1877	(Apr.)	Black	.50	
HS-OSC	187(?)		Black	.50	
HS-OSD	1877		Black	.50	

B. The Adhesive Seals of the Dead Letter Office.

The three designs were each from a plate of fifty stamps, arranged in a single pane. The imprint on the first seal was at the sides of the plate, in type V, which is well known on the Small Queen stamps. (See page 282).

The later seals, all by the American Bank Note Co. have the type IX imprint at the top over the fifth and sixth stamps of the sheet. (See page 318).

We have seen the following proofs:

REFERENCE LIST

DIE PROOFS

(On India, die sunk on card)

D-OS1a GREEN.
D-OS2a Black on card. Die No. "C11".
D-OS3a Black on card. "CANADA-G-O-32"—"210F".

On Card Cut to Stamp Size (Rare)

D-OS1b Black.
D-OS2b Black.

PLATE PROOFS
(Scarce)

P-OS1a Brown on India.
P-OS2b Black on blue.

We have seen a block of six (2 x 3) of P-OS2b with manuscript note "Approved as to paper and color RMC" (R. M. Coulter, Dep. P.M.G.). The back is a circular handstamp in dark blue "Postage Stamp Branch/P. O. Dept. Canada/ Superintendent Feb. 28, 1902".

Official Seals of the Dead Letter Office

OS1   1875-1901.

CS4.   1913-29.

OS2, OS3.   1902-1912.
This design adopted from the $5.00 Law Stamp of 1897.

The Adhesive Seals of the Dead Letter Office.

#	Description	Issued	Plates	Unused	Used	Notes
OS1	Brown Perf 11½x12	1875	1 of 50 (5x10)	5.00	10.00	Type V imprint Approximately 20,000 issued
a	Perf 12			x		
b	Imperf.			x		
OS2	Black on blue (Victoria)	1902	1 of 50 (10x5)	15.00	25.00	Type IX imprint. 10,000 issued Vignette Engraved by Charles Skinner
OS3	Black (Victoria)	1907	From same plate as 1902 Seal	2.50	5.00	50,000 issued
OS4	Black brown (Bi-lingual)	1913	1 of 50 (5x10)	1.00	2.50	Type IX imprint. 60,000 issued .

All on stout wove paper.

Various forms of type set gummed labels have been used to seal letters and packets that have opened or become damaged in transit.

Seals on covers are worth twice the price given for used copies.

Chapter XLI

A. THE HANDSTRUCK OFFICIAL STAMPS.

Although Canada has never issued any adhesive Official stamps, the Franking privilege has been given to certain officials at various times, and letters were struck with several types of markings to indicate that they were transmitted free of any postage charges.

Prior to the Post Office being transferred to Provincial Control on April 6, 1851, the regulations of the British Post Office concerning free letters applied. However, this was of little practical use to Canada, as only members of the British Parliament had the privilege under certain regulations and even this restricted use was abolished in 1840.

The desire of the local legislatures to have the Franking privilege resulted in both houses of the legislature in Upper Canada passed a franking act in April 1837. Under the terms of this act members were authorized to send letters free during the sitting of the legislature.

An Early Post Office Frank. 1848. (HS-PO-I)

The Governor General, the Earl of Gosford urged that the correspondence of the Governor General and his civil secretary be exempt from postage charges. The Deputy Postmaster General, Stayner, objected to all attempts to deprive his office any revenue, on various grounds, chiefly that such granting of the franking privilege was open to abuses, (which was a well known fact), and that the Post Office being under Imperial control could not be affected by the acts of the local legislatures.

Nevertheless at various times prior to April 1851 what is commonly referred to as the franking privilege was granted by statute or regulations made thereunder to Members of Parliament, Government Departments, Certain Classes of officials and to a limited extent to the public generally. The extent to which the privilege was granted varied from time to time depending upon the view point of the Parliament of the day. Under this privilege the persons referred to were permitted to send mail matter free from postage rates and in the case of the public they were allowed to send letters to certain Government Departments free of charge. Under appropriate regulations all postmasters were advised as to these franking privileges and when letters or other mail matter suitably designated were posted the postmaster stamped thereon the word "Free". In the case of Members of Parliament this was done in the post office at the Parliament Buildings and in all other cases in the post office where the letters were posted. The Postmasters themselves had the franking privilege on their *personal* mail in addition to official correspondence.

With the transfer to Provincial control, however, the Franking privilege was abolished, except of course for the Post Office Department itself.

In July 1855, however, an act passed on the 19th of May, granted the franking privilege as follows:

"IV. All letters and other mailable matter addressed to or sent by the Governor of this Province, or sent to or by any Public Department at the seat of Government, shall be free of Provincial Postage under such regulations as may be directed by the Governor in Council."

"V. All letters and other mailable matter addressed to or sent by the Speaker or Chief Clerk of the Legislative Council or of the Legislative Assembly, or by or to any member of either of said branches of the Legislature during any Session of the Legislature, shall be free of Provincial Postage."

After Federation in 1867, only the Federal Departments had the Franking privilege, the Provincial Legislatures being permitted to send only documents, open at the ends, free.

It should be understood that correspondence relating to Post Office Business was at all times handled Free, and still is.

We are of the opinion that nearly all of the "Free" correspondence prior to July 1855 is Post Office Business.

a. THE IMPERIAL AND PROVINCIAL.

Post Office Business Franks

HS-PO I   Black (See page 721)   20.00

1. "Free" Handstamps. (See Appendix B #7)

	HS-01 "FREE"	HS-02 Black	Blue
HS-O1	20x4-4½ mm. (1838-51)	1.00	
HS-O2	20x5-5½ mm. (1838-51)	1.25	x

	1860 HS-03 "FREE"	1861 HS-04	1863 HS-05 Black	Red	Blue
HS-O3	21x5½ mm.		1.00	1.50	
HS-O4	17x3½ mm.		2.00	3.00	3.00
HS-O5	22x5½ mm		5.00		

	HS-015a "FREE"	HS-015b	HS-015c Black	Red	HS-016 Blue
HS-O15a,b,c	General use (1856)[1]		1.00	1.00	1.50
HS-O16	Ottawa, Goderich		2.00	2.50	

	HS-017 "FREE"	HS-018	HS-019 Black	Red	HS-020 Blue
HS-O17	1862	Sarnia	2.00	2.00	3.00
HS-O18	1862	Sandwich	5.00		
HS-O19	1863	Hamilton	2.00		
HS-O20	1868	Beaverton	2.00		

1. See Appendix F, Table B.

2. The Handstruck Legislative Franks.

HS-06

HS-07 HS-08

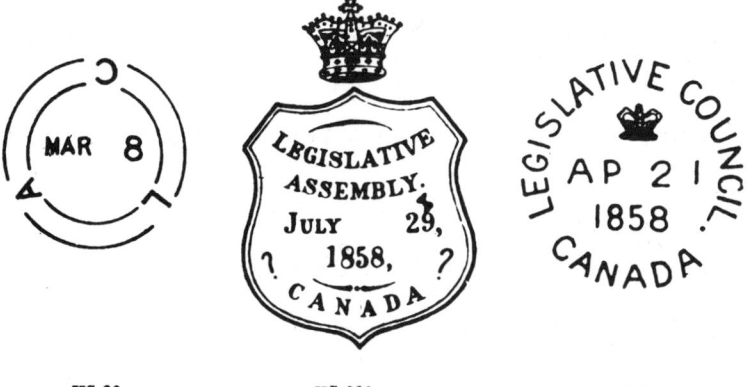

HS-09 HS-010 HS-011

HS-O12

HS-O13

See Note 1.

Cover, with 7½p, to Scotland Struck with HS-O10 in red. Since this was sent outside of Canada, the postage had to be paid. Signed "O Mowat M. P. P" who later became P.M.G.

The types illustrated on pages 723-24 (Nos. HS-O6 to HS-O13) were used on mail franked by Members of Parliament or by Government Departments and are usually on stampless covers. Letters carrying postage stamps mailed at the Parliament Buildings were also stamped with these postmarks. All were used prior to Confederation.

Reference List of the Handstruck Legislative Franks to 1868.

			Black	Red	Blue
HS-O6	1849	Legislative Assembly Canada, oval	—	—	5.00
HS-O7	1857	Legislative Assembly Canada, circular	—	—	10.00
HS-O8	1860	Legislative Council, Double circle	—	10.00	
HS-O9	1858	"L—A—C" circluar	x		
HS-O10	1858	Shield Type		12.50	12.50
HS-O11	1858	Legislative Council, circular			5.00
HS-O12	1863	Legislative Council, circular	2.50	2.50	
HS-O13	1864	Legislative Assembly, circular	2.50	2.50	

1. A typical handstamp of one of the Provincial Legislatures. These are outside the scope of this book.

b. DOMINION HANDSTAMPS.

1. General.

(HS-O15c)

HS-O21

HS-O22

		Black
HS-O21	"FREE" in circle (1880)	1.00[2]
HS-O22	"Ottawa-Canada Free" (1886)	1.00
(HS-O15c)	"FREE" (1880)	1.00[3]

2. Senate Franks.

HS-O23

HS-O24

(b)

(a)

HS-O25

	Black	Blue
HS-O23 1875	1.50	2.00

---

2. The contractors supplied 20 of these markings in April 1880.
3. In November 1880 the contractors furnished some "Free" hand stamps very similar to Type HS-O15c to the P.O.D.

	Black	Red	Violet
HS-O24 Jan. 1882	2.00	2.00	2.00
HS-O25a 1882	1.50		
HS-O25b Jan. 1882 (with date)	2.50	3.00	

There are a number of types of these, varying in the size of the crown, lettering, etc.

3. House of Commons Franks.

HS-O26

HS-O27, O28

HS-O29

HS-O30

HS-O31

		Black	Blue	Red
HS-O26	1867 Shield and crown			12.50
HS-O27	1868 Oval (30 x 22 mm.)	1.50		
HS-O28	1868 Oval without "Free" (50 x 40 mm.)	1.25		
HS-O29	1874 With date		2.00	
HS-O30	1872 Double circle		2.00	
HS-O31	1880 Single outer circle	1.00		

There are a number of sub-types of the above.

In addition to the listed types for the Legislative bodies, there are a number of handstamps used by the various government departments, such as, Finance Department, Indian Department, Marine & Fisheries, Crown Lands Department (C. L. D.) etc.

The data on these is incomplete, and by the early years of the 20th century have been replaced to a great extent by printed forms, similar to the "Penalty" envelopes of the United States. Metered mail is also commonly used.

B. THE ADHESIVE STAMPS PUNCHED "OHMS".
1920-44.

Adhesive stamps punched "O.H.M.S." first appeared late in 1920 and were used exclusively by the Receiver General's Office, Ottawa, and the Assistant Receiver General's Offices in the various provinces.

The issues up to July 1, 1939, were punched at the Receiver General's Office by a machine having five holes in the vertical strokes of the "H" and "M".

An Order in Council of June 29, 1939 directed that all Canadian stamps for official use be punched, and that it be done by the Post Office Department. Stamps so punched have four holes in the vertical strokes of the "H" and "M" as compared with five of the machines at the Receiver General's office.

Since the work is manually perforated there are inverted, reversed, pair one without punching, etc.

The stamps known with the five hole punch are; Boggs #
102, 106, 107, 117, 119, 121, 122, 124, 115, 117, 118, 129, 151, 154, 158, 159, 164, 165, 166, 167, 168, 171, 178, 180, 181, 182, 189, 192, 193, 194, 196, 198, 208, 209, 211, 216, 217, 218, 219, 220, 221, 222, 222a, 223, 224, 225, 226, 261, 264, 265, 270, 271.

The four hole punch is known on: 211, 216, 217, 218, 219, 220, 221, 222, 222a, 223, 224, 225, 226, 230, 231, 232, 233, 234, 235, 236, 237, 238, 239, 240, 241, 242, 243, AM1, AM6, AM7, AM8, SD10, SD11.

2c Small Queen on a Wrapper, Group 4 Precancel. Used in 1876.

CHAPTER XLII

PRECANCELLED STAMPS

Stamps Cancelled Before Affixing to Mail Matter

The Forerunners

The first precancelling was done at the Ottawa Post Office in 1888, complete sheets of the 1c, 2c, 3c, and 5c stamps being struck with the "killer" then in use, which consisted of the numeral "1" in a circle made of nineteen horizontal lines. Later in the same year the St. John office applied its "killer," which was the numeral "1" in a circle, surrounded by a vertical oval made up of fourteen horizontal lines, to the 1c denomination. It is believed that in 1889 the Montreal office used the old "21" roller which had been used on the 1851, 1859 and rarely on the 1868 issue. This was applied to 1c, 2c, 3c, 6c, and 10c values. Toronto precancelled the 1c, 2c, and 3c denominations by ruling lines with a pen across each row of stamps.

These forerunners while unofficial are nevertheless of historic interest, and should form the opening pages of every precancel collection.

1888-89 Forerunners (On Small Queens)

Factors of Value

Type	City	1c	2c	3c	5c	6c	10c
PF1	Ottawa	100	100	100	100	—	—
PF2	St. John	100	—	—	—	—	—
PF3	Montreal	100	125	150	—	100	100
PF4	Toronto	100	100	100	—	—	—

PF1 and PF2 can only be distinguished when in pair or blocks such examples showing no town date and mark. PF3 was only used as a precancel on the 1888-9 issues. PF4 can only be told when on a cover used by a firm known to have used the privilege of precancellation. In all cases of these forerunner types being on covers the stamps of course will not be "tied" by the cancellation.

The Early Line Types—Prepared at Ottawa (1890-94)

Beginning in 1889 the Department took official cognizance of the practical value of precancels as a method of saving labor and expediting the mail. A revolving self-inking roller, which precancelled a row at a time, was used to prepare sheets of the ½c, 1c, 2c, 3c, and 5c stamps. Later, in 1892, the 6c and 10c were precancelled and in 1893-94 the 8c, 15c, 20c and 50c were treated in this manner. It was in 1892 that precancels were first allowed on parcels.

The Line Types being applied by hand show numerous varieties, such as double, diagonal, vertical, eac., which while interesting to the specialist do not warrant separate listing. They are divisible into three groups, viz: (On Small Queen Stamps).
 1. 3 to 6 thick lines (1890) ½c, 1c, 3c.
 2. 6 to 8 thin lines (1890) ½c, 1c, 2c, 3c, 5c, 6c, 8c, 10c.
 3. 2 to 8 lines of diagonal dashes (1891) 1c, 3c.

The theory that the third group was the result of a series of rubber bands on a tube, the twists in the bands accounted for the dashes is rather far fetched. The ink on these precancels is the usual cancelling inks, or printers ink, which does not work properly on rubber surfaces. It is more likely that a roller with twisted wire was used, or the cancelling ridges were deliberately cut to make dashes.

Group 1 occurs in black and violet, the other groups only in black.

Group 4.

During 1892 the wavy line between straight lines type was introduced. This was applied to sheets by a self inking hand roller ten stamps wide. Blocks are known showing various differences between the adjoining rows showing that the so called types occured on the same roller. This type was used on all the Small Queen designs, as well as the 15c large Queen, and the later issues to 1903.

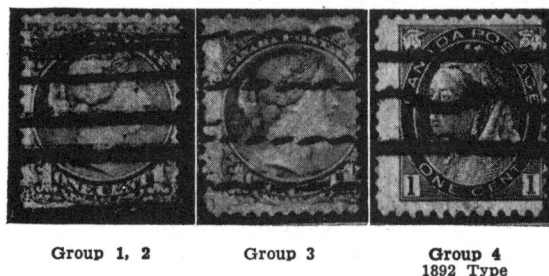

Group 1, 2   Group 3   Group 4
                            1892 Type

The Electro Type. (1895-1903)

In 1895 a standard type was adopted, which was used from that time until the city types were introduced.

This was printed a sheet at a time from an electro, and the squared off curves of the wavy line is characteristic of this type. In use until the city types of 1903 were introduced.

The City Types—Prepared at Ottawa (1903-1935)

Beginning in 1903 all precancellation was done with electrotypes which cancelled one hundred stamps at a time. Over fifty cities used this type of precancellation in which the name of the city appears with bars in various combinations.

The type for these electros was cast on a Ludlow machine in rows of ten, and this is repeated to make up a plate of 100 subjects. It can thus be seen how the "BRIBGEBURG" (for BRIDGEBURG) error occurs on the extreme right vertical row of the sheet on all stamps overprinted by the Bridgeburg electro.

The printing was done on a press secured in 1903 from the Toronto Type and Foundry Co. especially for precancelling stamps.

It is interesting to note some of the electros were in use for nearly thirty years, notably Victoria, Brandon, Calgary, and Peterboro.

The "Bribgeburg" Error

General City Types (1903-1944)

(Used in Two or More Cities)

Type A
Wavy lines above, between and below lines.

Type B
"ONTARIO" 3mm below lines. "A" wide, "O" Narrow No wavy lines.

Type C
"ONTARIO" 2mm below lines. "A" Narrow, "O" wide No wavy lines.

Type D
Serifed caps, wavy lines above and below lines. Province name abbreviated.

Type E
City name in upper and lower case. Wavy lines above and below lines.

Type F
No wavy lines. Straight lines and lettering thin sans serif caps. Lines 3mm from city and province name.

Type G
Lettering thicker and 2mm above and below lines. Smaller than type C

Type H
3 lines between city and province name.

Type J
City name in serifed caps. Wavy lines above and below lines.

Type K
City name in upper and lower case. Wavy lines as type J.

Type L
City name in tall thin serifed caps. Dotted lines above and below lines.

Type T
"For Third Class Matter"

732

Specific City Types (1903-1944)

These types are peculiar to their respective cities. They are noted as type "S"—(Specific).

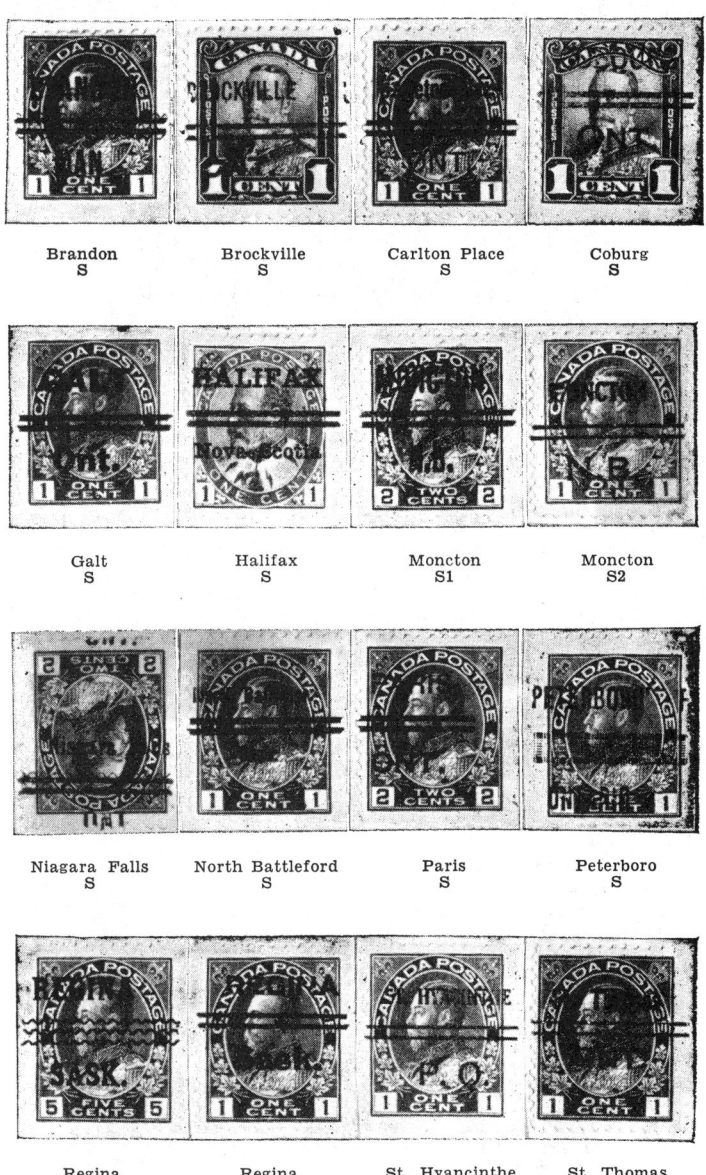

| Toronto | Toronto | Toronto | Truro |
| S1 | S2 | S3 | S |

| Walkerville | Winnipeg | Winnipeg |
| S | S1 | S2 |

NOTE: Montreal and Toronto used a special type on the 50c Widows Weeds design. It occurs only on that stamp.

Of the general city electros there were twelve types, each used by two or more cities. In addition certain cities had electros of their own, Toronto having three such types. A total of 23 specific city types are known. This makes a total of thirty-five city types. Previous to the general use of city names, however, Toronto, and Montreal each used an electro to precancel the 50c Widows Weeds design. It is peculiar to this stamp. All of the electros were made and the precancelling done at Ottawa by the Kings Printer.

The Money Order Office Number System

In 1931 a uniform style consisting of a number between parallel double lines was introduced. The number used corresponds to the particular post office's number in the Money Order System. This type gradually replaced the city name types in all but the smaller offices which are supplied with the parallel **double line type.**

Prior to the adoption of this method of precancelling stamps, essays were made on the King George Admiral Type 3c carmine stamp, about 1928. The experimental electro differs from the issued types in that the numrals are slightly taller, and the closely spaced double lines are 10 mm. apart.

| Type I | Type II | Type III |

The issued types we illustrate above, and note the differences as follows:

	Numerals	Serifs	Spacing of Lines
Type I	3mm. tall	slight	9½mm.
Type II	2½mm. tall	none	10mm.
Type III	2½mm. tall	yes	10mm.

The double lines of type I are very close.
Types I, and II are by the British American Bank Note Co., III by the Canadian Bank Note Co.

Block of Four of Essay for Numeral Precancels

Money Order Office Number

M. O. Office #	Post Office		
XO30	Charlottetown, P. E. I.	3800	Niagara Falls, Ont.
X275	Halifax, N. S.	3893	Oshawa, Ont.
X592	Lennoxville, Que.	3900	Ottawa, Ont.
O700	Montreal, Que.	3975	Owen Sound, Ont.*
X899	Moncton, N. B.	4004	Paris, Ont.*
X910	St. John, N. B.	4035	Peterborough, Ont.
X945	Sackville, N. B.	4260	St. Thomas, Ont.
1050	Quebec, Que.	4530	Toronto, Ont.
1142	Rock Island, Que.*	4900	Weston, Ont.*
1470	St. Hyacinthe, Que.*	4940	Windsor, Ont.
1810	Sherbrooke, Que.*	4970	Woodstock, Ont.*
2186	Beamsville, Ont.*	5099	Brandon, Man.
2310	Brantford, Ont.	5850	Winnipeg, Man.
2342	Brockville, Ont.	7120	Moose Jaw, Sask.
2450	Carleton Pl., Que.*	7420	Regina, Sask.
2575	Cobourg, Ont.	7550	Saskatoon, Sask.
2980	Galt, Ont.*	7977	Yorkton, Sask.
3080	Guelph, Ont.	8160	Calgary, Alta.
3100	Hamilton, Ont.	8360	Edmonton, Alta.
3340	Kingston, Ont.	8605	Lethbridge, Alta.*
3366	Kitchener, Ont.	8802	Red Deer, Alta.
3445	Lindsay, Ont.	9500	New Westminster, B. C.*
3070	London, Ont. (error)	9780	Vancouver, B. C.
3470	London, Ont.	9890	Victoria, B. C.

* These cities now are only authorized to use the general line type.

The 1923 Line Types

With the elimination of minimum requirements as to quantity in 1923 a special electrotype consisting merely of groups of parallel lines was made so that smaller offices could avail themselves of the precancel privilege.

The first type has thick lines, and was by the Canadian Bank Note Co., from electros. When the British American Bank Note Co. began printing the stamps it used a similar arrangement of lines, but the electro had thinner lines, and the space between each pair is wider.

When the Canadian Bank Note Co. again secured the contract, the third type of line precancels was introduced. These are printed from machine set plates instead of electros, and as the metal is melted down after each printing, every new setting produces various varieties of spacing.

The Line Precancels

Type I   Type II   Type III
Electra, C. B. N. Co   Electro, B. A. B. N.. Co.   Type Set, C. B. N. Co.

The precancelled stamps of Canada have always been under the strict supervision of the Post Office Department, and from 1889 on have only been produced at Ottawa, thereby occupying a position somewhat analagous to United States Bureau Prints. At first precancels were issued to any office with an annual revenue of $3,000 or more. In 1904 the use of these stamps was limited to mailings of 25,000 pieces or more at a time. About six weeks later the requirements were reduced to 10,000 pieces at a mailing. See Appendix B #59.

Chapter XLIII

THE MACHINE IMPRINTED POSTAGE STAMPS
(Postage Meters and Postage Machines)

A. Meters

The impressing of stamps on envelopes or strips of gummed paper, such impressions being made by patented machines, under rigid rules and regulations of the Postal Officials, was first permitted in Norway as early as 1903, followed by New Zealand in 1905. The system attracted little attention from other Post Office Administrations, although various machines were patented and tested, only to be rejected by the authorities.

In January 1914 an experiment was made by the United States Post Office Department which permitted several users to try the Pitney Postage Meter. Further improvements, delayed by World War I, finally resulted in the definite approval of Metered Mail in November 1920.

The success in the United States, and Great Britain shortly thereafter, of this form of prepayment of postage was studied by the Canada Post Office Department, which in July 1923 authorized the use of Postage Meters.

The device and its advantages are briefly described herewith:

"The Postage Meter machine is a device for metering and printing postage directly on mail matter. The postage imprint is a combination of postage stamp cancellation, and postmark. The meter is a detachable unit and is taken to the post office to be set for postage as required, payment being made at the time of setting.

"The postage meter is in no way similar to the many devices of affixing adhesive postage stamps, nor should it be confused with the numerous appliances placed on the market for printing permit indicia on identical pieces of mail. It is the first machine authorized by the Post Office Department conforming to the special rules and regulations governing the use of a device having detachable printing and recording mechanism to be set by the postmaster and which automatically locks when impressions paid for are exhausted.

"Metered mail is not subject to the restrictions governing the acceptance of ordinary permit mail imprinted by any of the various appliances now on the market. Being paid for in advance, per piece, through settings of the meter, metered mail is accepted by the post office in any quantity, and may vary in size, weight and content. It goes direct to the sorters when it reaches the post office, without delay for verification of count and collecting of postage.

"By eliminating the delay for facing and cancelling (post office operations required on ordinary stamped mail) the postage meter expedites the transit of commercial mail from one to twenty-four hours. It establishes a perfect system of safeguarding and accounting for postage. As a labor saver it is invaluable to every concern doing a large mailing.

"The meter is a small printing and recording mechanism, detachable from the machine which operates it so that it may be taken to the post office for setting. It has two registers, both inaccessible to the user, but visible through small glass windows. The upper register is an ascending total indicating the amount of postage used, accumulating to one million when it automatically re-sets to zero. The lower register is a descending total indicating the stamp impressions paid for and unused. It has a capacity of 100,000 imprints. Each imprint increases the upper register one unit and decreases the lower register correspondingly. When the lower register entirely discharges, the printing head automatically locks and will not function until the meter is taken to the post office and re-set for additional postage. It is unnecessary to completely discharge the meter before having it re-set.

"The printing die is engraved steel. It prints the user's post office license number and the registered number of the meter. The die is permanently attached to the meter, and will not print unless the meter is in proper position on the machine. It is mechanically impossible to waste metered postage, as the register will not record unless an imprint is made on a piece of mail. A set of interchangeable steel type for the date and hour of mailing is furnished with each meter.

"In general construction and design the machine operating the meter is largely a modification of the postmarking and cancelling machines in use in the post offices of this and many foreign countries.

"There is no limit on mailings of first class matter bearing postage meter indicia. Any number of pieces may be presented at one mailing and the pieces need not be identical as to size, contents or weight. Mail matter bearing this indicia may be addressed to any post office in Canada or abroad."

It can thus be seen that the impression of these meters is accepted as a POSTAGE STAMP, by the Universal Postal Union on the same basis as adhesive stamps and postal stationery.

Meter Terminology.

There is a special terminology used in discussing these impressions and listed below are some of the terms used, and their definitions.

Device: The entire apparatus, including all attachments.

Register: The detachable, portable part of the device, containing the arrangements for setting by the postmaster the total amount of postage asked and paid for.

Town-cancel or Town-mark: The name of town and province, as well as the date.

Indicia: That part of the meter which represents—and is—the *postage stamp*.

Meter: The imprint upon the envelope of the indicia and town-cancel, replacing respectively the stamp and the cancellation.

Design: The form and shape of the indicia.

Denomination or value: The amount of postage represented by the figure or figures in the indicia.

Single Denomination: Signifies that the register is built for imprinting one given denomination only.

Fixed Denomination: Signifies that the register is built so that the denomination can be changed by removing one die and inserting another as needed.

Multi-Denomination: Signifies that the register is built to imprint, by turning a knob or button, one of a certain number of different denominations, such as, for instance, a 10c, a 5c and a 3c to make up the registry fee of 18c.

Omni-Denomination: Signifies that the register is built so that, by indicating the postage required on the keyboard, the amount is imprinted in one operation, such as, for instance 1:33. Some of these machines imprint an amount up to 9.99 others up to 99.99.

The first Canadian Metered Mail dispatch was by Pitney Bowes Agent, August 7, 1923, and the first commercial installation was at the T. Eaton Co., September 29, 1923, both from Toronto.

The first meters were single denomination meters. In 1926 the Universal Postal Frankers Midget Model from Great Britain was introduced. This was a fixed value meter, employing three denominations. The Pitney-Bowes Fixed value model was introduced in 1928, and was the first to print either on tape or envelope.

Six years later (1934) a multi-denomination meter was introduced capable of printing ten denominations, by the turn of a knob.

Omni-denomination models came into use in 1936, although experiments began as early as 1933.

An improved Omni-denomination meter was placed in service in 1940.

The Mailomat

The Mailomat, a mechanical Post Office was experimentally operated in Toronto in 1938, and in 1944 an installation was made in Ottawa. We consider the Mailomat a most important development in the metered mail field, which promises in time to curtail the printing and sale of adhesive postage stamps to a considerable extent.

We do not give this output of the Postage Meter Co. a new type number, for the simple reason that the indicia is not a new type, and therefore merely note it as "The Mailomat".

For detailed description, etc., we quote from a Pitney Bowes Postage Meter Co. circular, such portions as we deem of interest adapted to our purpose.

"A revolutionary method of using the mails was made available to the general public, when a new, coin-operated postage meter mailing machine and automatic letter box, called the 'Mailomat', was installed for an extended official test in the lobby of the Toronto Post Office."

"The 'Mailomat' enables the public, without the use of adhesive postage stamps, to deposit coins up to 60c at a time, dial from this prepaid credit any postage value or denominations, insert letters or postcards, and thus simultaneously prepay postage and deposit letters in a simple, automatic operation.

"The available amount of the mailer's coin deposit is always visible to him through a glass window, and one or more letters can be mechanically stamped and mailed just as fast as the mailer can insert them in a guided slot or track."

"Postal officials consider the public service possibilities of the new machine both wide and important. By combining a multi-denomination postage meter, operative by coins, with a mail depository having the function of a street letter box for mail collections, the 'Mailomat' automatically makes one operation of purchasing postage and mailing letters. It serves, unattended, as a miniature post office, selling postage of all rates, and mechanically depositing letters for scheduled collection by postal workers."

"At the twist of a dial, the exact postage denomination is available for any letter—in a single imprinted metered mail stamp, whether 1c for a post card, 3c for a regular letter, 5c for a foreign letter, 8c for a domestic air mail letter, 16c for out-of-town special delivery."

"One of the outstanding advantages of metered mail, which the 'Mailomat' now for first time brings to the general public, is the expedition of mail in despatch from the outgoing post office. Mail bearing adhesive stamps or enclosed in Government stamped envelopes must be delayed in the outgoing post office for cancelling and postmarking. The 'Meter Stamps' which the Mailomat prints, contain the date of mailing and need no other postmarking or cancellation, consequently mail bearing Meter Stamps skips these operations, saves time in the outgoing post office and may be received from one to twenty-four hours earlier.

"The 'Mailomat' is the culmination of many years of experimental research and development."

"The machine has obvious advantages over the stamp vending machines such as those familiar to drug store patrons."

"It is impossible for this machine, incorporating a postage meter, to "run-out" of any one value or denomination of stamp. There is no need to make provision for reloading coils or reels of stamps because no stamp, as such, are used; and any postage value is available at the twist of a dial and the dropping of a coin or coins."

"No premium is charged for postage. Full postage value is given for all coins, since the machine is designed for regular post office service."

"In addition, both the post office and the public are protected by means of an automatic coin detector. And the machine will accept no letter for mailing which has not passed through the coin-paid metering device. There is basic protection, too, in that the machine sells or dispenses nothing that can be taken away from it by the mailer."

"Another feature of the 'Mailomat' is its flexibility. It will accept oversize letters as large as 12 inches by 6, and up to 3/8 inches in thickness. It is equipped with regulation post office time cards, similar to those on corner mailboxes, showing schedule of mail collections by regular postal workers."

Types of Meter Indicia.

Type 1. "Cents".
(a) With Licence No.
(b) Without License No.

Type 2. "Midget" Type.

Type 2. "Midget" Type. (This is a rectangular indicia, very severe and without ornamentation. Similar to U. S. Meters of the "D" group.)

Type 3. "Cents" "Midget".
Shield Type—25 mm. High.

Type 4. "Cents" Pitney-Bowes Shield Type
23 mm. High.

Types 5 to 9, and 12 "Scroll Type.

Types 10 and 13. "Crown" Type.

Types 11 and 14. Maple Leaf Type.

Indicia are usually in red which is according to the U.P.U. regulations. Impressions are known in colors corresponding to the color of the adhesive of the same denomination, that is, 1c green, 5c blue, etc.

Meter Slogans

Meter slogans came into use on postage meters simultaneously with the appearance of multi-denominational machines, about 1924. Since then they have developed into one of the principal features of metered mail. To collectors of them they furnish endless possibilities for specializing and, taken as a whole, they reflect the "passing show" more accurately than any other form of postal marking.

Metered Mail Indicia

Type	Design	Date	Series	Machine	Notes
1	"Cents"	1923	400	Pitney-Bowes Model C, M, or H.	Single denomination. (a) With (b) without license number.
2	"Cents"	1926	500	Universal Postal Frankers "Midget" Model	Fixed value. Popularly known as "Midget". Obsolete 1938.
3	"Cents"	1926		Universal Postal Frankers "Midget" Model	Fixed value. With "Meter" or "Metre", or with number only, sometimes preceded by "M". Now obsolete shield design.
4	"Cents" Scroll	1928	40,000 – 48,000	Pitney-Bowes Model C, M, or H.	Shield design, "Meter".
5	"Cents" Scroll	1934	40,000 – 48,000	Pitney-Bowes Model C, M, or H.	Multi-denomination. Scroll type, "Metre". Similar to current adhesives.
6	Scroll	1934	82,400 up	Pitney-Bowes Model H	Limited value. "Meter No"; "Metre"; or "Meter-Compteur".
7	Scroll	1936	54,000 up	Pitney-Bowes Model CV	Limited value "Meter" or "Meter-Compteur".
8	Scroll	1934	O4,000 up	Pitney-Bowes Model C, M, or H.	Single denomination "Meter No."; "Metre" or "M-C".
9	Scroll	1933-6	1021-5	Pitney-Bowes	Omni-denomination. Experimental. Obsolete.
10	Crown	1936	94,000	Pitney-Bowes Model JD	Omni-denomination "Metre"; or "M-C".
11	Maple Leaf	1940	140,000 up	Pitney-Bowes	Omni-denomination.
12	Scroll		9922/3	National Postal Meter	"Compteur", or "M-C".
13	Crown	1938	101	Mailomat	Pitney-Bowes machine, used at Toronto. Obsolete.
14	Maple Leaf	1944	51,000 – 51,010	Mailomat	Pitney-Bowes machine, used at Toronto, Ottawa. Obsolete.

B. Postage Machines

About the middle of 1925 Postal Register Machines of the cash register type were authorized by the Canadian Post Office Department for the prepayment of postage on parcels of printed matter, parcel post, and bulky matter prepaid at the letter rate.

The National Cash Register Co. of Dayton, Ohio, manufactures the machines which produce a gummed label with an impression of the amount of postage paid. This label is affixed to each item of mail matter at the upper right-hand corner where stamps are usually placed.

The first three registers installed were: T. Eaton Co., Toronto, permit No. 100, Sept. 3, 1925. Postal Terminal "A", Toronto, Permit No. 105; Sept 28, 1925. Adelaide Station Post Office, Toronto, permit No. 104, Sept. 30, 1925.

All impressions show the inscription "Canada Postage Paid," the machine (or permit) number, town of origin, year, date and a serial number.

The labels can be divided into two distinct groups, as two models of machine were used. (A) 28x85 mm.; (B) 54x46 mm.

GROUP A (28 x 85 mm.)

The impression consists of two parts, namely, the fixed indicia comprising "Canada Postage Paid," machine number, town name and year; and the changeable numerals indicating postage, date and serial number. There are three different arrangements in existence viz:

Type a	Type b	Type c
CANADA POSTAGE PAID	date, serial No.	CANADA POSTAGE PAID
denomination	CANADA POSTAGE PAID	date, serial No.
No.	denomination & letter	denomination
town		No.
year	No.	town
serial No., date	town	year
	year	denomination (4 figures of value)

There are several variations from the above arrangements, notably:

No. 734 Winnipeg "Canada Post Office".
No. 112 Toronto, Town omitted.
No. 862 Saskatoon, No. Town, and year repeated.

While the above vary from the standard arrangement for various reasons, two other varieties were for special purposes: Type a No. 149 top: "Canada Postage / PAID / House of Assembly / P. O.," register installed at the post office in the House of Assembly, Toronto, Ont., and Type c No. 137 top: "CANADA/ POSTAGE DUE" (boxed) used as postage due register at Postal Terminal "A", Toronto, Ont.

While the special types on No. 137 and 149 have been in use for some time, some of the other varieties were used only temporarily as No. 112 exists also in the regular arrangement. Even changes from one arrangement to another on the same permit No. can be noticed as for instance No. 811 exists in both b & c arrangements.

Registers installed in the Province of Quebec are bi-lingual. The following arrangements are known:

Type a, top:

    CANADA/Postage Paid/Port Paye—Nos. 501, 514, 517, 523.
    CANADA/POSTAGE PAID/Port Paye—No. 520.
    Canada/Postage Paid/Port Paye—No. 508.
    CANADA POSTAGE/PAID/PORT PAYE—No. 524.
    CANADA/POSTAGE/PAID/PORT PAYE—No. 221.

Type b, upper center:

    CANADA/Postage Paid/Port Paye—No. 50?

All impressions found are in purple except two early Winnipeg items used in 1926/7 (Nos. 710, 715), in blue. The postage due labels from No. 137 always show red prints in order to distinguish this from ordinary postage.

Early machines used plain white paper, in the years 1926 and 1927; but an impression as late as January, 1929, exists on white paper (No. 311). A special safety paper with a grey background soon became standard, showing the maple leaf, CANADA POSTAGE, and crown continuously repeated. The color of the background was changed to pale pink apparently in 1933. Various shades of pink can be found, and labels with inverted background are frequent, as the paper rolls could be inserted in the machine either way. While the pink paper is still generally used, some labels with green background are known. The postage due machine No. 137 always used this kind of paper and it is also known on prints from Registers No. 221 and 341.

Group B—(54 x 46 mm.)

In 1931 the National Cash Register Co. introduced a new register model which was especially adapted for the prepayment of postage. While this model went into use in the United States in January, 1931, it made its first appearance in Canada somewhat later, but at least by May 1932 (No. 404).

The artistic design of the almost square label of Group B is a definite improvement over the plain lettering of Group A.

Four different arrangements can be noted:

    Type a—2 figures of value, 3 figure serial number.
    Type b—2 figures of value, 4 figure serial number.
    Type c—3 figures of value, 3 figure serial number.
    Type d—3 figures of value, 4 figures serial number.

Type b and c are standard and only very few registers of the other two arrangements have been used. The most popular b outnumbering c by a large margin.

While most figures of value on arrangement c are much smaller than on d, a few machines used the larger b numerals such as Nos. 739, 812, 841.

Ordinarily town and province names appear at the bottom of the indicia, the province name usually being abbreviated. No. 116 exists without province name, Nos. 109, 172 and 180 with "CAN." instead of the province name, etc.,

The earliest labels are orange paper which is in use on all NCR registers installed in the U. S. These labels are not common. Early in 1934 the same pink safety paper used in Group A was put into general use.

The impression is always purple. Only No. 983 has been found in a greenish discoloration of the indicia frame with all numerals printed in the normal purple.

Various styles can be found on the meter number. Early machines seem to favor small sized figures, later medium and large sizes became popular. Often all these varieties can be found on the same meter number during several years of use.

The numbers known show that the register number was continued even when NCR A was superseded by NCR B, as the register numbers are identical with the postal permit numbers.

Town	NCR A			NCR B			
Type ☞ a	b	c	a	b	c	d
Georgetown							1
Woodstock 1							
Oshawa				2			2
Halifax 22	21			22			
Truro 41							
Moncton				78			
St. John	81						
Toronto 102, 103, 108, 109, 110, 111, 116. 117, 118, 119, 121, 122, 124, 126, 130, 131, 132, 133, 143, 145, 150, 152, 153, 154	104, 105, 112	137	158	100, 103, 104, 109, 110, 111, 116, 150, 157, 159, 161, 164, 165, 168, 169, 172, 180		
Sherbrooke 221							
Brantford	256						
Hamilton 311a,312	311				311		
Kitchener ..341							
London	361						
Ottawa	401, 403			404	404		
Montreal 501, 508, 514, 517, 520, 523, 524				528			
Windsor	601, 602				603		
Simcoe 621							
Paris (631).							
Winnipeg 702, 707, 708, 710, 712, 713, 714, 715, 720, 724, 726, 728, 734, 737				733, 738	739		
Moose Jaw	811	811			812		
Regina	841, 848			850, 851, 860, 866, 867	841		
Calgary	881						
Edmonton ..902	901						
Vancouver ..963, 965	961, 967			965	968		
Victoria 981	982				982, 983		

Both Georgetown and Woodstock use No. 1 at the same time which does not seem to be in line with the usual procedure.

For further details concerning this class of postage stamps we refer collector's to "A Handbook of United States Postage Meters" including Meter Slogans, Second edition, 1940, by William C. Steiger, Stephen G. Rich Pub.

Chapter XLIV

BOGUS AND QUESTIONABLE ITEMS

We have called attention to counterfeits several times in this work, but there is a class of material which is not counterfeit or fake, but merely bogus; the product of a vivid imagination with the assistance of various printing devices. We note those we have seen but there are no doubt others of this ilk.

The Surcharged "Pence" Stamps

The ½p surcharged with a large "1"—probably for "1" cent, and the same stamp with surcharge "8d STG", both in black, were known as early as 1875. These are obviously bogus, and were made to deceive the collectors of those innocent days, when there were few varieties of stamps to collect and novelties were eagerly sought for.

The largest number of items of this class, however, were the product of a certain Henry Hechler of Halifax whose "bisects" have already been discussed (pages 302-4).

We give herewith a brief note concerning the "Official" overprints.

The "Hechler" Overprints on Dominion Envelopes. 1884-89.

A **Service.**

B **Service.**

Enlargements of the two types of "Service" overprints used by Hechler in overprinting stationery.

In 1884-85 Louis Riel led another abortive rebellion in the Northwest Provinces. The government sent troops out, and among them were the "53rd Rifles" from Halifax, of which Henry Hechler was Captain. This enterprising gentleman was also interested in philately, and took the opportunity to have envelopes and post cards overprinted "Service" with various additional legends. These were un-official and without sanction from the Post Office Department, but the overprinting did not affect the postal value, and used copies are frequently seen.

The first type of overprint (Type A) was made late in 1884. There is some reason to believe that it was done at Winnipeg. There are at least two settings:

On Stamp	At Top Center	At Lower Left	
1. "Service"	Coat of Arms	"Head Quarters 63 Rifles"	all in black
2. "Service"	Coat of Arms	"63rd Rifles"	all in red

Later about 1886-1887 he had another batch overprinted, probably in Halifax. The second type of overprint (Type B), is decidedly different in character. We have seen only one setting of this, reading:

On Stamp	At Top Center	At Lower Left
"Service"	Coat of Arms	"On M. S. only".

In black, red, and blue.

The remainders of the "Winnipeg" (Type A) overprints were again overprinted with the "Halifax" (Type B) overprints!

The varieties we have seen are as follows:

Date	Overprint Type	Color	Stamped Envelope (E) or Card (C)
1884	A-1	Black	1c Blue (E)
	A-1	Black	3c Red (E)
	A-2	Red	1c Blue (E)
	A-1	Black	1c Gray blue (C)
	A-2	Red	1c Gray blue (C)
1887	B	Black	1c Blue (E)
	B	Blue	1c Blue (E)
	Var. Double overprint		1c Blue (E)
	B	Red	1c Blue (E)
	B	Blue	3c Red (E)
	B	Red	1c Blue (C)

Double overprints on 1c blue envelopes

1887-9   A-1 and B, both in black.
         A-1 in black, and B in red.
         A-1 in black, and B in blue.

One cover we examined had Type A-1 overprint in black, on 1c blue envelope, bearing two 1c orange yellow adhesives, with diagonal manuscript "Service" in black (by Mr. Hechler), cancelled "Winnipeg Apr. 27, 1885", to Mrs. Hechler—with details as to his Battalion going on to Swift Current. By May 5 he was at Swift Current, from which he wrote again to Mrs. Hechler, using a 3c red envelope overprinted Type A-1 in black.

Diagonal overprint in black.   "O. S. in violet."

There is also reason to believe that the ½c to 10c, Small Queen, and 12½c and 15c Large Queen adhesives, overprinted "OFFICIAL" in black, diagonally from lower left to upper right were done by Hechler, in Halifax.

We have seen another bogus overprint, (origin unknown, but possibly an early Hechler effort) "O.S." in violet on 3c Small Queen, 2nd Ottawa Printing.

"3" on Two Cents Registered Letter Stamp

A more plausible effort is the 2c registered letter stamp surcharged "3".

This is doubtful. There is an outside possibility that owing to a shortage of regular 3c a P. M. may have surcharged a few 2c registry stamps, as they were approximately the same color as the regular 3c. Another possibilty is that with the registry rate set at 5c the "3" may indicate an addition of 3c+2c=5c in order to use up a small remaining supply of 2c registry stamps. Further copies of this might solve the question.

Bogus Cancellations

We are very doubtful of some types of fancy cancellations reported on the Small Queen stamps particularly the 3c. Two in particular, which have been examined by us; the coat of arms of Nicaragua, and a cartoon-like figure of a small policeman with a helmet, vintage of 1890.

In our opinion both of these are the results of playfulness; the results of using a set of rubber stamps on a few 3c Small Queens. Nearly every stamp magazine in the period of 1880-1900 carried advertisements of rubber stamps of various kinds, and sets of coats of arms, etc., were frequently offered.

The policeman is one of the figures from the famous Palmer Cox's Brownies, a comic strip of great popularity when dad or grand dad was a boy. Sets of rubber stamps were commonly sold so that children could make up their own "Brownie Adventures".

BIBLIOGRAPHY

This study has been an attempt to give the story of Canada's postal development, and to discuss the postage stamps issued by the Post Office Department, and the correlative material in the way of postal markings.

As will be observed we have relied almost exclusively on original sources, much of which we have given in Volume II, as well as extensive excerpts throughout Volume I. Some of the material in Volume II has never previously been published anywhere before, while much other data was buried in the various reports of the Postmaster General.

Some of the information is from sources which must for the present remain confidential, but we are grateful for the permission to publish it.

As far as philatelic sources are concerned we have referred throughout our text to such where we have used them, but generally speaking we have been sparing in our use of such sources. We have, however, carefully searched the files of the leading philatelic magazines for material, as well as particularly examining all the Canadian Philatelic Periodicals available.

We give herewith a brief list of the non-philatelic books and articles which have been of assistance to us, aside from those already referred to in the text, or the acknowledgements.

GENERAL WORKS

THE ENCYCLOPAEDIA OF CANADA. Edited by W. Stewart Wallace, M. A. (Oxon), F. R. S. C. Librarian, University of Canada. Published by University Associates of Canada, Toronto, 1936.

SELECT DOCUMENTS IN CANADIAN ECONOMIC HISTORY 1497-1783 by H. A. Innes. Toronto, 1929.

HISTORY OF THE POST OFFICE IN BRITISH NORTH AMERICA. 1639-1870 by William Smith, Cambridge University Press, 1920.

DEVELOPMENT OF RATES OF POSTAGE by A. D. Smith, 1918.

SANFORD FLEMING, EMPIRE BUILDER by J. Lawrence Burpee. Humphrey Milford, Oxford University Press, 1915.

GOVERNMENT DOCUMENTS

REPORT OF THE POSTMASTER GENERAL for the years 1852 to 1942 inclusive.

OFFICIAL POSTAL GUIDES for various years.

SEMI-OFFICIAL

THE CANADA DIRECTORY for 1851-2 by Robert S. W. Mackay. John Lovell, Montreal 1852.

CANADIAN GEOGRAPHY AND STAMPS by A. Stanley Deaville, Canadian Geographical Journal, Vol. XIII, #5, Sept. 1936. P222.

PHILATELIC PUBLICATIONS

We list below the Philatelic Publications referred to

STANDARD POSTAGE STAMP CATALOGUE, Scott Publications, and Predecessors, New York. Many editions.

STANLEY GIBBONS PRICED CATALOGUE OF POSTAGE STAMPS, Stanley Gibbons, London, Eng. Many editions.

THE REGENT ENCYCLOPAEDIA OF EMPIRE POSTAGE STAMPS, 1935 and supplements. Robson Lowe, London, Eng.

THE POSTAGE STAMPS, ENVELOPES, WRAPPERS, AND POST CARDS OF THE NORTH AMERICAN COLONIES OF GREAT BRITAIN. The Philatelic Society of London, 1889.

GROSSER GANZSACHEN KATALOG. Edited by Dr. Ascher, Robert Noske, Leipzig, 1925.

In addition, complete files of the following magazines were thoroughly searched for material:

American Journal of Philately, First Series 1871 to 1879. (U. S.)
American Journal of Philately, Second Series 1880 to 1905. (U. S.)
American Philatelist. (U. S.)
Chambers Stamp Journal. (U. S.)
Collectors Club Philatelist. (Eng.)
Godden's Gazette. (Eng).
London Philatelist. (Eng.)
Mekeel's Weekly Stamp News, particularly the articles by H. Huber. (U.S.)
Morley's Philatelic Journal. (Eng.)
Philatelic Classics, by Charles J. Phillips. (U. S.)
Philatelic Journal of Great Britain. (Eng.)
Philatelic Magazine. (Eng.)
Philatelic Record. (Eng.)
Stamps Magazine. (U. S.)
Stamp Collecting. (Eng.)
Stamp Collector's Fortnightly. (Eng).
Stanley Gibbons Monthly Journal (Old and New Series). (Eng.)
Stanley Gibbons Weekly. (Eng).
Stamp Collectors Magazine. (Eng).
Montreal Philatelist. (Can.)
Halifax Philatelist. (Can.)
Dominion Philatelist. (Can.)
Canadian Philatelist. (Can.)
    Both magazises of that name.
Postman's Knock. (Can.)

The catalogues of the principal auction sales, especially of such sales as the Mirabaud, Seybold, Worthington, Ferrari, Hind, Brown and Pack collections. In addition numerous other Philatelic periodicals were refered to in part.

INDEX

Numbers refer to pages, and body of text, except when followed by "n" which indicates reference to a footnote.

Abbreviations, Month, 563
Acts, Legislative, See Legislative Acts
Admiral Type. See King George V 1911-28.
Airmails, 497-502. Semi-Official ix. Description, 497, 499. Special Delivery, 500, 502. Reference List, 501, 502.
"Alexander, Pirie & Sons", Watermark (see "Paper").
Allen, Hugh, Founder of Canadian Line, 686.
Altered Relief, (See Relief).
American Bank Note Co., 91, 92, 94, Organized 101-109, Prints 1859 issue 181, Prints 1897-1929 issues 315.
Amherst, Sir Jeffrey, Gage writes, 3.
Arch and Maple Leaf Issue. See King George V 1930-31.
Arrangement, Plate. (See Plate).
Arrow. (See Plate).

Booklet Pane xxii, 440-455. Contract Prices 441. Bantam 455. King Geo. V, Admiral type 376-7, 443, 445, 447, 448. King Edward VIII, 443, 444, 446. King Geo. V Scroll, 449-450. Arch, 450, 451. Medallion, 451-452. King Geo. V "Dated Die", 452, 453. King Geo. VI, 543-55. Essay for 442. Tete-beches, 377, 440, 448.
Both sides, Printed on. See (Printing).
"Bothwell, E & G Clutha Mills" watermark (See Paper).
Bradbury, Wilkinson & Co. Essays, 151, 151n19. For 1868, 240.
Brazer, Dr. Clarence W. 89n, 115, 175n2, 240n10.
Break, Relief. (See Relief).
British American Bank Note Co. Organization, 109-115, 181, 151, 221. Advertising sheet, 223, 225. Proposal of 1867, 227. Correspondence, 43H, 44H, 2O. Issues of 1930-35, 391-402, 429-436.
Broken Relief. See Relief).
Burland & L'Africain. Proposal of 1867, 227.
Bald, J Dorsey, Engraver, 101.
Bibliography, 750-751.
Bi-colored, xxv.
Bishop Henry (P.M.G. of G.B.), 22n.
Bishop Marks, 22.

Bliss, Frederick E., Engraver, 101.
Bond Paper. See Paper.
Bogus and Questionable items, 747-749.
Calder, Senator James A., xxiii, 185, 185n11.
Canada Bank Note Engraving Organization & Printing Co. 115-116, Contract of 1891, 230. Essay by, 300-301.
Canada-U. S. Postal Relations. See Postal Relations, Canada and the United States.
Canadian Bank Note Co., 91, 91n3, Subsidiary of American Bank Note Co 315.
Cancellations. See Handstruck Stamps, Obliterations, Postal Markings.
"CaPOD" Watermark. See Paper.
Carpenter, Charles T., Engraver, 101.
Carpenter, Samuel H. Jr., Engraver, 101.
Cartier, Georges, 1931, 400-401. 1914 unissued, 422-424.
Cartier Jacques. Claims Canada for France 1. On 10d, 185. 1934 Issue, 430-432, 435.
Cartier, 1934, 430-432, 435. Design 430, 431. Wide gutter 431, 432. Proofs 432. Listing 435.
Champlain, Samuel de. Makes first permanent settlement 1.
Chrominum plating. See Plate.
"Clutha Mills, E & G Bothwell". See Paper.
Coils. General xxii. Plate numbers xxii. Provisional 353, 355. Experimental 356. Auto Vending 356-60. Admiral Type 377-78, 380, 382. Scholl Issue 1928-29, 390.
Collectors of Canada, Fundamental Information for, xvii-xxxi.
Color. Shade,xxiv. Trials, xxv.
Commemoratives. Jubilee 1897, 317-320. Imperial Penny Postage 1899, 339-342. 20th Century, 415-439. Quebec 1908, 416-421. Unissued 1914, 422-424. Confederation 1917-27, 424-428. Historical 1927, 426-428. Imperial Conference 1932, 428-429. U. P. U. 1933, 427, 435. Grain Conference 1933, 429, 430, 435. Royal William 1933, 430, 435. Cartier 1934, 430-432, 435. U. E. L. 1934, 432-435. New Brunswick 1934, 434-436. Sil-

ver Jubilee 1935, 436-437, 439. Coronation 1937, 437-439. Royal Visit, 1939, 438-439.
Commissions, Rate of Postmasters, 3.
Compound perforation. See perforation. Envelopes. See Envelopes.
Concentric Ring Obliterations. See Postal Markings.
Confederation 1917-27, 424-428. 1917 design, 424. Plates, 425. Engraver, 425. Proofs, 425. Listing, 425. Exhausted, 425. 1927 Dies approved 425. Listing, 427. Proofs, 428.
Contractors for Cancellations, Francis. See Francis, John.
Contract for Engraving and Printing Stamps. Rawdon, Wright, Hatch, & Edson, 7H. British American Bank Note Co, 228. American Bank Note Co., 315.
Coronation 1937, 437, 439.
Cost of Printing Stamps. 1851-59 Issues, 123. 7H. 1868-97 Issues, 230. 1897-1929 Issues, 315, 316. Booklet Issues, 441. Provincial Envelopes, 507. Dominion Envelopes, 523. Post Cards, 230, 541n, 542n.
Courier service, 1, 3, 4, 6, 6n, 7, 8, 10.
Cousland, William. Engraver, 101.
Cracked Plate. See Plate.
Cuppage, William, Railway Mail Clerk, 658.

Danford, Edward J., Engraver, 101.
Danford, Mosley I., Designer, 101.
Darley, F. O. C., Designer, 107.
Dated Die Issues. King Geo. V, 403-407. King Geo. VI, 408-410. War Effort, 411-414. Envelopes, 531. Post Cards, 537, 554-5.
Day, Dr. Kenneth. Student, 221.
Dead Letter Office. See also Official Seals. History of, 715-16. Handstruck Markings, 716-718.
Decimal Currency Issue 1859, 181-219. Reasons for issue, 181. Order for, 181. Delivery, 181. Origin of design, 181. Proofs, 182, 215. Specimens, 182-183. Paper, 183. Perforations, 183. Plates, 185, 188. Imprint, 185. Re-entries, 187-194, 197-201. Flaws, 187, 188, 194-7, 201-03. Short Transfers, 187, 197. Bisects, 206-209. Counterfeits, 209. Fakes, 209, 210. Trade Samples, 214, 215. Correspondence regarding, 29H, et Seq. Listing, 211-213.
Decimal Currency Issue. 1c, Origin of design, 181. Proofs, 182, 215. Specimens, 182. Paper, 183. Perforation, 184. Multiples, 185, 186, 203. Imprint, 185. Plates, 185. Re-entries, 187. Flaws, 187. Short Transfers, 187. Combinations, 203. Soldiers Letters, 206. Bisects, 206-7. See also general references to this issue.
Decimal Currency Issue. 2c, Origin of design, 181. Proofs, 182, 215. Specimens, 182. Paper, 183. Perforation, 184. Plates, 185. Multiples, 180. Frame lines, 187-188. Flaws, 188. See also general references to this issue.
Decimal Currency Issue 5c, Origin of design, 181. Proofs, 182, 215. Specimens, 182. Paper, 183. Perforation, 184. Multiples, 184, 186, 204. Plates, 185, 188. Major re-entry, 188, 204. Re-entries, 188-194. Flaws, 194-7. Bisects, 206-7. See also general references to this issue.
Decimal Currency Issue. 10c, Origin of design, 181. Proofs, 182, 215. Specimens, 182. Paper, 183. Perforation, 184. Plates, 185. Multiples, 180. Re-entries, 197. Flaws, 197. Short Transfers, 197. Bisects, 206, 208-9. See also general references to this issue.
Decimal Currency Issue. 12½c, Origin of design, 181. Proofs, 182, 215. Specimens, 182-183. Paper, 183. Perforation, 184. Plates, 185. Multiples, 180, 185. Re-entries, 198. Re-entries, 198. Flaws, 198. Short Transfers, 198. See also general references to this issue.
Decimal Currency Issue. 17c, Origin of design. 181. Proofs, 182, 215. Specimens, 182. Paper, 183. Perforation, 184. Plates, 185. Multiples, 180, 185, 205. Re-entries, 198-201. Flaws, 201-203. Short Transfers, 203. Combinations, 203. See also general references to this issue.
Defective relief. See Relief.
Designers. F. O. C. Darley, Moseley I. Danforth, Henry Earle, Sr. See under name of designer.
Diamond Jubilee Issue 1897, 317-320. Plates, 318. Bisects, 318. Proofs and Specimens, 319.
Die, xx. Proof, xxvi.
Dominion of Canada. Seal, 220. Brief discussion of formation, 220.
Dot, Position. See Plate.
Double Entry. See Plate, double entry. Impression, xxv, 232, see also Print. Paper, xxvii. Perforation,

xxix, see also perforation. Transfer, xxi, see also Plate, re-entry.
Draper, Robert. Engraver, 101.
Dues, Postage, xi. Handstruck, 481-485, see also Handstruck Stamps. Adhesive, 486-490. Listings, 489-490. Proofs, 488.
Durand, Cyrus. Engraver, 90.

Earle, Henry, Sr., Engraver and Designer, 111. Biography, 112, 114, 221.
Earle, John. Inventor, 112.
Edson, Tracy R., Engraver, 91, 92. Biography, 95, 101.
1859 Issue. See Decimal Currency Issue.
1868 Issue. See Large Queen Designs and Introduction to Queen's Head designs.
1870-97 Issue. See Introduction to Queen's Head Designs also Small Queen Designs.
1897 Maple Leaf Issue. See Maple Leaf Issue 1897.
1898 Numerals. See Numeral Issue 1898.
Electrotype, xxvi. See also Printing.
Engraved, Re-, xxi. See also Printing.
Engravers. See under individual names.
Engraving Firms. See under individual concerns.
Engraving, Line, xx. See also Printing.
Entry, Double. See also Plate. Fresh, see also Plate. Re-, xxi. See also Plate.
Envelopes, xxx, 507-531. Compound, 522, 530. Nesbitt, 505-515. British American Bank Note, 518. Dominion, 517-531. See also Postal Stationery.
Essay, xxvi. See also individual issues.
Express Company. Franks, 527n. Cancellations, 647.
Exchange Markings, 46-50.
Explanation of Terms, xx-xxxi.
Express. First, 6, 6n10. Yearly, 9.

Factor Value, x, xvi.
Finlay, Hugh, xxx. Appointed by Franklin, 3. Deputy P. M. G., 7. Report of 1766, 4. Dismissed, 9. Death, 9.
Flat Plate. See Plate.
Fleming, Sanford. Designs first stamp, 119. Portrait, 120. Essay for 3d, 1s, 121. Biographical notes, 121n7.
Foxcraft, William (DP.M.G.), with Franklin, 3.
Francis, John (London, Eng.) Contractor for Cancellations, 23.

Franklin, Benjamin, xxx, (D.P.M.G.) Appoints Finlay P.M. of Quebec, 3.
"Free", xxx. See also Postal Markings.
French Control of Postal Service, 1, 2.
Fundamental Information for Collectors of Canada, xvii-xxxi.

Gage, General Thomas, 2, 3.
Gavit, John E., Engraver, 101.
Gauge, xxvii.
General Post Office, London, Control of 1763-1851, 3.
Gobrecht, Christian. Inventor of the lathe, 90.
Goodall, Albert G., Engraver, 101.
Grain Conference 1933, 429, 430, 435.
Grummer, A. K. Student, 221.
Guide lines, xx, xxii. See also Plate.
Gutter, xxii. See also Plate arrangement. Block, xxii.

Handstruck Postage Stamps, x. Paid, 23-34. General, 23-25, 27-29. Dues, 35-40, 42, 481-486. City, 25-26, 29, 30. Ocean Mail, 41-42. Decimal, 30-33. United States, 33-34, 48-50, 61, 67-68. Crowned Circle, 25-26, 26n, 66, 70, 72-73, 75.
Harrison, J. A. C., Engraver. Engraved King Edward VII die for Perkins, Bacon, 345.
Hatch, George Whitfield. Engraver. Biography, 95, 101.
Hay, De Witt C., Engraver, 101.
Hechler, Henry, 302, 304, 747-748.
Heviot, George (D.P.M.G.) Appointed, 9. Administration, 10. Resigned, 10.
Hidden Plate Number, xxii. 1911-21, 380-382.
Historical Issue 1927, 426-428. Designs, 426. Listing, 427. Proofs, 428.
Howes, Clifton A., Student, ix.
Horizontal Imperforate, xxix.

Imperforate, xxix. Horizontally, xxix, Vertically, xxix. Between, xxix.
Imeprial Conference 1932, 428-429.
Imperial Penny Postage 1898, Reason, 339. Designed by, 339. Source of Motto, 339. Issued, 339. Plates, 339, 342. Re-entries, 339, 341-342. Listing, 341-342.
Impression, Double, xxv.
Imprint, xxii.
India Paper. See Paper.
Information for Collectors of Canana. Fundamental, xvii-xxxi.
Ink. Inking the plate, xxiii. Recipe for colors, 274-275.

Intaglio Engraving. See also Printing. Line engraving, xx.
Inverted Center, xxvi.
Ivy Mills. Made paper for pence issue, 125. Illustration, 124.

Jeens, Charles Henry, Engraver, Portrait, 221.
Jocelyn, Nathaniel. Engraver, 101.
Jocelyn, Simeon S., Jr., Engraver, 101.
Joint Line Pair, xxii.
Jones, Alfred. Engraver, 101. Biography, 112. Engraver 3d, 121. Engraved Queen vignette, 240. For Essay Letter, 222, 20.
Jubilee Issue 1897. Reason for Issue, 317. Designers, 317. Proposed Quantities, 317. Plates, 318. Bisects, 318. Issued, 318. Proofs, 319. Specimens, 319. Counterfeits, 319. Reference List, 320.

King Edward VII Issue, 345-60. Official notice, 345. Issued, 345. Design, 345. Essay, 345-46. Plate, 346. Imprints, 346-350. Hairlines, 351. Re-entries, 352. Booklets, 443-44, 446. Proofs, 353. Specimens, 353. Coils—Provisional, 353, 355. Expermental, 356. Auto-Vending, 356-60. Imperforates, 353-355, 319. Listing, 354. Shaes, 355. Perforations for, 411.
King Geo. V 1911-28 (Amiral Type), 361-386. Booklets, 376-7, 443, 45, 47-48. Design, 361. Dies, 361-68. Differences, 366-67. Essays, 368, 385. Proofs, 368. Imprints, 369. Marginal patterns, 371-73. Plate varities, 374-75. Recuts, 375. Etching, 375. Printing, 375-6. Paper, 376. Gum, 376. Coils, 377-78, 380, 382. Listing, 379-83, 386. Provisionals, 378, 384-86. Part perforates, 383-4. Tetebeche, 377.
King George V 1928-29 "Scroll Issue", 387-90. Booklets, 449-450. Designs, 387. Plates, 387. Imprints, 387. Die Proofs, 388. Listing, 389-90. Coils, 390.
King George V 1930-31 Arch and Maple Leaf Issue, 391-399. Booklets, 450-51. Contract, 391. Essay, 392. Proofs, 392. Plates, 393-95. Listing, 397-399. Plates, 393, 395. Re-entry, 393-94. Dies, 395. Colors, 396. Paper, 396. Perforation, 396.
King George V 1932 Medallion Issue, 401-2. Booklets, 451-52. Reason for issue, 401. Plates, 401. Printing, 401. Dies, 402. Listing, 402. Coils, 402.
King George V 1935 "Dated Dies", 403-407. Booklets, 452-53. Reason for issue, 403. Printing, 403-405. Listing, 407. Plates, 405. Dates, location of, 404. Alignment on coils, 405. Re-entry on 50c, 405. Dies, 406. Perforation varieties, 406. Imprint, 406.
King George VI "Dated Die" 1937-38, 408-410. Booklets, 453-55. Reason for issue, 408. Designs, 408. Dates, location of, 409. Plates, 410. Imprint, 410. Proofs, 410. Listing, 410.
Knife, Envelope, 503-04, 511-11, 526.

Laid Paper, xxvii. See also Paper.
Lanoullier, Nicholas. Proposed postal system, 2.
Large Queen Design 1868, 237-265. Issued, 237. Rates of 1868, 239. Combinations, 238-39. Essays, 240-42. Plates, 243-44, 244n9. Imprints, 243-44, 244n8. Counters, 244, 246. Bisects, 260-61. Counterfeits, 261. 6c plates, 245, 245n9. Sample sheet, 223. Listing, 262-65. Multiples, 243-44, 246, 248-49. Re-entry 2c, 248, 257n8a. Paper, 251-54, 259, 8P., 9P. Watermark, 255-56. Perforation, 257, 259. Gum, 257, 259.
Legislative Acts. Rates—9th of Anne (1710) 3. Regulation of Post 9th of Anne, 5.
Letter Cards, 557-558. See also Postal Stationery.
Limitations, ix.
Lindsley, Joseph C. Designer. Designed Essay 1868, 240.
Line Engraving (Intaglio, Recess), xx. See also Printing.
Line. Engraved, xx. Guide, xx, xxii. Pair, xxii. Laid, xxvii. See also Paper, and Plate.
Lithography, xxv. See also Printing.
Locals, ix.

MacDonald-Cartier Issue 1914, 422-24.
Machine Imprinted Stamps, 737-45. Meters, 737-42. Postage Machines, 743-45. Terminology, 738. Mailomat, 739. Indicia Table, 742. Machine numbers, 745.
Maisohnerve, Founds Montreal, 1.
Major, James Parsons. Designer, 94, Biography, 95-7. Supervised designing of Peace issue, 121.
Mandel, Henry, 173n.
Manila, Paper, xxvii.

Manuscript Markings. See Postal markings.
Map Stamp 1893. See Imperial Penny Postage Issue.
Maple Leaf Issue 1897. Design, 321. Method of production, 321. Plates, 321. Official circular, 321. Re-entries, 323. Proofs, 324-25. Listing, 327.
Marginal Marks. See Marks, Marginal. See Plate.
Marks, Marginal, xx. Register. See also Plate, Imprint, Number, Arrow.
Marking, Plate, xxi, xxii. Registry, xxii. Postal, xxx-xxxi. See also Imprint, Plate Numbers, Arrows.
Markings, Manuscript. See Postal Markings.
Mathews, George, 89, 91, 104, 107n.
Mathews & Smillie. Proposal of 1867, 227.
Medallion Issue. See King George V, 1932.
Metered Mail, ix, xxxi, 737-42. See also Machine Imprinted Stamps.
Military Covers, 162, 206. Postal Service 1760-63, 2, 3. Markings, 642-46. Regulations concerning, 24B et. seq.
"Money Letter". See Registered Letter Stamps.
Montreal, City of. Maisonnerve, founds, 1. Gage, Gevernor, 2. Quebec Route, 1, 2, 3, 5, 7.
Morris, James. 1st P.M.G. of Canada. Portrait, 13.
Morris, Thes. F., Jr., Student, 90.
National Bank Note Co., 116-17. Essay for 1868 Issue, 240.
Northwest, Postal History of, 689-700. List of Post Offices, 700-714.
Numbering and Classification, System explained, xv.
Numeral Issue 1898. Reason for, 329. Production, 329. Proofs, 329-30. 2c Types, 330. Re-entries, 332. Listing, 332-33.

Obliterations, xxx, 559-642, 583-642. See also Postal Markings and Handstruck Stamps.
Ocean Mail Stamps, Handstruck, 41-2.
Official Seals, ix, 718-720. See also Dead Letter Office.
Official Stamps, 721-727. Handstruck, 721-726. Adhesive, 727.
Offset. See printed on both sides.
"OHMS". See Official Stamps, 727.
Order, Printing, xxiii.
Overprint, xxvi. See Surcharge.

Pack, Charles L. Student, 221.
Packet Marking, xxxi. See Postal Markings.
"Paid", xxxi. See Postal Markings, Handstruck Stamps.
Pair, line, xxii. Joint, xxii. Paste-up, xxii.
Pane, xxi. Booklet, xxii.
Paper, General notes, xxvii. Bothwell, E & G, Clutha Mills, xxviii, 251, 253, 255. Alexander Pirie & Sons, xxviii, 251, 254, 256. "CaPod" xxviii. See also Watermarks.
Part Perforate, xxix.
Paste-up Pair, xxii.
Pelure. See Paper.
Penny Post, In Quebec, 5.
Pence Issue 1851-57, 119-179, 216-219. Laid Paper, 119-139. Wove Paper, 140-167, 152, 3. Perforated, 167-172. Proofs, Contemporary, 123, 151-52. Post Contemporary, 173-76. Counterfeits, 176-78. Preparation of, 121, 123, 149. "Specimens", 123-24, 152. Paper, 125. Plates, 126, 153, 216. Listing, 139, 148. Wove Paper varieties, 143-44. Imprint, 145-47, 153. Essays, 119, 121, 151. Bisects, 165-67. Trade Samples, 175-6. Similitudes, 177-8. Fakes, 176-77.
Pence Issue. 1d Essay, 151.
Pence Issue. ½d. Preparation, 149. Origin of design, 149. Purpose, 149. Multiples, 150, 159, 162, 179. Specimen, 152. Paper, 152. Quantities, 152. Imprint, 153. Re-entries, 157. Short Transfers, 158. Shades, 158. Combinations, 160, 163. Counterfeits, 176.
Pence Issue. 3d. Essays, 119, 121. Criticism of, 121. Relief Break, 126. Plate varieties, 127-8. Multiple pieces, 122, 130, 140-42, 168, 170. Other varieties, 127-8. Ribbed Paper, 140-41, 143, 143n12. Flaws, 140. Imprint, 145-47. Counterfeits, 176. Fakes, 143n12, 176-77. Handmade Paper, 143. Machine Made Paper, 143. Shades, 146. Bisects, 148, 165-67. Quantities, 123, 143. Combinations, 157, 159-60. 163. Perforated, 167-72. Rouletted, 167-68, 172.
Pence Issue. 6d. Varieties, 129. Multiple pieces, 122, 160, 172. Shades, 147. Essays, 151. Quantities, 123, 143. Imprint, 145-47. Combinations, 160, 204. Bisects, 165-7. Perforated, 170-72. Proofs, 123, 174. Specimens, 123. Counterfeits, 176-7.

Pence Issue. 7½d. Wide and narrow, 152-3. Imprint, 153. Re-entries, 156-57. Shades, 158. Combinations, 157, 159, 161, 163. Proofs, 152, 173. Counterfeits, 176. Similitudes, 177-8. Preparation, 149. Origin of design, 149. Purpose, 149. Multiples, 150, 159. Specimens, 152. Paper, 152, Quantities, 152.

Pence Issue. 10d. Earliest mention, 149. Design, 149. Purpose, 149. Essays, 151. Re-entries, 153-55. Specimens, 152. Paper, 152. Quantities, 152. Multiples, 155, 160-61. Wide and narrow, 152-3. Short Transfers, 156. Shades, 158. Combinations, 160-61. Counterfeits, 176. Similitudes, 177-8.

Pence Issue. 6d Sterling. See 7½d.

Pence Issue. 12d. Varieties, 129, 133-4. Paper, 129, 131, 133. Plate, 133. Covers, 136-38. Quantity, 129-30, 135. Pair, 122. Distribution, 135. Essays, 119, 121. Shades, 133.

Penny Post. First, 5, 5n6.

Perforation, xxix. Pence Issues, 167-72. Decimal Issue, 183. 1868-97 Issues, 257, 276-79, 287, 292, 299. Vending machine, 356-60, 378. Guage, xxix, Rough, xxix, Compound, xxix, Double, xxix, Part, xxix.

Perkins, Jacob. Inventor, 89-91. Null and die process, 89-90. Other Inventors, 91.

Perkins, Bacon & Co. Engraved die for King Edward VII Issue, 345.

"Pirie & Sons, Alexander. See Paper.

Plate, xx-xxvii. Cancelled, 308.

Plating, Chromium, xx, xxiii.

Port Hood Provisionals 1898, 335-37. Reason, 335. Validity, 335-36. Listing, 336.

Position Dot, xx. See Plate. Plate, method of numbering, xxi.

Post, Card, 535-556. Houses 2. Road, 2, Routes, 1-8. Runners, 6, 6n9, 7. Penny P. 5, 5n, 6. Offices opened, 9.

Postage Dues, ix, 35-40. French, 2. Early British, 3-4. Bet. Canada and U. S., 43-6. Adhesive, 486-490. Handstruck, 481-86. More-to-pay, 481. Reference List, 489-90. Reason for Issue, 487.

Postage Rates. See Rates.

Postal Bands, 532-33. See Postal Stationery.

Postal Cards. See Postal Stationery.

Postal History, Early, 1 et seq. Service, Military 1760-63, 2, 3. G.P.O. London, 3. Map, xxxvi.

Postal Markings, xxx-xxxi. Early, 15, 22. Paid, 23-34. Bishop marks, 21-22. Ferriage, 59. Triangular, 22. Manuscript, 15. "Money Letter", 75, 80. "Registered", 457-62, 629. "Too Late", 578-79. Postage Due, 35-40, 42. Concentric ring, 583-89. Numerals, 4 ring, 593-605. 2 ring, 610-618. others, 603-05, 619-24. Townmarks, 567-78, 625. "Late Fee", 578. "Advertised", 580. "Forwarded", 580-81. "Missest", 581-82. Target Cancellations, 590-92. Crown Cancellations, 626-28. Obliterations and Cancellations, 559-60. Introductory, 559. Postmarks, 560. Abbreviations of Months, 561. Post Offices in 1840, 561-66. Imperial and Provincial, 567-607. Straight line, 15-19, 567. Types of Circular Town Marks, 567-77. Duplex Town Marks, 573-74, 625. Colored postmarks, 577-78. Dominion Postmarks and Cancellations, 609-29. Non-Official Obliterators, 630-41. Military Markings, 642-46. Express Markings, 647. Railway Post Marks, 649-80. Provincial Railway Marks, 649-58. Dominion Railway Marks, 658-80. Steamboat and Steamship Markings, 681-87. Northwest, 689-714. Alberta, 701-03. Assiniboia, 703-06. Keewatin, 706, Northwest Terr., 707-08. Saskatchewan, 709. Manitoba, 710-12. Yukon, 713. Pembina, 714. Bogus, 749. Regulation Marks, 578-582.

Postal Relations between Canada and the United States, 9, 43-87. First convention between, 43. Canada P. O. as U. S. Agent, 43. Commission to D. P. M. G., 43. Legal situation, 43. U. S. Act of 1845, 43. Rates between, 43, 52-58. Discontinuance of collecting U. S. Postage, 43. Convention between U. S. and G. B., 45. Provincial Control, 45. Ferriage, 45. Postal arrangement of 1875, 45. Exchange Markings, 45-52. U. S. Postmasters of Canada, 58. Illustrations, 59-87. Rates, 53-57.

Postal Routes, Early, xxxvi, 1-8, 10.

Postal Stationery, 503-5. Introduction, 503. Knives, 503-04, 510-11, 526. Nesbitt, 505-515. Reference List, 508-09, 527-31. British American Bank Note Co., 518. American Bank Note Co., 517-19. Dominion, 517-31.

Printing and Stationery Dept., 522. Essay, 508, 517-18. Registered, 522, 531. Postal Bands, 532-33. Wrappers, 532-34. Post Cards, 535-556. Envelopes, 507-31.
Post Cards, 535-556. Origin, 535. Issued, 535, 538. Domestic, 537. United Kingdom, 537. Proofs, 537. U.P.U., 537-38. Sizes, 539. Listing of Line Engraved, 540. U. P. U., 541. Typographed, 542-556. Inscriptions, 545 Listing, 543-44, 546-550, 553-56. Official view cards, 551-52. Letter Cards, 557-558.
Post Offices, Early, 1-4, List of in 1840, 561-64.
Precancels, xxxi, 728-36. Forerunners, 729. Early line types, 729. City types, 730-34. Money Order #'s, 734-36. Line type, 737.
Printers of Canadian Stamps and Postal Stationery, 89-117. See also individual issues. See also names of firms.
Printed or Printing, xxiii-xxvi.
Proclamation of Governor General on Province Assuming Control of the P. O., 118.
Proofs. See Die, and Plate.
Provincial Issues, 119-219. Epilogue to, 216-19. See also Pence Issues, Decimal Currency Issue.
Provisionals, Port Hood, 335-36. 2c on 3c, 343. Coils, 353-55. 2c on 3c 1926, 378, 384-86. See also individual Issues.
Publisher's Wrappers, Listing, 534.

Quebec, City of, Founded, 1. Montreal Route, 1-3, 5. x
Quebec Issue 1908, 416-421. Reason for Issue, 417. Designs, 417. Engravers, 417. Essays, 417-18. Proofs, 417-18. Varieties, 419. Listing, 420-21.
Queen Head Issue 1868-97. Introduction, 221-36. Large Queen designs, 1868, 237-65. Small Queen designs, 266-314. See also under individual Issues. Plates, 224-26. Advertising sheet, 225. Impressions, 226, 226n6, 228n10a. Proposals for printing, 227-8. Summary of Contracts, 230. Reason for Small Queen design, 231. Printing varieties, 231, 234-5. Double Prints, 232-233. "Kisses" 232-33. Shades, 232. Perforations, 232, 234.

Railroad Postmarks, xxx, 649-680. Provincial, 649-58. Dominion, 658-80. List of, 660-77. Registered, 679-80.
Rates, Postage, French, 2. Early British, 3-4. Between Canada and U. S., 43, 53-57. Markings, Canadian, 23-42, on U. S., 51-52. Payment of U. S.-Canada, 54. During Pence Issue, 119, 149. Registered Letter, 457- 8.
Rawdon, Freeman. Engraver, Biography, 94, 101.
Rawdon, Ralph. Engraver, 91, Biography, 93-4.
Rawdon, Wright, Hatch & Edson. Engravers, 91-2, 97-9. Appendix H #1-86.
Receiving Marks, xxxi.
Recess, Engraving, xx. Perkins process, 89. See also printing.
Re-Entry, xxi. See Re-cut. Of 3d, 127-8. 12d, 133-4. 10d, 154-55. 7½d, 156. ½d, 157-8. 1859 5c, 188-194. 10c, 197. 12½c, 198. 17c, 198-99. 1868 2c, 247. 1887-97 2c, 296. 6c, 295, 297. 1897, 326, 331. 1903, 352. 1911, 374. 1930, 394.
Reford, Dr. Lewis L., Student, 183, 221.
Relief, xx. Altered, xx, Defective, xx, Broken, xx, Method, 89.
Recut, xxi. See Re-entry.
Re-engraved, Plate, xxi.
Register Marks, xxii.
Registry Markings, xxii. See Register Marks.
Registered Letter Stamps, 457-74. Handstruck, 457-62. Money Letters, 457-58. Essays of 1865, 463-68. Adhesive Registered Letter Stamps, 469-74. Listing, 474. Envelopes, 522, 531. Official, 462. City Types, 461. 3c on 2c, 749.
Re-touching, Re-touched Die, xxi.
Revenues, used for postage, 491.
Roll, Transfer, xx.
Ronaldson, Douglas. Engraver, Biographical note, 117. Frame for 1868 Essay, 240.
Rotary Press, Printing, xxvi.
Rough perforation, xxix.
Roulette, xxix.
Route, Early Postal, Map, xxxvi. Guebec-Montreal, 1-3, 7. Other, 6-10.
Royal Visit 1939, 438-39. Proofs, 438. Plate No. Combinations, 438.
Royal William 1933, 430, 435.
Runners, Post, 6-7.

Saulnier, Henry E., Siderographer, 101.
Savage, Robert. Engraver. Engraved King George V, Admiral Issue, 366, 366n1.
Scroll Issue. See King George V, 1928-29.
Semi-Official Airmails, ix.
Sheet, xxi.
"Ship" Postmarks, xxxi.
Shoemaker, L. D., Student, 221.
Short Transfer, xxi.
Siderographers. Henry E. Saulnier, Neziah Wright. See under individual names.
Sills, S. First Express, 6, 6n10.
Silver Jubilee 1935, 436-37, 439. Reason for Issue, 427. Proofs, 437. "Weeping Princess" variety, 437. Listing, 439.
Skinner, Charles. Engraver. Engraved Maple Leaf Issue, 321. Engraved Numeral Issue, 329. Engraved King Edward VII Issue, 346.
Small Queen Design 1870-93. Reason for, 231. Essay, 269-70. Proofs, 271. Plates, 224-26.
Small Queen First Ottawa Printing 1870-74, 273-82. Plates, 273. Listing, 280. Re-entries, 273, 276. Perforations, 276-79. 12½ perforation, 277-79. 11½ x 12 perforation, 279. Gum, 281
Small Queen Montreal Printing 1874-87, 282-90. Plate varieties, 283. Plates, 282-87. Perforations, 287. Paper, 288. Gum, 288. Listing, 289.
Small Queen Second Ottawa Printing 1887-97. Plates, 291-2, 294. Perforations, 292. Paper, 292-93. Gum, 293. Specimens, 293-94. Re-entries, 295-98. 5c on 6c, 297-8.
Small Queen Additional Values of 1893, 299. Listing, 312-13. Bisects, 301-4. Imperforates, 305-07. Cancelled Plates, 308. Plate, Production of, 309. Shoemaker's Classification, 310. Summary of Printing, 311.
Smillie, William C., 62, 67, 110. Biography, 109, 111-12, 221, 221n3. Proposal of 1867, 227-8. Joins Canada B. N. & Printing, 230.
Spencer, Asa. Perfector of Gobrecht's Lathe, 90.
Special Delivery, 475-480. Reference List, 479-80. Description, 475, 477. Air Mail, 500-02.
Stayner, Thomas Allen, D. P. M. G. Appointed 1827, 11. New Routes, 11. N. B. transfered to U. S., 12. System under his control, 12. Montreal P. O. during his administration, 12-13. Registration introduced, 13. Basis for rating letter changed, 13. Steamboat Letter, 13. Last order, 13. Succeeded by James Morris, 13. Commissions from U. S. P. O. D., 43. Acts as Postmaster for U. S., 58.
Steamboat and Steamships, Markings, 681-87. Allen Line, 686.
Stitch Watermark, xxviii.
Surcharge, xxvi. See overprint. 3c on 2c, 1932, 400-01.
Sutherland, Daniel, D. P. M. G. Appointed 1816, 10. Offices opened, 11. Legal position during his administration, 11. Retired 1827, 11.
System of Numbering and Classification Explained, xv. Tabular Information and Factor Explained, xvi.

Target Cancellation, xxxi. See also Concentric Ring Cancels, Obliteratiins, Postal Markings.
Tete-Beches. See Booklets.
Tied, Tied on, xxxi.
Terms, Explanation of, xx-xxxi.
Texture, Paper, xxvii.
Three Pence. See Pence Issue.
Toppan, Charles. Engraver, 101.
Transfer, xx-xxi. Double, xxi. See Re-entry. Roll, xx. Short, xxi. Triple, xxi. Press, 89.
2c on 3c Provisionals. Reason for Issue, 343. Methods of surcharging, 343. Listing, 343.
Type-Set, xxiv. See also electrotype.

Unissued 1914 Commemoratives. Centenary of Peace, 422. MacDonald-Cartier, 422-24.
United Empire Loyalists 1934, 432-35. Historical background, 432-34. Listing, 435. Proofs, 434.
United States. Postal arrangements with. See Postal relations between Canada and United States. Handstruck Stamps, 33-34. Rate Markings, 51-52.
Universal Postal Union 1933, 429, 435.
"US Po D" Watermark, xxviii.

Value Factors, x, xvi.
Van Zandt, C. L., Printer, 107.
Vertical, Imperforate, xxi.

War Effort Issue 1942, 411-14. Designs, 411-12. Listing, 413. Proofs, 413. Dates, location of, 414.
War Tax Stamps, 491-95. Reason for Issue, 491. Dies, 492-93. Proofs, 492. Reference List, 495.
Watermarks, xxvii. Stitch, xxvii. "E & G Bothwell, Clutha Mills", xxviii, 251, 253, 255. Origin of, 8P. "Alexander, Pirie & Sons", xxviii, 251, 254, 256. "CPCO.", 527. "CaPoD", xxviii, 509. "USPOD", xxviii, 508.
"Way", xxxi.
Wellstood, John G., Engraver, 101.
Welsh, Charles. Engraver, 101.
Whiting, William H., Engraver, 101.
Willcox, James. Owner of Ivy Paper Mills, 125.
Wove, Paper, xxiii.
Wrappers, Publishers, 532-34. See Postay Stationery.
Wright, Neziah. Engraver and Siderographer, Biography, 94, 101, 107.

VOLUME II
Abridged

APPENDIX A
LEGISLATIVE ENACTMENTS CONCERNING THE POSTAL SERVICE
1765-1899

Rates of 1765

#1

Upon the establishment of the Post Office in Canada by the British authorities in 1765 the rates were as established by the British Parliament as follows:

	Up to 60 Miles	60 to 100 Miles	100 to 200 Miles	Every Extra 100 Miles
Single sheet of paper Less than 1 oz.	4d stg. 4½d cy.	6d stg. 7d cy.	8d stg. 9d cy.	2d stg. 2d cy.

Change of 1801

#2

The Act of 1801 repealed all the rates enacted by the Acts of 1710 and 1765, and set new rates for Great Britain, but neglected to set Colonial rates. As a result there were no legal rates in Canada from 1801 to 1834[1].

History of the Transfer of the Post Office to Provincial Control.

#3

The agitation for control of the postal affairs by the various provinces had long been under way. Upon the arrival of Lord Elgin as Governor General the Colonists were invited (as per instructions to Lord Elgin) "to assume control and management of the internal Post Office."

Similar propositions were made to the other Provincial Governments so that in 1847 a conference was held in Canada of the representatives of Canada, Nova Scotia, and New Brunswick for a discussion of the organization of the Colonial Posts. The representatives made various recommendations to their respective legislatures, and on June 10, 1848, a Committee of the Executive Council of Canada reported "the arrival in this Province and at the Seat of Government of the Hon. Mr. Uniacke, from the sister Province of Nova Scotia," bearing "a memorandum[2] explanatory of the intentions and opinions of the Government of Nova Scotia." Among the suggestions was "Postage stamps for prepayment be allowed, and Colonial stamps to be engraved[3]."

On June 14, 1848, Lord Elgin sent home a minute of a Committee of the Executive Council containing their suggestions and those of a deputation from Nova Scotia on the future arrangements of the Post Office in British North America.

This minute was referred by the Colonial Secretary, Lord Grey, to the Treasury and the General Post Office expressing the hope that there might be no objection entertained to the proposals of the local Governments.

The Postmaster General, Lord Clanricarde, on Dec. 8, 1848, sent his private secretary to the Colonial Office to explain why it was necessary that *legal* steps should be taken for the transfer of the control of the Post Office.

Four days later the Treasury stated they would take care that proper steps were taken for bringing a bill into Parliament on the basis of the Executive Council's Minute.

---
1. Act of 4 Will IV Cap. 7 (1834), permitted colonists to establish their own rates, but the administration remained under control of the G.P.O., London.
2. Journals of the Assembly of Nova Scotia, 1849, Appendix 5, p. 91. It can thus be seen that Nova Scotia deserves the credit for suggesting adhesive stamps.
3. Journals of the Legislative Assembly of Canada, Session of 1849, Appendix B.B.B.

On December 15, 1848, Lord Grey informed Lord Elgin he had lost no time in communicating with the Department here and that His Majesty's Government were prepared to carry into effect the proposals for having the British North American Colonies to manage their own Post Offices, but that the Law Officers had advised that this could not be done without the authority of an Imperial Act, and that application would therefore be made to Parliament for this purpose in the ensuing session.

Accordingly on July 28, 1849, an Act of Parliament was passed for enabling Colonial Legislatures to establish inland Posts. A copy of this Act was forwarded to Lord Elgin on August 10, 1849. (See #4.)

But between the date of Lord Grey's despatch (Dec. 5, 1848) and the date of passing the Imperial Act (July 28, 1849) the Legislature of Canada had passed an Act, which anticipating the Imperial Act, authorized the Governor General to enter into arrangements and to make regulations for the management of the Post Office until the end of the next Session of the Provincial Legislature. (See also #5.)

#3A

RESOLUTIONS

To be proposed by Mr. Blake, in Committee of the Whole, on Monday, the 21st day of May.

Mr. Blake moves to resolve, as the opinion of this Committee:—

1. That whereas it is expedient that a uniform and cheap rate of Postage should be established throughout British America: And whereas the Imperial Government has signified to His Excellency the Governor General its readiness to relinquish the management of this Department so soon as a uniform System of Postage should have been agreed upon by the different local Governments: And whereas the different local Governments of British America have agreed upon the following propositions, namely:—

"That there be one uniform rate of threepence, Provincial currency, throughout British North America:

"That no transit postage between the Provinces be allowed;

"That two pence sterling the half ounce shall continue as the rate in operation as regards letters by British Mails, to be extended to countries having postal convention with Great Britain (unless Her Majesty's Government shall see fit to permit this rate to be changed to three pence currency):

"That the pre-payment of postage shall be optional.

"That each Province shall retain the amount of postage it collects.

"That the packet postage shall be paid in England, the Provincial rate of two pence sterling to belong to the Province which collects it, and if pre-paid in England, to be credited to the Province to which the letter is addressed;

"That no privilege of franking be allowed;

"That postage stamps for pre-payment be allowed, and colonial stamps be engraved.

"That newspaper, pamphlet and magazine postage be allowed to remain at the present rates, with power to each Legislature to send them free of charge:

"And that the rate of remuneration for the transport of British mails by express through the Provinces of Nova Scotia and New Brunswick, be left for future arrangement."

And whereas the Imperial Government has approved the said propositions, but, nevertheless, legislative action is necessary to enable Her Majesty's Government to give effect to the proposed arrangements:

And whereas it is expedient to enable the Governor General in Council to give effect to such arrangements as he may deem right for the establishment of a uniform rate of postage, so soon as the necessary enactment may have been passed by the Imperial Legislature:—

It is therefore expedient that the Governor in Council be empowered to enter into such arrangements with the Imperial Government, and with the Provincial Governments of the other British North American Provinces, as shall, in the opinion of the Governor in Council, be expedient to secure a uniform and cheap rate of postage; and that the Governor in Council be authorized to make all such regulations for the management of the Post Office Department and the officers thereof, and of all matters thereunto belonging, as to him may seem meet, and from time to time to alter the same, which regulations shall have the same force and effect as if embodied in this Act, until the expiration of the next Session of Parliament.

2. That it is expedient that such regulations as shall be then in force, be laid before both Houses of the Provincial Parliament within ten days after the opening of the next Session of the said Parliament, and that the same shall remain permanently in force as law, unless it shall be otherwise provided in some Act to be passed during the said Session.

3. That it is expedient that the Governor in Council be authorized to pay out of the Consolidated Revenue Fund such sums (if any) as may be required to make up any deficiency in the funds arising from the revenue of the Post Office Department to meet the expenses thereof.

#4

This is the enabling act referred to on Page 2-A—for the transfer of the Post Office to Provincial Control.
We quote the principal provisions from what is known as

The Post Office Act.
13° & 14° Victoriae., Cap. XVII

An Act to provide for the transfer of the management of the Inland Posts to the Provincial Government, and for the regulation of the said Department.

I. Whereas by the Act of the Parliament of the United Kingdom, passed in the Session held in the twelfth and thirteenth years of Her Majesty's Reign, and entitled, *An Act for enabling Colonial Legislatures to establish Inland Posts*[1] the Legislatures or proper legislative authorities of Her Majesty's Colonies are empowered. . . . to make such provisions as [they] may think fit for and concerning the establishment, maintenance, and regulation of Posts and Post Communications within such Colonies respectively, and for charging rates of postage for the conveyance of letters by such Posts and Post Communications, and for appropriating the Revenue to be derived therefrom. . . . And whereas it is expedient that a uniform and cheap rate of postage should be established throughout the several Colonies of British North America, and with a view to the establishment thereof, the Local Governments of the said Colonies have agreed upon certain conditions hereinafter mentioned and forming a part of the provisions of this Act, and it is therefore expedient to exercise the powers so vested as aforesaid in the Legislature of this Province: . . . .

II. And be it enacted, That the Inland Posts and Post Communications in the Province shall, so far as may be consistent with the Acts of the Parliament of the United Kingdom in force in this Province, be exclusively under Provincial management and control; the Revenue arising from the duties of postage and other dues receivable by the Officers employed in managing such Posts and Post Communications shall form part of the Provincial Revenue, unless such moneys belong of right to the United Kingdom or to some other Colony, or to some foreign state; and the expenses of management shall be defrayed out of Provincial Funds, and that the Act passed in the Eighth of Her Majesty's Reign, and entitled An Act to provide for the management of the Customs, and shall apply to the said Posts and Post Communications, and to the officers and persons employed in managing the same, or in collecting or accounting for the duties and dues aforesaid, except in so far as any provision of the said Act may be insusceptible of such application, or may be inconsistent with any provision of this Act.

x x x x x x x x

V. And be it enacted, That the Provincial Post Master General shall be appointed by Commission under the Great Seal of the Province, and to hold his office during pleasure, but the Post Masters and other Officers of the Department shall be appointed and may be removed by letter from the proper Officer communicating the Governor's pleasure.

VI. [*All privileges, powers and authority of Her Majesty's Deputy Post Master General are transferred to and vested in the Provincial Post Master General.*]

x x x x x x x x

VIII. And in conformity to the agreement made as aforesaid between the Local Governments of the several Colonies of British North America, Be it enacted, That the Provincial Postage on letters and packets not being of Newspapers or Printed Pamphlets, Magazines or Books, entitled to pass at lower rate, shall not exceed the rate of three pence currency, per half ounce, for any distance whatsoever

---
1. 12, 13 Vict. Cap 66. Passed July 28, 1849.

3-A

within this Province, any fraction of a half ounce being chargeable as a half ounce; that no transit postage shall be charged on any letter or packet passing through this Province or any part thereof to any other Colony in British North America, unless it be posted in this Province and the sender choose to pre-pay it; nor on any letter or packet from any such Colony if pre-paid there; that two pence sterling the half ounce shall remain as the rate in operation as regards letters by British Mails, to be extended to Countries having postal conventions with the United Kingdom, unless Her Majesty's Government in the United Kingdom shall see fit to allow this rate to be changed to three pence currency:

That the pre-payment of Provincial Postage shall be optional:

That all Provincial Postage received within the Province shall be retained as belonging to it, and that all Provincial Postage received within any other of the British North American Colonies, may be retained as belonging to such Colony:

That the British Packet Postage and other British Postage collected in this Province shall be accounted for and paid over to the proper authorities in the United Kingdom; but the Colonial Postage on the same letters or packets shall belong to the Colony collecting it, or if prepaid to the British Post Office, it may be credited to the Colony to which such letters or packets are addressed:

That no privilege of franking be allowed as regards Provincial Postage:

That Provincial Stamps for the pre-payment of postage may be prepared under the orders of the Governor in Council, which stamps shall be evidence of the pre-payment of Provincial Postage to the amount mentioned on such stamp, and that such stamps prepared under the direction of the proper authorities in the other British North American Colonies, shall be allowed in this Province as evidence of the pre-payment of Provincial Postage in such other Colonies respectively, on the letters or packets to which they are affixed and which have been mailed there:

That the Provincial Postage on Newspapers, Pamphlets, Magazines and Printed Books, shall remain such as it now is until it be altered by regulation under this Act. . . . Provided always, that one copy of each newspaper published in this Province may be sent free from postage to any Publisher of another Newspaper in this Province, that all printed documents addressed to the Publisher of any Newspaper in this Province shall be delivered to him free, and that all Newspapers published in this Province and addressed to Subscribers in the United States, shall pass free to the Provincial line, under such regulations as the Governor in Council shall make to prevent the abuse of the privileges hereby granted:

And, subject to the foregoing provisions of this section and to the other express provisions of this act, the Governor in Council shall have full power and authority . . . . for establishing the rates of postage on Newspapers and Printed Pamphlets, Magazines and Books, and for declaring what shall be deemed such, or directing that in any case or class of cases they be free of postage, either in the first instance or the case of their being re-mailed . . . *(for the preparing and distributing of Provincial stamps for pre-payment)* for limiting the weight and dimensions of letters or packets to be sent by Post . . . . for prescribing the conditions and circumstances under which letters, accounts and papers relating solely to the business of the Post Office, and addressed to or sent by some officer thereof, shall be free from Provincial Postage, ... for providing, when he shall think it expedient, means for avoiding the risk of transmitting small sums of money through the Post, by establishing a system of money orders to be granted by one Post Master or officer of the Department on another, and fixing the terms on which such orders may be obtained, for establishing a system for the Registering of letters and the charge be made for such registration, ... for the delivery of letters and packets in the larger and more populous Cities and Towns, at the residences of parties to whom they are addressed, and fixing the limits within which such delivery shall take place, and the rates to be paid by the parties who shall prefer to have their letters and packets so delivered, rather than apply for them at the Post Office: .... and generally to make such regulations as may Postal business and arrangements, and for carrying this ⁂Act fully into effect:

IX. And be it enacted, That subject always to the provisions and regulations aforesaid, the Provincial Post Master General shall have the sole and exclusive privilege of conveying, receiving, collecting, sending and delivering letters within this Province; and that any person or party who shall (except in the cases hereinafter excepted) collect, send, convey or deliver, or undertake to convey or deliver any letter within this Province, or who shall receive or have in his possession any letter for the purpose of conveying or delivering it, otherwise than in conformity with this Act, shall for each and every letter so unlawfully conveyed or undertaken to be conveyed, received, delivered or found in his possession, incur a penalty not exceeding five pounds currency: [*exceptions are letters taken by friends journeying, by special messengers, Court Commissions, etc.*]

x   x   x   x   x   x   x   x

XI. And be it enacted, That as well the Colonial, British or Foreign as the Provincial Postage on any letter or packet shall (if not prepaid) be payable to the Provincial Post Master General by the party to whom the same shall be addressed, or who may lawfully receive such a letter or packet, which may be detained until the same be paid: .... and if any letter or packet be refused, or if the party to whom it is addressed cannot be found, then such postage shall be recoverable by the Provincial Post Master General from the sender or such letter or packet: .... and that all postage may be recovered with costs, by civil action in any Court having jurisdiction to the amount, or in any way in which duties are recoverable.

XII. *And for avoiding doubts, and preventing inconvenient delay in the delivery of letters,* Be it declared and enacted, That no Post Master shall be bound to give change, but the exact amount of the postage on any letter or packet shall be tendered or paid to him in current coin or in Provincial Postage stamps.

x   x   x   x   x   x   x   x

XIV. [*Letters of Soldiers, Seamen, etc., shall be charged a certain fixed sum in place of all British or Provincial postage.*] (That is 1d per ½ oz.)

XV. [*Posted letters to be property of party addressed.*]

XVI. .... To forge, counterfeit or imitate any Postage Stamp issued or used under the authority of this Act, or by or under the authority of the Government or proper authority of the United Kingdom, or of any British North American Province, or of any Foreign Country, or knowingly to use any such forged, counterfeit or imitated stamp, or to engrave, cut, sink or make any plate, die or other thing whereby to forge, counterfeit or imitate such stamp or any part or portion thereof, except by the permission in writing of the Provincial Post Master General, or of some officer or person who under the regulations to be made in that behalf, may lawfully grant such permission, or to have possession of any such plate, die or other thing as aforesaid, without such permission as aforesaid, or to forge, counterfeit, or unlawfully imitate, use or affix to or upon any letter or packet, any stamp, signature, initials, or other mark or sign purporting that such letter or packet ought to pass free of postage, or at a lower rate of postage, or that the postage thereon or any part thereof hath been pre-paid or ought to be paid by or charged to any person, department or party whomsoever, shall be felony, punishable by imprisonment in the Provincial Penitentiary for life.

This Act was passed August 10, 1850, by the Canadian Legislature.

The terms of this Act were not to take effect until April 6, 1851. Nevertheless, the Governor in Council had authority to enter into engagements, order stamps, and to make any other necessary arrangements for the transfer of the Postal Service to the provincial authorities during the interim between Aug. 10, 1850, and April 6, 1851.

Continuation of the History of the Transfer of the Post Office to Provincial Control.

Lord Elgin's letters of 1850.

#5

The public feeling was expressed by Lord Elgin in a letter to the Colonial Office enclosing the Post Office Act on August 16, 1850. He stated: "Public expectation on the subject is, however, very much excited and I earnestly hope that nothing may interfere to prevent the transfer of this Department from Imperial to Provincial Control in the month of October as suggested by your Lordship" (Kincardine).

#6

The Governor General's anxiety was again expressed in a letter written Christmas Eve, 1850:

Gov't House
Toronto
24 Dec 1850

...*I much fear that great dissatisfaction will be excited in this Province if the boon of a low and uniform rate of postage which the Provincial Govt. and Legislature have made every effort in their power to secure for the people be longer withheld from them in consequence of delays attending the transfer of the accounts from the P. O. in England to that of Canada.*

I need hardly remind you that when I came to the country four years ago I was instructed to invite the Colonists to assume control and management of the internal Post Office. On these subsequent occasions on which I have addressed the Legislature I have informed them that arrangements for effecting this object were in progress, and I should consider it greatly to be regretted if I were compelled again to meet Parliament without being able to state they were completed.

If further delay in completing these arrangements should be inevitable, which I sincerely trust may not be the case, I would venture respectfully to suggest that it might be expedient that H.M. P.M.G. should instruct his Deputy[4] *in this Province to adopt at once the low and uniform rate of threepence per ½ oz. without waiting the close of the negotiations for transfer.*

(Signed) Elgin.

The reply to this letter was satisfactory for on April 5, 1851, the Governor General issued a proclamation announcing the transfer of the Post Office to the Provincial Authorities.

---

4. T. A. Stayner.

Enactments by the Provincial Legislature.

#7

CARRIER SYSTEM ESTABLISHED AND CARRIER FEE SET AT ½D.
14° & 15° Vict. Cap. LXXI.

x x x x x x x x
XV. And be it enacted, That the Post Master General shall be authorized, whenever the same may be proper for the accommodation of the public in any city, to employ Letter Carriers for the delivery of letters received at the Post Office in such city, excepting such as persons to whom they are addressed may have requested, in writing addressed to the Postmaster, to be retained in the Post Office, and for the receipt of letters at such places in the said city as the Postmaster General may direct, and for the deposit of the same in the Post Office, and for the delivery by Carrier of each letter received from the Post Office, the person to whom the same is delivered shall pay not exceeding Half-penny, and for every letter received by a Carrier to be deposited in the Post Office, there shall be paid to him, at the time of the receipts, not exceeding One Half-penny:—all of which receipts, by the Carriers in any city, shall, if the Postmaster General so direct, be accounted for to the Postmaster of the said city, to constitute a fund for the compensation of the said Carriers, and to be paid to them in such proportions and manner as the Postmaster General may direct.

#8

RATE OF EXCHANGE BETWEEN HALIFAX, STERLING AND UNITED STATES CURRENCIES ESTABLISHED.
16° Vict. Cap. CLVIII.

An Act to regulate the Currency. (Assented to 14th June, 1853.)

x x x x x x x x
II. And be it enacted, That the denominations of money in the Currency of this Province, shall be pounds, dollars, shillings, pence, cents and mills: the pound, shilling and penny shall have, respectively, the same proportionate values as they now have, the dollar shall be one-fourth of a pound, the cent shall be one-hundredth of a dollar, and the mill one-tenth of a cent. . . .

III. And be it enacted, That the Pound Currency shall be held to be equivalent to and to represent one hundred and one grains and three hundred and twenty-one thousandths of a grain. Troy weight of Gold of the Standard of fineness now prescribed by Law for the Gold Coins of the United Kingdom; and the Dollar Currency shall be held to be equivalent to and to represent one-fourth part of the weight aforesaid of Gold of the said Standard. . . .

IV. And be it enacted, That the Pound Sterling shall be held to be equal to one pound, four shillings and four pence, or four dollars, eighty-six cents and two-thirds of a cent, Currency. . . .

x x x x x x x x
IX. And be it enacted, That . . . . the Gold Eagle of the United States, coined after (1st July, 1834), ... and weighing ten penny weights, eighteen grains, Troy weight, shall pass current and be a legal tender in this Province for ten Dollars or two pounds ten shillings currency. . . .

#9
ESTABLISHMENT OF DECIMAL SYSTEM AS THE SOLE MONETARY SYSTEM IN CANADA.

22° VICT. CAP. XVII
An Act to amend the Post Office Laws.
[*Assented to 4th May, 1859.*]

Whereas it is expedient to amend the Post Office Laws, in the manner hereinafter provided: Therefore, Her Majesty, by and with the advice and consent of the Legislative Council and Assembly of Canada, enacts as follows:

1. There shall be payable on all Newspapers sent by Post in Canada, except "Exchange Papers" addressed to Editors and Publishers of Newspapers, such rate of Postage, not exceeding one cent on each such Newspaper, as the Governor in Council shall from time to time direct by regulation, and such rate shall be payable on all such Newspapers posted on or after the first day of July next.

2. So much of any Act as provides that Newspapers posted within this Province shall pass free of Postage, in cases other than those in which they will be free under this Act, is hereby repealed.

3. In order to adapt the operations of the Post Office to the Decimal Currency, the internal letter postage rate shall be changed from three pence to its equivalent of five cents per half ounce—the charge for advertising a dead letter from three farthings to two cents—the charge for returning a dead letter to the writer, from one penny to three cents; and in all cases where a one half-penny or penny rate of Postage is chargeable, these rates shall be changed to one cent and two cents respectively.

4. To promote simplicity and economy in the business of the Post Office, all letters posted in Canada for any place within the Province, and not prepaid, shall be charged seven instead of five cents per half ounce on delivery; and on letters posted for the British Mails, for the other British North American Provinces, or for the United States, when not prepaid, there shall be charged such addition to the ordinary rate, not in any case exceeding a double rate, as the Post Master General may agree upon with the Post Office Authorities of those Countries, for the purpose of enforcing prepayment.

5. The Post Master General may establish a Parcel Post and parcels other than letters and not containing letters, may be sent by such Parcel Post, and when so sent shall be liable to such charges for conveyance and to such regulations as the Governor in Council shall from time to time see fit to make.

See Appendix B #31.

#10
RATE OF DISCOUNT TO STAMP AGENTS, STREET LETTER BOXES, ETC.

29°—30° VICT. CAP. XI
An Act to amend the Post Office Act.
[*Assented to 15th August, 1866.*]

Whereas the more effectually to prevent frauds upon the Post Office Revenue, it is expedient to amend the Post Office Act: Therefore, Her Majesty, by and with the consent of the Legislative Council and Assembly of Canada, enacts as follows:

1. If any person uses or attempts to use in payment of postage on any letter or mailable thing posted in this Province, any postage stamp which has been before used for a like purpose, such person shall be subjected to a penalty of not less than Ten and not exceeding Forty dollars for every such offense, and the letter or other mailable thing on which such stamp has been so improperly used may be detained, or in

the discretion of the Postmaster General forwarded to its destination charged with double the postage to which it would have been liable if posted unpaid.

x x x x x x x x

3. The Postmaster General may grant licenses, revocable at pleasure, to Agents, other than Postmasters, for the sale to the Public, of Postage Stamps and Stamped envelopes, and may allow to such Agents a commission not exceeding five per cent on the amount of their sales;— and it shall not be lawful for any person to exercise the business of selling Postage Stamps or Stamped envelopes to the Public unless duly licensed to do so by the Postmaster General and under such conditions as he may prescribe: and any person who shall violate this provision by selling Postage Stamps or Stamped envelopes to the public without a license from the Postmaster General, shall on conviction before a Justice of the Peace, incur a penalty of not exceeding forty dollars for each offense.

x x x x x x x x

5. The Postmaster General may, when in his judgment the public convenience requires it, establish Street Letter Boxes or Pillar Boxes for the reception of letters and other mailable matter in the streets of any City or Town in this Province, and from the time that a letter is deposited in any such Street Letter Box or Pillar Box it shall be deemed to be a Post Letter within the meaning of the Post Office Act.

x x x x x x x x

8. The Governor in Council may, by regulations to be from time to time made, provide for the transmission through the Mails of this Province, of patterns and samples of merchandise and goods for sale, and of packages of seeds, cuttings, bulbs, roots and scions or grafts, on such terms and conditions as may be set forth in such regulations.

9. [*Wilfully destroying, damaging or detaining any of above articles is a misdemeanor.*]

Although Toronto had had street letter boxes as early as 1859 apparently no letter deposited in these boxes was considered a post letter until it reached the post office. This Act made such letters mail matter as soon as dropped in a letter box. See Appendix L #39 and #42.

Enactments by the Dominion Parliament.

#11

THE DOMINION POST OFFICE ACT.

Known as the Post Office Act of 1867—preliminary to the Large Cents Issue. Extract from:

31° VICT. CAP. X
An Act for the regulation of the Postal Service.
(Assented to 21st. December, 1867)

Her Majesty, by and with the advice and consent of the Senate and House of Commons of Canada, enacts as follows:

PRELIMINARY—INTERPRETATION.

1. This Act shall be known and may be cited as *The Post Office Act* 1867; and the following terms and expressions therein shall be held to have the meaning hereinafter assigned to them. . . .

The term "Letter" includes Packets of Letters;

The term "Postage" means the duty or sum chargeable for the conveyance of Post Letters, Packets and other things by Post;

The term "Foreign Country" means any country not included in the dominions of Her Majesty;

The term "Foreign Postage" means the postage on the conveyance of Letters, Packets or other things, within any Foreign Country or payable to any Foreign Government;

The term "Canada Postage" means the postage on the conveyance of Letters, Packets and other things by Post within the Dominion of Canada or by Canada Mail Packet;

The term "Mail" includes every conveyance by which Post Letters are carried, whether it be by land or by water;

The term "British Packet Postage" means the postage due on the conveyance of letters by British North America;—And the term "British Postage" includes all Postage not being Foreign, Colonial or Canadian;

The term "Post Letter" means any letter transmitted or deposited in any Post Office to be transmitted by the Post;—And a letter shall be deemed a Post Letter from the time of its being so deposited or delivered at a Post Office, to the time of its being delivered to the party to whom it is addressed. . . .

2. All Laws in force in the Provinces of Canada, Nova Scotia or New Brunswick, at the Union thereof on the first of July, one thousand eight hundred and sixty-seven, in respect to the Postal Service, and continued in force by the "British North America Act 1867," shall be and the same are hereby repealed.

x   x   x   x   x   x   x   x

Under the terms of this Act the following regulations were laid down:

ORGANIZATION AND GENERAL PROVISIONS.

7. There shall be at the seat of Government of Canada a Post Office Department for the superintendence and management of the Postal Service of Canada, under the direction of a Postmaster General.

8. The Postmaster General shall be appointed by Commission under the Great Seal of Canada, and shall hold his office during pleasure.

10. The Postmaster General may, subject to the provisions of this Act:

1. Establish and close Post Offices and Post Routes;

x   x   x   x   x   x   x   x

3. Enter into and enforce all contracts relating to the conveyance of the Mails or other business of the Post Office;

4. [*Make regulations concerning mailable matter and limits of weight and dimensions of such.*]

x   x   x   x   x   x   x   x

6. Cause to be prepared and distributed Postage Stamps, necessary for the prepayment of Postages under this Act, also stamped envelopes for the like purpose;

7. [*Make arrangements concerning Posts and Postal business with postal authorities outside of Canada.*]

x   x   x   x   x   x   x   x

11. Prescribe and enforce such Regulations as to letters directed to be registered as to him may seem necessary, in respect to the registration of letters and other matter passing by Mail, as well between places in Canada, as between Canada and the United Kingdom, any British Possession, the United States or any other Foreign Country, and to the charge to be made for the same; and also in respect to the registration by the officers of the Post Office of letters unquestionably containing money or other valuable enclosure when posted without registration by the senders of the same, and to imposing a rate of two cents registration charge upon such letters;

x   x   x   x   x   x   x   x

14. Establish and provide Street Letter Boxes or Pillar Boxes or Boxes of any other description for the receipt of letters and such other mailable matter as he may deem expedient, in the streets of any City or Town in Canada, or at any Railway Station or other public place where he may consider such Letter Boxes to be necessary;

15. Grant Licenses revocable at pleasure, to Agents other than Postmasters, for the sale to the Public of Postage Stamps and Stamped Envelopes, and allow to such Agents a commission of not exceeding five per cent. on the amount of their sales.

x　x　x　x　x　x　x　x

Rates of Postage

19. On all letters transmitted by Post for any distance within Canada, except in cases herein otherwise specially provided for, there shall be charged and paid one uniform rate of three cents per half ounce in weight, any fraction of an ounce being chargeable as a half ounce, provided that such three cents postage rate be prepaid by postage stamps or in current coin at the time of posting such letters; and when such letters are posted without prepayment being made thereon, then and in such case it shall be lawful to charge upon letters so posted unpaid a rate of five cents per half ounce.

20. On letters not transmitted through the mails, but posted and delivered at the same Post Office, commonly known as local or drop letters, the rate shall be one cent, to be in all cases prepaid by postage stamp affixed to such letters.

21. [*Seamen and Soldiers, etc., in Her Majesty's service, entitled to receive and send letters on payment of a certain special sum (2c per ½ oz.) of all British Postage, shall be freed likewise from Canadian Postage.*]

22. The rate of postage upon newspapers printed and published in Canada, and issued not less frequently than once a week, from a known office of publication, and sent to regular subscribers in Canada by mail, shall be as follows: upon each such newspaper, when issued once a week, the rate for each quarter of a year, commencing on the first of January, first of April, first of July, or first of October of each year, shall be five cents, when issued twice a week, ten cents, when issued three times a week, fifteen cents when issued six times a week, thirty cents and in that proportion, adding one rate of five cents for each issue more frequent than once a week; and such postage must be prepaid in advance from the first day of the quarter from which the payment commences, for a term of not less than a quarter of a year; .... provided, nevertheless, that *Exchange Papers*, addressed by one editor or publisher of a newspaper to another editor or publisher, may be sent by Post free of charge.

23. On all newspapers sent by Post in Canada, except in the cases hereinbefore expressly provided for, there shall be payable a rate not exceeding two cents each, and when such newspapers are posted in Canada this rate shall in all cases be prepaid by postage stamp affixed to the same.

24. For the purpose of this Act, the word "Newspapers" shall be held to mean periodicals published not less frequently than once in each week, and containing notices of passing events.

25. The rate of postage upon periodical publications, other than newspapers, shall be one cent per four ounces, or half a cent per number, when such periodicals weigh less than one ounce and are posted singly, and when such periodical publications are posted in Canada, these rates shall in all cases be prepaid by postage stamps affixed to the same.

26. On books, pamphlets, occasional publications, printed circulars, prices current, handbills, book and newspaper manuscript, printers' proof sheets whether corrected or not, maps, prints, drawings, engravings, photographs when not on glass, in cases containing glass, sheet music whether printed or written, packages of seeds, cuttings, bulbous roots, scions or grafts, patterns or samples of merchandize or goods, the rate of postage shall be one cent per ounce; provided that no letter or other communication intended to serve the purpose of a letter be sent or enclosed therein, and that the same be sent in covers open at the ends or sides or otherwise so put up as to admit of inspection by the Officers of the Post Office to ensure compliance with this provision—and this postage rate shall be prepaid by postage stamps in all cases when such articles are posted in Canada.

11-A

27. [*Foregoing rates subject to such conditions as may be agreed upon between Canada and any other country.*]

x   x   x   x   x   x   x

29. In all cases where letters and other mailable matter are posted for places without the limits of Canada, on which stamps for prepayment are affixed of less value than the true rate of Postage to which such letters are liable,—or when stamps for prepayment are affixed to letters addressed to any place as aforesaid for which prepayment cannot be taken in Canada,—the Postmaster General may forward such letters, charged with postage, as if no stamp had been affixed.

30. And for avoiding doubts, and preventing inconvenient delay in the posting and delivery of letters,—no Postmaster shall be bound to give change, but the exact amount of the postage on any letter or other mailable matter shall be tendered or paid to him in current coin as respects letters or other things delivered, and in current coin or postage stamps as the case may require in respect to the letters or other things posted.

31. [*The Postmaster General may make reasonable compensation to Masters of vessels not Post Office Packets for conveyance of ship letters from foreign ports to Canada.*]

32. The Post Office is a monopoly. *$20 penalty for infraction.* (See 13°—14° Vict. Cap. XVII, Sec. 9.)

35. [*The Postmaster General may employ Letter Carriers, and charge two cents for delivery of a letter and one cent for a newspaper or pamphlet.* (See 14°—15° Vict. Cap. LXXI. Sec. 15)]

36. It shall be lawful for the Postmaster General, with the consent of the Governor in Council, to establish in any city, when he shall deem it expedient, a system of free delivery by Letter Carrier of letters brought by mail and he may direct that from the time that such system is established, no charge shall be made for the delivery of such letters by Letter Carriers in such city, and further that on drop or local letters when delivered by Letter Carrier in such city, one cent only per half ounce shall be charged in addition to the ordinary local or drop letter rate.

37. [*Postmaster General may establish a parcel post.* (See 22° Vict. Cap. XVII. Sec. 5.)]

x   x   x   x   x   x   x

40. Letters or other articles, which from any cause remain undelivered in any Post Office, or which having been posted, cannot be forwarded by post, shall under such regulations as the Postmaster General may make, be transmitted by Postmasters to the Post Office Department as Dead Letters, there to be opened and returned to the writers on payment of any postage due thereon, with five cents additional on each Dead Letter to defray the costs of returning the same, or such Dead Letters may in any case or class of cases be otherwise disposed of as the Postmaster General may direct.

x   x   x   x   x   x   x   x

77. [*Stealing mail matter or forging stamps, etc.,* (see 13°-14° Vict. Cap. XVII, Sec. 16) *is a felony. Stealing or damaging printed matter, package of merchandise, etc., or enclosing a letter in other mail matter, or obstructing mails is a misdemeanor.*]

Sub. sec. 16. To remove with fradulent intent from any letter, newspaper or other mailable matter, sent by Post, any postage stamp which shall have been affixed thereon, or wilfully, with intent aforesaid remove from any postage stamp which shall have been made thereon at any Post Office, shall be a misdemeanor.

x   x   x   x   x   x   x   x

81. If any person uses or attempts to use in prepayment of postage on any letter or other mailable matter posted in this Province, any postage stamp which has been before used for a like purpose, such person shall be subject to a penalty of not less than Ten and not exceeding Forty dollars for every such offense, and the letter or other mailable

matter on which such stamp has been so improperly used may be detained, or in the discretion of the Postmaster General forwarded to its destination charged with double postage.

x   x   x   x   x   x   x

91. This Act shall come into operation on the first day of April, one thousand eight hundred and sixty-eight.

See Appendix B #40.

#12

THE UNIVERSAL POSTAL UNION AND 5c LETTER RATE TO THE UNITED KINGDOM

A treaty for the formation of a General Postal Union, and for the adoption of uniform postage rates and regulations for International correspondence, was arranged and signed at Berne, Switzerland, in October, 1874, by the representatives of the Post Offices of the chief Nations of the world. This agreement took effect between all the countries which were directly parties to the Treaty, in July last. *The Treaty did not include the British Possessions beyond the sea,* but Canada has, with the concurrence of the Imperial Government, applied for admission as a member of this Postal Union. Meanwhile the letter rate of postage between Canada and the United Kingdom has, by arrangement with the Imperial Post Office, been reduced to the International rate of 2½ pence sterling—5 cents currency, established by the Union regulations; and this reduction has also been made applicable to correspondence passing by way of New York, making the rate between Canada and the United Kingdom uniform at 5 cents by whatever route conveyed.

#13

THE POST OFFICE ACT OF 1875

Compulsory prepayment enacted.

The Act passed in the last Session of Parliament for the regulation of the Postal Service of Canada, came wholly into force on the 1st October, 1875.

This Act shall be known and may be cited as "The Post Office Act, 1875," etc., etc.

1. Letters passing by mail at 3 cents per ½ oz.
2. Local or drop letters at 1 cent per ½ oz.
3. Post Cards 1 cent each.
4. Canadian Newspapers and periodicals, from office of publication at 1 cent per pound of bulk weight.
5. Transient newspapers and periodicals, circulars, books, pamphlets, etc., open, 1 cent per 4 oz.
6. Newspapers or periodicals weighing less than 1 oz. each, when posted singly, ½ cent each.
7. Closed parcels not containing letters, 12½ cents per 8 oz.

10.—6. Cause to be prepared and distributed postage and registration stamps necessary for the prepayment of postages and registration charges, under this act; also stamped envelopes for the like purpose and post-cards and stamped post bands or wrappers for newspapers, or other mailable articles not being post letters.

19. [*Letter rate of 3 cents per ½ oz.*]; and such postage rate of three cents shall be *pre-paid by postage stamp or stamps at the time of posting the letter,* otherwise such letter shall not be forwarded by post, except that letters addressed to any place in Canada and on which one full rate of three cents has been so pre-paid, shall be forwarded to their destination charged with double the amount of the postage thereon not so prepaid, which amount shall be collected on delivery.

20. [*Drop letter rate restricted to* "one cent per half ounce weight."]

13-A

22. The rate of postage on newspaper and periodical publications printed and published in Canada, and issued not less frequently than once a month from a known office of publication or news agency, and addressed and posted by and from the same to regular subscribers or news agents, shall be one cent for each pound weight, or any fraction of a pound weight, to be prepaid by postage stamps or otherwise as the Postmaster General may, from time to time, direct; and such newspapers and periodicals shall be put into packages and delivered into the post office, and the postage rate thereon prepaid by the sender thereof, under such regulations as the Postmaster General may, from time to time, direct.

23. Newspapers and periodicals weighing less than one ounce each may be posted singly at a postage rate of half a cent each, which must be in all cases prepaid by postage stamp affixed to each.

24. On all newspapers and periodicals posted in Canada, except in the cases hereinbefore expressly provided for, and on books, etc., etc., [*repeats Sec. 26 of Act of 1867*], the rate of postage shall be one cent for each four ounces or fraction of four ounces, ... and this postage rate shall be prepaid by postage stamps or stamped post bands or wrappers. . . .

27. [*Repeats Sec. 29 of Act of 1867*] And when any letter or other mailable matter is posted in Canada without prepayment, or insufficiently prepaid, in any case in which prepayment is by this Act made obligatory, the Postmaster General may detain the same, and cause it to be returned, when practicable, to the sender.

28. [*Replaces Sec. 30 of Act of 1867*] And for avoiding doubts, and preventing inconvenient delay in the posting and delivery of letters,—no Postmaster shall be bound to give change, but the exact amount of the postage on any letter or other mailable matter shall be tendered or paid to him in current coin as respects letters or other things delivered, bearing unpaid postage, as shall also the exact value in current coin as respects postage stamps, registration stamps, stamped envelopes or post cards, post bands or wrappers, purchased from any Postmaster and the exact amount of postage payable to any letter-carrier on any letter or mailable matter delivered by him.

38. [*Repeats Sec. 40 of Act of 1867 concerning dead letters, but lowers the charge for returning to three cents and allows for deduction of postage prepaid in the case of insufficiently prepaid matter.*]

87. The foregoing sections of this Act shall come into force and effect on the first day of October, in the present year one thousand eight hundred and seventy-five, except only in so far as they relate to the rates of postage on newspapers and periodicals sent to the United States, as to which they shall come into force on the first day of May now next. . . .

See Appendix B #43.

#14

CANADA ADMITTED TO THE U. P. U.

At the meeting of the International Postal Congress, which, under the provisions of the Postal Treaty of Berne, concluded in October, 1874, took place at Paris in May, 1878, Canada was admitted to be a member of the General Postal Union from the 1st July, 1878, and in consequence the rate of letter postage between Canada and all Europe became one uniform charge of 5 cents per half ounce. Newspapers and other printed matter, and samples and patterns of merchandise also became subject to uniform postage rates and regulations for all destinations in Europe. Existing postal arrangements between the United States and Canada were, by mutual agreement, allowed to remain undisturbed by the entry of Canada into the Union, under a provision of the General Postal Union Treaty applicable to such a case.

#15

RATE MADE 3c PER OZ.

By Act of May 2, 1889. See APPENDIX B #50.

#16

2c POSTAGE, JANUARY 1, 1899.

Order in Council,
   Post Office Department.

By Proclamation dated the 29th day of December, 1898, in virtue of the Act further to amend the Post Office Act (61 Victoria, chapter 20) and of an Order in Council in accordance therewith, it was declared that the postage rate payable on all letters originating in and transmitted by post for any distance in Canada for delivery in Canada, should be one uniform rate of two cents per ounce weight, from the 1st January, 1899.

See also Appendix B #53, and #56.

APPENDIX F

TABULATIONS OF ORDERS
for
HANDSTRUCK STAMPS, REGULATION MARKINGS, ETC.
Compiled from the official records
1851-1867

Table A

Marking	FRANCIS Orders First	FRANCIS Orders Last	FRANCIS No. of Orders	FRANCIS Quantity	BERRI Orders First	BERRI Orders Last	BERRI No. of Orders	BERRI Quantity	ELLIS Orders First	ELLIS Orders Last	ELLIS No. of Orders	ELLIS Quantity	Totals Orders	Totals Quantity
PAID	6/53	10/54	2	350	7/56	7/58	4	300	—	—	—	—	6	650
PAID 3d	9/52	—	1	200	7/56	6/58	5	275	—	—	—	—	6	475
PAID 6d	—	—	—	—	7/58	8/58	5	275	—	—	—	—	5	275
PAID 9d	6/53	—	1	6	—	—	—	—	—	—	—	—	1	6
PAID d¹	9/52	—	1	200	—	—	—	—	—	—	—	—	1	200
PAID ½d	6/53	—	1	2	—	—	—	—	—	—	—	—	1	2
PAID 1d	6/53	—	1	2	—	—	—	—	—	—	—	—	1	2
PAID 3	—	—	—	—	5/55	3/56	3	175	—	—	—	—	3	175
PAID 6	—	—	—	—	12/55	3/55	2	150	—	—	—	—	2	150
PAID 6d stg	—	—	—	—	7/56	4/58	2	37	—	—	—	—	2	37
PAID 8d stg	—	—	—	—	7/56	4/58	2	50	—	—	—	—	2	50
PAID 5	—	—	—	—	6/59	4/67	4	400	12/59	1/62	5	350	9	750
PAID 10	—	—	—	—	7/59	1/61	2	15	6/64	—	1	25	3	40

¹ (This marking had a space so that amount could be inserted by hand).

NOTE—Although the first order to Ellis in the records was dated July 1859, the report of the P.M.G. for 1855 shows that Ellis was paid £34-16-0 in the quarter ending June 30, 1854, for engraving cancellations for the Toronto Post Office.

Table A (Con't.)

Marking	FRANCIS				BERRI				ELLIS				Totals	
	Orders First	Last	No. of Orders	Quantity	Orders First	Last	No. of Orders	Quantity	Orders First	Last	No. of Orders	Quantity	Orders	Quantity
6d stg	3/54	—	1	80	7/56	—	1	12	—	—	—	—	2	92
8d stg	3/54	—	1	80	7/56	—	1	25	—	—	—	—	2	105
7½d cy	3/54	—	1	40	—	—	—	—	—	—	—	—	1	40
10d cy	3/54	—	1	40	—	—	—	—	—	—	—	—	1	40
3	9/52	—	1	500	12/55	3/56	2	225	—	—	—	—	3	725
6	9/52	—	1	50	3/56	—	1	100	—	—	—	—	2	150
½d	9/52	—	1	500	—	—	—	—	—	—	—	—	1	500
1d	9/52	—	1	500	—	—	—	—	—	—	—	—	1	500
2d	9/52	—	1	500	—	—	—	—	—	—	—	—	1	500
3d	—	—	—	—	12/56	7/58	3	400	—	—	—	—	3	400
4d	—	—	—	—	4/59	—	1	10	—	—	—	—	1	10
6d	—	—	—	—	12/56	7/58	3	400	—	—	—	—	3	400
1/5 cy	—	—	—	—	4/59	—	1	10	—	—	—	—	1	10
2/3 cy	—	—	—	—	—	—	—	—	12/60	—	1	6	1	10
1/-	—	—	—	—	—	—	—	—	4/60	—	1	1	1	6
4	—	—	—	—	6/59	4/67	4	400	1/60	1/62	4	250	1	1
7	—	—	—	—	—	—	—	—	7/59	1/61	2	15	8	650
14	—	—	—	—	—	—	—	—	7/59	—	1	5	2	15
25	—	—	—	—	—	—	—	—	4/60	—	1	5	1	5
29	—	—	—	—	—	—	—	—	—	—	—	—	1	5

Table B

Marking	FRANCIS Orders First	FRANCIS Orders Last	FRANCIS No. of Orders	FRANCIS Quantity	BERRI Orders First	BERRI Orders Last	BERRI No. of Orders	BERRI Quantity	ELLIS Orders First	ELLIS Orders Last	ELLIS No. of Orders	ELLIS Quantity	Totals Orders	Totals Quantity
Forwarded	6/53	5/54	2	150	12/56	2/67	4	125	—	—	—	—	6	275
MISSENT	5/54	—	1	100	—	—	—	—	—	—	—	—	1	100
REFUSED	5/54	—	1	50	12/56	6/59	3	100	—	—	—	—	4	150
RETURNED FOR BETTER DIRECTION	5/54	—	1	50	2/58	—	1	25	—	—	—	—	2	75
RETURNED FOR POSTAGE	5/54	—	1	50	8/58	—	1	25	—	—	—	—	2	75
Advertised and Not called for	5/54	—	1	50	8/58	—	1	25	—	—	—	—	2	75
Advertised	6/53	—	1	50	7/56	8/58	3	75	—	—	—	—	4	125
MISSENT TO	—	—	—	—	12/56	6/59	3	100	1/61	—	1	25	4	125
Free	—	—	—	—	3/56	8/58	4	150	—	—	—	—	4	150
UNCLAIMED	—	—	—	—	2/67	—	1	1	—	—	—	—	1	1
DEAD LETTER OFFICE	—	—	—	—	8/67	—	1	1	—	—	—	—	1	1

Table B (Con't)

REGULATION STAMP

Marking	FRANCIS Orders First	FRANCIS Orders Last	FRANCIS No. of Orders	FRANCIS Quantity	BERRI Orders First	BERRI Orders Last	BERRI No. of Orders	BERRI Quantity	ELLIS Orders First	ELLIS Orders Last	ELLIS No. of Orders	ELLIS Quantity	Totals Orders	Totals Quantity
MONEY LETTER	6/53	5/54	2	350	—	—	—	—	—	—	—	—	2	350
REGISTERED	—	—	—	—	5/55	6/64	4	1275	1/61	—	1	25	5	1300
TOO LATE	—	—	—	—	3/56	4/67	5	167	1/61	—	1	25	6	192
MORE TO PAY	—	—	—	—	3/56	7/57	2	50	—	—	—	—	2	50
UNPAID 5	—	—	—	—	10/61	—	1	1	7/59	—	1	2	2	3
UNPAID 25	—	—	—	—	10/66	—	1	1	—	—	—	—	1	1
UNPAID 30	—	—	—	—	10/66	—	1	1	—	—	—	—	1	1
SHORT PAID HALF FINE	—	—	—	—	4/62	—	1	8	—	—	—	—	1	8

Table C

EXCHANGE MARKINGS

These are the curved markings provided by R.W.H.&E. (See Appendix H #17).

Marking	Orders First	Orders Last	No. of Orders	Quantity (18)
CANADA	4/51	—	1	3
CANADA 10 CTS	6/53	—	1	74
CANADA PAID 10 CTS	6/53	—	1	2
PAID CANADA 10 CTS	—	—	1	12
CANADA PAID 10 CTS	—	—	1	25
CANADA UNPAID 10	6/64	—	1	25

APPENDIX J

Tables Showing
QUANTITIES OF POSTAGE STAMPS ORDERED
March 27, 1851, to August 4, 1870, Inclusive
Also Quantities Issued of Postage Stamps, and Postal Stationery 1870-1910

#1
Table A. Orders for the Pence Issues

Order of	½d	3d	6d	7½d	10d	12d
		Hand Made Laid Paper				
1 Mar. 27, 1851	—	250,000[1]	100,000	—	—	50,000
2 April 9, 1851	—	250,000	—	—	—	—
		Hand Made Wove Paper				
3 Mar. 16, 1852	—	250,000[2]	—	—	—	—
4 Aug. 31, 1853	—	250,000	—	—	—	—
5 May 30, 1854	—	250,000	—	—	—	—
6 Nov. 13, 1854	—	—	—	—	100,080	—
7 Feb. 14, 1855	—	—	50,000	—	—	—
8 Mar. 7, 1855	—	300,000	—	—	—	—
9 Jan. 25, 1856	—	300,000[3]	—	—	—	—
10 Apr. 14, 1856	—	—	50,000	—	—	—
11 Oct. 9, 1856	—	300,000	—	—	—	—
12 Mar. 23, 1857	—	—	—	100,080	—	—
13 April 2, 1857	—	—	50,000	—	—	—
14 April 14, 1857	—	300,000	—	—	—	—
15 June 29, 1857	200,000[4]	—	—	—	—	—
16 July 29, 1857	480,000	—	—	—	—	—
17 Aug. 11, 1857	240,000	—	—	—	—	—
18 Aug. 21, 1857	480,000	—	—	—	—	—
19 Sept. 17, 1857	—	300,000	—	—	—	—
20 Dec. 4, 1857	—	—	50,000	—	—	—
		Machine Made Wove Paper				
21 Feb. 4, 1858	600,000	—	—	—	—	—
22 Mar. 4, 1858	—	300,000	—	—	—	—
23 June 14, 1858	600,000	—	50,000	—	—	—
24 July 20, 1858	—	300,000	—	—	72,120	—
		Perforated				
25 Oct. 12, 1858	600,000	300,000	—	—	—	—
26 Dec. 10, 1858	—	—	50,000	—	—	—
27 Apr. 4, 1859	250,000	150,000	—	—	—	—
28 May 3, 1859	—	—	20,000	—	—	—
Totals ordered	3,450,000	3,800,000	420,000	100,080	172,200	50,000
28 Orders	8	14	8	1	2	1
Plus Extra Sheets Amounting to	—	200[5]	400[6]	—	—	1,000[7]
Totals sent	3,450,000	3,800,200	420,400	100,080	172,200	51,000
Remainders destroyed	60,660	21,700	17,578	17,680	31,200	49,490
Issue	3,389,340	3,778,500	402,822	82,400	141,000	1,510[8]

2 Two shipments. April 15, and 25, 1851, 100,000, and 150,000 respectively.
3 Two Shipments. Feb. 22, and Mar. 1, 1856, 100,000 and 200,000 respectively.
5 Appendix H #10.
6 Appendix H #10.
7 Appendix H #10.
8 1510 were distributed to postmasters, sixty were returned, so that postmasters sold 1450, Appendix C #28.

#2

Table B. Summary of Orders for Pence Issues.

	On Laid	Perforated	Wove	Total
3d	500,200	450,000	2,850,000	3,800,200
6d	100,400	70,000	250,000	420,400
12d	50,000		1,200	51,200
½d		850,000	2,600,000	3,450,000
7½d			100,080	100,080
10d			172,200	172,200
Totals	650,600	1,370,000	5,973,480	7,994,080

	½d	3d	6d
Howes[8] estimated the perforated issue as follows	789,440	428,000	52,422
Deliveries were	850,000	450,000	70,000
Remainders in P.O. Dept. June 30, 1859, and destroyed (Probably all perf.)	60,660	21,700	17,578
Leaving	789,340	428,300	52,422

Mr. Howes was out only 100 stamps for the ½d, 300 stamps for the 3d, correct for the 6d. A remarkable example of deductive reasoning!

[8] Clifford A. Howes in "CANADA, Its Postage Stamps and Postal Stationery," New England Stamp Co., Boston, 1911.

#7A

REGISTRATION STAMPS

	2c	5c	8c
1876	937,200	231,800	71,950
1877	1,408,250	135,150	17,200
1878	1,541,950	140,350	9,400
1879	1,575,200	149,800	25
1880	1,744,450	181,995	
1881	1,875,100	212,730	
1882	2,005,200	260,240	
1883	2,139,100	320,500	
1884	2,293,550	359,050	
1885	2,427,300	340,000	
1886	2,604,500	354,100	
1887	2,671,950	387,200	
1888	2,858,900	345,600	
1889	2,808,400	514,700	
1890	601,750	1,466,950	
1891	14,850	2,154,350	
1892	100	2,252,200	
1893		2,259,450	
1894		307,900	
1896	400		

#3

A. Orders and Quantities in Thousands for the 1859 Issue.

Perforated 11¾ x 11¾

	1c	2c	5c	10c	12½c	17c
Mar. 16, 1859	1,000	—	1,000	100	100	50
July 12, 1859	—	—	—	100	100	—
Aug. 3, 1859	500	—	500	—	—	—
Nov. 9, 1859	—	—	—	100	—	—
Nov. 29, 1859	—	—	500	—	—	—
Jan. 4, 1860	500	—	—	—	—	—
Jan. 10, 1860	—	—	—	—	—	50
Jan. 27, 1860	—	—	500	—	100	—
Feb. 10, 1860	—	—	—	200	—	—
Mar. 28, 1860	1,000	—	1,000	—	—	—
July 2, 1860	—	—	—	—	200	—
Sept. 29, 1860	1,000	—	1,000	200	—	—
Dec. 26, 1860	—	—	1,000	—	—	—
Mar. 6, 1861	1,000	—	—	200	100	50
Apr. 9, 1861	—	—	1,000	—	—	—
Aug. 13, 1861	1,000	—	1,000	200	200	—
Nov. 26, 1861	500	—	1,000	—	—	50
Jan. 23, 1862	—	—	1,000	200	200	—
Feb. 13, 1862	1,000	—	1,000	—	—	—
May 31, 1862	500	—	—	200	100	—

Perforated 11¾ x 12 all except 5c or 12 x 11¾ 5c only

	1c	2c	5c	10c	12½c	17c
Sept. 2, 1862	500	—	1,000	100	—	—
Oct. 29, 1862	1,000	—	—	—	200	50
Dec. 17, 1862	—	—	1,000	200	—	—
Feb. 27, 1863	1,000	—	1,000	200	—	—
June 9, 1863	1,000	—	1,000	—	100	—
Aug. 10, 1863	—	—	—	—	—	50
Sept. 14, 1863	500	—	1,000	100	100	—
Nov. 21, 1863	500	—	1,000	200	200	—
Feb. 2, 1864	—	—	1,000	—	—	—
Mar. 1, 1864	1,000	—	—	200	100	—
Mar. 30, 1864	1,000	—	1,000	—	—	50
May 6, 1864	—	—	—	300	—	—
June 14, 1864	—	200	—	—	—	—
July 9, 1864	1,000	—	2,000	200	200	—

Perforated 12 x 12

	1c	2c	5c	10c	12½c	17c
Nov. 28, 1864	1,000	10	1,000	200	100	50
Jan. 28, 1865	1,000	50	2,000	200	200	—
April 22, 1865	2,000	200	3,000	300	300	50
Sept. 25, 1865	2,000	200	3,000	300	300	50
Mar. 24, 1866	—	—	2,000	—	—	—
April 24, 1866	—	—	—	300	—	—
July 27, 1866	2,000	100	2,000	400	—	—
Dec. 11, 1866	2,000	—	2,000	500	—	50
Feb. 22, 1867	2,000	100	2,000	100	300	50
Aug. 21, 1867	—	—	1,000	400	—	—
Dec. 4, 1867	—	5	1,300	—	—	—
	27,500	865	39,800	5,700	3,200	600
45 Orders	26 orders	8 orders	31 orders	26 orders	19 orders	12 orders

See Table 4B for analysis of quantities by perforations and denominations.

#4

Table B. Summary of Orders for 1859-68 Issue.

Denomination	Perf.	Orders	Dates	Quantities covered by the orders
1c	11¾	1 to 10	From 3/16/59 to 5/31/62	8,000,000
	12 x 11¾	11 to 19	From 9/2/62 to 7/9/64	7,500,000
	12	20 to 26	From 11/28/64 to 2/22/67	12,000,000
	Total—27,500,000.	Remainders—319,900.	Net issued—26,180,100.	
2c	12 x 11¾	1	6/14/64	200,000
	12	2 to 8	From 11/28/64 to 12/4/67	665,000
	Total—865,000.	Remainders—700.	Net issued—864,300.	
5c	11¾	1 to 12	From 3/16/59 to 5/31/62	10,500,000
	11¾ x 12	13 to 21	From 9/2/62 to 7/9/64	10,000,000
	12	22 to 31	From 11/28/64 to 12/4/67	19,300,000
	Total—39,800,000.	Remainders—138,400.	Net issued 39,661,600.	
10c	11¾	1 to 9	From 3/16/59 to 5/31/62	1,500,000
	12 x 11¾	10 to 17	From 9/2/62 to 7/9/64	1,500,000
	12	28 to 26	From 11/28/64 to 8/21/67	2,700,000
	Total—5,700,000.	Remainders—60,850.	Net issued—5,639,150.	
12½c	11¾	1 to 8	From 3/16/59 to 5/31/62	1,100,000
	12 x 11¾	9 to 14	From 10/29/62 to 7/9/64	900,000
	12	15 to 19	From 11/28/64 to 2/22/67	1,200,000
	Total—3,200,000.	Remainders—68,750.	Net issued—3,131,250.	
17c	11¾	1 to 4	From 3/16/59 to 11/26/61	200,000
	12 x 11¾	5, 6, 7	From 10/29/62 to 3/30/64	150,000
	12	8 to 12	From 11/28/64 to 2/22/67	250,000
	Total—600,000.	Remainders—33,876.	Net issued—566,124.	

The last two orders of the 17c show the "burr over shoulder" variety, especially those of the last half of the 12th order, which was for 50,000 stamps.

#5

Orders to B. A. B. N. Co. 1868 Issue (Large Queens) and Early Small Queens.

Order		½c	1c	2c	3c	6c	12½c	15c
1	1867 Dec. 23	500,000	2,000,000	2,000,000	6,000,000	2,000,000	500,000	
2	1868 May 22	1,000,000	2,000,000	2,000,000	3,000,000	1,000,000	500,000	100,000[1]
3	Oct. 8				3,000,000			
4	Oct. 23		2,000,000				500,000	500,000
5	1869 Jan. 2		3,000,000		3,000,000			
6	Mar. 31		3,000,000		4,000,000	2,000,000		
7	July 8			300,000	3,000,000		300,000	
8	Nov. 4		300,000		4,000,000	1,000,000		
9	Dec. 17			1,000,000	3,000,000			
10	1870 Mar. 6				2,000,000			
11	Mar. 14		2,000,000			1,000,000		
12	May 19							
13	Aug. 4		4,000,000	2,000,000	4,000,000	1,000,000		
Totals		1,500,000	12,000,000 LQ 6,300,000 SQ	7,300,000	25,000,000 LQ 13,000,000 SQ	7,000,000	1,800,000	600,000[1]
13 Orders		2 orders	5 LQ; 3 SQ 5 orders	7 LQ; 4 SQ 6 orders			4 orders	2 orders

6,000,000 of each color of the 1c—red and orange.

NOTES: Order 1—On Paper A. Order 2—On Papers A, B, and C. Included 2c pale green. Orders 3 and 4—On Papers B and D. Orders 5 to 8—Paper B. Included 1c orange and yellow. Order 9—Included the first small Queen design; 1c orange 300,000 and 3c dull red 4,000,000. The 12½c were dull blue. Some of the 3c were perforated 12½ x12½, and it is possible that some of the 1c of this order also were perforated 12½ x 12½, but none have been noted so far. Order 10—Was for 6c yellow brown. Orders 11 to 13—Included 1c and 3c small Queen design and 6c in light brown.

In order to complete the table above we give the quantities issued to the postmasters of the Large Queens from 1871 to 1899 inclusive, on the following page.

---

[1] There was a previous order for this stamp amounting to 212,500 stamps which does not appear in the records, but is in the Report of the P.M.G. Total 812,500.

#6

1868-97. Quantities of Stamps Issued to Postmasters. (Large Queens)

Year ending June 30.

	½c	5c	12½c	15c
1871	271,600		64,050	63,100
1872	434,400		69,950	85,000
1873	401,800		76,850	99,500
1874	484,600		77,450	101,000
1875	732,800		64,850	77,200
1876	563,800	1,250,000	72,100	53,950
1877	424,600	Super-	80,050	55,075
1878	478,100	seded by	84,150	46,650
1879	422,200	Small 5c	13,400	46,350
1880	361,100		4,950	63,750
1881	465,800		5,650	90,575
1882	437,894		5,150	91,100
1883	Super-		4,700	90,825
1884	seded		2,650	90,150
1885	by		1,400	99,575
1886	Small		450	110,400
1887	½		1,100	100,350
1888			No	81,150
1889			further	75,200
1890			Issues	80,550
1891			to P.M.	68,850
1892			after	45,000
1893			June 30,	49,650
1894			1888	55,150
1895				57,800
1896				21,350
1897				Discon-
1898				tinued
1899				Nov. 2,
1900				1899

Total quantities of each value of Large Queens therefore is about as follows:

½c— 6,707,000
1c—12,000,000
2c— 8,900,000
15c— 2,712,000
3c—25,000,000
6c— 8,160,000
12½c— 2,430,000

#7

1870-97. Quantities of Stamps Issued to Postmasters.
(Small Queens)

From the Reports of the Postmaster General
Year Ending June 30

	½c	1c	2c	3c	5c	6c	8c	10c
				First Ottawa Printings				
1870	—	1,300,000[1]	—	9,000,000[1]	—	—	—	—
1871	—	5,631,300	—	15,029,500	—	—	—	—
1872	—	5,528,600	1,447,500	16,361,600	—	1,500,000	—	—
1873	—	6,906,200	3,393,800	18,969,500	—	3,866,250	—	—
1874	—	8,312,700	3,929,800	21,066,700	—	4,196,350	—	—
			First Ottawa and Montreal Printings. Perf. 11½ x 12					
1875	—	10,212,700	4,183,000	24,508,900	—	3,136,300	—	85,550
				Montreal Printings				
1876	—	12,986,700	3,155,700	24,522,300	—	3,553,500	—	140,000
1877	—	14,384,700	2,293,900	32,038,800	1,294,050	362,650	—	141,950
1878	—	15,946,300	2,279,600	34,457,200	1,397,950	431,700	—	145,000
1879	—	16,272,100	2,038,100	33,945,700	1,304,050	388,150	—	111,200
1880	—	17,636,000	2,220,500	37,187,500	1,389,490	531,500	—	121,900
1881	—	19,182,500	2,277,500	39,961,000	1,528,300	560,600	—	141,550
1882	—	21,974,300	2,299,700	45,574,100	1,814,500	723,480	—	187,550
1883	594,800	25,045,000	2,468,100	49,177,100	2,073,350	763,000	—	200,050
1884	526,100	27,812,500	2,699,400	52,087,400	2,255,000	817,000	—	202,350
1885	511,400	29,309,700	2,744,100	52,249,700	2,165,550	849,050	—	198,300
1886	544,500	30,279,100	2,681,000	54,187,200	2,091,500	903,700	—	206,350
			Montreal and Second Ottawa Printings					
1887	554,800	33,691,500	2,744,600	57,447,100	2,208,750	947,500	—	218,050
				Second Ottawa Printings				
1888	565,700	36,172,100	2,889,800	61,014,000	2,293,200	958,850	—	217,800
1889	535,700	40,873,600	4,199,200	65,816,600	2,600,700	894,600	—	235,650
1890	508,800	34,356,300	9,625,800	66,688,300	2,776,450	575,600	—	190,150
1891	564,800	36,838,700	10,764,000	70,334,600	2,708,700	444,700	—	211,200
1892	728,400	37,874,900	11,337,700	73,810,400	2,756,850	409,500	—	211,150
1893	815,000	39,839,000	12,165,000	77,477,500	2,759,050	372,350	—	224,300
1894	860,100	41,236,300	12,138,500	76,573,200	3,003,900	346,100	1,398,350	211,300
1895	902,200	42,325,700	12,388,900	78,246,700	3,086,000	372,500	1,527,000	206,800
1896	846,500	45,234,900	12,925,100	81,674,800	3,072,450	372,950	1,522,450	225,650
1897	88,800	45,580,500	12,804,300	82,398,200	3,034,600	356,850	1,437,200	243,650
1898	—	—	—	—	—	—	775,000	—

[1] The report of the P.M.G. for 1870 shows that 2,300,000 1c and 11,300,000 3c were issued to postmasters, but of these amounts only 1,300,000 and 9,000,000 respectively were small queens.

See Page 2-J for Registration Stamps.

#8

1872-1910. Quantities of Postal Stationery Issued to Postmasters.
Envelopes and Cards.

	1c Env.	2c Env.	3c Envelope Size 1	3c Envelope Size 2	1c Cards	1c+1c Reply	2c U.P.U. Cards	2c U.K. Cards
1871	—	—	—	—	—	—	—	—
1872	—	—	—	—	—	—	—	—
1873	—	—	—	—	1,857,500	—	—	—
1874	—	—	—	—	2,642,900	—	—	—
1875	—	—	—	—	3,336,000	—	—	—
1876	—	—	—	—	4,464,000	—	—	—
1877	—	—	—	—	5,522,689	—	—	98,300[10]
1878	369,800	—	699,400	252,000	6,469,700	—	—	6,090
1879	125,900	—	258,900	78,100	7,120,600	—	27,300	13,680
1880	121,100	—	261,900	70,700	8,252,299	—	26,500	—
1881	138,600	—	222,200	113,300	9,776,100	—	26,300	—
1882	177,400	—	200,800	104,700	9,553,100 / 1,775,000[1]	—	32,346	—
1883	180,500	—	238,400	114,400	12,854,100	285,800	47,500	—
1884	201,500	—	178,300	116,100	13,424,400	85,500	46,350	—
1885	159,900	—	172,200	84,600	14,038,400	116,300	56,800	—
1886	189,700	—	164,700	87,800	15,078,300	135,150	47,700	—
1887	166,300	—	146,700	86,900	16,244,991	113,540	60,554	—
1888	149,000	—	158,200	130,700	16,813,000	122,200	52,400	—
1889	147,000	—	99,300	112,600	18,062,000	103,900	54,500	—
1890	62,000	—	90,500	130,900	18,591,000	106,450	55,900	—
1891	51,600	—	85,300	110,400	19,897,300	116,400	55,110	—
1892	42,800	—	80,000	71,700	20,956,600	135,650	67,400	—
1893	38,800	—	71,900	71,200	17,808,400[1a] / 4,983,900[2]	161,050	64,600	—
1894	31,200	—	62,900	89,100	23,705,100	151,500	49,400	—
1895	40,800	9,800	55,800	88,400	24,032,000	244,750	47,000	—
1896	25,500	33,870	54,000	85,500	24,322,500	182,000	46,000	—
1897	25,500	15,900	49,000	91,700	23,672,500	138,400	58,900	—
1898	28,200	26,600	54,600	37,900[3] / 67,900[4]	20,398,800	151,000	68,700	—
1899	83,600[5] / 1,900[6]	253,300[7] / 8,800[8]	—	112,100[9]	24,492,000	112,750	39,600	—
1900	55,700	429,300	—	—	21,909,000	112,800	36,700	—
1901	125,400	578,900	—	—	21,456,500	129,550	45,600	—
1902	98,100	756,200	—	—	21,855,300	149,850	28,200	—
1903	118,500	1,001,100	—	—	22,071,500	149,400	36,600	—
1904	141,100	1,226,500	—	—	22,249,500	166,700	42,700	—
1905	197,600	1,539,200	—	—	22,374,200	124,100	43,400	—
1906	346,600	1,949,200	—	—	23,824,700	174,050	49,700	—
1907	304,400	1,694,100	—	—	18,574,600	112,150	49,200	—
1908	352,000	2,577,900	—	—	24,747,600	182,250	108,600	—
1909	1,036,700	2,455,500	—	—	25,103,000	229,600	78,900	—
1910	1,360,100	2,928,400	—	—	26,093,500	455,400	79,400	—

1 Typographca cards.
1a Regular size cards.
2 New large size cards.
3 Old issue.
4 New issue.
5 @ $1.20 per 100.
6 @ $1.25 per 100.
7 @ $2.20 per 100.
8 @ $2.30 per 100.
9 @ $3.20 per 100.
10 Regular 2c U. K. card replaced by U.P.U. card in 1877.

#9

1875-1910. Quantities of Postal Stationery Issued to Postmasters. Postbands, Wrappers, Letter Cards, Etc.

Year	Post Bands	Wrappers	1c Letter Cards	2c Letter Cards	3c Letter Cards	Advertising Cards 1c Single	Sheets[1] of 8	Sheets[1] of 16
1875	52,000	—	—	—	—	—	—	—
1876	228,700	—	—	—	—	—	—	—
1877	243,980	—	—	—	—	—	—	—
1878	297,861	—	—	—	—	—	—	—
1879	280,100	—	—	—	—	—	—	—
1880	304,400	—	—	—	—	—	—	—
1881	369,300	—	—	—	—	—	—	—
1882	488,100	—	—	—	—	—	—	—
1883	518,200	—	—	—	—	—	—	—
1884	558,200	—	—	—	—	—	—	—
1885	546,100	—	—	—	—	—	—	—
1886	579,900	—	—	—	—	—	—	—
1887	559,200	—	—	—	—	—	—	—
1888	558,100	—	—	—	—	—	—	—
1889	530,400	—	—	—	—	—	—	—
1890	497,200	—	—	—	—	—	—	—
1891	514,200	—	—	—	—	—	—	—
1892	466,900	—	—	—	—	—	—	—
1893	448,700	—	265,350	—	—	—	—	—
1894	431,700	—	104,650	—	—	—	—	—
1895	421,900	—	77,750	—	—	—	—	—
1896	437,300	—	73,500 / 76,300	49,700 / 86,000	101,950 / 106,600	—	—	—
1897	368,700	—	80,200 / 75,650	38,100 / 92,150	111,950 / 95,350	—	—	—
1898	431,300	—	114,500 / 45,000	84,000 / 22,000	146,350 / 24,000	145,500	279,000	172,000
1899	365,600	—	102,200 / 31,000	160,400 / 64,000	76,300 / 19,500	257,800	629,000	262,000
1900	380,300	—	156,800	306,300	—	238,300	653,000	270,000
1901	408,100	—	211,500	287,900	—	278,300	775,000	260,000
1902	388,000	—	195,000	352,000	—	244,100	837,000	344,000
1903	384,000	—	—	—	—	259,600	992,000	352,000
1904	430,900	—	—	—	—	327,700	1,262,000	432,000
1905	374,700	—	—	—	—	321,400	1,360,000	472,000
1906	447,700	—	—	—	—	384,600	1,789,000	506,000
1907	357,900	—	—	—	—	301,200	1,299,000	366,000
1908	537,500	1,332,800	—	—	—	416,000	1,929,000	600,000
1909	549,900	854,800	—	—	—	415,300	1,989,000	676,000
1910	489,700	882,000	—	—	—	435,500	2,162,000	740,000

Wrappers

	2c	3c
1908	300,300	15,600
1909	280,246	52,190

[1] Figures are number of cards not sheets.

APPENDIX N

BIOGRAPHICAL, GEOGRAPHICAL, HISTORICAL
and Other Notes Concerning the
DESIGNS OF SOME OF THE STAMPS
of Canada
(In Order of Appearance)

#1

3d 1851 and 5c 1859

The beaver (castor fibre) is an aquatic mammal found in the northern parts of both hemispheres. It is now practically extinct in Europe, but is still common enough in Canada and the northern United States. The animal is about three and a half feet long when adult, and covered with a coat of long chestnut brown hair, except the flat paddle shaped tail, about a foot long, which is covered with a scaly coat, a modification of the hair of the rest of the body. The legs are short and strong, the hind feet being webbed. As with all rodents the teeth are very powerful and sharp, firmly set in jaws of enormous muscular strength.

The beaver is noteworthy for its gregariousness, and for the construction of dams and houses, displaying an admixture of instinct and reason that is a never-ending source of wonder to those who have observed their work.

Beavers secrete a musk known as "castoreum" from two glandular sacs near the base of the tail. This musk has a powerful attraction to all beavers and trappers frequently use it as a lure. It is commercially used in perfumery.

The Canadian National Shield has the beaver, as a symbol of sagacity and industry.

The beaver skin was a standard of exchange in the early days of the Hudson's Bay Company. Other skins were valued on the basis of the beaver skin. Later *(circa 1820)* brass tokens were made which passed as "Beavers" or fractional amounts, and by the time stamps were issued *(1851)* there were paper notes for 1sh., 5sh., and £1. Sandford Fleming undoubtedly had the "made beaver" in mind when he designed and engraved the Three Pence stamps.

#2

6d 1851 and 10c 1859

H.R.H. *Prince Albert,* Duke of Saxony, Prince of Coburg and Gotha, born August 26, 1819, died December 14, 1861; beloved husband of Queen Victoria, wise counselor, he was a conservative influence, and did much to smooth over various difficulties, political and diplomatic. He was particularly interested in arts and sciences, and was the originator of the great International Exhibitions, the first one being held in 1851, for which the Great Crystal Palace was erected. The portrait on the stamp is from a source as yet untraced.

#3

12d 1851, 7½d 1857 and 12½c 1859

Queen Victoria (1819-1901). Her Royal Highness Princess Victoria was the only daughter of Edward Duke of Kent, fourth son of King George III, was born at Kensington Palace, May 24, 1819. She succeeded to the throne on June 20, 1837, being crowned June 28, 1838, at Westminster Abbey. She married Albert, Duke of Saxony, Prince of Coburg and Gotha (q.v.), February 10, 1840, by whom she had nine children. Died January 22, 1901, after a glorious reign, the longest of any British monarch.

The portrait on the stamp shows the head of the young queen from the famous full length portrait of Her Majesty in Robes of State (see Frontispiece, Vol. I). It was painted by Alfred Edward Chalon, R.A[1]., at the command of the Queen, as a memento of her first visit to the House of Lords, July 17, 1837, and presented to the Duchess of Kent, the Queen's mother. It is curious to note that the official notice refers to the stamp as "One Shilling" whereas the value was expressed as "Twelve Pence." The reason for this being that in "Halifax Currency" fifteen pence were required to make one shilling Sterling. Add to this the fact that in New England the "shilling" was a current expression for 16 2/3 cents (10 pence currency), while in New York it represented 12½ cents (7½ pence currency) and we can readily see that in Canadian territory contiguous to these sections the number of pence to a "shilling" might often be a debatable quantity. As a matter of fact the French Canadians of Lower Canada made general use of the "shilling" as reckoned at 10 pence (20 cents) in the old currency, while the "York shilling" was extensively used in Upper Canada. "Twelve pence" was without doubt wholly intentional, therefore, as the designation of the stamp, and was a happy solution of any ambiguity in its use, even if it has proved a stumbling block to the understanding of latter day collectors.[2]

#4

10d 1855, 17c 1859, 1c 1908 and 3c 1934

Jacques Cartier (1491-Sept. 1, 1557). Famous navigator and explorer who laid the foundations of New France in North America. Born at St. Malo, Brittany, from which town he made his voyages of discovery. His first voyage, in 1534 resulted in the discovery of Canada, advancing as far west as Gaspe Basin, Chaleurs Bay, and the estuary of the St. Lawrence.

Upon his return the King (Francis I) offered him a commission to continue his explorations. In May, 1535, he set sail with three ships and 110 men determined to go up the great river as far as possible. He went as far as Hochelaga (Montreal) and returned to pass the winter at Stadacona (Quebec). He sailed for France in May, 1536, arriving at St. Malo July 16. Cartier made two more voyages, and in 1544 or 1545 retired to his manor at Limoilu where he stayed until his death.

The portrait on the Ten Pence stamp is a copy of a painting by Francois Riss, who was born in Moscow in 1804. Riss went to Paris, and according to Parkman executed this portrait in 1839. The last report has it that the painting is now in the Hotel-de-Ville, St. Malo.[3]

#5

½d 1857, 1c 1859, and 2c 1864

Queen Victoria. This was adapted from a 4d stamp of Great Britain (Appendix H #57) which in turn was an adaptation of the head on William Wyon's medal struck to commemorate Queen Victoria's visit to the city of London, 1837.

#6

½c to $5.00 1897

1897 Jubilee Issue. Portrait of Queen Victoria, shown on right was painted by *Heinrich von Angeli.* Hungarian painter, born 1840 at Odenburg, studied at

---

[1] CHALON, ALFRED EDWARD. Artist. Born February 15, 1781, at Geneva, Switzerland; died October 3, 1860, in London. A.R.A. 1812, R.A. 1816. Appointed painter in water-colours to Queen Victoria, and his portrait of Her Majesty in robes of State, July 17, 1837, was the source of the head on the Canadian Twelve pence stamp of 1851, as well as the New Zealand stamps of the first type which were engraved by Humphreys.

[2] This is quoted from Howe's book. Appendix H, shows that the designation "Twelve Pence" was intentional.

[3] See Also Appendix H. #34.

Vienna and Dusseldorf. Settled in Vienna 1862 as a portrait painter, and in 1877 became professor at the Vienna Academy. He visited Germany and Great Britain, painting the portraits of royalties of both countries. His portrait of Queen Victoria, painted by command, was copied for British Empire post card (1889), the Universal Postal Union card (1892), the 2, 3, and 5 rupees (1895), and the 3 pies (1899), of India, and Southern Nigeria (1901), as well as for the Canadian Jubilee Series of 1897.

The other portrait is the well known Chalon portrait, see #3.

#7

King Edward VII Issue, 1903, and 2c 1908

King Edward VII (1841-1910). His Most Excellent Majesty Edward the Seventh by the Grace of God of Great Britain, Ireland, and of the British Dominions beyond the Seas, King, Defender of the Faith, Emperor of India, eldest son of Her Majesty Queen Victoria and her Consort Prince Albert. Born November 9, 1841, and married on March 19, 1863, to H. R. H. Princess Alexandria of Denmark. Succeeded to the throne on January 22, 1901, and was crowned at Westminster Abbey on August 9, 1902. He died on May 6, 1910. From a photograph by Downey of London.

#8

½c 1908 and 3c 1935

The Princess of Wales (Later Queen Mary) (1867-194-). Her Serene Highness Princess Victoria Mary Augusta Louise Olga Pauline Claudine Agnes of Teck, born at Kensington Palace May 26, 1867. On July 6, 1893, she married George, Duke of York, only surviving son of Edward, Prince of Wales. On the accession of King Edward VII to the throne, January 22, 1901, she became the Princess of Wales, and on May 6, 1910, upon the death of King Edward VII, became Queen Consort to His Majesty King George V. From photographs.

#9

½c—1908 and Many Stamps to 1935

The Prince of Wales (Later King George V) (1865-1936). Born at Marlborough House June 3, 1865, only surviving son of King Edward VII and Queen Alexandria. Married July 6, 1893, Princess Victoria Mary of Teck. Succeeded to the throne as George V May 6, 1910, and was Crowned in Westminster Abbey June 22, 1911. Died Jan. 20, 1936. From photographs.

#10

1c 1908

Samuel de Champlain (c. 1567-1635). Born at Brouage, France, the son of a mariner from whom he inherited his love for the sea. In his early life he was a soldier, but in 1598 he began his career as a navigator and explorer. He made voyages to Mexico and the West Indies, was the first to suggest the uniting of the Atlantic and Pacific oceans by cutting the Isthmus of Panama.

In 1603 he made his first voyage to Canada, and penetrated as far as the Sault St. Louis. Finally on July 3, 1608, he laid the foundation of the "Abitation de Quebec." In the following year he discovered the lake which bears his name, and became involved in Indian wars. He continued his explorations in 1611, and again in 1613 reaching the shores of Lake Huron. In 1620 he was appointed Governor of New France. He was poorly supported by the home government, and finally had to capitulate to the English in 1629 after a year's siege. Quebec was restored to France, however, and Champlain was again appointed Governor in 1633. He died Christmas Day, 1635.

Champlain was an extensive writer and at least six works were published by him, mostly relating to his discoveries. See also #4.

#11

2c 1908

Queen Alexandria (1844-1925). Her Royal Highness Queen Alexandria Caroline Marie Charlotte Louise Julia, eldest daughter of King Christian IX of Denmark, born December 1, 1844. On March 10, 1863, she married His Royal Highness The Prince of Wales, who succeeded to the throne As King Edward VII on January 22, 1901. She survived King Edward by fifteen years, dying November 20, 1925. From a photograph by Downey of London. See also #7.

#11A

5c 1908

This design shows a view of the first settlement of Quebec, which was merely a fortified residence for the first settlers, with storehouse. The design is from a cut in Champlain's narrative of his voyage to New France, and the inscription "L'ABITATION DE QUEBECQ" is the title there given to it. The modern French word "habitation," anciently "abitation," may mean either a dwelling or a settlement, and hence the misdescription of the design as Champlain's House. Note the archaic spelling of Quebec, "Quebecq."

#12

7c 1908

General James Wolfe (1727-1759). Born in Kent, England, in 1727. He entered the army and rapidly rose from the ranks. He distinguished himself at the Siege of Louisburg in 1745, and by the time he was thirty had attained the rank of Lieutenant-General. He was the protege of William Pitt, "The Great Commoner" who, when in control of the affairs of state in 1757, placed Wolfe in supreme command of the forces sent to America to capture Quebec and seize control of New France. Arriving before Quebec in June, 1759, he made many unsuccessful attempts to capture the city. Finally in collaboration with Admiral Saunders, British Naval Commander in America, he succeeded in scaling the heights and on the morning of September 13, 1759, engaged Montcalm's troops in battle, defeating the French General. Wolfe was wounded three times and died on the field of battle, as Montcalm did.

The portrait is based on an engraving by Houston, from the original sketch by Harvey Smyth, Esq., who was General Wolfe's aide-de-camp at Quebec. Smyth was an amateur artist of considerable merit. The sketch is believed to be still in existence.

#13A

7c 1908

General Marquis de Pombal de Montcalm (1712-1759). Commander-in-Chief of the French forces in New France during the Seven Years War. He captured Forts Oswego and Ontario, and overthrew the British Army at Ticonderoga. With General Wolfe threatening Quebec Montcalm prepared to defend the city. By a ruse General Wolfe succeeded in scaling the heights and deployed his troops on the Plains of Abraham. In spite of his amazement Montcalm courageously attacked, but was defeated, losing his life on the field of battle as did his audacious opponent General Wolfe.

The portrait is from a painting that was long in the possession of the Montcalm family, and up to twenty years ago, at least, was at the Chateau D'Aveze, France. The artist is believed to be Baltazar Moncornet, an 18th Century painter.

#14

10c 1908

View of Quebec, 1700. This was adapted from Bacqueville de la Potheries "History de la Nouvelle France."

#15

15c 1908

This is a composite design inspired by a passage from Champlain's "Narrative," viz:—"With our canoes laden with provisions, our arms and some merchandise to be given as presents to the Indians, I started on Monday, May 27th, from the Isle of Sainte Helaine, accompanied by four Frenchmen and one Indian. A salute was given in my honour from some small pieces of artillery." This was one of Champlain's voyages of exploration into the then unknown west. The inscription includes another archaism the word "partment" being superseded by "depart."

#16

20c 1908

Arrival of Cartier at Quebec. The trio of vessels were "La Grand Hermione", 120 tons, "La Petit Hermione", 80 tons, and "La Hermionette", 40 tons.

NOTE: The descriptions of the later issues are of selected designs. Further details may easily be found in various reference works.

#17

1c and 12c 1927

Sir John Alexander MacDonald. One of the Fathers of the Confederation and a giant in Canadian politics. Born in Glasgow, Scotland, January 11, 1815, and when five years of age his family emigrated to Canada. He studied law and was called to the bar of Upper Canada in 1836. His political career began in 1844 when he was elected to the Legislative Assembly as representative for Kingston. Became Attorney General for Upper Canada in the McNabb-Morin Government. Was Prime Minister in 1857, which was short lived, but was appointed Postmaster General in 1858. This wasn't for long, however, his interest in Confederation being paramount. He took a foremost part in both the Quebec Conference of 1864, and the London Conference in 1866, which settled the details of the British North America Act.

In 1867 he was elected the first Prime Minister of the Dominion, and except for a brief period from 1873 to 1878 he held that position until his death in 1891 from a stroke of paralysis.

His brief eclipse (1873-78) was due to the "Pacific Scandal" concerning the construction of the transcontinental railway.

In 1867 he was made a K.C.B., and in 1884, a G.C.B. He was a member of the Privy Council from 1879. Honorary degrees were bestowed on him by Oxford and Cambridge Universities.

Sir Wilfred Laurier described him as "Canada's foremost citizen and statesman." No Canadian leader has dominated the political arena as did MacDonald, and although always an opportunist, and contributing little to political ethics, he achieved much that was fundamentally constructive and sound, achievements that have made possible the great Dominion of today.

#18

5c and 12c 1927

Sir Wilfrid Laurier. Born in St. Lin, L.C., near Montreal on Nov. 20, 1841, of French-Canadian parents, Laurier studied law at McGill University, Montreal, and was called to the bar in 1864. Although a Roman Catholic, his politics were Liberal, and in 1871 he was elected to the Provincial Assembly of Quebec as a member of that party. In 1874 he was elected to the Dominion Parliament, and during the temporary eclipse of MacDonald he served in 1877 in Prime Minister Mackenzie's cabinet when only thirty-six. When MacDonald returned to power, Laurier became the leader of the French-Canadian Liberals, and in 1884 was elected to the titular head of the party, and Leader of the Opposition.

The death of MacDonald in 1891 left the Conservatives without vigorous leadership, and in 1896 the Liberals came into power and Laurier was Prime Minister. As first French-Canadian Premier of Canada he retained that office for fifteen years. His chief claim to fame was his "Free Trade Within the Empire" policy, by which Great Britain was given preferential trade facilities with Canada.

He was made a G.C.M.G. in 1897 at the Diamond Jubilee, and was prominently associated with the Imperial Conference of 1907 and again in 1911, the year in which his government was defeated. He was also a member of the Legion of Honor of France.

He opposed conscription in 1914 to 1918, but served wholeheartedly, in the cause of the Allies. Death came in 1919 at the age of seventy-seven.

#19

5c 1927

Thomas D'Arcy McGee. One of the Fathers of the Confederation, was born in Carlingford, County Louth, Ireland, April 13, 1825. Emigrated to America, but returned to Ireland in 1845 and edited the Freeman's Journal of Dublin. This being too moderate he joined the "Nation" which was the organ of Young Ireland. His activities forced him to flee to America in 1848 disguised as a priest. In New York he founded "The Nation," and in 1850 went to Boston where he founded the "American Celt." In 1852 he moved his paper as well as himself to Buffalo, where he continued to publish his paper for five years. His youthful animosity to British rule cooling down, he moved to Montreal in 1857, where he founded "The New Era" which occupied his activities until 1858. In that year he was elected to the Legislative Assembly, and sat until 1867.

He was a delegate to the Charlottetown and Quebec Conferences in 1864, and labored unceasingly for two causes, reconciliation between the Roman Catholics and the Protestants, and Confederation. He was the "Magazine of Canadian Nationalism," and used his gift of oratory to proclaim the ideal of "one great nationality bound, like the shield of Achilles, by the blue rim of the ocean."

He incurred the enmity of the Fenian movement, and was assassinated at Ottawa on April 7, 1868, by a Fenian named Whalen, as he was returning from a late session of the House.

#20

20c 1927

Robert Baldwin. Born at York (Toronto), May 12, 1804. Studied law under his father, and was called to the bar of Upper Canada in 1825. Elected to the Legislative Assembly in 1829, but was defeated in the general election of 1830. His high character and ability early won for him general esteem. In 1836 he was appointed to the Executive Council of Upper Canada by Sir Francis Bond Head. This ended a month later. In 1841 he became Solicitor General, and in 1842 joined Lafontaine to form a ministry. He retired to private life in 1851, and died in Toronto in 1858, a comparatively young man.

#21

20c 1927

Sir Louis Hippolyte Lafontaine. Born at Boucherville, Chambly County, in 1807. Practiced law in Montreal, but owing to his connection with Louis Joseph Papineau left Canada in 1837. He returned in 1838 joining Robert Baldwin who put him in the Assembly where he represented various districts. In 1842 he joined the Baldwin-Lafontaine Ministry, and was Prime Minister 1848-1851. In 1854 he was made a baronet. He married twice and had two sons by his second wife, neither of which survived him, his title ceasing after his death in 1858.

#22

10c 1928

Mount Hurd. The picture of the mountain on this stamp was reproduced from an oil painting entitled "The Ice-Crowned Monarch of the Rockies," by Frederick M. Bell-Smith, an Englishman, who was at one time Director of the Toronto Art School. The original painting owned by Mr. R. D. Hume of Toronto, was loaned to the Government for reproduction. At either side is a Totem Pole of a bear fraternity belonging to a British Columbian tribe of Indians.

According to the Geographic Board of Canada

"HURD is a Mount and Pass south of confluence of Ottertail and Kicking Horse Rivers, Rocky Mountains, Kootenay district, B. C.

"Named after Major Hurd, a Canadian Pacific Railway Engineer; explored the Kananaskis and other rivers; name approved, 1904."

#23

12c 1928-29

Quebec Bridge. This magnificent cantilever structure with a central span of 640 feet, and a total length of 3,239 feet, is the largest of its kind in the world, and is an engineering marvel. The river channel between the piers is 1800 feet and at the highest tides the clearance is 150 feet, sufficient for the largest ocean vessels.

It is ten miles west of the city of Quebec and is used by the Canadian Pacific Railway which has a double line of tracks on it. The structure was completed in September, 1917, at a cost of $22,000,000. In 1929 a 16-foot highway and two sidewalks were added costing $5,000,000.

Almost as soon as railways began to expand the desirability of bridging the St. Lawrence near Quebec began to be broached. Several plans were made, and in 1899 the actual construction began. On August 29, 1907, however, the south cantilever arm collapsed, killing seventy men. In 1910 construction was resumed after new plans had been drawn up, and on September 11, 1916, disaster came again. The central span was being raised into place, when one of the hydraulic jacks slipped, sending the span into a corkscrew dive into the river, and causing the death of fourteen more men. Work was immediately started on completing the bridge, which was finally finished September 10, 1917.

#24

50c 1928-29

Schooner "Bluenose". This stamp has been acclaimed as the most beautiful stamp ever made. Certainly in the minds of many philatelists it holds first place. The design is from "Bluenose" and the United States contestant, "Columbia", from photographs taken on the occasion of the International Fishermen's Race off Halifax Harbor in the autumn of 1926 when she competed with the United States contestant "Columbia." The picture is a composite one, but in the arrangement care was taken that any variation in sailing points shown by the two vessels was within the bounds of practical off-shore sailing. It is perhaps needless to add that the race was won by the "Bluenose."

The Department, in selecting this subject, gave world-wide publicity to three important phases of Nova Scotian life and industry—fisheries, shipbuilding and seamanship.

The "Bluenose" was built at Lunenburg, Nova Scotia, in 1920-1921, by Smith and Rhuland. With the exception of the masts she is constructed throughout of Nova Scotian timber—spruce, oak, birch and pine. Notwithstanding her remarkable racing record she has been used as a practical fishing schooner year after year, with a crew of twenty men and a successful record of catches. She was on display at the Century of Progress Exhibition in Chicago in 1933, and proceeded to England in 1935, where she was in line at Spithead when the late King George V reviewed the British Fleet for the last time. It is rather curious, but *both* the vessels depicted are the "Bluenose"!

#25

50c 1930

Church at Grand Pré and Monument to Evangeline.—This is a composite picture of the Acadian home of Longfellow's fictive heroine, Evangeline, who seems so real as to be almost an historical personage. The little village is almost deserted now, but the church, a fairly modern structure at present used as a museum of Acadian relics, and the surrounding area, are maintained as a national institution and attract many visitors.

#26

$1.00 1930

Mt. Edith Cavell, in the Canadian Rockies, near Resplendent, British Columbia, which was named after the heroic Englishwoman who was executed by the German military authorities on the 13th of October, 1915 for activities which had exposed her to the extreme penalty. The noble mountain, over eleven thousand feet high, forms a dignified subject which has been well rendered by the engraver.

#27

10c 1931

Sir George Etienne Cartier. Born at St. Antoine, Vercheres County, September 6, 1814, probably a descendant of a collateral branch of the family of Jacques Cartier. Educated at St. Sulpice in Montreal, and was called to the bar in 1837. Joined the forces of Louis Joseph Papineau, and was forced, like Lafontaine, to take refuge in the United States. Returned to Canada in 1838 and ten years later was elected to the Legislative Assembly, where he represented Vercheres until 1861, when he was elected for Montreal which he served until his death in 1873. He was the leading French-Canadian member of the Great Coalition. He was created a baronet in 1868.

#28

5c 1932 and 5c 1935

The Prince of Wales (Now Duke of Windsor). His Royal Highness The Prince of Wales, Edward Albert Christian George Andrew Patrick David, eldest son of their majesties King George V and Queen Mary. Born June 23, 1894. On January 20, 1936, he succeeded to the throne on the death of his father, as King Edward VIII. He abdicated on December 10, 1936, in favor of his brother, now King George VI. From a photograph.

#29

5c 1933

Royal William. A vessel of 830 tons burthen, built at Cap Blanc, Quebec, by George Black and John Saxton Campbell for the run between Quebec and Halifax. Engines by Bennett & Henderson of Montreal. Length 176 feet, beam 27 feet 4 inches. Launched April 29, 1831.

At 5 a.m. on August 4, 1833, under the command of Captain McDougall, she left Quebec for London, via Pictou, taking 25 days in transit. In September, 1834, she was sold to the Spânish Government and re-named the Ysabel Segunda. In service against Don Carlos until 1837. Sent to London until claims against the Spanish Government by officers and crew were settled, late in 1837. Returned to Spain and soon afterwards was sent to Bordeaux. Timbers so decayed that she was converted into a hulk, after her engines had been placed in a new vessel, which was still in service in 1853.

Model in the Literary and Historical Society of Quebec (1895).

#30

10c 1934

United Empire Loyalists Issue. The central design is a reproduction of the United Empire Loyalist monument and is intended to perpetuate the memory of those colonists of New England who remained loyal to the British Government during the period of the American Revolutionary War, afterwards removing to what is now the Dominion of Canada, where they were given land on which to begin afresh. The Loyalists were all of the best class of law-abiding people in the Colonies, and were quite unused to the fearful hardships they had to bear in their new surroundings. They were the first English speaking people to settle in Upper Canada, and were undoubtedly a great factor in determining for all time the British connections which is now enjoyed in the Province of Ontario, and in all other parts of the Dominion of Canada.

The United Empire Loyalist Monument erected in Prince's Square in front of the Wentworth County Court House at Hamilton, Ontario, Canada, and unveiled May 23rd, 1929, Empire Day, was designed and executed by Mr. Sydney March, of Farnborough, Kent County, England, in the famous "Goddendene" studios of the March brothers, situated about fourteen miles from London, and in the same studios where the very handsome monument to Samuel de Champlain erected at Orillia, Ontario, was designed and executed by Mr. Vernon March.

The bronze plinth depicts the moment in the life of the Loyalist and his faithful partner when having drawn his lot number from the Government surveyor he and his wife are looking forward with satisfaction and keenness, not unmixed with curiosity, to the location of their new home in Canada after the turmoil of many years of warfare and after having lost all of their worldly possessions.

The pedestal of the monument, erected on a solid foundation of concrete, is constructed entirely and fittingly of Queenston dolomite stone from the quarries situated almost on the battlefield of Queenston Heights on the Canadian side of the Niagara River. The height of the stone pedestal is 7½ feet. The base measures 10½ feet by 18½ feet. The height of the loyalist is eight feet and the other figures are in proportion. The weight of the bronze group of four persons and the bronze base on which it stands is approximately three and a half tons. Two of the bronze panels attached to the sides of the pedestal and which tell the story of the loyalists, are three by six feet, while the remaining two are three by three feet.

The Front Panel Inscription (North), facing Main Street reads: "This monument is dedicated to the lasting memory of THE UNITED EMPIRE

LOYALISTS who, after the Declaration of Independence, came into British North America from the seceded American colonies and who, with faith and fortitude, and under great pioneering difficulties, largely laid the foundations of this Canadian nation as an integral part of the British Empire. Neither confiscation of their property, the pitiless persecution of their kinsmen in revolt, nor the galling chains of imprisonment could break their spirits or divorce them from a loyalty almost without parallel. 'No country ever had such founders— no country in the world—no, not since the days of Abraham.'—Lady Tennyson."

East Panel Inscription reads: "The United Empire Loyalists were distinguished for their devotion to principle, for their valour in battle during the American Revolution and for their loyalty and bravery in the war of 1812-1914 in defence of Canadian homes and hearths. They set the stamp of their character in the institutions of this country and handed them on to succeeding generations glorified by their sacrifices, enriched by their labours and made sure by their indomitable spirit."

West Panel Inscription reads: "Dedicated to the glory of God. Erected by Mr. and Mrs. Stanley Mills of Hamilton, in grateful memory of their United Empire Loyalist forebears and connections, the Davis, Gage, Hesse, Howell, Mills and Willson families. Unveiled Empire Day, May twenty-third, nineteen hundred and twenty-nine."

South Panel Inscription, facing Wentworth County Court House Building, reads: "For the unity of empire. The United Empire Loyalists, believing that a monarchy was better than a republic, and shrinking with abhorrence from a dismemberment of the empire, were willing, rather than lose the one and endure the other, to bear with temporary injustice. Taking up arms for the King, they passed through all the horrors of civil war and bore what was worse than death, the hatred of their fellow-countrymen, and, when the battle went against them, sought no compromise, but, forsaking every possession excepting their honour, set their faces toward the wilderness of British North America to begin, amid untold hardships, life anew under the flag they revered. 'They drew lots for their lands and with their axes cleared the forest and with their hoes planted the seed of Canada's future greatness.'—Elizabeth Bowman-Spohn."

#31

1c 1935 and 1939

Princess Elizabeth. Her Royal Highness Princess Elizabeth Alexandra Mary, born April 21, 1926. Upon her father's accession to the throne became Heiress-Apparent, and future Queen of Great Britain, and the British Commonwealth of Nations. From a photograph.

#32

2c 1935, and Many Stamps from 1937

The Duke of York (Now King George VI). His Royal Highness Albert Frederick Arthur George, Duke of York, Earl of Inverness, and Baron Killarney, was the second son of King George V and Queen Mary. Born December 14, 1895, and on April 26, 1922, married Lady Elizabeth Bowes-Lyon. Upon abdication of his brother, King Edward VIII, he became King George VI (December 11, 1936).

#33

10c 1935

Windsor Castle. Situated on a low but steep chalk cliff which rises abruptly from the Thames, it dominates the town and extensive flat region around it. It still preserves the original form as built by William the Conqueror, about 1080, in its division into a Lower Ward, containing chapels, cloisters, and deanery;

a Middle Ward, wholly occupied by the Round Tower; and an Upper Ward, surrounded by the apartments of the royal residence

Later monarchs, notably Henry III (1207-72) extended the castle, and Edward III who was born in the castle in 1312, rebuilt the whole on a more massive scale, the famous William of Wykeham being his architect. King David of Scotland, King John of France, and James I of Scotland were held captive; and the last espied from his prison bars Joan Beaufort, his future wife, walking in the garden below the Round Tower. The third great era of building of Windsor Castle dates from the time of George IV, when Sir Jeffrey Wyatville in 1824 began the extensive series of restorations and additions which were not finished until the reign of Queen Victoria, and left the majestic building as it is now.

Windsor Castle has seen little of actual war, though it was twice besieged during the reign of King John who was living there when he made his historic visit to Runnymede in 1215, while Prince Rupert made a futile attack on it in 1642. Edward the Black Prince, was married in the castle in 1361, and Henry VI (of Windsor) was born there in 1421.

A building as ancient as this has had many volumes of works, covering every aspect of its history, written by numerous authors, but it is hoped that this brief outline will be sufficient for our readers.

#34

10c 1935

Royal Canadian Mounted Police. This is a Constabulary force maintained by the Dominion Government in all provinces as far north as Ellsmere Land.

It was formed in 1873 as the North West Mounted Police, and in 1874 numbered only a little over 200 men. Its purpose was to police the vast prairie areas of the northwest territories. The rebellion of 1885 was too much for such a small number of men, but it undoubtedly prevented the uprising from becoming more serious.

The Mounted Police served in policing the Klondyke gold rush of 1898, and sent some members in the Canadian Contingent in the Boer War, 1899-1902.

In 1920, owing to the gradual elimination of many of its original reasons for existence, it was merged with the Dominion Police which protects Government property.

Discipline is semi-military and is commanded by a commissioner and deputy commissioner. At present it numbers about 2,500 men.

#35

20c 1935

Niagara Falls—Father Louis Hennepin is reputed to be the first white man to have seen the Falls of Niagara, December 6, 1678. Since then it has been a mecca for explorers, sightseers, and tourists in untold numbers. It has been described by numerous writers, and the subject of equally numerous artists. The stamp shows the Horseshoe or Canadian Falls. They are also on the United States 25c stamp of 1923-26.

#36

3c 1937 and 1939

Queen Elizabeth. Her Majesty Queen Elizabeth Angela Marguerite Bowes-Lyon was born August 4, 1900, the youngest of ten children of the Earl and Countess of Strathmore. She married His Royal Highness, King George VI, then Duke of York on April 26, 1922. Portrait from a photograph.

#37

10c 1938

Memorial Chamber, Souvenir Room, Peace Tower, Ottawa. The building completed in 1921. This room is built in beautiful Gothic architecture, with stained glass windows. Under the windows are several graven tablets bearing the names of all the members of the Canadian Expeditionary Forces and an inscription having the names of the 65,000 Canadian soldiers asleep in "Flanders Fields, where poppies grow; Between the crosses, Row on Row." In the foreground of the picture is the Alter of Sacrifices, "where there is kept the deathless roll of those who died in the Great War for Canada and the Empire." It is the Canadian "National Shrine," visited with the reverence that must perforce be attached to this beautiful dedication to the glory of a great virile Canada, growing steadily in the mature wisdom generously cast upon her by a gracious God.

#38

20c 1938

Fort Garry. Named after Nicholas Garry, Deputy Governor of Hudson's Bay Co., 1822-35. Built during the administration of Lord Selkirk in order to command the Red and Assiniboine Rivers, which made the fort a real gateway to the great prairie lands of the West. In 1870 a second and more substantial Fort, 240' x 280', was built to meet the needs of the settlement and the surrounding country. During this decade Louis Riel, a leader of the so-called Metis, led an abortive rebellion against the governor sent out to Manitoba. This was put down by troops under Colonel Wolseley.

The portion shown on the stamp is the north gate and is all that remains of the Fort that played so important a part in the Riel Rebellion. Sold to the city of Winnipeg in 1882 the remains are well covered with ivy and stand in the grounds of the Fort Garry Hotel, near the center of the city.

#39

50c 1938

Vancouver Harbor. The entrance to the famous land locked harbor of Vancouver at the head of Burrard Inlet, looking from the ocean, with the city of Vancouver in the background. First charted by Captain James Cook in 1778, it was explored by George Vancouver in 1791.

#40

$1.00 1938

Chateau de Ramezay, Montreal. This building was erected by Claude de Ramezay, Seigneur de la Gesse, eleventh governor of Montreal, in 1705. When Canada was ceded to the British in 1763, it became the official residence of the British Governors. When the Continental Army occupied Montreal during the American Revolution, Benjamin Franklin set up his printing press in the cellar. Benedict Arnold also was a resident in the chateau for a number of weeks. From 1841 to 1849 it was the Government Headquarters of both Upper and Lower Canada.

At present it is under the care of the Antiquarian and Numismatic Society of Montreal, who have made it into a museum. The architecture is typically early eighteenth century French.

#41

1c 1939

H. R. H. Princess Margaret Rose. The youngest child of their Royal Highnesses, born August 21, 1930. Upon her father becoming King George VI, she became second in line of succession to the throne. Portrait from a photograph.

#42

2c 1939

War Memorial, Ottawa. Designed and executed by the March Family of Farnborough, Kent, England. Unveiled by King George VI, May 15, 1939.

After the temporary erecting in Hyde Park, London, Eng., was shipped to Ottawa to await assembling.

Designed by Mr. Vernon March, who died before the actual construction was begun, it was carried to completion by his six brothers and his sister, and is without doubt one of the most impressive produced by the War. The memorial consists of a great archway of Laurentian granite surmounted by two figures allegorical of victory and liberty, the whole standing at a height of 60 feet. Through the archway itself passes a group of 19 figures, two of them mounted, and representing the various units of the Canadian Forces. These figures are 8 feet in height and are cast in bronze by a process which exposes all the ruggedness of the original modelling.

It has been the aim of the designers throughout to avoid anything in the nature of the glorification of war. It conveys afeeling of gratitude that out of the great conflict a new hope has sprung for future prosperity under conditions of lasting peace.

Mr. Vernon March is responsible for other monuments in Canada, notably that of Champlain, at Orillia, in Ontario, and the monument to the United Empire Loyalists who left the United States after the Revolution and settled in Canada.

#43

6c Air Mail—1938

This is a composite scene on the Mackenzie River. The stern wheel steamer is of a type which makes the trip from Forth Smith to Aklavik on the Arctic Ocean. The course of Mackenzie River was traced by Sir Alexander Mackenzie in 1789, hence its name. The river with its tributaries forms one of the principal means of communication into the North West Territories. The pontoon fitted airplane now carries the Arctic mail in this vast territory.

#44

Special Delivery. 20c, 1938; 10c, 1939. Arms of Canada

BY THE KING

A PROCLAMATION

Declaring His Majesty's Pleasure concerning the Ensigns Armorial of the Dominion of Canada

GEORGE R.I.

Whereas We have received a request from the Governor General in Council of Our Dominion of Canada that the Arms or Ensigns Armorial hereinafter described should be assigned to Our said Dominion.

We do hereby, by and with the advice of Our Privy Council, and in exercise of the powers conferred by the first Article of the Union with Ireland Act,

1800, appoint and declare that the Arms or Ensigns Armorial of the Dominion of Canada shall be Tierced in fesse the first and second divisions containing the quarterly coat following, namely, 1st Gules three lions passant guardant in pale or, 2nd, Or a lion rampant within a double tressure flory-caunter-flory gules, 3rd, Azure a harp or stringed argent, 4th, Azure three fleurs-de-lis or, and the third division Argent three maple leaves conjoined on one stem proper. And upon a Royal helmet mantled argent doubled gules the Crest, that is to say, On a wreath of the colours argent and gules a lion passant guardant or imperially crowned proper and holding in the dexter paw a maple leaf gules. And for Supporters On the dexter a lion rampant or holding a lance argent, point or, flying therefrom to the dexter the Union Flag, and on the sinister A unicorn argent armed chined and unguled or, gorged with a coronet composed of crosses-patée and fleurs-de-lis a chain affixed thereto reflexed of the last, and holding a like lance flying therefrom to the sinister a banner azure charged with three fleurs-de-lis or; the whole ensigned with the Imperial Crown proper and below the shield upon a wreath composed of roses, thistles, shamrocks and lillies a scroll azure inscribed with the motto—A mari usque ad mare, and Our Will and Pleasure further is that the Arms or Ensigns Armorial aforesaid shall be used henceforth, as far as conveniently may be, on all occasions wherein the said Arms or Ensigns Armorial of the Dominion of Canada ought to be used.

Given at Our Court at Buckingham Palace, this twenty-first day of November, in the year of Our Lord One thousand nine hundred and twenty-one, and in the twelfth year of Our Reign.

GOD SAVE THE KING

The motto is taken from the Latin version of the 72nd Psalm, "Et dominabitur *a mari usque ad mare,* et a flumine usque ad terminos orbis terrarum"; the translation reads, "He shall have dominion also *from sea to sea,* and from the river unto the ends of the earth."

APPENDIX P

Supplementary Notes and Correspondence on
PAPERS

#1

The Papers of the Pence Issues

Micrometric measurement of a large number of 3d and 6d stamps on laid and wove papers led to interesting conclusions.

We examined 150 3d and 50 6d on laid paper, and 350 3d and 100 6d on wove paper.

A. Summary of the Examination of the Papers of the 3d 1851 Stamp

We picked from the lot of some five hundred copies, well mixed, one hundred examples. Upon sorting they broke into the following groups—

(a) Laid paper .... 12 copies
(b) Wove paper .... 80 copies
(c) Ribbed paper .... 8 copies
                                                                      ———
                                                                      100 copies

Micrometric measurement showed;

(a) Laid: Extremes .00275″ to .00350″ variation., .00075″ or 27%
    60%   .00300″
    25%   .00275″
    ———
    85%

(b) Wove: Extremes .00220″ to .00450″ variation.
    50%   .00250″ to .00275″   .00230″, or 104%.
    20%   .00300″ to .00325″
    ———
    70%

Only 12% were extremely thin, or extremely thick.

(c) Ribbed Paper. Of the eight copies measured six were .0030″, one was .0032″, and the other .0028″. The extreme was only .0004″ or 14%, and this variation is very slight indeed.

Some consideration should be given to the impression, as the amount of ink used may give measurements .0002″ in difference, so that care should be taken to make due allowance for this factor. All the figures given above include the impression. We would also warn students that the translucency of the paper, its feel or crispness, and conversely the opacity, or the softness of a paper are not reliable indicia of the actual thickness of the paper. See also #2b, 3.

B. Summary of the Examination of the Papers of the 3d and 6d Stamps.

Total number of stamps examined 650. Results were as follows:

Laid Paper.
    Thinnest   .00275″
    Thickest   .00350″
    ————
    Difference .00075″ = 27% in range.
    Average = .00290″

Wove Paper.
  Thinnest .00220″
  Thickest .00450″

Difference .00230″=104% in range.
  60% were between .00225″ and .00275″
  28% were between .00300″ and .00375″

88% were between .00225″ and .00375″

Only 12% were either less than .00225″ or over .00375″ with the majority at the thin extreme. There was also a notable lack of specimens ranging between .00275″ and .00300″.

Ribbed wove.
  Thinnest .00280″
  Thickest .00320″

Extremes .00040″=14% in range.

82% measured .00300″; the remaining 18% being equally divided; 9% thinner than average; 9% thicker than average.

The cause of the ribbing was given to us by Dr. Dard Hunter, in answer to our letter enclosing two copies of the 3d on this paper.

November first mcmxliii

Dear Mr. Boggs:

The two Canadian stamps sent in your letter of October twenty-eighth are returned herewith.

In an examination of the paper upon which these stamps are printed it is our belief that the slight horizontal lines are the result of the actual paper manufacture. The lines were in all probability caused by the wires of the mould upon which the paper was formed. While the paper appears to be "wove" it is not unusual to find the wires of one direction a trifle more pronounced than the wires of the other direction. This would cause the very slight ribbing that appears in the stamps. We feel certain that these lines are in the paper and it is likely that there was no intention on the part of the papermaker to make the paper appear ribbed. It is difficult, of course, to arrive at a definite conclusion with such small bits of paper as postage stamps afford, but we feel that we have given you a proper diagnosis.

Very truly yours,
Dard Hunter Paper Museum of M. I. T.

The variation in the wove papers is not surprising as they were in use for over six years, there being twelve orders for the 3d, and seven orders for the 6d, from 1852 to 1859. (Appendix J #1).

The laid paper printings were probably all on the same lot of paper, the total being three reams, hence the comparatively little variation in thickness.

#2

Further data on the paper for the Pence and 1859 stamps.

Abstracts from a small book which is a reprint from *"The 'Records' of the American Catholic Historical Society"* of an article, "The Willcox Paper Mill (Ivy Mills), 1729-1866."

(a). P. 33ff. "After the year 1832 the mill was engaged almost wholly in making bank paper, until the death of James M. Willcox, which occurred on March 4th, 1854."

"From that time the mill was operated by his sons Mark, James, and Joseph Willcox, under the firm name of J. M. Willcox & Sons, until November 1859; when it passed into the possession of his youngest son, Henry B. Willcox. The latter continued to manufacture paper there until March, 1866, when the business of manufacturing hand made paper was abandoned."

"On October 20th, 1850, James M. Willcox sent a printed circular[1], with samples of bank paper, to all of the banks in the United States. In it he stated that he had made the manufacture of bank-note paper, for the last twenty years, almost an exclusive business. This referred only to the department of hand made paper; as he, at that time, owned two mills (in which paper was made on Fourdrinier machines), one erected in 1837, and the other in 1845, at Glen Mills, 2½ miles from Ivy Mills.

(b). P. 39. "The range in thickness of bank paper in former times varied from 12 to 18 pounds per 1,000 sheets; each sheet making 8 notes."

(c). P. 48. "Until about the year 1832 bank paper was made only in comparatively small lots, at Ivy Mills, to supply the orders from banks or bank-note engravers; but after that date, a large supply, of various kinds, was usually kept on hand, ready for immediate delivery."

(d). A partial list of the engravers and printers who bought Willcox paper is given on Pps. 53 and 54 of this book:

P. 53. "1826 Aug. 19th Tracy R. Edson, New York, N. Y.
"1828 Dec. 13th Rawdon, Wright & Co., New York, N. Y.
"1832 Apr. 20th Rawdon, Wright, Hatch & Co., New York, N. Y.
"1833 Apr. 30th New England Bank Note Co., Boston, Mass.
"1850 Oct. Rawdon, Wright, Hatch & Edson, New York, N. Y., and Cincinnati, O[2].

(e). P. 55. "The paper usually contracted in size, to the amount of three or four per cent, in the process of drying. Bank paper was made on foolscap moulds" (Foolscap 14¼ x 16¾")[3].

#3

Further evidence concerning the variation in handmade paper is given herewith.
Quotation from "PAPER MAKING" by Dard Hunter, published by Alfred A. Knopf. 1943. Pps. 304-305. (Italics ours.)

Aside from the deckle edges on the handmade paper, which make registration in printing difficult, unless the hand press with pin register is used, there are numerous other imperfections in handmade paper that cause difficulties to the printers who utilize paper of this kind. *Probably the most annoying of these defects is a disparity of thickness in the separate sheets,* as it is humanly impossible for a vat man to gauge each sheet of a ream so it will weigh exactly the same as every other sheet. In forming paper in a hand-mould the worker has only his sense of weight and balance to guide him, and the thickness of each individual sheet of paper depends entirely upon the skill of the craftsman. It would be rare indeed to find a workman who could always dip precisely the same amount of liquid pulp with his mould, for the weight of each sheet must be judged while the fibre is saturated with water. A newly formed sheet of moist rag fibre weighing several pounds might after drying weigh only as many ounces. Only a superhuman artisan could be expected to form all sheets of a ream identical in weight, but it is surprising how dextrous the vatman becomes after many years of practice. The difficulty of moulding paper, however, *does not lessen the trouble and worry involved in printing upon paper that is uneven in thickness and lacking in uniformity. If one sheet of paper is thin and another heavy, there is certain to be a difference of impression when the paper is put through the press. A far more exasperating defect, sometimes present in handmade paper, is that one portion of a single sheet is heavier than another. While this difficulty is not so common as variation in the weight of separate sheets, it is nevertheless prevalent to some extent in the finest handmade papers and the result is that undue hardship is caused the pressman when he prints upon it, either on a hand press or one operated by power.* Inasmuch as the weight and thickness of handmade paper is so irregular, paper of this kind is seldom sold by weight, the tendency being to list the paper as bulking so much to the ream.

---

1. See # 6 where this circular is quoted in full.
2 We are of the opinion that some of the paper in this order was used for the first Canadian stamps.
3 The plates for the pence issues had about 8" x 10" to 10" x 10" of engraved surface which with margins was about 9" x 11" to 11" x 11". A finished sheet after being trimmed would measure approximately 13" x 16". (See #8).

Another characteristic of handmade paper that makes for difficulty in printing is that the sheets are not always square. The moulds upon which the paper is formed are perfectly true, as well as the wooden deckle boundary rims, but it is seldom that the finished paper dries absolutely square and even at the four corners[1].

The variation in shade of the early pence printings is due in part to the vagaries of handmade paper.

#4

Pursuing our investigations further we directed our inquiries to Dr. Dard Hunter, the well-known authority on paper.

February 15, 1943.

My dear Dr. Hunter:—

I am preparing a book on the Postage Stamps and Postal History of Canada, and am at the stage of writing about the first issue which appeared in 1851.

These stamps were printed by the well known engraving firm of Rawdon, Wright, Hatch & Edson of New York. I have fairly definite information that the engravers bought their paper from the Ivy Mills run by Willcox. In your reference material have you any data about the Ivy Mills which would show that they made paper for Rawdon, Wright, Hatch & Edson, and their successors the American Bank Note Company?

If it is not imposing on you I would like to send you several copies of the first Canadian stamps for your opinion as to the paper, and how the "stitch" watermark occurs.

Anticipating the pleasure of hearing from you shortly, I remain

Very truly yours,
(Sgd.) Winthrop S. Boggs.

#5

Dr. Hunter's reply was most cordial and helpful.

February seventeenth mcmxliii

Dear Mr. Boggs:

In your letter of the fifteenth you ask if we can establish any connection with the Willcox Mill and the bank-note engraving firm of Rawdon, Wright, Hatch & Edson.

While we have considerable material relating to Ivy Mills we have not been able to trace directly a sale of paper for the 1851 issue of Canadian stamps. *We have, however, copied a few references which may be of help to you in showing that this paper mill actually made paper for the engravers in question.*

We have gone through a number of original letters written by Joseph Willcox, who assumed management of Ivy Mills sometime previous to 1858, but they reveal nothing about the paper for the Canadian postage stamps. We have various specimens of Willcox paper all through the 1840-66 period so if you would care to send a stamp or two we would be able to compare the paper.

Very truly yours,
Dard Hunter Paper Museum of M. I. T.
(Sgd.) Dard Hunter / m Curator

The most important reference is the circular quoted herewith:

#6

Circular issued in 1850 by James M. Wilcox (in Paper Museum of the Massachusetts Institute of Technology). Quoted through the courtesy of Dr. Dard Hunter, the curator of the museum.

Dear Sir:—

Inclosed are three samples of BANK-NOTE PAPER, each a quarter of a sheet, of different thicknesses, but made in the manner (handmade), and of the same material.

The subscriber has been a manufacturer of Bank-note paper for nearly a

---

1. This is overcome by trimming the paper.

half century, and for the last twenty years has made it almost an exclusive business.

After various experiments, he thinks he has succeeded in making a paper peculiarly adapted to that purpose. It is made of a material different from any heretofore used, being tough and flexible, having a surface not liable to crack or wear rough, and susceptible of receiving the finest steel or copper-plate impressions; of which the samples are specimens.

He has also in store a large quantity of Bank-note paper that is well seasoned, being from eight to ten years old, of which samples will be forwarded without delay when required. Every sheet is warranted perfect, and equal to sample.

The price of this paper is $22.50 per 1000 sheets, and is for SALE BY JAS. M. WILLCOX & CO., NO. 7 MINOR STREET, PHILADELPHIA, and at manufacturer's prices, by

Messrs. RAWDON, WRIGHT, HATCH & EDSON, Engravers and Copper-plate Printers, New York, New Orleans and Cincinnati.

NEW ENGLAND BANK-NOTE CO., Boston.

Messrs. TOPPAN, CARPENTER, CASILEAR & CO., Engravers and Copper-plate Printers, New York, Philadelphia and Cincinnati.

Messrs. DANFORTH, BALD & Co., Engravers and Copper-plate Printers, New York and Philadelphia.

Messrs. WELLSTOOD, BENSON & HANKS, Engravers and Copper-plate Printers, New York.

Messrs. DRAPER, WELSH & CO., Engravers and Copper-plate Printers, Philadelphia.

Very respectfully yours, &c.,
Ivy Mills, October 20, 1850.   JAMES M. WILLCCOX.

NOTE—The circular is printed in script and Gothic type on thin bank-note paper measuring 8¼ x 10½ inches. Observe that this is similar in size to the Pence plates, and also that in #2d, above, Rawdon, Wright, Hatch & Edson ordered paper in October, 1850, the date of the circular.

#7

In accordance with Dr. Hunter's suggestion we sent some 3d stamps for examination.

Dear Dr. Hunter:—   February 19, 1943.

Many thanks for your courteous reply to my recent letter asking for information concerning the Willcox Mills.

I take the liberty of enclosing herewith *ten copies of the 3d Canada 1858, a pair, a strip of three, and five singles.*

I would appreciate it if you could let me know if this is Willcox paper, and if so I presume it is handmade. *Furthermore in the case of the stitch watermark, I would be pleased to know how such a variety occurs.*

Yours very truly,
Winthrop S. Boggs.

#8

Dear Mr. Boggs: February twenty-fourth mcmxliii

Since receiving the Canadian stamps we have been able to compare this stamp paper with the Willcox product from the year 1850.

While it is impossible to state definitely, we have a paper dated 1850 that is a very close match for the Canadian stamp paper. This particular sheet is a specimen submitted to the trade in October, 1850. Another paper that very closely resembles the stamp paper is a half sheet written upon by Joseph Willcox. The letter was written April 17, 1916, and addressed to me. In its original size this sheet would have been 13 x 16 inches. The paragraph relating to this paper reads: "The paper I now write on is bank-note paper made by my father James M. Willcox in 1850." Postage stamps do not permit of much examination as they are so small and the paper covered to such an extent with the printing. *However, either of the two papers examined would be identical with the Canadian stamp paper you have sent.* We would not wish to state definitely that such was the case, but it appears likely. *The "stitch" marks should not be* taken too seriously as they appear to be nothing more than perhaps a mended mould.

The ten stamps are returned herewith. Should you ascertain anything further relative to the possible Willcox fabrication of this paper we would be glad to learn of your findings.

                  Very truly yours,
                  Dard Hunter Paper Museum of M. I. T.
                  Dard Hunter, Curator.

#9

In another letter Dr. Hunter referred us to Mr. R. C. Pierce of the Crane Paper Co., Dalton, Mass., which resulted in the following correspondence:

Mr. Ruben C. Pierce,   March 30, 1943.
Crane & Co.,
Dalton, Mass.
My Dear Mr. Pierce:—

Dr. Dard Hunter of the Massachusetts Institute of Technology has very kindly given me your name as one who may be able to answer a question of mine concerning early bank note papers.

I am writing a book on the Postage Stamps and Postal History of Canada, and as the issues from 1851 to 1868 were printed by Messrs. Rawdon, Wright, Hatch & Edson, and their successors the American Bank Note Company, the question of the papers used by these firms is a matter of some interest.

My investigations seem to show that until about late 1857 a handmade paper from the Willcox Mill was used. Early in 1858 or thereabouts the paper becomes much more uniform in texture and thickness, and takes a much better impression.

Dr. Hunter has informed me that the Crane Mill perfected a method of making bank note paper by machine about that time.

The question therefore is, *did the Crane Co. furnish paper to the various bank note companies in general and R. W. H. & E., and the A. B. N. in particular beginning in 1858?*

If necessary I would be glad to send a number of copies of these early stamps for identifications of the paper.

I trust that my inquiry is not of too confidential a nature as to preclude giving me some information.

Awaiting with interest your reply, and in the meantime thanking you for any courtesy you may be able to extend, I remain,
                  Sincerely yours,
                  Winthrop S. Boggs.

#10

Dear Sir: April 2, 1943.

I have received your letter of March 30th with reference to paper made for postage stamps early in 1858. I am afraid that I cannot give you any very definite information as to whether the paper you refer to was made by Crane & Co., or someone else. However, *we did start selling the American Bank Note Company in Philadelphia early in 1861 and previous to that we had sold Bank Note paper made on a fourdrinier machine to quite a number of concerns doing steel engraved printing.*

I think if you would be willing to send us some specimens of stamps printed about this time that you evidently refer to that we could perhaps match up the paper with some samples that we have in our museum.

At this time I have not made any search except through office records. If you wish to send up the stamps I will see that they are promptly returned to you with such information as may be of interest to you.
                  Yours very truly,
                  CRANE & CO., INC.
                  R. C. Pierce, Sec'y.

#11

Mr. R. C. Pierce,　　　　　　　　　　　　　　　　　　　　April 4, 1943.
Crane & Co.,
Dalton, Mass.
Dear Mr. Pierce:—
　　I take the liberty of enclosing herewith some of the early Three Pence stamps of Canada which were current from 1851 to 1859 inclusive.
　　The strips of four and three are from the early printings, and are, we believe, on a handmade paper by the Willcox people. About December, 1857, a much more even textured and whiter paper came into use which takes the impression from the plate much better.
　　The three pairs are from later printings, and it would be of great help to determine if possible the maker of this better paper.
　　The American Bank Note Co., as you probably know was formed in 1858, and Rawdon, Wright, Hatch & Edson were among the firms in the consolidation. This firm had the contract for printing the Canadian stamps, and the American Bank Note Company continued to do so until the formation of the Dominion in 1867 when the British American Bank Note Co. secured the contract and from April 1868 to 1897 printed all the Canadian stamps.
　　Would it be possible to let me know whether your firm supplied paper to the firms mentioned above and if so for what years?
　　Thanking you for your courtesy, and enclosing return postage and registration, I remain
　　　　　　　　　　　　　　　　　Yours very truly,
　　　　　　　　　　　　　　　　　Winthrop S. Boggs.

#12

Dear Mr. Boggs:　　　　　　　　　　　　　　　　　　　　April 21, 1943.
　　Replying to your letter of April 4th which was received together with the specimen Canadian postage stamps which you state were currently used from 1851 to 1859 inclusive.
　　I have just found time to make a search of samples that are now in our museum of paper made back during the period in question and *I am enclosing a swatch of the samples together with the return of the postage stamps which you sent. While there is quite a direct similarity in some of our paper to the better Canadian stamps it is pretty hard to definitely say whether they were printed on Crane's paper or not. I would say, however, that the small specimen marked 1858 and 1859 that micrometers .003 is very close to those, the thickness and general appearance of the paper is about the same.*
　　There is a question, however, as to whether the postage stamp is of quite as good a quality as our paper. It is awfully hard to determine the quality of paper without disintegrating the fibers and of course we would not want to do that with your postage stamps.
　　The small samples of paper which we are sending to you need not be returned as they have been clipped from larger sheets which we have on file in our museum.
　　　　　　　　　　　　　　　　　Yours very truly,
　　　　　　　　　　　　　　　　　　　CRANE & CO., INC.
　　　　　　　　　　　　　　　　　　　　　R. C. Pierce.

　　NOTE: Five samples of paper were enclosed as follows: 1854—.0020," 1857—.0035," 1858—.0030," 1859—.0030," 1850-60—.0025."

#13

Mr. R. C. Pierce,　　　　　　　　　　　　　　　　　　　　June 4, 1943.
Crane & Co.,
Dalton, Mass.
Dear Mr. Pierce:—
　　This is a somewhat belated letter of thanks for your most helpful letter of April 21, last. *Your micrometric measurements agree closely with mine, and in the case of the so-called ribbed paper the thickness is remarkably uniform, indicating a machine made product.*

7-P　　　　　　　　　　　　　　　　　　　　　　　　　　　815

Enclosed are three copies of the 3p beaver which you may use anyway you see fit, even complete destruction in order to determine if possible whether or not the paper is your product, or another mill's.

I believe I mentioned before that the early papers are apparently from the Ivy Mills of Chester, Pa., and in 1857 or 8 the paper becomes more uniform, and I suspect a machine made product of your mills.

Anticipating the pleasure of hearing from you at your convenience, and appreciating anything you can do to enlighten us on the paper of the 1851-58 issues of Canada, I remain

Yours very truly,
Winthrop S. Boggs.

#14

Dear Mr. Boggs: June 14, 1943.

I duly received your letter of June 4th and turned the specimen stamps over to our laboratory for their inspection and research.

Unfortunately, paper made so many years ago had characteristics that were different, of course, from what they are today and, while it could be said that we ought to know our own make of paper, it is an impossibility to make a definite statement as to whether Crane & Company made the paper on which these stamps were printed or not.

While I have no foundation for making such a statement, I feel that Crane & Company probably did not make that paper. *On the other hand, we were supplying paper to the people who were printing stamps at that time and whether it was used for stamps or other purposes we do not know.*

Regretting that I cannot enlighten you on the paper used in the issue of Canada stamps from 1851-58, I am

Yours very truly,
CRANE & CO., INC.
R. C. Pierce.

This last letter of Mr. Pierce is not conclusive, but since Crane & Co. "were supplying paper to the people who were printing stamps at that time" is some evidence that R.W.H. & E. used the regular bank note paper supplied by Crane for the printing of stamps. The difficulty Mr. Pierce speaks of in the second paragraph of the above letter is due in part to the effect of aging, and the chemical reaction of ink and gum on the paper. We feel it a reasonable assumption that the later printings of the Pence issues were on a paper supplied by Crane & Co.

The machines used for this type of paper were cylinder machines similar to those patented by John Dickinson, in England in 1809.

#15

Special Notes on Papers C, D and F of the 1868 Issue

Paper C. The watermark "E & G Bothwell—Clutha Mills" is in two lines of sans-serif letters. The upper line is 140 mm., and the lower line 120 mm. long. The capitals are 13 mm. high, while the other letters are 12½ mm. high. The two lines of watermark are spaced 11½mm. apart so that not more than twenty-two or less than fourteen stamps of each sheet can show portions of the watermark. Aside from normal the watermark may exist inverted, reversed, or inverted and reversed, but never vertically.

The paper bearing this watermark was made for Andrew Whyte & Son, of Edinburgh, and Glasgow, by Messrs. W. & J. Sommerville, Bitton Mills, Gloucester, England. The watermark is a coined *name* "E. & G." meaning "Edinburgh & Glasgow," "Bothwell" is from "Bothwell St., Glasgow," where a warehouse of Whyte & Son was located, while "Clutha" is an ancient name for the "Clyde." The last dandy roll with this watermark was destroyed in a fire in the 1890's. The dandy rolls were made by Messrs. T. & J. Marshall & Co., of Stoke Newington, England, which firm invented the "dandy roll" about 1830.

Paper D. Apparently a small lot of this paper was used late in 1868 possibly due to a shortage of the regular paper; to use up a small surplus stock discontinued; but what is more reasonable is that some of the laid paper intended to be used for correspondence by the firm after having the letterhead printed on it was inadvertently used in printing some of the 1c and 3c stamps. We have seen several letters dated in the 1870's bearing the B.A.B.N. Co.'s letterhead, on a laid paper, with the watermark of "Alex^r Pirie & Sons" in Old English letters! A careful search through the laid paper stamps may result in finding examples with part of the watermark. The laid lines are always horizontal and vary from 13 to 15 vergeures to 2 cm. Care should be taken to avoid wove paper stamps with faked laid lines. Alexander Pirie & Sons were a Scottish mill located at Stoneywood and from 1856 also at Culter, near Aberdeen. The firm is still in business under the title of the Culter Mills Paper Co. Ltd.

Paper F. This paper is rare and occurs only on the 15c value. We have examined seven copies and illustrate two. It is remarkably uniform in thickness. The watermark was handmade of bent wire, a method discontinued about 1875.

#16

Note on the Paper used for the Small Queen Issues 1870-1897.

In reply to our inquire enclosing a number of these stamps Dr. Hunter replied as follows:

Dear Mr. Boggs:

Your letter of the twenty-second of December has been forwarded to me from M. I. T., hence the delay in answering.

The paper used in printing these stamps would appear to be machine-made and as near as I can see from a casual examination they are made from rags. I do not like to destroy the stamps for a chemical examination, but it is doubtful if such an examination would reveal the presence of wood. From outward appearances I would suggest that the stock is linen and cotton which would be in keeping with the period. It is unlikely that handmade paper would have been used as late as 1868, especially in the United States or Canada.

The stamps are being returned intact.

Sincerely yours,
Dard Hunter

APPENDIX Q

Plate Diagrams

1. Plate of 200—10 x 10+10 x 10—two panes of 100 separated by a gutter 10-10½ mm. wide. 1851. 3d, 6d, 12d. 1st state.
    (a) Cut in half Oct. Dec. 1857, as shown by dotted arrows, and imprints added. 2nd state.

2. Plate of 120—12 x 10 one pane.
   ½d, 7½d, 10d. Imprints on ½d and 7½d. 1854.
   Second state of ½d plate had rows indicated by dotted arrows removed, by stoning, late 1858.

3. Plate of 100 (10 x 10). 1859.

4. Plate of 100 (10 x 10). Large Queens of 1868, also Small Queens of 1870. Imprints located as shown.
    (a) ½c Plate of 200 (10 x 10+10 x 10) two panes.
    (b) Plate of 200 (20 x 10) one pane.

5. Jubilee Plates of 1897, and Special Delivery Plates of 1898, 1920. Imprint at top only.
    (a) (10 x 10).
    (b) (5 x 10).

6. Maple Leaf Plates, 1898 (10 x 10 + 10 x 10).

7. Numeral Plates 1899.
    (a) Regular plate of 200 (10 x 10+10 x 10) two panes.
    (b) Booklet plate of 120 (6 x 20) twenty panes.

8. King Edward VII Plates, 1903.
    (a) Plate of 200 (10 x 10+10 x 10) two panes.
    (b) Plate of 400 (10 x 10+10 x 10+10 x 10+10 x 10) four panes, upper panes with imprint "TOP."
    (c) Booklet plate same as numeral booklet plate.

9. King George V Plates, 1912-26.
    (a) Plate of 400 (20 x 20) four panes, some separated by a gutter, other plates not.
    (b) Booklet plates same as numeral booklet plate.

10. King George V-VI 360 Subject Booklet Plate 1928-1944. Sixty Panes.

11. Registered Letter Stamp Plates. See Chapter on these stamps.

12. Special Delivery Plates.
    (a) Fifty subjects (5 x 10). Same as 50 subject Jubilee plates.
    (b) One hundred subjects (10 x 10). Same as 100 subject Jubilee plates.

13. Postage Due Plates. Similar to the regular issue plates, but owing to the horizontal format the imprints will be at sides or V.V. when compared with regular issues.

14. Official Seal Plate. Similar to 50 subject Registered Letter Plates.

The other plate layouts are fully covered in the respective chapters. The recent issues are so common in blocks and sheets that the location of the imprints, etc. is familiar to all collectors.

Plate Layout #1

(a) First State—Plate of 200 (10 x 10 + 10 x 10).
1851-57 3d, 6d and 12d.

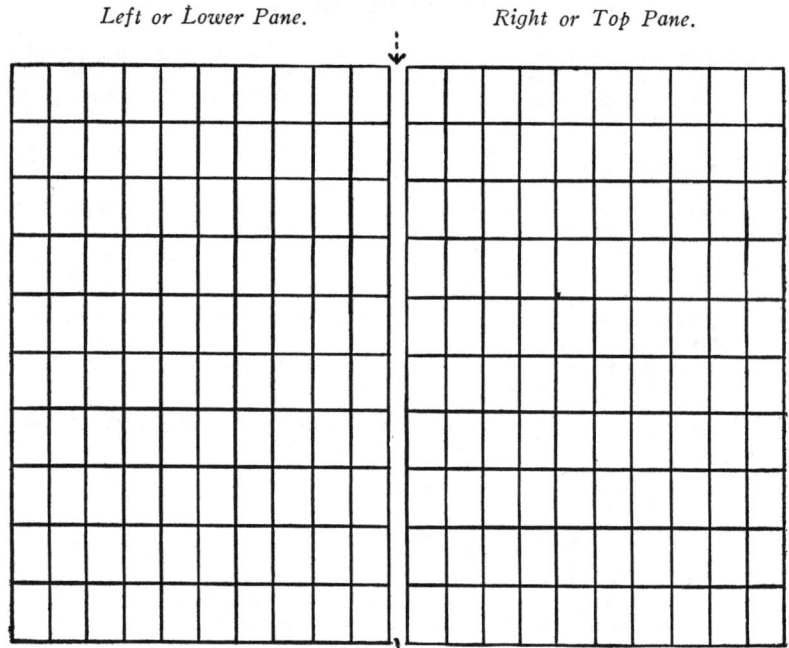

Left or Lower Pane.   *Right or Top Pane.*

GUTTER 10 - 10½ MM. WIDE

(b) Second State—Plates Cut in Half and Imprints Added.
1857-58 3d and 6d.

Plate Layout #2

Plate of 120 (12 x 10).

(a) 1854-57 ½d First State, 7½d and 10d.

(b) 1857 second state of ½d plate had two left rows stoned off as shown by the dotted arrows, making 100 subject sheets, for perforating.

Location of Imprints given in chapter on these issues.

Plate Layout #3
1859 Issue. Plate of 100 (10 x 10). All values.

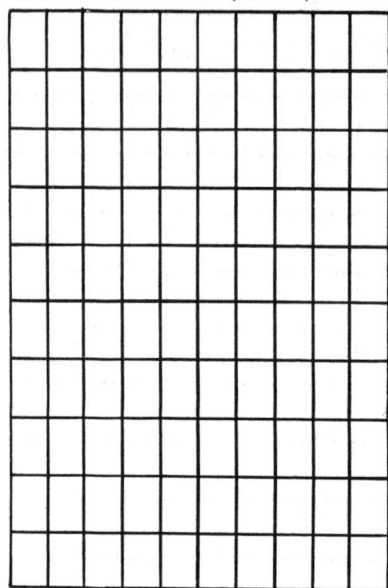

Imprints added in 1865. Location given in chapter on these issues.

Plate Layout #4
1868 Large Queens. Plate of 100 (10 x 10).

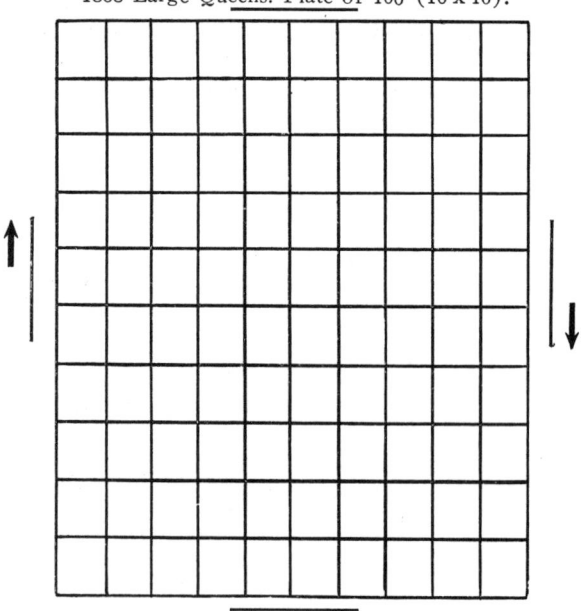

Plate Layout #4a

½c 1882

The Small Queen Plates.

The "Montreal and Ottawa" plates of 1870-74, the "Montreal" plates of 1875-88 and the 2c "Ottawa" plate of 100 were similar in the layout to the Large Queen plates, excepting of course the ½c of 1882. This was in two panes of 100 (10 x 10 + 10 x 10), shown herewith.

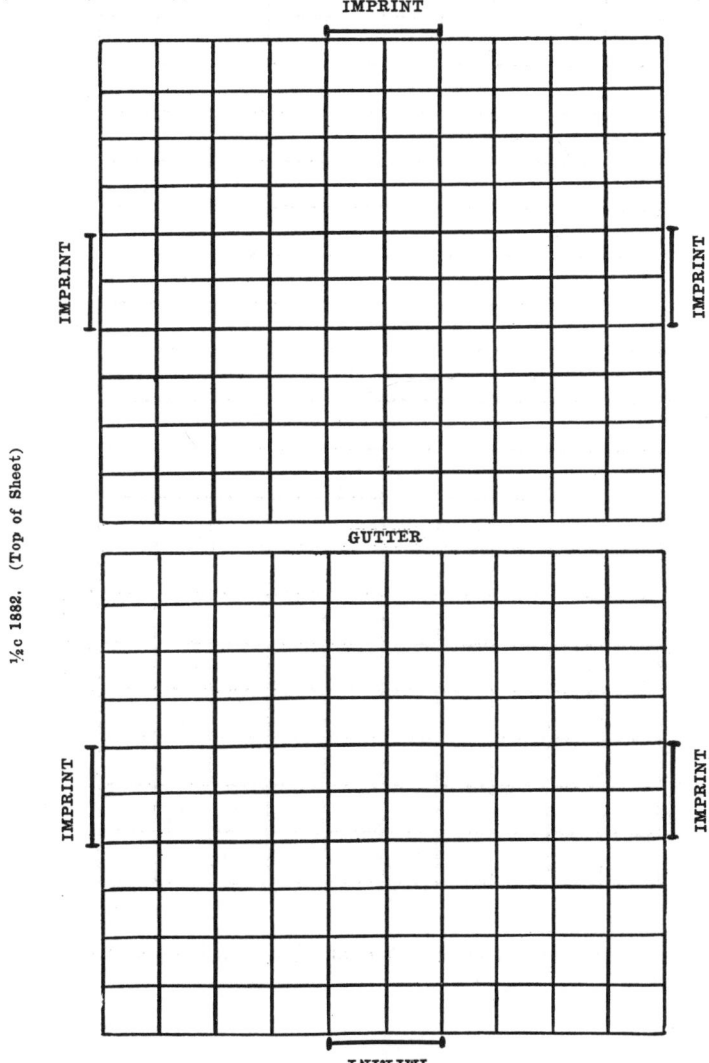

Imprints located as shown.

Plate Layout #4b

The 1892 "Ottawa" plates of 200 were of one pane. 1c, 2c, 3c only.

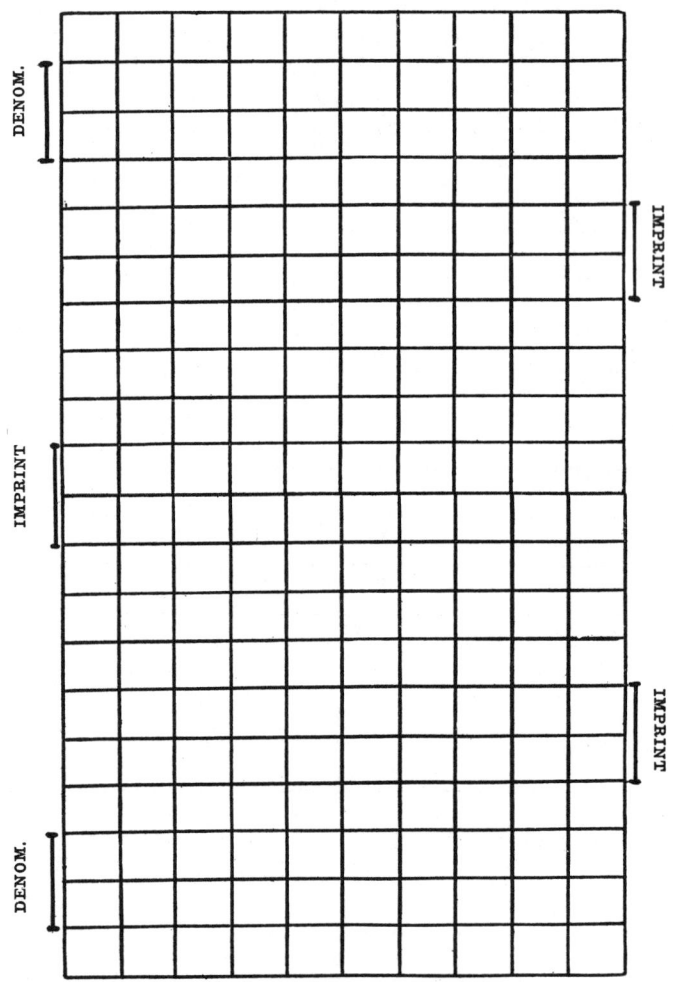

Imprint once at top and twice at bottom. Value in large letters at upper left and right.

Plate Layout #5
1897 Jubilee Issue.

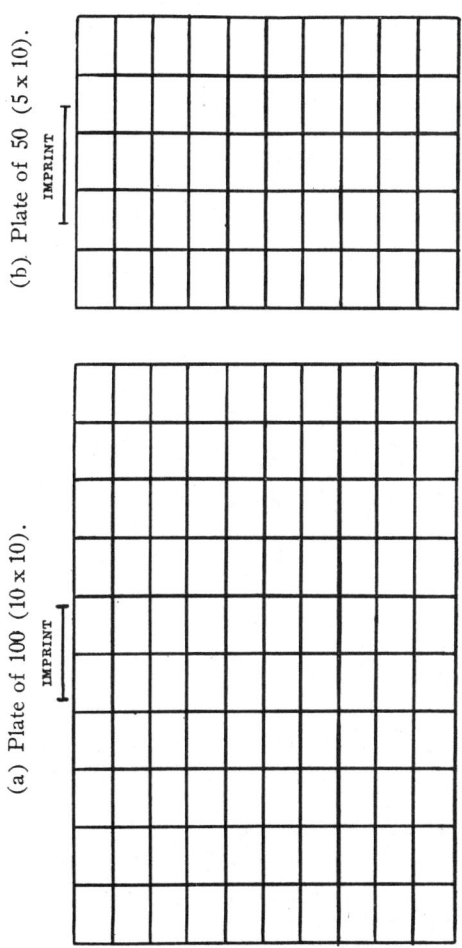

Also used for the Special Delivery Plates of 1898 and 1920.

Plate Layout #6

Maple Leaf Plates.

200 Subjects (10 x 10 + 10 x 10).

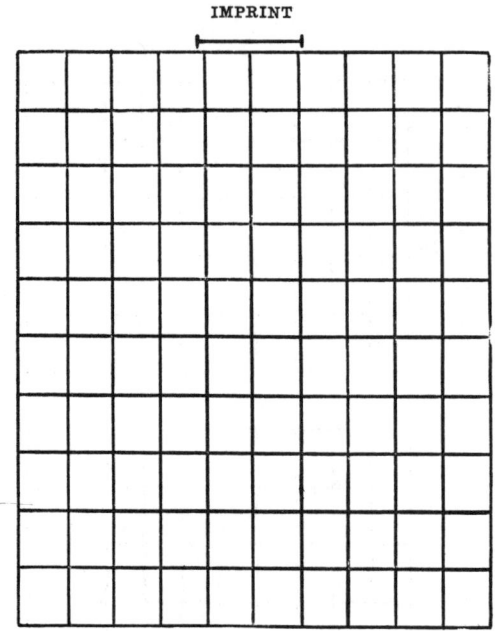

Diagiam of Pane of 100. Gutter 12-13 mm. Wide Between Panes.

Notes on the Diagrams on Pages Q-10 and Q-12 (Booklet Plates)

The panes of four were from plates of 240 subjects of similar layout but with the 3rd, 4th, 9th, 10th, and 15th and 16th vertical rows omitted.

The Arch and Maple Leaf Issues were from similar plates, but none of the stamps were tete-beche, and the left gutter of *each* group was for binding instead of the alternate gutters.

The Bantam Booklets of 1943 are probably from a similar layout but cut horizontally along every row instead of alternate rows.

Plate Layout #7a, 8a, b

For Numeral Issues, and 200 Subject Plates of King Edward VII Issues.

(a) Regular Plate of 200 (10 x 10 + 10 x 10).

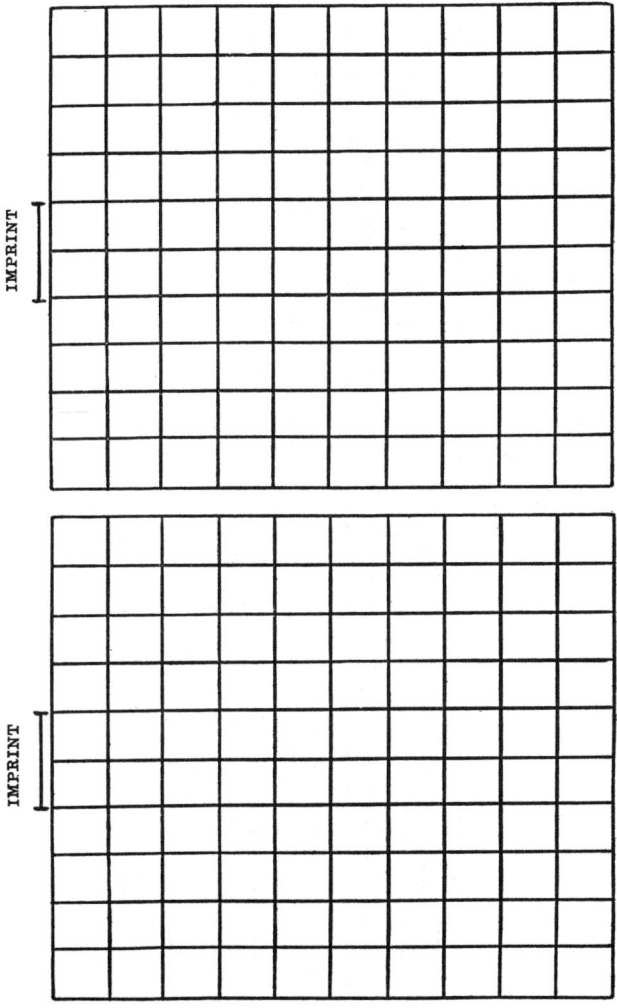

Imprint at top only.

(8b) The King Edward plates of 400 were arranged in a block of four pane separated by a gutter. The upper plates had the word "TOP" engraved in the margin near the imprint, 1c and 2c plates only.

Plate Layout #7b, 8c and 9b

Booklet Plate of 120 (6 x 20)—20 Panes of 6 (3 x 2).
Tete-beche as indicated by arrows. Used for all booklets—1899-1927.
2c Q. V. 1899, 2c K. E. 1903, and 1c, 2c, 3c K. G. 1912-26.

Binding Edge In Gutter.

The 1918 and subsequent panes of four were made from plates of similar lay out but the 3rd and 4th vertical rows were blank—thus producing a plate of 80—20 panes of four. (See Page Q-8).

Plate Layout #9a

King George V—1912-26.

400 Subject Plates (10x10+10x10+10x10+10x10).

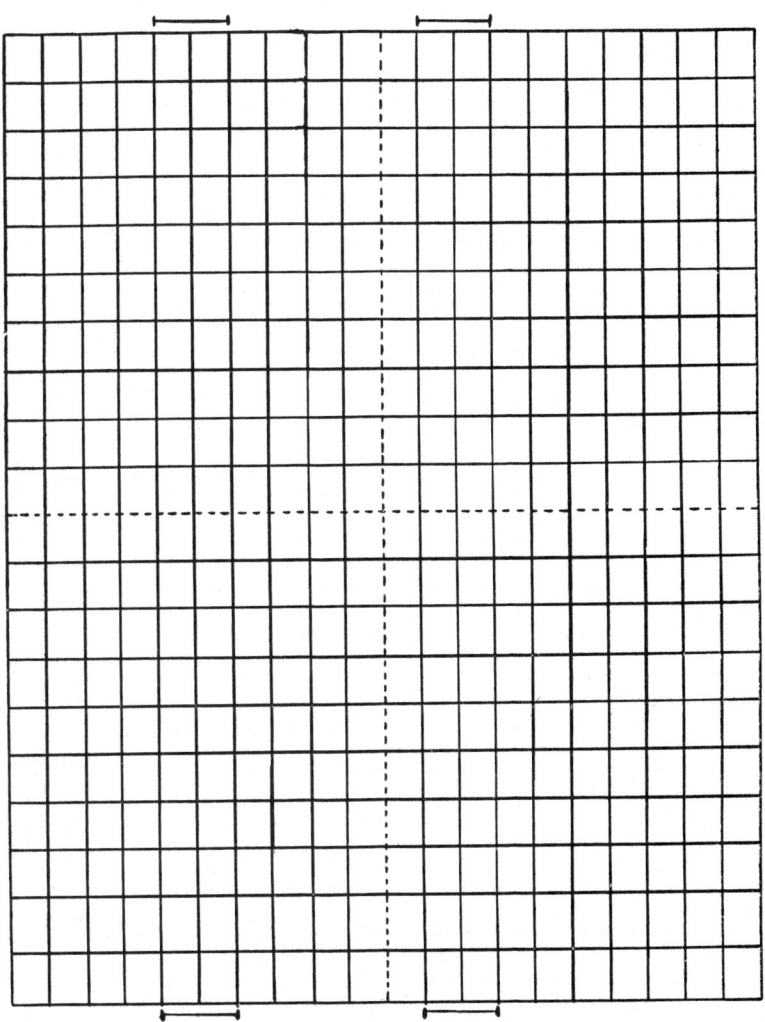

Dotted Lines Indicate Straight Edges.

Some of the early plates of the 1c and 2c were arranged similarly to the 400 subject plates of the K. E. issue, that is with a gutter between the panes.

NOTE: The imprint varies considerably in location but it is always at the top or bottom; never at the sides. It is sometimes inverted at bottom.

Plate Layout #10

Booklet Panes—Panes of 6—1928-29, 1935, 1937 and 1942.
360 Subjects—3 Groups of 120 (See Page Q-8)

AUTHOR'S REVISIONS

AUTHOR'S REVISIONS

PAGE	COMMENTS
xv	Insert AMS, Airmail Stationery.
xvi	Add "There will be occasions when the value factor will result in a fantastic valuation. This may be correct if scarcity alone is considered. However, demand and the state of the market also must be considered. The actual value will be the balance of all these considerations."
xxii	In para. 7, change first sentence to "Small panes (of three, four or six stamps, and strips of three) especially....."
xxvi	In para. 11, change date to 1864.
xxviii	In para. 1, change date after USPOD to "(1864)."
1	Change Fig. 1 caption to "....Mons. de Bourlamaque..."
2	Change heading at bottom of page to "...Service of 1759-1763." Change second line down from heading to "...on the 8th of September, 1760..." and change next line to ..."Quebec on September 13 of 1759." Delete "same year" on next line.
5	Answer to question in Footnote 6 is: no.
9	Add footnote 19a: There was an American P.O. in Montreal from Nov. 13, 1775 to June, 1776.
19	Insert PM17a, 1795-1800, black. Add PM21, Niagara with date, 1795-1807, black.
22	Add "The Bishop Mark was also apparently used in Montreal, September, 1784."
29	In H49, Post Office column, add "Quebec Apr. 1860, red, and June, 1859 Mount Elgin U.S., red."
30	In Single Rate group, item b, add note: "Quebec, Jan. 1, 1860, red."
33	Beside photograph add "without 'Paid' in black, 1818."
35	Under Type H75b drawing, add "Chatham U.C. Nov. '54, black; Raleigh U.C. Aug. '51 red; Cabourg U.C. Apr.'52, black."

PAGE	COMMENTS
37	For H96, Post Office column, add "Mount Elgin C.W., Feb. '55."
40	Change date beside H123 to "Dec. 1860." Add "Wallace Town" in Post Office column.
47	To Type IVg add "Jan. 1856."
48	To Type IIa add "similar but sans shield - 1852 - N.Y. State to Woodstock C.W. via London and Windsor."
51	Change date in (e) to 1847. Add "Aug. 1851" to (g) and add "1859" to (j).
72	Fig. 25 caption, third line up from bottom should read ...letters could be prepaid through only in and U.S. stamps..."
77	Add notation to Fig. 33: "Overpay 1c."
121	Change first two words of first para. to "An engraved.."
123	Under Contemporary Die Proofs section, add "vignette only, in black, on card, 6d, 12d."
124	Add to caption: "Founded 1729, refitted in 1829 and made bank note paper until 1861. It continued making other grades of hand-made paper until 1866 when it closed down completely. Historical Soc. of Pa. conclusively shows that R.W.H.&E. bought their paper exclusively from Wilcox Mills.
125	In S1a, Carmine column, add "h." In S1b, Carmine column, add "D." In S2e, Green column, add "V." Add new column "V. Blue", put "V" in this column opposite S3a.
144	In Plates section, second para., last date, change to "April 1857."
146	Under chart at top of page add "normal on 6d."
147	In Fig. 16 caption, change "blue" to "red" and "37" to "27" in first line.
151	Add "E4Ae, red violet." Add notation beside group: "in sheets of at least 9."
152	Add "P8c, 1/2 d claret" and "P8d, 1/2 d green." Insert "S7b, overprint" and "S7c, specimen with serifs."

PAGE	COMMENTS

152   Add "S8d 1/2d, deep rose, carmine overprint, vertical," and "S8e 1/2 orange, brown-black overprint, vertical."
Add to Footnote: "varies in shade to orange-red."

160   Change Fig. 34 caption to: "...of each, paying double rate by American packet to London. Checks rate via Boston." Delete "over...cy!"

162   Add to Fig. 37 caption: "This rate was established by Act of Parliament in Great Britain in 1795. In 1812 Canada extended the privilege to Canadians serving in the reserve forces."

173   Add P7f - vermilion, P7g - brown, P7h - dull blue, P7k - greenish blue, P7l - orange.
Add to Fig. 53 caption: "strictly speaking, a plate with two die impressions."

174   After word "black", first item, top list, add "varies in shade from gray black to deep black." Add new column "D^3 Laid", add an "x" on this same line. Add "g - dull red."
Under Plate Proofs add "1879 Goodall Proof in all 5 colors" and "12p in dull blue on India on card from this die."
Above Fig. 54 insert: "Goodall die proofs on India" and "12p - cancelled die, P3c-12p black, P3d - 12p vermilion, P3e - 12p green, P3d - 12p blue, P3e - 12p orange."

175   In Trade Samples section, add "(p) black" and the general notation "several shades of each color."
After (2) description, add "also bistre brown, blue."
Under footnote add "on wove blue chemical paper: 10p - ora orange, 1/2 p - orange, 1/2 p - black." ."

182   Add "P16e - yellow green." Add "P17e - brown, P17f - green, and P17g - vermilion." To S12a add "1c orange yellow, handstamped specimen with only one overprinted." Put "D" in S12a Carmine column. Add "S15c, 10c, brown black, Spec. D in carmine, V in carmine." Add comment to S15b: "brown card 'Specimen', vertically - color?"

PAGE	COMMENTS
183	Add to top of page: "The 2c dull rose has been seen handstamped 'specimen' in serifed caps 18 x 3 in orange red, H at bottom and V at R."
187	Under #77 add "#76, dash in right '2'."
206	Add to Fig. 11 caption: "also have seen 2c 'Quebec' Apr. 13, '66 to London, Eng."
	Add to Fig. 12 caption: "also 2c - Windsor to Hamilton Dec. 1865."
215	In 1879 chart put an "x" beside all items in the U-Black and V-Deep Green columns.
	In first sentence of Proofs para., change word green to blue.
	Beside B13c change "(green overprint)" to "(blue overprint)". Add "P13d - 2c dull rose 'specimen in red horizontally at bottom."
240	Add to Fig. 4 caption: "lathwork by Joseph Lindsley."
	Add E22e, 3c, pale blue. Under that add: "same but without colorless border." Add E22Aa, pale red, and E22Ab, dark green.
241	Beside Plate Proofs heading, add "in sheets of at least 9."
	Add to E18, "f - mauve, g - light blue, h - orange, j - rose, k - dark blue on stout wove, l - vermilion."
242	Additions to Table

	Die D On India	E Bond Paper	P On Card	G Glazed Wove	F Perf.& Gummed	N India
P18						
(a)		x				
(d) Carmine	x		x			
P19						
(a)		x				
(b)		x				
(c)		x				
(d)					x	
(f) Yellow		x				

PAGE	COMMENTS						
242	Additions to Table (continued)						
		Die D On India	E Bond Paper	P On Card	G Glazed Wove	F Perf.& Gummed	N India
P21							
(a)		x					
(b)		x	x		x		
(c)		x					
(d)	Blue	x	x				
(e)	Brown	x					
P22							
(a)		x					
(c)			x				
(d)		x					
(e)	Bright Red				x		
P23							
(b)		x					x
(c)		x	x				
(d)	also Deep Red	x					
(f)		x	x				
(h)	Brown						x
P24							
(a)		x					
(b)			x				
(d)		x					
(e)		x					
P26							
(d)			x				
(e)		x			x		
(f)	Brown						
P27							
(b)		x			x		
(c)		x					
(d)			x				
(e)	Orange-Yellow			x			

243 Add notation: "Specimen, 2c green 'specimen' hor. with black serifed caps (handstamped.)"

245 Footnote 8, second line, should read: "Ottawa, until late 1874..."

PAGE	COMMENTS
251	First words in Section A, Characteristics column, should read: "Thin to medium (.0021" to .0028") crisp..."
	Delete (1/2c?) in Section C, Values column.
	Above footnote add: "Stitch watermarks may occur on any of these papers; have seen 1/2c Paper A-Vert., 1c red Vert., 6c yellow-brown Vert."
262	In #18 section, C column, delete question mark under word "used."
270	Additions to Table

			D Die Proof On India	E Bond Paper
E38	(b)	Orange Red	x	
	(c)	Green	x	
	(d)	Blue	x	
E28	(b)	Black	x	
	(c)	Orange Red	x	
	(d)	Green	x	
	(e)	Blue	x	
E29	(a)	2c Blue	x	
E26	(d)	Black	x	
E27	(c)	Green		x
	(d)	Red	x	

271   Additions to Table

			D India	E Bond Paper	P Card	C Thin Wove
P38	(a)	1/2c Black		x	x	
	(b)	Brown			x	
P28	(b)	Yellow		x	x	
	(e)	Dull Red	x		x	
	(g)	Violet	x			
P29	(a)	2c Green	x	x	x	
	(b)	Black	x			
	(c)	Vermilion	x			
	(d)	Blue	x			
	(e)	Brown	x			
	(f)	Red				x

PAGE	COMMENTS				
271	Additions to Table (continued)				
		D India	E Bond Paper	P Card	C Thin Wove
	P30(a) 3c Vermilion	x		x	
	(b) Blue Green		x		
	(c) Blue	x		x	
	(d) Black	x			
	P35(a) 5c Olive		x	x	
	(b) Blue	x			
	(c) Dull Orange			x	x
	(d) Green	x			
	(e) Black	x			
	(f) Red Black	x			
	P31(a) 6c Yellow - Brown	x	x	x	
	(c) Vermilion	x			
	(d) Green	x			
	(e) Black	x		x	
	P47(c) Violet-Black			x	
	(d) Dull Dark Green				x
	(e) Black	x			
	(f) Greenish-Gray	x			
	(g) Claret	x			
	P38(a) 10c Pale Lilac		x	x	
	(b) Red Orange	x		x	
	(c) Brown Red			x	
	P48(a) 20c Vermilion	x		x	
	(b) Black	x			
	(c) Carmine	x			
	P49(b) Black	x			
	(c) Red	x			
	TRIAL COLORS 1c Dull Purple Perf. 12				
273	To Fig. 8 caption add: "seen on 1c, 3c, 6c."				
277	After Fig. 13 caption add: "known from St. Stephen NB. Apr. '70" and "known Feb. 2 from Halifax, also Apr. 20, 1870 from Truro."				

PAGE	COMMENTS
281	Add a new 1873-74 category, with 1 in Paper column, 2 in Perforation column, V in Gum column and 1c in last column.
282	After Fig. 21 caption add: "seen on 1/2 c, 1c, 3c, 5c, 6c, 10c."
287	Add beside letters and plates: "E^2 on 1c Montreal above imprint."
293	Add beside Watermarked Paper heading: "stitch wmk - 3c indian red."
297	In footnote, first sentence, change 1c to 2c and 2c to 1c.
300	Additions to Table

DIE PROOF
Vignette Only. (Very Rare). By Alfred Jones

add

    2c Brown on India

    2c Green on India

    2c Black on India

    2c Olive Green on India

PLATE PROOFS

under E41b 2c Yellow Green

add   2c Blue Green

under E41c 2c Green

add   2c Olive Green

add E41d 2c Orange

add E41e 2c Brown

    On Thin Bond Paper (Onion Skin) (Scarce)

add E41g, 2c Black on greenish-toned paper, ruled lines on back

add E41h, 2c orange red

| 301 | Add to Lithographed section: E41k, 2c Blue. |

    Add to Small Queen Bisects section: 2c - L.R. half, cut L.L. to U.R. with another 2c making 3c rate from Wilmot, N.S. to Bridgetown, April 19, 1873.

| 302 | Insert "6c, L.L. cut, U.L. to L.R. as 3c Wilmot to |

PAGE	COMMENTS
	Bridgetown."
312	In #40, add "c."
	In VII column, add an "x" in Unused column and a "?" in Used column.
319	TRIAL COLOR PLATE PROOFS
	add
	3c Black on India
	above Canada F-12
	imprint below
	Green on India
	Change TC53c to 3c Deep Purple
	add
	TC53e, 3c Blue
	TC53f, Pale Green
	TC53g, Dull Green
	Change caption in Column B from "On Soft Wove" to "On India."
	Add at bottom of page:
	Die Proofs on India
	Die Sunk on Card
	3c Bright Rose Ms "3c"
	Orange
	Grayish-Green
	Steel Blue - Ms "15c"
	Ultramarine - Ms "50c"
	Lake
	Deep Lake
	Purple
	Deep Purple
	Yellow Bistre
	Deep Violet
	Violet
323	In the second line above Fig. 2, delete #91 and insert #14.

PAGE	COMMENTS

324 Additions to Tables

REFERENCE LIST

under E66a add description:

3c Black on card - cross hatching on cheek and in veil unfinished; also at sides of oval around portrait; also earlier slate with wash in oval at sides. Black.

under #69d add:

Space painted in.

E69p, 3c Black on white card.

add to section "B" :

E66b, 1/2 c Black

E68a, 2c Red Violet on card

E68b, 2c Red Violet on white wove

Finished DIE PROOFS and Plate Proofs

Item	Die #	India	Notes
P 66	F 102		
P 67	F 103		
P 68	F 104		
P 69	F 105		
P 70	F 106		
P 70a		x	Plate 1
P 71	F 107		Plate 1
P 71a		x	
P 72	F 108		
P 72a		x	Plate 1
P 73	F 109		
P 73a			Plate 1

325 Corrections to Tables

Add to top of page: "3c Die Proof on card in shades of Red (8 known shades)."

Add to Trial Color Die Proofs section:

66TCa   1/2c Red Violet

68TCa   2c Violet on India

68TCb   2c Violet on white wove

PAGE	COMMENTS				
325	Corrections to Tables (continued)				
	68TCc	2c Blue on Yellowish wove			
	68TCd	2c Orange of Yellowish wove			
	69TCa	3c Black			
	b	3c Deep Olive Green			
	c	3c Dark Green			
	d	3c Blue Green			
	71TCa	6c Dull Violet on Green			
	Add to Trial Color Plate Proofs section:				
			<u>A.</u>	<u>B.</u>	<u>C.</u>
	68TCb	2c Blue	x		
	c	2c Orange	x		
	72TCa	8c Carmine	x	x	x (Imperf.)
	73TCa	10c Deep Red			x (Perforated)
	b	10c Orange	x		
327	In Section 68, Plates column, add "imperf. P13."				
	In Section 71, Notes column, delete #91 and insert #14.				
329	Under last line of page add: "D82d, 15c, dull yellow."				
330	In Without Die Number of Imprint section add:				
	D81c	8c Orange			
	D82a	10c Red			
	D82h	15c Orange			
	In White Wove Perforated and Gummed section add:				
	P78c	5c Brown Violet			
	P78b	5c Dull Red Violet			
332	In Section 75, Plates column, insert "Pl. 8" opposite "a".				
	In Section 79 add "b, imperf."				
333	In Section 80, Plates column, add "Pl. 2 has plate # reversed."				
341	On D88 line, change #F189-1/2 to #F139-1/2 and add "also cut close."				
343	In Section 90, underneath July 28, 1899, add "hor. stitch wmk."				

PAGE	COMMENTS
346	In middle of page, between words TOP and numbers, insert "Engraved." Add to this sentence: 60, 61, 62, 63, 64, 65, 66, 67. The next line should read: 1c - Plates 29, hand punched TOP on 1c, Pl. 32, 33, 34, 48, 47, 50, 51, 52, 55, 70 (op 71), 71, 72. The next line should read: 2c - Plate 17, 29, 62, hand punched top, 63, 64, 69, ...74 (inverted) 83, 84, 85, 86 op 71, 73.
353	Add to first sentence in DIE PROOF section, "...glazed paper die sunk on heavy fray card (very scarce)." Add to this section: Eb92 1c Black Ec Reddish Brown Ed Purple Ef Blue In ISSUED DESIGN, DIE PROOFS section, make sentence: "On White Card, Cut Close, also with large margins, Die # and imprint at bottom." Add above SPECIMEN section: Perforated - 2c Dull Red on Greenish paper; also, Plate Proof on India - P93a, 2c carmine.
355	In third line down from top, after Plate 1, 2 add: "13, 14."
356	In Experimental Coil section, add: "1c Green, uncalled, a paste up" and also "1c green, Ottawa parcel, cancel, a paste up."
360	Caption under the top two pictures should read: "Fig. 13 Type I Roulette."
368	To D100c, add "Die III" in Notes column. Insert D102a, 2c Green. In DIE PROOFS ON WHITE CARD section, insert "D100f, 1c Black, Die I." Add "Die F211" to D101e. Add to bottom of page:

PAGE	COMMENTS
368	(continued)
	Large Die Proof -
	2c Green, Die II, on soft yellowish wove
	2c Black, Die II, on soft yellowish wove
	7c Olive Brown in India
369	In first sentence, insert "Marker B" over 400; insert "Marker A" over 200. Add "Marker D" to end of third line.
371	Beside Pattern I at page bottom, add "Marker A."
372	Beside Pattern II picture, add "Marker B." Beside Pattern III picture, add "Marker C." Under Pattern V, Inverted picture, add "Marker D."
373	Additions to Tables

Pattern	1c Grn.	1c Yel.	2c Carm.	2c Grn.	3c Brn.	3c Carm.	4c Olive	5c Blue	5c Vio.
A - I									
B - II									
C - III	x		x	x					
D - IV			delete x						
D - V									

Pattern	7c Olive	7c r. Brn.	10c Plum	10c Blue	20c Grn.	50c Blk.	$1.00 Orange
A - I			x				
B - II			x				
C - III							
D - IV		x			x	x	
D - V					x		

379	Additions to Table						
#	Denom.& Color	Date Issued	Quantity Issued	Plates	Value Unused	Factor Used	Notes
100	Imperf			Delete A182, A186, A187. Add A170			
102	a-Imperf						

PAGE	COMMENTS						
379	Additions to Table (continued)						
#	Denom.& Color	Date Issued	Quantity Issued	Plates	Value Unused	Factor Used	Notes
103	a-imperf	Change to Dec. 29 1911					
104				Add A-5			All on damp paper- 7 positions Plates 1 & 2
105			Change to 146,700,000				
106			Change to 91,966,000				Pl. 1-7 damp; Pl. 6-7 8-9 dry
107							1-3 damp 4-dry

380	Additions to Table	
#	Date Issued	Quantity Issued
108 2 Plates		18,500,000
109 2 Plates		
110 no special plates		500,000
111 1 Plate		
112 12 Plates	Oct. 1912	18,050,000
113 1 Plate	Oct. 1912	
114 12 Plates, 1-12	Oct. 1912	
115 10 Plates, 1-10		

PAGE	COMMENTS

381	Additions to Table			
#	Date Issued	Quantity Issued	Plates	Notes
121	Dec. 18, 1923			
122	Mar. 1924 (?)		A132-A176	
123	July 7, 1922			1-4 wet paper 5-7 dry paper
124				All wet process except Plates 23, 24, 25
125		16,280,000		Early ptgs damp Later ptgs dry
126				Dry only
127		128,328,000	A13 - A22	A-13 damp A21-22 dry
128		89,713,000	A21 - A25	Dry only
129	July 22, 1923			Both damp & dry

Change Footnote 1 to: "Total was about 2,228,975.000."
Change Footnote 3 to: "Total was 184,650,000."
Add: Plates 19 and 20 retouched. Plates 165 to 176 were made but apparently not used.

382	Additions to Table		
#	Denom. & Color	Date Issued	Notes
130	Pl 11-14		
131	Die II- 15-17		
132		Dec. 1922	Plates 11 - 12
133		December	Plates 13 - 17
134		Dec. 1922	Plate 2
135		Apr. 9, 1924	Plates 11,12 damp
136		Apr. 9, 1924	Plates 13-15 dry

PAGE	COMMENTS
383	Additions to Table

#	Date Issued	Plates
137		11, 12
138		15, 16, 17
139		13, 14
140		15, 16, 17
141		11, 12
142	Oct. 6, 1924	
143	Oct. 6, 1924	
144	Jan. 23, 1924	

386 In section 148, write "a" before Double Surcharge, "b" before Triple Surcharge." Add "c, Quadruple Surcharge" and "d, double one inverted."

388 In D153 section, after 4c Bistre add: "X-G215" and change the date to 1/8/29.

389 Additions to Table

#	Plates
156	1, 2, 3
157	Pl. 1 imperf vert.
159	Pl. 3 imperf horiz.

392 In DIE PROOFS section, for E166a, 2c green add "also in orange, also in black." In E172a, change date to July 17. For E182a, change date to May 23. Add to E163a through E173b: "also known in black."

Add dates to DIE PROOFS OF ISSUED DESIGN section:

D166a, Sept. 4, 1928

D172a, Jan. 3, 1930

D173a, July 3, 1930

D178a, Jan. 9, 1930

D179a, Jan. 9, 1930

PAGE	COMMENTS

392 (continued)

D180a, Jan. 9, 1930

D181a, Jan. 9, 1930

D182a, Jan. 9, 1930

Change last sentence: We have also seen the 1c; 2c green, appd. Aug. 18, 1931; 2c deep red; 3c and 4c; 7c brown, Jan. 9, 1930; 8c blue, Jan. 9, 1930; cut close....

Add to bottom of page:

1c appd. 10/4/28

2c green, 10/1/29

2c red, 11/?/30, 4/17/31

3c red appd. 10/1/29 (6/15/29) Die I

398 Add the note: "10c, 12c, 20c, 50c and $1.00 exist imperforate."

400 In fifth line down, insert "imperf" by digit 1. Add above section C: "Plate Proof in Olive-Green. D189, 10c olive mounted on card. Appd. Aug. 17, 1931."

402 Add notes beside photo: "All exist imperforate." "Two dies of 3c, 1st Die 9/7/32." "Second die 11/28/32, issued 12/1/32. First die was damaged. First die - small die proof, deep red on white wove, mounted on card."

Additions to Table

#	Denom. & Color	Plates
192	Sept. 16, 1932 Small die on cards	1, 2, 6
193	11/9/32	
194	Die II	
195	7/16/32	
196	9/16/32	
197	9/16/32	
198	9/8/32	Plate 1 imperf

406 Beside photo add: "50c vignette engraved by Dawson."

PAGE	COMMENTS
406	(continued)

Additions to Table

D202a	3/21/25
D203a	3/4/35
D204a	4/3/35
D205a	3/21/35
D206a	3/21/35
D207a	3/29/35
D210a	TC Orange Red
D211b	Dark Blue
D212a	$1.00 Dull Yellow
D-E211a	50 c Black, unfinished lettering and slsy

Die Proof on white wove, 50c Blue

407 Add at bottom of page: "All the above exist imperforate."

408 Beside 10c photo add: "both shades and others exist imperforate."

410 Add to DIE PROOFS section:

1c Die XG 631
2c Die XG 651
3c XG 649
4c XG 633
5c XG 634
8c XG 635

All the above with HM King George VI below and the # Canadian Bank Note Company Limited.

Add "also in green" to D224a.
Add "also in blue" to D266a.

Corrections to Table

#	Denom. & Color	Plates
216		Delete 2
217		Delete 13 Add 14*
218		Delete 19 Add 23*

PAGE	COMMENTS
410	Corrections to Table (continued)

#	Donom. & Color	Plates
222		1 - 2
222a		1 - 2
224	20c unfinished at lower left. Die Proof in red brown.	

* Plates 9-10 were of 600 subjects in six panes.
  Plates 12-13 were of 600 subjects in six panes.

413 Add new section: Die Proofs, 1946 issue

In this section add:

8c large Die Proof XG-814

10c XG 821, imprint and number more high below design

14c XG 815

20c XG 818, imprint and number more high below design

50c XG 816

$1.00 XG 822, imprint and number more high below design

In DIE PROOFS section, insert "D241b - without value."

Additions to Issued Stamp Table:

#	
230	Pl 1-32
231	Pl 1-6
232	Pl 1-10
233	6, 7, 10-34
234	8,000,000
235	1-28, 30-50, 29 damaged (?)
236	1-4
237	1
238	1-6
239	1 - 4,000,000
240	1
241	1, 2
242	1
243	1

PAGE	COMMENTS
413	(continued)
	230 through 244 all imperf.
417	Change date after 20c Cartier's..... to 1535.
	Add to E250a:
	2c Black - 2 stages
	2c Canary - shading on portraits and around inscriptions incomplete
	20c Sepia, shading of clouds incomplete
	Additions to DIE PROOFS section:
	D250a, appd. July, 1908
	D253b, appd. June 27, 1908
	D255a, 10c Black
	D255b, appd. June 27, 1908
	D257b, appd. July 10, 1908, small die proofs, 39 x 27 mm set in normal colors
421	Change quantity to 500,000 in #255.
423	Add to Prince of Wales photo: "7c in red brown, 9 stages of die, have seen 6. Re-engraved in brown."
	At bottom of page add: "7c engraved by E.T. Loizeaux, re-engraved by Robert Savage."
424	Insert D254f, 7c Brown.
	Insert D257e, 50c Dull Orange.
425	Add to #258: "Plate 2 is inverted."
427	Add to #259: "Plate 2 imperforate vertically."
	Add to #264: "Plate 2 imperforate horizontally."
428	Add to #D259b: "Essay this design, 10c Green (12/18/25)"
429	Add note to top of page: "Small die on cards - 5c, 5/16/32' 13c, 5/27/32. Plate Proofs on card dated 3c, 5c, 13c."
	Add above B: "Large die proof - black on white wove, blue on white wove. Small die on card, Jan. 7, 1933. Die proof of vignette only, on surfaced white wove, dull blue."
	Add at bottom of page: "Over print proof, OK June 16,33.

PAGE	COMMENTS
430	Add beside 5c photo: "Small die on card 7/17/33. Die proof of vignette only. Blue on white wove. TC die proof, dull orange on white wove."
	Add beside 3c photo: "Small die proof on white wove, mounted on card. Handstamped in black, 'Assistant Deputy/ Mar. 9, 1934,' initialed 'S.G. Act P. Mg.' in blue."
434	Add to D274a: "Small die on card 5/8/34, BHBN."
435	Add to #270: "Plate 1 imperf."
	Add to #271: "Change quantity issued to 5,561,000."
	Add to #272: "Plate 1 imperf."
	Add to #273: "Plate 1 imperf."
	Add note at bottom of chart: All above exist imperf.
436	Add note beside top picture: "Die proof in brown red on white wove, mounted on card, Aug. 8/34."
437	Add above D276a: "Die Essays - 3c unfinished vignettes, pencil lining of leaves, on white card, deep red orange. 10c, clouds and water unfinished, on India, on card, dull green on white over dull green. Die proof 5c without stars in l. corner."
	Add to D278a: "Die XG 590."
	Add to D279a: "5c Black, XG 591."
	Add under D278a: "T.C. 2c - small die proofs on white wove, orange red. T.C. 13c - small die proof on dull violet."
438	Add to top of page: "Die proof XG 663, # and imprint below design."
	Add note beside 3c photo: "dark orange red. 1 issue known imperforate. Color photo models of issued design are known by WHC, dated 1/27/39.
	Add to D283a: "Die XG 685."
	Add to D285a: "Die XG 687."
439	Add note: Additional Commemoratives, 4c Bell, 25,000,000.
	Add 30,500,000 to #276.

PAGE	COMMENTS
439	(continued)
	Add 3,125,000 to #280.
	Add: "#282 is known imperforate. 283/5 are known imperforate. 276/285 are known imperforate."
443	Add note at top of page: "Original booklets are on horizontal mesh wove paper; falses from ordinary perf. or imperfs. are on vertical mesh wove paper - marker."
	Add March 11, 1907, to dates in 2nd line below Table BK II.
	Add note referring to word green in 2nd line below King George V heading: "22 Plates, 1-12, 15-16, Type X 168, 13-14, 17-22 Type X-252 Subs. Three plate arrangement."
	Add note referring to word yellow in next line: "Panes of 4, 1 plate, 3 groups - 56 subjects."
	Add note referring to Plates 1 and 2, 3rd line up from bottom: "Brown and carmine."
	Add note referring to Plates 3 and 4, same line: "Carmine."
448	Revisions to Table

#	Date Issued	Den	Description
BK6a	Jan 1912?		
BK7a			
BK8a			
BK4 Pl 1-20 1-14x 15-20x 11-12 not used			Carmine Red
BK5	early 1922		Dk. Brown
BK6	June 1922		Yellow(shades)
BK7	Aug. 1922	Pl 19-25	Green
BK6 Pl 1-56 subjects			Orange-Yellow
BK7		2 Plates	Yellow-Green

PAGE	COMMENTS
448	Revisions to Table (continued)

#	Date Issued	Den	Description
BK6 Pl 1-56 Subjects			Chrome Yellow
BK8	Mar. 30, 1923		Carmine Red

449   Revisions to Table

#	Den	Value Pane	Factor Book
BK12	Pls 1-2		
BK12a	Pls 1-2		Imprint "Top 916AA"
BK13a		Imprint Ottawa No. 1	

Add note by Rural Delivery Mail in next to last line on page: "Have seen this with 34 mm circular, 'Philatelic Div. Fin. Br. 1928, PO Dept. Ottawa - handstam.'"

458   In RH2 line, add "Quebec."

In RH4 line, change the date to 1845 and add "Quebec."

472   On the P-R2a line, P. Plate Proof column, delete green and add "blue green" and "yellow green."

Under Fig. 12 caption add: "We have seen a used copy with part gum of the 5c with the right half of a vertical pair of 2c Small Queens offset most distinctly."

478   To D-SD8a add "XG 673."

To D-SD5a add "11/3/32 BABN."

Under 1942 picture add: "1946 SD-XG 819, imprint and number below design, mm high."

479   Add "C, imperforate" to SD4 section.

480   Revisions to Table

#	Denom. & Color	Quantity Issued	Die #
SD6 brown imperf			
SD7 brown imperf			
SD 8 brown imperf	Diagonal 1/2 used as 10c on x	300,000	

PAGE	COMMENT

481	Revisions to Table (continued)			
	#	Denom. & Color	Quantity Issued	Die #
	SD9		200,000	
	SD10 brown imperf			
	SD11 brown imperf			X-G 752

488 Add to D-PD7a: "appd. June 6, 1928."
Add to D-PD8b: "appd. June 6, 1928."
Add to D-PD9b: "Jan. 3, 1930."
         10b: the same
         11b: the same
         12b: the same
         13b: the same
Add to D-PD15b: 2/6/35
        16b: 2/?/35
        17b: 4/3/35
        18b: 2/9/35

Delete D-DP13.

Under D-PD14b add: Small die on card 'BABN'". To this add: 1c, 4/19/34
     2c, 11/28/33
     4c, 11/28/33
     10c, 11/29/33

489 Add "A2" to #PD4, Plates column.

490 Add note: "#PD14 is imperf." Also add: "#s PD18, 19, 20 and 21 are imperf."

491 Add above chart: "Copies have been shen of all values over-printed 'sample' in purple script letters, generally between the stamps horizontally. These were probably so marked to indicate the package on which they were used contained samples and have no philatelic significance."

PAGE	COMMENT
492	Add note at top: "Essay War Tax. 1c black surch. Submitted when ITe was under consideration."

495

#	Date Issued	Plates
WT7	Aug. 16, 1916	
WT8		A 15, A-40, 42-46, 50, 55, 56

1. Add WT8 imperf., vert., Pl 3

499   Add E-AM1a, 5c black.

Add to D-AM6b: "in brown and in red orange."

Add to D-AMSD1b: "in violet red."

Add to D-AM2c: "appd. Jan. 9, 1930."

500   Add under 17c stamp photo: 1946, 7c air - V-G 820, imprint and number below design, mm high. 1946 A.S.D."

Add below this: " ∧accent X-G 817

∖accent X-G 817."

501   Add "A1" to AM3c, Plates column.

502   Revisions to Table

#	Denom. & Color	Plates	Quantity	Notes
AM5 imperf				
AM6 imperf				
AM7 imperf		1 - 2		
AM8 imperf		1 - 5		
imperf	16c blue			
imperf	17c blue		300,000	
	17c blue			accent corrected

506	Add notes:	Lanark	UC De 31, 1860	knife 2
		Theorold	UC Mr 12, 1860	knife 2
		Clinton	UC Fe(?), 1861	knife 2
		Seneca	UC Sp 22, 1860	knife 2
		(Toronto?)	CW Ap 27, 1860	knife 2

PAGE	COMMENTS
508	Under Essay heading, add EPS1b - 5c black on white wove, blue ruled lines. Add P-PSIIg, 10c violet on buff. Beside (very rare) add knife 5 - wmkd POD/US with patent lines.

#	A. White	C. White	D. Buff	E. Blue
PPSIf				x
PPSIIa	also without lines			
PPSIId		delete	delete	
PPSIIe		50.00	50.00	
PPSIIf	also ruled lines on back			

Add E-PSIIa - on blue.

519	Add E-PS2e, 3c red on white wove and E-PS2f - Essay of knife, red on white laid - Flap at top with tongued tip. Change date in footnote 4 to 1920.
522	Add note at bottom: "The 1933 designs were engraved by the BABN Die Proofs of 1c, 2c, 3c.
523	Add note at top: "Essay for 1898 (Type III) by De La Rue, 3c carmine on white wove; 'Canada' much thicker than on issued envs. Add to A: "Also 'Old Berkshire Mills 1881' in double line serifed caps and lower case in 4 lines. This is a Crane paper."
524	Add note under Type V: "Die Proof, 1c green on bond paper, 2c carmine on bond paper."
525	Add note under Type VIII: "Die Proof 1c - 29 Nov 32; 2c - 28 Nov 1932; 3c - 28 Nov 1932 by BABN. Electrotypes by Public Printing Stationery Office."
526	Knife 1 .... 146x79 Knife 2 .... 152x86 Knife 4 .... 152x89 Knife 5 .... 165x92 Knife 5a 165x92

PAGE	COMMENTS
526	(Continued)
	Knife 6 .... 241x105
	Change dimensions on tables.
527	Knife 1, 1a (140x79 mm)
	Knife 2 (152x85 mm)
	Footnote 2. 25mm tall. This is a Crane Paper Co. water mark and its ....
528	Knife 2, 152x85 mm
	Knife 3, 146x89
	Knife 5, 165x92
529	Add to surcharges section: "This surcharge has been seen on the Essay envelope #E-PS2f."
	Knife 4, 152x89
	Knife 5, 165x92
	Knife 6, 241x105
	Knife 8, 162x85
	Knife 9, 237x106
530	Change Knife 6 to 5.
	Change Knife 7 to 6, 241x105.
531	Add PS46 between 45 and 47.
	Change Knife 5 to 6, Knife 7 to 6.
538	Add note above photo: "D-UPC-1 Die Proof on white wove 2c green.
539	Add note at top: "Essay for 1c card - 1897. Typographed - black on thick cream wove paper."
542	Add under 3 lines of dates: "Proofs 1c black, 2c black, typographed white wove, perf 12 stamp sized gummed."

546		B. Mimeo	
		Unused	Used
	PC42	x	x

547	Inscription	B. Mimeo	
		Unused	Used
	PC54	x	x
	PC59	x	x
	PC70 Djng & Dcfmh		

859

PAGE	COMMENTS
551	Change 542 to 452 and 543 to 453.
552	70 designs - 5 occur three times 8 occur twice 57 occur once
557	Add note to bottom: Maple Leaf Die Proofs, 1c black on thin paper imperf 1c black on thick white wove paper - Perf 12 gum 1c orange 2c green 3c dull orange
561	Change Berthier, L.C. date to 1791.
562	Change Cornwall, U.C. and Kingston U.D. dates to 1791.
563	Change Niagara, U.C. and Port Trent U.C. dates to 1791.
564	Change Three Rivers L.C. date to 1791. Add to footnote 5a "in 1857." Add to footnote 6 "until 1815."
566	Revise and complete list: Augusta L.C., Est. 1789, became Prescott 1815; Bastard U.C. 1820; Beverly 1831; Delta 1857; Caldwell Manor 1820; Charlottenburg, U.C. Hallowell U.C. 1820; Picton 1839; Long Point U.C. 1817; Vittoria 1821; Monahan U.C. 1829 Mount Pleasant U.C. 1823-4 Mount Mohawk 1837 Niagara - Newark U.C. 1789 Newcastle U.C. 1814 New Johnston U.C. - 1789 - Cornwall Pointe Olivier L.C. 1826

PAGE	COMMENTS
566	(Continued)
	St. Mathias 1829
	Shefford L.C. 1825
	Shipton L.C. 1817
	Richmond 1820
	Yarmouth U.C. 1829
568	Type Ie and also "D" above 23.
571	Change 1843 in list to 1840.
572	Add note to Type IIIa - "Ms. up to 1835 at least."
	Add note to Type IIIb - "Add LaPrarie 1831."
574	Insert Erin U.S., IVd - type set date, struck separately 2 Jan 1860.
	Industry IIIc - red, Nov 1842
	IIIc - 1834 Rawdon, red
	Add to Prescott, IIIa, April 1839.
575	Insert: Bondhead Jy 1864, IVe
	Delhi Dec 1862, IVg
	Dunnville Mr 66, IVe
	Morpeth U.C. Mar 66, IVg
	Lefroy Dec 1860, IVe
	Add to Barrie, IVd, Ap 66
	Add IVd, 1840 red, St. Anne de la Perade
	Change date in Georgeville to 39, add red
	Add to Griffith, Aug 1860, IVl
	Add to Hamilton, Sep 1862, IVl
	Add to London, Mar 1860, IVg
	Add to Montebello, Ja 1863
576	Add: Owen Sound Dec 1860, IVl
	Oil Springs Sep 1862, IVl
	Point-Aux-Trembles-Quebec Ju 1867, IVg
	Point Levi L.C. Sp 1856, IVg
	St. Andrews 1833, black, IVa
	St. Benoit July 1855, black, IVd
	Simcoe Sep 67, IVl

PAGE	COMMENTS
576	(Continued)
	Add: Tavistock Fe 61, IVg
	Thornhill, C.W. Oc 1860, IVg
	St. Johns 1837, IVa
	Add Oc 1853 to St. Hilaire
	Ja 64 to Stratford
	Ap 1867 to Tamworth
	IVd 1862 to Vercheres
	IVg July 1860 to Windsor
	IVa, '62 to Woodstock
578	Insert Ornistown, 58 in Column G.
580	Add at top: Three Rivers Nov 1795 (?), larger serif type, black.
	Change 1859 May to 1855.
581	1. Change to Nov. 1841, Quebec, red
	3. Add: "also Woodstock U.C. Feb 1855."
584	Change type 7 to type 8. Add note: "black on 3c, in red on 6c, 1868."
585	Change first 4 words on page to "the two 5c are two.....
587	Revisions to Table

Type	Color	6d	1c red	1c yellow
1a	Red		x	
to	Blue		x	x
1c	Green	On thick white wove		
2b	Black		x	

588 Revisions to Table

Type	2c	3c	5c	12½c	15c	3c
to	x	x	x	x		
(blank)					25 Lawrenceville Mar 1874	
2a	x				x	
2d	x					

PAGE	COMMENTS
589	Revisions to Table

Type	1868	
	3c	1c
4d		x
7	x	
	also 6c	

592 Revisions to Table

Change 5c (1868) to 6c

Type	3c	6c
2d		x
2e		x
3d	x	

595 Revisions to Table

#	1859 Issues	1868	
	5c	1c Red	1c Yellow
1			x
2	1½		
3			x
7			x
17		x-B	

596 Put an "x" in the 3c(1868) column for #7.

597 Revisions to Table

#	1859	1868
	2c	1c Red
19		x
25	x	

598 Revisions to Table

#	LARGE CENTS			
	2c	3c	12½c	15c
20	x			x
23				x
25		x		
26			x	

PAGE	COMMENTS				
599	Revisions to Table				
	#	Post Office	1859 Issues 2c 10c	Large Cents 1c Red	
	31		Green		
	34	delete "Port"		Also on 5c Nesbitt env.	
	39		x		
600	Revisions to Table				
	#	Large Cents Issue 2c 3c 6c			
	34	x x			
	35	x			
	39	x x			
	40	x			
601	Revisions to Table				
	#	1859 Issues 2c	Large Cents Issue 1c Red 1c Yellow		
	47		x		
	52		x x		
	516	x			
602	Revisions to Table				
	#	Large Cents 2c 3c 6c			
	41	x x x			
	42	x			
	45	x B			
	48	x			
	50	x			
	52	x			
604	Revisions to Table				
	#	Pence Issues 7½d 10d	1859 Issues 2c 17c	Large Cents 1c Red	
	16A	x x			
	21		x x		
	37B		x	x	

PAGE	COMMENTS						
604	Revisions to Table (continued)						

#	Large Cents			Small Cents			
	3c	5c	15c	10c			
21				x			
37A		3	x				
37B	delete 3						

605 Revisions to Table

#	Post Office	Large		Cents			Small Cents
		1c Yel	2c	3c	6c	15c	3c
15			x	x	x	x	delete 8
23					x		x
51	Brockville				x		
17					x		

611 Revisions to Table

#	Large Cents	
	½c	1c Yel
5	3 R4	
8		x

612 Revisions to Table

#	Large Cents					Small Cents
	2c	3c	5c	6c	15c	1c
2	1½ B					
5					x	
7			x			
8	x					
9					x	
13						x
14				x		
16		x				

PAGE	COMMENTS						
613	Revisions to Table						
	#	Post Office		1859 Issues 1c		Large Cents 1c Red	1c Yellow
	18			x			
	22						x
	31	Oshawa					
	32					xB	2B
614	Revisions to Table						
	#	Large Cents 2c 3c 12½c 15c				Small Cents 1c 3c	
	19						x
	21					x	x
	22		x				
	25	x			x		
	32	B4					
615	Revisions to Table						
	#	Post Office		1859 Issues 1c		Large Cents 1c Yellow	
	34	delete Branchton, insert Chatham, N.B.				x	
	37					x	
	48			x			
616	Revisions to Table						
	#	Large Cents 2c 5c 6c			Small Cents 1c 3c		
	37				x		
	40		x				
	42	x			x	x	
	48	x	x				
617	Revisions to Table						
	#	Large Cents 1c Yellow					
	56	x					

PAGE	COMMENTS

618 Revisions to Table

#	Large Cents			Small Cents
	2c	5c	15c	6c
53		x		
54		x		
58				x
59	x			
60			x	

621 Revisions to Table

Type	Large Cents		
	1c Yellow	5c	15c
1a	x	x	x

1b (change to (Nov. 1875)

622 Revisions to Table

Type	Large Cents				Small Cents
	1c Yellow	3c	5c	6c	3c
1			x		x	delete "3"
1a	x		x		

624 Revisions to Table

Type	Large Cents	
	6c	12½c
3	x	
5	x	
15		x

628 Revisions to Table

Type	Small Cents
	½c
3	x

629 Add new sentence to text under Type 4: "In 1920(?) a new type of Registry Mark was introduced."

630 Change Type 9 caption to: "Napanee 'B' 1878."

632 Change H4 to H3a. Change H5 to H3b. Add notation: "Types of H occurring in the Halifax bar cancel.

Change H6 to H4, H7 to H5, H9 to H8 and add notation: "H.D. Beveridge P.M., Andover, N.B."

Add notation to J2: "Probably bogus(?)"

PAGE	COMMENTS
633	Beside M7 add "1880. Northern Vidal Piedmont Q. Also Marlsvesey Victoria Harbour O."
	Beside N4 add: "Probably York St. Sta., Toronto."
	Under bottom picture delete "L" and insert "B.H.J.-P.M.'s initials."
634	To O3 add: "on 6c Sq. Port Perry, Aug. 1872."
	To O5 add: "probably bogus(?)"
635	To B1 add: "On 1c yell., BC, 12½c."
	To C1 add: "Ottawa. Also on 15c L.Q."
	Change H8 to H6.
	To T1 add: "1c yellow red, also on 6c, 12½c."
	Change L4 to "WHL - P.M., W.H. LaPinotiere." Also add: "on 6c L.D."
636	To top picture add: "'B, initial of town."
	To Type 14 add: "On 6c LQ 2c."
637	To Type 3, Four Pointed Stars, add: "New T" and "2LQ, 6LQ."
	To Type 3, Five Pointed Stars, add: "Stewart Bay, Ont., May 1888."
638	To Type 8b add: "Apr 1877 afl 2c LQ, 1c LQ, 2c Reg., Apr 1871."
639	To top middle picture add: "On 2c, 115c."
	To extreme right, center group under Leaf Cancels, add: "1 Orange, SQ."
645	Change date under top picture to April 3. Add to following text: "Another type of this marking has been noted, reading Canadian Contingent En Route and dated January, 1900."
657	To Island Pond and Montreal route, Type 15b, add: "Clerk #6."
	In Quebec & Riviere DuLoup route, Date column, change 1863 to Apr 1862.
669	Change date in Medicine Hat & Nelson Route, Type II column to 1947.

PAGE	COMMENTS
669	(Continued) Change date in Midway & Nelson route, Type II column, to 1947.
674	Add to Footnote 5: "127 miles."
677	Insert Halifax & Proctor, H. & PR, Type I, 2/26/70. Change Midland Railway, Type I column, to "No. 2 South, Ap 10, '78." G.B. & L.E. means "Green Bay & Lake Erie."
684	In first line under middle photo, change Type I to Type IV.
686	Complete Type III date: Jul. 1842. Change Type IV date to Sept 1850. In Type V, insert "Black 1855" in black column. In Type V(b) insert "Black 1855" in black column. To Type V(b) add 1, 3, 4. To Type V(c) add Clerk Nos. 5, 6 or 8.
687	Add Type VII, 1817, Three Rivers, strip letter.
704	To Grenfell, Type I column, add Aug 14, 1897.
705	To Oakley, date Est. column, add Jun 9, 1893.
706	To Tiree, Type I column, add Jy 22, '86.
707	Insert Rainy River. Insert Moosomin.
708	Change Shell River, Date Est. date to Nov 1, 1880.
709	Add to Saskatchewan Landing, Date Est. column, Mar 1, 1888.
711	The Date Est. for Lower Fort Garry is Jul 1, 1875.
712	The Date Est. for St. Agathe through St. Ann's is Jul 1. Date Est. for Springfield is Jul 1, 1875.
713	In table at bottom, Forty Mile Post Office, Canc. date is Apr 26, 1895, Type I.
718	Insert E-0S1a, incomplete engraving on India, brown. Insert D-0S1 b, black. Insert D0-S1 c, green. Insert D-0S4b, black.
720	To #0S2 description add "imperforate."

PAGE	COMMENTS
725	To HS-024 drawing add: "12 Ju 1871."
726	Change date in HS-029 to 1872 in chart at bottom of page.
727	In Section, para. 4, change to read "....without punching, double etc." and add "One row of stamps are punched at a time."
	Add to next para: 104, 123, 126, 127, 128, 150, 156, 160, 191, 231, 267.
	Add to last para: 189, 208, 209, 263, 265, 261, 268, 270, 271, 282, 283, 284, 285, SD8, AMSD1, AMSD2.
728	Last word in caption should be 1896.
740	Add Sept 1923 under Type 1 photo.
	Add under Type 2 description: Meter #s 503, 507, 509, 512, 513, all except one in Montreal.
743	Change first 4 words to page to "In October."